# Java™ Cookbook™

# Other Java™ resources from O'Reilly

**Related titles**  Java™ in a Nutshell  Learning Java™
Head First Java™  Better, Faster, Lighter Java™
Head First EJB™  Java™ Servlet and JSP™
Programming Jakarta Struts  Cookbook™
Tomcat: The Definitive Guide  Hardcore Java™
JavaServer™ Pages

**Java Books**
**Resource Center**  *java.oreilly.com* is a complete catalog of O'Reilly's books on Java and related technologies, including sample chapters and code examples.

*OnJava.com* is a one-stop resource for enterprise Java developers, featuring news, code recipes, interviews, weblogs, and more.

**Conferences**  O'Reilly brings diverse innovators together to nurture the ideas that spark revolutionary industries. We specialize in documenting the latest tools and systems, translating the innovator's knowledge into useful skills for those in the trenches. Visit *conferences.oreilly.com* for our upcoming events.

Safari Bookshelf (*safari.oreilly.com*) is the premier online reference library for programmers and IT professionals. Conduct searches across more than 1,000 books. Subscribers can zero in on answers to time-critical questions in a matter of seconds. Read the books on your Bookshelf from cover to cover or simply flip to the page you need. Try it today with a free trial.

SECOND EDITION

# Java™ Cookbook™

*Ian F. Darwin*

O'REILLY®

Beijing · Cambridge · Farnham · Köln · Paris · Sebastopol · Taipei · Tokyo

**Java™ Cookbook™, Second Edition**
by Ian F. Darwin

Copyright © 2004, 2001 O'Reilly Media, Inc. All rights reserved.
Printed in the United States of America.

Published by O'Reilly Media, Inc., 1005 Gravenstein Highway North, Sebastopol, CA 95472.

O'Reilly books may be purchased for educational, business, or sales promotional use.
Online editions are also available for most titles (*safari.oreilly.com*). For more information, contact our corporate/institutional sales department: (800) 998-9938 or *corporate@oreilly.com*.

| | |
|---|---|
| **Editors:** | Mike Loukides and Debra Cameron |
| **Production Editor:** | Marlowe Shaeffer |
| **Cover Designer:** | Hanna Dyer |
| **Interior Designer:** | David Futato |

**Printing History:**

| | |
|---|---|
| June 2001: | First Edition. |
| June 2004: | Second Edition. |

 This book uses RepKover™, a durable and flexible lay-flat binding.

ISBN: 0-596-00701-9
ISBN13: 978-0-596-00701-0
[M]                                                                            [1/07]

# Table of Contents

# Preface

## Preface to the Second Edition

JDK 1.5, code-named Tiger, is an exciting change to the Java landscape. It introduces several major new facilities, such as generic types for better data structuring, metadata for annotating Java™ classes in a flexible but well-defined manner, new pattern-based mechanisms for reading data, and a new mechanism for formatted printing. In addition, a much larger number of smaller but important changes add up to a new release that is a must for Java developers. It will be quite some time before these mechanisms are fully understood and in wide circulation, but you will want to know about them right away.

I wrote in the Afterword to the first edition that "writing this book has been a humbling experience." I should add that maintaining it has been humbling, too. While many reviewers and writers have been lavish with their praise—one very kind reviewer called it "arguably the best book ever written on the Java programming language"—I have been humbled by the number of errors and omissions in the first edition. In preparing this edition, I have endeavored to correct these.

At the same time I have added a number of new recipes and removed a smaller number of old ones. The largest single addition is Chapter 8, which covers generic types and enumerations, features that provide increased flexibility for containers such as Java Collections. Now that Java includes a regular expressions API, Chapter 4 has been converted from the Apache Regular Expressions API to JDK 1.4 Regular Expressions.

I have somewhat hesitantly removed the chapter on Network Web, including the JabaDot Web Portal Site program. This was the longest single program example in the book, and it was showing signs of needing considerable refactoring (in fact, it needed a complete rewrite). In writing such a web site today, one would make much greater use of JSP tags, and almost certainly use a web site framework such as Struts (*http://jakarta.apache.org/struts*), SOFIA (*http://www.salmonllc.com/*), or the Spring Framework (*http://www.springframework.org/*) to eliminate a lot of the tedious coding. Or, you might use an existing package such as the Java Lobby's JLCP. Material on Servlets and JavaServer pages can be found in O'Reilly's *Java Servlet & JSP Cookbook* by Bruce W. Perry. Information on Struts itself can be found in Chuck Cavaness's *Programming Jakarta Struts* (O'Reilly). Information on SOAP-based web services is included in O'Reilly's *Java Web Services* by Dave Chappell and Tyler Jewell, so this topic is not covered here.

While I've tested the examples on a variety of systems and provide Ant scripts to rebuild everything, I did most of the new development and writing for this edition using Mac OS X, which truly is "Unix for the masses," and which provides one of the best-supported out-of-the-box Java experiences. Mac OS X Java does, however, suffer a little from "new version lag" and, since 1.5 was not available for the Mac by the time this edition went to press, the JDK 1.5 material was developed and tested on Linux and Windows.

I wish to express my heartfelt thanks to all who sent in both comments and criticisms of the book after the first English edition was in print. Special mention must be made of one of the book's German translators,* Gisbert Selke, who read the first edition cover to cover during its translation and clarified my English. Gisbert did it all over again for the second edition and provided many code refactorings, which have made this a far better book than it would be otherwise. Going beyond the call of duty, Gisbert even contributed one recipe (Recipe 26.4) and revised some of the other recipes in the same chapter. Thank you, Gisbert! The second edition also benefited from comments by Jim Burgess, who read large parts of the book. Comments on individual chapters were received from Jonathan Fuerth, Kim Fowler, Marc Loy, and Mike McCloskey. My wife Betty and teenaged children each proofread several chapters as well.

The following people contributed significant bug reports or suggested improvements from the first edition: Rex Bosma, Rod Buchanan, John Chamberlain, Keith Goldman, Gilles-Philippe Gregoire, B. S. Hughes, Jeff Johnston, Rob Konigsberg, Tom Murtagh, Jonathan O'Connor, Mark Petrovic, Steve Reisman, Bruce X. Smith, and Patrick Wohlwend. My thanks to all of them, and my apologies to anybody I've missed.

My thanks to the good guys behind the O'Reilly "bookquestions" list for fielding so many questions. Thanks to Mike Loukides, Deb Cameron, and Marlowe Shaeffer for editorial and production work on the second edition.

---

\* The first edition is available today in English, German, French, Polish, Russian, Korean, Traditional Chinese, and Simplified Chinese. My thanks to all the translators for their efforts in making the book available to a wider audience.

# Preface to the First Edition

If you know a little Java, great. If you know more Java, even better! This book is ideal for anyone who knows some Java and wants to learn more. If you don't know *any* Java yet, you should start with one of the more introductory books from O'Reilly, such as *Head First Java* or *Learning Java* if you're new to this family of languages, or *Java in a Nutshell* if you're an experienced C programmer.

I started programming in C in 1980 while working at the University of Toronto, and C served me quite well through the 1980s and into the 1990s. In 1995, as the nascent language Oak was being renamed Java, I had the good fortune to be told about it by my colleague J. Greg Davidson. I sent an email to the address Greg provided, and got this mail back from James Gosling, Java's inventor, in March 1995:

```
> Hi. A friend told me about WebRunner(?), your extensible network
> browser. It and Oak(?) its extension language, sounded neat. Can
> you please tell me if it's available for play yet, and/or if any
> papers on it are available for FTP?

Check out http://java.sun.com
(oak got renamed to java and webrunner got renamed to
  hotjava to keep the lawyers happy)
```

I downloaded HotJava and began to play with it. At first I wasn't sure about this newfangled language, which looked like a mangled C/C++. I wrote test and demo programs, sticking them a few at a time into a directory that I called *javasrc* to keep it separate from my C source (because often the programs would have the same name). And as I learned more about Java, I began to see its advantages for many kinds of work, such as the automatic memory reclaim and the elimination of pointer calculations. The *javasrc* directory kept growing. I wrote a Java course for Learning Tree,* and the directory grew faster, reaching the point where it needed subdirectories. Even then, it became increasingly difficult to find things, and it soon became evident that some kind of documentation was needed.

In a sense, this book is the result of a high-speed collision between my *javasrc* directory and a documentation framework established for another newcomer language. In O'Reilly's *Perl Cookbook,* Tom Christiansen and Nathan Torkington worked out a very successful design, presenting the material in small, focused articles called "recipes." The original model for such a book is, of course, the familiar kitchen cookbook. Using the term "cookbook" to refer to an enumeration of how-to recipes relating to computers has a long history. On the software side, Donald Knuth applied the "cookbook" analogy to his book *The Art of Computer Programming* (Addison Wesley), first published in 1968. On the hardware side, Don Lancaster

---

* One of the world's leading high-tech, vendor-independent training companies; see *http://www.learningtree. com/.*

wrote *The TTL Cookbook* (Sams, 1974). (Transistor-transistor logic, or TTL, was the small-scale building block of electronic circuits at the time.) Tom and Nathan worked out a successful variation on this, and I recommend their book for anyone who wishes to, as they put it, "learn more Perl." Indeed, the work you are now reading strives to be the book for the person who wishes to "learn more Java."

The code in each recipe is intended to be largely self-contained; feel free to borrow bits and pieces of any of it for use in your own projects. The code is distributed with a Berkeley-style copyright, just to discourage wholesale reproduction.

## Who This Book Is For

I'm going to assume that you know the basics of Java. I won't tell you how to `println` a string and a number at the same time, or how to write a class that extends `Applet` and prints your name in the window. I'll presume you've taken a Java course or studied an introductory book such as O'Reilly's *Head First Java*, *Learning Java*, or *Java in a Nutshell*. However, Chapter 1 covers some techniques that you might not know very well and that are necessary to understand some of the later material. Feel free to skip around! Both the printed version of the book and the electronic copy are heavily cross-referenced.

## What's in This Book?

Unlike my Perl colleagues Tom and Nathan, I don't have to spend as much time on the oddities and idioms of the language; Java is refreshingly free of strange quirks. But that doesn't mean it's trivial to learn well! If it were, there'd be no need for this book. My main approach, then, is to concentrate on the Java APIs. I'll teach you by example what the APIs are and what they are good for.

Like Perl, Java is a language that grows on you and with you. And, I confess, I use Java most of the time nowadays. Things I'd once done in C are now—except for device drivers and legacy systems—done in Java.

But Java is suited to a different range of tasks than Perl. Perl (and other scripting languages, such as awk and Python) are particularly suited to the "one-liner" utility task. As Tom and Nathan show, Perl excels at things like printing the 42nd line from a file. While it can certainly do these things, Java, because it is a compiled, object-oriented language, seems more suited to "development in the large" or enterprise applications development. Indeed, much of the API material added in Java 2 was aimed at this type of development. However, I will necessarily illustrate many techniques with shorter examples and even code fragments. Be assured that every line of code you see here has been compiled and run.

Many of the longer examples in this book are tools that I originally wrote to automate some mundane task or another. For example, MkIndex (described in Chapter 17) reads the top-level directory of the place where I keep all my Java example source code and builds a browser-friendly *index.html* file for that directory. For another example, the body of the first edition was partly composed in XML, a simplification that builds upon many years of experience in SGML (the parent standard that led to the tag-based syntax of HTML). It is not clear at this point if XML will primarily be useful as a publishing format or as a data manipulation format, or if its prevalence will further blur that distinction, although it seems that the blurring of distinctions is more likely. However, I used XML here to type in and mark up the original text of some of the chapters of this book. The text was then converted to the publishing software format by the XmlForm program. This program also handles—by use of another program, GetMark—full and partial code insertions from the source directory. XmlForm is discussed in Recipe 21.7.

Let's go over the organization of this book. I start off Chapter 1, *Getting Started: Compiling, Running, and Debugging,* by describing some methods of compiling your program on different platforms, running them in different environments (browser, command line, windowed desktop), and debugging. Chapter 2, *Interacting with the Environment*, moves from compiling and running your program to getting it to adapt to the surrounding countryside—the other programs that live in your computer.

The next few chapters deal with basic APIs. Chapter 3, *Strings and Things*, concentrates on one of the most basic but powerful data types in Java, showing you how to assemble, dissect, compare, and rearrange what you might otherwise think of as ordinary text.

Chapter 4, *Pattern Matching with Regular Expressions*, teaches you how to use the powerful regular expressions technology from Unix in many string-matching and pattern-matching problem domains. JDK 1.4 was the first release to include this powerful technology; I also mention several third-party regular expression packages.

Chapter 5, *Numbers*, deals both with built-in types such as int and double, as well as the corresponding API classes (Integer, Double, etc.) and the conversion and testing facilities they offer. There is also brief mention of the "big number" classes. Since Java programmers often need to deal in dates and times, both locally and internationally, Chapter 6, *Dates and Times*, covers this important topic.

The next two chapters cover data processing. As in most languages, *arrays* in Java are linear, indexed collections of similar-kind objects, as discussed in Chapter 7, *Structuring Data with Java*. This chapter goes on to deal with the many "Collections" classes: powerful ways of storing quantities of objects in the java.util package.

A new chapter was added in this section of the second edition. JDK 1.5 introduced a new dimension to the notion of data structuring, by adapting the C++ notion of templates to the Java Collections; the result known as Generics is the main subject of Chapter 8, *Data Structuring with Generics, foreach, and Enumerations (JDK 1.5)*.

Despite some syntactic resemblance to procedural languages such as C, Java is at heart an object-oriented programming language. Chapter 9, *Object-Oriented Techniques*, discusses some of the key notions of OOP as it applies to Java, including the commonly overridden methods of `java.lang.Object` and the important issue of Design Patterns.

The next few chapters deal with aspects of traditional input and output. Chapter 10, *Input and Output*, details the rules for reading and writing files. (Don't skip this if you think files are boring, as you'll need some of this information in later chapters: you'll read and write on serial or parallel ports in Chapter 12 and on a socket-based network connection in Chapter 16!) Chapter 11, *Directory and Filesystem Operations*, shows you everything else about files—such as finding their size and last-modified time—and about reading and modifying directories, creating temporary files, and renaming files on disk. Chapter 12, *Programming External Devices: Serial and Parallel Ports*, shows how you can use the `javax.comm` API to read/write on serial and parallel ports using a standard Java API.

Chapter 13, *Graphics and Sound*, leads us into the GUI development side of things. This chapter is a mix of the lower-level details, such as drawing graphics and setting fonts and colors, and very high-level activities, such as controlling a video clip or movie. In Chapter 14, *Graphical User Interfaces*, I cover the higher-level aspects of a GUI, such as buttons, labels, menus, and the like—the GUI's predefined components. Once you have a GUI (really, before you actually write it), you'll want to read Chapter 15, *Internationalization and Localization*, so your programs can work as well in Akbar, Afghanistan, Algiers, Amsterdam, or Angleterre as they do in Alberta, Arkansas, or Alabama....

Since Java was originally promulgated as "the programming language for the Internet," it's only fair that we spend some of our time on networking in Java. Chapter 16, *Network Clients*, covers the basics of network programming from the client side, focusing on sockets. We'll then move to the server side in Chapter 17, *Server-Side Java: Sockets*. In Chapter 18, *Network Clients II: Applets and Web Clients*, you'll learn more client-side techniques. Programs on the Net often need to generate electronic mail, so this section ends with Chapter 19, *Java and Electronic Mail*.

Chapter 20, *Database Access*, covers the essentials of the Java Database Connectivity (JDBC) and Java Data Objects (JDO) packages, showing how you can connect to local or remote relational databases, store and retrieve data, and find out information about query results or about the database.

Another form of storing and exchanging data is XML. Chapter 21, *XML,* discusses XML's formats and some operations you can apply using SAX and DOM, two standard Java APIs.

Chapter 22, *Distributed Java: RMI,* takes the distributed notion one step further and discusses Remote Method Invocation, Java's standard remote procedure call mechanism. RMI lets you build clients, servers, and even "callback" scenarios, using a standard Java mechanism—the Interface—to describe the contract between client and server.

Chapter 23, *Packages and Packaging,* shows how to create packages of classes that work together. This chapter also talks about "deploying" or distributing and installing your software.

Chapter 24, *Threaded Java,* tells you how to write classes that appear to do more than one thing at a time and let you take advantage of powerful multiprocessor hardware.

Chapter 25, *Introspection, or "A Class Named Class",* lets you in on such secrets as how to write API cross-reference documents mechanically ("become a famous Java book author in your spare time!") and how web browsers are able to load any old applet—never having seen that particular class before—and run it.

Sometimes you already have code written and working in another language that can do part of your work for you, or you want to use Java as part of a larger package. Chapter 26, *Using Java with Other Languages,* shows you how to run an external program (compiled or script) and also interact directly with "native code" in C/C++ or other languages.

There isn't room in an 800-page book for everything I'd like to tell you about Java. The *Afterword* presents some closing thoughts and a link to my online summary of Java APIs that every Java developer should know about.

No two programmers or writers will agree on the best order for presenting all the Java topics. To help you find your way around, I've included extensive cross-references, mostly by recipe number.

## Platform Notes

Java has gone through five major versions. The first official release was JDK 1.0, and its last bug-fixed version was 1.0.2. The second major release is Java JDK 1.1, and the latest bug-fixed version is 1.1.9, though it may be up from that by the time you read this book. The third major release, in December 1998, was to be known as JDK 1.2, but somebody at Sun abruptly renamed JDK 1.2 at the time of its release to Java 2, and the implementation is known as Java 2 SDK 1.2. The current version as of the writing of the first edition of this book was Java 2 SDK 1.3 (JDK 1.3), which was released in 2000.

As the first edition of this book went to press, Java 2 Version 1.4 was about to appear; it entered beta (which Sun calls "early access") around the time of the book's completion so I could mention it only briefly. The second edition of this book looks to have better timing; Java 2 Version 1.5 is in beta as I am updating the book.

This book is aimed at the fifth version, Java 2 Standard Edition, Version 1.5. By the time of publication, I expect that all Java projects in development will be using JDK 1.4, with a very few wedded to earlier versions for historical reasons. I have used several platforms to test this code for portability. I've tested with Sun's Linux JDK. For the mass market, I've tested many of the programs on Sun's Win32 (Windows 2000/XP/2003) implementation. And, "for the rest of us," I've done most of my recent development using Apple's Mac OS X Version 10.2.x and later. However, since Java is portable, I anticipate that the vast majority of the examples will work on any Java-enabled platform, except where extra APIs are required. Not every example has been tested on every platform, but all have been tested on at least one—and most on more than one.

The Java API consists of two parts: core APIs and noncore APIs. The core is, by definition, what's included in the JDK that you download for free from *http://java.sun.com/*. Noncore is everything else. But even this "core" is far from tiny: it weighs in at around 50 packages and well over 2,000 public classes, averaging around 12 public methods each. Programs that stick to this core API are reasonably assured of portability to any Java platform.

The noncore APIs are further divided into standard extensions and nonstandard extensions. All standard extensions have package names beginning with javax.* (and reference implementations are available from Sun). A Java licensee (such as Apple or IBM) is not required to implement every standard extension, but if it does, the interface of the standard extension should be adhered to. This book calls your attention to any code that depends on a standard extension. Little code here depends on nonstandard extensions, other than code listed in the book itself. My own package, com.darwinsys, contains some utility classes used here and there; you will see an import for this at the top of any file that uses classes from it.

In addition, two other *platforms*, the J2ME and the J2EE, are standardized. Java 2 Micro Edition is concerned with small devices such as handhelds (PalmOS and others), cell phones, fax machines, and the like. Within J2ME are various "profiles" for different classes of devices. At the high end, the Java 2 Enterprise Edition (J2EE) is concerned with building large, scalable, distributed applications. Servlets, JavaServer Pages, JavaServer Faces, CORBA, RMI, JavaMail, Enterprise JavaBeans™ (EJBs), Transactions, and other APIs are part of the J2EE. J2ME and J2EE packages normally begin with "javax" as they are not core J2SE packages. This book does not

---

* Note that not all packages named javax. are extensions: javax.swing and its subpackages—the Swing GUI packages—used to be extensions, but are now core.

cover J2ME at all but includes a few of the J2EE APIs that are also useful on the client side, such as RMI and JavaMail. As mentioned earlier, coverage of Servlets and JSPs from the first edition of this book has been removed as there is now a *Servlet and JSP Cookbook*.

## Other Books

A lot of useful information is packed into this book. However, due to the breadth of topics, it is not possible to give book-length treatment to any one topic. Because of this, the book also contains references to many web sites and other books. This is in keeping with my target audience: the person who wants to learn more about Java.

O'Reilly publishes, in my opinion, the best selection of Java books on the market. As the API continues to expand, so does the coverage. You can find the latest versions and ordering information on O'Reilly's Java books online at *http://java.oreilly.com*, and you can buy them at most bookstores, both physical and virtual. You can also read them online through a paid subscription service; see *http://safari.oreilly.com*. While many are mentioned at appropriate spots in the book, a few deserve special mention here.

First and foremost, David Flanagan's *Java in a Nutshell* offers a brief overview of the language and API and a detailed reference to the most essential packages. This is handy to keep beside your computer. *Head First Java* offers a much more whimsical introduction to the language and is recommended for the less experienced developer.

A definitive (and monumental) description of programming the Swing GUI is *Java Swing* by Marc Loy, Robert Eckstein, Dave Wood, James Elliott, and Brian Cole.

*Java Virtual Machine*, by Jon Meyer and Troy Downing, will intrigue the person who wants to know more about what's under the hood. This book is out of print but can be found used and in libraries.

*Java Network Programming* and *Java I/O*, both by Elliotte Rusty Harold, and *Database Programming with JDBC and Java*, by George Reese, are also useful references.

There are many more; see the O'Reilly web site for an up-to-date list.

## Other Java Books

You should not consider releasing a GUI application unless you have read Sun's official *Java Look and Feel Design Guidelines* (Addison Wesley). This work presents the views of a large group of human factors and user-interface experts at Sun who have worked with the Swing GUI package since its inception; they tell you how to make it work well.

## General Programming Books

Donald E. Knuth's *The Art of Computer Programming* has been a source of inspiration to generations of computing students since its first publication by Addison Wesley in 1968. Volume 1 covers *Fundamental Algorithms*, Volume 2 is *Seminumerical Algorithms*, and Volume 3 is *Sorting and Searching*. The remaining four volumes in the projected series are still not completed. Although his examples are far from Java (he invented a hypothetical assembly language for his examples), many of his discussions of algorithms—of how computers ought to be used to solve real problems—are as relevant today as they were years ago.[*]

Though somewhat dated now, the book *The Elements of Programming Style*, by Kernighan and Plauger, set the style (literally) for a generation of programmers with examples from various structured programming languages. Kernighan and Plauger also wrote a pair of books, *Software Tools* and *Software Tools in Pascal*, which demonstrated so much good advice on programming that I used to advise all programmers to read them. However, these three books are dated now; many times I wanted to write a follow-on book in a more modern language, but instead defer to *The Practice of Programming*, Brian's follow-on—co-written with Rob Pike—to the *Software Tools* series. This book continues the Bell Labs (now part of Lucent) tradition of excellence in software textbooks. In Recipe 3.13, I have even adapted one bit of code from their book.

See also *The Pragmatic Programmer* by Andrew Hunt and David Thomas (Addison Wesley).

## Design Books

Peter Coad's *Java Design* (PTR-PH/Yourdon Press) discusses the issues of object-oriented analysis and design specifically for Java. Coad is somewhat critical of Java's implementation of the observable-observer paradigm and offers his own replacement for it.

One of the most famous books on object-oriented design in recent years is *Design Patterns,* by Gamma, Helm, Johnson, and Vlissides (Addison Wesley). These authors are often collectively called "the gang of four," resulting in their book sometimes being referred to as "the GOF book." One of my colleagues called it "the best book on object-oriented design ever," and I agree; at the very least it's among the best.

*Refactoring*, by Martin Fowler, covers a lot of "coding cleanups" that can be applied to code to improve readability and maintainability. Just as the GOF book introduced new terminology that helps developers and others communicate about how

---

[*] With apologies for algorithm decisions that are less relevant today given the massive changes in computing power now available.

code is to be designed, Fowler's book provided a vocabulary for discussing how it is to be improved. Many of the "refactorings" now appear in the Refactoring Menu of the Eclipse IDE (see Recipe 1.3).

Two important streams of methodology theories are currently in circulation. The first is collectively known as Agile Methods, and its best-known member is Extreme Programming. XP (the methodology, not last year's flavor of Microsoft's OS) is presented in a series of small, short, readable texts led by its designer, Kent Beck. A good overview of all the Agile methods is Highsmith's *Agile Software Development Ecosystems*. The first book in the XP series is *Extreme Programming Explained*.

Another group of important books on methodology, covering the more traditional object-oriented design, is the UML series led by "the Three Amigos" (Booch, Jacobson, and Rumbaugh). Their major works are the *UML User Guide*, *UML Process*, and others. A smaller and more approachable book in the same series is Martin Fowler's *UML Distilled*.

# Conventions Used in This Book

This book uses the following conventions.

## Programming Conventions

I use the following terminology in this book. A *program* means either an applet, a servlet, or an application. An *applet* is for use in a browser. A *servlet* is similar to an applet but for use in a server. An *application* is any other type of program. A desktop application (a.k.a. *client*) interacts with the user. A server program deals with a client indirectly, usually via a network connection.

The examples shown are in two varieties. Those that begin with zero or more import statements, a Javadoc comment, and a public class statement are complete examples. Those that begin with a declaration or executable statement, of course, are excerpts. However, the full versions of these excerpts have been compiled and run, and the online source includes the full versions.

Recipes are numbered by chapter and number, so, for example, Recipe 7.5 refers to the fifth recipe in Chapter 7.

## Typesetting Conventions

The following typographic conventions are used in this book:

*Italic*

    Used for commands, filenames, and URLs. It is also used to define new terms when they first appear in the text.

`Constant width`

> Used in code examples to show partial or complete Java source code program listings. It is also used for class names, method names, variable names, and other fragments of Java code.

**`Constant width bold`**

> Used for user input, such as commands that you type on the command line.

 This icon signifies a tip, suggestion, or general note.

 This icon indicates a warning or caution.

Many programs are accompanied by an example showing them in action, run from the command line. These will usually show a prompt ending in either $ for Unix or > for Windows, depending on which computer I was using that day. Text before this prompt character can be ignored; it will be a pathname or a hostname, again depending on the system.

## Comments and Questions

As mentioned earlier, I've tested all the code on at least one of the reference platforms, and most on several. Still, there may be platform dependencies, or even bugs, in my code or in some important Java implementation. Please report any errors you find, as well as your suggestions for future editions, by writing to:

> O'Reilly Media, Inc.
> 1005 Gravenstein Highway North
> Sebastopol, CA 95472
> (800) 998-9938 (in the United States or Canada)
> (707) 829-0515 (international or local)
> (707) 829-0104 (fax)

To ask technical questions or comment on the book, send email to:

> *bookquestions@oreilly.com*

An O'Reilly web site for the book lists errata, examples, and any additional information. You can access this page at:

> *http://www.oreilly.com/catalog/javacook2/*

I also have a personal web site for the book:

> *http://javacook.darwinsys.com/*

Both sites list errata and plans for future editions. You'll also find the source code for all the Java code examples to download; *please* don't waste your time typing them again! For specific instructions, see the next section.

## Getting the Source Code

From my web site *http://javacook.darwinsys.com*, just follow the Downloads link. You are presented with three choices:

1. Download the entire source archive as a single large zip file.
2. Download individual source files, indexed alphabetically as well as by chapter.
3. Download the binary JAR file for the com.darwinsys.* package needed to compile many of the other programs.

Most people will choose either option 1 or 2, but anyone who wants to compile my code will need option 3. See Recipe 1.5 for information on using these files.

Downloading the entire source archive yields a large zip file with all the files from the book (and more). This archive can be unpacked with *jar* (see Recipe 23.4), the free zip program from Info-ZIP, the commercial WinZip or PKZIP, or any compatible tool. The files are organized into subdirectories by topic, with one for strings (Chapter 3), regular expressions (Chapter 4), numbers (Chapter 5), and so on. The archive also contains the index by name and index by chapter files from the download site, so you can easily find the files you need.

Downloading individual files is easy, too: simply follow the links either by file/subdirectory name or by chapter. Once you see the file you want in your browser, use File → Save or the equivalent, or just copy and paste it from the browser into an editor or IDE.

The files are updated periodically, so if there are differences between what's printed in the book and what you get, be glad, for you'll have received the benefit of hindsight.

## Acknowledgments

My life has been touched many times by the flow of the fates bringing me into contact with the right person to show me the right thing at the right time. Steve Munroe, with whom I've long since lost touch, introduced me to computers—in particular an IBM 360/30 at the Toronto Board of Education that was bigger than a living room, had 32 or 64K of memory, and had perhaps the power of a PC/XT—in 1970. Herb Kugel took me under his wing at the University of Toronto while I was learning about the larger IBM mainframes that came later. Terry Wood and Dennis Smith at the University of Toronto introduced me to mini- and micro-computers before there was an IBM PC. On evenings and weekends, the Toronto Business Club of Toast-masters International (*http://www.toastmasters.org*) and Al Lambert's Canada SCUBA School allowed me to develop my public speaking and instructional abilities. Several people at the University of Toronto, but especially Geoffrey Collyer, taught me the features and benefits of the Unix operating system at a time when I was ready to learn it.

Greg Davidson of UCSD taught the first Learning Tree course I attended and welcomed me as a Learning Tree instructor. Years later, when the Oak language was about to be released on Sun's web site, Greg encouraged me to write to James Gosling and find out about it. James's reply of March 29th, 1995, that the lawyers had made them rename the language to Java and that it was "just now" available for download, is the prized first entry in my saved Java mailbox. Mike Rozek took me on as a Learning Tree course author for a Unix course and two Java courses. After Mike's departure from the company, Francesco Zamboni, Julane Marx, and Jennifer Urick in turn provided product management of these courses. Jennifer also arranged permission for me to "reuse some code" in this book that had previously been used in my Java course notes. Finally, thanks to the many Learning Tree instructors and students who showed me ways of improving my presentations. I still teach for "The Tree" and recommend their courses for the busy developer who wants to zero in on one topic in detail over four days. Their web site is *http://www.learningtree.com*.

Closer to this project, Tim O'Reilly believed in "the little Lint book" when it was just a sample chapter, enabling my early entry into the circle of O'Reilly authors. Years later, Mike Loukides encouraged me to keep trying to find a Java book idea that both he and I could work with. And he stuck by me when I kept falling behind the deadlines. Mike also read the entire manuscript and made many sensible comments, some of which brought flights of fancy down to earth. Jessamyn Read turned many faxed and emailed scratchings of dubious legibility into the quality illustrations you see in this book. And many, many other talented people at O'Reilly helped put this book into the form in which you now see it.

I also must thank my first-rate reviewers for the first edition, first and foremost my dear wife Betty Cerar, who still knows more about the caffeinated beverage that I drink while programming than the programming language I use, but whose passion for clear expression and correct grammar has benefited so much of my writing during our life together. Jonathan Knudsen, Andy Oram, and David Flanagan commented on the outline when it was little more than a list of chapters and recipes, and yet were able to see the kind of book it could become, and to suggest ways to make it better. Learning Tree instructor Jim Burgess read most of the first edition with a very critical eye on locution, formulation, and code. Bil Lewis and Mike Slinn (*mslinn@mslinn.com*) made helpful comments on multiple drafts of the book. Ron Hitchens (*ron@ronsoft.com*) and Marc Loy carefully read the entire final draft of the first edition. I am grateful to Mike Loukides for his encouragement and support throughout the process. Editor Sue Miller helped shepherd the manuscript through the somewhat energetic final phases of production. Sarah Slocombe read the XML chapter in its entirety and made many lucid suggestions; unfortunately time did not permit me to include all of them in the first edition. Each of these people made this book better in many ways, particularly by suggesting additional recipes or revising existing ones. The faults that remain are my own.

I used a variety of tools and operating systems in preparing, compiling, and testing the first edition. The developers of OpenBSD (*http://www.openbsd.org*), "the proactively secure Unix-like system," deserve thanks for making a stable and secure Unix clone that is also closer to traditional Unix than other freeware systems. I used the *vi* editor (*vi* on OpenBSD and *vim* on Windows) while inputting the original manuscript in XML, and Adobe FrameMaker to format the documents. Each of these is an excellent tool in its own way, but I must add a caveat about FrameMaker. Adobe had four years from the release of OS X until I started this book revision cycle during which they could have produced a current Macintosh version of FrameMaker. They did not do so, requiring me to do the revision in the increasingly ancient Classic environment. Strangely enough, their Mac sales of FrameMaker dropped steadily during this period, until, during the final production of this book, Adobe officially announced that it would no longer be producing any Macintosh versions of this excellent publishing software, ever.

No book on Java would be complete without a quadrium[*] of thanks to James Gosling for inventing the first Unix Emacs, the *sc* spreadsheet, the NeWS window system, and Java. Thanks also to his employer Sun Microsystems (NASDAQ SUNW) for creating not only the Java language but an incredible array of Java tools and API libraries freely available over the Internet.

Thanks to Tom and Nathan for the *Perl Cookbook*. Without them I might never have come up with the format for this book.

Willi Powell of Apple Canada provided Mac OS X access in the early days of OS X; I currently have an Apple notebook of my own. Thanks also to Apple for basing OS X on BSD Unix, making Apple the world's largest-volume commercial Unix company.

Thanks to the Tim Horton's Donuts in Bolton, Ontario for great coffee and for not enforcing the 20-minute table limit on the geek with the computer.

To each and every one of you, my sincere thanks.

---

[*] It's a good thing he only invented four major technologies, not five, or I'd have to rephrase that to avoid infringing on an Intel trademark.

# CHAPTER 1

# Getting Started: Compiling, Running, and Debugging

## 1.0 Introduction

This chapter covers some entry-level tasks that you need to know how to do before you can go on—it is said you must crawl before you can walk, and walk before you can ride a bicycle. Before you can try out anything in this book, you need to be able to compile and run your Java code, so I start there, showing several ways: the JDK way, the Ant way, and the Integrated Development Environment (IDE) way. Another issue people run into is setting CLASSPATH correctly, so that's dealt with next. Then I'll discuss a few details about applets, in case you are working on them. Deprecation warnings come next, as you're likely to meet them in maintaining "old" Java code.[*] The chapter ends with some general information about conditional compilation, unit testing, assertions, and debugging.

If you're already happy with your IDE, you may wish to skip some or all of this material. It's here to ensure that everybody can compile and debug their programs before we move on.

## 1.1 Compiling and Running Java: JDK

### Problem

You need to compile and run your Java program.

### Solution

This is one of the few areas where your computer's operating system impinges on Java's portability, so let's get it out of the way first.

---

[*] There is humor in the phrase "old Java code," which should be apparent when you realize that Java had been in circulation for under five years at the time of this book's first edition.

## JDK

Using the command-line Java Development Kit (JDK) may be the best way to keep up with the very latest improvements from Sun. This is not the fastest compiler available by any means; the compiler is written in Java and interpreted at compile time, making it a sensible bootstrapping solution, but not necessarily optimal for speed of development. Nonetheless, using Sun's JDK, the commands are javac to compile and java to run your program (and, on Windows only, javaw to run a program without a console window). For example:

```
C:\javasrc>javac HelloWorld.java

C:\javasrc>java HelloWorld
Hello, World

C:\javasrc>
```

As you can see from the compiler's (lack of) output, this compiler works on the Unix "no news is good news" philosophy: if a program was able to do what you asked it to, it shouldn't bother nattering at you to say that it did so. Many people use this compiler or one of its clones.

There is an optional setting called CLASSPATH, discussed in Recipe 1.4, that controls where Java looks for classes. CLASSPATH, if set, is used by both javac and java. In older versions of Java you had to set your CLASSPATH to include ".", even to run a simple program from the current directory; this is no longer true on Sun's current Java implementations. It may be true on some of the clones.

### Command-line alternatives

Sun's *javac* compiler is the official reference implementation. But it is itself written in Java, and hence must be interpreted at runtime. Some other Java compilers are written in C/C++, so they are quite a bit faster than an interpreted Java compiler. In order to speed up my compilations, I have used Jikes, which is fast (C++), free, and available both for Windows and for Unix. It's also easy to install and is included with the Mac OS X Developer Tools package. For Windows, Linux, and other Unix systems, you can find binaries of the current version on IBM's Jikes web site. If you are using OpenBSD, NetBSD, or FreeBSD, you should only need to run something like:

```
cd /usr/ports/lang/jikes; sudo make install
```

or just download the package file and use pkg_add to get it installed. Visit *http://oss. software.ibm.com/developerworks/projects/jikes/* for Jikes information and downloads.

What I really like about Jikes is that it gives much better error messages than the JDK compiler does. It alerts you to slightly misspelled names, for example. Its messages are often a bit verbose, but you can use the +E option to make it print them in a shorter format. Jikes has many other command-line options, many that are the same as the JDK compiler's, but some that go beyond them. See Jikes's online documentation for details.

Another alternative technology is Kaffe, a product that Transvirtual licenses but also makes available in open source form (at *http://www.kaffe.org/*) under the GNU Public License. Kaffe aims to be a complete JDK replacement, though it has moved rather slowly and is not quite a complete, up-to-date Java 2 clone as of this writing. Again, Kaffe is available for BSD Unix and for Linux in RPM format. Visit the Kaffe web site for the latest information on Kaffe.

Other freeware programs include Japhar, a Java runtime clone, available from *http://www.hungry.com/old-hungry/products/japhar/*, and the IBM Jikes Runtime from the same site as Jikes.

If you really want to get away from the mainstream, consider investigating JNODE, the Java New Operating system Development Idea, at *http://www.jnode.org/*. JNODE is a complete operating system written in Java, a kind of proof of concept. At this point JNODE is probably not something you would use for your main desktop—I've booted it only under Virtual PC on Mac OS X—but it could become that someday.

### Mac OS X

The JDK is pure command-line. At the other end of the spectrum in terms of keyboard-versus-visual, we have the Apple Macintosh. Books have been written about how great the Mac user interface is, and I won't step into that debate. Mac OS X (Release 10.x of Mac OS) is a new technology base built upon a BSD Unix base. As such, it has a regular command line (the Terminal application, hidden away under */Applications/Utilities*), as well as all the traditional Mac tools. It features a full Java implementation, including two GUI packages, Sun's Swing and Apple's own Cocoa. JDK 1.4.2 has been released for Mac OS 10.3 as of this writing; the latest version is always available from Software Update.

Mac OS X users can use the command-line JDK tools as above or Ant (see Recipe 1.7). Compiled classes can be packaged into "clickable applications" using the Jar Packager discussed in Recipe 23.7. Alternately, Mac fans can use one of the many full IDE tools discussed in Recipe 1.3.

## 1.2  Editing and Compiling with a Color-Highlighting Editor

### Problem

You are tired of command-line tools but not ready for an IDE.

### Solution

Use a color-highlighting editor.

## Discussion

It's less than an IDE (see the next recipe), but more than a command line. What is it? It's an editor with Java support. Tools such as TextPad (*http://www.textpad.com*), Visual Slick Edit, and others are low-cost windowed editors (primarily for Windows) that have some amount of Java recognition built-in and the ability to compile from within the editor. TextPad recognizes quite a number of file types, including batch files and shell scripts, C, C++, Java, JSP, JavaScript, and many others. For each of these, it uses color highlighting to show which part of the file being edited comprises keywords, comments, quoted strings, and so on. This is very useful in spotting when part of your code has been swallowed up by an unterminated /* comment or a missing quote. While this isn't the same as the deep understanding of Java that a full IDE might possess, experience has shown that it definitely aids programmer productivity. TextPad also has a "compile Java" command and a "run external program" command. Both of these have the advantage of capturing the entire command output into a window, which may be easier to scroll than a command-line window on some platforms. On the other hand, you don't see the command results until the program terminates, which can be most uncomfortable if your GUI application throws an exception before it puts up its main window. Despite this minor drawback, TextPad is a very useful tool. Other editors that include color highlighting include *vim* (an enhanced version of the Unix tool *vi*, available for Windows and Unix platforms from *http://www.vim.org*), the ever-popular Emacs editor, and many others.

And speaking of Emacs, since it is so extensible, it's natural that people have built enhanced Java capabilities for it. One example is JDEE (Java Development Environment for Emacs), an Emacs "major mode" (jde-mode, based on c-mode) with a set of menu items such as Generate Getters/Setters. You could say that JDEE is in between using a Color-Highlighting Editor and an IDE. The URL for JDEE is *http://jdee.sunsite.dk/*.

Even without JDEE, Emacs features dabbrev-expand, which does class and method name completion. It is, however, based on what's in your current edit buffers, so it doesn't know about classes in the standard API or in external Jars. For that level of functionality, you have to turn to a full-blown IDE, such as those discussed in Recipe 1.3.

# 1.3 Compiling, Running, and Testing with an IDE

## Problem

Several tools are too many.

---

## Solution

Use an integrated development environment.

## Discussion

Many programmers find that using a handful of separate tools—a text editor, a compiler, and a runner program, not to mention a debugger (see Recipe 1.13)—is too many. An *integrated development environment* (IDE[*]) incorporates all of these into a single toolset with a (hopefully consistent) graphical user interface. Many IDEs are available, ranging all the way up to fully integrated tools with their own compilers and virtual machines. Class browsers and other features of IDEs round out the purported ease-of-use feature-sets of these tools. It has been argued many times whether an IDE really makes you more productive or if you just have more fun doing the same thing. However, even the JDK maintainers at Sun admit (perhaps for the benefit of their advertisers) that an IDE is often more productive, although it hides many implementation details and tends to generate code that locks you into a particular IDE. Sun's Java Jumpstart CD (part of *Developer Essentials*) said, at one time:

> The JDK software comes with a minimal set of tools. Serious developers are advised to use a professional Integrated Development Environment with JDK 1.2 software. Click on one of the images below to visit external sites and learn more.

This is followed by some (presumably paid) advertising links to various commercial development suites. I do find that IDEs with "incremental compiling" features—which note and report compilation errors as you type, instead of waiting until you are finished typing—do provide somewhat increased productivity for most programmers. Beyond that, I don't plan to debate the IDE versus the command-line process; I use both modes at different times and on different projects. I'm just going to show a few examples of using a couple of the Java-based IDEs.

One IDE that runs on both Windows and Unix platforms is NetBeans, which is a free download. Originally created by NetBeans.com, this IDE was so good that Sun bought the company and now distributes the IDE in two versions that share a lot of code: NetBeans (formerly called Forte, distributed as open source), and Sun One Studio (commercial, not open sourced). There is a plug-in API; some *.nbm* files will work either on the free or the Studio version while others work only on one or the other. You can download the free version and extension modules from *http://www.netbeans.org*; the commercial version can be had from *http://www.sun.com/*.

NetBeans comes with a variety of templates. In Figure 1-1, I have opted for the Swing JFrame template.

---

[*] It takes too long to say, or type, Integrated Development Environment, so I'll use the term IDE from here on. I know you're good at remembering acronyms, especially TLAs.

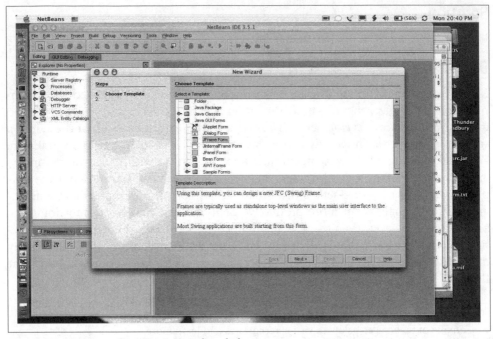

Figure 1-1. NetBeans: New From Template dialog

In Figure 1-2, NetBeans lets me specify a class name and package name for the new program I am building.

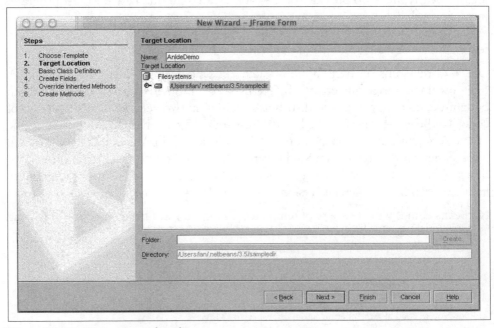

Figure 1-2. NetBeans: Name that class

In Figure 1-3, I am building the GUI using NetBeans' GUI builder. Select a visual component in the upper right, and click on the form where you want it. While there are several things about NetBeans that most people find quirky, I do like the fact that it defaults to using a BorderLayout; some other IDEs default to using no layout at all, and the resulting GUIs do not resize gracefully.

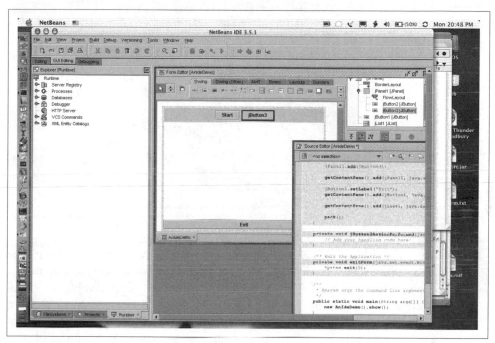

*Figure 1-3. NetBeans: GUI building*

I also like the way NetBeans handles GUI action handlers (see Recipe 14.4). You simply double click on the GUI control you want to handle actions for, and NetBeans creates an action handler for it and puts you into the editor to type the code for the action handler. In this case, I made a deliberate typing error to show the effects; when I click the Build Project menu item, the offending line of code is highlighted in bright red, both in the source code and in the error listing from the compiler (see Figure 1-4).

Another popular cross-platform, open source IDE for Java is Eclipse, originally from IBM. Just as NetBeans is the basis of Sun Studio, so Eclipse is the basis of IBM's WebSphere Studio Application Developer.[*] Eclipse tends to have more options than NetBeans; see for example, its New Java Class wizard shown in Figure 1-5. It also features a number of refactoring capabilities, shown in Figure 1-6.

---

[*] WebSphere Studio Application Developer describes itself, in its online help, as "IBM's implementation of Eclipse" and gives a link to *http://www.eclipse.org/*.

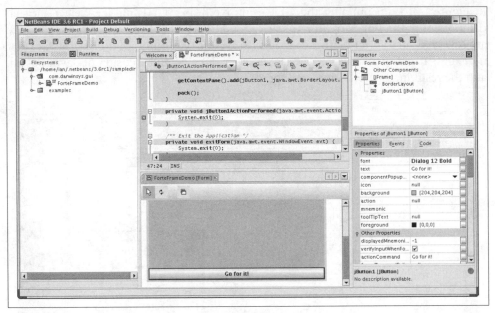

*Figure 1-4. NetBeans: Compilation error highlighted*

Of these two major open source IDEs, many people like NetBeans and many like Eclipse. Many other IDEs are available for Java, especially on Windows, and almost everybody who uses one has a favorite, such as Borland JBuilder, WebGain Visual Cafe, Sun Studio, or IBM WebSphere Studio Application Developer. Most of them have a free version and/or a trial version as well as a Pro version. For up-to-date comparisons, you may want to consult the glossy magazines, since IDEs are updated relatively often.

Mac OS X includes Apple's Developer Tools. The main IDE is Xcode in 10.3 (shown in Figure 1-7). Unlike most IDEs, Apple's IDE does not include a GUI builder; a separate program, called Interface Builder, handles this task. Both tools can be used with a variety of programming languages, including C/C++, Objective C, and Java. While the Interface Builder is one of the nicer GUI builder tools around, at present it builds only Cocoa applications, not Swing applications. Figure 1-8 shows Xcode running a trivial application built using its default frame-based template.

How do you choose an IDE? Given that all the major IDEs can be downloaded free (Eclipse, NetBeans), "free" but without source, or at least in free trial versions, you should try a few and see which one best fits the kind of development you do. Regardless of what platform you use to develop Java, if you have a Java runtime, you should have plenty of IDEs from which to choose.

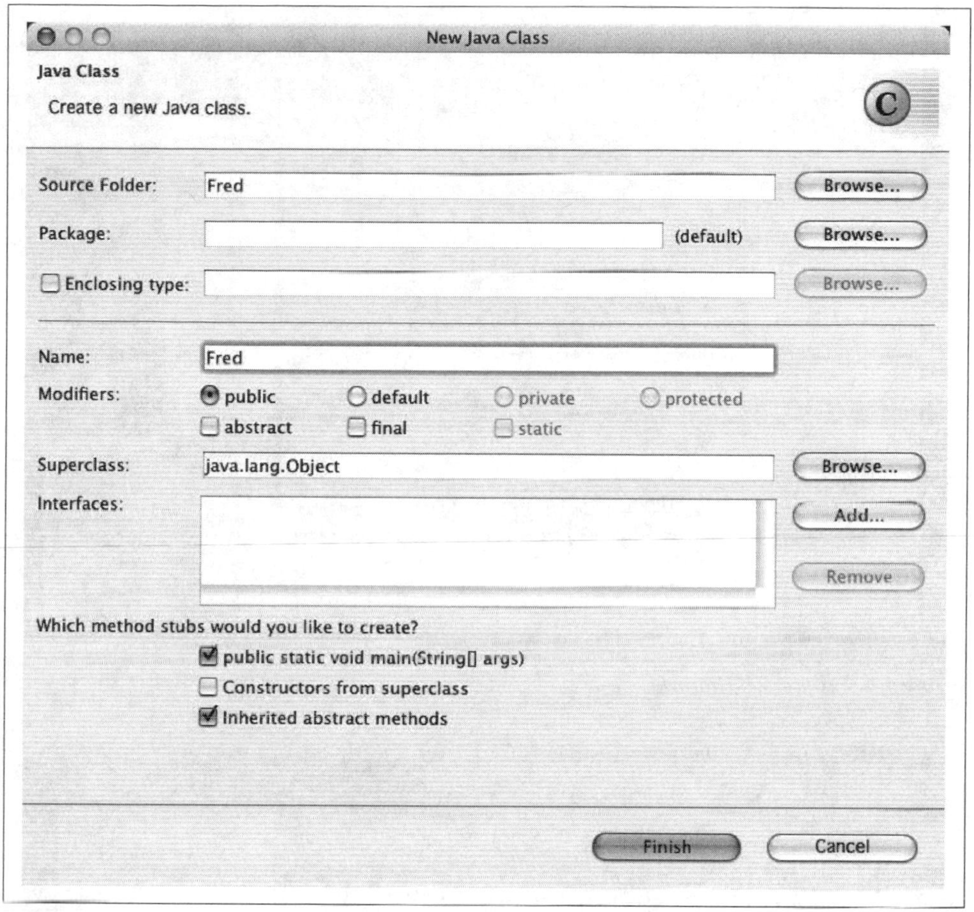

Figure 1-5. Eclipse: New Java Class

## See Also

For NetBeans, see *NetBeans: The Definitive Guide* by Tim Boudreau, Jesse Glick, Simeon Greene, Vaughn Spurlin, and Jack J. Woehret (O'Reilly). For Eclipse, see *Eclipse Cookbook* by Steve Holzner (O'Reilly) or *The Java Developer's Guide to Eclipse* by Sherry Shavor, Jim D'Anjou, Scott Fairbrother, Dan Kehn, John Kellerman, and Pat McCarthy (Addison Wesley). Both IDEs are extensible; if you're interested in extending Eclipse, the book *Contributing to Eclipse: Principles, Patterns, and Plugins* (Addison Wesley) was written by noted OO theorists Erich Gamma (lead author of *Design Patterns*) and Kent Beck (author of *Extreme Programming Explained*).

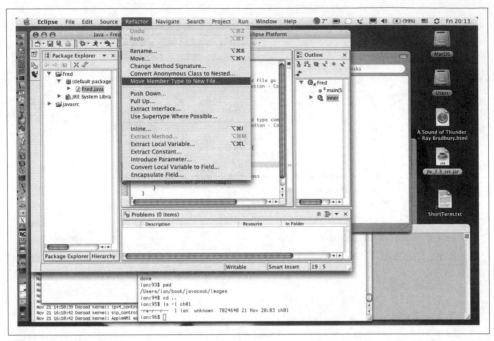

*Figure 1-6. Eclipse: Refactoring*

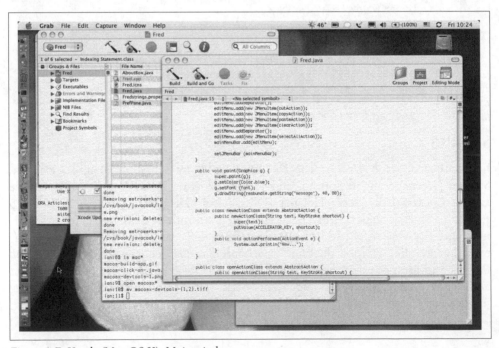

*Figure 1-7. Xcode (Mac OS X): Main windows*

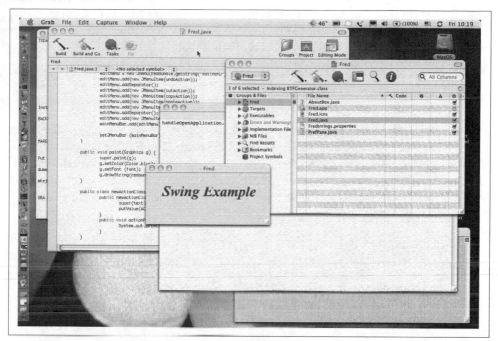

*Figure 1-8. Xcode IDE (Mac OS X): Application built and running*

## 1.4    Using CLASSPATH Effectively

### Problem

You need to keep your class files in a common directory, or you're wrestling with CLASSPATH.

### Solution

Set CLASSPATH to the list of directories and/or JAR files that contain the classes you want.

### Discussion

CLASSPATH is one of the more "interesting" aspects of using Java. You can store your class files in any of a number of directories, JAR files, or zip files. Just like the PATH your system uses for finding programs, the CLASSPATH is used by the Java runtime to find classes. Even when you type something as simple as *java Hello-World*, the Java interpreter looks in each of the places named in your CLASSPATH until it finds a match. Let's work through an example.

The CLASSPATH can be set as an environment variable on systems that support this (Unix, including Mac OS X, and Windows). You set it the same way you set other environment variables, such as your PATH environment variable.

Alternatively, you can specify the CLASSPATH for a given command on its command line:

```
java -classpath \c:\ian\classes MyProg
```

Suppose your CLASSPATH were set to *C:\classes;*. on Windows or *~/classes:*. on Unix (on the Mac, you can set the CLASSPATH with JBindery). Suppose you had just compiled a file named *HelloWorld.java* into *HelloWorld.class* and tried to run it. On Unix, if you run one of the kernel tracing tools (trace, strace, truss, ktrace), you would probably see the Java program open (or stat, or access) the following files:

- Some file(s) in the JDK directory
- Then *~/classes/HelloWorld.class*, which it probably wouldn't find
- And *./HelloWorld.class*, which it would find, open, and read into memory

The vague "some file(s) in the JDK directory" is release-dependent. On Sun's JDK it can be found in the system properties:

```
sun.boot.class.path = C:\JDK1.4\JRE\lib\rt.jar;C:\JDK1.4\JRE\lib\i18n.jar;C:\JDK1.4\
JRE\classes
```

The file *rt.jar* is the runtime stuff; *i18n.jar* is the internationalization; and *classes* is an optional directory where you can install additional classes.

Suppose you had also installed the JAR file containing the supporting classes for programs from this book, *darwinsys.jar*. You might then set your CLASSPATH to *C:\classes;C:\classes\darwinsys.jar;*. on Windows or *~/classes:~/classes/darwinsys.jar:*. on Unix. Notice that you *do* need to list the JAR file explicitly. Unlike a single class file, placing a JAR file into a directory listed in your CLASSPATH does not suffice to make it available.

Note that certain specialized programs (such as a web server running Java Servlets) may not use either bootpath or CLASSPATH as shown; these application servers typically provide their own ClassLoader (see Recipe 25.4 for information on class loaders).

Another useful tool in the JDK is *javap*, which, by default, prints the external face of a class file: its full name, its public methods and fields, and so on. If you ran a command like *javap HelloWorld* under kernel tracing, you would find that it opened, looked around in, and read from a file *\jdk\lib\tools.jar*, and then got around to looking for your HelloWorld class, as previously. Yet there is no entry for this in your CLASSPATH setting. What's happening here is that the *javap* command sets its CLASSPATH internally to include the *tools.jar* file. If it can do this, why can't you? You can, but not as easily as you might expect. If you try the obvious first attempt at doing a setProperty("java.class.path") to itself, plus the delimiter, plus *jdk/lib/ tools.jar*, you won't be able to find the JavaP class (sun.tools.java.JavaP); the CLASSPATH is set in the java.class.path at the beginning of execution, before your program starts. You can try it manually and see that it works if you set it beforehand:

```
C:\javasrc>java -classpath /jdk1.4/lib/tools.jar sun.tools.javap.JavaP
Usage: javap <options> <classes>...
```

If you need to do this in an application, you can either set it in a startup script, as we did here, or write C code to start Java, which is described in Recipe 26.6.

How can you easily store class files in a directory in your CLASSPATH? The *javac* command has a -d dir option, which specifies where the compiler output should go. For example, using -d to put the HelloWorld class file into my */classes* directory, I just type:

```
javac -d /classes HelloWorld.java
```

As long as this directory remains in my CLASSPATH, I can access the class file regardless of my current directory. That's one of the key benefits of using CLASS-PATH.

Managing CLASSPATH can be tricky, particularly when you alternate among several JVMs (as I do) or when you have multiple directories in which to look for JAR files. You may want to use some sort of batch file or shell script to control this. Here is part of the script that I use. It was written for the Korn shell on Unix, but similar scripts could be written in the C shell or as a DOS batch file.

```
# These guys must be present in my classpath...
export CLASSPATH=/home/ian/classes/darwinsys.jar:

# Now a for loop, testing for .jar/.zip or [ -d ... ]
OPT_JARS="$HOME/classes $HOME/classes/*.jar
    ${JAVAHOME}/jre/lib/ext/*.jar
    /usr/local/antlr-2.6.0"

for thing in $OPT_JARS
do
    if [ -f $thing ]; then        //must be either a file...
        CLASSPATH="$CLASSPATH:$thing"
    else if [ -d $thing ]; then       //or a directory
        CLASSPATH="$CLASSPATH:$thing"
    fi
done
CLASSPATH="$CLASSPATH:."
```

This builds a minimum CLASSPATH out of *darwinsys.jar*, then goes through a list of other files and directories to check that each is present on this system (I use this script on several machines on a network), and ends up adding a dot (.) to the end of the CLASSPATH.

## 1.5 Using the com.darwinsys API Classes from This Book

### Problem

You want to try out my example code and/or use my utility classes.

### Solution

I have built up a fairly sizeable collection of reusable classes into my own API, which I use in my own Java projects. I use example code from it throughout this book, and I use classes from it in many of the other examples. So, if you're going to be downloading and compiling the examples individually, you should first download the file *darwinsys.jar* and include it in your CLASSPATH. Note that if you are going to build all of my source code (as in Recipe 1.6), you can skip this download because the top-level Ant file starts off by building the JAR file for this API.

### Discussion

I have split the `com.darwinsys.util` package from the first edition of this book into about a dozen `com.darwinsys` packages, listed in Table 1-1. I have also added many new classes; these packages now include approximately 50 classes and interfaces. You can peruse the documentation online at *http://javacook.darwinsys.com/docs/api*.

*Table 1-1. The com.darwinsys packages*

| Package name | Package description |
| --- | --- |
| com.darwinsys.database | Classes for dealing with databases in a general way |
| com.darwinsys.html | Classes (only one so far) for dealing with HTML |
| com.darwinsys.io | Classes for input and output operations, using Java's underlying I/O classes |
| com.darwinsys.lang | Classes for dealing with standard features of Java |
| com.darwinsys.macosui | Classes for dealing with Swing GUIs slightly differently under Mac OS X |
| com.darwinsys.mail | Classes for dealing with e-mail, mainly a convenience class for sending mail |
| com.darwinsys.sql | Classes for dealing with SQL databases |
| com.darwinsys.swingui | Classes for helping construct and use Swing GUIs |
| com.darwinsys.swingui.layout | A few interesting LayoutManager implementations |
| com.darwinsys.util | A few miscellaneous utility classes |

Many of these classes are used as examples in this book; just look for files whose first line is:

```
package com.darwinsys.nnn;
```

You'll also find that many examples have imports from the `com.darwinsys` packages.

# 1.6 Compiling the Source Code Examples from This Book

## Problem

You want to try out my examples.

## Solution

Download the latest archive of the book source files, unpack it, edit *build.properties*, and run Ant (see Recipe 1.7) to compile the files.

## Discussion

You can download the latest version of the source code for all the examples in this book from the book's web site, *http://javacook.darwinsys.com/*. You can get it all as one large file containing all the source code, in a file called *javacooksrc.jar*, which you should unzip into an empty directory someplace convenient, wherever you like to keep source code. You should then edit the file *build.properties*, specifying the locations of some jar files. Editing *build.properties* and then running ant in this directory first creates a file called *darwinsys.jar*\* containing the com.darwinsys API described in Recipe 1.5 (you will probably want to add this file to your CLASS-PATH—see Recipe 1.4—or to your *JDKHOME/jre/lib/ext* directory). Ant goes on to build as many of the other examples as it can given the settings in *build.properties*, your Java runtime, and your operating system. The files are roughly organized in per-chapter directories, but there is a lot of overlap and cross-referencing. Because of this, I have prepared a cross-reference file named *index-bychapter.html*. A mechanically generated file called *index-byname.html* can be used if you know the name of the file you want (and remember that Java source files almost always have the same name as the public class they contain). The canonical index file, *index.html*, links to both these files.

If you have JDK 1.3 or 1.4 instead of 1.5, a few files will not compile, but the compiler prints a comment about needing 1.4 or 1.5. And the "native code" examples may not compile at all. Most everything else should compile correctly.

If you're not using Ant, well, you should! But if you can't, or won't, after you've set your CLASSPATH, you should compile what you need. You will need the *darwinsys.jar* file; you should probably just download it. In some directories you can simply say *javac \*.java* or *jikes \*.java*. But in others, you have to set your CLASSPATH manually; if some files that you need won't compile, you'll have to look in the Ant file *build.xml* to see what jar files are needed. I no longer provide Makefiles; Ant has simply become the dominant build tool for Java developers.

---

\* If you have a file called *com-darwinsys-util.jar*, that file contains the old API described in the first edition and will not work with the examples in this book.

There may also be times when you don't want to download the entire archive—if you just need a bit of code in a hurry—so you can access those index files and the resulting directory, for "anyplace, anytime access" on the same web site, *http:// javacook.darwinsys.com/*

### A caveat

One of the practices of Extreme Programming is Continuous Refactoring—the ability to improve any part of the code base at any time. Don't be surprised if the code in the online source directory is different from what appears in the book; it is a rare week that I don't make some improvement to the code, and the results are put online quite often.

# 1.7   Automating Compilation with Ant

## Problem

You get tired of typing *javac* and *java* commands.

## Solution

Use the Ant program to direct your compilations.

## Discussion

The intricacies of Makefiles have led to the development of a pure Java solution for automating the build process. Ant is free software; it is available in source form or ready-to-run from the Apache Foundation's Jakarta Project web site, at *http:// jakarta.apache.org/ant/*. Like *make*, Ant uses a file or files—written in XML—listing what to do and, if necessary, how to do it. These rules are intended to be platform-independent, though you can of course write platform-specific recipes if necessary.

To use Ant, you must create a 15 to 30 line file specifying various options. This file should be called *build.xml*; if you call it anything else, you'll have to give a special command-line argument every time you run Ant. Example 1-1 shows the build script used to build the files in the *starting* directory. See Recipe 21.0 for a discussion of the XML syntax. For now, note that the <!-- tag begins an XML comment, which extends to the --> tag.

*Example 1-1. Ant example file (build.xml)*

```
<project name="Java Cookbook Examples" default="compile" basedir=".">

  <!-- Set global properties for this build -->
  <property name="src" value="."/>
  <property name="build" value="build"/>
  <!-- Specify the compiler to use.
```

*Example 1-1. Ant example file (build.xml) (continued)*

```
    Using jikes is supported but requires rt.jar in classpath. -->
  <property name="build.compiler" value="modern"/>

  <target name="init">
    <!-- Create the time stamp -->
    <tstamp/>
    <!-- Create the build directory structure used by compile -->
    <mkdir dir="${build}"/>
  </target>

  <!-- Specify what to compile. This builds everything -->
  <target name="compile" depends="init">

    <!-- Compile the java code from ${src} into ${build} -->
    <javac srcdir="${src}" destdir="${build}"
           classpath="../darwinsys.jar"/>
  </target>

</project>
```

When you run Ant, it produces a reasonable amount of notification as it goes:

```
$ ant compile
Buildfile: build.xml
Project base dir set to: /home/ian/javasrc/starting
Executing Target: init
Executing Target: compile
Compiling 19 source files to /home/ian/javasrc/starting/build
Performing a Modern Compile
Copying 22 support files to /home/ian/javasrc/starting/build
Completed in 8 seconds
$
```

## See Also

The sidebar "make Versus Ant"; *Ant: The Definitive Guide* by Jesse E. Tilly and Eric M. Burke (O'Reilly).

# 1.8    Running Applets

## Problem

You want to run an applet.

## Solution

Write a class that extends java.applet.Applet; write some HTML and point a browser at it.

# make Versus Ant

*make* is another build tool used in Unix and C/C++ development. *make* and Ant each have advantages; I'll try to stay neutral, although I admit I have been using *make* far longer than I have Ant.

*Makefiles* are shorter. No contest. *make* has its own language instead of using XML, so it can be a lot more terse. *make* runs faster; it's written in C. However, Ant has the ability to run many Java tasks at once—such as the built-in Java compiler, *jar/war/tar/zip* files, and many more—to the extent that it may be more efficient to run several Java compilations in one Ant process than to run the same compilations using make. That is, once the JVM that is running Ant itself is up and running, it doesn't take long at all to run the Java compiler and run the compiled class. This is Java as it was meant to be!

Ant files can do more. The *javac* task in Ant, for example, automatically finds all the *\*.java* files in subdirectories. With *make*, a sub-*make* is normally required. And the `include` directive for subdirectories differs between GNU *make* and BSD *make*.

Ant has special knowledge of CLASSPATH, making it easy to set a CLASSPATH in various ways for compile time. See the CLASSPATH setting in Example 1-1. You may have to duplicate this in other ways—shell scripts or batch files—for manually running or testing your application.

*make* is simpler to extend, but harder to do so portably. You can write a one-line *make* rule for getting a CVS archive from a remote site, but you may run into incompatibilities between GNU *make*, BSD *make*, etc. There is a built-in Ant task for getting an archive from CVS using Ant; it was written as a Java source file instead of just a series of command-line commands.

*make* has been around much longer. There are millions (literally) more *Makefiles* than Ant files. Non-Java developers have typically not heard of Ant; they almost all use *make*. Almost all non-Java open source projects use *make*.

*make* is easier to start with. Ant's advantages make more sense on larger projects. Yet of the two, only *make* has been used on the really large projects. For example, *make* is used for telephone switch source code, which consists of hundreds of thousands of source files containing tens or hundreds of millions of lines of source code. By contrast, Tomcat 4 is about 340,000 lines of code, and the JBoss J2EE server about 560,000 lines. The use of Ant is growing steadily, particularly now that most of the widely used Java IDEs (JBuilder, Eclipse, NetBeans, and others) have interfaces to Ant. Effectively all Java open source projects use Ant.

*make* is included with most Unix and Unix-like systems and shipped with many Windows IDEs. Ant is not included with any operating system but is included with many open source Java packages.

To sum up, although *make* and Ant are both good tools, new Java projects should use Ant.

# Discussion

An *applet* is simply a Java class that extends java.applet.Applet, and in doing so inherits the functionality it needs to be viewable inside a web page in a Java-enabled web browser.* All that's necessary is an HTML page referring to the applet. This HTML page requires an applet tag with a minimum of three *attributes*, or modifiers: the name of the applet itself and its onscreen width and height in screen dots or pixels. This is not the place for me to teach you HTML syntax—there is some of that in Recipe 18.1—but I'll show my HTML applet template file. Many of the IDEs write a page like this if you use their "build new applet" wizards:

```
<html>
<head><title>A Demonstration</title></head>
<body>
<h1>My TEMPLATE Applet</h1>
<applet code="CCC"  width="200" height="200">
</applet>
</body>
</html>
```

You can probably intuit from this just about all you need to get started. For a little more detail, see Recipe 18.1. Once you've created this file (replacing the CCC with the fully qualified class name of your applet—e.g., code="com.foo.MyApplet") and placed it in the same directory as the class file, you need only tell a Java-enabled web browser to view the HTML page, and the applet should be included in it.

All right, so the applet appeared and it even almost worked. Make a change to the Java source and recompile. Click the browser's Reload button. Chances are you're still running the old version! Browsers aren't very good at debugging applets. You can sometimes get around this by holding down the Shift key while you click Reload. But to be sure, use AppletViewer, a kind of mini-browser included in the JDK. You need to give it the HTML file, just like a regular browser. Sun's AppletViewer (shown in Figure 1-9 under Windows) has an explicit Reload button that actually reloads the applet. And it has other features, such as debugging hooks, and other information displays. It also has a View → Tag option that lets you resize the window until the applet looks best, and then you can copy and paste the tag—including the adjusted width and height attributes—into a longer HTML document.

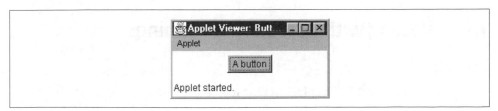

*Figure 1-9. Sun JDK AppletViewer*

---

* Includes Netscape/Mozilla, Apple Safari, MS Internet Explorer, KDE Konqueror, and most others.

The Mac OS X runtime includes both the standard AppletViewer from Sun and Apple's own implementation (available as */Applications/Utilities/Java/Applet Launcher*, shown in Figure 1-10), which is more colorful but slightly different. It has no Reload item in its menu; you close the Applet's window and press the Launch button to reload. It also lets you load a new HTML file by typing in the URL field (or pressing Open... and browsing), which is more efficient than closing and restarting the traditional AppletViewer when the HTML file changes or when you want to invoke a different file.

*Figure 1-10. Apple Mac OS X applet launcher*

Neither the Sun version nor the Apple version is a full applet runtime; features such as jumping to a new document do not work. But they are very good tools for debugging applets. Learn to use the AppletViewer that comes with your JDK or IDE.

## See Also

The bad news about applets is that they either can't use features of current Java versions or they run into the dreaded browser-incompatibility issue. In Recipe 23.6, I show how to use the Java Plug-in to get around this. In Recipe 23.13, I talk about Java Web Start, a relatively new technique for distributing applications over the Web in a way similar to how applets are downloaded; with JWS, programs are downloaded using HTTP but stored as, and run as, regular applications on your system's local disk.

# 1.9   Dealing with Deprecation Warnings

## Problem

Your code used to compile cleanly, but now it gives deprecation warnings.

## Solution

You must have blinked. Either live—dangerously—with the warnings or revise your code to eliminate them.

## Discussion

Each new release of Java includes a lot of powerful new functionality, but at a price: during the evolution of this new stuff, Java's maintainers find some old stuff that wasn't done right and shouldn't be used anymore because they can't really fix it. In building JDK 1.1, for example, they realized that the java.util.Date class had some serious limitations with regard to internationalization. Accordingly, many of the Date class methods and constructors are marked "deprecated." To *deprecate* something means, according to the *American Heritage Dictionary*, to "express disapproval of; deplore." Java's developers are therefore disapproving of the old way of doing things. Try compiling this code:

```
import java.util.Date;

/** Demonstrate deprecation warning */
public class Deprec {

    public static void main(String[] av) {

        // Create a Date object for May 5, 1986
        // EXPECT DEPRECATION WARNING
        Date d = new Date(86, 04, 05);          // May 5, 1986
        System.out.println("Date is " + d);
    }
}
```

What happened? When I compile it, I get this warning:

```
C:\javasrc>javac Deprec.java
Note: Deprec.java uses or overrides a deprecated API.  Recompile with
"-deprecation" for details.
1 warning
C:\javasrc>
```

So, we follow orders. Recompile with -deprecation (if using Ant, use <javac deprecation= 'true '...>) for details:

```
C:\javasrc>javac -deprecation Deprec.java
Deprec.java:10: warning: constructor Date(int,int,int) in class java.util.Date has
been deprecated
            Date d = new Date(86, 04, 05);          // May 5, 1986
                     ^
1 warning

C:\javasrc>
```

The warning is simple: the Date constructor that takes three integer arguments has been deprecated. How do you fix it? The answer is, as in most questions of usage, to refer to the Javadoc documentation for the class. In Java 2, the introduction to the Date page says, in part:

The class Date represents a specific instant in time, with millisecond precision.

Prior to JDK 1.1, the class Date had two additional functions. It allowed the interpretation of dates as year, month, day, hour, minute, and second values. It also allowed the formatting and parsing of date strings. Unfortunately, the API for these functions was not amenable to internationalization. As of JDK 1.1, the Calendar class should be used to convert between dates and time fields and the DateFormat class should be used to format and parse date strings. The corresponding methods in Date are deprecated.

And more specifically, in the description of the three-integer constructor, it says:

Date(int year, int month, int date)

Deprecated. As of JDK version 1.1, replaced by Calendar.set(year + 1900, month, date) or GregorianCalendar(year + 1900, month, date).

As a general rule, when something has been deprecated, you should not use it in any new code and, when maintaining code, strive to eliminate the deprecation warnings.

The main areas of deprecation warnings in the standard API are Date (as mentioned), JDK 1.0 event handling, and some methods—a few of them important—in the Thread class.

You can also deprecate your own code. Put in a doc comment (see Recipe 23.2) with the @deprecated tag immediately before the class or method you wish to deprecate.

# 1.10  Conditional Debugging Without #ifdef

## Problem

You want conditional compilation and Java doesn't seem to provide it.

## Solution

Use constants, command-line arguments, or assertions (Recipe 1.12), depending upon the goal.

## Discussion

Some older languages such as C, PL/I, and C++ provide a feature known as *conditional compilation*. Conditional compilation means that parts of the program can be included or excluded at compile time based upon some condition. One thing it's often used for is to include or exclude debugging print statements. When the program appears to be working, the developer is struck by a fit of hubris and removes all the error checking. A more common rationale is that the developer wants to make the finished program smaller—a worthy goal—or make it run faster by removing conditional statements.

### Conditional compilation?

Although Java lacks any explicit conditional compilation, a kind of conditional compilation is implicit in the language. All Java compilers must do *flow analysis* to ensure that all paths to a local variable's usage pass through a statement that assigns it a value first, that all returns from a function pass out via someplace that provides a return value, and so on. Imagine what the compiler will do when it finds an if statement whose value is known to be false at compile time. Why should it even generate code for the condition? True, you say, but how can the results of an if statement be known at compile time? Simple: through final boolean variables. Further, if the value of the if condition is known to be false, then the body of the if statement should not be emitted by the compiler either. Presto—instant conditional compilation!

```
// IfDef.java
final boolean DEBUG = false;
System.out.println("Hello, World ");
if (DEBUG) {
        System.out.println("Life is a voyage, not a destination");
}
```

Compilation of this program and examination of the resulting class file reveals that the string "Hello" does appear, but the conditionally printed epigram does not. The entire println has been omitted from the class file. So Java does have its own conditional compilation mechanism.

```
darian$ jr IfDef
 jikes +E  IfDef.java
 java IfDef
Hello, World
darian$ strings IfDef.class | grep Life # not found!
darian$ javac IfDef.java # try another compiler
darian$ strings IfDef.class | grep Life # still not found!
darian$
```

What if we want to use debugging code similar to this but have the condition applied at runtime? We can use System.properties (Recipe 2.2) to fetch a variable. Recipe 1.11 uses my Debug class as an example of a class whose entire behavior is controlled this way.

But this is as good a place as any to interject about another feature—inline code generation. The C/C++ world has a language keyword inline, which is a hint to the compiler that the function (method) is not needed outside the current source file. Therefore, when the C compiler is generating machine code, a call to the function marked with inline can be replaced by the actual method body, eliminating the overhead of pushing arguments onto a stack, passing control, retrieving parameters, and returning values. In Java, making a method final enables the compiler to know that it can be inlined, or emitted in line. This is an optional optimization that the compiler is not obliged to perform, but may for efficiency.

## See Also

Recipe 1.12.

# 1.11 Debugging Printouts

## Problem

You want to have debugging statements left in your code enabled at runtime.

## Solution

Use my Debug class.

## Discussion

Instead of using the conditional compilation mechanism of Recipe 1.10, you may want to leave your debugging statements in the code but enable them only at runtime when a problem surfaces. This is a good technique for all but the most compute-intensive applications, because the overhead of a simple if statement is not all that great. Let's combine the flexibility of runtime checking with the simple if statement to debug a hypothetical fetch( ) method (part of Fetch.java):

```
String name = "poem";
if (System.getProperty("debug.fetch") != null) {
    System.err.println("Fetching " + name);
}
value = fetch(name);
```

Then, we can compile and run this normally and the debugging statement is omitted. But if we run it with a -D argument to enable debug.fetch, the printout occurs:

```
> java Fetch          # See? No output
> java -Ddebug.fetch Fetch
Fetching poem
>
```

Of course this kind of if statement is tedious to write in large quantities, so I have encapsulated it into a Debug class, which is part of my com.darwinsys.util package. Debug.java appears in full in Recipe 1.17 at the end of this chapter. My Debug class also provides the string "debug." as part of the argument to System.getProperty( ), so we can simplify the previous Fetch example as follows (code in *FetchDebug.java*):

```
String name = "poem", value;
Fetch f = new Fetch( );
Debug.println("fetch", "Fetching " + name);
value = f.fetch(name);
```

Running it behaves identically to the original Fetch:

```
> java FetchDebug     # again, no output
> java -Ddebug.fetch FetchDebug
Fetching poem
>
```

## See Also

Some more comprehensive and flexible "debug printout" mechanisms—including ones that can log across a network connection—are covered in Recipes 17.7, 17.8, and 17.9.

# 1.12  Maintaining Program Correctness with Assertions

## Problem

You want to leave tests in your code but not have runtime checking overhead until you need it.

## Solution

Use the JDK 1.4 Assertions mechanism.

## Discussion

JDK 1.4 introduced a new keyword into the language: assert. The assert keyword takes two arguments separated by a colon (by analogy with the conditional operator): an expression that is asserted by the developer to be true, and a message to be included in the exception that is thrown if the expression is false. To provide for backward compatibility with programs that might have used "assert" as an identifier name on prior JDK versions, JDK 1.4 requires a command-line switch (-source 1.4) that must be provided for assert to be recognized as a keyword. Normally, assertions are meant to be left in place (unlike quick and dirty print statements, which are often put in during one test and then removed). To reduce runtime overhead, assertion checking is not enabled by default; it must be enabled explicitly with the -enableassertions (or -ea) command-line flag. Here is a simple demo program that shows the use of the assertion mechanism:

```
ian:147$  cd testing;
ian:148$ cat AssertDemo.java
public class AssertDemo {
        public static void main(String[] args) {
                int i = 4;
                if (args.length == 1) {
                        i = Integer.parseInt(args[0]);
                }
                assert i > 0 : "i is non-positive";
                System.out.println("Hello after an assertion");
        }
}
ian:149$ javac -source 1.4 AssertDemo.java   # will not compile without 1.4 flag
ian:150$ java AssertDemo   -1
```

```
Hello after an assertion
ian:151$ java -ea  AssertDemo  -1
Exception in thread "main" java.lang.AssertionError: i is non-positive
        at AssertDemo.main(AssertDemo.java:15)
ian:152$
```

# 1.13   Debugging with JDB

## Problem

The use of debugging printouts and assertions in your code is still not enough.

## Solution

Use a debugger, preferably the one that comes with your IDE.

## Discussion

The JDK includes a command-line-based debugger, *jdb*, and any number of IDEs include their own debugging tools. If you've focused on one IDE, learn to use the debugger that it provides. If you're a command-line junkie, you may want to learn at least the basic operations of *jdb*.

Here is a buggy program. It intentionally has bugs introduced so that you can see their effects in a debugger:

```java
/** This program exhibits some bugs, so we can use a debugger */
public class Buggy {
    static String name;

    public static void main(String[] args) {
        int n = name.length();      // bug # 1

        System.out.println(n);

        name += "; The end.";     // bug #2
        System.out.println(name); // #3
    }
}
```

Here is a session using *jdb* to find these bugs:

```
ian> java Buggy
Exception in thread "main" java.lang.NullPointerException
        at Buggy.main(Compiled Code)
ian> jdb Buggy
Initializing jdb...
0xb2:class(Buggy)
> run
run Buggy
running ...
main[1]
```

```
Uncaught exception: java.lang.NullPointerException
        at Buggy.main(Buggy.java:6)
        at sun.tools.agent.MainThread.runMain(Native Method)
        at sun.tools.agent.MainThread.run(MainThread.java:49)

main[1] list
2          public class Buggy {
3                  static String name;
4
5                  public static void main(String[] args) {
6     =>                  int n = name.length();  // bug # 1
7
8                          System.out.println(n);
9
10                         name += "; The end.";   // bug #2
main[1] print Buggy.name
Buggy.name = null
main[1] help
** command list **
threads [threadgroup]      -- list threads
thread <thread id>         -- set default thread
suspend [thread id(s)]     -- suspend threads (default: all)
resume [thread id(s)]      -- resume threads (default: all)
where [thread id] | all    -- dump a thread's stack
wherei [thread id] | all   -- dump a thread's stack, with pc info
threadgroups               -- list threadgroups
threadgroup <name>         -- set current threadgroup

print <id> [id(s)]         -- print object or field
dump <id> [id(s)]          -- print all object information

locals                     -- print all local variables in current stack frame

classes                    -- list currently known classes
methods <class id>         -- list a class's methods

stop in <class id>.<method>[(argument_type,...)] -- set a breakpoint in a method
stop at <class id>:<line> -- set a breakpoint at a line
up [n frames]              -- move up a thread's stack
down [n frames]            -- move down a thread's stack
clear <class id>.<method>[(argument_type,...)]   -- clear a breakpoint in a method
clear <class id>:<line>    -- clear a breakpoint at a line
step                       -- execute current line
step up                    -- execute until the current method returns to its caller
stepi                      -- execute current instruction
next                       -- step one line (step OVER calls)
cont                       -- continue execution from breakpoint

catch <class id>           -- break for the specified exception
ignore <class id>          -- ignore when the specified exception

list [line number|method] -- print source code
use [source file path]     -- display or change the source path
```

```
memory                      -- report memory usage
gc                          -- free unused objects

load classname              -- load Java class to be debugged
run <class> [args]          -- start execution of a loaded Java class
!!                          -- repeat last command
help (or ?)                 -- list commands
exit (or quit)              -- exit debugger
main[1] exit
ian>
```

Many other debuggers are available; a look in the current Java magazines will inform you of them. Many of them work remotely since the Java Debugger API (that which the debuggers use) is network-based.

# 1.14  Unit Testing: Avoid the Need for Debuggers

## Problem

You don't want to have to debug your code.

## Solution

Use unit testing to validate each class as you develop it.

## Discussion

Stopping to use a debugger is time-consuming; it's better to test beforehand. The methodology of *unit testing* has been around for a long time but has been overshadowed by newer methodologies. Unit testing is a tried and true means of getting your code tested in small blocks. Typically, in an OO language like Java, unit testing is applied to individual classes, in contrast to "black box" testing where the entire application is tested.

I have long been an advocate of this very basic testing methodology. Indeed, developers of the software methodology known as Extreme Programming (XP for short; see *http://www.extremeprogramming.org*) advocate writing the unit tests *before* you write the code, and they also advocate running your tests almost every time you compile. This group of extremists has some very well-known leaders, including Gamma and Beck of *Design Patterns* fame. I definitely go along with their advocacy of unit testing.

Indeed, many of my classes come with a "built-in" unit test. Classes that are not main programs in their own right often include a main method that just tests out the functionality of the class. Here is an example:

```
/** A simple class used to demonstrate unit testing. */
public class Person {
    protected String fullName;
    protected String firstName, lastName;
```

```
/** Construct a Person using his/her first+last names. */
public Person(String firstName, String lastName) {
    this.firstName = firstName;
    this.lastName = lastName;
}

/** Get the person's full name */
public String getFullName() {
    if (fullName != null)
        return fullName;
    return firstName + " " + lastName;
}

/** Simple test program. */
public static void main(String[] argv) {
    Person p = new Person("Ian", "Darwin");
    String f = p.getFullName();
    if (!f.equals("Ian Darwin"))
        throw new IllegalStateException("Name concatenation broken");
    System.out.println("Fullname " + f + " looks good");
}
}
```

What surprised me is that, before encountering XP, I used to think I did this often, but an actual inspection of two projects indicated that only about a third of my classes had test cases, either internally or externally. Clearly what is needed is a uniform methodology. That is provided by JUnit.

JUnit is a Java-centric methodology for providing test cases. You can freely download JUnit from the obvious web site, *http://www.junit.org*. JUnit is a very simple but useful testing tool. It is easy to use—you just write a test class that has a series of methods whose names begin with test. JUnit uses introspection (see Chapter 25) to find all these methods, and then it runs them for you! Extensions to JUnit handle tasks as diverse as load testing and testing Enterprise JavaBeans (EJBs); the JUnit web site provides links to these extensions.

How do you get started using JUnit? All that's necessary is to write a test. Here I have excerpted the test from my Person class and placed it into a class PersonTest. Note the obvious naming pattern.

```
import junit.framework.*;

/** A simple test case for Person */
public class PersonTest extends TestCase {

    /** JUnit test classes require this constructor */
    public PersonTest(String name) {
        super(name);
    }

    public void testNameConcat() {
        Person p = new Person("Ian", "Darwin");
```

```
            String f = p.getFullName( );
            assertEquals(f, "Ian Darwin");
        }

    }
```

To run it, I need only compile the test and invoke the test harness junit:

```
daroad.darwinsys.com$ javac PersonTest.java
daroad.darwinsys.com$ java junit.textui.TestRunner PersonTest
.
Time: 0.188

OK (1 tests)

daroad.darwinsys.com$
```

The use of a full class name is a bit tedious, so I have a script named *jtest* that invokes it; I just say *jtest Person* and it runs the previous command for me.

```
#!/bin/sh

exec java junit.textui.TestRunner ${1}Test
```

In fact, even that is tedious, so I usually have a *regress* target in my Ant scripts. There is a junit task in Ant's "Optional Tasks" package.[*] Using it is easy:

```
<target  name="regress" depends="build">
    <junit>
            <test name="PersonTest" />
    </junit>
</target>
```

## See Also

If you prefer flashier GUI output, several JUnit variants (built using Swing and AWT; see Chapter 14) will run the tests with a GUI.

JUnit offers classes for building comprehensive test suites and comes with considerable documentation of its own; download the program from the web site listed earlier.

Also, for testing graphical components, I have developed a simple component tester, described in Recipe 13.2.

Remember: *Test early and often!*

# 1.15   Getting Readable Tracebacks

## Problem

You're getting an exception stack trace at runtime, but most of the important parts don't have line numbers.

---

[*] In some versions of Ant, you may need an additional download for this to function.

---

## Solution

Be sure you have compiled with debugging enabled. On older systems, disable JIT and run it again, or use the current HotSpot runtime.

## Discussion

When a Java program throws an exception, the exception propagates up the call stack until there is a catch clause that matches it. If none is found, the Java interpreter program that invoked your main( ) method catches the exception and prints a stack traceback showing all the method calls that got from the top of the program to the place where the exception was thrown. You can print this traceback yourself in any catch clause: the Throwable class has several methods called printStackTrace( ).

The traceback includes line numbers only if they were compiled in. When using Sun's javac, this is the default. When using Ant's javac task, this is not the default; you must be sure you have used <javac debug="true" ...> in your *build.xml* file if you want line numbers.

The Just-In-Time (JIT) translation process consists of having the Java runtime convert part of your compiled class file into machine language so that it can run at full execution speed. This is a necessary step for making Java programs run under interpretation and still be acceptably fast. However, in the early days of Java, its one drawback was that it generally lost the line numbers. Hence, when your program died, you still got a stack traceback but it no longer showed the line numbers where the error occurred. So we have the trade-off of making the program run faster, but harder to debug. Modern versions of Sun's Java runtime include the HotSpot Just-In-Time translator, which doesn't have this problem.

If you're still using an older (or non-Sun) JIT, there is a way around this. If the program is getting a stack traceback and you want to make it readable, you need only disable the JIT processing. How you do this depends upon what release of Java you are using. On JDK 1.2 and above, you need only set the environment variable JAVA_COMPILER to the value NONE, using the appropriate *set* command:

```
C:\> set JAVA_COMPILER=NONE # DOS, Windows
setenv JAVA_COMPILER NONE   # Unix Csh
export JAVA_COMPILER=NONE # Unix Ksh, modern sh
```

To make this permanent, you would set it in the appropriate configuration file on your system; on recent versions of Windows, you can also set environment variables through the Control Panel.

An easier way to disable JIT temporarily, and one that does not require changing the setting in your configuration files or Control Panel, is the -D command-line option, which updates the system properties. Just set java.compiler to NONE on the command line:

```
java -Djava.compiler=NONE  myapp
```

Note that the -D command-line option overrides the setting of the JAVA_COMPILER environment variable.

As mentioned, Sun's HotSpot JIT runtime—included in most modern Java releases—generally provides tracebacks, even with JIT mode enabled.

# 1.16   Finding More Java Source Code

## Problem

You want even more Java code examples to look at.

## Solution

Use The Source, Luke.

## Discussion

Java source code is everywhere. As mentioned in the Preface, all the code examples from this book can be downloaded from the O'Reilly site (*http://java.oreilly.com/*). What I didn't tell you, but what you might have realized by extension, is that the source examples from *all* the O'Reilly Java books are available there, too: the examples from *Java Examples in a Nutshell*, *Java Swing*—all of them.

Another valuable resource is the source code for the Java API. You may not have realized it, but the source code for all the public parts of the Java API are included with each release of the Java Development Kit. Want to know how `java.util.ArrayList` actually works? You have the source code. Got a problem making a `JTable` behave? Sun's JDK includes the source for all the public classes! Look for a file called *src.zip* or *src.jar*; some versions unzip this and some do not.

If that's not enough, you can get the source for the whole JDK for free over the Internet, just by committing to the Sun Java Community Source License and downloading a large file. This includes the source for the public and non-public parts of the API, as well as the compiler (written in Java) and a large body of code written in C/C++ (the runtime itself and the interfaces to the native library). For example, `java.io.Reader` has a method called `read( )`, which reads bytes of data from a file or network connection. This is written in C because it actually calls the `read( )` system call for Unix, Windows, Mac OS, BeOS, or whatever. The JDK source kit includes the source for all this stuff.

And ever since the early days of Java, there have been a number of web sites set up to distribute free software or open source Java, just as with most other modern "evangelized" languages, such as Perl, Python, Tk/Tcl, and others. (In fact, if you need native code to deal with some oddball filesystem mechanism in a portable way, beyond the material in Chapter 11 of this book, the source code for these runtime systems might be a good place to look.)

---

I'd like to mention several web sites of lasting value:

- Gamelan has been around almost forever (in Java time). The URL *http://www. gamelan.com* still worked the last I checked, but the site has been (naturally) commercialized, and it is now part of *http://www.developer.com*.

- Java.Net is a collaboration between Sun and O'Reilly, and it contains a number of interesting Java projects.

- The Giant Java Tree is more recent and is limited to code that is covered by the GNU Public License. There is a great deal of source code stored there, all of which can be freely downloaded. See *http://www.gjt.org*.

- The CollabNet open source marketplace is not specific to Java but offers a meeting place for people who want open source code written and those willing to fund its development. See *http://www.collab.net*.

- SourceForge, also not specific to Java, offers free public hosting of open source projects. See *http://sourceforge.net*.

- Finally, the author of this book maintains a small Java site at *http://www. darwinsys.com/java/*, which may be of value. It includes a listing of Java resources and material related to this book.

As with all free software, please be sure that you understand the ramifications of the various licensing schemes. Code covered by the GPL, for example, automatically transfers the GPL to any code that uses even a small part of it. And even once looking at Sun's Java implementation details (the licensed download mentioned previously) may prevent you from ever working on a "clean-room" reimplementation of Java, the free software Kaffe, or any commercial implementation. Consult a lawyer. Your mileage may vary. Despite these caveats, the source code is an invaluable resource to the person who wants to learn more Java.

# 1.17 Program: Debug

Most of the chapters of this book end with a "Program" recipe that illustrates some aspect of the material covered in the chapter. Example 1-2 is the source code for the Debug utility mentioned in Recipe 1.11.

*Example 1-2. Debug.java*

```
package com.darwinsys.util;

/** Utilities for debugging
 */
public class Debug {
    /** Static method to see if a given category of debugging is enabled.
     * Enable by setting e.g., -Ddebug.fileio to debug file I/O operations.
     * Use like this:<BR>
     * if (Debug.isEnabled("fileio"))<BR>
```

*Example 1-2. Debug.java (continued)*

```
 *       System.out.println("Starting to read file " + fileName);
 */
public static boolean isEnabled(String category) {
    return System.getProperty("debug." + category) != null;
}

/** Static method to println a given message if the
 * given category is enabled for debugging.
 */
public static void println(String category, String msg) {
    if (isEnabled(category))
        System.out.println(msg);
}
/** Same thing but for non-String objects (think of the other
 * form as an optimization of this).
 */
public static void println(String category, Object stuff) {
    println(category, stuff.toString( ));
}
}
```

# CHAPTER 2

# Interacting with the Environment

## 2.0    Introduction

This chapter describes how your Java program can deal with its immediate surroundings, with what we call the *runtime environment*. In one sense, everything you do in a Java program using almost any Java API involves the environment. Here we focus more narrowly on things that directly surround your program. Along the way we'll meet the System class, which knows a lot about your particular system.

Two other runtime classes deserve brief mention. The first, java.lang.Runtime, lies behind many of the methods in the System class. System.exit( ), for example, just calls Runtime.exit( ). It is technically part of "the environment," but the only time we use it directly is to run other programs, which is covered in Recipe 26.1. The java.awt.Toolkit object is also part of the environment and is discussed in Chapter 13.

## 2.1    Getting Environment Variables

### Problem

You want to get the value of "environment variables" from within your Java program.

### Solution

Don't (JDK 1.4 and earlier). Go ahead, but be careful (JDK 1.5).

### Discussion

The seventh edition of Unix, released in 1979, had an exciting new feature known as *environment variables*. Environment variables are in all modern Unix systems (including Mac OS X) and in most later command-line systems, such as the DOS subsystem underlying Windows, but are not in some older platforms or other Java runtimes. Environment variables are commonly used for customizing an individual computer user's runtime environment, hence the name. To take one familiar example, on Unix or DOS the environment variable PATH determines where the system looks for executable programs. So of course the issue comes up: "How do I get at environment variables from my Java program?"

The answer is that you can do this in some versions of Java, but you shouldn't. Java is designed to be a portable runtime environment. As such, you should not depend on operating system features that don't exist on every single Java platform. I just mentioned several Java platforms that don't have environment variables.

## 1.4 and earlier

Oh, all right, if you insist. Let's try it out using a static method called getenv( ) in class java.lang.System. But remember, you made me do it. First, the code. All we need is the little program shown in Example 2-1.

*Example 2-1. GetEnv.java*

```
public class GetEnv {
    public static void main(String[] argv) {
        System.out.println("System.getenv(\"PATH\") = " + System.getenv("PATH"));
    }
}
```

Let's try compiling it:

```
C:\javasrc>javac GetEnv.java
Note: GetEnv.java uses or overrides a deprecated API. Recompile with -deprecation for
details.
```

That message is seldom welcome news. We'll do as it says:

```
C:\javasrc>javac -deprecation GetEnv.java
GetEnv.java:9: Note: The method java.lang.String getenv(java.lang.String) in class
java.lang.System has been deprecated.
System.out.println("System.getenv(\"PATH\") = " + System.getenv("PATH"));
                                                                ^
Note: GetEnv.java uses or overrides a deprecated API.  Please consult the
documentation for a better alternative.
1 warning
```

But it's only a warning, right? What the heck. Let's try running the program!

```
C:\javasrc>java  GetEnv
Exception in thread "main" java.lang.Error: getenv no longer supported, use
properties and -D instead: PATH
        at java.lang.System.getenv(System.java:602)
        at GetEnv.main(GetEnv.java:9)
```

Well, of all the non-backward-compatible things! It used to work, in JDK 1.1, but it really and truly doesn't work anymore in later versions. I guess we'll just have to do what the error message tells us, which is to learn about "properties and -D instead." In fact, that's our very next recipe.

### Back to the future: 1.5

In Java 1.5, the getenv( ) method is no longer deprecated, although it still carries the warning that System Properties (Recipe 2.2) should be used instead. Even among systems that support them, environment variable names are case-sensitive on some platforms and case-insensitive on others. However, if you insist, run a program like GetEnv above, and you'll get output like the following:

```
C:\javasrc>java GetEnv
C:\windows\bin;c:\j2sdk1.5\bin;c:\documents and settings\ian\bin
C:\javasrc>
```

In another addition in 1.5, the no-argument form of the method System.getenv( ) returns *all* the environment variables, in the form of a non-modifiable String Map. You can iterate through this list and access all the user's settings or retrieve multiple environment settings.

Both forms of getenv( ) require you to have permissions to access the environment, so they typically do not work in restricted environments such as applets.

# 2.2    System Properties

## Problem

You need to get information from the system properties.

## Solution

Use System.getProperty( ) or System.getProperties( ).

## Discussion

What is a *property* anyway? A property is just a name and value pair stored in a java.util.Properties object, which we discuss more fully in Recipe 7.7. So if I chose to, I could store the following properties in a Properties object called ian:

```
name=Ian Darwin
favorite_popsicle=cherry
favorite_rock group=Fleetwood Mac
favorite_programming_language=Java
pencil color=green
```

The Properties class has several forms of its retrieval method. You could, for example, say ian.getProperty("pencil color") and get back the string "green". You can also provide a default: say ian.getProperty("pencil color", "black"), and, if the property has not been set, you get the default value "black".

For now, we're concerned with the System class and its role as keeper of the particular Properties object that controls and describes the Java runtime. The System class has a static Properties member whose content is the merger of operating system specifics (os.name, for example), system and user tailoring (java.class.path), and properties defined on the command line (as we'll see in a moment). Note that the use of periods in these names (like os.arch, os.version, java.class.path, and java.lang.version) makes it look as though there is a hierarchical relationship similar to that for class names. The Properties class, however, imposes no such relationships: each key is just a string, and dots are not special.

To retrieve one system-provided property, use System.getProperty( ). If you want them all, use System.getProperties( ). Accordingly, if I wanted to find out if the System Properties had a property named "pencil color", I could say:

```
String color = System.getProperty("pencil color");
```

But what does that return? Surely Java isn't clever enough to know about everybody's favorite pencil color? Right you are! But we can easily tell Java about our pencil color (or anything else we want to tell it) using the -D argument.

The -D option argument is used to predefine a value in the system properties object. It must have a name, an equals sign, and a value, which are parsed the same way as in a properties file (see below). You can have more than one -D definition between the java command and your class name on the command line. At the Unix or Windows command line, type:

```
java -D"pencil color=Deep Sea Green" SysPropDemo
```

Using an IDE, put the variable's name and value in the appropriate dialog box when running the program. The SysPropDemo program is short; its essence is this one line:

```
System.getProperties( ).list(System.out);
```

When run this way, the program prints about 50 lines, looking something like:

```
java.library.path=/usr/local/linux-jdk1.2/jre/lib/i386/...
java.vm.specification.vendor=Sun Microsystems Inc.
sun.io.unicode.encoding=UnicodeLittle
pencil color=Deep Sea Green
file.encoding=ANSI_X3.4-1968
java.specification.vendor=Sun Microsystems Inc.
user.language=en
```

The program also has code to extract just one or a few properties, so you can say:

```
$ java SysPropDemo os.arch
os.arch = x86
```

Which reminds me—this is a good time to mention system-dependent code. Recipe 2.3 talks about release-dependent code, and Recipe 2.4 talks about OS-dependent code.

## See Also

Recipe 7.7 lists more details on using and naming your own Properties files. The Javadoc page for java.util.Properties lists the exact rules used in the load( ) method, as well as other details.

## 2.3    Writing JDK Release-Dependent Code

### Problem

You need to write code that depends on the JDK release.

### Solution

Don't do this.

### Discussion

Although Java is meant to be portable, Java runtimes have some significant variations. Sometimes you need to work around a feature that may be missing in older runtimes, but you want to use it if it's present. So one of the first things you want to know is how to find out the JDK release corresponding to the Java runtime. This is easily obtained with System.getProperty( ):

```
System.out.println(System.getProperty("java.specification.version"));
```

Accordingly, you may want to test for the presence or absence of particular classes. One way to do this is with Class.forName("class"), which throws an exception if the class cannot be loaded—a good indication that it's not present in the runtime's library. Here is code for this, from an application wanting to find out whether the JDK 1.1 or later components are available. It relies on the fact that the class java.lang.reflect.Constructor was added in 1.1 but was not present in 1.0. (The Javadoc for the standard classes reports the version that a given class was added to the Java standard, under the heading "Since." If there is no such heading, it normally means that the class has been present since the beginning—i.e., JDK 1.0.)

```
/** Test for JDK >= 1.1 */
public class TestJDK11 {
    public static void main(String[] a) {
        // Check for JDK >= 1.1
        try {
            Class.forName("java.lang.reflect.Constructor");
        } catch (ClassNotFoundException e) {
            String failure =
                "Sorry, but this version of MyApp needs \n" +
                "a Java Runtime based on Java JDK 1.1 or later";
            System.err.println(failure);
            throw new IllegalArgumentException(failure);
        }
        System.out.println("Happy to report that this is JDK1.1");
        // rest of program would go here...
        return;
    }
}
```

To check if the runtime includes the Swing components with their final names,* you could use:

```
Class.forName("javax.swing.JButton");
```

It's important to distinguish between testing this at compile time and at runtime. In both cases, this code must be compiled on a system that includes the classes you are testing for—JDK 1.1 and Swing, respectively. These tests are only attempts to help the poor backwater Java runtime user trying to run your up-to-date application. The goal is to provide this user with a message more meaningful than the simple "class not found" error that the runtime gives. It's also important to note that this test becomes unreachable if you write it inside any code that depends on the code you are testing for. The check for Swing won't ever see the light of day on a JDK 1.0 system if you write it in the constructor of a JPanel subclass (think about it). Put the test early in the main flow of your application, before any GUI objects are constructed. Otherwise the code just sits there wasting space on newer runtimes and never gets run on Java 1.0 systems.

As for what the class Class actually does, we'll defer that until Chapter 25.

## 2.4    Writing Operating System-Dependent Code

### Problem

You need to write code that depends on the underlying operating system.

### Solution

Again, don't do this. Or, if you must, use System.properties.

### Discussion

While Java is designed to be portable, some things aren't. These include such variables as the filename separator. Everybody on Unix knows that the filename separator is a slash character (/) and that a backward slash, or backslash (\), is an escape character. Back in the late 1970s, a group at Microsoft was actually working on Unix—their version was called Xenix, later taken over by SCO—and the people working on DOS saw and liked the Unix filesystem model. MS-DOS 2.0 didn't have directories, it just had "user numbers" like the system it was a clone of, Digital Research CP/M (itself a clone of various other systems). So the Microsoft folk set out to clone the Unix filesystem organization. Unfortunately, they had already committed the slash character for use as an option delimiter, for which Unix had used a dash (-); and the PATH separator (:) was also used as a "drive letter" delimiter, as in C: or A:. So we now have commands like this:

---

* Old-timers will remember that on the preliminary Swing releases, the name of this class was com.sun.java.swing.JButton.

| System | Directory list command | Meaning | Example PATH setting |
|--------|------------------------|---------|----------------------|
| Unix | *ls -R /* | Recursive listing of /, the top-level directory | *PATH=/bin:/usr/bin* |
| DOS | *dir/s \* | Directory with subdirectories option (i.e., recursive) of \, the top-level directory (but only of the current drive) | *PATH=C:\windows; D:\mybin* |

Where does this get us? If we are going to generate filenames in Java, we need to know whether to put a / or a \ or some other character. Java has two solutions to this. First, when moving between Unix and Microsoft systems, at least, it is *permissive*: either / or \ can be used,* and the code that deals with the operating system sorts it out. Second, and more generally, Java makes the platform-specific information available in a platform-independent way. First, for the file separator (and also the PATH separator), the java.io.File class (see Chapter 11) makes available some static variables containing this information. Since the File class is platform-dependent, it makes sense to anchor this information here. The variables are:

| Name | Type | Meaning |
|------|------|---------|
| separator | static String | The system-dependent filename separator character—e.g., / or \. |
| separatorChar | static char | The system-dependent filename separator character—e.g., / or \. |
| pathSeparator | static String | The system-dependent path separator character, represented as a string for convenience. |
| pathSeparatorChar | static char | The system-dependent path separator character. |

Both filename and path separators are normally characters, but they are also available in String form for convenience.

A second, more general, mechanism is the system Properties object mentioned in Recipe 2.2. You can use this to determine the operating system you are running on. Here is code that simply lists the system properties; it can be informative to run this on several different implementations:

```
import java.util.*;
/**
 * Demonstrate System Properties
 */
public class SysPropDemo {
    public static void main(String argv[]) {
        System.out.println("System Properties:");
        Properties p = System.getProperties();
        p.list(System.out);
    }
}
```

---

* When compiling strings for use on Windows, remember to double them, since \ is an escape character in most places other than the MS-DOS command line: String rootDir = "C:\\";.

Some OSes, for example, provide a mechanism called "the null device" that can be used to discard output (typically used for timing purposes). Here is code that asks the system properties for the "os.name" and uses it to make up a name that can be used for discarding data. If no null device is known for the given platform, we return the name *junk*, which means that on such platforms, we'll occasionally create, well, junk files. I just remove these files when I stumble across them.

```
/** Some things that are System dependent.
 * All methods are static, like java.lang.Math.
 */
public class SysDep {
    /** Return the name of the Null device on platforms which support it,
     * or the string "junk" otherwise.
     */
    public static String getDevNull() {
        String sys = System.getProperty("os.name");
        if (sys==null)
            return "junk";
        if (sys.startsWith("Windows"))
            return "NUL:";
        return "/dev/null";
    }
}
```

In one case you do need to check for the OS. Mac OS X has a number of GUI goodies that can be used only on that OS and yet should be used to make your GUI application look more like a "native" Mac application. Recipe 14.16 explores this issue in more detail. In brief, Apple says to look for the string `mrj.version` to determine whether you are running on OS X:

```
boolean isMacOS = System.getProperty("mrj.version") != null;
```

# 2.5  Using Extensions or Other Packaged APIs

## Problem

You have a JAR file of classes you want to use.

## Solution

Simply copy the JAR into *JDKHOME/jre/lib/ext/*.

## Discussion

The Java API has grown by leaps and bounds since its first public release in 1995. It is now considered sufficiently functional for writing robust applications, but the areas to which it is being applied continue to grow. Some specialized APIs may require more resources than you have on a given Java platform. Many of the new

APIs from Sun are in the form of *standard extensions*, which is indicated by their package names beginning in javax.. Classes in packages named java. or javax. are treated as built-in classes by a web browser for purposes of applet security, for example. Each extension is distributed in the form of a JAR file (see Recipe 23.4).

If you have a Java runtime that does not support this feature, you may need to add each JAR file to your CLASSPATH, as in Recipe 1.4.

As you accumulate these and other optional APIs contained in JAR files, you can simply drop these JAR files into the Java Extensions Mechanism directory, typically something like *\jdk1.4\jre\lib\ext.*, instead of listing each JAR file in your CLASS-PATH variable and watching CLASSPATH grow and grow and grow. The runtime looks here for any and all JAR and zip files, so no special action is needed. In fact, unlike many other system changes, you do not even need to reboot your computer; this directory is scanned each time the JVM starts up. You may, however, need to restart a long-running program such as an IDE for it to notice the change. Try it and see first.

## 2.6   Parsing Command-Line Arguments

### Problem

You need to parse command-line options. Java doesn't provide an API for it.

### Solution

Look in the args array passed as an argument to main. Or use my GetOpt class.

### Discussion

The Unix folk have had to deal with this longer than anybody, and they came up with a C-library function called getopt.* getopt processes your command-line arguments and looks for single-character options set off with dashes and optional arguments. For example, the command:

```
sort -n -o outfile myfile1 yourfile2
```

runs the standard *sort* program. The -n tells it that the records are numeric rather than textual, and the -o outfile tells it to write its output into a file named *outfile*. The remaining words, *myfile1* and *yourfile2*, are treated as the input files to be sorted. On Windows, command arguments are sometimes set off with slashes (/). We use the Unix form—a dash—in our API, but feel free to change the code to use slashes.

---

\* The Unix world has several variations on getopt; mine emulates the original AT&T version fairly closely, with some frills such as long-name arguments.

Each GetOpt parser is constructed to recognize a particular set of arguments; this is sensible since a given program normally has a fixed set of arguments that it accepts. You can construct an array of GetOptDesc objects that represent the allowable arguments. For the sort program shown previously, you might use:

```
GetOptDesc options[] = {
    new GetOptDesc('n', "numeric", false},
    new GetOptDesc('o', "output-file", true),
});
Map optionsFound = new GetOpt(options).parseArguments(argv);
if (optionsFound.get("n") != null)
    sortType = NUMERIC;
} else  if (optionsFound.get("o")){
...
```

The simple way of using GetOpt is to call its parseArguments method.

For backward compatibility with people who learned to use the Unix version in C, the getopt() method can be used normally in a while loop. It returns once for each valid option found, returning the value of the character that was found or the constant DONE when all options (if any) have been processed.

Here is a complete program that uses my GetOpt class just to see if there is a -h (for help) argument on the command line:

```
import com.darwinsys.util.GetOpt;

/** Trivial demonstration of GetOpt. If -h present, print help.
 */
public class GetOptSimple {
    public static void main(String[] args) {
        GetOpt go = new GetOpt("h");
        char c;
        while ((c = go.getopt(args)) !=GetOpt.DONE) {
            switch(c) {
            case 'h':
                helpAndExit(0);
                break;
            default:
                System.err.println("Unknown option in " +
                    args[go.getOptInd( )-1]);
                helpAndExit(1);
            }
        }
        System.out.println( );
    }

    /** Stub for providing help on usage
     * You can write a longer help than this, certainly.
     */
    static void helpAndExit(int returnValue) {
        System.err.println("This would tell you how to use this program");
        System.exit(returnValue);
    }
}
```

This longer demo program has several options:

```java
import com.darwinsys.lang.GetOpt;
import com.darwinsys.lang.GetOptDesc;
import java.util.*;

/** Demonstrate the modern way of using GetOpt. This allows a subset of
 * <pre>Unix sort options: sort -n -o outfile infile1 infile2</pre>
 * which means: sort numerically (-n), writing to file "outfile" (-o
 * outfile), sort from infile1 and infile2.
 */
public class GetOptDemoNew {
    public static void main(String[] argv) {
        boolean numeric_option = false;
        boolean errs = false;
        String outputFileName = null;

        GetOptDesc options[] = {
            new GetOptDesc('n', "numeric", false),
            new GetOptDesc('o', "output-file", true),
        };
        GetOpt parser = new GetOpt(options);
        Map optionsFound = parser.parseArguments(argv);
        Iterator it = optionsFound.keySet().iterator();
        while (it.hasNext()) {
            String key = (String)it.next();
            char c = key.charAt(0);
            switch (c) {
                case 'n':
                    numeric_option = true;
                    break;
                case 'o':
                    outputFileName = (String)optionsFound.get(key);
                    break;
                case '?':
                    errs = true;
                    break;
                default:
                    throw new IllegalStateException(
                    "Unexpected option character: " + c);
            }
        }
        if (errs) {
            System.err.println("Usage: GetOptDemo [-n][-o file][file...]");
        }
        System.out.print("Options: ");
        System.out.print("Numeric: " + numeric_option + ' ');
        System.out.print("Output: " + outputFileName + "; ");
        System.out.print("Inputs: ");
        List files = parser.getFilenameList();
        for (int i = 0; i < files.size(); i++) {
            System.out.print(files.get(i));
            System.out.print(' ');
```

```
        }
        System.out.println( );
    }
}}
```

If we invoke it several times with different options, including both single-argument
and long-name options, here's how it behaves:

```
> java GetOptDemoNew
Options: Numeric: false Output: null; Inputs:
> java GetOptDemoNew -M
Options: Numeric: false Output: null; Inputs: -M
> java GetOptDemoNew -n a b c
Options: Numeric: true Output: null; Inputs: a b c
> java GetOptDemoNew -numeric a b c
Options: Numeric: true Output: null; Inputs: a b c
> java GetOptDemoNew -numeric -output-file /tmp/foo a b c
Options: Numeric: true Output: /tmp/foo; Inputs: a b c
```

A longer example exercising all the ins and outs of this version of GetOpt can be
found in the online source under *darwinsys/src/regress*. The source code for GetOpt
itself is shown in Example 2-2.

*Example 2-2. Source code for GetOpt*

```java
package com.darwinsys.lang;

import com.darwinsys.util.Debug;

import java.util.Map;
import java.util.HashMap;
import java.util.List;
import java.util.ArrayList;
import java.util.Iterator;

/** A class to implement Unix-style (single-character) command-line argument
 * parsing. Originally patterned after (but not using code from) the Unix
 * getopt(3) program, this has been redesigned to be more Java-friendly.
 * <p>
 * This is <em>not</em> threadsafe; it is expected to be used only from main( ).
 * <p>
 * For another way of dealing with command lines, see the
 * <a href="http://jakarta.apache.org/commons/cli/">Jakarta Commons
 * Command Line Interface</a>.
 * @author Ian F. Darwin, ian@darwinsys.com
 * @version $Id: ch02,v 1.4 2004/05/04 20:11:12 ian Exp $
 */
public class GetOpt {
    /** The list of file names found after args */
    protected List fileNameArguments;
    /** The set of characters to look for */
    protected GetOptDesc[] options;
    /** Where we are in the options */
    protected int optind = 0;
    /** Public constant for "no more options" */
    public static final int DONE = 0;
```

*Example 2-2. Source code for GetOpt (continued)*

```java
/** Internal flag - whether we are done all the options */
protected boolean done = false;
/** The current option argument. */
protected String optarg;

/** Retrieve the current option argument */
public String optarg( ) {
    return optarg;
}

/* Construct a GetOpt parser, given the option specifications
 * in an array of GetOptDesc objects. This is the preferred constructor.
 */
public GetOpt(GetOptDesc[] options) {
    this.options = options;
}

/* Construct a GetOpt parser, storing the set of option characters.
 * This is a legacy constructor for backward compatibility.
 */
public GetOpt(String patt) {
    // Pass One: just count the letters
    int n = 0;
    for (int i = 0; i<patt.length( ); i++) {
        if (patt.charAt(i) != ':')
            ++n;
    }
    if (n == 0)
        throw new IllegalArgumentException(
            "No option letters found in " + patt);

    // Pass Two: construct an array of GetOptDesc objects.
    options = new GetOptDesc[n];
    for (int i = 0, ix = 0; i<patt.length( ); i++) {
        char c = patt.charAt(i);
        boolean argTakesValue = false;
        if (i < patt.length( ) - 1 && patt.charAt(i+1) == ':') {
            argTakesValue = true;
            ++i;
        }
        options[ix++] = new GetOptDesc(c, null, argTakesValue);
        Debug.println("getopt",
            "CONSTR: options[" + ix + "] = " + c + ", " + argTakesValue);
    }
}

/** Reset this GetOpt parser */
public void rewind( ) {
    fileNameArguments = null;
    done = false;
    optind = 0;
}
```

*Example 2-2. Source code for GetOpt (continued)*

```java
/** Array used to convert a char to a String */
private static char[] strConvArray = { 0 };

/**
 * Modern way of using GetOpt: call this once and get all options.
 * <p>
 * This parses the options and returns a Map whose keys are the found options.
 * Normally followed by a call to getFilenameList().
 * @return a Map whose keys are Strings of length 1 (containing the char
 * from the option that was matched) and whose value is a String
 * containing the value, or null for a non-option argument.
 */
public Map parseArguments(String[] argv) {
    Map optionsAndValues = new HashMap();
    fileNameArguments = new ArrayList();
    for (int i = 0; i < argv.length; i++) {
        Debug.println("getopt", "parseArg: i=" + i + ": arg " + argv[i]);
        char c = getopt(argv);
        if (c != DONE) {
            strConvArray[0] = c;
            optionsAndValues.put(new String(strConvArray), optarg);
            // If this arg takes an option, we must skip it here.
            if (optarg != null)
                ++i;
        } else {
            fileNameArguments.add(argv[i]);
        }
    }
    return optionsAndValues;
}

/** Get the list of filename-like arguments after options */
public List getFilenameList() {
    if (fileNameArguments == null) {
        throw new IllegalArgumentException(
            "Illegal call to getFilenameList() before parseOptions()");
    }
    return fileNameArguments;
}

/** The true heart of getopt, whether used old way or new way:
 * returns one argument; call repeatedly until it returns DONE.
 */
public char getopt(String argv[]) {
    Debug.println("getopt",
        "optind=" + optind + ", argv.length="+argv.length);

    if (optind == (argv.length)-1) {
        done = true;
    }

    // If we are (now) finished, bail.
    if (done) {
```

*Example 2-2. Source code for GetOpt (continued)*

```
            return DONE;
        }

        // TODO - two-pass, 1st check long args, 2nd check for
        // char, may be multi char as in "-no outfile" == "-n -o outfile".

        // Pick off the next command-line argument; check if it starts "-".
        // If so, look it up in the list.
        String thisArg = argv[optind++];
        if (thisArg.startsWith("-")) {
            optarg = null;
            for (int i=0; i<options.length; i++) {
                if ( options[i].argLetter == thisArg.charAt(1) ||
                    (options[i].argName != null &&
                     options[i].argName == thisArg.substring(1))) { // found it
                    // If it needs an option argument, get it.
                    if (options[i].takesArgument) {
                        if (optind < argv.length) {
                            optarg = argv[optind];
                            ++optind;
                        } else {
                            throw new IllegalArgumentException(
                                "Option " + options[i].argLetter +
                                " needs value but found end of arg list");
                        }
                    }
                    return options[i].argLetter;
                }
            }
            // Began with "-" but not matched, so must be error.
            return '?';
        } else {
            // Found non-argument non-option word in argv: end of options.
            done = true;
            return DONE;
        }
    }

    /** Return optind, the index into args of the last option we looked at */
    public int getOptInd( ) {
        return optind;
    }
}
```

## See Also

GetOpt is an adequate tool for processing command-line options. You may come up with something better and contribute it to the Java world; this is left as an exercise for the reader.

For another way of dealing with command lines, see the Jakarta Commons Command Line Interface, which can be found at *http://jakarta.apache.org/commons/cli/*.

# CHAPTER 3
# Strings and Things

## 3.0    Introduction

Character strings are an inevitable part of just about any programming task. We use them for printing messages for the user; for referring to files on disk or other external media; and for people's names, addresses, and affiliations. The uses of strings are many, almost without number (actually, if you need numbers, we'll get to them in Chapter 5).

If you're coming from a programming language like C, you'll need to remember that String is a defined type (class) in Java. That is, a string is an object and therefore has methods. It is not an array of characters and should not be thought of as an array. Operations like fileName.endsWith(".gif") and extension.equals(".gif") (and the equivalent ".gif".equals(extension)) are commonplace.

Notice that a given String object, once constructed, is immutable. That is, once I have said String s = "Hello" + yourName; then the particular object that reference variable s refers to can never be changed. You can assign s to refer to a different string, even one derived from the original, as in s = s.trim( ). And you can retrieve characters from the original string using charAt( ), but it isn't called getCharAt( ) because there is not, and never will be, a setCharAt( ) method. Even methods like toUpperCase( ) don't change the String; they return a new String object containing the translated characters. If you need to change characters within a String, you should instead create a StringBuilder* (possibly initialized to the starting value of the String), manipulate the StringBuilder to your heart's content, and then convert that to String at the end, using the ubiquitous toString( ) method.

How can I be so sure they won't add a setCharAt( ) method in the next release? Because the immutability of strings is one of the fundamentals of the Java Virtual

---

* StringBuilder is new in JDK 1.5. It is functionally equivalent to the older StringBuffer. We will delve into the details in Recipe 3.3.

Machine. Remember that Java is the one language that takes security and multiprocessing (threads) seriously. Got that in mind? Good. Now think about applets, which are prevented from accessing many local resources. Consider the following scenario: Thread A starts up another Thread B. Thread A creates a string called s containing a filename, saves a reference s2 to it, and passes s to some method that requires permission. This method will certainly call the Java Virtual Machine's SecurityManager* object, if one is installed (as it certainly will be in an applet environment). Then, in the nanoseconds between the time the SecurityManager passes its approval on the named file and the time the I/O system actually gets around to opening the file, Thread B changes the string referred to by s2 to refer to a system file. Poof! If you could do this, the entire notion of Java security would be a joke. But of course, they thought of that, so you can't. While you can, at any time, assign a new String reference to s, this never has any effect on the string that s used to refer to. Except, of course, if s were the only reference to that String, it is now eligible for garbage collection—it may go up the pipe!

Remember also that the String is a very fundamental type in Java. Unlike most of the other classes in the core API, the behavior of strings is not changeable; the class is marked final so it cannot be subclassed. So you can't declare your own String subclass. Think if you could—you could masquerade as a String but provide a setCharAt( ) method! Again, they thought of that. If you don't believe me, try it out:

```
/**
 * If this class could be compiled, Java security would be a myth.
 */
public class WolfInStringsClothing extends java.lang.String {
    public void setCharAt(int index, char newChar) {
        // The implementation of this method
        // is left as an exercise for the reader.
        // Hint: compile this code exactly as-is before bothering!
    }
}
```

Got it? They thought of that!

Of course you do need to be able to modify strings. Some methods extract part of a String; these are covered in the first few recipes in this chapter. And StringBuilder is an important set of classes that deals in characters and strings and has many methods for changing the contents, including, of course, a toString( ) method. Reformed C programmers should note that Java strings are not arrays of chars as in C, so you must use methods for such operations as processing a string one character at a time; see Recipe 3.4. Figure 3-1 shows an overview of String, StringBuilder, and C-language strings.

---

* SecurityManager is a class that is consulted about whether the current application is allowed to do certain things, such as open local disk files, open arbitrary network connections, etc. Applets run with a more restrictive security manager than do normal applications, for example.

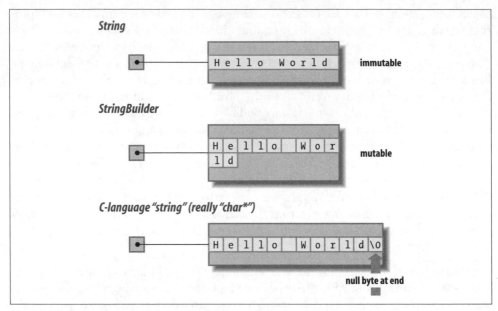

*Figure 3-1. String, StringBuilder, and C-language strings*

While we haven't discussed the details of the java.io package yet (we will, in Chapter 10), you need to be able to read text files for some of these programs. Even if you're not familiar with java.io, you can probably see from the examples that read text files that a BufferedReader allows you to read "chunks" of data, and that this class has a very convenient readLine( ) method.

We won't show you how to sort an array of strings here; the more general notion of sorting a collection of objects is discussed in Recipe 7.8.

# 3.1  Taking Strings Apart with Substrings

## Problem

You want to break a string apart into substrings by position.

## Solution

Use the String object's substring( ) method.

## Discussion

The substring( ) method constructs a new String object made up of a run of characters contained somewhere in the original string, the one whose substring( ) you called. The name of this method, substring( ), violates the stylistic dictum that words should be capitalized; if Java were 100.0% consistent, this method would be named subString. But it's not—it's substring. The substring method is overloaded: both forms require a starting index. The one-argument form returns from startIndex to the end. The two-argument form takes an ending index (not a length, as in some languages), so that an index can be generated by the String methods indexOf( ) or lastIndexOf( ). Note that the end index is one beyond the last character!

```
// File SubStringDemo.java
public static void main(String[] av) {
    String a = "Java is great.";
    System.out.println(a);
    String b = a.substring(5);     // b is the String "is great."
    System.out.println(b);
    String c = a.substring(5,7);// c is the String "is"
    System.out.println(c);
    String d = a.substring(5,a.length( ));// d is "is great."
    System.out.println(d);
}
```

When run, this prints the following:

```
> java SubStringDemo
Java is great.
is great.
is
is great.
>
```

# 3.2   Taking Strings Apart with StringTokenizer

## Problem

You need to take a string apart into words or tokens.

## Solution

Construct a StringTokenizer around your string and call its methods hasMoreTokens( ) and nextToken( ). Or, use Regular Expressions (see Chapter 4).

The StringTokenizer methods implement the Iterator design pattern (see Recipe 7.4):

```
// StrTokDemo.java
StringTokenizer st = new StringTokenizer("Hello World of Java");

while (st.hasMoreTokens( ))
    System.out.println("Token: " + st.nextToken( ));
```

StringTokenizer also implements the Enumeration interface directly (also in Recipe 7.4), but if you use the methods thereof you need to cast the results to String.

A StringTokenizer normally breaks the String into tokens at what we would think of as "word boundaries" in European languages. Sometimes you want to break at some other character. No problem. When you construct your StringTokenizer, in addition to passing in the string to be tokenized, pass in a second string that lists the "break characters." For example:

```
// StrTokDemo2.java
StringTokenizer st = new StringTokenizer("Hello, World|of|Java", ", |");

while (st.hasMoreElements())
    System.out.println("Token: " + st.nextElement());
```

But wait, there's more! What if you are reading lines like:

```
FirstName|LastName|Company|PhoneNumber
```

and your dear old Aunt Begonia hasn't been employed for the last 38 years? Her "Company" field will in all probability be blank.[*] If you look very closely at the previous code example, you'll see that it has two delimiters together (the comma and the space), but if you run it, there are no "extra" tokens. That is, the StringTokenizer normally discards adjacent consecutive delimiters. For cases like the phone list, where you need to preserve null fields, there is good news and bad news. The good news is you can do it: you simply add a second argument of true when constructing the StringTokenizer, meaning that you wish to see the delimiters as tokens. The bad news is that you now get to see the delimiters as tokens, so you have to do the arithmetic yourself. Want to see it? Run this program:

```
// StrTokDemo3.java
StringTokenizer st =
    new StringTokenizer("Hello, World|of|Java", ", |", true);

while (st.hasMoreElements())
    System.out.println("Token: " + st.nextElement());
```

and you get this output:

```
C:\javasrc>java  StrTokDemo3
Token: Hello
Token: ,
Token:
Token: World
Token: |
Token: of
Token: |
Token: Java
```

This isn't how you'd like StringTokenizer to behave, ideally, but it is serviceable enough most of the time. Example 3-1 processes and ignores consecutive tokens, returning the results as an array of Strings.

---

[*] Unless, perhaps, you're as slow at updating personal records as I am.

*Example 3-1. StrTokDemo4.java (StringTokenizer)*

```java
import java.util.*;

/** Show using a StringTokenizer including getting the delimiters back */
public class StrTokDemo4 {
    public final static int MAXFIELDS = 5;
    public final static String DELIM = "|";

    /** Processes one String; returns it as an array of Strings */
    public static String[] process(String line) {
        String[] results = new String[MAXFIELDS];

        // Unless you ask StringTokenizer to give you the tokens,
        // it silently discards multiple null tokens.
        StringTokenizer st = new StringTokenizer(line, DELIM,  true);

        int i = 0;
        // stuff each token into the current slot in the array
        while (st.hasMoreTokens()) {
            String s = st.nextToken();
            if (s.equals(DELIM)) {
                if (i++>=MAXFIELDS)
                    // This is messy: See StrTokDemo4b which uses
                    // a Vector to allow any number of fields.
                    throw new IllegalArgumentException("Input line " +
                        line + " has too many fields");
                continue;
            }
            results[i] = s;
        }
        return results;
    }

    public static void printResults(String input, String[] outputs) {
        System.out.println("Input: " + input);
        for (int i=0; i<outputs.length; i++)
            System.out.println("Output " + i + " was: " + outputs[i]);
    }

    public static void main(String[] a) {
        printResults("A|B|C|D", process("A|B|C|D"));
        printResults("A||C|D", process("A||C|D"));
        printResults("A|||D|E", process("A|||D|E"));
    }
}
```

When you run this, you will see that A is always in Field 1, B (if present) is in Field 2, and so on. In other words, the null fields are being handled properly:

```
Input: A|B|C|D
Output 0 was: A
Output 1 was: B
Output 2 was: C
```

```
Output 3 was: D
Output 4 was: null
Input: A||C|D
Output 0 was: A
Output 1 was: null
Output 2 was: C
Output 3 was: D
Output 4 was: null
Input: A|||D|E
Output 0 was: A
Output 1 was: null
Output 2 was: null
Output 3 was: D
Output 4 was: E
```

## See Also

Now that Java includes Regular Expressions (as of JDK 1.4), many occurrences of StringTokenizer can be replaced with Regular Expressions (see Chapter 4) with considerably more flexibility. For example, to extract all the numbers from a String, you can use this code:

```
Matcher toke = Pattern.compile("\\d+").matcher(inputString);
  while (toke.find( )) {
        String courseString = toke.group(0);
        int courseNumber = Integer.parseInt(courseString);
        ...
```

This allows user input to be more flexible than you could easily handle with a StringTokenizer. Assuming that the numbers represent course numbers at some educational institution, the inputs "471,472,570" or "Courses 471 and 472, 570" or just "471 472 570" should all give the same results.

# 3.3   Putting Strings Together with +, StringBuilder (JDK 1.5), and StringBuffer

## Problem

You need to put some String pieces (back) together.

## Solution

Use string concatenation: the + operator. The compiler implicitly constructs a StringBuilder for you and uses its append( ) methods. Better yet, construct and use it yourself.

## Discussion

An object of one of the StringBuilder classes basically represents a collection of characters. It is similar to a String object, but, as mentioned, Strings are immutable.

StringBuilders are mutable and designed for, well, building Strings. You typically construct a StringBuilder, invoke the methods needed to get the character sequence just the way you want it, and then call toString() to generate a String representing the same character sequence for use in most of the Java API, which deals in Strings.

StringBuffer is historical—it's been around since JDK 1.1. Some of its methods are synchronized (see Recipe 24.5), which involves unneeded overhead in a single-threaded application. In 1.5, this class was "split" into StringBuffer (which is synchronized) and the new StringBuilder (which is not synchronized); thus, it is faster and preferable for single-threaded use. Another new class, AbstractStringBuilder, is the parent of both. In the following discussion, I'll use "the StringBuilder classes" to refer to all three, since they mostly have the same methods. My example code uses StringBuffer instead of StringBuilder since most people have not yet migrated to 1.5. Except for the fact that StringBuilder is not threadsafe, these classes are identical and can be used interchangeably.

The StringBuilder classes have a variety of methods for inserting, replacing, and otherwise modifying a given StringBuilder. Conveniently, the append() method returns a reference to the StringBuilder itself, so that statements like the .append(...).append(...) are fairly common. You might even see this third way in a toString() method. Example 3-2 shows the three ways of concatenating strings.

*Example 3-2. StringBufferDemo.java*

```
/**
 * StringBufferDemo: construct the same String three different ways.
 */
public class StringBufferDemo {
    public static void main(String[] argv) {
        String s1 = "Hello" + ", " + "World";
        System.out.println(s1);

        // Build a StringBuffer, and append some things to it.
        StringBuffer sb2 = new StringBuffer();
        sb2.append("Hello");
        sb2.append(',');
        sb2.append(' ');
        sb2.append("World");

        // Get the StringBuffer's value as a String, and print it.
        String s2 = sb2.toString();
        System.out.println(s2);

        // Now do the above all over again, but in a more
        // concise (and typical "real-world" Java) fashion.

        StringBuffer sb3 = new StringBuffer().append("Hello").
            append(',').append(' ').append("World");
        System.out.println(sb3.toString());
```

*Example 3-2. StringBufferDemo.java (continued)*

```
            // Exercise for the reader: do it all again but without
            // creating ANY temporary variables.
    }
}
```

In fact, all the methods that modify more than one character of a StringBuilder's contents—append( ), delete( ), deleteCharAt( ), insert( ), replace( ), and reverse( )—return a reference to the object to facilitate this style of coding.

To show that StringBuilder is, as Sun claims, a (non-threadsafe) "drop-in replacement for StringBuffer," here is StringBuilderDemo, a copy of StringBufferDemo converted to use StringBuilder. Its output is identical to StringBufferDemo:

```
/**
 * StringBuilderDemo: construct the same String three different ways.
 */
public class StringBuilderDemo {

    public static void main(String[] argv) {

        String s1 = "Hello" + ", " + "World";
        System.out.println(s1);

        // Build a StringBuilder, and append some things to it.
        StringBuilder sb2 = new StringBuilder( );
        sb2.append("Hello");
        sb2.append(',');
        sb2.append(' ');
        sb2.append("World");

        // Get the StringBuilder's value as a String, and print it.
        String s2 = sb2.toString( );
        System.out.println(s2);

        // Now do the above all over again, but in a more
        // concise (and typical "real-world" Java) fashion.

        StringBuilder sb3 = new StringBuilder( ).append("Hello").
            append(',').append(' ').append("World");
        System.out.println(sb3.toString( ));
    }
}
```

As another example of using a StringBuilder, consider the need to convert a list of items into a comma-separated list, like this:

```
StringBuffer sb = new StringBuffer( );
while (st.hasMoreElements( )) {
    sb.append(st.nextToken( ));
    if (st.hasMoreElements( ))
        sb.append(", ");
}
return sb.toString( );
```

This pattern relies on the fact that you can call the informational method hasMoreElements() in the Enumeration (or hasNext() in an Iterator, as discussed in Recipe 7.4) more than once on each element. But it works, and it avoids getting an extra comma after the last element of the list.

# 3.4  Processing a String One Character at a Time

## Problem

You want to process the contents of a string, one character at a time.

## Solution

Use a for loop and the String's charAt() method.

## Discussion

A string's charAt() method retrieves a given character by index number (starting at zero) from within the String object. To process all the characters in a String, one after another, use a for loop ranging from zero to String.length()-1. Here we process all the characters in a String:

```
// StrCharAt.java
String a = "A quick bronze fox leapt a lazy bovine";
for (int i=0; i < a.length(); i++)
    System.out.println("Char " + i + " is " + a.charAt(i));
```

A *checksum* is a numeric quantity representing and confirming the contents of a file. If you transmit the checksum of a file separately from the contents, a recipient can checksum the file—assuming the algorithm is known—and verify that the file was received intact. Example 3-3 shows the simplest possible checksum, computed just by adding the numeric values of each character. Note that on files, it does not include the values of the newline characters; to fix this, retrieve System.getProperty("line.separator"); and add its character value(s) into the sum at the end of each line. Or give up on line mode and read the file a character at a time.

*Example 3-3. CheckSum.java*

```
/** CheckSum one file, given an open BufferedReader. */
    public int process(BufferedReader is) {
        int sum = 0;
        try {
            String inputLine;

            while ((inputLine = is.readLine()) != null) {
                int i;
                for (i=0; i<inputLine.length(); i++) {
                    sum += inputLine.charAt(i);
                }
            }
```

*Example 3-3. CheckSum.java (continued)*

```
            is.close( );
        } catch (IOException e) {
            System.out.println("IOException: " + e);
    } f
    return sum;
}
```

## 3.5    Aligning Strings

### Problem

You want to align strings to the left, right, or center.

### Solution

Do the math yourself, and use `substring` (Recipe 3.1) and a `StringBuilder` (Recipe 3.3). Or, just use my `StringAlign` class, which is based on the `java.text.Format` class.

### Discussion

Centering and aligning text comes up surprisingly often. Suppose you want to print a simple report with centered page numbers. There doesn't seem to be anything in the standard API that will do the job fully for you. But I have written a class called `StringAlign` that will. Here's how you might use it:

```
/* Align a page number on a 70-character line. */
public class StringAlignSimple {

    public static void main(String[] args) {
        // Construct a "formatter" to center strings.
        StringAlign formatter = new StringAlign(70, StringAlign.JUST_CENTER);
        // Try it out, for page "i"
        System.out.println(formatter.format("- i -"));
        // Try it out, for page 4. Since this formatter is
        // optimized for Strings, not specifically for page numbers,
        // we have to convert the number to a String
        System.out.println(formatter.format(Integer.toString(4)));
    }
}
```

If we compile and run this class, it prints the two demonstration line numbers centered, as shown:

```
> jikes +E -d . StringAlignSimple.java
> java StringAlignSimple
                              - i -
                               4

>
```

Example 3-4 is the code for the StringAlign class. Note that this class extends a class called Format. In the package java.text, there is a series of Format classes that all have at least one method called format( ). It is thus in a family with numerous other formatters, such as DateFormat, NumberFormat, and others, that we'll meet in upcoming chapters.

*Example 3-4. StringAlign.java*

```java
/** Bare-minimum String formatter (string aligner). */
public class StringAlign extends Format {
    /* Constant for left justification. */
    public static final int JUST_LEFT = 'l';
    /* Constant for centering. */
    public static final int JUST_CENTRE = 'c';
    /* Centering Constant, for those who spell "centre" the American way. */
    public static final int JUST_CENTER = JUST_CENTRE;
    /** Constant for right-justified Strings. */
    public static final int JUST_RIGHT = 'r';

    /** Current justification */
    private int just;
    /** Current max length */
    private int maxChars;

        /** Construct a StringAlign formatter; length and alignment are
         * passed to the Constructor instead of each format( ) call as the
         * expected common use is in repetitive formatting e.g., page numbers.
         * @param nChars - the length of the output
         * @param just - one of  JUST_LEFT, JUST_CENTRE or JUST_RIGHT
         */
    public StringAlign(int maxChars, int just) {
        switch(just) {
        case JUST_LEFT:
        case JUST_CENTRE:
        case JUST_RIGHT:
            this.just = just;
            break;
        default:
            throw new IllegalArgumentException("invalid justification arg.");
        }
        if (maxChars < 0) {
            throw new IllegalArgumentException("maxChars must be positive.");
        }
        this.maxChars = maxChars;
    }

        /** Format a String.
         * @param input _ the string to be aligned
         * @parm where - the StringBuffer to append it to.
         * @param ignore - a FieldPosition (may be null, not used but
         * specified by the general contract of Format).
         */
```

*Example 3-4. StringAlign.java (continued)*

```java
    public StringBuffer format(
        Object obj, StringBuffer where, FieldPosition ignore)  {

        String s = (String)obj;
        String wanted = s.substring(0, Math.min(s.length( ), maxChars));

        // Get the spaces in the right place.
         switch (just) {
            case JUST_RIGHT:
                pad(where, maxChars - wanted.length( ));
                where.append(wanted);
                break;
            case JUST_CENTRE:
                int startPos = where.length( );
                pad(where, (maxChars - wanted.length( ))/2);
                where.append(wanted);
                pad(where, (maxChars - wanted.length( ))/2);
                // Adjust for "rounding error"
                pad(where, maxChars - (where.length( ) - startPos));
                break;
            case JUST_LEFT:
                where.append(wanted);
                pad(where, maxChars - wanted.length( ));
                break;
            }
        return where;
    }

    protected final void pad(StringBuffer to, int howMany) {
        for (int i=0; i<howMany; i++)
            to.append(' ');
    }

    /** Convenience Routine */
    String format(String s) {
        return format(s, new StringBuffer( ), null).toString( );
    }

    /** ParseObject is required, but not useful here. */
    public Object parseObject (String source, ParsePosition pos)  {
        return source;
    }

}
```

# See Also

The alignment of numeric columns is considered in Chapter 5.

# 3.6 Converting Between Unicode Characters and Strings

## Problem

You want to convert between Unicode characters and Strings.

## Solution

Since both Java char values and Unicode characters are 16 bits in width, a char can hold any Unicode character. The charAt( ) method of String returns a Unicode character. The StringBuilder append( ) method has a form that accepts a char. Since char is an integer type, you can even do arithmetic on chars, though this is not necessary as frequently as in, say, C. Nor is it often recommended, since the Character class provides the methods for which these operations were normally used in languages such as C. Here is a program that uses arithmetic on chars to control a loop, and also appends the characters into a StringBuilder (see Recipe 3.3):

```java
/**
 * Conversion between Unicode characters and Strings
 */
public class UnicodeChars {
    public static void main(String[] argv) {
        StringBuffer b = new StringBuffer();
        for (char c = 'a'; c<'d'; c++) {
            b.append(c);
        }
        b.append('\u00a5');    // Japanese Yen symbol
        b.append('\u01FC');    // Roman AE with acute accent
        b.append('\u0391');    // GREEK Capital Alpha
        b.append('\u03A9');    // GREEK Capital Omega

        for (int i=0; i<b.length(); i++) {
            System.out.println("Character #" + i + " is " + b.charAt(i));
        }
        System.out.println("Accumulated characters are " + b);
    }
}
```

When you run it, the expected results are printed for the ASCII characters. On my Unix system, the default fonts don't include all the additional characters, so they are either omitted or mapped to irregular characters (Recipe 13.3 shows how to draw text in other fonts):

```
C:\javasrc\strings>java  UnicodeChars
Character #0 is a
Character #1 is b
Character #2 is c
Character #3 is %
```

```
Character #4 is |
Character #5 is
Character #6 is )
Accumulated characters are abc%|)
```

My Windows system doesn't have most of those characters either, but at least it prints the ones it knows are lacking as question marks (Windows system fonts are more homogenous than those of the various Unix systems, so it is easier to know what won't work). On the other hand, it tries to print the Yen sign as a Spanish capital Enye (N with a ~ over it). Amusingly, if I capture the console log under Windows into a file and display it under Unix, the Yen symbol now appears:

```
Character #0 is a
Character #1 is b
Character #2 is c
Character #3 is ¥
Character #4 is ?
Character #5 is ?
Character #6 is ?
Accumulated characters are abc¥???
```

## See Also

The Unicode program in this book's online source displays any 256-character section of the Unicode character set. Documentation listing every character in the Unicode character set can be downloaded from the Unicode Consortium at *http://www.unicode.org*.

# 3.7   Reversing a String by Word or by Character

## Problem

You wish to reverse a string, a character, or a word at a time.

## Solution

You can reverse a string by character easily, using a StringBuilder. There are several ways to reverse a string a word at a time. One natural way is to use a StringTokenizer and a *stack*. Stack is a class (defined in java.util; see Recipe 7.14) that implements an easy-to-use last-in, first-out (LIFO) stack of objects.

## Discussion

To reverse the characters in a string, use the StringBuilder reverse( ) method:

```
// StringRevChar.java
String sh = "FCGDAEB";
System.out.println(sh + " -> " + new StringBuffer(sh).reverse( ));
```

The letters in this example list the order of the sharps in the key signatures of Western music; in reverse, it lists the order of flats. Alternately, of course, you could reverse the characters yourself, using character-at-a-time mode (see Recipe 3.4).

A popular *mnemonic*, or memory aid, for the order of sharps and flats consists of one word for each sharp instead of just one letter, so we need to reverse this one word at a time. Example 3-5 adds each one to a Stack (see Recipe 7.14), then processes the whole lot in LIFO order, which reverses the order.

*Example 3-5. StringReverse.java*

```
String s = "Father Charles Goes Down And Ends Battle";

// Put it in the stack frontward
Stack myStack = new Stack();
StringTokenizer st = new StringTokenizer(s);
while (st.hasMoreTokens()) myStack.push(st.nextElement());

// Print the stack backward
System.out.print('"' + s + '"' + " backwards by word is:\n\t\"");
while (!myStack.empty()) {
    System.out.print(myStack.pop());
    System.out.print(' ');
}
System.out.println('"');
```

# 3.8   Expanding and Compressing Tabs

## Problem

You need to convert space characters to tab characters in a file, or vice versa. You might want to replace spaces with tabs to save space on disk, or go the other way to deal with a device or program that can't handle tabs.

## Solution

Use my Tabs class or its subclass EnTab.

## Discussion

Example 3-6 is a listing of EnTab, complete with a sample main program. The program works a line at a time. For each character on the line, if the character is a space, we see if we can coalesce it with previous spaces to output a single tab character. This program depends on the Tabs class, which we'll come to shortly. The Tabs class is used to decide which column positions represent tab stops and which do not. The code also has several Debug printouts. (Debug was introduced in Recipe 1.11.)

*Example 3-6. Entab.java*

```java
/**
 * EnTab: replace blanks by tabs and blanks. Transmuted from K&R Software Tools
 * book into C. Transmuted again, years later, into Java. Totally rewritten to
 * be line-at-a-time instead of char-at-a-time.
 *
 * @author Ian F. Darwin, http://www.darwinsys.com/
 * @version $Id: ch03,v 1.3 2004/05/04 18:03:14 ian Exp $
 */
public class EnTab {
    /** The Tabs (tab logic handler) */
    protected Tabs tabs;

    /**
     * Delegate tab spacing information to tabs.
     *
     * @return
     */
    public int getTabSpacing() {
        return tabs.getTabSpacing();
    }

    /**
     * Main program: just create an EnTab object, and pass the standard input
     * or the named file(s) through it.
     */
    public static void main(String[] argv) throws IOException {
        EnTab et = new EnTab(8);
        if (argv.length == 0) // do standard input
            et.entab(
                new BufferedReader(new InputStreamReader(System.in)),
                System.out);
        else
            for (int i = 0; i < argv.length; i++) { // do each file
                et.entab(
                    new BufferedReader(new FileReader(argv[i])),
                    System.out);
            }
    }

    /**
     * Constructor: just save the tab values.
     *
     * @param n
     *              The number of spaces each tab is to replace.
     */
    public EnTab(int n) {
        tabs = new Tabs(n);
    }

    public EnTab() {
        tabs = new Tabs();
    }
```

*Example 3-6. Entab.java (continued)*

```java
/**
 * entab: process one file, replacing blanks with tabs.
 *
 * @param is A BufferedReader opened to the file to be read.
 * @param out a PrintWriter to send the output to.
 */
public void entab(BufferedReader is, PrintWriter out) throws IOException {
    String line;
    int c, col = 0, newcol;

    // main loop: process entire file one line at a time.
    while ((line = is.readLine()) !- null) {
        out.println(entabLine(line));
    }
}
/**
 * entab: process one file, replacing blanks with tabs.
 *
 * @param is A BufferedReader opened to the file to be read.
 * @param out A PrintStream to write the output to.
 */
public void entab(BufferedReader is, PrintStream out) throws IOException {
    entab(is, new PrintWriter(out));
}

/**
 * entabLine: process one line, replacing blanks with tabs.
 *
 * @param line -
 *              the string to be processed
 */
public String entabLine(String line) {
    int N = line.length(), outCol = 0;
    StringBuffer sb = new StringBuffer();
    char ch;
    int consumedSpaces = 0;

    for (int inCol = 0; inCol < N; inCol++) {
        ch = line.charAt(inCol);
        // If we get a space, consume it, don't output it.
        // If this takes us to a tab stop, output a tab character.
        if (ch == ' ') {
            Debug.println("space", "Got space at " + inCol);
            if (!tabs.isTabStop(inCol)) {
                consumedSpaces++;
            } else {
                Debug.println("tab", "Got a Tab Stop "+ inCol);
                sb.append('\t');
                outCol += consumedSpaces;
                consumedSpaces = 0;
            }
            continue;
        }
```

*Example 3-6. Entab.java (continued)*

```
                // We're at a non-space; if we're just past a tab stop, we need
                // to put the "leftover" spaces back out, since we consumed
                // them above.
                while (inCol-1 > outCol) {
                    Debug.println("pad", "Padding space at "+ inCol);
                    sb.append(' ');
                    outCol++;
                }

                // Now we have a plain character to output.
                sb.append(ch);
                outCol++;

            }
            // If line ended with trailing (or only!) spaces, preserve them.
            for (int i = 0; i < consumedSpaces; i++) {
                Debug.println("trail", "Padding space at end # " + i);
                sb.append(' ');
            }
            return sb.toString( );
        }
    }
```

As the comments state, this code was patterned after a program in Kernighan and Plauger's classic work, *Software Tools*. While their version was in a language called *RatFor* (Rational Fortran), my version has since been through several translations. Their version actually worked one character at a time, and for a long time I tried to preserve this overall structure. For this edition of the book, I finally rewrote it to be a line-at-a-time program.

The program that goes in the opposite direction—putting tabs in rather than taking them out—is the DeTab class shown in Example 3-7; only the core methods are shown.

*Example 3-7. DeTab.java*

```
public class DeTab {
    Tabs ts;        // iniitialized in Constructor

    public static void main(String[] argv) throws IOException {
        DeTab dt = new DeTab(8);
        dt.detab(new BufferedReader(new InputStreamReader(System.in)),
                new PrintWriter(System.out));
    }

    /** detab one file (replace tabs with spaces)
     * @param is - the file to be processed
     * @param out - the updated file
     */
    public void detab(BufferedReader is, PrintWriter out) throws IOException {
        String line;
```

*Example 3-7. DeTab.java (continued)*

```
        char c;
        int col;
        while ((line = is.readLine()) != null) {
            out.println(detabLine(line));
        }
    }

    /** detab one line (replace tabs with spaces)
     * @param line - the line to be processed
     * @return the updated line
     */
    public String detabLine(String line) {
        char c;
        int col;
        StringBuffer sb = new StringBuffer();
        col = 0;
        for (int i = 0; i < line.length(); i++) {
            // Either ordinary character or tab.
            if ((c = line.charAt(i)) != '\t') {
                sb.append(c); // Ordinary
                ++col;
                continue;
            }
            do { // Tab, expand it, must put >=1 space
                sb.append(' ');
            } while (!ts.isTabStop(++col));
        }
        return sb.toString();
    }
}
```

The Tabs class provides two methods, settabpos( ) and istabstop( ). Example 3-8 lists the source for the Tabs class.

*Example 3-8. Tabs.java*

```
public class Tabs {
    /** tabs every so often */
    public final static int DEFTABSPACE =    8;
    /** the current tab stop setting. */
    protected int tabSpace = DEFTABSPACE;
    /** The longest line that we worry about tabs for. */
    public final static int MAXLINE  = 250;
    /** the current tab stops */
    protected boolean[] tabstops;

    /** Construct a Tabs object with a given tab stop settings */
    public Tabs(int n) {
        if (n <= 0)
            n = 1;
        tabstops = new boolean[MAXLINE];
        tabSpace = n;
```

*Example 3-8. Tabs.java (continued)*

```
        settabs();
    }

    /** Construct a Tabs object with a default tab stop settings */
    public Tabs() {
        this(DEFTABSPACE);
    }

    /** settabs - set initial tab stops */
    private void settabs() {
        for (int i = 0; i < tabstops.length; i++) {
            tabstops[i] = ((i+1) % tabSpace) == 0;
            Debug.println("tabs", "Tabs[" + i + "]=" + tabstops[i]);
        }
    }

    /**
     * @return Returns the tabSpace.
     */
    public int getTabSpacing() {
        return tabSpace;
    }

    /** isTabStop - returns true if given column is a tab stop.
     * If current input line is too long, we just put tabs wherever,
     * no exception is thrown.
     * @param col - the current column number
     */
    public boolean isTabStop(int col) {
        if (col > tabstops.length-1) {
            tabstops = new boolean[tabstops.length * 2];
            settabs();
        }
        return tabstops[col];
    }
}
```

# 3.9   Controlling Case

## Problem

You need to convert strings to uppercase or lowercase, or to compare strings without regard for case.

## Solution

The String class has a number of methods for dealing with documents in a particular case. toUpperCase( ) and toLowerCase( ) each return a new string that is a copy of the current string, but converted as the name implies. Each can be called either with no arguments or with a Locale argument specifying the conversion rules; this is necessary because of internationalization. Java provides significantly more internationalization and localization features than ordinary languages, a feature that is covered in Chapter 15. While the equals( ) method tells you if another string is exactly the same, equalsIgnoreCase( ) tells you if all characters are the same regardless of case. Here, you can't specify an alternate locale; the system's default locale is used:

```
// Case.java
String name = "Java Cookbook";
System.out.println("Normal:\t" + name);
System.out.println("Upper:\t" + name.toUpperCase( ));
System.out.println("Lower:\t" + name.toLowerCase( ));
String javaName - "java cookBook"; // As if it were Java identifiers :-)
if (!name.equals(javaName))
    System.err.println("equals( ) correctly reports false");
else
    System.err.println("equals( ) incorrectly reports true");
if (name.equalsIgnoreCase(javaName))
    System.err.println("equalsIgnoreCase( ) correctly reports true");
else
    System.err.println("equalsIgnoreCase( ) incorrectly reports false");
```

If you run this, it prints the first name changed to uppercase and lowercase, then it reports that both methods work as expected.

```
C:\javasrc\strings>java Case
Normal: Java Cookbook
Upper:  JAVA COOKBOOK
Lower:  java cookbook
equals( ) correctly reports false
equalsIgnoreCase( ) correctly reports true
```

## See Also

Regular expressions make it simpler to ignore case in string searching (see Chapter 4).

# 3.10   Indenting Text Documents

## Problem

You need to indent (or "undent" or "dedent") a text document.

## Solution

To indent, either generate a fixed-length string and prepend it to each output line, or use a for loop and print the right number of spaces:

```
// Indent.java
/** the default number of spaces. */
static int nSpaces = 10;
```

```
        while ((inputLine = is.readLine()) != null) {
            for (int i=0; i<nSpaces; i++) System.out.print(' ');
            System.out.println(inputLine);
        }
```

A more efficient approach to generating the spaces might be to construct a long string of spaces and use substring( ) to get the number of spaces you need.

To undent, use substring to generate a string that does not include the leading spaces. Be careful of inputs that are shorter than the amount you are removing! By popular demand, I'll give you this one, too. First, though, here's a demonstration of an Undent object created with an undent value of 5, meaning remove up to five spaces (but don't lose other characters in the first five positions):

```
$ java Undent
Hello World
Hello World
 Hello
Hello
     Hello
Hello
      Hello
 Hello

^C
$
```

I test it by entering the usual test string "Hello World", which prints fine. Then "Hello" with one space, and the space is deleted. With five spaces, exactly the five spaces go. With six or more spaces, only five spaces go. A blank line comes out as a blank line (i.e., without throwing an Exception or otherwise going berserk). I think it works!

```
import java.io.*;

/** Undent - remove up to 'n' leading spaces
 */
public class Undent {
    /** the maximum number of spaces to remove. */
    protected int nSpaces;

    Undent(int n) {
        nSpaces = n;
    }

    public static void main(String[] av) {
        Undent c = new Undent(5);
        switch(av.length) {
            case 0: c.process(new BufferedReader(
                            new InputStreamReader(System.in))); break;
            default:
            for (int i=0; i<av.length; i++)
                try {
```

```
            c.process(new BufferedReader(new FileReader(av[i])));
        } catch (FileNotFoundException e) {
            System.err.println(e);
        }
    }
}

/** process one file, given an open BufferedReader */
public void process(BufferedReader is) {
    try {
        String inputLine;

        while ((inputLine = is.readLine()) != null) {
            int toRemove = 0;
            for (int i=0; i<nSpaces && i < inputLine.length(); i++)
                if (Character.isSpace(inputLine.charAt(i)))
                    ++toRemove;
            System.out.println(inputLine.substring(toRemove));
        }
        is.close();
    } catch (IOException e) {
        System.out.println("IOException: " + e);
    }
}
}
```

# 3.11   Entering Nonprintable Characters

## Problem

You need to put nonprintable characters into strings.

## Solution

Use the backslash character and one of the Java string escapes.

## Discussion

The Java string escapes are listed in Table 3-1.

*Table 3-1. String escapes*

| To get: | Use: | Notes |
|---------|------|-------|
| Tab | \t | |
| Linefeed (Unix newline) | \n | See System.getProperty("line.separator"), which gives you the platform's line end. |
| Carriage return | \r | |
| Form feed | \f | |
| Backspace | \b | |

Table 3-1. String escapes (continued)

| To get: | Use: | Notes |
|---------|------|-------|
| Single quote | \' | |
| Double quote | \" | |
| Unicode character | \u*NNNN* | Four hexadecimal digits (no \x as in C/C++). See *http://www.unicode.org* for codes. |
| Octal(!) character | \*NNN* | Who uses octal (base 8) these days? |
| Backslash | \\ | |

Here is a code example that shows most of these in action:

```
// StringEscapes.java
System.out.println("Java Strings in action:");
// System.out.println("An alarm or alert: \a");    // not supported
System.out.println("An alarm entered in Octal: \007");
System.out.println("A tab key: \t(what comes after)");
System.out.println("A newline: \n(what comes after)");
System.out.println("A Unicode character: \u0207");
System.out.println("A backslash character: \\");
```

If you have a lot of non-ASCII characters to enter, you may wish to consider using Java's input methods, discussed briefly in the JDK online documentation.

# 3.12   Trimming Blanks from the End of a String

## Problem

You need to work on a string without regard for extra leading or trailing spaces a user may have typed.

## Solution

Use the String class trim( ) method.

## Discussion

Example 3-9 uses trim( ) to strip an arbitrary number of leading spaces and/or tabs from lines of Java source code in order to look for the characters //+ and //-. These strings are special Java comments I use to mark the parts of the programs in this book that I want to include in the printed copy.

*Example 3-9. GetMark.java (trimming and comparing strings)*

```
/** the default starting mark. */
public final String startMark = "//+";
/** the default ending mark. */
public final String endMark = "//-";
/** True if we are currently inside marks. */
protected boolean printing = false;
```

*Example 3-9. GetMark.java (trimming and comparing strings) (continued)*

```
      try {
        String inputLine;

    while ((inputLine = is.readLine()) != null) {
        if (inputLine.trim().equals(startMark)) {
            printing = true;
        } else if (inputLine.trim().equals(endMark)) {
            printing = false;
        } else if (printing)
            System.out.println(inputLine);
            }
            is.close();
        } catch (IOException e) {
          // not shown
        }
    }
```

# 3.13   Parsing Comma-Separated Data

## Problem

You have a string or a file of lines containing comma-separated values (CSV) that you need to read. Many Windows-based spreadsheets and some databases use CSV to export data.

## Solution

Use my CSV class or a regular expression (see Chapter 4).

## Discussion

CSV is deceptive. It looks simple at first glance, but the values may be quoted or unquoted. If quoted, they may further contain escaped quotes. This far exceeds the capabilities of the StringTokenizer class (Recipe 3.2). Either considerable Java coding or the use of regular expressions is required. I'll show both ways.

First, a Java program. Assume for now that we have a class called CSV that has a no-argument constructor and a method called parse() that takes a string representing one line of the input file. The parse() method returns a list of fields. For flexibility, the fields are returned as a List, from which you can obtain an Iterator (see Recipe 7.4). I simply use the Iterator's hasNext() method to control the loop and its next() method to get the next object:

```
import java.util.*;

/* Simple demo of CSV parser class.
 */
public class CSVSimple {
```

```
public static void main(String[] args) {
    CSV parser = new CSV();
    List  list = parser.parse(
        "\"LU\",86.25,\"11/4/1998\",\"2:19PM\",+4.0625");
    Iterator it = list.iterator( );
    while (it.hasNext( )) {
        System.out.println(it.next( ));
    }
}
}
```

After the quotes are escaped, the string being parsed is actually the following:

```
"LU",86.25,"11/4/1998","2:19PM",+4.0625
```

Running CSVSimple yields the following output:

```
> java CSVSimple
LU
86.25
11/4/1998
2:19PM
+4.0625
>
```

But what about the CSV class itself? The code in Example 3-10 started as a translation of a CSV program written in C++ by Brian W. Kernighan and Rob Pike that appeared in their book *The Practice of Programming* (Addison Wesley). Their version commingled the input processing with the parsing; my CSV class does only the parsing since the input could be coming from any of a variety of sources. And it has been substantially rewritten over time. The main work is done in parse( ), which delegates handling of individual fields to advquoted( ) in cases where the field begins with a quote; otherwise, to advplain( ).

*Example 3-10. CSV.java*

```
import java.util.*;

import com.darwinsys.util.Debug;

/** Parse comma-separated values (CSV), a common Windows file format.
 * Sample input: "LU",86.25,"11/4/1998","2:19PM",+4.0625
 * <p>
 * Inner logic adapted from a C++ original that was
 * Copyright (C) 1999 Lucent Technologies
 * Excerpted from 'The Practice of Programming'
 * by Brian W. Kernighan and Rob Pike.
 * <p>
 * Included by permission of the http://tpop.awl.com/ web site,
 * which says:
 * "You may use this code for any purpose, as long as you leave
 * the copyright notice and book citation attached." I have done so.
 * @author Brian W. Kernighan and Rob Pike (C++ original)
 * @author Ian F. Darwin (translation into Java and removal of I/O)
```

*Example 3-10. CSV.java (continued)*

```java
 * @author Ben Ballard (rewrote advQuoted to handle '"""' and for readability)
 */
public class CSV {

    public static final char DEFAULT_SEP = ',';

    /** Construct a CSV parser, with the default separator (','). */
    public CSV( ) {
        this(DEFAULT_SEP);
    }

    /** Construct a CSV parser with a given separator.
     * @param sep The single char for the separator (not a list of
     * separator characters)
     */
    public CSV(char sep) {
        fieldSep = sep;
    }

    /** The fields in the current String */
    protected List list = new ArrayList( );

    /** the separator char for this parser */
    protected char fieldSep;

    /** parse: break the input String into fields
     * @return java.util.Iterator containing each field
     * from the original as a String, in order.
     */
    public List parse(String line)
    {
        StringBuffer sb = new StringBuffer( );
        list.clear( );              // recycle to initial state
        int i = 0;

        if (line.length( ) == 0) {
            list.add(line);
            return list;
        }

        do {
            sb.setLength(0);
            if (i < line.length( ) && line.charAt(i) == '"')
                i = advQuoted(line, sb, ++i);    // skip quote
            else
                i = advPlain(line, sb, i);
            list.add(sb.toString( ));
            Debug.println("csv", sb.toString( ));
            i++;
        } while (i < line.length( ));

        return list;
    }
```

*Example 3-10. CSV.java (continued)*

```java
/** advQuoted: quoted field; return index of next separator */
protected int advQuoted(String s, StringBuffer sb, int i)
{
    int j;
    int len= s.length( );
    for (j=i; j<len; j++) {
        if (s.charAt(j) == '"' && j+1 < len) {
            if (s.charAt(j+1) == '"') {
                j++; // skip escape char
            } else if (s.charAt(j+1) == fieldSep) { //next delimiter
                j++; // skip end quotes
                break;
            }
        } else if (s.charAt(j) == '"' && j+1 == len) { // end quotes at end of line
            break; //done
        }
        sb.append(s.charAt(j));    // regular character.
    }
    return j;
}

/** advPlain: unquoted field; return index of next separator */
protected int advPlain(String s, StringBuffer sb, int i)
{
    int j;

    j = s.indexOf(fieldSep, i); // look for separator
    Debug.println("csv", "i = " + i + ", j = " + j);
    if (j == -1) {                    // none found
        sb.append(s.substring(i));
        return s.length( );
    } else {
        sb.append(s.substring(i, j));
        return j;
    }
}
}
```

In the online source directory, you'll find *CSVFile.java*, which reads a text file and runs it through parse( ). You'll also find Kernighan and Pike's original C++ program.

We haven't discussed regular expressions yet (we will in Chapter 4). However, many readers are familiar with regexes in a general way, so the following example demonstrates the power of regexes, as well as providing code for you to reuse. Note that this program replaces *all* the code* in both *CSV.java* and *CSVFile.java*. The key to understanding regexes is that a little specification can match a lot of data.

---

* With the caveat that it doesn't handle different delimiters; this could be added using GetOpt and constructing the pattern around the delimiter.

```java
import java.io.BufferedReader;
import java.io.IOException;
import java.io.InputStreamReader;
import java.util.ArrayList;
import java.util.List;
import java.util.regex.Matcher;
import java.util.regex.Pattern;

/* Simple demo of CSV matching using Regular Expressions.
 * Does NOT use the "CSV" class defined in the Java CookBook, but uses
 * a regex pattern simplified from Chapter 7 of <em>Mastering Regular
 * Expressions</em> (p. 205, first edn.)
 * @version $Id: ch03,v 1.3 2004/05/04 18:03:14 ian Exp $
 */
public class CSVRE {
    /** The rather involved pattern used to match CSV's consists of three
     * alternations: the first matches aquoted field, the second unquoted,
     * the third a null field.
     */
    public static final String CSV_PATTERN = "\"([^\"]+?)\",?|([^,]+),?|,";
    private static Pattern csvRE;

    public static void main(String[] argv) throws IOException {
        System.out.println(CSV_PATTERN);
        new CSVRE().process(new BufferedReader(new InputStreamReader(System.in)));
    }

    /** Construct a regex-based CSV parser. */
    public CSVRE() {
        csvRE = Pattern.compile(CSV_PATTERN);
    }

    /** Process one file. Delegates to parse() a line at a time */
    public void process(BufferedReader in) throws IOException {
        String line;

        // For each line...
        while ((line = in.readline()) != null) {
            System.out.println("line = `" + line + "'");
            List l = parse(line);
            System.out.println("Found " + l.size() + " items.");
            for (int i = 0; i < l.size(); i++) {
                System.out.print(l.get(i) + ",");
            }
            System.out.println();
        }
    }

    /** Parse one line.
     * @return List of Strings, minus their double quotes
     */
    public List parse(String line) {
        List list = new ArrayList();
        Matcher m = csvRE.matcher(line);
```

```
        // For each field
        while (m.find()) {
            System.out.println(m.groupCount());
            String match = m.group();
            if (match == null)
                break;
            if (match.endsWith(",")) {// trim trailing ,
                match = match.substring(0, match.length() - 1);
            }
            if (match.startsWith("\"")) { // assume also ends with
                match = match.substring(1, match.length() - 1);
            }
            if (match.length() == 0)
                match = null;
            list.add(match);
        }
        return list;
    }
}
```

It is sometimes "downright scary" how much mundane code you can eliminate with a single, well-formulated regular expression.

## 3.14  Program: A Simple Text Formatter

This program is a very primitive text formatter, representative of what people used on most computing platforms before the rise of standalone graphics-based word processors, laser printers, and, eventually, desktop publishing, word processors, and desktop office suites. It simply reads words from a file—previously created with a text editor—and outputs them until it reaches the right margin, when it calls println( ) to append a line ending. For example, here is an input file:

```
It's a nice
day, isn't it, Mr. Mxyzzptllxy?
I think we should
go for a walk.
```

Given the above as its input, the Fmt program prints the lines formatted neatly:

```
It's a nice day, isn't it, Mr. Mxyzzptllxy? I think we should go for a
walk.
```

As you can see, it fits the text we gave it to the margin and discards all the line breaks present in the original. Here's the code:

```
import java.io.*;
import java.util.*;

/**
 * Fmt - format text (like Berkeley Unix fmt).
 */
```

```java
public class Fmt {
    /** The maximum column width */
    public static final int COLWIDTH=72;
    /** The file that we read and format */
    BufferedReader in;

    /** If files present, format each, else format the standard input. */
    public static void main(String[] av) throws IOException {
        if (av.length == 0)
            new Fmt(System.in).format();
        else for (int i=0; i<av.length; i++)
            new Fmt(av[i]).format();
    }

    /** Construct a Formatter given a filename */
    public Fmt(String fname) throws IOException {
        in = new BufferedReader(new FileReader(fname));
    }

    /** Construct a Formatter given an open Stream */
    public Fmt(InputStream file) throws IOException {
        in = new BufferedReader(new InputStreamReader(file));
    }

    /** Format the File contained in a construcLed Fmt object */
    public void format() throws IOException {
        String w, f;
        int col = 0;
        while ((w = in.readLine()) != null) {
            if (w.length() == 0) {      // null line
                System.out.print("\n");         // end current line
                if (col>0) {
                    System.out.print("\n");     // output blank line
                    col = 0;
                }
                continue;
            }

            // otherwise it's text, so format it.
            StringTokenizer st = new StringTokenizer(w);
            while (st.hasMoreTokens()) {
                f = st.nextToken();

                if (col + f.length() > COLWIDTH) {
                    System.out.print("\n");
                    col = 0;
                }
                System.out.print(f + " ");
                col += f.length() + 1;
            }
        }
        if (col>0) System.out.print("\n");
        in.close();
    }
}
```

A slightly fancier version of this program, Fmt2, is in the online source for this book. It uses "dot commands"—lines beginning with periods—to give limited control over the formatting. A family of "dot command" formatters includes Unix's *roff, nroff, troff*, and *groff*, which are in the same family with programs called *runoff* on Digital Equipment systems. The original for this is J. Saltzer's *runoff*, which first appeared on Multics and from there made its way into various OSes. To save trees, I did not include Fmt2 here; it subclasses Fmt and overrides the format( ) method to include additional functionality.

## 3.15   Program: Soundex Name Comparisons

The difficulties in comparing (American-style) names inspired the development of the Soundex algorithm, in which each of a given set of consonants maps to a particular number. This was apparently devised for use by the Census Bureau to map similar-sounding names together on the grounds that in those days many people were illiterate and could not spell their family names consistently. But it is still useful today—for example, in a company-wide telephone book application. The names Darwin and Derwin, for example, map to D650, and Darwent maps to D653, which puts it adjacent to D650. All of these are historical variants of the same name. Suppose we needed to sort lines containing these names together: if we could output the Soundex numbers at the beginning of each line, this would be easy. Here is a simple demonstration of the Soundex class:

```
/** Simple demonstration of Soundex.  */
public class SoundexSimple {

    /** main */
    public static void main(String[] args) {
        String[] names = {
            "Darwin, Ian",
            "Davidson, Greg",
            "Darwent, William",
            "Derwin, Daemon"
        };
        for (int i = 0; i< names.length; i++)
            System.out.println(Soundex.soundex(names[i]) + ' ' + names[i]);
    }
}
```

Let's run it:

```
> jikes +E -d . SoundexSimple.java
> java SoundexSimple | sort
D132 Davidson, Greg
D650 Darwin, Ian
D650 Derwin, Daemon
D653 Darwent, William
>
```

As you can see, the Darwin-variant names (including Daemon Derwin*) all sort together and are distinct from the Davidson (and Davis, Davies, etc.) names that normally appear between Darwin and Derwin when using a simple alphabetic sort. The Soundex algorithm has done its work.

Here is the Soundex class itself: it uses Strings and StringBuilders to convert names into Soundex codes. A JUnit test (see Recipe 1.14) is also online as *SoundexTest.java*.

```
import com.darwinsys.util.Debug;
/**
 * Soundex - the Soundex Algorithm, as described by Knuth
 * <p>
 * This class implements the soundex algorithm as described by Donald
 * Knuth in Volume 3 of <I>The Art of Computer Programming</I>.  The
 * algorithm is intended to hash words (in particular surnames) into
 * a small space using a simple model which approximates the sound of
 * the word when spoken by an English speaker.  Each word is reduced
 * to a four character string, the first character being an upper case
 * letter and the remaining three being digits. Double letters are
 * collapsed to a single digit.
 *
 * <h2>EXAMPLES</h2>
 * Knuth's examples of various names and the soundex codes they map
 * to are:
 * <b>Euler, Ellery -> E460
 * <b>Gauss, Ghosh -> G200
 * <b>Hilbert, Heilbronn -> H416
 * <b>Knuth, Kant -> K530
 * <b>Lloyd, Ladd -> L300
 * <b>Lukasiewicz, Lissajous -> L222
 *
 * <h2>LIMITATIONS</h2>
 * As the soundex algorithm was originally used a <B>long</B> time ago
 * in the United States of America, it uses only the English alphabet
 * and pronunciation.
 * <p>
 * As it is mapping a large space (arbitrary length strings) onto a
 * small space (single letter plus 3 digits) no inference can be made
 * about the similarity of two strings which end up with the same
 * soundex code.  For example, both "Hilbert" and "Heilbronn" end up
 * with a soundex code of "H416".
 * <p>
 * The soundex() method is static, as it maintains no per-instance
 * state; this means you never need to instantiate this class.
 *
 * @author Perl implementation by Mike Stok (<stok@cybercom.net>) from
 * the description given by Knuth.  Ian Phillips (<ian@pipex.net>) and
 * Rich Pinder (<rpinder@hsc.usc.edu>) supplied ideas and spotted
 * mistakes.
 */
```

---

* In Unix terminology, a *daemon* is a server. The word has nothing to do with demons but refers to a helper or assistant. Derwin Daemon is actually a character in Susannah Coleman's "Source Wars" online comic strip; see *http://darby.daemonnews.org*.

```
public class Soundex {

    /* Implements the mapping
     * from: AEHIOUWYBFPVCGJKQSXZDTLMNR
     * to:   000000001111122222222334556
     */
    public static final char[] MAP = {
        //A  B   C   D   E   F   G   H   I   J   K   L   M
        '0','1','2','3','0','1','2','0','0','2','2','4','5',
        //N  O   P   W   R   S   T   U   V   W   X   Y   Z
        '5','0','1','2','6','2','3','0','1','0','2','0','2'
    };

    /** Convert the given String to its Soundex code.
     * @return null if the given string can't be mapped to Soundex.
     */
    public static String soundex(String s) {

        // Algorithm works on uppercase (mainframe era).
        String t = s.toUpperCase();

        StringBuffer res = new StringBuffer();
        char c, prev = '?';

        // Main loop: find up to 4 chars that map.
        for (int i=0; i<t.length() && res.length() < 4 &&
            (c = t.charAt(i)) != ','; i++) {

            // Check to see if the given character is alphabetic.
            // Text is already converted to uppercase. Algorithm
            // handles only ASCII letters; do NOT use Character.isLetter()!
            // Also, skip double letters.
            if (c>='A' && c<='Z' && c != prev) {
                prev = c;

                // First char is installed unchanged, for sorting.
                if (i==0)
                    res.append(c);
                else {
                    char m = MAP[c-'A'];
                    Debug.println("inner", c + " --> " + m);
                    if (m != '0')
                        res.append(m);
                }
            }
        }
        if (res.length() == 0)
            return null;
        for (int i=res.length(); i<4; i++)
            res.append('0');
        return res.toString();
    }
}
```

# CHAPTER 4

# Pattern Matching with Regular Expressions

## 4.0    Introduction

Suppose you have been on the Internet for a few years and have been very faithful about saving all your correspondence, just in case you (or your lawyers, or the prosecution) need a copy. The result is that you have a 50-megabyte disk partition dedicated to saved mail. And let's further suppose that you remember that somewhere in there is an email message from someone named Angie or Anjie. Or was it Angy? But you don't remember what you called it or where you stored it. Obviously, you have to look for it.

But while some of you go and try to open up all 15,000,000 documents in a word processor, I'll just find it with one simple command. Any system that provides regular expression support allows me to search for the pattern in several ways. The simplest to understand is:

```
Angie|Anjie|Angy
```

which you can probably guess means just to search for any of the variations. A more concise form ("more thinking, less typing") is:

```
An[^ dn]
```

to search in all the files. The syntax will become clear as we go through this chapter. Briefly, the "A" and the "n" match themselves, in effect finding words that begin with "An", while the cryptic [^ dn] requires the "An" to be followed by a character other than a space (to eliminate the very common English word "an" at the start of a sentence) or "d" (to eliminate the common word "and") or "n" (to eliminate Anne, Announcing, etc.). Has your word processor gotten past its splash screen yet? Well, it doesn't matter, because I've already found the missing file. To find the answer, I just typed the command:

```
grep 'An[^ dn]' *
```

*Regular expressions*, or regexes for short, provide a concise and precise specification of patterns to be matched in text.

As another example of the power of regular expressions, consider the problem of bulk-updating hundreds of files. When I started with Java, the syntax declaring array references was baseType arrayVariableName[]. For example, a method with an array argument, such as every program's main method, was commonly written as:

```
public static void main(String args[]) {
```

But as time went by, it became clear to the stewards of the Java language that it would be better to write it as baseType[] arrayVariableName, e.g.:

```
public static void main(String[] args) {
```

This is better Java style because it associates the "array-ness" of the type with the type itself, rather than with the local argument name, and the compiler now accepts both modes. I wanted to change all occurrences of main written the old way to the new way. I used the pattern 'main(String [a-z]' with the *grep* utility described earlier to find the names of all the files containing old-style main declarations, that is, main(String followed by a space and a name character rather than an open square bracket. I then used another regex-based Unix tool, the stream editor *sed*, in a little shell script to change all occurrences in those files from 'main(String \([a-z][a-z]*\ )\[\]' to 'main(String[] \1' (the syntax used here is discussed later in this chapter). Again, the regex-based approach was orders of magnitude faster than doing it interactively, even using a reasonably powerful editor such as vi or emacs, let alone trying to use a graphical word processor.

Unfortunately, the syntax of regexes has changed as they get incorporated into more tools* and more languages, so the exact syntax in the previous examples is not exactly what you'd use in Java, but it does convey the conciseness and power of the regex mechanism.

As a third example, consider parsing an Apache web server log file, where some fields are delimited with quotes, others with square brackets, and others with spaces. Writing *ad-hoc* code to parse this is messy in any language, but a well-crafted regex can break the line into all its constituent fields in one operation (this example is developed in Recipe 4.10).

These same time gains can be had by Java developers. Prior to 1.4, Java did not include any facilities for describing regular expressions in text. This is mildly surprising given how powerful regular expressions are, how ubiquitous they are on the Unix operating system (where Java was first brewed), and how powerful they are in modern scripting languages like *sed*, *awk*, Python, and Perl. Table 4-1 lists about half a

---

* Non-Unix fans fear not, for you can do this on Win32 using one of several packages. One is an open source package alternately called CygWin (after Cygnus Software) or GnuWin32 (*http://sources.redhat.com/cygwin/*). Another is Microsoft's own Unix Services for Windows. Or you can use my Grep program in Recipe 4.6 if you don't have grep on your system. Incidentally, the name *grep* comes from an ancient Unix line editor command g/RE/p, the command to find the regex globally in all lines in the edit buffer and print the lines that match—just what the *grep* program does to lines in files.

dozen regular expression packages for Java. I even wrote my own at one point; it worked well enough but was too slow for production use. The Apache Jakarta Regular Expressions and ORO packages are widely used.

*Table 4-1. Some Java regex packages*

| Package | Notes | URL |
| --- | --- | --- |
| JDK 1.4 API | Package `java.util.regex` | *http://java.sun.com/* |
| Richard Emberson's | Unknown license; not being maintained | None; posted to *advanced-java@berkeley.edu* in 1998 |
| Ian Darwin's regex | Simple, but slow. Incomplete; didactic | *http://www.darwinsys.com/java/* |
| Apache Jakarta RegExp (original by Jonathan Locke) | Apache (BSD-like) license | *http://jakarta.apache.org/regexp/* |
| Apache Jakarta ORO (original by Daniel Savarese) | Apache license; more comprehensive than Jakarta RegExp | *http://jakarta.apache.org/oro/* |
| GNU Java Regexp | Lesser GNU Public License | *http://www.cacas.org/java/gnu/regexp/* |

With JDK 1.4 and later, regular expression support is built into the standard Java runtime. The advantage of using the JDK 1.4 package is its integration with the runtime, including the standard class `java.lang.String` and the "new I/O" package. In addition to this integration, the JDK 1.4 package is one of the fastest Java implementations. However, code using any of the other packages still works, and you will find existing applications using some of these packages for the next few years since the syntax of each package is slightly different and it's not necessary to convert. Any new development, though, should be based on the JDK 1.4 regex package.

The first edition of this book focused on the Jakarta RegExp package; this edition covers the JDK 1.4 Regular Expressions API and does not cover any other package. The syntax of regexes themselves is discussed in Recipe 4.1, and the syntax of the Java API for using regexes is described in Recipe 4.2. The remaining recipes show some applications of regex technology in JDK 1.4.

## See Also

*Mastering Regular Expressions* by Jeffrey E. F. Friedl (O'Reilly), now in its second edition, is the definitive guide to all the details of regular expressions. Most introductory books on Unix and Perl include some discussion of regexes; *Unix Power Tools* (O'Reilly) devotes a chapter to them.

# 4.1  Regular Expression Syntax

## Problem

You need to learn the syntax of JDK 1.4 regular expressions.

# Solution

Consult Table 4-2 for a list of the regular expression characters.

# Discussion

These pattern characters let you specify regexes of considerable power. In building patterns, you can use any combination of ordinary text and the *metacharacters*, or special characters, in Table 4-2. These can all be used in any combination that makes sense. For example, a+ means any number of occurrences of the letter a, from one up to a million or a gazillion. The pattern Mrs?\. matches Mr. or Mrs.. And .* means "any character, any number of times," and is similar in meaning to most command-line interpreters' meaning of the * alone. The pattern \d+ means any number of numeric digits. \d{2,3} means a two- or three-digit number.

*Table 4-2. Regular expression metacharacter syntax*

| Subexpression | Matches | Notes |
|---|---|---|
| **General** | | |
| ^ | Start of line/string | |
| $ | End of line/string | |
| \b | Word boundary | |
| \B | Not a word boundary | |
| \A | Beginning of entire string | |
| \z | End of entire string | |
| \Z | End of entire string (except allowable final line terminator) | See Recipe 4.9 |
| . | Any one character (except line terminator) | |
| [...] | "Character class"; any one character from those listed | |
| [^...] | Any one character not from those listed | See Recipe 4.2 |
| **Alternation and grouping** | | |
| (...) | Grouping (capture groups) | See Recipe 4.3 |
| \| | Alternation | |
| (?:*re*) | Noncapturing parenthesis | |
| \G | End of the previous match | |
| \\*n* | Back-reference to capture group number "*n*" | |
| **Normal (greedy) multipliers** | | |
| {*m,n*} | Multiplier for "from *m* to *n* repetitions" | See Recipe 4.4 |
| {*m,*} | Multiplier for "*m* or more repetitions" | |
| {*m*} | Multiplier for "exactly *m* repetitions" | See Recipe 4.10 |
| {*,n*} | Multiplier for 0 up to *n* repetitions | |
| * | Multiplier for 0 or more repetitions | Short for {0,} |
| + | Multiplier for 1 or more repetitions | Short for {1,}; see Recipe 4.2 |

*Table 4-2. Regular expression metacharacter syntax (continued)*

| Subexpression | Matches | Notes |
|---|---|---|
| ? | Multiplier for 0 or 1 repetitions (i.e, present exactly once, or not at all) | Short for {0,1} |
| **Reluctant (non-greedy) multipliers** | | |
| {*m*,*n*}? | Reluctant multiplier for "from *m* to *n* repetitions" | |
| {*m*,}? | Reluctant multiplier for "*m* or more repetitions" | |
| {,*n*}? | Reluctant multiplier for 0 up to *n* repetitions | |
| *? | Reluctant multiplier: 0 or more | |
| +? | Reluctant multiplier: 1 or more | See Recipe 4.10 |
| ?? | Reluctant multiplier: 0 or 1 times | |
| **Possessive (very greedy) multipliers** | | |
| {*m*,*n*}+ | Possessive multiplier for "from *m* to *n* repetitions" | |
| {*m*,}+ | Possessive multiplier for "*m* or more repetitions" | |
| {,*n*}+ | Possessive multiplier for 0 up to *n* repetitions | |
| *+ | Possessive multiplier: 0 or more | |
| ++ | Possessive multiplier: 1 or more | |
| ?+ | Possessive multiplier: 0 or 1 times | |
| **Escapes and shorthands** | | |
| \ | Escape (quote) character: turns most metacharacters off; turns subsequent alphabetic into metacharacters | |
| \Q | Escape (quote) all characters up to \E | |
| \E | Ends quoting begun with \Q | |
| \t | Tab character | |
| \r | Return (carriage return) character | |
| \n | Newline character | See Recipe 4.9 |
| \f | Form feed | |
| \w | Character in a word | Use \w+ for a word; see Recipe 4.10 |
| \W | A non-word character | |
| \d | Numeric digit | Use \d+ for an integer; see Recipe 4.2 |
| \D | A non-digit character | |
| \s | Whitespace | Space, tab, etc., as determined by java.lang.Character. isWhitespace( ) |
| \S | A nonwhitespace character | See Recipe 4.10 |
| **Unicode blocks (representative samples)** | | |
| \p{InGreek} | A character in the Greek block | (simple block) |
| \P{InGreek} | Any character not in the Greek block | |
| \p{Lu} | An uppercase letter | (simple category) |
| \p{Sc} | A currency symbol | |

*Table 4-2. Regular expression metacharacter syntax (continued)*

| Subexpression | Matches | Notes |
|---|---|---|
| **POSIX-style character classes (defined only for US-ASCII)** | | |
| \p{Alnum} | Alphanumeric characters | [A-Za-z0-9] |
| \p{Alpha} | Alphabetic characters | [A-Za-z] |
| \p{ASCII} | Any ASCII character | [\x00-\x7F] |
| \p{Blank} | Space and tab characters | |
| \p{Space} | Space characters | [ \t\n\x0B\f\r] |
| \p{Cntrl} | Control characters | [\x00-\x1F\x7F] |
| \p{Digit} | Numeric digit characters | [0-9] |
| \p{Graph} | Printable and visible characters (not spaces or control characters) | |
| \p{Print} | Printable characters | Same as \p{Graph} |
| \p{Punct} | Punctuation characters | One of !"#$%&'( )*+,-./:;<=> ?@[\]^_`{|}~ |
| \p{Lower} | Lowercase characters | [a-z] |
| \p{Upper} | Uppercase characters | [A-Z] |
| \p{XDigit} | Hexadecimal digit characters | [0-9a-fA-F] |

Regexes match anyplace possible in the string. Patterns followed by a *greedy* multiplier (the only type that existed in traditional Unix regexes) consume (match) as much as possible without compromising any subexpressions which follow; patterns followed by a *possessive* multiplier match as much as possible without regard to following subexpressions; patterns followed by a *reluctant* multiplier consume as few characters as possible to still get a match.

Also, unlike regex packages in some other languages, the JDK 1.4 package was designed to handle Unicode characters from the beginning. And the standard Java escape sequence \u*nnnn* is used to specify a Unicode character in the pattern. We use methods of java.lang.Character to determine Unicode character properties, such as whether a given character is a space.

To help you learn how regexes work, I provide a little program called REDemo.* In the online directory *javasrc/RE*, you should be able to type either ant REDemo, or javac REDemo followed by java REDemo, to get the program running.

In the uppermost text box (see Figure 4-1), type the regex pattern you want to test. Note that as you type each character, the regex is checked for syntax; if the syntax is OK, you see a checkmark beside it. You can then select Match, Find, or Find All. Match means that the entire string must match the regex, while Find means the regex must be found somewhere in the string (Find All counts the number of occurrences

---

* REDemo was inspired by (but does not use any code from) a similar program provided with the Jakarta Regular Expressions package mentioned in the Introduction to Chapter 4.

that are found). Below that, you type a string that the regex is to match against. Experiment to your heart's content. When you have the regex the way you want it, you can paste it into your Java program. You'll need to escape (backslash) any characters that are treated specially by both the Java compiler and the JDK 1.4 regex package, such as the backslash itself, double quotes, and others (see the sidebar "Remember This!").

---

### Remember This!

Remember that because a regex compiles strings that are also compiled by *javac*, you usually need two levels of escaping for any special characters, including backslash, double quotes, and so on. For example, the regex:

```
"You said it\."
```

has to be typed like this to be a Java language `String`:

```
"\"You said it\\.\""
```

I can't tell you how many times I've made the mistake of forgetting the extra backslash in \d+, \w+, and their kin!

---

In Figure 4-1, I typed qu into the REDemo program's Pattern box, which is a syntactically valid regex pattern: any ordinary characters stand as regexes for themselves, so this looks for the letter q followed by u. In the top version, I typed only a q into the string, which is not matched. In the second, I have typed quack and the q of a second quack. Since I have selected Find All, the count shows one match. As soon as I type the second u, the count is updated to two, as shown in the third version.

Regexes can do far more than just character matching. For example, the two-character regex ^T would match beginning of line (^) immediately followed by a capital T—i.e., any line beginning with a capital T. It doesn't matter whether the line begins with *Tiny trumpets*, *Titanic tubas*, or *Triumphant slide trombones*, as long as the capital T is present in the first position.

But here we're not very far ahead. Have we really invested all this effort in regex technology just to be able to do what we could already do with the java.lang.String method startsWith( )? Hmmm, I can hear some of you getting a bit restless. Stay in your seats! What if you wanted to match not only a letter T in the first position, but also a vowel (a, e, i, o, or u) immediately after it, followed by any number of letters in a word, followed by an exclamation point? Surely you could do this in Java by checking startsWith("T") and charAt(1) == 'a' || charAt(1) == 'e', and so on? Yes, but by the time you did that, you'd have written a lot of very highly specialized code that you couldn't use in any other application. With regular expressions, you can just give the pattern ^T[aeiou]\w*!. That is, ^ and T as before, followed by a *character class* listing the vowels, followed by any number of word characters (\w*), followed by the exclamation point.

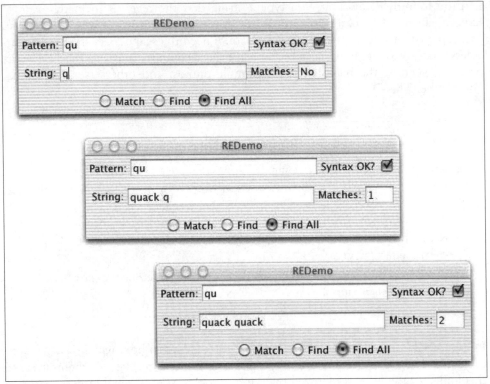

*Figure 4-1. REDemo with simple examples*

"But wait, there's more!" as my late, great boss Yuri Rubinsky used to say. What if you want to be able to change the pattern you're looking for *at runtime*? Remember all that Java code you just wrote to match T in column 1, plus a vowel, some word characters, and an exclamation point? Well, it's time to throw it out. Because this morning we need to match Q, followed by a letter other than u, followed by a number of digits, followed by a period. While some of you start writing a new function to do that, the rest of us will just saunter over to the RegEx Bar & Grille, order a ^Q[^u]\d+\.. from the bartender, and be on our way.

OK, the [^u] means "match any one character that is not the character u." The \d+ means one or more numeric digits. The + is a *multiplier* or *quantifier* meaning one or more occurrences of what it follows, and \d is any one numeric digit. So \d+ means a number with one, two, or more digits. Finally, the \.? Well, . by itself is a metacharacter. Most single metacharacters are switched off by preceding them with an escape character. Not the ESC key on your keyboard, of course. The regex "escape" character is the backslash. Preceding a metacharacter like . with escape turns off its special meaning. Preceding a few selected alphabetic characters (e.g., n, r, t, s, w) with escape turns them into metacharacters. Figure 4-2 shows the ^Q[^u]\d+\.. regex in action. In the first frame, I have typed part of the regex as ^Q[^u and, since there is an unclosed square bracket, the Syntax OK flag is turned off; when I complete the regex, it will be turned back on. In the second frame, I have finished the regex and typed the string as QA577 (which you should expect to match the ^Q[^u]\d+, but not the period since I haven't typed it). In the third frame, I've typed the period so the Matches flag is set to Yes.

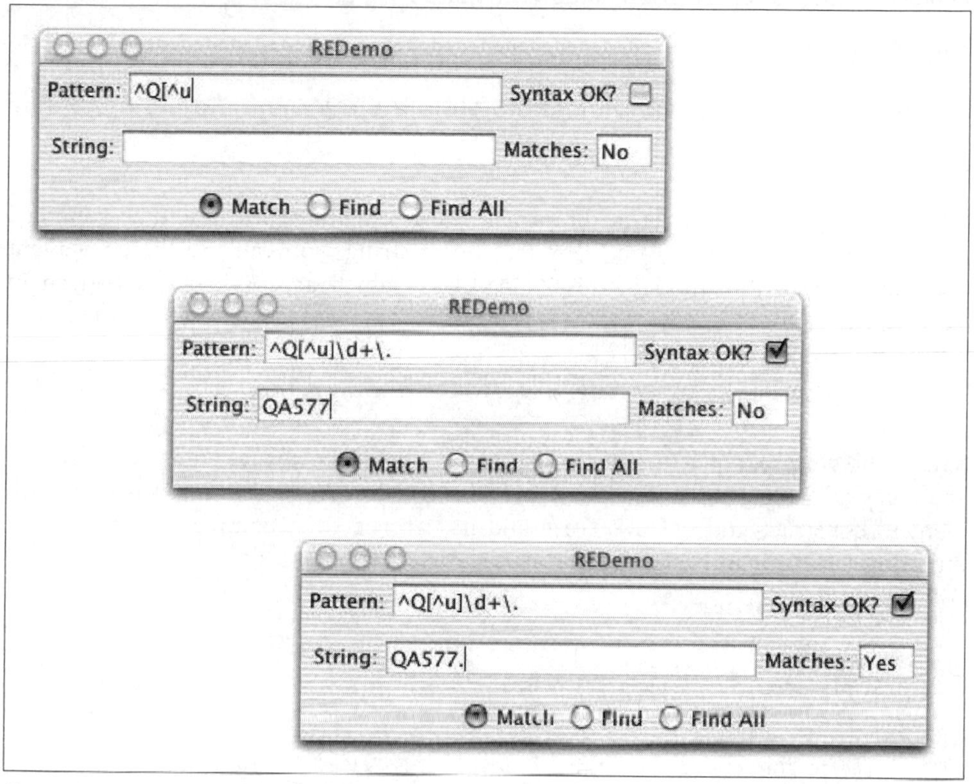

*Figure 4-2. REDemo with ^Q[^u]\d+\. example*

One good way to think of regular expressions is as a "little language" for matching patterns of characters in text contained in strings. Give yourself extra points if you've already recognized this as the design pattern known as *Interpreter*. A regular expression API is an interpreter for matching regular expressions.

So now you should have at least a basic grasp of how regexes work in practice. The rest of this chapter gives more examples and explains some of the more powerful topics, such as capture groups. As for how regexes work in theory—and there is a lot of theoretical details and differences among regex flavors—the interested reader is referred to the book *Mastering Regular Expressions*. Meanwhile, let's start learning how to write Java programs that use regular expressions.

# 4.2 Using regexes in Java: Test for a Pattern

## Problem

You're ready to get started using regular expression processing to beef up your Java code by testing to see if a given pattern can match in a given string.

## Solution

Use the Java Regular Expressions Package, `java.util.regex`.

## Discussion

The good news is that the Java API for regexes is actually easy to use. If all you need is to find out whether a given regex matches a string, you can use the convenient boolean `matches()` method of the `String` class, which accepts a regex pattern in String form as its argument:

```
if (inputString.matches(stringRegexPattern)) {
    // it matched... do something with it...
}
```

This is, however, a convenience routine, and convenience always comes at a price. If the regex is going to be used more than once or twice in a program, it is more efficient to construct and use a `Pattern` and its `Matcher`(s). A complete program constructing a `Pattern` and using it to match is shown here:

```
import java.util.regex.*;

/**
 * Simple example of using regex class.
 */
public class RESimple {
    public static void main(String[] argv) throws PatternSyntaxException {
        String pattern = "^Q[^u]\\d+\\.";
        String input = "QA777. is the next flight. It is on time.";

        Pattern p = Pattern.compile(pattern);

        boolean found = p.matcher(input).lookingAt();

        System.out.println("'" + pattern + "'" +
            (found ? " matches '" : " doesn't match '") + input + "'");
    }
}
```

The `java.util.regex` package consists of two classes, `Pattern` and `Matcher`, which provide the public API shown in Example 4-1.

*Example 4-1. Regex public API*

```java
/** The main public API of the java.util.regex package.
 * Prepared by javap and Ian Darwin.
 */

package java.util.regex;

public final class Pattern {
    // Flags values ('or' together)
    public static final int
        UNIX_LINES, CASE_INSENSITIVE, COMMENTS, MULTILINE,
        DOTALL, UNICODE_CASE, CANON_EQ;
    // Factory methods (no public constructors)
    public static Pattern compile(String patt);
    public static Pattern compile(String patt, int flags);
    // Method to get a Matcher for this Pattern
    public Matcher matcher(CharSequence input);
    // Information methods
    public String pattern();
    public int flags();
    // Convenience methods
    public static boolean matches(String pattern, CharSequence input);
    public String[] split(CharSequence input);
    public String[] split(CharSequence input, int max);
}


public final class Matcher {
    // Action: find or match methods
    public boolean matches();
    public boolean find();
    public boolean find(int start);
    public boolean lookingAt();
    // "Information about the previous match" methods
    public int start(),
    public int start(int whichGroup);
    public int end();
    public int end(int whichGroup);
    public int groupCount();
    public String group();
    public String group(int whichGroup);
    // Reset methods
    public Matcher reset();
    public Matcher reset(CharSequence newInput);
    // Replacement methods
    public Matcher appendReplacement(StringBuffer where, String newText);
    public StringBuffer appendTail(StringBuffer where);
    public String replaceAll(String newText);
    public String replaceFirst(String newText);
    // information methods
    public Pattern pattern();
}
```

*Example 4-1. Regex public API (continued)*

```
/* String, showing only the regex-related methods */
public final class String {
    public boolean matches(String regex);
    public String replaceFirst(String regex, String newStr);
    public String replaceAll(String regex, String newStr)
    public String[] split(String regex)
    public String[] split(String regex, int max);
}
```

This API is large enough to require some explanation. The normal steps for regex matching in a production program are:

1. Create a Pattern by calling the static method Pattern.compile( ).

2. Request a Matcher from the pattern by calling pattern.matcher(CharSequence) for each String (or other CharSequence) you wish to look through.

3. Call (once or more) one of the finder methods (discussed later in this section) in the resulting Matcher.

The CharSequence interface, added to java.lang with JDK 1.4, provides simple read-only access to objects containing a collection of characters. The standard implementations are String and StringBuffer (described in Chapter 3), and the "new I/O" class java.nio.CharBuffer.

Of course, you can perform regex matching in other ways, such as using the convenience methods in Pattern or even in java.lang.String. For example:

```
// StringConvenience.java  -- show String convenience routine for "match"
String pattern = ".*Q[^u]\\d+\\..*";
String line = "Order QT300. Now!";
if  (line.matches(pattern)) {
    System.out.println(line + " matches \"" + pattern + "\"");
} else {
    System.out.println("NO MATCH");
}
```

But the three-step list just described is the "standard" pattern for matching. You'd likely use the String convenience routine in a program that only used the regex once; if the regex were being used more than once, it is worth taking the time to "compile" it, since the compiled version runs faster.

As well, the Matcher has several finder methods, which provide more flexibility than the String convenience routine match( ). The Matcher methods are:

match( )
> Used to compare the entire string against the pattern; this is the same as the routine in java.lang.String. Since it matches the entire String, I had to put .* before and after the pattern.

lookingAt( )
> Used to match the pattern only at the beginning of the string.

---

find()

>    Used to match the pattern in the string (not necessarily at the first character of the string), starting at the beginning of the string or, if the method was previously called and succeeded, at the first character not matched by the previous match.

Each of these methods returns boolean, with true meaning a match and false meaning no match. To check whether a given string matches a given pattern, you need only type something like the following:

```
Matcher m = Pattern.compile(patt).matcher(line);
if (m.find()) {
    System.out.println(line + " matches " + patt)
}
```

But you may also want to extract the text that matched, which is the subject of the next recipe.

The following recipes cover uses of this API. Initially, the examples just use arguments of type String as the input source. Use of other CharSequence types is covered in Recipe 4.5.

# 4.3  Finding the Matching Text

## Problem

You need to find the text that the regex matched.

## Solution

Sometimes you need to know more than just whether a regex matched a string. In editors and many other tools, you want to know exactly what characters were matched. Remember that with multipliers such as *, the length of the text that was matched may have no relationship to the length of the pattern that matched it. Do not underestimate the mighty .*, which happily matches thousands or millions of characters if allowed to. As you saw in the previous recipe, you can find out whether a given match succeeds just by using find() or matches(). But in other applications, you will want to get the characters that the pattern matched.

After a successful call to one of the above methods, you can use these "information" methods to get information on the match:

start(), end()

>    Returns the character position in the string of the starting and ending characters that matched.

groupCount()

>    Returns the number of parenthesized capture groups if any; returns 0 if no groups were used.

```
group(int i)
```
Returns the characters matched by group *i* of the current match, if *i* is less than or equal to the return value of groupCount( ). Group 0 is the entire match, so group(0) (or just group( )) returns the entire portion of the string that matched.

The notion of parentheses or "capture groups" is central to regex processing. Regexes may be nested to any level of complexity. The group(int) method lets you retrieve the characters that matched a given parenthesis group. If you haven't used any explicit parens, you can just treat whatever matched as "level zero." For example:

```java
// Part of REmatch.java
String patt = "Q[^u]\\d+\\.";
Pattern r = Pattern.compile(patt);
String line = "Order QT300. Now!";
Matcher m = r.matcher(line);
if (m.find()) {
    System.out.println(patt + " matches \"" +
        m.group(0) +
        "\" in \"" + line + "\"");
} else {
    System.out.println("NO MATCH");
}
```

When run, this prints:

```
Q[^u]\d+\. matches "QT300." in "Order QT300. Now!"
```

An extended version of the REDemo program presented in Recipe 4.2, called REDemo2, provides a display of all the capture groups in a given regex; one example is shown in Figure 4-3.

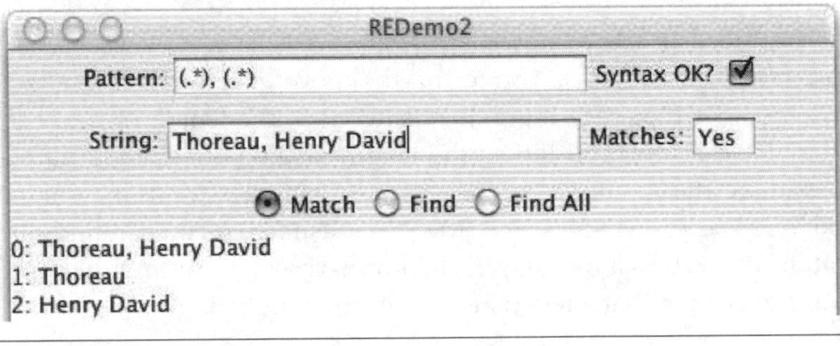

*Figure 4-3. REDemo2 in action*

It is also possible to get the starting and ending indexes and the length of the text that the pattern matched (remember that terms with multipliers, such as the \d+ in this example, can match an arbitrary number of characters in the string). You can use these in conjunction with the String.substring( ) methods as follows:

```java
// Part of regexsubstr.java -- Prints exactly the same as REmatch.java
Pattern r = Pattern.compile(patt);
String line = "Order QT300. Now!";
```

```
Matcher m = r.matcher(line);
if (m.find()) {
    System.out.println(patt + " matches \"" +
        line.substring(m.start(0), m.end(0)) +
        "\" in \"" + line + "\"");
} else {
        System.out.println("NO MATCH");
    }
}
```

Suppose you need to extract several items from a string. If the input is:

```
Smith, John
Adams, John Quincy
```

and you want to get out:

```
John Smith
John Quincy Adams
```

just use:

```
// from REmatchTwoFields.java
// Construct a regex with parens to "grab" both field1 and field2
Pattern r = Pattern.compile("(.*), (.*)");
Matcher m = r.matcher(inputLine);
 if (!m.matches())
    throw new IllegalArgumentException("Bad input: " + inputLine);
System.out.println(m.group(2) + ' ' + m.group(1));
```

# 4.4   Replacing the Matched Text

As we saw in the previous recipe, regex patterns involving multipliers can match a lot
of characters with very few metacharacters. We need a way to replace the text that
the regex matched without changing other text before or after it. We could do this
manually using the String method substring(). However, because it's such a common requirement, the JDK 1.4 Regular Expression API provides some substitution
methods. In all these methods, you pass in the replacement text or "right-hand side"
of the substitution (this term is historical: in a command-line text editor's substitute
command, the left-hand side is the pattern and the right-hand side is the replacement text). The replacement methods are:

replaceAll(newString)
> Replaces all occurrences that matched with the new string.

appendReplacement(StringBuffer, newString)
> Copies up to before the first match, plus the given newString.

appendTail(StringBuffer)
> Appends text after the last match (normally used after appendReplacement).

Example 4-2 shows use of these three methods.

*Example 4-2. ReplaceDemo.java*

```
// class ReplaceDemo
// Quick demo of substitution: correct "demon" and other
// spelling variants to the correct, non-satanic "daemon".

// Make a regex pattern to match almost any form (deamon, demon, etc.).
String patt = "d[ae]{1,2}mon";  // i.e., 1 or 2 'a' or 'e' any combo

// A test string.
String input = "Unix hath demons and deamons in it!";
System.out.println("Input: " + input);

// Run it from a regex instance and see that it works
Pattern r = Pattern.compile(patt);
Matcher m = r.matcher(input);
System.out.println("ReplaceAll: " + m.replaceAll("daemon"));

// Show the appendReplacement method
m.reset();
StringBuffer sb = new StringBuffer();
System.out.print("Append methods: ");
while (m.find()) {
    m.appendReplacement(sb, "daemon");  // Copy to before first match,
                                        // plus the word "daemon"

}
m.appendTail(sb);                       // copy remainder
System.out.println(sb.toString());
```

Sure enough, when you run it, it does what we expect:

```
Input: Unix hath demons and deamons in it!
ReplaceAll: Unix hath daemons and daemons in it!
Append methods: Unix hath daemons and daemons in it!
```

# 4.5    Printing All Occurrences of a Pattern

## Problem

You need to find all the strings that match a given regex in one or more files or other sources.

## Solution

This example reads through a file one line at a time. Whenever a match is found, I extract it from the line and print it.

This code takes the group( ) methods from Recipe 4.3, the substring method from the CharacterIterator interface, and the match( ) method from the regex and simply puts them all together. I coded it to extract all the "names" from a given file; in running the program through itself, it prints the words "import", "java", "until", "regex", and so on:

---

```
> jikes +E -d . ReaderIter.java
> java ReaderIter ReaderIter.java
import
java
util
regex
import
java
io
Print
all
the
strings
that
match
given
pattern
from
file
public
```

I interrupted it here to save paper. This can be written two ways, a traditional "line at a time" pattern shown in Example 4-3 and a more compact form using "new I/O" shown in Example 4-4 (the "new I/O" package is described in Chapter 10).

*Example 4-3. ReaderIter.java*

```java
import java.util.regex.*;
import java.io.*;

/**
 * Print all the strings that match a given pattern from a file.
 */
public class ReaderIter {
    public static void main(String[] args) throws IOException {
        // The regex pattern
        Pattern patt = Pattern.compile("[A-Za-z][a-z]+");
        // A FileReader (see the I/O chapter)
        BufferedReader r = new BufferedReader(new FileReader(args[0]));

        // For each line of input, try matching in it.
        String line;
        while ((line = r.readLine()) != null) {
            // For each match in the line, extract and print it.
            Matcher m = patt.matcher(line);
            while (m.find()) {
                // Simplest method:
                // System.out.println(m.group(0));

                // Get the starting position of the text
                int start = m.start(0);
                // Get ending position
                int end = m.end(0);
```

*Example 4-3. ReaderIter.java (continued)*

```
                    // Print whatever matched.
                    System.out.println("start=" + start + "; end=" + end);
                    // Use CharSequence.substring(offset, end);
                    System.out.println(line.substring(start, end));
            }
        }
    }
}
```

*Example 4-4. GrepNIO.java*

```java
import java.io.*;
import java.nio.*;
import java.nio.channels.*;
import java.nio.charset.*;
import java.util.regex.*;

/* Grep-like program using NIO, but NOT LINE BASED.
 * Pattern and file name(s) must be on command line.
 */
public class GrepNIO {
    public static void main(String[] args) throws IOException {

        if (args.length < 2) {
            System.err.println("Usage: GrepNIO patt file [...]");
            System.exit(1);
        }

        Pattern p = Pattern.compile(args[0]);
        for (int i=1; i<args.length; i++)
            process(p, args[i]);
    }

    static void process(Pattern pattern, String fileName) throws IOException {

        // Get a FileChannel from the given file.
        FileChannel fc = new FileInputStream(fileName).getChannel();

        // Map the file's content
        ByteBuffer buf = fc.map(FileChannel.MapMode.READ_ONLY, 0, fc.size());

        // Decode ByteBuffer into CharBuffer
        CharBuffer cbuf =
            Charset.forName("ISO-8859-1").newDecoder().decode(buf);

        Matcher m = pattern.matcher(cbuf);
        while (m.find()) {
            System.out.println(m.group(0));
        }
    }
}
```

The NIO version shown in Example 4-4 relies on the fact that an NIO `Buffer` can be used as a `CharSequence`. This program is more general in that the pattern argument is taken from the command-line argument. It prints the same output as the previous example if invoked with the pattern argument from the previous program on the command line:

```
java GrepNIO " [A-Za-z][a-z]+"  ReaderIter.java
```

You might think of using `\w+` as the pattern; the only difference is that my pattern looks for well-formed capitalized words while `\w+` would include Java-centric oddities like `theVariableName`, which have capitals in nonstandard positions.

Also note that the NIO version will probably be more efficient since it doesn't reset the `Matcher` to a new input source on each line of input as `ReaderIter` does.

# 4.6    Printing Lines Containing a Pattern

## Problem

You need to look for lines matching a given regex in one or more files.

## Solution

Write a simple *grep*-like program.

## Discussion

As I've mentioned, once you have a regex package, you can write a *grep*-like program. I gave an example of the Unix *grep* program earlier. *grep* is called with some optional arguments, followed by one required regular expression pattern, followed by an arbitrary number of filenames. It prints any line that contains the pattern, differing from Recipe 4.5, which prints only the matching text itself. For example:

```
grep "[dD]arwin" *.txt
```

searches for lines containing either `darwin` or `Darwin` in every line of every file whose name ends in *.txt.*[*] Example 4-5 is the source for the first version of a program to do this, called `Grep0`. It reads lines from the standard input and doesn't take any optional arguments, but it handles the full set of regular expressions that the `Pattern` class implements (it is, therefore, not identical with the Unix programs of the same name). We haven't covered the `java.io` package for input and output yet (see Chapter 10), but our use of it here is simple enough that you can probably intuit it. The online source includes `Grep1`, which does the same thing but is better structured (and therefore longer). Later in this chapter, Recipe 4.12 presents a `Grep2` program that uses my `GetOpt` (see Recipe 2.6) to parse command-line options.

---

[*] On Unix, the shell or command-line interpreter expands *.txt to match all the filenames, but the normal Java interpreter does this for you on systems where the shell isn't energetic or bright enough to do it.

*Example 4-5. Grep0.java*

```java
import java.io.*;
import java.util.regex.*;

/** Grep0 - Match lines from stdin against the pattern on the command line.
 */
public class Grep0 {
    public static void main(String[] args) throws IOException {
        BufferedReader is =
            new BufferedReader(new InputStreamReader(System.in));
        if (args.length != 1) {
            System.err.println("Usage: Grep0 pattern");
            System.exit(1);
        }
        Pattern patt = Pattern.compile(args[0]);
        Matcher matcher = patt.matcher("");
        String line = null;
        while ((line = is.readLine()) != null) {
            matcher.reset(line);
            if (matcher.find()) {
                System.out.println("MATCH: " + line);
            }
        }
    }
}
```

# 4.7    Controlling Case in Regular Expressions

## Problem

You want to find text regardless of case.

## Solution

Compile the Pattern passing in the flags argument Pattern.CASE_INSENSITIVE to indicate that matching should be case-independent ("fold" or ignore differences in case). If your code might run in different locales (see Chapter 15), add Pattern. UNICODE_CASE. Without these flags, the default is normal, case-sensitive matching behavior. This flag (and others) are passed to the Pattern.compile() method, as in:

```java
// CaseMatch.java
Pattern  reCaseInsens = Pattern.compile(pattern, Pattern.CASE_INSENSITIVE |
Pattern.UNICODE_CASE);
reCaseInsens.matches(input);         // will match case-insensitively
```

This flag must be passed when you create the Pattern; as Pattern objects are immutable, they cannot be changed once constructed.

The full source code for this example is online as *CaseMatch.java*.

## 4.8 Matching "Accented" or Composite Characters

### Problem

You want characters to match regardless of the form in which they are entered.

### Solution

Compile the Pattern with the flags argument Pattern.CANON_EQ for "canonical equality."

### Discussion

Composite characters can be entered in various forms. Consider, as a single example, the letter e with an acute accent. This character may be found in various forms in Unicode text, such as the single character é (Unicode character \u00e9) or as the two-character sequence e´ (e followed by the Unicode combining acute accent, \u0301).

To allow you to match such characters regardless of which of possibly multiple "fully decomposed" forms are used to enter them, the regex package has an option for "canonical matching," which treats any of the forms as equivalent. This option is enabled by passing CANON_EQ as (one of) the flags in the second argument to Pattern. compile( ). This program shows CANON_EQ being used to match several forms:

```
import java.util.regex.*;

/**
 * CanonEqDemo - show use of Pattern.CANON_EQ, by comparing varous ways of
 * entering the Spanish word for "equal" and see if they are considered equal
 * by the regex-matching engine.
 */
public class CanonEqDemo {
    public static void main(String[] args) {
        String pattStr = "\u00e9gal"; // égal
        String[] input = {
                "\u00e9gal", // égal - this one had better match :-)
                "e\u0301gal", // e + "Combining acute accent"
                "e\u02cagal", // e + "modifier letter acute accent"
                "e'gal", // e + single quote
                "e\u00b4gal", // e + Latin-1 "acute"
        };
        Pattern pattern = Pattern.compile(pattStr, Pattern.CANON_EQ);
        for (int i = 0; i < input.length; i++) {
            if (pattern.matcher(input[i]).matches()) {
                System.out.println(pattStr + " matches input " + input[i]);
            } else {
                System.out.println(pattStr + " does not match input " + input[i]);
            }
        }
    }
}
```

When you run this program on JDK 1.4 or later, it correctly matches the "combining accent" and rejects the other characters, some of which, unfortunately, look like the accent on a printer, but are not considered "combining accent" characters.

```
égal matches input égal
égal matches input e?gal
égal does not match input e?gal
égal does not match input e'gal
égal does not match input e´gal
```

For more details, see the character charts at *http://www.unicode.org/*.

# 4.9   Matching Newlines in Text

## Problem

You need to match newlines in text.

## Solution

Use \n or \r.

See also the flags constant `Pattern.MULTILINE`, which makes newlines match as beginning-of-line and end-of-line (^ and $).

## Discussion

While line-oriented tools from Unix such as *sed* and *grep* match regular expressions one line at a time, not all tools do. The *sam* text editor from Bell Laboratories was the first interactive tool I know of to allow multiline regular expressions; the Perl scripting language followed shortly. In the Java API, the newline character by default has no special significance. The `BufferedReader` method `readLine( )` normally strips out whichever newline characters it finds. If you read in gobs of characters using some method other than `readLine( )`, you may have some number of \n, \r, or \r\n sequences in your text string.[*] Normally all of these are treated as equivalent to \n. If you want only \n to match, use the `UNIX_LINES` flag to the `Pattern.compile( )` method.

In Unix, ^ and $ are commonly used to match the beginning or end of a line, respectively. In this API, the regex metacharacters ^ and $ ignore line terminators and only match at the beginning and the end, respectively, of the entire string. However, if you pass the `MULTILINE` flag into `Pattern.compile( )`, these expressions match just after or just before, respectively, a line terminator; $ also matches the very end of the string. Since the line ending is just an ordinary character, you can match it with . or similar expressions, and, if you want to know exactly where it is, \n or \r in the pattern match it as well. In other words, to this API, a newline character is just another character with no special significance. See the sidebar "Pattern.compile( ) Flags". An example of newline matching is shown in Example 4-6.

*Example 4-6. NLMatch.java*

```
import java.util.regex.*;

/**
 * Show line ending matching using regex class.
 * @author Ian F. Darwin, ian@darwinsys.com
 * @version $Id: ch04,v 1.4 2004/05/04 20:11:27 ian Exp $
 */
public class NLMatch {
    public static void main(String[] argv) {

        String input = "I dream of engines\nmore engines, all day long";
        System.out.println("INPUT: " + input);
        System.out.println( );
```

---

[*] Or a few related Unicode characters, including the next-line (\u0085), line-separator (\u2028), and paragraph-separator (\u2029) characters.

*Example 4-6. NLMatch.java (continued)*

```
    String[] patt = {
        "engines.more engines",
        "engines$"
    };

    for (int i = 0; i < patt.length; i++) {
        System.out.println("PATTERN " + patt[i]);

        boolean found;
        Pattern p1l = Pattern.compile(patt[i]);
        found = p1l.matcher(input).find( );
        System.out.println("DEFAULT match " + found);

        Pattern pml = Pattern.compile(patt[i],
            Pattern.DOTALL|Pattern.MULTILINE);
        found = pml.matcher(input).find( );
        System.out.println("MultiLine match " + found);
        System.out.println( );
    }
  }
}
```

If you run this code, the first pattern (with the wildcard character .) always matches, while the second pattern (with $) matches only when MATCH_MULTILINE is set.

```
> java NLMatch
INPUT: I dream of engines
more engines, all day long

PATTERN engines
more engines
DEFAULT match true
MULTILINE match: true

PATTERN engines$
DEFAULT match false
MULTILINE match: true
```

# 4.10  Program: Apache Logfile Parsing

The Apache web server is the world's leading web server and has been for most of the web's history. It is one of the world's best-known open source projects, and one of many fostered by the Apache Foundation. But the name Apache is a pun on the origins of the server; its developers began with the free NCSA server and kept hacking at it or "patching" it until it did what they wanted. When it was sufficiently different from the original, a new name was needed. Since it was now "a patchy server," the name Apache was chosen. One place this patchiness shows through is in the log file format. Consider this entry:

```
123.45.67.89 - - [27/Oct/2000:09:27:09 -0400] "GET /java/javaResources.html HTTP/1.0"
200 10450 "-" "Mozilla/4.6 [en] (X11; U; OpenBSD 2.8 i386; Nav)"
```

The file format was obviously designed for human inspection but not for easy parsing. The problem is that different delimiters are used: square brackets for the date,
quotes for the request line, and spaces sprinkled all through. Consider trying to use a
StringTokenizer; you might be able to get it working, but you'd spend a lot of time
fiddling with it. However, this somewhat contorted regular expression* makes it easy
to parse:

```
^([\d.]+) (\S+) (\S+) \[([\w:/]+\s[+\-]\d{4})\] "(.+?)" (\d{3}) (\d+) "([^"]+)"
"([^"]+)"
```

You may find it informative to refer back to Table 4-2 and review the full syntax used
here. Note in particular the use of the non-greedy quantifier +? in \"(.+?)\" to match
a quoted string; you can't just use .+ since that would match too much (up to the
quote at the end of the line). Code to extract the various fields such as IP address,
request, referer URL, and browser version is shown in Example 4-7.

*Example 4-7. LogRegExp.java*

```java
import java.util.regex.*;

/**
 * Parse an Apache log file with Regular Expressions
 */
public class LogRegExp implements LogExample {

    public static void main(String argv[]) {

        String logEntryPattern =
            "^([\\d.]+) (\\S+) (\\S+) \\[([\\w:/]+\\s[+\\-]\\d{4})\\] \"(.+?)\" (\\d{3}) 
(\\d+) \"([^\"]+)\" \"([^\"]+)\"";

        System.out.println("Using regex Pattern:");
        System.out.println(logEntryPattern);

        System.out.println("Input line is:");
        System.out.println(logEntryLine);

        Pattern p = Pattern.compile(logEntryPattern);
        Matcher matcher = p.matcher(logEntryLine);
        if (!matcher.matches() ||
            NUM_FIELDS != matcher.groupCount()) {
            System.err.println("Bad log entry (or problem with regex?):");
            System.err.println(logEntryLine);
            return;
        }
```

---

* You might think this would hold some kind of world record for complexity in regex competitions, but I'm
sure it's been outdone many times.

*Example 4-7. LogRegExp.java (continued)*

```
        System.out.println("IP Address: " + matcher.group(1));
        System.out.println("Date&Time: " + matcher.group(4));
        System.out.println("Request: " + matcher.group(5));
        System.out.println("Response: " + matcher.group(6));
        System.out.println("Bytes Sent: " + matcher.group(7));
        if (!matcher.group(8).equals("-"))
            System.out.println("Referer: " + matcher.group(8));
        System.out.println("Browser: " + matcher.group(9));
    }
}
```

The `implements` clause is for an interface that just defines the input string; it was used in a demonstration to compare the regular expression mode with the use of a `StringTokenizer`. The source for both versions is in the online source for this chapter. Running the program against the sample input shown above gives this output:

```
Using regex Pattern:
^([\d.]+) (\S+) (\S+) \[(([\w:/]+\s[+\-]\d{4})\] "(.+?)" (\d{3}) (\d+) "([^"]+)"
"([^"]+)"
Input line is:
123.45.67.89 - - [27/Oct/2000:09:27:09 -0400] "GET /java/javaResources.html HTTP/1.0"
200 10450 "-" "Mozilla/4.6 [en] (X11; U; OpenBSD 2.8 i386; Nav)"
IP Address: 123.45.67.89
Date&Time: 27/Oct/2000:09:27:09 -0400
Request: GET /java/javaResources.html HTTP/1.0
Response: 200
Bytes Sent: 10450
Browser: Mozilla/4.6 [en] (X11; U; OpenBSD 2.8 i386; Nav)
```

The program successfully parsed the entire log file format with one call to `matcher.matches( )`.

## 4.11 Program: Data Mining

Suppose that I, as a published author, want to track how my book is selling in comparison to others. This information can be obtained for free just by clicking on the page for my book on any of the major bookseller sites, reading the sales rank number off the screen, and typing the number into a file—but that's too tedious. As I wrote in the book that this example looks for, "computers get paid to extract relevant information from files; people should not have to do such mundane tasks." This program uses the Regular Expressions API and, in particular, newline matching to extract a value from an HTML page on the hypothetical *QuickBookShops.web* web site. It also reads from a URL object (see Recipe 18.7). The pattern to look for is something like this (bear in mind that the HTML may change at any time, so I want to keep the pattern fairly general):

```
<b>QuickBookShop.web Sales Rank: </b>
26,252
</font><br>
```

As the pattern may extend over more than one line, I read the entire web page from the URL into a single long string using my `FileIO.readerToString()` method (see Recipe 10.8) instead of the more traditional line-at-a-time paradigm. I then plot a graph using an external program (see Recipe 26.1); this could (and should) be changed to use a Java graphics program (see Recipe 13.13 for some leads). The complete program is shown in Example 4-8.

*Example 4-8. BookRank.java*

```
// Standard imports not shown
import com.darwinsys.io.FileIO;
import com.darwinsys.util.FileProperties;

/** Graph of a book's sales rank on a given bookshop site.
 * @author Ian F. Darwin, http://www.darwinsys.com/, Java Cookbook author,
 *     originally translated fairly literally from Perl into Java.
 * @author Patrick Killelea <p@patrick.net>: original Perl version,
 *     from the 2nd edition of his book "Web Performance Tuning".
 * @version $Id: ch04,v 1.4 2004/05/04 20:11:27 ian Exp $
 */
public class BookRank {
    public final static String DATA_FILE = "book.sales";
    public final static String GRAPH_FILE = "book.png";

    /** Grab the sales rank off the web page and log it. */
    public static void main(String[] args) throws Exception {

        Properties p = new FileProperties(
            args.length == 0 ? "bookrank.properties" : args[1]);
        String title = p.getProperty("title", "NO TITLE IN PROPERTIES");
        // The url must have the "isbn=" at the very end, or otherwise
        // be amenable to being string-catted to, like the default.
        String url = p.getProperty("url", "http://test.ing/test.cgi?isbn=");
        // The 10-digit ISBN for the book.
        String isbn = p.getProperty("isbn", "0000000000");
        // The regex pattern (MUST have ONE capture group for the number)
        String pattern = p.getProperty("pattern", "Rank: (\\d+)");

        // Looking for something like this in the input:
        //      <b>QuickBookShop.web Sales Rank: </b>
        //      26,252
        //      </font><br>

        Pattern r = Pattern.compile(pattern);

        // Open the URL and get a Reader from it.
        BufferedReader is = new BufferedReader(new InputStreamReader(
            new URL(url + isbn).openStream() ));
        // Read the URL looking for the rank information, as
        // a single long string, so can match regex across multi-lines.
        String input = FileIO.readerToString(is);
        // System.out.println(input);
```

*Example 4-8. BookRank.java (continued)*

```
            // If found, append to sales data file.
            Matcher m = r.matcher(input);
            if (m.find( )) {
                PrintWriter pw = new PrintWriter(
                    new FileWriter(DATA_FILE, true));
                String date = // 'date +'%m %d %H %M %S %Y'`;
                    new SimpleDateFormat("MM dd hh mm ss yyyy ").
                    format(new Date( ));
                // Paren 1 is the digits (and maybe ','s) that matched; remove comma
                Matcher noComma = Pattern.compile(",").matcher(m.group(1));
                pw.println(date + noComma.replaceAll(""));
                pw.close( );
            } else {
                System.err.println("WARNING: pattern `" + pattern +
                    "' did not match in `" + url + isbn + "'!");
            }

            // Whether current data found or not, draw the graph, using
            // external plotting program against all historical data.
            // Could use gnuplot, R, any other math/graph program.
            // Better yet: use one of the Java plotting APIs.

            String gnuplot_cmd =
                "set term png\n" +
                "set output \"" + GRAPH_FILE + "\"\n" +
                "set xdata time\n" +
                "set ylabel \"Book sales rank\"\n" +
                "set bmargin 3\n" +
                "set logscale y\n" +
                "set yrange [1:60000] reverse\n" +
                "set timefmt \"%m %d %H %M %S %Y\"\n" +
                "plot \"" + DATA_FILE +
                    "\" using 1:7 title \"" + title + "\" with lines\n"
                ;

            Process proc = Runtime.getRuntime( ).exec("/usr/local/bin/gnuplot");
            PrintWriter gp = new PrintWriter(proc.getOutputStream( ));
            gp.print(gnuplot_cmd);
            gp.close( );
    }
}
```

# 4.12  Program: Full Grep

Now that we've seen how the regular expressions package works, it's time to write
Grep2, a full-blown version of the line-matching program with option parsing.
Table 4-3 lists some typical command-line options that a Unix implementation of
*grep* might include.

---

Table 4-3. Grep command-line options

| Option | Meaning |
|---|---|
| -c | Count only: don't print lines, just count them |
| -C | Context; print some lines above and below each line that matches (not implemented in this version; left as an exercise for the reader) |
| -f pattern | Take pattern from file named after -f instead of from command line |
| -h | Suppress printing filename ahead of lines |
| -i | Ignore case |
| -l | List filenames only: don't print lines, just the names they're found in |
| -n | Print line numbers before matching lines |
| -s | Suppress printing certain error messages |
| -v | Invert: print only lines that do NOT match the pattern |

We discussed the GetOpt class in Recipe 2.6. Here we use it to control the operation of an application program. As usual, since main( ) runs in a static context but our application main line does not, we could wind up passing a lot of information into the constructor. Because we have so many options, and it would be inconvenient to keep expanding the options list as we add new functionality to the program, we use a kind of Collection called a BitSet to pass all the true/false arguments: true to print line numbers, false to print filenames, etc. (Collections are covered in Chapter 7.) A BitSet is much like a Vector (see Recipe 7.3) but is specialized to store only Boolean values and is ideal for handling command-line arguments.

The program basically just reads lines, matches the pattern in them, and, if a match is found (or not found, with -v), prints the line (and optionally some other stuff, too). Having said all that, the code is shown in Example 4-9.

*Example 4-9. Grep2.java*

```java
import com.darwinsys.util.*;
import java.io.*;
import java.util.*;

/** A command-line grep-like program. Accepts some options and takes a pattern
 * and a list of text files.
 */
public class Grep2 {
    /** The pattern we're looking for */
    protected Matcher pattern;
    /** The Reader for the current file */
    protected BufferedReader d;
    /** Are we to only count lines, instead of printing? */
    protected boolean countOnly = false;
    /** Are we to ignore case? */
    protected boolean ignoreCase = false;
    /** Are we to suppress printing of filenames? */
    protected boolean dontPrintFileName = false;
```

*Example 4-9. Grep2.java (continued)*

```java
/** Are we to only list names of files that match? */
protected boolean listOnly = false;
/** are we to print line numbers? */
protected boolean numbered = false;
/** Are we to be silent about errors? */
protected boolean silent = false;
/** are we to print only lines that DONT match? */
protected boolean inVert = false;

/** Construct a Grep object for each pattern, and run it
 * on all input files listed in argv.
 */
public static void main(String[] argv) throws RESyntaxException {

    if (argv.length < 1) {
        System.err.println("Usage: Grep2 pattern [filename...]");
        System.exit(1);
    }
    String pattern = null;

    GetOpt go = new GetOpt("cf:hilnsv");
    BitSet args = new BitSet();

    char c;
    while ((c = go.getopt(argv)) != 0) {
        switch(c) {
            case 'c':
                args.set('C');
                break;
            case 'f':
                try {
                    BufferedReader b = new BufferedReader
                            (new FileReader(go.optarg()));
                    pattern = b.readLine();
                    b.close();
                } catch (IOException e) {
                    System.err.println("Can't read pattern file " +
                            go.optarg());
                    System.exit(1);
                }
                break;
            case 'h':
                args.set('H');
                break;
            case 'i':
                args.set('I');
                break;
            case 'l':
                args.set('L');
                break;
            case 'n':
                args.set('N');
```

*Example 4-9. Grep2.java (continued)*

```
                    break;
                case 's':
                    args.set('S');
                    break;
                case 'v':
                    args.set('V');
                    break;
            }
        }

        int ix = go.getOptInd( );

        if (pattern == null)
            pattern = argv[ix-1];

        Grep2 pg = new Grep2(pattern, args);

        if (argv.length == 1x)
            pg.process(new InputStreamReader(System.in), "(standard input)");
        else
            for (int i=ix; i<argv.length; i++) {
                try {
                    pg.process(new FileReader(argv[i]), argv[i]);
                } catch(Exception e) {
                    System.err.println(e);
                }
            }
    }

    /** Construct a Grep2 object.
     */
    public Grep2(String patt, BitSet args)  {
        // compile the regular expression
        if (args.get('C'))
            countOnly - true;
        if (args.get('H'))
            dontPrintFileName = true;
        if (args.get('I'))
            ignoreCase = true;
        if (args.get('L'))
            listOnly = true;
        if (args.get('N'))
            numbered = truc;
        if (args.get('S'))
            silent = true;
        if (args.get('V'))
            inVert = true;
        int caseMode = ignoreCase ? Pattern.UNICODE_CASE | Pattern.CASE_INSENSITIVE : 0;
        pattern = Pattern.compile(patt, caseMode);
        matcher = pattern.matcher("");
    }
```

*Example 4-9. Grep2.java (continued)*

```java
/** Do the work of scanning one file
 * @param     ifile     Reader      Reader object already open
 * @param     fileName String       Name of the input file
 */
public void process(Reader ifile, String fileName) {

    String line;
    int matches = 0;

    try {
        d = new BufferedReader(ifile);

        while ((line = d.readLine()) != null) {
            if (pattern.match(line)) {
                if (countOnly)
                    matches++;
                else {
                if (!dontPrintFileName)
                    System.out.print(fileName + ": ");
                System.out.println(line);
                }
            } else if (inVert) {
                System.out.println(line);
            }
        }
        if (countOnly)
            System.out.println(matches + " matches in " + fileName);
        d.close();
    } catch (IOException e) { System.err.println(e); }
}
}
```

# CHAPTER 5

# Numbers

## 5.0 Introduction

Numbers are basic to just about any computation. They're used for array indexes, temperatures, salaries, ratings, and an infinite variety of things. Yet they're not as simple as they seem. With floating-point numbers, how accurate is accurate? With random numbers, how random is random? With strings that should contain a number, what actually constitutes a number?

Java has several built-in types that can be used to represent numbers, summarized in Table 5-1. Note that unlike languages such as C or Perl, which don't specify the size or precision of numeric types, Java—with its goal of portability—specifies these exactly and states that they are the same on all platforms.

*Table 5-1. Numeric types*

| Built-in type | Object wrapper | Size of built-in (bits) | Contents |
| --- | --- | --- | --- |
| byte | Byte | 8 | Signed integer |
| short | Short | 16 | Signed integer |
| int | Integer | 32 | Signed integer |
| long | Long | 64 | Signed integer |
| float | Float | 32 | IEEE-754 floating point |
| double | Double | 64 | IEEE-754 floating point |
| char | Character | 16 | Unsigned Unicode character |

As you can see, Java provides a numeric type for just about any purpose. There are four sizes of signed integers for representing various sizes of whole numbers. There are two sizes of floating-point numbers to approximate real numbers. There is also a type specifically designed to represent and allow operations on Unicode characters.

When you read a string from user input or a text file, you need to convert it to the appropriate type. The object wrapper classes in the second column have several functions, but one of the most important is to provide this basic conversion functionality—replacing the C programmer's *atoi/atof* family of functions and the numeric arguments to *scanf*.

Going the other way, you can convert any number (indeed, anything at all in Java) to a string just by using string concatenation. If you want a little bit of control over numeric formatting, Recipe 5.8 shows you how to use some of the object wrappers' conversion routines. And if you want full control, it also shows the use of NumberFormat and its related classes to provide full control of formatting.

As the name *object wrapper* implies, these classes are also used to "wrap" a number in a Java object, as many parts of the standard API are defined in terms of objects. Later on, Recipe 10.16 shows using an Integer object to save an int's value to a file using *object serialization*, and retrieving the value later.

But I haven't yet mentioned the issues of floating point. Real numbers, you may recall, are numbers with a fractional part. There is an infinity of possible real numbers. A floating-point number—what a computer uses to approximate a real number—is not the same as a real number. The number of floating-point numbers is finite, with only $2^{32}$ different bit patterns for floats, and $2^{64}$ for doubles. Thus, most real values have only an approximate correspondence to floating point. The result of printing the real number 0.3 works correctly, as in:

```
// RealValues.java
System.out.println("The real value 0.3 is " + 0.3);
```

results in this printout:

```
The real value 0.3 is 0.3
```

But the difference between a real value and its floating-point approximation can accumulate if the value is used in a computation; this is often called a *rounding error*. Continuing the previous example, the real 0.3 multiplied by 3 yields:

```
The real 0.3 times 3 is 0.89999999999999991
```

Surprised? More surprising is this: you'll get the same output on any conforming Java implementation. I ran it on machines as disparate as a Pentium with OpenBSD, a Pentium with Windows and Sun's JDK, and on Mac OS X with JDK 1.4.1. Always the same answer.

And what about random numbers? How random are they? You have probably heard the expression "pseudo-random numbers." All conventional random number generators, whether written in Fortran, C, or Java, generate pseudo-random numbers. That is, they're not truly random! True randomness comes only from specially built hardware: an analog source of Brownian noise connected to an analog-to-digital converter, for example.[*] This is not your average PC! However, pseudo-random number

---

[*] For a low-cost source of randomness, check out *http://www.lavarand.org*. These folks use digitized video of 1970s "lava lamps" to provide "hardware-based" randomness. Fun!

generators (PRNG for short) are good enough for most purposes, so we use them. Java provides one random generator in the base library java.lang.Math, and several others; we'll examine these in Recipe 5.13.

The class java.lang.Math contains an entire "math library" in one class, including trigonometry, conversions (including degrees to radians and back), rounding, truncating, square root, minimum, and maximum. It's all there. Check the Javadoc for java.lang.Math.

The package java.Math contains support for "big numbers"—those larger than the normal built-in long integers, for example. See Recipe 5.19.

Java works hard to ensure that your programs are reliable. The usual ways you'd notice this are in the common requirement to catch potential exceptions—all through the Java API—and in the need to "cast" or convert when storing a value that might or might not fit into the variable you're trying to store it in. I'll show examples of these.

Overall, Java's handling of numeric data fits well with the ideals of portability, reliability, and ease of programming.

## See Also

The *Java Language Specification*. The Javadoc page for java.lang.Math.

# 5.1 Checking Whether a String Is a Valid Number

## Problem

You need to check whether a given string contains a valid number, and, if so, convert it to binary (internal) form.

## Solution

Use the appropriate wrapper class's conversion routine and catch the NumberFormatException. This code converts a string to a double:

```
// StringToDouble.java
public static void main(String argv[]) {
    String aNumber = argv[0];     // not argv[1]
    double result;
    try {
        result = Double.parseDouble(aNumber);
    } catch(NumberFormatException exc) {
        System.out.println("Invalid number " + aNumber);
        return;
    }
    System.out.println("Number is " + result);
}
```

## Discussion

Of course, that lets you validate only numbers in the format that the designers of the wrapper classes expected. If you need to accept a different definition of numbers, you could use regular expressions (see Chapter 4) to make the determination.

There may also be times when you want to tell if a given number is an integer number or a floating-point number. One way is to check for the characters ., d, e, or f in the input; if one of these characters is present, convert the number as a double. Otherwise, convert it as an int:

```
// Part of GetNumber.java
private static Number NAN = new Double(Double.NaN);

/* Process one String, returning it as a Number subclass
 */
public Number process(String s) {
    if (s.matches(".*[.dDeEfF]")) {
        try {
            double dValue = Double.parseDouble(s);
            System.out.println("It's a double: " + dValue);
            return new Double(dValue);
        } catch (NumberFormatException e) {
            System.out.println("Invalid a double: " + s);
            return NAN;
        }
    } else // did not contain . d e or f, so try as int.
        try {
            int iValue = Integer.parseInt(s);
            System.out.println("It's an int: " + iValue);
            return new Integer(iValue);
        } catch (NumberFormatException e2) {
            System.out.println("Not a number:" + s);
            return NAN;
        }
}
```

## See Also

A more involved form of parsing is offered by the DecimalFormat class, discussed in Recipe 5.8.

JDK 1.5 also features the Scanner class; see Recipe 10.5.

# 5.2    Storing a Larger Number in a Smaller Number

## Problem

You have a number of a larger type and you want to store it in a variable of a smaller type.

## Solution

Cast the number to the smaller type. (A *cast* is a type listed in parentheses before a value that causes the value to be treated as though it were of the listed type.)

For example, to cast a long to an int, you need a cast. To cast a double to a float, you also need a cast.

## Discussion

This causes newcomers some grief, as the default type for a number with a decimal point is double, not float. So code like:

```
float f = 3.0;
```

won't even compile! It's as if you had written:

```
double tmp = 3.0;
float f = tmp;
```

You can fix it by making f a double, by making the 3.0 a float, by putting in a cast, or by assigning an integer value of 3:

```
double f = 3.0;
float f = 3.0f;
float f = 3f;
float f = (float)3.0;
float f = 3;
```

The same applies when storing an int into a short, char, or byte:

```
// CastNeeded.java
public static void main(String argv[]) {
    int i;
    double j = 2.75;
    i = j;              // EXPECT COMPILE ERROR
    i = (int)j;         // with cast; i gets 2
    System.out.println("i =" + i);
    byte b;
    b = i;              // EXPECT COMPILE ERROR
    b = (byte)i;     // with cast, i gets 2
    System.out.println("b =" + b);
}
```

The lines marked EXPECT COMPILE ERROR do not compile unless either commented out or changed to be correct. The lines marked "with cast" show the correct forms.

# 5.3 Converting Numbers to Objects and Vice Versa

## Problem

You need to convert numbers to objects and objects to numbers.

## Solution

Use the Object Wrapper classes listed in Table 5-1 at the beginning of this chapter.

## Discussion

Often you have a primitive number and you need to pass it into a method where an `Object` is required. This frequently happens when using the Collection classes (see Chapter 7) in 1.4 and earlier (in 1.5 you can use AutoBoxing, described in Recipe 8.4).

To convert between an `int` and an `Integer` object, or vice versa, you can use the following:

```
// IntObject.java
// int to Integer
Integer i1 = new Integer(42);
System.out.println(i1.toString()); // or just i1

// Integer to int
int i2 = i1.intValue();
System.out.println(i2);
```

# 5.4  Taking a Fraction of an Integer Without Using Floating Point

## Problem

You want to multiply an integer by a fraction without converting the fraction to a floating-point number.

## Solution

Multiply the integer by the numerator and divide by the denominator.

This technique should be used only when efficiency is more important than clarity, as it tends to detract from the readability—and therefore the maintainability—of your code.

## Discussion

Since integers and floating-point numbers are stored differently, it may sometimes be desirable and feasible, for efficiency purposes, to multiply an integer by a fractional value without converting the values to floating point and back, and without requiring a "cast":

```
/** Compute the value of 2/3 of 5 */
public class FractMult {
    public static void main(String u[]) {
```

```
        double d1 = 0.666 * 5;     // fast but obscure and inaccurate: convert
        System.out.println(d1);   // 2/3 to 0.666 in programmer's head

        double d2 = 2/3 * 5;      // wrong answer - 2/3 == 0, 0*5 = 0
        System.out.println(d2);

        double d3 = 2d/3d * 5;    // "normal"
        System.out.println(d3);

        double d4 = (2*5)/3d;     // one step done as integers, almost same answer
        System.out.println(d4);

        int i5 = 2*5/3;                // fast, approximate integer answer
        System.out.println(i5);
    }
}
```

Running it looks like this:

```
$ java  FractMult
3.33
0.0
3.333333333333333
3.3333333333333335
3
$
```

# 5.5   Ensuring the Accuracy of Floating-Point Numbers

## Problem

You want to know if a floating-point computation generated a sensible result.

## Solution

Compare with the INFINITY constants, and use isNaN( ) to check for "not a number."

Fixed-point operations that can do things like divide by zero result in Java notifying you abruptly by throwing an exception. This is because integer division by zero is considered a *logic error*.

Floating-point operations, however, do not throw an exception because they are defined over an (almost) infinite range of values. Instead, they signal errors by producing the constant POSITIVE_INFINITY if you divide a positive floating-point number by zero, the constant NEGATIVE_INFINITY if you divide a negative floating-point value by zero, and NaN (Not a Number), if you otherwise generate an invalid result. Values for these three public constants are defined in both the Float and the Double wrapper classes. The value NaN has the unusual property that it is not equal to itself, that is, NaN != NaN. Thus, it would hardly make sense to compare a (possibly suspect) number against NaN, because the expression:

```
x == NaN
```

can never be true. Instead, the methods Float.isNaN(float) and Double.isNaN(double) must be used:

```
// InfNaN.java
public static void main(String argv[]) {
    double d = 123;
    double e = 0;
    if (d/e == Double.POSITIVE_INFINITY)
        System.out.println("Check for POSITIVE_INFINITY works");
    double s = Math.sqrt(-1);
    if (s == Double.NaN)
        System.out.println("Comparison with NaN incorrectly returns true");
    if (Double.isNaN(s))
        System.out.println("Double.isNaN() correctly returns true");
}
```

Note that this, by itself, is not sufficient to ensure that floating-point calculations have been done with adequate accuracy. For example, the following program demonstrates a contrived calculation—Heron's formula for the area of a triangle—both in float and in double. The double values are correct, but the floating-point value comes out as zero due to rounding errors. This happens because, in Java, operations involving only float values are performed as 32-bit calculations. Related languages such as C automatically promote these to double during the computation, which can eliminate some loss of accuracy.

```
/** Compute the area of a triangle using Heron's Formula.
 * Code and values from Prof W. Kahan and Joseph D. Darcy.
 * See http://www.cs.berkeley.edu/~wkahan/JAVAhurt.pdf.
 * Derived from listing in Rick Grehan's Java Pro article (October 1999).
 * Simplified and reformatted by Ian Darwin.
 */
public class Heron {
    public static void main(String[] args) {
        // Sides for triangle in float
        float af, bf, cf;
        float sf, areaf;

        // Ditto in double
        double ad, bd, cd;
        double sd, aread;

        // Area of triangle in float
        af = 12345679.0f;
        bf = 12345678.0f;
        cf = 1.01233995f;
```

```
        sf = (af+bf+cf)/2.0f;
        areaf = (float)Math.sqrt(sf * (sf - af) * (sf - bf) * (sf - cf));
        System.out.println("Single precision: " + areaf);

        // Area of triangle in double
        ad = 12345679.0;
        bd = 12345678.0;
        cd = 1.01233995;

        sd = (ad+bd+cd)/2.0d;
        aread =        Math.sqrt(sd * (sd - ad) * (sd - bd) * (sd - cd));
        System.out.println("Double precision: " + aread);
    }
}
```

Let's run it. To ensure that the rounding is not an implementation artifact, I'll try it both with Sun's JDK and with Kaffe:

```
$ java Heron
Single precision: 0.0
Double precision: 972730.0557076167
$ kaffe Heron
Single precision: 0.0
Double precision: 972730.05570761673
```

If in doubt, use `double`!

To ensure consistency of very large magnitude double computations on different Java implementations, Java provides the keyword `strictfp`, which can apply to classes, interfaces, or methods within a class.[*] If a computation is Strict-FP, then it must always, for example, return the value `INFINITY` if a calculation would overflow the value of `Double.MAX_VALUE` (or underflow the value `Double.MIN_VALUE`). Non-Strict-FP calculations—the default—are allowed to perform calculations on a greater range and can return a valid final result that is in range even if the interim product was out of range. This is pretty esoteric and affects only computations that approach the bounds of what fits into a double.

# 5.6   Comparing Floating-Point Numbers

## Problem

You want to compare two floating-point numbers for equality.

## Solution

Based on what we've just discussed, you probably won't just go comparing two floats or doubles for equality. You might expect the floating-point wrapper classes,

---

[*] Note that an expression consisting entirely of compile-time constants, like `Math.PI * 2.1e17`, is also considered to be Strict-FP.

Float and Double, to override the equals( ) method, which they do. The equals( ) method returns true if the two values are the same bit for bit, that is, if and only if the numbers are the same or are both NaN. It returns false otherwise, including if the argument passed in is null, or if one object is +0.0 and the other is –0.0.

If this sounds weird, remember that the complexity comes partly from the nature of doing real number computations in the less-precise floating-point hardware, and partly from the details of the IEEE Standard 754, which specifies the floating-point functionality that Java tries to adhere to, so that underlying floating-point processor hardware can be used even when Java programs are being interpreted.

To actually compare floating-point numbers for equality, it is generally desirable to compare them within some tiny range of allowable differences; this range is often regarded as a tolerance or as *epsilon*. Example 5-1 shows an equals( ) method you can use to do this comparison, as well as comparisons on values of NaN. When run, it prints that the first two numbers are equal within epsilon:

```
$ java FloatCmp
True within epsilon 1.0E-7
$
```

*Example 5-1. FloatCmp.java*

```
}/**
 * Floating-point comparisons.
 */
public class FloatCmp {
    final static double EPSILON = 0.0000001;
    public static void main(String[] argv) {
        double da = 3 * .3333333333;
        double db = 0.99999992857;

        // Compare two numbers that are expected to be close.
        if (da == db) {
            System.out.println("Java considers " + da + "==" + db);
        // else compare with our own equals method
        } else if (equals(da, db, 0.0000001)) {
            System.out.println("True within epsilon " + EPSILON);
        } else {
            System.out.println(da + " != " + db);
        }

        // Show that comparing two NaNs is not a good idea:
        double d1 = Double.NaN;
        double d2 = Double.NaN;
        if (d1 == d2)
            System.err.println("Comparing two NaNs incorrectly returns true.");
        if (!new Double(d1).equals(new Double(d2)))
            System.err.println("Double(NaN).equal(NaN) incorrectly returns false.");
    }
```

*Example 5-1. FloatCmp.java (continued)*

```
/** Compare two doubles within a given epsilon */
public static boolean equals(double a, double b, double eps) {
    if (a==b) return true;
    // If the difference is less than epsilon, treat as equal.
    return Math.abs(a - b) < eps;
}

/** Compare two doubles, using default epsilon */
public static boolean equals(double a, double b) {
    if (a==b) return true;
    // If the difference is less than epsilon, treat as equal.
    return Math.abs(a - b) < EPSILON * Math.max(Math.abs(a), Math.abs(b));
}
}
```

Note that neither of the System.err messages about "incorrect returns" prints. The point of this example with NaNs is that you should always make sure values are not NaN before entrusting them to Double.equals( ).

# 5.7   Rounding Floating-Point Numbers

## Problem

You need to round floating-point numbers to integers or to a particular precision.

## Solution

If you simply cast a floating value to an integer value, Java truncates the value. A value like 3.999999 cast to an int or long becomes 3, not 4. To round floating-point numbers properly, use Math.round( ). It has two forms: if you give it a double, you get a long result; if you give it a float, you get an int.

What if you don't like the rounding rules used by round? If for some bizarre reason you wanted to round numbers greater than 0.54 instead of the normal 0.5, you could write your own version of round( ):

```
/*
 * Round floating values to integers.
 * @Return the closest int to the argument.
 * @param d A non-negative values to be rounded.
 */
static int round(double d) {
    if (d < 0) {
        throw new IllegalArgumentException("Value must be non-negative");
    }
    int di = (int)Math.floor(d);    // integral value below (or ==) d
    if ((d - di) > THRESHOLD) {
        return di + 1;
```

```
        } else {
            return di;
        }
    }
```

If you need to display a number with less precision than it normally gets, you probably want to use a `DecimalFormat` object or a `Formatter` object.

## 5.8 Formatting Numbers

### Problem

You need to format numbers.

### Solution

Use a `NumberFormat` subclass.

Java has not traditionally provided a C-style *printf*/*scanf* functions because they tend to mix together formatting and input/output in a very inflexible way. Programs using *printf*/*scanf* can be very hard to internationalize, for example.

Java has an entire package, `java.text`, full of formatting routines as general and flexible as anything you might imagine. As with *printf*, it has an involved formatting language, described in the Javadoc page. Consider the presentation of long numbers. In North America, the number one thousand twenty-four and a quarter is written 1,024.25, in most of Europe it is 1 024,25, and in some other part of the world it might be written 1.024,25. Not to mention how currencies and percentages are formatted! Trying to keep track of this yourself would drive the average small software shop around the bend rather quickly.

Fortunately, the `java.text` package includes a `Locale` class, and, furthermore, the Java runtime automatically sets a default `Locale` object based on the user's environment; e.g., on the Macintosh and Windows, the user's preferences; on Unix, the user's environment variables. (To provide a nondefault locale, see Recipe 15.8.) To provide formatters customized for numbers, currencies, and percentages, the `NumberFormat` class has static *factory methods* that normally return a `DecimalFormat` with the correct pattern already instantiated. A `DecimalFormat` object appropriate to the user's locale can be obtained from the factory method `NumberFormat.getInstance()` and manipulated using set methods. Surprisingly, the method `setMinimumIntegerDigits()` turns out to be the easy way to generate a number format with leading zeros. Here is an example:

```
import java.text.*;
import java.util.*;

/*
 * Format a number our way and the default way.
 */
```

```
public class NumFormat2 {
    /** A number to format */
    public static final double data[] = {
        0, 1, 22d/7, 100.2345678
    };

    /** The main (and only) method in this class. */
    public static void main(String av[]) {
        // Get a format instance
        NumberFormat form = NumberFormat.getInstance( );

        // Set it to look like 999.99[99]
        form.setMinimumIntegerDigits(3);
        form.setMinimumFractionDigits(2);
        form.setMaximumFractionDigits(4);

        // Now print using it.
        for (int i=0; i<data.length; i++)
            System.out.println(data[i] + "\tformats as " +
                form.format(data[i]));
    }
}
```

This prints the contents of the array using the NumberFormat instance form:

```
$ java NumFormat2
0.0        formats as 000.00
1.0        formats as 001.00
3.142857142857143      formats as 003.1429
100.2345678      formats as 100.2346
$
```

You can also construct a DecimalFormat with a particular pattern or change the pattern dynamically using applyPattern( ). Some of the more common pattern characters are shown in Table 5-2.

Table 5-2. DecimalFormat pattern characters

| Character | Meaning |
| --- | --- |
| # | Numeric digit (leading zeros suppressed) |
| 0 | Numeric digit (leading zeros provided) |
| . | Locale-specific decimal separator (decimal point) |
| , | Locale-specific grouping separator (comma in English) |
| - | Locale-specific negative indicator (minus sign) |
| % | Shows the value as a percentage |
| ; | Separates two formats: the first for positive and the second for negative values |
| ' | Escapes one of the above characters so it appears |
| Anything else | Appears as itself |

The NumFormatTest program uses one DecimalFormat to print a number with only two decimal places and a second to format the number according to the default locale:

```
// NumFormatTest.java
/** A number to format */
public static final double intlNumber = 1024.25;
/** Another number to format */
public static final double ourNumber = 100.2345678;
NumberFormat defForm = NumberFormat.getInstance();
NumberFormat ourForm = new DecimalFormat("##0.##");
// toPattern() shows the combination of #0., etc
// that this particular local uses to format with
System.out.println("defForm's pattern is " +
    ((DecimalFormat)defForm).toPattern());
System.out.println(intlNumber + " formats as " +
    defForm.format(intlNumber));
System.out.println(ourNumber + " formats as " +
    ourForm.format(ourNumber));
System.out.println(ourNumber + " formats as " +
    defForm.format(ourNumber) + " using the default format");
```

This program prints the given pattern and then formats the same number using several formats:

```
$ java NumFormatTest
defForm's pattern is #,##0.###
1024.25 formats as 1,024.25
100.2345678 formats as 100.23
100.2345678 formats as 100.235 using the default format
$
```

## See Also

Chapter 17; O'Reilly's *Java I/O* by Elliotte Rusty Harold.

# 5.9   Converting Between Binary, Octal, Decimal, and Hexadecimal

## Problem

You want to display an integer as a series of bits—for example, when interacting with certain hardware devices. You want to convert a binary number or a hexadecimal value into an integer.

## Solution

The class java.lang.Integer provides the solutions. Use toBinaryString() to convert an integer to binary. Use valueOf() to convert a binary string to an integer:

```
// BinaryDigits.java
String bin = "101010";
```

```
System.out.println(bin + " as an integer is " + Integer.valueOf(bin, 2));
int i = 42;
System.out.println(i + " as binary digits (bits) is " +
    Integer.toBinaryString(i));
```

This program prints the binary as an integer, and an integer as binary:

```
$ java BinaryDigits
101010 as an integer is 42
42 as binary digits (bits) is 101010
$
```

## Discussion

Integer.valueOf( ) is more general than binary formatting. It also converts a string number from any radix to int, just by changing the second argument. Octal is base 8, decimal is 10, hexadecimal 16. Going the other way, the Integer class includes toBinaryString( ), toOctalString( ), and toHexString( ).

The String class itself includes a series of static methods, valueOf(int), valueOf(double), and so on, that also provide default formatting. That is, they return the given numeric value formatted as a string.

# 5.10 Operating on a Series of Integers

## Problem

You need to work on a range of integers.

## Solution

For a contiguous set, use a for loop.

## Discussion

To process a contiguous set of integers, Java provides a for loop.* Loop control for the for loop is in three parts: initialize, test, and change. If the test part is initially false, the loop will never be executed, not even once.

For discontinuous ranges of numbers, use a java.util.BitSet.

The following program demonstrates all of these techniques:

```
import java.util.BitSet;

/** Operations on series of numbers */
public class NumSeries {
    public static void main(String[] args) {
```

---

* If the set of numbers is in an array or collection (see Chapter 7), use a "foreach" loop (see Recipe 8.2).

```
// When you want an ordinal list of numbers, use a for loop
// starting at 1.
for (int i = 1; i <= months.length; i++)
    System.out.println("Month # " + i);

// When you want a set of array indexes, use a for loop
// starting at 0.
for (int i = 0; i < months.length; i++)
    System.out.println("Month " + months[i]);

// For a discontiguous set of integers, try a BitSet

// Create a BitSet and turn on a couple of bits.
BitSet b = new BitSet();
b.set(0);    // January
b.set(3);    // April

// Presumably this would be somewhere else in the code.
for (int i = 0; i<months.length; i++) {
    if (b.get(i))
        System.out.println("Month " + months[i] + " requested");
    }
}
/** The names of the months. See Dates/Times chapter for a better way */
protected static String months[] = {
    "January", "February", "March", "April",
    "May", "June", "July", "August",
    "September", "October", "November", "December"
};
}
```

# 5.11   Working with Roman Numerals

## Problem

You need to format numbers as Roman numerals. Perhaps you've just written the next *Titanic* or *Star Wars* episode and you need to get the copyright date correct. Or, on a more mundane level, you need to format page numbers in the front matter of a book.

## Solution

Use my RomanNumberFormat class:

```
// RomanNumberSimple.java
RomanNumberFormat nf = new RomanNumberFormat();
int year = Calendar.getInstance().get(Calendar.YEAR);
System.out.println(year + " -> " + nf.format(year));
```

The use of Calendar to get the current year is explained in Recipe 6.1. Running RomanNumberSimple looks like this:

```
+ jikes +E -d . RomanNumberSimple.java
+ java RomanNumberSimple
2004 -> MMIV
```

## Discussion

Nothing in the standard API formats Roman numerals. However, the java.text. Format class is designed to be subclassed for precisely such unanticipated purposes, so I have done just that and developed a class to format numbers as Roman numerals. Here is a better and complete example program of using it to format the current year. I can pass a number of arguments on the command line, including a "-" where I want the year to appear (note that these arguments are normally not quoted; the "-" must be an argument all by itself, just to keep the program simple). I use it as follows:

```
$ java RomanYear   Copyright (c) - Ian Darwin
Copyright (c) MMIV Ian Darwin
$
```

The code for the RomanYear program is simple, yet it correctly puts spaces around the arguments:

```
import java.util.*;

/** Print the current year in Roman Numerals */
public class RomanYear {

    public static void main(String[] argv) {

        RomanNumberFormat rf = new RomanNumberFormat();
        Calendar cal = Calendar.getInstance();
        int year = cal.get(Calendar.YEAR);

        // If no arguments, just print the year.
        if (argv.length == 0) {
            System.out.println(rf.format(year));
            return;
        }

        // Else a micro-formatter: replace "-" arg with year, else print.
        for (int i=0; i<argv.length; i++) {
            if (argv[i].equals("-"))
                System.out.print(rf.format(year));
            else
                System.out.print(argv[i]);    // e.g., "Copyright"
            System.out.print(' ');
        }
        System.out.println();
    }
}
```

Now here's the code for the RomanNumberFormat class. I did sneak in one additional class, java.text.FieldPosition. A FieldPosition simply represents the position of one numeric field in a string that has been formatted using a variant of NumberFormat. format(). You construct it to represent either the integer part or the fraction part (of course, Roman numerals don't have fractional parts). The FieldPosition methods getBeginIndex() and getEndIndex() indicate where in the resulting string the given field wound up.

Example 5-2 is the class that implements Roman number formatting. As the comments indicate, the one limitation is that the input number must be less than 4,000.

*Example 5-2. RomanNumberFormat.java*

```java
import java.text.*;
import java.util.*;

/**
 * Roman Number class. Not localized, since Latin's a Dead Dead Language
 * and we don't display Roman Numbers differently in different Locales.
 * Filled with quick-n-dirty algorithms.
 */
public class RomanNumberFormat extends Format {

    /** Characters used in "Arabic to Roman", that is, format() methods. */
    static char A2R[][] = {
            { 0, 'M' },
            { 0, 'C', 'D', 'M' },
            { 0, 'X', 'L', 'C' },
            { 0, 'I', 'V', 'X' },
    };

    /** Format a given double as a Roman Numeral; just truncate to a
     * long, and call format(long).
     */
    public String format(double n) {
        return format((long)n);
    }

    /** Format a given long as a Roman Numeral. Just call the
     * three-argument form.
     */
    public String format(long n) {
        if (n <=  0 || n >= 4000)
            throw new IllegalArgumentException(n + " must be > 0 && < 4000");
        StringBuffer sb = new StringBuffer();
        format(new Integer((int)n), sb, new FieldPosition(NumberFormat.INTEGER
                FIELD));
        return sb.toString();
    }

    /* Format the given Number as a Roman Numeral, returning the
     * Stringbuffer (updated), and updating the FieldPosition.
     * This method is the REAL FORMATTING ENGINE.
     * Method signature is overkill, but required as a subclass of Format.
     */
    public StringBuffer format(Object on, StringBuffer sb, FieldPosition fp) {
        if (!(on instanceof Number))
            throw new IllegalArgumentException(on + " must be a Number object");
```

*Example 5-2. RomanNumberFormat.java (continued)*

```
        if (fp.getField( ) != NumberFormat.INTEGER_FIELD)
            throw new IllegalArgumentException(fp +
                            " must be FieldPosition(NumberFormat.INTEGER_FIELD");
        int n = ((Number)on).intValue( );    // TODO check for in range here

        // First, put the digits on a tiny stack. Must be 4 digits.
        for (int i=0; i<4; i++) {
            int d=n%10;
            push(d);
            // System.out.println("Pushed " + d);
            n=n/10;
        }

        // Now pop and convert.
        for (int i=0; i<4; i++) {
            int ch = pop( );
            // System.out.println("Popped " + ch);
            if (ch==0)
                continue;
            else if (ch <= 3) {
                for(int k=1; k<=ch; k++)
                    sb.append(A2R[i][1]); // I
            }
            else if (ch == 4) {
                sb.append(A2R[i][1]);    // I
                sb.append(A2R[i][2]);    // V
            }
            else if (ch == 5) {
                sb.append(A2R[i][2]);    // V
            }
            else if (ch <= 8) {
                sb.append(A2R[i][2]);    // V
                for (int k=6; k<=ch; k++)
                    sb.append(A2R[i][1]);    // I
            }
            else { // 9
                sb.append(A2R[i][1]);
                sb.append(A2R[i][3]);
            }
        }
        // fp.setBeginIndex(0);
        // fp.setEndIndex(3);
        return sb;
    }

    /** Parse a generic object, returning an Object */
    public Object parseObject(String what, ParsePosition where) {
        throw new IllegalArgumentException("Parsing not implemented");
        // TODO PARSING HERE
        // return new Long(0);
    }
```

*Example 5-2. RomanNumberFormat.java (continued)*

```
    /* Implement a toy stack */
    protected int stack[] = new int[10];
    protected int depth = 0;

    /* Implement a toy stack */
    protected void push(int n) {
        stack[depth++] = n;
    }
    /* Implement a toy stack */
    protected int pop( ) {
        return stack[--depth];
    }
}
```

Several of the public methods are required because I wanted it to be a subclass of Format, which is abstract. This accounts for some of the complexity, like having three different format methods.

Note that the parseObject( ) method is also required, but we don't actually implement parsing in this version. This is left as the usual exercise for the reader.

## See Also

*Java I/O* (O'Reilly) has an entire chapter on NumberFormat and develops an ExponentialNumberFormat subclass.

The online source for this book has ScaledNumberFormat, which prints numbers with a maximum of four digits and a computerish scale factor (B for bytes, K for kilo-, M for mega-, and so on).

# 5.12  Formatting with Correct Plurals

## Problem

You're printing something like "We used " + n + " items", but in English, "We used 1 items" is ungrammatical. You want "We used 1 item."

## Solution

Use a ChoiceFormat or a conditional statement.

Use Java's ternary operator (cond ? trueval : falseval) in a string concatenation. Both zero and plurals get an "s" appended to the noun in English ("no books, one book, two books"), so we test for n==1.

```
    // FormatPlurals.java
    public static void main(String argv[]) {
        report(0);
        report(1);
        report(2);
```

```
    }
    /** report -- using conditional operator */
    public static void report(int n) {
        System.out.println("We used " + n + " item" + (n==1?"":"s"));
    }
```

Does it work?

```
$ java FormatPlurals
We used 0 items
We used 1 item
We used 2 items
$
```

The final println statement is short for:

```
if (n==1)
    System.out.println("We used " + n + " item");
else
    System.out.println("We used " + n + " items");
```

This is a lot longer, in fact, so the ternary conditional operator is worth learning.

The ChoiceFormat is ideal for this. It is actually capable of much more, but here I'll show only this simplest use. I specify the values 0, 1, and 2 (or more), and the string values to print corresponding to each number. The numbers are then formatted according to the range they fall into:

```
import java.text.*;
/**
 * Format a plural correctly, using a ChoiceFormat.
 */
public class FormatPluralsChoice extends FormatPlurals {
        static double[] limits = { 0, 1, 2 };
        static String[] formats = { "items", "item", "items"};
        static ChoiceFormat myFormat = new ChoiceFormat(limits, formats);

        /** report -- using conditional operator */
        public static void report(int n) {
                System.out.println("We used " + n + " " + myFormat.format(n));
        }

        public static void main(String[] argv) {
                report(0);
                report(1);
                report(2);
        }
}
```

This generates the same output as the basic version. It is slightly longer, but more general, and lends itself better to internationalization.

## 5.13 Generating Random Numbers

### Problem

You need to generate random numbers in a hurry.

### Solution

Use `java.lang.Math.random( )` to generate random numbers. There is no claim that the random values it returns are very *good* random numbers, however. This code exercises the `random( )` method:

```
// Random1.java
// java.lang.Math.random( ) is static, don't need to construct Math
System.out.println("A random from java.lang.Math is " + Math.random( ));
```

Note that this method only generates double values. If you need integers, you need to scale and round:

```
/** Generate random ints by asking Random( ) for
 * a series of random integers from 1 to 10, inclusive.
 *
 * @author Ian Darwin, http://www.darwinsys.com/
 * @version $Id: ch05,v 1.5 2004/05/04 20:11:35 ian Exp $
 */
public class RandomInt {
    public static void main(String[] a) {
        Random r = new Random( );
        for (int i=0; i<1000; i++)
            // nextInt(10) goes from 0-9; add 1 for 1-10;
            System.out.println(1+Math.round(r.nextInt(10)));
    }
}
```

To see if it was really working well, I used the Unix tools *sort* and *uniq*, which, together, give a count of how many times each value was chosen. For 1,000 integers, each of 10 values should be chosen about 100 times:

```
C:> java RandomInt | sort -n | uniq -c
110 1
106 2
 98 3
109 4
108 5
 99 6
 94 7
 91 8
 94 9
 91 10
C:>
```

## See Also

Recipe 5.14 shows easier and better ways to get random integers and doubles. Also see the Javadoc documentation for java.lang.Math and the warning in this chapter's Introduction about pseudo-randomness versus real randomness.

# 5.14 Generating Better Random Numbers

## Problem

You need to generate better random numbers.

## Solution

Construct a java.util.Random object (not just any old random object) and call its next*( ) methods. These methods include nextBoolean( ), nextBytes( ) (which fills the given array of bytes with random values), nextDouble( ), nextFloat( ), nextInt( ), and nextLong( ). Don't be confused by the capitalization of Float, Double, etc. They return the primitive types boolean, float, double, etc., not the capitalized wrapper objects. Clear enough? Maybe an example will help:

```
// Random2.java
// java.util.Random methods are non-static, so need to construct
Random r = new Random( );
for (int i=0; i<10; i++)
    System.out.println("A double from java.util.Random is " + r.nextDouble( ));
for (int i=0; i<10; i++)
    System.out.println("An integer from java.util.Random is " + r.nextInt( ));
```

You can also use the java.util.Random nextGaussian( ) method, as shown next. The nextDouble( ) methods try to give a "flat" distribution between 0 and 1.0, in which each value has an equal chance of being selected. A Gaussian or normal distribution is a bell-curve of values from negative infinity to positive infinity, with the majority of the values around zero (0.0).

```
// Random3.java
Random r = new Random( );
for (int i=0; i<10; i++)
    System.out.println("A gaussian random double is " + r.nextGaussian( ));
```

To illustrate the different distributions, I generated 10,000 numbers first using nextRandom( ) and then using nextGaussian( ). The code for this is in *Random4.java* (not shown here) and is a combination of the previous programs with code to print the results into files. I then plotted histograms using the R statistics package (see *http://www.r-project.org*). The results are shown in Figure 5-1.

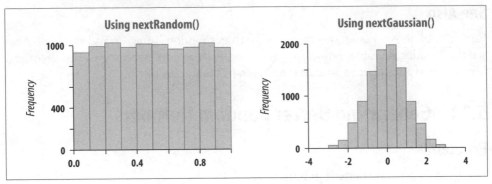

*Figure 5-1. Flat (left) and Gaussian (right) distributions*

## See Also

The Javadoc documentation for `java.util.Random`, and the warning in the Introduction about pseudo-randomness versus real randomness.

For cryptographic use, see class `java.security.SecureRandom`, which provides cryptographically strong pseudo-random number generators (PRNG).

# 5.15  Calculating Trigonometric Functions

## Problem

You need to compute sine, cosine, and other trigonometric functions.

## Solution

Use the trig functions in `java.lang.Math`. Like `java.lang.Math.random( )`, all the methods of the `Math` class are static, so no `Math` instance is necessary. This makes sense, as none of these computations maintains any state. Note that the arguments for trigonometric functions are in radians, not in degrees. Here is a program that computes a few (mostly) trigonometric values and displays the values of e and PI that are available in the math library:

```
// Trig.java
System.out.println("Java's PI is " + Math.PI);
System.out.println("Java's e is " + Math.E);
System.out.println("The cosine of 1.1418 is " + Math.cos(1.1418));
```

The `java.lang.StrictMath` class, introduced in JDK 1.3, is intended to perform the same operations as `java.lang.Math` but with greater cross-platform repeatability.

# 5.16 Taking Logarithms

## Problem

You need to take the logarithm of a number.

## Solution

For logarithms to base e, use `java.lang.Math`'s `log( )` function:

```
// Logarithm.java
double someValue;
// compute someValue...
double log_e = Math.log(someValue);
```

For logarithms to other bases, use the identity that:

$$\log_n(x) = \frac{\log_e(x)}{\log_e(n)}$$

where x is the number whose logarithm you want, n is any desired base, and e is the natural logarithm base. I have a simple LogBase class containing code that implements this functionality:

```
// LogBase.java
public static double log_base(double base, double value) {
    return Math.log(value) / Math.log(base);
}
```

## Discussion

My `log_base` function allows you to compute logs to any positive base. If you have to perform a lot of logs to the same base, it is more efficient to rewrite the code to cache the `log(base)` once. Here is an example of using `log_base`:

```
// LogBaseUse.java
public static void main(String argv[]) {
    double d = LogBase.log_base(10, 10000);
    System.out.println("log10(10000) = " + d);
}
C:> java LogBaseUse
log10(10000) = 4.0
```

# 5.17 Multiplying Matrices

## Problem

You need to multiply a pair of two-dimensional arrays, as is common in mathematical and engineering applications.

## Solution

Use the following code as a model.

## Discussion

It is straightforward to multiply an array of a numeric type. The code in Example 5-3 implements matrix multiplication.

*Example 5-3. Matrix.java*

```java
/**
 * Multiply two matrices.
 * Only defined for int:
 * for long, float, and double.
 */
public class Matrix {

    /* Matrix-multiply two arrays together.
     * The arrays MUST be rectangular.
     * @author Tom Christiansen & Nathan Torkington, Perl Cookbook version.
     */
    public static int[][] multiply(int[][] m1, int[][] m2) {
        int m1rows = m1.length;
        int m1cols = m1[0].length;
        int m2rows = m2.length;
        int m2cols = m2[0].length;
        if (m1cols != m2rows)
            throw new IllegalArgumentException(
                "matrices don't match: " + m1cols + " != " + m2rows);
        int[][] result = new int[m1rows][m2cols];

        // multiply
        for (int i=0; i<m1rows; i++)
            for (int j=0; j<m2cols; j++)
                for (int k=0; k<m1cols; k++)
                    result[i][j] += m1[i][k] * m2[k][j];

        return result;
    }

    public static void mprint(int[][] a) {
        int rows = a.length;
        int cols = a[0].length;
        System.out.println("array["+rows+"]["+cols+"] = {");
        for (int i=0; i<rows; i++) {
            System.out.print("{");
            for (int j=0; j<cols; j++)
                System.out.print(" " + a[i][j] + ",");
            System.out.println("},");
        }
        System.out.println(":;");
    }
}
```

Here is a program that uses the `Matrix` class to multiply two arrays of ints:

```
// MatrixUse.java
int x[][] = {
    { 3, 2, 3 },
    { 5, 9, 8 },
};
int y[][] = {
    { 4, 7 },
    { 9, 3 },
    { 8, 1 },
};
int z[][] = Matrix.multiply(x, y);
Matrix.mprint(x);
Matrix.mprint(y);
Matrix.mprint(z);
```

## See Also

Consult a book on numerical methods for more things to do with matrices; one of our reviewers recommends *Numerical Recipes in Fortran* by Teukolsky, Flannery, et al., available as a PDF from *http://www.library.cornell.edu/nr/bookfpdf.html*. Commercial software packages can do some of these calculations for you, including the Visual Numerics libraries, which can be downloaded from *http://www.vni.com*.

# 5.18  Using Complex Numbers

## Problem

You need to manipulate complex numbers, as is common in mathematical, scientific, or engineering applications.

## Solution

Java does not provide any explicit support for dealing with complex numbers. You could keep track of the real and imaginary parts and do the computations yourself, but that is not a very well-structured solution.

A better solution, of course, is to use a class that implements complex numbers. I provide just such a class. First, an example of using it:

```
// ComplexDemo.java
Complex c = new Complex(3,  5);
Complex d = new Complex(2, -2);
System.out.println(c + ".getReal( ) = " + c.getReal( ));
System.out.println(c + " + " + d + " = " + c.add(d));
System.out.println(c + " + " + d + " = " + Complex.add(c, d));
System.out.println(c + " * " + d + " = " + c.multiply(d));
```

Example 5-4 is the complete source for the Complex class and shouldn't require much explanation. To keep the API general, I provide—for each of add, subtract, and multiply—both a static method that works on two complex objects and a nonstatic method that applies the operation to the given object and one other object.

*Example 5-4. Complex.java*

```
/** A class to represent Complex Numbers. A Complex object is
 * immutable once created; the add, subtract and multiply routines
 * return newly created Complex objects containing the results.
 *
 */
public class Complex {
    /** The real part */
    private double r;
    /** The imaginary part */
    private double i;
    /** Construct a Complex */
    Complex(double rr, double ii) {
        r = rr;
        i = ii;
    }
    /** Display the current Complex as a String, for use in
     * println() and elsewhere.
     */
    public String toString() {
        StringBuffer sb = new StringBuffer().append(r);
        if (i>0)
            sb.append('+');     // else append(i) appends - sign
        return sb.append(i).append('i').toString();
    }
    /** Return just the Real part */
    public double getReal() {
        return r;
    }
    /** Return just the Real part */
    public double getImaginary() {
        return i;
    }
    /** Return the magnitude of a complex number */
    public double magnitude() {
        return Math.sqrt(r*r + i*i);
    }

    /** Add another Complex to this one */
    public Complex add(Complex other) {
        return add(this, other);
    }
    /** Add two Complexes */
    public static Complex add(Complex c1, Complex c2) {
        return new Complex(c1.r+c2.r, c1.i+c2.i);
    }
```

*Example 5-4. Complex.java (continued)*

```
    /** Subtract another Complex from this one */
    public Complex subtract(Complex other) {
        return subtract(this, other);
    }
    /** Subtract two Complexes */
    public static Complex subtract(Complex c1, Complex c2) {
        return new Complex(c1.r-c2.r, c1.i-c2.i);
    }

    /** Multiply this Complex times another one */
    public Complex multiply(Complex other) {
        return multiply(this, other);
    }
    /** Multiply two Complexes */
    public static Complex multiply(Complex c1, Complex c2) {
        return new Complex(c1.r*c2.r - c1.i*c2.i, c1.r*c2.i + c1.i*c2.r);
    }
    /** Divide c1 by  c2.
     * @author Gisbert Selke.
     */
    public static Complex divide(Complex c1, Complex c2) {
        return new Complex(
        (c1.r*c2.r+c1.i*c2.i)/(c2.r*c2.r+c2.i*c2.i),
        (c1.i*c2.r-c1.r*c2.i)/(c2.r*c2.r+c2.i*c2.i));
    }
}
```

# 5.19   Handling Very Large Numbers

## Problem

You need to handle integer numbers larger than Long.MAX_VALUE or floating-point values larger than Double.MAX_VALUE.

## Solution

Use the BigInteger or BigDecimal values in package java.math:

```
// BigNums.java
System.out.println("Here's Long.MAX_VALUE: " + Long.MAX_VALUE);
BigInteger bInt = new BigInteger("3419229223372036854775807");
System.out.println("Here's a bigger number: " + bInt);
System.out.println("Here it is as a double: " + bInt.doubleValue());
```

Note that the constructor takes the number as a string. Obviously you couldn't just type the numeric digits since by definition these classes are designed to represent numbers larger than will fit in a Java long.

## Discussion

Both `BigInteger` and `BigDecimal` objects are immutable; that is, once constructed, they always represent a given number. That said, a number of methods return new objects that are mutations of the original, such as negate( ), which returns the negative of the given `BigInteger` or `BigDecimal`. There are also methods corresponding to most of the Java language built-in operators defined on the base types int/long and float/double. The division method makes you specify the rounding method; consult a book on numerical analysis for details. Example 5-5 is a simple stack-based calculator using `BigDecimal` as its numeric data type.

*Example 5-5. BigNumCalc*

```java
import java.math.BigDecimal;
import java.util.Stack;

/** A trivial reverse-polish stack-based calculator for big numbers */
public class BigNumCalc {

    /** an array of Objects, simulating user input */
    public static Object[] testInput = {
        new BigDecimal("3419229223372036854775807.23343"),
        new BigDecimal("2.0"),
        "*",
    };

    public static void main(String[] args) {
        BigNumCalc calc = new BigNumCalc();
        System.out.println(calc.calculate(testInput));
    }

    Stack s = new Stack();

    public BigDecimal calculate(Object[] input) {
        BigDecimal tmp;
        for (int i = 0; i < input.length; i++) {
            Object o = input[i];
            if (o instanceof BigDecimal)
                s.push(o);
            else if (o instanceof String) {
                switch (((String)o).charAt(0)) {
                // + and * are commutative, order doesn't matter
                case '+':
                    s.push(((BigDecimal)s.pop()).add((BigDecimal)s.pop()));
                    break;
                case '*':
                    s.push(((BigDecimal)s.pop()).multiply((BigDecimal)s.pop()));
                    break;
                // - and /, order *does* matter
                case '-':
                    tmp = (BigDecimal)s.pop();
                    s.push(((BigDecimal)s.pop()).subtract(tmp));
                    break;
```

*Example 5-5. BigNumCalc (continued)*

```
                case '/':
                    tmp = (BigDecimal)s.pop( );
                    s.push(((BigDecimal)s.pop( )).divide(tmp,
                        BigDecimal.ROUND_UP));
                    break;
                default:
                    throw new IllegalStateException("Unknown OPERATOR popped");
                }
            } else {
                throw new IllegalStateException("Syntax error in input");
            }
        }
        return (BigDecimal)s.pop( );
    }
}
```

Running this produces the expected (very large) value:

```
> jikes +E -d . BigNumCalc.java
> java BigNumCalc
68384584467440737095516146.466860
>
```

The current version has its inputs hard-coded, as does the JUnit test program, but in real life you can use regular expressions to extract words or operators from an input stream (as in Recipe 4.5), or you can use the StreamTokenizer approach of the simple calculator (Recipe 10.4). The stack of numbers is maintained using a java.util. Stack (Recipe 7.14).

BigInteger is mainly useful in cryptographic and security applications. Its method isProbablyPrime( ) can create prime pairs for public key cryptography. BigDecimal might also be useful in computing the size of the universe.

# 5.20  Program: TempConverter

The program shown in Example 5-6 prints a table of Fahrenheit temperatures (still used in daily life weather reporting in the United States) and the corresponding Celsius temperatures (used in science everywhere, and in daily life in most of the world).

*Example 5-6. TempConverter.java*

```
import java.text.*;

/* Print a table of Fahrenheit and Celsius temperatures
 */
public class TempConverter {

    public static void main(String[] args) {
        TempConverter t = new TempConverter();
```

*Example 5-6. TempConverter.java (continued)*

```
            t.start();
            t.data();
            t.end();
    }

    protected void start() {
    }

    protected void data() {
        for (int i=-40; i<=120; i+=10) {
            float c = (i-32)*(5f/9);
            print(i, c);
        }
    }

    protected void print(float f, float c) {
        System.out.println(f + " " + c);
    }

    protected void end() {
    }
}
```

This works, but these numbers print with about 15 digits of (useless) decimal fractions! The second version of this program subclasses the first and uses a DecimalFormat to control the formatting of the converted temperatures (Example 5-7).

*Example 5-7. TempConverter2.java*

```
import java.text.*;

/* Print a table of fahrenheit and celsius temperatures, a bit more neatly.
 */
public class TempConverter2 extends TempConverter {
    protected DecimalFormat df;

    public static void main(String[] args) {
        TempConverter t = new TempConverter2();
        t.start();
        t.data();
        t.end();
    }

    // Constructor
    public TempConverter2() {
        df = new DecimalFormat("#0.00");
    }

    protected void print(float f, float c) {
        System.out.println(f + " " + df.format(c));
    }
}
```

*Example 5-7. TempConverter2.java (continued)*

```
protected void start( ) {
    System.out.println("Fahr    Centigrade.");
}

protected void end( ) {
    System.out.println("--------------------");
}
}
```

This works, and the results are better than the first version's, but still not right:

```
C:\javasrc\numbers>java  TempConverter2
Fahr    Centigrade.
-40.00 -40.00
-30.00 -34.44
-20.00 -28.89
-10.00 -23.33
0.00 -17.78
10.00 -12.22
20.00 -6.67
30.00 -1.11
40.00 4.44
50.00 10.00
60.00 15.56
70.00 21.11
80.00 26.67
90.00 32.22
100.00 37.78
110.00 43.33
120.00 48.89
```

It would look neater if we lined up the decimal points, but Java had nothing in its standard API for doing this. This is deliberate! They wanted to utterly break the ties with the ancient IBM 1403 line printers and similar monospaced devices such as typewriters, "dumb" terminals,* and DOS terminal windows. However, with a bit of simple arithmetic, the FieldPosition from Recipe 5.11 can be used to figure out how many spaces need to be prepended to line up the columns; the arithmetic is done in print( ), and the spaces are put on in prependSpaces( ). The result is much prettier:

```
C:\javasrc\numbers>java  TempConverter3
Fahr    Centigrade.
 -40    -40
 -30    -34.444
 -20    -28.889
 -10    -23.333
   0    -17.778
  10    -12.222
  20     -6.667
```

---

* My children are quick to remind me that "dumb" means "incapable of speech." Nobody who has used, say, a TTY33 or a DecWriter 100 dumb terminal will claim that they are incapable of speech. Intelligible speech yes, but they certainly did talk at you while they were printing....

```
        30    -1.111
        40     4.444
        50    10
        60    15.556
        70    21.111
        80    26.667
        90    32.222
       100    37.778
       110    43.333
       120    48.889
       ------------------
```

And the code (Example 5-8) is only ten lines longer!

*Example 5-8. TempConverter3.java*

```java
import java.text.*;

/* Print a table of Fahrenheit and Celsius temperatures, with decimal
 * points lined up.
 */
public class TempConverter3 extends TempConverter2 {
    protected FieldPosition fp;
    protected DecimalFormat dff;

    public static void main(String[] args) {
        TempConverter t = new TempConverter3();
        t.start();
        t.data();
        t.end();
    }

    // Constructor
    public TempConverter3() {
        super();
        dff = new DecimalFormat("##.#");
        fp = new FieldPosition(NumberFormat.INTEGER_FIELD);
    }

    protected void print(float f, float c) {
        String fs = dff.format(f, new StringBuffer(), fp).toString();
        fs = prependSpaces(4 - fp.getEndIndex(), fs);

        String cs = df.format(c, new StringBuffer(), fp).toString();
        cs = prependSpaces(4 - fp.getEndIndex(), cs);

        System.out.println(fs + "   " + cs);
    }

    protected String prependSpaces(int n, String s) {
        String[] res = {
            "", " ", "  ", "   ", "    ", "     "
        };
        if (n<res.length)
```

*Example 5-8. TempConverter3.java (continued)*

```
            return res[n] + s;
        throw new IllegalStateException("Rebuild with bigger \"res\" array.");
    }
}
```

Remember, though, that the fields line up only if you use a fixed-width font, such as Courier or LucidaSansTypewriter. If you want to line it up in a graphical display, you'll need to use Java's font capability (see Chapter 13) or a JTable (see the Javadoc for javax.swing.JTable or the O'Reilly book *Java Swing*).

# 5.21   Program: Number Palindromes

My wife, Betty, recently reminded me of a theorem that I must have studied in high school but whose name I have long since forgotten: that any positive integer number can be used to generate a palindrome by adding to it the number comprised of its digits in reverse order. Palindromes are sequences that read the same in either direction, such as the name "Anna" or the phrase "Madam, I'm Adam" (ignoring spaces and punctuation). We normally think of palindromes as composed of text, but the concept can be applied to numbers: 13531 is a palindrome. Start with the number 72, for example, and add to it the number 27. The results of this addition is 99, which is a (short) palindrome. Starting with 142, add 241, and you get 383. Some numbers take more than one try to generate a palindrome. 1951 + 1591 yields 3542, which is not palindromic. The second round, however, 3542 + 2453, yields 5995, which is. The number 17,892, which my son Benjamin picked out of the air, requires 12 rounds to generate a palindrome, but it does terminate:

```
C:\javasrc\numbers>java  Palindrome 72 142 1951 17892
Trying 72
72->99
Trying 142
142->383
Trying 1951
Trying 3542
1951->5995
Trying 17892
Trying 47763
Trying 84537
Trying 158085
Trying 738936
Trying 1378773
Trying 5157504
Trying 9215019
Trying 18320148
Trying 102422529
Trying 1027646730
Trying 1404113931
17892->2797227972

C:\javasrc\numbers>
```

If this sounds to you like a natural candidate for recursion, you are correct. *Recursion* involves dividing a problem into simple and identical steps, which can be implemented by a function that calls itself and provides a way of termination. Our basic approach, as shown in method findPalindrome, is:

```
long findPalindrome(long num) {
    if (isPalindrome(num))
        return num;
    return findPalindrome(num + reverseNumber(num));
}
```

That is, if the starting number is already a palindromic number, return it; otherwise, add it to its reverse, and try again. The version of the code shown here handles simple cases directly (single digits are always palindromic, for example). We won't think about negative numbers, as these have a character at the front that loses its meaning if placed at the end, and hence are not strictly palindromic. Further, palindromic forms of certain numbers are too long to fit in Java's 64-bit long integer. These cause underflow, which is trapped. As a result, an error message like "too big" is reported.[*] Having said all that, Example 5-9 shows the code.

*Example 5-9. Palindrome.java*

```
/** Compute the Palindrome of a number by adding the number composed of
 * its digits in reverse order, until a Palindrome occurs.
 * e.g., 42->66 (42+24); 1951->5995 (1951+1591=3542; 3542+2453=5995).
 */
public class Palindrome {
    public static void main(String[] argv) {
        for (int i=0; i<argv.length; i++)
            try {
                long l = Long.parseLong(argv[i]);
                if (l < 0) {
                    System.err.println(argv[i] + " -> TOO SMALL");
                    continue;
                }
                System.out.println(argv[i] + "->" + findPalindrome(l));
            } catch (NumberFormatException e) {
                System.err.println(argv[i] + "-> INVALID");
            } catch (IllegalStateException e) {
                System.err.println(argv[i] + "-> TOO BIG(went negative)");
            }
    }

    /** find a palindromic number given a starting point, by
     * calling ourself until we get a number that is palindromic.
     */
    static long findPalindrome(long num) {
        if (num < 0)
            throw new IllegalStateException("went negative");
```

---

[*] Certain values do not work; for example, Ashish Batia reported that this version gets an exception on the value 8989 (which it does).

*Example 5-9. Palindrome.java (continued)*

```
        if (isPalindrome(num))
            return num;
        System.out.println("Trying " + num);
        return findPalindrome(num + reverseNumber(num));
    }

    /** The number of digits in Long.MAX_VALUE */
    protected static final int MAX_DIGITS = 19;

    // digits array is shared by isPalindrome and reverseNumber,
    // which cannot both be running at the same time.

    /* Statically allocated array to avoid new-ing each time. */
    static long[] digits = new long[MAX_DIGITS];

    /** Check if a number is palindromic. */
    static boolean isPalindrome(long num) {
        if (num >= 0 && num <= 9)
            return true;
        int nDigits = 0;
        while (num > 0) {
            digits[nDigits++] = num % 10;
            num /= 10;
        }
        for (int i=0; i<nDigits/2; i++)
            if (digits[i] != digits[nDigits - i - 1])
                return false;
        return true;
    }

    static long reverseNumber(long num) {
        int nDigits = 0;
        while (num > 0) {
            digits[nDigits++] = num % 10;
            num /= 10;
        }
        long ret = 0;
        for (int i=0; i<nDigits; i++) {
            ret *= 10;
            ret += digits[i];
        }
        return ret;
    }
}
```

## See Also

People using Java in scientific or large-scale numeric computing should check out the Java Grande Forum (*http://www.javagrande.org*), a working group that aims to work with Sun to ensure Java's usability in these realms.

# CHAPTER 6

# Dates and Times

## 6.0  Introduction

From its earliest releases, Java included a class called Date designed for representing and operating upon dates. Its problems were that it was Anglocentric—like much of Java 1.0—and that its dates began with the Unix time epoch: January 1, 1970. The year was an integer whose minimum value 70 represented 1970, so 99 was 1999, 100 was 2000, and so on. This led to the problem that those of us ancient enough to have been born before that venerable year of 1970 in the history of computing—the time when Unix was invented—found ourselves unable to represent our birthdates, and this made us grumpy and irritable.

The Anglocentricity and 1970-centricity were partly vanquished with Java 1.1. A new class, Calendar, was devised, with hooks for representing dates in any date scheme such as the Western (Christian) calendar, the Hebrew calendar, the Islamic calendar, the Chinese calendar, and even Star Trek Star Dates. Unfortunately, there wasn't enough time to implement any of these. In fact, only the GregorianCalendar class appears in Java 1.1, and subsequent Java versions have done little to solve the problem (though 1.2 did repair the Date class to allow it to represent years before 1970.) You may have to go to other sources to get additional calendar classes; one source is listed in Recipe 6.3.

The Calendar class can represent any date, BC or AD, in the Western calendar. A separate Java int variable, with 32 bits of storage, is allocated for each item such as year, month, day, and so on. Years are signed, with negative numbers meaning before the calendar epoch and positive numbers after it. The term *epoch* means the beginning of recorded time. In the Western world, our calendar epoch is the year 1, representing the putative birth year of Jesus Christ. This is such an important event in Western society that the years before it are called Before Christ or BC, and dates since then are called…well, not After Christ, but the Latin *anno domini*, "in the year of our Lord." Because that takes too long to say and write, we use the acronym AD, thus proving that computerists take no blame whatsoever for inventing the use of acronyms. In the modern spirit of political correctness, these terms have been renamed to BCE (Before Common Era) and CE (Common Era), but to most English speakers born before about 1980, they will always be BC and AD. The GregorianCalendar class, intended to represent Western or Christian dates, also uses BC and AD.

Where was I? Oh yes, Java. As ints in Java are 32 bits, that allows $2^{31}$, or 2,147,483,648, years. Let's say roughly two billion years. I, for one, am not going to worry about this new Y2B menace—even if I'm still around, I'm sure they'll have gone to a 64-bit integer by then.

Fortunately, in JDK 1.2, the Date class was changed to use long values, and it can now represent a much wider range of dates. And what about the DateFormat class? Well, it provides a great deal of flexibility in the formatting of dates. Plus, it's bidirectional—it can parse dates too. We'll see it in action in Recipes 6.2 and 6.5.

Note also that some of these classes are in package java.text, while others are in java.util. Package java.text contains classes and interfaces for handling text, dates, numbers, and messages in a manner independent of natural languages, while java.util contains the collections framework and legacy collection classes (see Chapter 7), event model, date and time facilities, internationalization, and miscellaneous utility classes. You'll need imports from both packages in most date-related programs.

# 6.1 Finding Today's Date

## Problem

You want to find today's date.

## Solution

Use a Date object's toString( ) method.

## Discussion

The quick and simple way to get today's date and time is to construct a Date object with no arguments in the constructor call, and call its toString( ) method:

```
// Date0.java
System.out.println(new java.util.Date( ));
```

However, for reasons just outlined, we want to use a Calendar object. Just use Calendar.getInstance( ).getTime( ), which returns a Date object (even though the name makes it seem like it should return a Time value*) and prints the resulting Date object, using its toString( ) method or preferably a DateFormat object. You might be

---

* Just to be clear: Date's getTime( ) returns the time in milliseconds while Calendar's getTime( ) returns a Date.

tempted to construct a GregorianCalendar object, using the no-argument constructor, but if you do this, your program will not give the correct answer when non-Western locales get Calendar subclasses of their own (which might occur in some future release of Java). The static factory method Calendar.getInstance( ) returns a localized Calendar subclass for the locale you are in. In North America and Europe it will likely return a GregorianCalendar, but in other parts of the world it might (someday) return a different kind of Calendar.

Do *not* try to use a GregorianCalendar's toString( ) method; the results are truly impressive, but not very interesting. Sun's implementation prints all its internal state information; Kaffe's inherits Object's toString( ), which just prints the class name and the hashcode. Neither is useful for our purposes.

```
C> java Date1
java.util.
GregorianCalendar[time=932363506950,areFieldsSet=true,areAllFieldsSet=true,lenient=tr
ue,zone=java.util.SimpleTimeZone[id=America/Los_Angeles,offset=-
28800000,dstSavings=3600000,useDaylight=true,startYear=0,startMode=3,startMonth=3,sta
rtDay=1,startDayOfWeek=1,startTime=7200000,endMode=2,endMonth=9,endDay=-
1,endDayOfWeek=1,endTime=7200000],firstDayOfWeek=1,minimalDaysInFirstWeek=1,ERA=1,YEA
R=1999,MONTH=6,WEEK_OF_YEAR=30,WEEK_OF_MONTH=4,DAY_OF_MONTH=18,DAY_OF_YEAR=199,DAY_
OF_WEEK=1,DAY_OF_WEEK_IN_MONTH=3,AM_PM=1,HOUR=10,HOUR_OF_
DAY=22,MINUTE=51,SECOND=46,MILLISECOND=950,ZONE_OFFSET=-28800000,DST_OFFSET=3600000]
```

Calendar's getTime( ) returns a Date object, which can be passed to println( ) to print today's date (and time) in the traditional (but non-localized) format:

```
// Date2.java
System.out.println(Calendar.getInstance( ).getTime( ));
```

To print the date in any other format, use java.text.DateFormat, which you'll meet in Recipe 6.2.

# 6.2   Printing Date/Time in a Given Format

## Problem

You want to print the date and/or time in a locale-sensitive or otherwise-specified format.

## Solution

Use java.text.DateFormat.

## Discussion

To print the date in the correct format for whatever locale your software lands in, simply use the default DateFormat formatter, which is obtained by calling DateFormat.getInstance( ):

---

```
import java.util.*;
import java.text.*;

public class DateFormatBest {
        public static void main(String[] args) {
                Date today = new Date( );

                DateFormat df = DateFormat.getInstance( );
                System.out.println(df.format(today));

                DateFormat df_fr =
                        DateFormat.getDateInstance(DateFormat.FULL, Locale.FRENCH);
                System.out.println(df_fr.format(today));
        }
}
```

When I run this, it prints:

```
3/3/04 12:17 PM
mercredi 3 mars 2004
```

You can ask for a default date and time formatter (df in the example), or a TimeFormatter or DateFormatter that extracts just the time or date portion of the Date object (df_fr in the example). You can also request a nondefault Locale (df_fr in the example). Five codes—FULL, LONG, MEDIUM, SHORT and DEFAULT—can be passed to describe how verbose a format you want.

Suppose you want the date printed, but instead of the default format, you want it printed like "Sun 2004.07.18 at 04:14:09 PM PDT". A look at the Javadoc page for SimpleDateFormat—the only nonabstract subclass of DateFormat—reveals that it has a rich language for specifying date and time formatting. Be aware that in so doing you are presuming to know the correct format in all locales; see Chapter 15 for why this may be a bad idea.

To use a default format, of course, we can just use the Date object's toString( ) method, and for a localized default format, we use DateFormat.getInstance( ). But to have full control and get the "Sun 2004.07.18 at 04:14:09 PM PDT", we construct an instance explicitly, like so:

```
new SimpleDateFormat ("E yyyy.MM.dd 'at' hh:mm:ss a zzz");
```

E means the day of the week; yyyy, MM, and dd are obviously year, month, and day. The quoted string 'at' means the string "at". hh:mm:ss is the time; a means A.M. or P.M., and zzz means the time zone. Some of these are more memorable than others; I find the zzz tends to put me to sleep. Here's the code:

```
// DateDemo.java
Date dNow = new Date( );

/* Simple, Java 1.0 date printing */
System.out.println("It is now " + dNow.toString( ));
```

```
// Use a SimpleDateFormat to print the date our way.
SimpleDateFormat formatter
    = new SimpleDateFormat ("E yyyy.MM.dd 'at' hh:mm:ss a zzz");
System.out.println("It is " + formatter.format(dNow));
```

There are many format symbols; a list is shown in Table 6-1.

*Table 6-1. SimpleDateFormat format codes*

| Symbol | Meaning | Presentation | Example |
|--------|---------|--------------|---------|
| G | Era designator | Text | AD |
| y | Year | Number | 2001 |
| M | Month in year | Text and Number | July or 07 |
| d | Day in month | Number | 10 |
| h | Hour in A.M./P.M. (1~12) | Number | 12 |
| H | Hour in day (0~23) | Number | 0 |
| m | Minute in hour | Number | 30 |
| s | Second in minute | Number | 43 |
| S | Millisecond | Number | 234 |
| E | Day in week | Text | Tuesday |
| D | Day in year | Number | 360 |
| F | Day of week in month | Number | 2 (second Wed. in July) |
| w | Week in year | Number | 40 |
| W | Week in month | Number | 1 |
| a | A.M./P.M. marker | Text | PM |
| k | Hour in day (1~24) | Number | 24 |
| K | Hour in A.M./P.M. (0~11) | Number | 0 |
| z | Time zone | Text | Eastern Standard Time |
| ' | Escape for text | Delimiter | |
| " | Single quote | Literal | ' |

You can use as many of the given symbols as needed. Where a format can be used either in text or numeric context, you can set it to a longer form by repetitions of the character. For codes marked Text, four or more pattern letters cause the formatter to use the long form; fewer cause it to use the short or abbreviated form if one exists. Thus, E might yield Mon, whereas EEEE would yield Monday. For those marked Number, the number of repetitions of the symbol gives the minimum number of digits. Shorter numbers are zero-padded to the given number of digits. The year is handled specially: yy yields an ambiguous* two-digit year (98, 99, 00, 01...), whereas

---

* Remember Y2K? Use a four-digit year!

yyyy yields a valid year (2001). For those marked Text and Number, three or more symbols causes the formatter to use text, while one or two make it use a number: MM might yield 01, while MMM would yield January.

# 6.3   Representing Dates in Other Epochs

## Problem

You need to deal with dates in a form other than the Gregorian Calendar used in the Western world.

## Solution

Download the IBM calendar classes.

## Discussion

The only nonabstract Calendar subclass is the GregorianCalendar, as mentioned previously. However, other calendar classes do exist. IBM has a set of calendars— Hebrew, Islamic, Buddhist, Japanese, and even an Astronomical Calendar class—that covers most of the rest of the world. This work has been open sourced and is now part of a project called International Components for Unicode for Java, which can be found at *http://oss.software.ibm.com/icu4j/*.

The calendar classes in ICU4J work in a similar fashion to the standard GregorianCalendar class, but they have constants for month names and other information relevant to each particular calendar. They are not subclassed from java.util. Calendar, however, so they must be referred to by their full class name:

```
import java.util.Locale;
import com.ibm.icu.util.Calendar;
import java.text.DateFormat;
import com.ibm.icu.util.IslamicCalendar;

public class IBMCalDemo {
        public static void main(String[] args) {
                Locale ar_loc = new Locale("ar");
                Calendar c = new com.ibm.icu.util.IslamicCalendar( );
                DateFormat d = DateFormat.getDateInstance(DateFormat.LONG, ar_loc);
                System.out.println(d.format(c.getTime( )));
        }
}
```

I can't include the textual output because of font limitations. The icu4j package includes a multicalendar demo application whose output is shown in Figure 6-1.

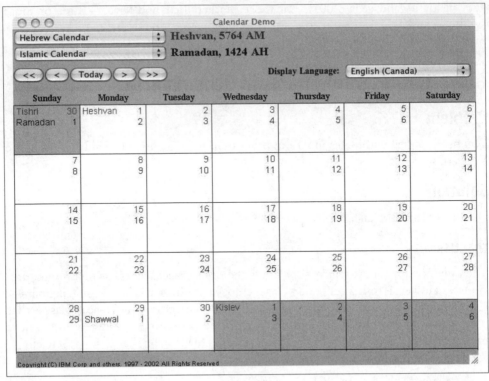

*Figure 6-1. IBMCalDemo in action*

# 6.4 Converting YMDHMS to a Calendar or Epoch Seconds

## Problem

You have year, month, day, hour, minute, and maybe even seconds, and you need to convert it to a Calendar or a Date.

## Solution

Use the Calendar class's set(y,m,d,h,m[,s]) method, which allows you to set the date/time fields to whatever you wish. Note that when using this form and providing your own numbers, or when constructing either a Date or a GregorianCalendar object, the month value is zero-based while all the other values are true-origin. Presumably, this is to allow you to print the month name from an array without having to remember to subtract one, but it is still confusing.

```
// GregCalDemo.java
GregorianCalendar d1 = new GregorianCalendar(1986, 04, 05); // May 5
GregorianCalendar d2 = new GregorianCalendar();    // today
Calendar d3 = Calendar.getInstance();    // today
```

```
System.out.println("It was then " + d1.getTime( ));
System.out.println("It is now " + d2.getTime( ));
System.out.println("It is now " + d3.getTime( ));
d3.set(Calendar.YEAR, 1915);
d3.set(Calendar.MONTH, Calendar.APRIL);
d3.set(Calendar.DAY_OF_MONTH, 12);
System.out.println("D3 set to " + d3.getTime( ));
```

This prints the dates as shown:

```
It was then Mon May 05 00:00:00 EDT 1986
It is now Thu Mar 25 16:36:07 EST 2004
It is now Thu Mar 25 16:36:07 EST 2004
D3 set to Mon Apr 12 16:36:07 EST 1915
```

# 6.5    Parsing Strings into Dates

## Problem

You need to convert user input into Date or Calendar objects.

## Solution

Use a DateFormat.

## Discussion

The DateFormat class introduced in Recipe 6.2 has some additional methods, notably parse( ), which tries to parse a string according to the format stored in the given DateFormat object:

```
// DateParse1.java
SimpleDateFormat formatter
    = new SimpleDateFormat ("yyyy-MM-dd");
String input = args.length == 0 ? "1818-11-11" : args[0];
System.out.print(input + " parses as ");
Date t;
try {
    t = formatter.parse(input);
    System.out.println(t);
} catch (ParseException e) {
    System.out.println("unparseable using " + formatter);
}
```

This program parses any date back to Year Zero and well beyond Year 2000.

What if the date is embedded in an input string? You could, of course, use the string's substring( ) method to extract it, but there is an easier way. The ParsePosition object from java.text is designed to represent (and track) the position of an imaginary cursor in a string. Suppose we have genealogical data with input strings representing the times of a person's life:

```
BD: 1913-10-01 Vancouver, B.C.
DD: 1983-06-06 Toronto, ON
```

This lists one person's birth date (BD) and place, and death date (DD) and place. We can parse these using `String.indexOf(' ')` to find the space after the : character, `DateFormat parse()` to parse the date, and `String.substring()` to get the city and other geographic information. Here's how:

```
// DateParse2.java
SimpleDateFormat formatter =
    new SimpleDateFormat ("yyyy-MM-dd");
String input[] = {
    "BD: 1913-10-01 Vancouver, B.C.",
    "MD: 1948-03-01 Ottawa, ON",
    "DD: 1983-06-06 Toronto, ON" };
for (int i=0; i<input.length; i++) {
    String aLine = input[i];
    String action;
    switch(aLine.charAt(0)) {
        case 'B': action = "Born"; break;
        case 'M': action = "Married"; break;
        case 'D': action = "Died"; break;
        // others...
        default: System.err.println("Invalid code in " + aLine);
        continue;
    }
    int p = aLine.indexOf(' ');
    ParsePosition pp = new ParsePosition(p);
    Date d = formatter.parse(aLine, pp);
    if (d == null) {
        System.err.println("Invalid date in " + aLine);
        continue;
    }
    String location = aLine.substring(pp.getIndex());
    System.out.println(
        action + " on " + d + " in " + location);
}
```

This works like I said it would:

```
Born on Wed Oct 01 00:00:00 PDT 1913 in  Vancouver, B.C.
Married on Mon Mar 01 00:00:00 PST 1948 in  Ottawa, ON
Died on Mon Jun 06 00:00:00 PDT 1983 in  Toronto, ON
```

Note that the polymorphic form of `parse()` that takes one argument throws a `ParseException` if the input cannot be parsed, while the form that takes a `ParsePosition` as its second argument returns `null` to indicate failure.

# 6.6   Converting Epoch Seconds to DMYHMS

## Problem

You need to convert a number of seconds since 1970 into a Date.

## Solution

Just use the Date constructor.

## Discussion

"The Epoch" is the beginning of time as far as modern operating systems go. Unix time, and some versions of Windows time, count off inexorably the seconds since the epoch. On systems that store this in a 32-bit integer, time is indeed running out. Let's say we wanted to find out when the Unix operating system, whose 32-bit versions use a 32-bit date, will get into difficulty. We take a 32-bit integer of all ones, and construct a Date around it. The Date constructor needs the number of milliseconds since 1970, so we multiply by 1,000:

```
/** When does the UNIX date get into trouble? */

public class Y2038 {
    public static void main(String[] a) {

        // This should yield 2038AD, the hour of doom for the
        // last remaining 32-bit UNIX systems (there will be
        // millions of 64-bit UNIXes by then).

        long expiry = 0x7FFFFFFFL;

        System.out.println("32-bit UNIX expires on " +
            Long.toHexString(expiry) + " or " +
            new java.util.Date(expiry  * 1000));
    }
}
```

Sure enough, the program reports that 32-bit Unixes will expire in the year 2038 (you might think I knew that in advance if you were to judge by the name I gave the class; in fact, my web site has carried the Y2038 warning to Unix users for several years now). At least Unix system managers have more warning than most of the general public had for the original Y2K problem.

```
> java Y2038
32-bit UNIX expires on 7fffffff or Mon Jan 18 22:14:07 EST 2038
>
```

At any rate, if you need to convert seconds since 1970 to a date, you know how.

# 6.7   Adding to or Subtracting from a Date or Calendar

## Problem

You need to add or subtract a fixed amount to or from a date.

## Solution

As we've seen, Date has a getTime( ) method that returns the number of seconds since the epoch as a long. To add or subtract, you just do arithmetic on this value. Here's a code example:

```
// DateAdd.java
/** Today's date */
Date now = new Date( );

long t = now.getTime( );

t -= 700L*24*60*60*1000;

Date then = new Date(t);

System.out.println("Seven hundred days ago was " + then);
```

## Discussion

A cleaner variant is to use the Calendar's add( ) method. There is no corresponding subtraction method; you just add a negative value to make time run backward:

```
import java.text.*;
import java.util.*;

/** DateCalAdd -- compute the difference between two dates.
 */
public class DateCalAdd {
    public static void main(String[] av) {
        /** Today's date */
        Calendar now = Calendar.getInstance( );

        /* Do "DateFormat" using "simple" format. */
        SimpleDateFormat formatter
            = new SimpleDateFormat ("E yyyy/MM/dd 'at' hh:mm:ss a zzz");
        System.out.println("It is now " +
            formatter.format(now.getTime( )));

        now.add(Calendar.YEAR, - 2);
        System.out.println("Two years ago was " +
            formatter.format(now.getTime( )));
    }
}
```

Running this reports the current date and time, and the date and time two years ago:

```
> java DateCalAdd
It is now Tue 2003/11/25 at 09:14:26 AM EST
Two years ago was Sun 2001/11/25 at 09:14:26 AM EST
```

A method called roll( ) does not change "larger" fields. For example, rolling the month up from January 31, 2051 results in February 28, 2051.

---

# 6.8    Difference Between Two Dates

## Problem

You need to compute the difference between two dates.

## Solution

Convert to Date objects if necessary, call their getTime( ) methods, and subtract. Format the result yourself.

## Discussion

The API has no general mechanism for computing the difference between two dates. This is surprising, given how often it comes up in some types of commercial data processing. However, it's fairly simple to implement this yourself:

```
import java.util.*;

/** DateDiff -- compute the difference between two dates. */
public class DateDiff {
        public static void main(String[] av) {
                /** The date at the end of the last century */
                Date d1 = new GregorianCalendar(2000,11,31,23,59).getTime( );

                /** Today's date */
                Date today = new Date( );

                // Get msec from each, and subtract.
                long diff = today.getTime() - d1.getTime( );

                System.out.println("The 21st century (up to " + today +
                        ") is " + (diff / (1000*60*60*24)) + " days old.");
        }
}
```

I'm editing this recipe in November of 2003; the 20th Century AD ended at the end of 2000, so the value should be about $3\ ^{11}/_{12}$ years, and it is:

```
> java DateDiff
The 21st century (up to Tue Nov 25 09:20:15 EST 2003) is 1058 days old.
>
```

You saw Calendar's add( ) method in Recipe 6.7, but that only adds to the day, month, or year (or any other field) in the Calendar object; it does not add two Calendar dates together.

# 6.9    Comparing Dates

## Problem

You need to compare two dates.

## Solution

If the dates are in Date objects, compare with equals( ) and one of before( ) or after( ).
If the dates are in longs, compare with == and either < or >.

## Discussion

While Date implements equals( ) like any good class, it also provides before(Date)
and after(Date), which compare one date with another to see which happened first.
This can be used to determine the relationship among any two dates, as in
Example 6-1.

*Example 6-1. CompareDates.java*

```java
import java.util.*;
import java.text.*;

public class CompareDates {
    public static void main(String[] args) throws ParseException {

        DateFormat df = new SimpleDateFormat ("yyyy-MM-dd");

        // Get Date 1
        Date d1 = df.parse(args[0]);

        // Get Date 2
        Date d2 = df.parse(args[1]);

        String relation;
        if (d1.equals(d2))
            relation = "the same date as";
        else if (d1.before(d2))
            relation = "before";
        else
            relation = "after";
        System.out.println(d1 + " is " + relation + ' ' + d2);
    }
}
```

Running CompareDates with two close-together dates and the same date reveals that it
seems to work:

```
> java CompareDates 2000-01-01 1999-12-31
Sat Jan 01 00:00:00 EST 2000 is after Fri Dec 31 00:00:00 EST 1999
> java CompareDates 2000-01-01 2000-01-01
Sat Jan 01 00:00:00 EST 2000 is the same date as Sat Jan 01 00:00:00 EST 2000
```

It would be interesting to see if DateFormat.parse( ) really does field rolling, as the
documentation says. Apparently so!

```
> javaCompareDates 2001-02-29 2001-03-01
Thu Mar 01 00:00:00 EST 2001 is the same date as Thu Mar 01 00:00:00 EST 2001
>
```

Sometimes the API gives you a date as a `long`. For example, the `File` class has methods (detailed in Recipe 11.1) to give information such as when the last time a file on disk was modified. Example 6-2 shows a program similar to Example 6-1, but using the `long` value returned by the File's `lastModified()` method.

*Example 6-2. CompareFileDates.java*

```java
import java.util.*;
import java.io.File;

public class CompareFileDates {
    public static void main(String[] args) {
        // Get the timestamp from file 1
        String f1 = args[0];
        long d1 = new File(f1).lastModified();

        // Get the timestamp from file 2
        String f2 = args[1];
        long d2 = new File(f2).lastModified();

        String relation;
        if (d1 == d2)
            relation = "the same age as";
        else if (d1 < d2)
            relation = "older than";
        else
            relation = "newer than";
        System.out.println(f1 + " is " + relation + ' ' + f2);
    }
}
```

Running `CompareFileDates` on its source and class reveals that the class file is newer (that is, more up-to-date). Comparing a directory with itself gives the result of "the same age," as you'd expect:

```
> java CompareFileDates CompareFileDates.java CompareFileDates.class
CompareFileDates.java is older thanCompareFileDates.class
> java CompareFileDates . .
. is the same age as .
```

# 6.10  Day of Week/Month/Year or Week Number

## Problem

You have a date and need to find what day of the week, month, or year that date falls on.

## Solution

Use the `Calendar` class's `get()` method, which has constants for retrieving most such values.

## Discussion

The Calendar class can return most of these:

```java
// CalendarDemo.java
Calendar c = Calendar.getInstance();    // today
System.out.println("Year: " + c.get(Calendar.YEAR));
System.out.println("Month: " + c.get(Calendar.MONTH));
System.out.println("Day: " + c.get(Calendar.DAY_OF_MONTH));
System.out.println("Day of week = " + c.get(Calendar.DAY_OF_WEEK));
System.out.println("Day of year = " + c.get(Calendar.DAY_OF_YEAR));
System.out.println("Week in Year: " + c.get(Calendar.WEEK_OF_YEAR));
System.out.println("Week in Month: " + c.get(Calendar.WEEK_OF_MONTH));
System.out.println("Day of Week in Month: " +
          c.get(Calendar.DAY_OF_WEEK_IN_MONTH));
System.out.println("Hour: " + c.get(Calendar.HOUR));
System.out.println("AM or PM: " + c.get(Calendar.AM_PM));
System.out.println("Hour (24-hour clock): " +
          c.get(Calendar.HOUR_OF_DAY));
System.out.println("Minute: " + c.get(Calendar.MINUTE));
System.out.println("Second: " + c.get(Calendar.SECOND));
```

This chatty program shows most of the fields in the Calendar class. Note that months start at zero (for indexing an array of Strings), while the other values start at 1:

```
Year: 2005
Month: 6
Day: 19
Day of week = 2
Day of year = 200
Week in Year: 30
Week in Month: 4
Day of Week in Month: 3
Hour: 3
AM or PM: 1
Hour (24-hour clock): 15
Minute: 18
Second: 42
```

# 6.11  Creating a Calendar Page

## Problem

You want a calendar for a given month of a given year, or of the current month and year.

## Solution

Use Calendar.get( ) to find what day of the week the first of the month falls on and format accordingly.

## Discussion

Like the output of the Unix *cal* command, it is often convenient to view a month in compact form. The basic idea is to find what day of the week the first of the month is and print blank columns for the days of the week before the month begins. Then, print the numbers from 1 to the end of the month, starting a new row after you get to the last day of each week.

Here's my program, compared to the Unix *cal* command:

```
daroad.darwinsys.com$ java CalendarPage 6 2000
June 2000
Su Mo Tu We Th Fr Sa
             1  2  3
 4  5  6  7  8  9 10
11 12 13 14 15 16 17
18 19 20 21 22 23 24
25 26 27 28 29 30
daroad.darwinsys.com$ cal 6 2000
     June 2000
Su Mo Tu We Th Fr Sa
             1  2  3
 4  5  6  7  8  9 10
11 12 13 14 15 16 17
18 19 20 21 22 23 24
25 26 27 28 29 30
```

The source code is simple and straightforward (Example 6-3).

*Example 6-3. CalendarPage.java*

```java
import java.util.*;
import java.text.*;

/** Print a month page.
 * Only works for the Western calendar.
 */
public class CalendarPage {

    /** The names of the months */
    String[] months = {
        "January", "February", "March", "April",
        "May", "June", "July", "August",
        "September", "October", "November", "December"
    };

    /** The days in each month. */
    public final static int[] dom = {
            31, 28, 31, 30,    /* jan feb mar apr */
            31, 30, 31, 31, /* may jun jul aug */
            30, 31, 30, 31    /* sep oct nov dec */
    };
```

*Example 6-3. CalendarPage.java (continued)*

```java
/** Compute which days to put where, in the Cal panel */
public void print(int mm, int yy) {
    /** The number of days to leave blank at the start of this month */
    int leadGap = 0;

    System.out.print(months[mm]);        // print month and year
    System.out.print(" ");
    System.out.print(yy);
    System.out.println();

    if (mm < 0 || mm > 11)
        throw new IllegalArgumentException("Month " + mm + " bad, must be 0-11");
    GregorianCalendar calendar = new GregorianCalendar(yy, mm, 1);

    System.out.println("Su Mo Tu We Th Fr Sa");

    // Compute how much to leave before the first.
    // get(DAY_OF_WEEK) returns 0 for Sunday, which is just right.
    leadGap = calendar.get(Calendar.DAY_OF_WEEK)-1;

    int daysInMonth = dom[mm];
    if (calendar.isLeapYear(calendar.get(Calendar.YEAR)) && mm == 1)
        ++daysInMonth;

    // Blank out the labels before 1st day of month
    for (int i = 0; i < leadGap; i++) {
        System.out.print("   ");
    }

    // Fill in numbers for the day of month.
    for (int i = 1; i <= daysInMonth; i++) {

        // This "if" statement is simpler than fiddling with NumberFormat
        if (i<=9)
            System.out.print(' ');
        System.out.print(i);

        if ((leadGap + i) % 7 == 0)        // wrap if end of line.
            System.out.println();
        else
            System.out.print(' ');
    }
    System.out.println();
}

/** For testing, a main program */
public static void main(String[] av) {
    int month, year;

    CalendarPage cp = new CalendarPage();
```

*Example 6-3. CalendarPage.java (continued)*

```
        // print the current month.
        if (av.length == 2) {
            cp.print(Integer.parseInt(av[0])-1, Integer.parseInt(av[1]));
        } else {
            Calendar c = Calendar.getInstance();
            cp.print(c.get(Calendar.MONTH), c.get(Calendar.YEAR));
        }
    }
}
```

# 6.12   Measuring Elapsed Time

## Problem

You need to time how long it takes to do something.

## Solution

Call System.currentTimeMillis( ) twice, or System.nanoTime( ), and subtract the first result from the second result.

## Discussion

Needing a timer is such a common thing that, instead of making you depend on some external library, the developers of Java have built it in. The System class contains two static methods for times. currentTimeMillis( ) returns the current time (since 1970) in milliseconds, and nanoTime( ) (new in 1.5) returns the relative time in nanoseconds. To time some event, use this:

```
long start = System.currentTimeMillis( );
method_to_be_timed( );
long end - System.currentTimeMillis( ); l
ong elapsed = end - start;     // time in milliseconds
```

or:

```
long start = System.nanoTime( );
method_to_be_timed( );
long end = System.nanoTime( ); l
ong elapsed = end - start;     // time in nanoseconds
```

Be aware that the millisecond timer works on almost all platforms. The nanosecond timer is always available, but some operating systems and/or hardware combinations may not really provide nanosecond resolution; beware of reading too much into small differences in the values it returns, unless you know that your system is providing, and the JVM is using, a good high-resolution timer.

Here is a short example to measure how long it takes a user to press return. We divide the time in milliseconds by 1,000 to get seconds and print it nicely using a NumberFormat:

```
// Timer0.java
long t0, t1;
System.out.println("Press return when ready");
t0=System.currentTimeMillis();
int b;
do {
    b = System.in.read();
} while (b!='\r' && b != '\n');

t1=System.currentTimeMillis();
double deltaT = t1-t0;
System.out.println("You took " +
    DecimalFormat.getInstance().format(deltaT/1000.) + " seconds.");
```

This longer example uses the same technique but computes a large number of square roots and writes each one to a discard file. It uses the getDevNull() method from Recipe 2.4 to measure how long the computation takes:

```
import java.io.*;
import java.text.*;

/**
 * Timer for processing sqrt and I/O operations.
 */
public class TimeComputation {
    public static void main(String argv[]) {
        try {
            new Timer().run();
        } catch (IOException e) {
            System.err.println(e);
        }
    }
    public void run() throws IOException {

        DataOutputStream n = new DataOutputStream(
            new BufferedOutputStream(new FileOutputStream(SysDep.getDevNull())));
        long t0, t1;
        System.out.println("Java Starts at " + (t0=System.currentTimeMillis()));
        double k;
        for (int i=0; i<100000; i++) {
            k = 2.1 * Math.sqrt((double)i);
            n.writeDouble(k);
        }
        System.out.println("Java Ends at " + (t1=System.currentTimeMillis()));
        double deltaT = t1-t0;
        System.out.println("This run took " +
            DecimalFormat.getInstance().format(deltaT/1000.) + " seconds.");
    }
}
```

This code shows a simpler, but less portable, technique for formatting a "delta t", or time difference. It works only for the English locale (or any other where the number one-and-a-half is written "1.5"), but it's simple enough to write the code inline. I show it here as a method for completeness, and I confess to having used it this way on occasion:

```
/** QuickTimeFormat.java - Convert a long ("time_t") to seconds and thousandths. */
public static String msToSecs(long t) {
    return Double.toString(t/1000D);
}
```

## 6.13   Sleeping for a While

### Problem

You need to sleep for a while.

### Solution

Use Thread.sleep( ).

### Discussion

You can sleep for any period of time from one millisecond up to the lifetime of your computer. As I write this, for example, I have a chicken on the barbecue. My wife has instructed me to check it every five minutes. Since I'm busy writing, time tends to fly. So, I needed a reminder service and came up with this in a jiffy:

```
// Reminder.java
while (true) {
    System.out.println(new Date( ) + "\007");
    Thread.sleep(5*60*1000);
}
```

The 007 is not a throwback to the Cold War espionage thriller genre, but the ASCII character for a bell code, or beep. It's probably preferable to use \b for this, but then I couldn't make that 007 joke. Had I written the program as a windowed application using a frame, I could have called Toolkit.beep( ) instead, and, by toggling the state of setVisible( ), a pop up would appear every five minutes.

With a bit more work, you could have a series of events and wait until their due times, making a sort of minischeduler entirely in Java. In fact, we'll do that in Recipe 6.14.

## 6.14   Program: Reminder Service

The ReminderService program provides a simple reminder service. The load( ) method reads a plain text file containing a list of appointments like the ones shown here, using a SimpleDateFormat:

```
2004 03  06  22  00 Get some sleep!
2004 11  26  01  27 Finish this program
2004 11  25  01  29 Document this program
```

The program is based around java.util.Timer, which runs a threaded timer (threads
are discussed in Chapter 24) and starts each TimerTask at the scheduled time. In my
version, the TimerTask simply prints the message and displays it in a Swing pop up.
Example 6-4 shows the full program.

*Example 6-4. ReminderService.java*

```java
import java.io.*;
import java.text.*;
import java.util.*;
import javax.swing.JOptionPane;

/** Read a file of reminders, run each when due using java.util.Timer. */

public class ReminderService {

    /** The Timer object */
    Timer timer = new Timer( );

    class Item extends TimerTask {
        String message;
        Item(String m) {
            message = m;
        }
        public void run( ) {
            message(message);
        }
    }

    public static void main(String[] argv) throws IOException {
        new ReminderService().load( );
    }

    protected void load( ) throws IOException {

        BufferedReader is = new BufferedReader(
            new FileReader("ReminderService.txt"));
        SimpleDateFormat formatter =
            new SimpleDateFormat ("yyyy MM dd hh mm");
        String aLine;
        while ((aLine = is.readLine( )) != null) {
            ParsePosition pp = new ParsePosition(0);
            Date date = formatter.parse(aLine, pp);
            if (date == null) {
                message("Invalid date in " + aLine);
                continue;
            }
            String mesg = aLine.substring(pp.getIndex( ));
            timer.schedule(new Item(mesg), date);
```

*Example 6-4. ReminderService.java (continued)*

```
        }
        is.close( );
    }

    /** Display a message on the console and in the GUI.
     * Used both by Item tasks and by mainline parser.
     */
    void message(String message) {
        System.out.println("\007" + message);
        JOptionPane.showMessageDialog(null,
            message,
            "Timer Alert",                  // titlebar
            JOptionPane.INFORMATION_MESSAGE);   // icon
    }
}
```

I create a nested class Item to store one notification, scheduling it at its due date and time whilst constructing an Item object to display the message when it's due. The load( ) method reads the file containing the data and converts it, using the date parsing from Recipe 6.5. When invoked, the run( ) method in each Item object displays the reminder, as shown in Figure 6-2, both on the standard output (for debugging) and in a dialog window using the Swing JOptionPane class (see Recipe 14.7). The message( ) method consolidates both displays, allowing you to add a control to use only standard output or only the dialog (this is left as an exercise for the reader).

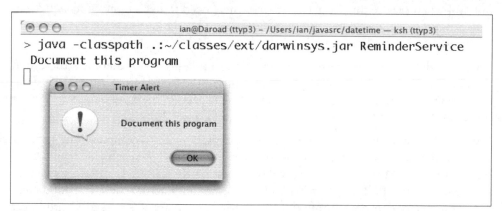

*Figure 6-2. ReminderService in action*

## See Also

You could implement the functionality of this reminder program without using the Timer class; see ReminderServiceOld in the online source.

# CHAPTER 7

# Structuring Data with Java

## 7.0    Introduction

Almost every application beyond "Hello World" needs to keep track of a certain amount of data. A simple numeric problem might work with three or four numbers only, but most applications have groups of similar data items. A GUI-based application may need to keep track of a number of dialog windows. A personal information manager or PIM needs to keep track of a number of, well, persons. An operating system needs to keep track of who is allowed to log in, who is currently logged in, and what those users are doing. A library needs to keep track of who has books checked out and when they're due. A network server may need to keep track of its active clients. A pattern emerges here, and it revolves around variations of what has traditionally been called *data structuring*.

There are data structures in the memory of a running program; there is structure in the data in a file on disk, and there is structure in the information stored in a database. In this chapter, we concentrate on the first aspect: in-memory data. We'll cover the second aspect in Chapter 10 and the third in Chapter 20.

If you had to think about in-memory data, you might want to compare it to a collection of index cards in a filing box, or to a treasure hunt where each clue leads to the next. Or you might think of it like my desk—apparently scattered, but actually a very powerful collection filled with meaningful information. Each of these is a good analogy for a type of data structuring that Java provides. An array is a fixed-length linear collection of data items, like the card filing box: it can only hold so much, then it overflows. The treasure hunt is like a data structure called a *linked list*. Until JDK 1.2, Java had no standard linked list class, but you could (and still can) write your own "traditional data structure" classes. The complex collection represents Java's Collection classes. A document entitled *Collections Framework Overview,* distributed with the Java Development Kit documentation (and stored as file *jdk1.x/docs/guide/collections/overview.html*), provides a detailed discussion of the Collections Framework. The framework aspects of Java collections are summarized in Recipe 7.16.

Beware of some typographic issues. The word Arrays (in constant width font) is short for the class java.util.Arrays, but in the normal typeface, the word "arrays" is simply the plural of "array" (and will be found capitalized at the beginning of a sentence). Also, note that HashMap and HashSet, added in JDK 1.2, follow the rule of having a "midcapital" at each word boundary, while the older Hashtable does not (the "t" is not capitalized).

Several classes in java.util are not covered in this chapter. All the classes whose names begin with Abstract are, in fact, abstract, and we discuss their nonabstract subclasses. BitSet is used less frequently than some of the classes discussed here and is simple enough to learn on your own; I have examples of it in Recipes 2.6 and 5.10. The StringTokenizer class is covered in Recipe 3.2.

We start our discussion of data structuring techniques with one of the oldest structures, the array. Then we'll go through a variety of fancier structuring techniques using classes from java.util. At the end, we discuss the overall structure of the java.util's Collections Framework.

# 7.1 Using Arrays for Data Structuring

## Problem

You need to keep track of a fixed amount of information and retrieve it (usually) sequentially.

## Solution

Use an array.

## Discussion

Arrays can be used to hold any linear collection of data. The items in an array must all be of the same type. You can make an array of any built-in type or any object type. For arrays of built-ins, such as ints, booleans, etc., the data is stored in the array. For arrays of objects, a reference is stored in the array, so the normal rules of reference variables and casting apply. Note in particular that if the array is declared as Object[], object references of any type can be stored in it without casting, although a valid cast is required to take an Object reference out and use it as its original type. I'll say a bit more on two-dimensional arrays in Recipe 7.15; otherwise, you should treat this as a review example:

```
import java.util.Calendar;

/** Review examples of arrays: shows array allocation, processing,
 * storing objects in Arrays, two-dimensional arrays, and lengths.
 *
 * @author Ian Darwin
 * @version $Id: ch07,v 1.5 2004/05/04 20:11:49 ian Exp $
 */
```

```java
public class Array1 {
    public static void main(String[] argv) {
        int[] monthLen1;              // declare a reference
        monthLen1 = new int[12];         // construct it
        int[] monthLen2 = new int[12];     // short form
        // even shorter is this initializer form:
        int[] monthLen3 = {
                31, 28, 31, 30,
                31, 30, 31, 31,
                30, 31, 30, 31,
        };

        final int MAX = 10;
        Calendar[] days = new Calendar[MAX];
        for (int i=0; i<MAX; i++) {
            // Note that this actually stores GregorianCalendar
            // etc. instances into a Calendar Array
            days[i] = Calendar.getInstance();
        }

        // Two-Dimensional Arrays
        // Want a 10-by-24 array
        int[][] me = new int[10][];
        for (int i=0; i<10; i++)
            me[i] = new int[24];

        // Remember that an array has a ".length" attribute
        System.out.println(me.length);
        System.out.println(me[0].length);

    }
}
```

Arrays in Java work nicely. The type checking provides reasonable integrity, and array bounds are always checked by the runtime system, further contributing to reliability.

The only problem with arrays is: what if the array fills up and you still have data coming in? See the Solution in Recipe 7.2.

# 7.2   Resizing an Array

## Problem

The array filled up, and you got an ArrayIndexOutOfBoundsException.

## Solution

Make the array bigger.

---

## Discussion

One approach is to allocate the array at a reasonable size to begin with, but if you find yourself with more data than will fit, reallocate a new, bigger array and copy the elements into it.* Here is code that does so:

```
import java.util.Calendar;
/** Re-allocate an array, bigger... */
public class Array2 {
    public static void main(String argv[]) {
        int nDates = 0;
        final int MAX = 10;
        Calendar[] dates = new Calendar[MAX];
        Calendar c;
        while ((c=getDate()) != null) {

            // if (nDates >= dates.length) {
            //     System.err.println("Too Many Dates! Simplify your life!!");
            //     System.exit(1);  // wimp out
            // }

            // better: reallocate, making data structure dynamic
            if (nDates >= dates.length) {
                Calendar[] tmp - new Calendar[dates.length + 10];
                System.arraycopy(dates, 0, tmp, 0, dates.length);
                dates - tmp;     // copies the array reference
                // old array will be garbage collected soon...
            }
            dates[nDates++] = c;
        }
        System.out.println("Array size = " + dates.length);
    }

    static int n;
    /* Dummy method to return a sequence of 21 Calendar references,
     * so the array should be sized >= 21.
     */
    public static Calendar getDate() {
        if (n++ > 21)
            return null;
        return Calendar.getInstance();
    }
}
```

This technique works reasonably well for simple linear collections of data. For data with a more variable structure, you probably want to use a more dynamic approach, as in Recipe 7.3.

---

* You could copy it yourself using a for loop if you wish, but System.arrayCopy() is likely to be faster because it's implemented in native code.

# 7.3   Like an Array, but More Dynamic

## Problem

You don't want to worry about storage reallocation; you want a standard class to handle it for you.

## Solution

Use an ArrayList.

## Discussion

ArrayList is a standard class that encapsulates the functionality of an array but allows it to expand automatically. You can just keep on adding things to it, and each addition behaves the same. If you watch *really* closely, you might notice a brief extra pause once in a while when adding objects as the ArrayList reallocates and copies. But you don't have to think about it.

However, because ArrayList is a class and isn't part of the syntax of Java, you can't use Java's array syntax; you must use methods to access the ArrayList's data. It has methods to add objects, retrieve objects, find objects, and tell you how big the List is and how big it can become without having to reallocate (note that the ArrayList class is but one implementation of the List interface; more on that later). Like the collection classes in java.util, ArrayList's storing and retrieval methods are defined in terms of java.lang.Object. But since Object is the ancestor of every defined type, you can store objects of any type in a List (or any collection) and cast it when retrieving it. If you need to store a small number of built-ins (like int, float, etc.) into a collection containing other data, use the appropriate wrapper class (see the Introduction to Chapter 5). To store booleans, either store them directly in a java.util.BitSet (see the online documentation) or store them in a List using the Boolean wrapper class.

Table 7-1 shows some of the most important methods of ArrayList. Equally important, those listed are also methods of the List interface, which we'll discuss shortly. This means that the same methods can be used with the older Vector class and several other classes.

*Table 7-1. List access methods*

| Method signature | Usage |
| --- | --- |
| add(Object o) | Add the given element at the end |
| add(int i, Object o) | Insert the given element at the specified position |
| clear() | Remove all element references from the Collection |
| contains(Object o) | True if the List contains the given Object |
| get(int i) | Return the object reference at the specified position |

*Table 7-1. List access methods (continued)*

| Method signature | Usage |
| --- | --- |
| indexOf(Object o) | Return the index where the given object is found, or −1 |
| remove(Object o)<br>remove(int i) | Remove an object by reference or by position |
| toArray( ) | Return an array containing the objects in the Collection |

ArrayListDemo stores data in an ArrayList and retrieves it for processing:

```
List al = new ArrayList( );

// Create a source of Objects
StructureDemo source = new StructureDemo(15);

// Add lots of elements to the ArrayList.
al.add(source.getDate( ));
al.add(source.getDate( ));
al.add(source.getDate( ));

// First print them out using a for loop.
System.out.println("Retrieving by index:");
for (int i = 0; i<al.size( ); i++) {
    System.out.println("Element " + i + " - " + al.get(i));
}
```

The older Vector and Hashtable classes predate the Collections framework, so they provide additional methods with different names: Vector provides addElement( ) and elementAt( ). In new code, you should use the Collections methods add( ) and get( ) instead. Another difference is that the methods of Vector are *synchronized*, meaning that they can be accessed from multiple threads (see Recipe 24.5). This does mean more overhead, though, so in a single-threaded application it may be faster to use an ArrayList (see timing results in Recipe 7.17).

# 7.4   Using Iterators for Data-Independent Access

## Problem

You want to write your code so that users don't have to know whether you store it in an array, a Vector, an ArrayList, or even a doubly linked list of your own choosing.

## Solution

Use the Iterator interface.

## Discussion

If you are making collections of data available to other classes, you may not want the other classes to depend upon how you have stored the data so that you can revise your class easily at a later time. Yet you need to publish a method that gives these classes access to your data. It is for this very purpose that the Enumeration and Iterator interfaces were included in the java.util package. These provide a pair of methods that allow you to *iterate*, or step through, all the elements of a data structure without knowing or caring how the data is stored. The newer Iterator interface also allows deletions, though classes that implement the interface are free either to implement the use of deletions or to throw an UnsupportedOperationException.

Here is IteratorDemo, the previous ArrayList demo rewritten to use an Iterator to access the elements of the data structure:

```java
import java.util.List;
import java.util.ArrayList;
import java.util.Iterator;

/** Iterator used to walk through a List.
 * @version $Id: ch07,v 1.5 2004/05/04 20:11:49 ian Exp $
 */
public class IteratorDemo {

    public static void main(String[] argv) {

        List l = new ArrayList( );
        StructureDemo source = new StructureDemo(15);

        // Add lots of elements to the list...
        l.add(source.getDate( ));
        l.add(source.getDate( ));
        l.add(source.getDate( ));

        int i = 0;

        Iterator it = l.iterator( );

        // Process the data structure using an iterator.
        // This part of the code does not know or care
        // if the data is an an array, a List, a Vector, or whatever.
        while (it.hasNext( )) {
            Object o = it.next( );
            System.out.println("Element " + i++ + " = " + o);
        }
    }
}
```

To demystify the Iterator and show that it's actually easy to build, we create our own Iterator in Recipe 7.13.

# 7.5    Structuring Data in a Linked List

## Problem

Your data isn't suitable for use in an array.

## Solution

Write your own data structure(s).

## Discussion

Anybody who's taken Computer Science 101 (or any computer science course) should be familiar with the concepts of data structuring, such as linked lists, binary trees, and the like. While this is not the place to discuss the details of such things, I'll give a brief illustration of the common linked list. A linked list is commonly used when you have an unpredictably large number of data items, you wish to allocate just the right amount of storage, and usually want to access them in the same order that you created them. Figure 7-1 is a diagram showing the normal arrangement.

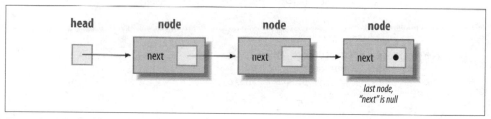

*Figure 7-1. Linked list structure*

Here is code that implements a simple linked list:

```
/**
 * Linked list class, written out in full using Java.
 */
public class LinkList {
    public static void main(String argv[]) {
        System.out.println("Here is a demo of a Linked List in Java");
        LinkList l = new LinkList();
        l.add(new Object());
        l.add("Hello");
        System.out.println("Here is a list of all the elements");
        l.print();
        if (l.lookup("Hello"))
            System.err.println("Lookup works");
        else
            System.err.println("Lookup does not work");
    }

    /* A TNode stores one node or item in the linked list. */
```

```
class TNode {
    TNode next;
    Object data;
    TNode(Object o) {
        data = o;
        next = null;
    }
}
protected TNode root;
protected TNode last;

/** Construct a LinkList: initialize the root and last nodes. */
LinkList( ) {
    root = new TNode(this);
    last = root;
}

 /** Add one object to the end of the list. Update the "next"
  * reference in the previous end, to refer to the new node.
  * Update "last" to refer to the new node.
  */
void add(Object o) {
    last.next = new TNode(o);
    last = last.next;
}

public boolean lookup(Object o) {
    for (TNode p=root.next; p != null; p = p.next)
        if (p.data==o || p.data.equals(o))
            return true;
    return false;
}

void print( ) {
    for (TNode p=root.next; p != null; p = p.next)
        System.out.println("TNode" + p + " = " + p.data);
}
}
```

This approach works reasonably well. But it turns out that many applications use linked lists. Why should each programmer have to provide his or her own linked list class, each with a slightly different set of bugs? You don't have to provide your own square root function or write your own Remote Method Invocation services. Accordingly, Java has a LinkedList class; here is a similar program that uses it:

```
import java.util.*;

/**
 * Demo 1.2 java.util.LinkedList; same example as my older LinkList class.
 */
public class LinkedListDemo {
    public static void main(String argv[]) {
```

```
System.out.println("Here is a demo of Java 1.2's LinkedList class");
LinkedList l = new LinkedList();
l.add(new Object());
l.add("Hello");

System.out.println("Here is a list of all the elements");
// ListIterator is discussed shortly.
ListIterator li = l.listIterator(0);
while (li.hasNext())
    System.out.println(li.next());

if (l.indexOf("Hello") < 0)
    System.err.println("Lookup does not work");
else
    System.err.println("Lookup works");
    }
}
```

As you can see, it does pretty much the same thing as my LinkList but uses the existing class java.util.LinkedList instead of having you roll your own. The ListIterator used here is a subinterface of an Iterator, which was discussed in Recipe 7.4.

# 7.6    Mapping with Hashtable and HashMap

## Problem

You need a one-way mapping from one data item to another.

## Solution

Use a HashMap or the older Hashtable.

## Discussion

HashMap (added in JDK 1.2) and Hashtable provide a one-way mapping from one set of object references to another. They are completely general purpose. I've used them to map AWT push buttons (see Recipe 14.4) to the URL to jump to when the button is pushed, to map names to addresses, and to implement a simple in-memory cache in a web server. You can map from anything to anything. Here we map from company names to addresses; the addresses here are String objects, but in real life they'd probably be Address objects:

```
// HashMapDemo.java
// Construct and load the HashMap. This simulates loading a database
// or reading from a file, or wherever the data is from.

// The hashtable maps from company name to company address.
// In a real application these would be Address objects.
HashMap h = new HashMap();
```

```
h.put("Adobe", "Mountain View, CA");
h.put("IBM", "White Plains, NY");
h.put("Learning Tree", "Los Angeles, CA");
h.put("O'Reilly Media, Inc.", "Sebastopol, CA");
h.put("Netscape", "Mountain View, CA");
h.put("Sun", "Mountain View, CA");

        // Two versions of the "retrieval" phase.
        // Version 1: get one pair's value given its key
        // (presumably the key would really come from user input):
        String queryString = "O'Reilly & Associates";
        System.out.println("You asked about " + queryString + ".");
        String resultString = (String)h.get(queryString);
        System.out.println("They are located in: " + resultString);
        System.out.println( );

        // Version 2: get ALL the keys and pairs
        // (maybe to print a report, or to save to disk)
        Iterator it = h.keySet( ).iterator( );
        while (it.hasNext( )) {
            String key = (String) it.next( );
            System.out.println("Company " + key + "; " +
                "Address " + h.get(key));
        }
    }
}
```

## 7.7   Storing Strings in Properties and Preferences

### Problem

You need to store keys and values that are both strings, possibly with persistence across runs of a program—for example, program customization.

### Solution

Use a java.util.Prefs.Preferences object (JDK 1.4 and above) or a java.util. Properties object.

### Discussion

Here are three approaches to customization based on the user's environment. Java offers Preferences and Properties for cross-platform customizations; for Windows only deployments, a Java-based commercial product can do the trick.

## Preferences

The Preferences class java.util.prefs.Preferences (added in SDK 1.4) is intended to provide an easier-to-use mechanism for storing user customizations in a system-dependent way (which might mean dot files on Unix, a preferences file on the Mac, or the registry on Windows systems). This new class provides a hierarchical set of nodes representing a user's preferences. Data is stored in the system-dependent storage format but can also be exported to or imported from an XML format. Here is a simple demonstration of Preferences:

```
// PrefsDemo.java

// Set up the Preferences for this application, by class.
Preferences prefs = Preferences.userNodeForPackage(PrefsDemo.class);

// Retrieve some preferences previously stored, with defaults in case
// this is the first run.
String text    = prefs.get("textFontName", "lucida-bright");
String display = prefs.get("displayFontName", "lucida-blackletter");
System.out.println(text);
System.out.println(display);

// Assume the user chose new preference values: Store them back.
prefs.put("textFontName", "times-roman");
prefs.put("displayFontName", "helvetica");
```

When you run the PrefsDemo program the first time, of course, it doesn't find any settings, so the calls to preferences.get( ) return the default values:

```
> javac  PrefsDemo.java
> java PrefsDemo
lucida-bright
lucida-blackletter
```

On subsequent runs, it finds and returns the "user provided" settings:

```
> java PrefsDemo
times-roman
helvetica
>
```

## Properties

The Properties class is similar to a HashMap or Hashtable (it extends the latter), but with methods defined specifically for string storage and retrieval and for loading/saving. Properties objects are used throughout Java, for everything from setting the platform font names to customizing user applications into different Locale settings as part of internationalization and localization. When stored on disk, a Properties object looks just like a series of name=value assignments, with optional comments.

Comments are added when you edit a Properties file by hand, ignored when the Properties object reads itself, and lost when you ask the `Properties` object to save itself to disk. Here is an example of a Properties file that could be used to internationalize the menus in a GUI-based program:

```
# Default properties for MenuIntl
program.title=Demonstrate I18N (MenuIntl)
program.message=Welcome to an English-localized Java Program
#
# The File Menu
#
file.label=File Menu
file.new.label=New File
file.new.key=N
file.open.label=Open...
file.open.key=O
file.save.label=Save
file.save.key=S
file.exit.label=Exit
file.exit.key=Q
```

Here is another example, showing some personalization properties:

```
name=Ian Darwin
favorite_popsicle=cherry
favorite_rock group=Fleetwood Mac
favorite_programming_language=Java
pencil color=green
```

A `Properties` object can be loaded from a file. The rules are flexible: either =, :, or spaces can be used after a key name and its values. Spaces after a non-space character are ignored in the key. Backslash can be used to continue lines or to escape other characters. Comment lines may begin with either # or !. Thus, a Properties file containing the previous items, if prepared by hand, could look like this:

```
# Here is a list of properties
! first, my name
name Ian Darwin
favorite_popsicle = cherry
favorite_rock\ group \
 Fleetwood Mac
favorite_programming_language=Java
pencil\ color green
```

Fortunately, when a `Properties` object writes itself to a file, it uses the simple format:

```
key=value
```

Here is an example of a program that creates a `Properties` object and adds into it the list of companies and their locations from Recipe 7.6. It then loads additional properties from disk. To simplify the I/O processing, the program assumes that the Properties file to be loaded is contained in the standard input, as would be done using a command-line redirection on either Unix or DOS:

```
import java.util.*;

public class PropsCompanies {
    public static void main(String argv[]) throws java.io.IOException {
        Properties props = new Properties();

        // Get my data.
        props.setProperty("Adobe", "Mountain View, CA");
        props.setProperty("IBM", "White Plains, NY");
        props.setProperty("Learning Tree", "Los Angeles, CA");
        props.setProperty("O'Reilly & Associates", "Sebastopol, CA");
        props.setProperty("Netscape", "Mountain View, CA");
        props.setProperty("Sun", "Mountain View, CA");

        // Now load additional properties
        props.load(System.in);

        // Now list the merged Properties, using System.out
        props.list(System.out);
    }
}
```

JDK 1.2 added setProperty(); prior to that, the put() method of parent class Hashtable was used.

Running it as:

**java PropsCompanies < PropsDemo.dat**

produces the following output:

```
-- listing properties --
Sony=Japan
Sun=Mountain View, CA
IBM=White Plains, NY
Netscape=Mountain View, CA
Nippon_Kogaku=Japan
Acorn=United Kingdom
Adobe=Mountain View, CA
Ericsson=Sweden
O'Reilly & Associates=Sebastopol, CA
Learning Tree=Los Angeles, CA
```

In case you didn't notice in either the HashMap or the Properties examples, the order that the outputs appear in these examples is neither sorted nor in the same order we put them in. The hashing classes and the Properties subclass make no claim about the order in which objects are retrieved. If you need them sorted, see Recipe 7.8.

As a convenient shortcut, my FileProperties class includes a constructor that takes a filename, as in:

```
import com.darwinsys.util.FileProperties;
...
Properties p = new FileProperties("PropsDemo.dat");
```

Note that constructing a FileProperties object causes it to be loaded, and therefore the constructor may throw a checked exception of class IOException.

### Commercial solution for Windows registry access

Though it is platform-specific, Cogent Logic produces a JNDI (Java Naming and Directory Interface) service provider for accessing the Windows registry, which can also be used for preferences. JNDI is a general naming and directory lookup that, like `java.util.prefs.Preference`, is better suited than `Properties` for dealing with hierarchical data. Cogent Logic's product gives you both local and (subject to security arrangements) remote access to preferences on a Windows system. See *http://cogentlogic.com/jndi/*.

# 7.8   Sorting a Collection

## Problem

You put your data into a collection in random order or used a `Properties` object that doesn't preserve the order, and now you want it sorted.

## Solution

Use the static method `Arrays.sort( )` or `Collections.sort( )`, optionally providing a `Comparator`.

## Discussion

If your data is in an array, you can sort it using the static `sort( )` method of the `Arrays` utility class. If it is in a `Collection`, you can use the static `sort( )` method of the `Collections` class. Here is a set of strings being sorted, first in an `Array` and then in a `Vector`:

```
public class SortArray {
    public static void main(String[] unused) {
        String[] strings = {
            "painful",
            "mainly",
            "gaining",
            "raindrops"
        };
        Arrays.sort(strings);
        for (int i=0; i<strings.length; i++)
            System.out.println(strings[i]);
    }
}

public class SortCollection {
    public static void main(String[] unused) {
        List l ist = new ArrayList();
        list.add("painful");
        list.add("mainly");
        list.add("gaining");
        list.add("raindrops");
```

```
            Collections.sort(list);
            for (int i=0; i<list.size(); i++)
                System.out.println(list.elementAt(i));
        }
    }
```

What if the default sort order isn't what you want? Well, you can create an object that implements the Comparator interface and pass that as the second argument to sort. Fortunately, for the most common ordering next to the default, you don't have to: a public constant String.CASE_INSENSITIVE_ORDER can be passed as this second argument. The String class defines it as "a Comparator that orders String objects as by compareToIgnoreCase." But if you need something fancier, you probably need to write a Comparator. Suppose that, for some strange reason, you need to sort strings using all but the first character of the string. One way to do this would be to write this Comparator:

```
public class SubstringComparator  implements Comparator {
    public int compare(Object o1, Object o2) {
        String s1 = o1.toString().substring(1);
        String s2 = o2.toString().substring(1);
        return s1.compareTo(s2);
        // or, more concisely:
        // return o1.toString().substring(1).equals(o2toString()..substring(1));
    }
}
```

Using it is just a matter of passing it as the Comparator argument to the correct form of sort(), as shown here:

```
import java.util.*;

public class SubstrCompDemo {
    public static void main(String[] unused) {
        String[] strings = {
            "painful",
            "mainly",
            "gaining",
            "raindrops"
        };
        Arrays.sort(strings);
        dump(strings, "Using Default Sort");
        Arrays.sort(strings, new SubstringComparator());
        dump(strings, "Using SubstringComparator");

    }
    static void dump(String[] args, String title) {
        System.out.println(title);
        for (int i=0; i<args.length; i++)
            System.out.println(args[i]);
    }
}
```

Here is the output of running it:

```
$ java SubstrCompDemo
Using Default Sort
gaining
mainly
painful
raindrops
Using SubstringComparator
raindrops
painful
gaining
mainly
```

And this is all as it should be.

On the other hand, you may be writing a class and want to build in the comparison functionality so that you don't always have to remember to pass the Comparator with it. In this case, you can directly implement the java.lang.Comparable interface. The String class; the wrapper classes Byte, Character, Double, Float, Long, Short, and Integer, BigInteger and BigDecimal from java.math; File from java.io; java.util. Date; and java.text.CollationKey all implement this interface, so arrays or Collections of these types can be sorted without providing a Comparator. Classes that implement Comparable are said to have a "natural" ordering. The documentation strongly recommends that a class's natural ordering be consistent with its equals() method, and it is consistent with equals() if and only if e1. compareTo((Object)e2)==0 has the same Boolean value as e1.equals((Object)e2) for every instance e1 and e2 of the given class. This means that if you implement Comparable, you should also implement equals(), and the logic of equals() should be consistent with the logic of the compareTo() method. Here, for example, is part of the appointment class Appt from a hypothetical scheduling program:

```java
public class Appt implements Comparable {
    // much code and variables omitted - see online version

    //-------------------------------------------------------------------
    //    METHODS - COMPARISON
    //-------------------------------------------------------------------
    /** compareTo method, from Comparable interface.
     * Compare this Appointment against another, for purposes of sorting.
     * <P>Only date and time participate, not repetition!
     * Consistent with equals().
     * @return -1 if this<a2, +1 if this>a2, else 0.
     */
    public int compareTo(Object o2) {
        Appt a2 = (Appt) o2;
        if (year < a2.year)
            return -1;
        if (year > a2.year)
            return +1;
        if (month < a2.month)
            return -1;
```

```
            if (month > a2.month)
                return +1;
            if (day < a2.day)
                return -1;
            if (day > a2.day)
                return +1;
            if (hour < a2.hour)
                return -1;
            if (hour > a2.hour)
                return +1;
            if (minute < a2.minute)
                return -1;
            if (minute > a2.minute)
                return +1;
            return target.compareTo(a2.target);
        }


        /** Compare this appointment against another, for equality.
         * Consistent with compareTo( ). For this reason, only
         * date & time participate, not repetition.
         * @returns true if the objects are equal, false if not.
         */
        public boolean equals(Object o2) {
            Appt a2 = (Appt) o2;
            if (year != a2.year ||
                month != a2.month ||
                day != a2.day ||
                hour != a2.hour ||
                minute != a2.minute)
                return false;
            return target.equals(a2.target);
        }
```

If you're still confused between Comparable and Comparator, you're probably not alone. This table summarizes the two "comparison" interfaces:

| Interface name | Description | Method(s) |
| --- | --- | --- |
| java.lang.Comparable | Provides a natural order to objects. Used in the class whose objects are being sorted. | int compareTo(Object o); boolean equals(Object c2) |
| java.util.Comparator | Provides total control over sorting objects of another class. Standalone; pass to sort( ) method or Collection constructor. Implements Strategy Design Pattern. | int compare(Object o1, Object o2); |

# 7.9   Avoiding the Urge to Sort

## Problem

Your data needs to be sorted, but you don't want to stop and sort it periodically.

## Solution

Not everything that requires order requires an explicit *sort* operation. Just keep the data sorted at all times.

## Discussion

You can avoid the overhead and elapsed time of an explicit sorting operation by ensuring that the data is in the correct order at all times. You can do this manually or, as of JDK 1.2, by using a TreeSet or a TreeMap. First, here is some code from a call tracking program that I first wrote on JDK 1.0 to keep track of people I had extended contact with. Far less functional than a Rolodex, my CallTrak program maintained a list of people sorted by last name and first name. It also had the city, phone number, and email address of each person. Here is a very small portion of the code surrounding the event handling for the New User push button:

```
/** The list of Person objects. */
protected List usrList = new ArrayList();

/** The scrolling list */
protected java.awt.List visList = new java.awt.List();

/** Add one (new) Person to the list, keeping the list sorted. */
protected void add(Person p) {
    String lastName = p.getLastName();
    int i;
    for (i=0; i<usrList.size(); i++)
        if (lastName.compareTo(((Person)(usrList.get(i))).getLastName()) <= 0)
            break;
    usrList.add(i, p);
    visList.add(p.getName(), i);
    visList.select(i);          // ensure current
}
```

This code uses the String class compareTo(String) routine.

If I were writing this code today, I might well use a TreeSet (which keeps objects in order) or a TreeMap (which keeps the keys in order and maps from keys to values; the keys would be the name and the values would be the Person objects). Both insert the objects into a tree in the correct order, so an Iterator that traverses the tree always returns the objects in sorted order. In addition, they have methods such as headSet() and headMap(), which give a new Set or Map of objects of the same class, containing the objects lexically before a given value. The tailSet() and tailMap() methods, similarly, return objects greater than a given value, and subSet() and subMap() return a range. The first() and last() methods retrieve the obvious components from the collection. The following program uses a TreeSet to sort some names:

```
// TreeSetDemo.java
/* A TreeSet keeps objects in sorted order. We use a
 * Comparator published by String for case-insensitive
 * sorting order.
 */
```

```
TreeSet tm = new TreeSet(String.CASE_INSENSITIVE_ORDER);
tm.add("Gosling");
tm.add("da Vinci");
tm.add("van Gogh");
tm.add("Java To Go");
tm.add("Vanguard");
tm.add("Darwin");
tm.add("Darwin");        // TreeSet is Set, ignores duplicate. See Recipe 7.10.

// Since it is sorted we can ask for various subsets
System.out.println("Lowest (alphabetically) is " + tm.first());
// Print how many elements are greater than "k"
System.out.println(tm.tailSet("k").toArray().length +
    " elements higher than \"k\"");

// Print the whole list in sorted order
System.out.println("Sorted list:");
java.util.Iterator t = tm.iterator();
while (t.hasNext())
    System.out.println(t.next());
```

One last point to note is that if you have a Hashtable or HashMap, you can convert it to a TreeMap, and therefore get it sorted, just by passing it to the TreeMap constructor:

```
TreeMap sorted = new TreeMap(unsortedHashMap);
```

# 7.10  Eschewing Duplication

## Problem

You want to ensure that only one copy of each unique value is stored in a collection.

## Solution

Use a Set.

## Discussion

The Set interface is a collection that maintains only one instance of each value. If you add into it an object that is equal (as defined by the equals( ) method) to another object, only one of the objects is maintained. By definition, it does not matter to you which of the two objects it keeps—the one in the collection or the one being added—since your objects' equals( ) method indicates they are both equal:

```
// SetDemo.java
HashSet h = new HashSet();
h.add("One");
h.add("Two");
h.add("One"); // DUPLICATE
h.add("Three");
```

```
Iterator it = h.iterator();
while (it.hasNext()) {
    System.out.println(it.next());
}
```

Not surprisingly, only the three distinct values are printed.

# 7.11  Finding an Object in a Collection

## Problem

You need to see whether a given collection contains a particular value.

## Solution

Ask the collection if it contains an object of the given value.

## Discussion

If you have created the contents of a collection, you probably know what is in it and what is not. But if the collection is prepared by another part of a large application, or even if you've just been putting objects into it and now need to find out if a given value was found, this recipe's for you. There is quite a variety of methods, depending on which collection class you have. The following methods can be used:

| Method(s) | Meaning | Implementing classes |
|---|---|---|
| binarySearch() | Fairly fast search | Arrays, Collections |
| contains() | Linear search | ArrayList, HashSet, Hashtable, LinkList, Properties, Vector |
| containsKey(), containsValue() | Checks if the collection contains the object as a Key or as a Value | HashMap, Hashtable, Properties, TreeMap |
| indexOf() | Returns location where object is found | ArrayList, LinkedList, List, Stack, Vector |
| search() | Linear search | Stack |

This example plays a little game of "find the hidden number" (or "needle in a haystack"): the numbers to look through are stored in an array. As games go, it's fairly pathetic: the computer plays against itself, so you probably know who's going to win. I wrote it that way so I would know that the data array contains valid numbers. The interesting part is not the generation of the random numbers (discussed in Recipe 5.13). The array to be used with Arrays.binarySearch() must be in sorted order, but since we just filled it with random numbers, it isn't initially sorted. Hence we call Arrays.sort() on the array. Then we are in a position to call Arrays.binarySearch(), passing in the array and the value to look for. If you run the program with a number, it runs that many games and reports on how it fared overall. If you don't bother, it plays only one game:

```java
import java.util.*;

/** Array Hunt "game" (pathetic: computer plays itself).
 */
public class ArrayHunt  {
    protected final static int MAX    = 4000; // how many random ints
    protected final static int NEEDLE = 1999; // value to look for
    int haystack[];
    Random r;

    public static void main(String argv[]) {
        ArrayHunt h = new ArrayHunt();
        if (argv.length == 0)
            h.play();
        else {
            int won = 0;
            int games = Integer.parseInt(argv[0]);
            for (int i=0; i<games; i++)
                if (h.play())
                    ++won;
            System.out.println("Computer won " + won +
                " out of " + games + ".");
        }
    }

    /** Construct the hunting ground */
    public ArrayHunt() {
        haystack = new int[MAX];
        r = new Random();
    }

    /** Play one game. */
    public boolean play() {
        int i;
        // Fill the array with random data (hay?)
        for (i=0; i<MAX; i++) {
            haystack[i] = (int)(r.nextFloat() * MAX);
        }

        // Precondition for binarySearch() is that array be sorted!
        Arrays.sort(haystack);

        // Look for needle in haystack. :-)
        i = Arrays.binarySearch(haystack, NEEDLE);

        if (i >= 0) {    // found it - hurray, we win!
            System.out.println("Value " + NEEDLE +
                " occurs at haystack[" + i + "]");
            return true;
        } else {           // not found, we lose.
            System.out.println("Value " + NEEDLE +
                " does not occur in haystack; nearest value is " +
                haystack[-(i+2)] + " (found at " + -(i+2) + ")");
            return false;
```

```
            }
        }
    }
```

The `Collections.binarySearch( )` works almost exactly the same way, except it looks in a `Collection`, which must be sorted (presumably using `Collections.sort`, as discussed in Recipe 7.8).

## 7.12   Converting a Collection to an Array

### Problem

You have a `Collection` but you need a Java language array.

### Solution

Use the `Collection` method `toArray( )`.

### Discussion

If you have an `ArrayList` or other `Collection` and you need a Java language array, you can get it just by calling the `Collection`'s `toArray( )` method. With no arguments, you get an array whose type is `Object[]`. You can optionally provide an array argument, which is used for two purposes:

1. The type of the array argument determines the type of array returned.
2. If the array is big enough (and you can ensure that it is by allocating the array based on the `Collection`'s `size( )` method), then this array is filled and returned. If the array is not big enough, a new array is allocated instead. If you provide an array and objects in the `Collection` cannot be casted to this type, you get an `ArrayStoreException`.

Example 7-1 shows code for converting an `ArrayList` to an array of type `Object`.

*Example 7-1. ToArray.java*

```
import java.util.*;

/** ArrayList to array */
public class ToArray {
    public static void main(String[] args) {
        ArrayList al = new ArrayList( );
        al.add("Blobbo");
        al.add("Cracked");
        al.add("Dumbo");
        // al.add(new Date( ));    // Don't mix and match!

        // Convert a collection to Object[], which can store objects
        // of any type.
```

*Example 7-1. ToArray.java (continued)*

```
        Object[] ol = al.toArray( );
        System.out.println("Array of Object has length " + ol.length);

        // This would throw an ArrayStoreException if the line
        // "al.add(new Date( ))" above were uncommented.
        String[] sl = (String[]) al.toArray(new String[0]);
        System.out.println("Array of String has length " + sl.length);
    }
}
```

# 7.13 Rolling Your Own Iterator

## Problem

You have your own data structure, but you want to publish the data as an `Iterator` to provide generic access to it.

## Solution

You need to write your own `Iterator`. Just implement (or provide an inner class that implements) the `Iterator` (or `Enumeration`) interface.

## Discussion

To make data from one part of your program available in a storage-independent way to other parts of the code, generate an `Iterator`. Here is a short program that constructs, upon request, an `Iterator` for some data that it is storing—in this case, in an array. The `Iterator` interface has only three methods: `hasNext( )`, `next( )`, and `remove( )`:

```
package com.darwinsys.util;

import java.util.Iterator;

/** De-mystify the Iterator interface, showing how
 * to write a simple Iterator for an Array of Objects.
 * @author    Ian Darwin, http://www.darwinsys.com/
 * @version    $Id: ch07,v 1.5 2004/05/04 20:11:49 ian Exp $
 */
public class ArrayIterator implements Iterator {
    /** The data to be iterated over. */
    protected Object[] data;

    protected int index = 0;

    /** Construct an ArrayIterator object.
     * @param data The array of objects to be iterated over.
     */
```

```java
    public ArrayIterator(Object[] data) {
        setData(data);
    }

    /** (Re)set the data array to the given array, and reset the iterator.
     * @param data The array of objects to be iterated over.
     */
    public void setData(Object[] data) {
        this.data = data;
        index = 0;
    }

    /**
     * Tell if there are any more elements.
     * @return true if not at the end, i.e., if next() will succeed.
     * @return false if next() will throw an exception.
     */
    public boolean hasNext() {
        return (index < data.length);
    }

    /** Returns the next element from the data */
    public Object next() {
        if (hasNext()) {
            return data[index++];
        }
        throw new IndexOutOfBoundsException("only " + data.length + " elements");
    }

    /** Remove the object that next() just returned.
     * An Iterator is not required to support this interface,
     * and we certainly don't!
     */
    public void remove() {
        throw new UnsupportedOperationException(
            "This demo does not implement the remove method");
    }

    /** Simple tryout */
    protected String[] data = { "one", "two", "three" };
    public static void main(String unused[]) {
        ArrayIterator it = new ArrayIterator(data);
        while (it.hasNext())
            System.out.println(it.next());
    }
}
```

The comments above the remove( ) method remind me of an interesting point. This interface introduces something new to Java, the *optional method*. Since there is no syntax for this, and they didn't want to introduce any new syntax, the developers of the Collections Framework decided on an implementation using existing syntax. If they are not implemented, the optional methods are required to throw an

UnsupportedOperationException if they ever get called. My remove() method does this. Note that UnsupportedOperationException is subclassed from RunTimeException, so it is not required to be declared or caught.

This code is unrealistic in several ways, but it does show the syntax and how the Iterator interface works. In real code, the Iterator and the data are usually separate objects (the Iterator might be an inner class from the data store class). Also, you don't even need to write this code for an array; you can just construct an ArrayList object, copy the array elements into it, and ask it to provide the Iterator. However, I believe it's worth showing this simple example of the internals of an Iterator so that you can understand both how it works and how you could provide one for a more sophisticated data structure, should the need arise.

# 7.14 Stack

## Problem

You need to process data in "last-in, first-out" (LIFO) or "most recently added" order.

## Solution

Write your own code for creating a stack; it's easy. Or, use a java.util.Stack.

## Discussion

You need to put things into a holding area quickly and retrieve them in last-in, first-out order. This is a common data structuring operation and is often used to reverse the order of objects. The basic operations of any stack are push( ) (add to stack), pop( ) (remove from stack), and peek( ) (examine top element without removing). ToyStack is a simple class for stacking only ints:

```
/** Toy Stack. */
public class ToyStack {

    /** The maximum stack depth */
    protected int MAX_DEPTH = 10;
    /** The current stack depth */
    protected int depth = 0;
    /* The actual stack */
    protected int[] stack = new int[MAX_DEPTH];

    /* Implement a toy stack version of push */
    protected void push(int n) {
        stack[depth++] = n;
    }
    /* Implement a toy stack version of pop */
    protected int pop() {
        return stack[--depth];
```

```
    }
    /* Implement a toy stack version of peek */
    protected int peek() {
        return stack[depth - 1];
    }
}
```

If you are not familiar with the basic idea of a stack, you should work through the code here; if you are familiar with it, you can skip ahead. While looking at it, of course, think about what happens if pop( ) or peek( ) is called when push( ) has never been called, or if push( ) is called to stack more data than will fit.

The java.util.Stack operation behaves in a similar fashion. However, instead of being built just for one type of primitive, such as Java int, the methods of java.util. Stack are defined in terms of java.lang.Object so that any kind of object can be put in and taken out. A cast is needed when popping objects, if you wish to call any methods defined in a class below Object. (In JDK 1.5, you can avoid the cast; see Recipe 8.1.)

For an example of a java.util.Stack in operation, Recipe 5.19 provides a simple stack-based numeric calculator.

# 7.15  Multidimensional Structures

## Problem

You need a two-, three-, or more dimensional array or ArrayList.

## Solution

No problem. Java supports this.

## Discussion

As mentioned back in Recipe 7.1, Java arrays can hold any reference type. Since an array is a reference type, it follows that you can have arrays of arrays or, in other terminology, *multidimensional* arrays. Further, since each array has its own length attribute, the columns of a two-dimensional array, for example, do not all have to be the same length (see Figure 7-2).

Here is code to allocate a couple of two-dimensional arrays, one using a loop and the other using an initializer. Both are selectively printed:

```
/** Show Two-Dimensional Array of Objects */
public class ArrayTwoDObjects {

    /** Return list of subscript names (unrealistic; just for demo). */
    public static String[][] getArrayInfo() {
        String info[][];
        info = new String[10][10];
```

```
    for (int i=0; i < info.length; i++) {
        for (int j = 0; j < info[i].length; j++) {
            info[i][j] = "String[" + i + "," + j + "]";
        }
    }
    return info;
}

/** Return list of allowable parameters (Applet method). */
public static String[][] getParameterInfo() {
    String param_info[][] = {
        {"fontsize",   "9-18",    "Size of font"},
        {"URL",        "-",       "Where to download"},
    };
    return param_info;
}

/** Run both initialization methods and print part of the results */
public static void main(String[] args) {
    print("from getArrayInfo", getArrayInfo());
    print("from getParameterInfo", getParameterInfo());
}

/** Print selected elements from the 2D array */
public static void print(String tag, String[][] array) {
    System.out.println("Array " + tag + " is " + array.length + " x " +
        array[0].length);
    System.out.println("Array[0][0] = " + array[0][0]);
    System.out.println("Array[0][1] = " + array[0][1]);
    System.out.println("Array[1][0] = " + array[1][0]);
    System.out.println("Array[0][0] = " + array[0][0]);
    System.out.println("Array[1][1] = " + array[1][1]);
}
}
```

Running it produces this output:

```
> java ArrayTwoDObjects
Array from getArrayInfo is 10 x 10
Array[0][0] = String[0,0]
Array[0][1] = String[0,1]
Array[1][0] = String[1,0]
Array[0][0] = String[0,0]
Array[1][1] = String[1,1]
Array from getParameterInfo is 2 x 3
Array[0][0] = fontsize
Array[0][1] = 9-18
Array[1][0] = URL
Array[0][0] = fontsize
Array[1][1] = -
>
```

The same kind of logic can be applied to any of the Collections. You could have an ArrayList of ArrayLists, or a Vector of linked lists, or whatever your little heart desires.

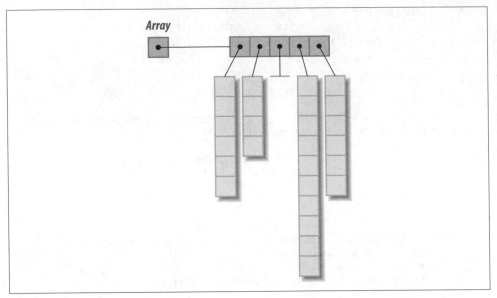

*Figure 7-2. Multidimensional arrays*

As Figure 7-2 shows, it is not necessary for the array to be "regular." That is, it's possible for each column of the 2D array to have a different height. That is why I used array[0].length for the length of the first column in the code example.

# 7.16  Finally, Collections

## Problem

You're having trouble keeping track of all these lists, sets, and iterators.

## Solution

There's a pattern to it. See Figure 7-3 and Table 7-2.

## Discussion

Figure 7-3, in the fashion of the package-level class diagrams in the O'Reilly classic *Java in a Nutshell*, shows the collection-based classes from package java.util.

## See Also

The Javadoc documentation on Collections, Arrays, List, Set, and the classes that implement them provides more details than there's room for here. Table 7-2 may further help you to absorb the regularity of the Collections Framework.

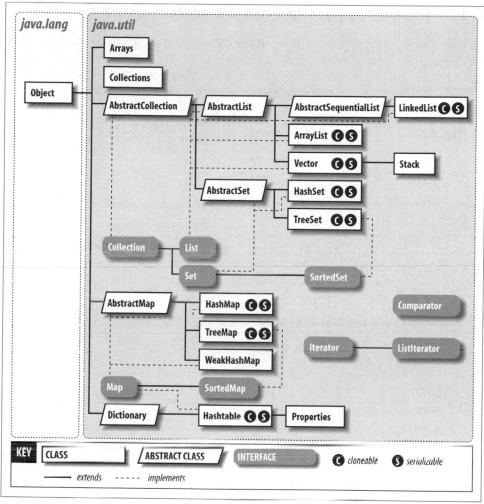

Figure 7-3. The Collections Framework

Table 7-2. Java collections

| Implementations | | | | |
| --- | --- | --- | --- | --- |
| Interfaces | Resizable array | Hashed table | Linked list | Balanced tree |
| Set | | HashSet | | TreeSet |
| List | ArrayList, Vector | | LinkList | |
| Map | | HashMap, HashTable | | TreeMap |

# 7.17  Program: Timing Comparisons

New developers sometimes worry about the overhead of these collections and think they should use arrays instead of data structures. To investigate, I wrote a program that creates and accesses 250,000 objects, once through a Java array and again through an ArrayList. This is a lot more objects than most programs use. First the code for the Array version:

```java
import com.darwinsys.util.MutableInteger;

/** Time a bunch of creates and gets through an Array */
public class Array {
    public static final int MAX = 250000;
    public static void main(String[] args) {
        System.out.println(new Array().run());
    }
    public int run() {
        MutableInteger list[] = new MutableInteger[MAX];
        for (int i=0; i<list.length; i++) {
            list[i] = new MutableInteger(i);
        }
        int sum = 0;
        for (int i=0; i<list.length; i++) {
            sum += list[i].getValue();
        }
        return sum;
    }
}
```

And the ArrayList version:

```java
import java.util.ArrayList;

import com.darwinsys.util.MutableInteger;

/** Time a bunch of creates and gets through an Array */
public class ArrayLst {
    public static final int MAX = 250000;
    public static void main(String[] args) {
        System.out.println(new ArrayLst().run());
    }
    public int run() {
        ArrayList list = new ArrayList();
        for (int i=0; i<MAX; i++) {
            list.add(new MutableInteger(i));
        }
        int sum = 0;
        for (int i=0; i<MAX; i++) {
            sum += ((MutableInteger)list.get(i)).getValue();
        }
        return sum;
    }
}
```

The Vector-based version, ArrayVec, is sufficiently similar that I don't feel the need to kill a tree reprinting its code—it's online.

How can we time this? As covered in Recipe 25.5, you can either use the operating system's *time* command, if available, or just use a bit of Java that times a run of your main program. To be portable, I chose to use the latter on an older, slower machine. Its exact speed doesn't matter since the important thing is to compare only versions of this program running on the same machine.

Finally (drum roll, please), the results:

```
$ java Time Array
Starting class class Array
1185103928
runTime=4.310
$ java Time ArrayLst
Starting class class ArrayLst
1185103928
runTime=5.626
$ java Time ArrayVec
Starting class class ArrayVec
1185103928
runTime=6.699
$
```

Notice that I have ignored one oft-quoted bit of advice that recommends giving a good initial estimate on the size of the ArrayList. I did time it that way as well; in this example, it made a difference of less than four percent in the total runtime.

The bottom line is that the efficiency of ArrayList is not totally awful compared to arrays. Obviously there is more overhead in calling a "get" method than in retrieving an element from an array. The overhead of objects whose methods actually do some computation probably outweighs the overhead of fetching and storing objects in an ArrayList rather than in an Array. Unless you are dealing with large numbers of objects, you may not need to worry about it. Vector is slightly slower but still only about two-thirds the speed of the original array version. If you are concerned about the time, once the "finished" size of the ArrayList is known, you can convert the ArrayList to an array (see Recipe 7.12).

# CHAPTER 8

# Data Structuring with Generics, foreach, and Enumerations (JDK 1.5)

## 8.0   Introduction

JDK 1.5 introduced two new concepts, Generics and AutoBoxing/Unboxing, and two new language features, "foreach" and typesafe enumerations; these features are covered in this chapter.

Generics allow a class to be tailored for a variety of argument/return types at compile time. It provides similar functionality to the Templates mechanism that has been in C++ for some years. When used with the Collections classes (see Chapter 7), Generics significantly increase type safety and remove the requirement for downcasting every object that is retrieved from a Collection (either directly or via an Iterator).

Recipe 5.3 discussed the "Wrapper" classes; these classes provide Objects that represent primitive values. Autoboxing automates the conversion from primitive to Object and vice versa.

The new "foreach" mechanism does not give Java a new keyword; the "for" keyword is still used. However, the syntax is changed slightly to resemble the "for value in list" construct in languages such as the Unix Bourne Shell and the Awk scripting language. This makes it much easier to use Collections, often eliminating the need to obtain an Iterator.

Finally, the Typesafe Enumerations feature provides a mechanism for dealing with a small list of discrete values, such as months, colors, and the like. It combines the enum syntax from Java's predecessor, C, with the Typesafe Enumeration design pattern, giving JDK 1.5 the best of both worlds.

These represent, for the most part, changes to the compiler and the class libraries, rather than changes to the underlying Java Virtual Machine; the changes were implemented by having the compiler map from new constructions to calls on classes, rather than by perturbing the JVM. Because of this, in order to maintain backward compatibility (so that the 1.5 compiler can compile 1.4-level code), these new mechanisms are not enabled by default. So get very used to typing the magical incantation:

```
javac -source 1.5 file.java
```

For without this, the examples in this chapter will universally fail to compile. You have been warned!

You do not, at least, need any special options to the *java* command that invokes the JVM to interpret your class file because, as mentioned, the changes are in the compiler, not in the JVM itself. This does not mean that most of this chapter's material can be compiled on 1.5 and run on 1.4; because of the need for extra methods in the Java runtime, you can't run most of the generated code under 1.4.

## See Also

The compiler techniques used in compiling these new constructs in a backward compatible way include erasure and bridging, topics discussed in an article by O'Reilly author William Grosso, which can be read online at *http://today.java.net/ pub/a/today/2003/12/02/explorations.html*.

# 8.1   Using Generic Collections

## Problem

You want to store your data in one of the Collection classes defined in Chapter 7 but have it treated as though it were homogeneous.

## Solution

Use the JDK 1.5 Generic Types mechanism, and declare the Collection with reference to the given type. The type name appears in angle brackets after the declaration and instantiation. For example, to declare an ArrayList for holding String object references:

```
List<String> myList = new ArrayList<String>();
```

## Discussion

When you instantiate a Collection (or any other class using Generic Types), the class appears to be instantiated with the type given in angle brackets becoming the type of arguments passed in, values returned, and so on. Recipe 8.3 provides some details on the implementation. As an example, consider the code in Example 8-1, which creates and uses an ArrayList specialized to contain String objects.

*Example 8-1. ArrayListGenericDemo.java*

```
import java.util.*;

public class ArrayListGenericDemo {
    public static void main(String[] args) {
        ArrayList<String> data = new ArrayList<String>();
        data.add("hello");
        data.add("goodbye");
```

*Example 8-1. ArrayListGenericDemo.java (continued)*

```
        // data.add(new Date()); This won't compile!

        Iterator<String> it = data.iterator();
        while (it.hasNext()) {
            String s = it.next();
            System.out.println(s);
        }
    }
}
```

As you know from the ArrayList example in Recipe 7.3, prior to Generics, the references obtained from a Collection or Iterator would have to be downcasted to their specific type, often after testing with the instanceof operator. A key benefit of Generic Types is that they obviate this testing and downcasting by doing more work at compile time.

You can still instantiate classes such as ArrayList without using a specific type. In this case, they behave as in 1.4—that is, the objects returned from a Collection or Iterator are typed as java.lang.Object and must be downcasted before use.

As a further example, consider the Map interface mentioned in Chapter 7. A Map requires Keys and Values in its put( ) method. A Map, therefore, has two parameterized types. To set up a Map whose keys are Person objects and whose values are Address objects (assuming these two classes exist in your application), you could define it as:

```
    Map<Person, Address> addressMap = new HashMap<Person, Addresss>();
```

This Map would expect a Person as its key and an Address as its value in the put( ) method; the get( ) method would return an Address object. The keySet( ) method would return Set<Person>—a Set specialized for Person objects—and so on.

# 8.2   Using "foreach" Loops

## Problem

You want a convenient means of accessing all the elements of an array or collection.

## Solution

Use the JDK 1.5 "foreach" construction. For example:

```
    for (String s : myList)
```

This form of for is always read as "foreach" and is referred to that way in the documentation and the compiler messages; the colon (:) is always pronounced as "in" so that the above statement is read as "foreach String s in myList." The String named s will be given each value from myList (which is presumed to be declared as an array or Collection of String references).

## Discussion

The foreach construction can be used on Java arrays and on collection classes. The compiler turns it into an iteration, typically using an Iterator object where Collection classes are involved. Example 8-2 shows foreach on an array; in a slightly longer example, Example 8-3 shows foreach on a Collection.

*Example 8-2. ForeachArray.java*

```
public class ForeachArray {
    public static void main(String args[]) {
        String[] data = { "Toronto", "Stockholm" };
        for (String s : data) {
            System.out.println(s);
        }
    }
}
```

*Example 8-3. ForeachDemo.java*

```
import java.util.Collection;
import java.util.List;
import java.util.ArrayList;

public class ForeachDemo {
    static void iterate(Collection<String> c) {
        for (String s: c)
            System.out.println(s);
    }
    public static void main(String args[]) {
        List<String> l = new ArrayList<String>();
        l.add("Toronto");
        l.add("Stockholm");
        iterate(l);
    }
}
```

# 8.3   Avoid Casting by Using Generics

## Problem

You wish to define your own container classes using the Generic Type mechanism to avoid needless casting.

## Solution

Define a class using *<TypeName>* where the type is declared and *TypeName* where it is used.

# Discussion

Consider the very simple Stack class in Example 8-4. This class has been parameterized to take a type whose local name is T. This type T will be the type of the argument of the push( ) method, the return type of the pop( ) method, and so on. Because of this return type—more specific than the Object return type of the original Collections—the return value from pop( ) does not need to be downcasted. In 1.5, the Collections Framework classes have been modified similarly.

*Example 8-4. MyStack.java*

```java
/** A  lax Stack implementation. */
public class MyStack<T> {
    private int ix = 0;
    public final int MAX = 10;
    private T[] data = (T[])new Object[MAX];

    public void push(T obj) {
        data[ix++] = obj;
    }

    public boolean hasNext( ) {
        return ix > 0;
    }

    public boolean hasRoom( ) {
        return ix <  MAX;
    }

    public T pop( ) {
        if (hasNext( )) {
            return data[--ix];
        }
        throw new ArrayIndexOutOfBoundsException(-1);
    }
}
```

The association of a particular type is done at the time the class is instantiated. For example, to instantiate a MyStack specialized for holding BankAccount objects, one would need to code only the following:

```java
MyStack<BankAccount>  theAccounts = new MyStack<BankAccount>( );
```

Note that if you do not provide a specific type, this class defaults to the most general behavior, that is, type T is treated as java.lang.Object. So this toy collection, like the real ones in java.util, will behave as they did in 1.4—accepting input arguments of any type, returning java.lang.Object from getter methods, and requiring downcasting—as their default, backward-compatible behavior. Example 8-5 shows a program that creates two instances of MyStack, one specialized for Strings and one left general. The general one, called m2, is loaded up with the same two String objects as m1 but also includes a Date object. The printing code is now "broken", as it will throw a

ClassCastException: a Date is not a String. I handle this case specially for pedantic purposes: it is illustrative of the kinds of errors you can get into when using nonparameterized container classes.

*Example 8-5. MyStackDemo.java*

```
public class MyStackDemo {
    public static void main(String[] args) {
        MyStack<String> ms1 = new MyStack<String>();
        ms1.push("billg");
        ms1.push("scottm");

        while (ms1.hasNext()) {
            String name = ms1.pop();
            System.out.println(name);
        }

        // Old way of using Collections: not type safe.
        MyStack ms2 = new MyStack();
        ms2.push("billg");
        ms2.push("scottm");
        ms2.push(new java.util.Date());

        // Show that it is broken
        try {
            String bad = (String)ms2.pop();
            System.err.println("Didn't get expected exception!");
        } catch (ClassCastException cx) {
            System.out.println("Did get expected exception.");
        }

        // Removed the brokenness, print rest of it.
        while (ms2.hasNext()) {
            String name = (String)ms2.pop();
            System.out.println(name);
        }
    }
}
```

Because of this potential for error, the 1.5 compiler warns that you have unchecked raw types. Like the Deprecation warnings discussed in Recipe 1.9, by default, these warnings are not printed in detail. You must ask for them, with the rather lengthy option -Xlint:unchecked:

```
C:> javac -source 1.5 MyStackDemo.java
Note: MyStackDemo.java uses unchecked or unsafe operations.
Note: Recompile with -Xlint:unchecked for details.
C:> javac -source 1.5 -Xlint:unchecked MyStackDemo.java
MyStackDemo.java:14: warning: unchecked call to push(T) as a member of the raw
type MyStack
            ms2.push("billg");
               ^
```

```
MyStackDemo.java:15: warning: unchecked call to push(T) as a member of the raw
type MyStack
                ms2.push("scottm");
                   ^
MyStackDemo.java:16: warning: unchecked call to push(T) as a member of the raw
type MyStack
                ms2.push(new java.util.Date( ));
                   ^

3 warnings
C:>
```

# 8.4    Let Java Convert with AutoBoxing and AutoUnboxing

## Problem

You are tired of typing code like new Integer(i) and intObj.intValue( ) to convert back and forth between primitives and Object Wrappers.

## Solution

Use the JDK 1.5 compiler; it will AutoBox and AutoUnbox for you.

## Discussion

There's a reason they call it automatic boxing: you don't have to do any work. The 1.5 compiler is finally able to figure out how to convert back and forth between primitives and their wrappers. Example 8-6 shows converting from a primitive int value to an Integer needed in a method call.

*Example 8-6. AutoboxDemo.java*

```java
public class AutoboxDemo {
    public static void main(String[] args) {
        int i = 42;
        foo(i);
    }

    public static void foo(Integer i) {
        System.out.println("Object = " + i);
    }
}
```

This code compiles and runs on JDK 1.5 (but only with the -source 1.5 option). Notice what happens when we omit that option:

```
C:\ian\javasrc\structure1.5>javac AutoboxDemo.java
AutoboxDemo.java:4: foo(java.lang.Integer) in AutoboxDemo cannot be applied to (int)
                foo(i);
                   ^
```

```
1 error

C:\ian\javasrc\structure1.5>javac -source 1.5 AutoboxDemo.java

C:\ian\javasrc\structure1.5>java AutoboxDemo
Object = 42

C:\ian\javasrc\structure1.5>
```

The resulting class file does not run in a JDK 1.4 implementation because it depends on a new method signature in the Integer class, notably valueOf(int i).

# 8.5   Using Typesafe Enumerations

## Problem

You need to manage a small list of discrete values within a program.

## Solution

Use the JDK 1.5 enum mechanism.

## Discussion

To enumerate means to list all the values. You often know that a small list of possible values is all that's wanted in a variable, such as the months of the year, the suits or ranks in a deck of cards, the primary and secondary colors, and so on. The C programming language provided an enum keyword:

```
enum  { BLACK, RED, ORANGE} color;
```

Java has been criticized since the earliest releases for its lack of enumerations, which many developers have wished for. Many have had to develop custom classes to implement the "enumeration pattern."

But C enumerations are not "typesafe"; they simply define constants that can be used in any integer context. For example, this code compiles without warning, even on gcc 3 with -Wall (all warnings), while a C++* compiler catches the error:

```
enum { BLACK, RED, ORANGE} color;
enum { READ, UNREAD } state;

/*ARGSUSED*/
int main(int argc, char *argv[]) {
        color = RED;
        color = READ;
        return 0;
}
```

---

* For Java folks not that familiar with C/C++, C is the older, non-OO language; C++ is an OO derivative of C; and Java is in part a portable, more strongly typesafe derivative of C++.

To replicate this mistake in Java, one needs only to define a series of `final int` values; it will still not be typesafe. By typesafe I mean that you can not accidentally use values other than those defined for the given enumeration. The definitive statement on the "typesafe enumeration pattern" is probably the version defined in Item 21 of Joshua Bloch's book *Effective Java* (Addison Wesley). Bloch was one of the authors of the Typesafe Enumeration specification for JDK 1.5, so you can be sure the book does a good job of implementing his pattern. These enums are implemented as Classes, subclassed (transparently, by the compiler) from the new class `java.lang.Enum`. Unlike C, and unlike the "series of final int" implementation, JDK 1.5 typesafe enumerations:

- Are printable (they print as the name, not as an underlying `int` implementation).
- Are almost as fast as `int` constants, but the code is more readable.
- Can be easily iterated over.
- Utilize a separate namespace for each enum type, so you don't have to prefix each with some sort of constant name, like ACCOUNT_SAVINGS, ACCOUNT_CHECKING, etc.

Enum constants are not compiled into clients, giving you the freedom to reorder the constants within your enum without recompiling the client classes. Normally this works correctly and, even if you blow it and remove a constant that a client depends on, you'll get an informative message instead of a cryptic crash. Additionally, an enum type is a class so it can, for example, implement arbitrary interfaces, and you can add arbitrary fields and methods to an enum class.

Compared to Bloch's Typesafe Enum pattern in the book:

- JDK 1.5 enums are simpler to use and more readable (those in the book require a lot of methods, making them cumbersome to write).
- Enums can be used in switch statements.

So there are many benefits and few pitfalls.

The new enum keyword is at the same level as the keyword `class` in declarations. That is, an enum may be declared in its own file with public or default access. It may also be declared inside classes, much like nested or inner classes (see Recipe 9.6). *Media.java*, shown in Example 8-7, is a code sample showing the definition of a typesafe enum.

*Example 8-7. Media.java*

```
public enum Media {
    book, music_cd, music_vinyl, movie_vhs, movie_dvd;
}
```

Notice that an enum is a class; see what *javap* thinks of the Media class:

```
C:> javap Media
Compiled from "Media.java"
```

```
public class Media extends java.lang.Enum{
    public static final Media book;
    public static final Media music_cd;
    public static final Media music_vinyl;
    public static final Media movie_vhs;
    public static final Media movie_dvd;
    public static final Media[] values();
    public static Media valueOf(java.lang.String);
    public Media(java.lang.String, int);
    public int compareTo(java.lang.Enum);
    public int compareTo(java.lang.Object);
    static {};
}
(:>
```

*Product.java*, shown in Example 8-8, is a code sample that uses the Media enum.

*Example 8-8. Product.java*

```
import com.darwinsys.util.Debug;

public class Product {
    String title;
    String artist;
    Media   media;

    public Product(String artist, String title, Media media) {
        this.title = title;
        this.artist = artist;
        switch (media) {
        case book:
            Debug.println("media", title + " is a book");
            break;
        case music_cd:
            Debug.println("media", title + " is a CD");
            break;
        case music_vinyl:
            Debug.println("media", title + " is a relic");
            break;
        case movie_vhs:
            Debug.println("media", title + " is on tape");
            break;
        case movie_dvd:
            Debug.println("media", title + " is on DVD");
            break;
        default:
            Debug.println("media", "Warning: " + title +
                ": Unknown media " + media);
            break;
        }
        this.media = media;
    }
}
```

In Example 8-9, MediaFancy shows how operations (methods) can be added to enumerations; the toString( ) method is overridden for the "book" value of this enum.

*Example 8-9. MediaFancy.java*

```
public enum MediaFancy {
    book {
        public String toString() { return "Book"; }
    },
    music_cd, music_vinyl, movie_vhs, movie_dvd;

    public static void main(String[] args) {
        MediaFancy[] data = { book, movie_dvd, music_vinyl };
        for (MediaFancy mf : data) {
            System.out.println(mf);
        }
    }
}
```

Running the MediaFancy program produces this output:

```
Book
movie_dvd
music_vinyl
```

That is, the Book values print in a "user-friendly" way compared to the default way the other values print. You'd want to extend this to all the values in an Enumeration.

Finally, EnumList, in Example 8-10, shows how to list all the possible values that a given enum can take on; simply iterate over the array returned by the class's values( ) method.

*Example 8-10. EnumList.java*

```
/** Simple demo to print all the types of an enum. */
public class EnumList {
    public static void main(String[] args) {
        enum State { ON, OFF, UNKNOWN };
        for (State i : State.values()) {
            System.out.println(i);
        }
    }
}
```

The output of the EnumList program is, of course:

```
ON
OFF
UNKNOWN
```

# 8.6    Program: MediaInvoicer

This sketch of an invoicing program demonstrates several of these concepts. MediaFactory is a class that takes a String (or int) and returns the corresponding Media enum constant:

```
/*
 * MediaFactory - give out Media enumeration constants
 * @verion $Id: ch08,v 1.5 2004/05/04 20:11:57 ian Exp $
 */
public class MediaFactory {

    public static void main(String[] args) {

        System.out.println(MediaFactory.getMedia("Book"));
    }
    public static Media getMedia(String s) {
        return Enum.valueOf(Media.class, s.toLowerCase());
    }
    public static Media getMedia(int n){
        return Media.values()[n];
    }
}
```

This program uses the valueOf( ) method inherited from java.lang.Enum by all user-defined enumerations. The MediaFactory is used in the main class's getInvoice() method to get the correct enum constant for a given String read from the *invoices* file, a sample of which looks like this:

```
# Lines beginning with # are comments, ignored by the program
# I invoice# cust#
# M    media item# quantity
M Book 2074 1
M MUSIC_VINYL 107 1
M MUSIC_CD 5102 5
M book 2100 1
```

As you can see, the data entry people have been careless about case, but the MediaFactory class turns the strings into lowercase before looking them up. The main program pulls these lines apart with a StringTokenizer and parses the ints with Integer.parseInt( ).

The main class uses two helper classes, Invoice and Item. An invoice can have one or more line items in it, so the Invoice object contains an array of Item objects.

Example 8-11 is the code for the main MediaInvoicer class and the helper classes.

*Example 8-11. MediaInvoicer.java*

```
import java.io.BufferedReader;
import java.io.IOException;
import java.io.InputStreamReader;
import java.io.InputStream;
```

*Example 8-11. MediaInvoicer.java (continued)*

```java
import java.io.PrintStream;
import java.util.ArrayList;
import java.util.List;
import java.util.StringTokenizer;

/**
 * MediaInvoicer - Simple applicatin of Media, MediaFactory &c.
 *
 * @author ian
 * @version $Id: ch08,v 1.5 2004/05/04 20:11:57 ian Exp $
 */
public class MediaInvoicer {

    public static void main(String[] args) throws IOException {
        MediaInvoicer mi = new MediaInvoicer(System.in);
        Invoice i = mi.getInvoice();
        i.print(System.out);
    }
    BufferedReader myFile;
    public MediaInvoicer(InputStream is) {
        myFile = new BufferedReader(new InputStreamReader(is));
    }

    public Invoice getInvoice() throws IOException {
        String line;
        List < Item > items = new ArrayList < Item > ();
        while ((line = myFile.readLine()) != null) {
            if (line.startsWith("#")) {
                continue;
            }
            StringTokenizer st = new StringTokenizer(line);
            st.nextToken();
            Media m = MediaFactory.getMedia(st.nextToken());
            int stock = Integer.parseInt(st.nextToken());
            int qty = Integer.parseInt(st.nextToken());
            Item tmp = new Item(m, stock, qty);
            items.add(tmp);
        }
        return new Invoice(1, 3,
            (Item[]) items.toArray(new Item[items.size()]));
    }

    /** Inner class for line order item */
    class Item {
        Media product;
        int stockNumber;
        int quantity;
        /**
         * @param product
         * @param stockNumber
         * @param quantity
         */
```

*Example 8-11. MediaInvoicer.java (continued)*

```
    public Item(Media product, int stockNumber, int quantity) {
        super( );
        this.product = product;
        this.stockNumber = stockNumber;
        this.quantity = quantity;
    }
    public String toString( ) {
        return "Item[" + product + " " + stockNumber + "]";
    }
}
/** Inner class for one invoice */
class Invoice {
    int orderNumber;
    int custNumber;
    Item[] items;

    public Invoice(int orderNumber, int custNumber, Item[] items) {
        super( );
        this.orderNumber = orderNumber;
        this.custNumber = custNumber;
        this.items = items;
    }
    public void print(PrintStream ps) {
        ps.println("*** Invoice ***");
        ps.println("Customer: " + custNumber + ")");
        ps.println("Our order number: " + orderNumber);
        for (int i = 0; i < items.length; i++) {
            Item it = items[i];
            ps.println(it);
        }
    }
}
}
```

Running the program with the sample file shown in Example 8-11 produces this output:

```
*** Invoice ***
Customer number: 1
Our order number: 3
Item[book 2074]
Item[music_vinyl 107]
Item[music_cd 5102]
Item[book 2100]
```

This demonstrates a bit of the ease of use of Java enumerations—they print as themselves—and the use of a List customized to hold Item objects—the list named items in the getInvoice( ) method.

# CHAPTER 9
# Object-Oriented Techniques

## 9.0  Introduction

Java is an object-oriented (OO) language in the tradition of Simula-67, SmallTalk, and C++. It borrows syntax from C++ and ideas from SmallTalk. The Java API has been designed and built on the OO model. *Design Patterns* (see the book of the same name), such as Factory and Delegate, are used throughout; an understanding of these patterns will help you better understand the use of the API and improve the design of your own classes.

### Advice, or Mantras

There are any number of short bits of advice that I could give. A few recurring themes arise when learning the basics of Java, and then when learning more Java.

#### Use the API

I can't say this often enough. A lot of the things you need to do have already been done by the good folks at JavaSoft. And this grows with most releases: 1.2 added the Collections API, and 1.4 added the Regular Expressions API discussed in Chapter 4. Learning the API well is a good grounds for avoiding that deadly "reinventing the flat tire" syndrome—coming up with a second-rate equivalent of a first-rate product that was available to you the whole time. In fact, part of this book's mission is to prevent you from reinventing what's already there. One example of this is the Collections API in `java.util`, discussed in Chapter 7. The Collections API has a high degree of generality and regularity, so there is usually very little reason to invent your own data structuring code.

#### Generalize

There is a trade-off between generality (and the resulting reusability), which is emphasized here, and the convenience of application specificity. If you're writing one small part of a very large application designed according to OO design techniques, you'll have in mind a specific set of *use cases*. On the other hand, if you're writing "toolkit-style" code, you should write classes with few assumptions about how they'll be used. Making code easy to use from a variety of programs is the route to writing reusable code.

### Read and write Javadoc

You've no doubt looked at the Java online documentation in a browser, in part because I just told you to learn the API well. Do you think Sun hired millions of tech writers to produce all that documentation? No. That documentation exists because the developers of the API took the time to write Javadoc comments, those funny /** comments you've seen in code. So, one more bit of advice: use Javadoc. We finally have a good, standard mechanism for API documentation. And use it as you write the code—don't think you'll come back and write it in later. That kind of tomorrow never comes.

See Recipe 23.2 for details on using Javadoc.

### Use subclassing and delegation

I can't say this one enough either. Use subclassing. Use subclassing. Use subclassing. It is the best basis not only for avoiding code duplication, but for developing software that works. See any number of good books on the topic of object-oriented design and programming for more details.

An alternative to subclassing is the Design Pattern (see below) known as delegation. For example, instead of subclassing NameAndAddress to make Supplier and Customer, make Supplier and Customer have instances of NameAndAddress. That is a clearer structure and also makes it easier for a Customer to have both a billing address and a shipping address.

### Use design patterns

In the Preface, I listed *Design Patterns* (Addison Wesley) as one of the Very Important Books on object-oriented programming. It provides a powerful catalog of things that programmers often reinvent. It is as important for giving a standard vocabulary of design as it is for its clear explanations of how the basic patterns work and how they can be implemented.

Here are some examples from the standard API:

| Pattern name | Meaning | Examples in Java API |
| --- | --- | --- |
| Factory Method | One class makes up instances for you, controlled by subclasses | `getInstance` (in `Calendar`, `Format`, `Locale`...); socket constructor; `RMI InitialContext` |
| Iterator | Loop over all elements in a collection, visiting each exactly once | `Iterator`; older `Enumeration`; `java.sql.ResultSet` |

| Pattern name | Meaning | Examples in Java API |
|---|---|---|
| Singleton | Only one instance may exist | `java.lang.Runtime,`<br>`java.awt.Toolkit` |
| Memento | Capture and externalize an object's state for later reconstruction | Object serialization |
| Command | Encapsulate requests, allowing queues of requests, undoable operations, etc. | `javax.swing.Action;`<br>`javax.swing.undo.UndoableEdit` |
| Model-View-Controller | Model represents data; View is what the user sees; Controller responds to user request | `Observer/Observable;`<br>used internally by all visible Swing components |

# 9.1 Printing Objects: Formatting with toString( )

## Problem

You want your objects to have a useful default format.

## Solution

Override the `toString()` method inherited from `java.lang.Object`.

## Discussion

Whenever you pass an object to `System.out.println()` or any equivalent method, or involve it in string concatenation, Java automatically calls its `toString()` method. Java "knows" that every object has a `toString()` method since `java.lang.Object` has one and all classes are ultimately subclasses of `Object`. The default implementation, in `java.lang.Object`, is neither pretty nor interesting: it just prints the class name, an @ sign, and the object's `hashCode()` value (see Recipe 9.3). For example, if you run this code:

```
/* Demonstrate toString( ) without an override */
public class ToStringWithout {
    int x, y;

    /** Simple constructor */
    public ToStringWithout(int anX, int aY) {
        x = anX; y = aY;
    }

    /** Main just creates and prints an object */
    public static void main(String[] args) {
        System.out.println(new ToStringWithout(42, 86));
    }
}
```

you might see this uninformative output:

```
ToStringWithout@990c747b
```

To make it print better, you should provide an implementation of toString() that prints the class name and some of the important states in all but the most trivial classes. This gives you formatting control in println(), in debuggers, and anywhere your objects get referred to in a String context. Here is the previous program rewritten with a toString() method:

```
/* Demonstrate toString() with an override */
public class ToStringWith {
    int x, y;

    /** Simple constructor */
    public ToStringWith(int anX, int aY) {
        x = anX; y = aY;
    }

    /** Override toString */
    public String toString() {
        return "ToStringWith[" + x + "," + y + "]";
    }
    /** Main just creates and prints an object */
    public static void main(String[] args) {
        System.out.println(new ToStringWith(42, 86));
    }
}
```

This version produces the more useful output:

```
ToStringWith[42,86]
```

# 9.2    Overriding the Equals Method

## Problem

You want to be able to compare objects of your class.

## Solution

Write an equals() method.

## Discussion

How do you determine equality? For arithmetic or Boolean operands, the answer is simple: you test with the equals operator (==). For object references, though, Java provides both == and the equals() method inherited from java.lang.Object. The equals operator can be confusing, as it simply compares two object references to see if they refer to the same object. This is not the same as comparing the objects themselves.

The inherited equals() method is also not as useful as you might imagine. Some people seem to start their life as Java developers thinking that the default equals() magically does some kind of detailed, field-by-field or even binary comparison of objects. But it does *not* compare fields! It just does the simplest possible thing: it returns the value of an == comparison on the two objects involved! So, for any major classes you write, you probably have to write an equals method. Note that both the equals and hashCode methods are used by hashes (Hashtable, HashMap; see Recipe 7.6). So if you think somebody using your class might want to create instances and put them into a hash, or even compare your objects, you owe it to them (and to yourself!) to implement equals( ) properly.

Here are the rules for an equals( ) method:

1. It is reflexive: x.equals(x) must be true.

2. It is symmetrical: x.equals(y) must be true if and only if y.equals(x) is also true.

3. It is transitive: if x.equals(y) is true and y.equals(z) is true, then x.equals(z) must also be true.

4. It is repeatable: multiple calls on x.equals(y) return the same value (unless state values used in the comparison are changed, as by calling a set method).

5. It is cautious: x.equals(null) must return false rather than accidentally throwing a NullPointerException.

Here is a class that endeavors to implement these rules:

```java
public class EqualsDemo {
    int int1;
    SomeClass obj1;

    /** Constructor */
    public EqualsDemo(int i, SomeClass o) {
        int1 = i;
        if (o == null) {
            throw new IllegalArgumentException("Object may not be null");
        }
        obj1 = o;
    }

    /** Default Constructor */
    public EqualsDemo() {
        this(0, new SomeClass());
    }

    /** Typical run-of-the-mill Equals method */
    public boolean equals(Object o) {
        if (o == this)                    // optimization
            return true;

        // Castable to this class? (false if == null)
        if (!(o instanceof EqualsDemo))
            return false;

        EqualsDemo other = (EqualsDemo)o;    // OK, cast to this class

        // compare field-by-field
        if (int1 != other.int1)              // compare primitives directly
            return false;
```

```
        if (!obj1.equals(other.obj1))    // compare objects using their equals
            return false;
        return true;
    }
}
```

And here is a JUnit test file (see Recipe 1.14) for the EqualsDemo class:

```
import junit.framework.*;
/** some junit test cases for EqualsDemo
 * writing a full set is left as "an exercise for the reader".
 * Run as: $ java junit.textui.TestRunner EqualsDemoTest
 */
public class EqualsDemoTest extends TestCase {

    /** an object being tested */
    EqualsDemo d1;
    /** another object being tested */
    EqualsDemo d2;

    /** init( ) method */
    public void setUp( ) {
        d1 = new EqualsDemo( );
        d2 = new EqualsDemo( );
    }

    /** constructor plumbing for junit */
    public EqualsDemoTest(String name) {
        super(name);
    }

    public void testSymmetry( ) {
        assert(d1.equals(d1));
    }

    public void testSymmetric( ) {
        assert(d1.equals(d2) && d2.equals(d1));
    }

    public void testCaution( ) {
        assert(!d1.equals(null));
    }
}
```

With all that testing, what could go wrong? Well, some things still need care. What if the object is a *subclass* of EqualsDemo? We cast it and…compare only our fields! You probably should test explicitly with getClass( ) if subclassing is likely. And subclasses should call super.equals( ) to test all superclass fields.

What else could go wrong? Well, what if either obj1 or other.obj1 is null? You might have just earned a nice shiny new NullPointerException. So you also need to test for any possible null values. Good constructors can avoid these NullPointerExceptions, as I've tried to do in EqualsDemo, or else test for them explicitly.

# 9.3    Overriding the hashCode Method

## Problem

You want to use your objects in a HashMap, HashSet, Hashtable, or other Collection, and you need to write a hashCode( ) method.

## Discussion

The hashCode( ) method is supposed to return an int that should uniquely identify different objects.

A properly written hashCode( ) method will follow these rules:

1. It is repeatable: hashCode(x) must return the same int when called repeatedly, unless set methods have been called.

2. It is consistent with equality: if x.equals(y), then x.hashCode( ) must == y.hashCode( ).

3. If !x.equals(y), it is not required that x.hashCode( ) != y.hashCode( ), but doing so may improve performance of hash tables; i.e., hashes may call hashCode( ) before equals( ).

The default hashCode( ) on Sun's JDK returns a machine address, which conforms to Rule 1. Conformance to Rules 2 and 3 depends, in part, upon your equals( ) method. Here is a program that prints the hashcodes of a small handful of objects:

```
/** Display hashCodes from some objects */
public class PrintHashCodes {

    /** Some objects to hashCode( ) on */
    protected static Object[] data = {
        new PrintHashCodes( ),
        new java.awt.Color(0x44, 0x88, 0xcc),
        new SomeClass( )
    };

    public static void main(String[] args) {
        System.out.println("About to hashCode " + data.length + " objects.");
        for (int i=0; i<data.length; i++) {
            System.out.println(data[i].toString() + " --> " +
                data[i].hashCode());
        }
        System.out.println("All done.");
    }
}
```

What does it print?

```
> jikes +E -d . PrintHashCodes.java
> java PrintHashCodes
About to hashCode 3 objects.
```

```
PrintHashCodes@982741a0 --> -1742257760
java.awt.Color[r=68,g=136,b=204] --> -12285748
SomeClass@860b41ad --> -2046082643
All done.
>
```

The hashcode value for the Color object is interesting. It is actually computed as something like:

```
alpha<<24 + r<<16 + g<<8 + b
```

In this formula, r, g, and b are the red, green, and blue components respectively, and alpha is the transparency. Each of these quantities is stored in 8 bits of a 32-bit integer. If the alpha value is greater than 128, the "high bit" in this word—having been set by shifting into the sign bit of the word—causes the integer value to appear negative when printed as a signed integer. Hashcode values are of type int, so they are allowed to be negative.

# 9.4    The Clone Method

## Problem

You want to clone yourself. Or at least your objects.

## Solution

Override Object.clone( ).

## Discussion

To *clone* something is to make a duplicate of it. The clone( ) method in Java makes an exact duplicate of an object. Why do we need cloning? Think about what happens when you call a method passing it an argument you have created. Java's method-calling semantics are call-by-reference—a reference to your object is passed—which allows the called method to modify the state of your carefully constructed object! Cloning the input object before calling the method allows you to pass a copy of the object, keeping your original safe.

How can you clone? Cloning is not "enabled" by default in classes that you write:

```
Object o = new Object( );
Object o2 = o.clone( );
```

If you try calling clone( ) without any special preparation, as in this excerpt from *Clone0.java*, you will see a message like this (from the Jikes compiler; the *javac* message may not be as informative):

```
Clone0.java:4:29:4:37: Error: Method "java.lang.Object clone( );" in class "java/lang/
Object" has protected or default access. Therefore, it is not accessible in class
"Clone0" which is in a different package.
```

You must take two steps to make your class cloneable:

1. Override Object's clone( ) method.
2. Implement the empty Cloneable interface.

## Using cloning

The class java.lang.Object declares its clone method *protected* and *native*. Protected methods can be called by a subclass or those in the same package (i.e., java.lang), but not by unrelated classes. That is, you can call Object.clone( )—the native method that does the magic of duplicating the object—only from within the object being cloned. Here is a simple example of a class with a clone method and a tiny program that uses it:

```
public class Clone1 implements Cloneable {

    /** Clone this object. Just call super.clone() to do the work */
    public Object clone()  {
        try {
            return super.clone();
        } catch (CloneNotSupportedException ex) {
            throw new InternalError(ex.toString());
        }
    }

    int x;
    transient int y;     // will be cloned, but not serialized

    public static void main(String[] args) {
        Clone1 c = new Clone1();
        c.x = 100;
        c.y = 200;
        try {
            Object d = c.clone();
            System.out.println("c=" + c);
            System.out.println("d=" + d);
        } catch (Exception ex) {
            System.out.println("Now that's a surprise!!");
            System.out.println(ex);
        }
    }

    /** Display the current object as a string */
    public String toString() {
        return "Clone1[" + x + "," + y + "]";
    }
}
```

The clone( ) method in Object throws CloneNotSupportedException. This handles the case of inadvertently calling clone( ) on a class that isn't supposed to be cloned. Since most of the time you don't need to do anything with this exception, a clone method could declare this exception in its throws clause and let the calling code deal with it. But CloneNotSupportedException is a checked exception, and it's generally unlikely, so it's often simpler to have your clone( ) method catch it and rethrow it as an unchecked exception, as this code does.

Calling Object's clone( ) creates a stateful, shallow copy down inside the JVM. That is, it creates a new object, and copies all the fields from the old object into the new. It then returns the new reference as an Object; you need to cast it to the appropriate object type. So if that's all there is, why do you even have to write this method? The reason is to give you a chance to do any preservation of state that is required in cloning your objects. For example, if your class has any references to other objects (and most real-world classes do), you may well want to clone them as well! The default clone method simply copies all the object's state so that you now have two references to each object. Or you might have to close and reopen files to avoid having two threads (see Chapter 24) reading from or writing into the same file. In effect, what you have to do here depends on what the rest of your class does.

Now suppose that you clone a class containing an array of objects. You now have two references to objects in the array, but further additions to the array will be made only in one array or the other. Imagine a Vector, Stack, or other collection class being used in your class, and your object gets cloned!

The bottom line is that most object references need to be cloned.

Even if you don't need clone( ), your subclasses may! If you didn't provide clone( ) in a class subclassed from Object, your subclasses will probably get the Object version, which causes problems if there are collections or other mutable objects referred to. As a general rule, you should provide clone( ) even if only your own subclasses would need it.

### Difficulty in the standard API

The java.util.Observable class (designed to implement the Model-View-Controller pattern with AWT or Swing applications) contains a private Vector but no clone method to deep-clone it. Thus, Observable objects cannot safely be cloned, ever!

# 9.5   The Finalize Method

## Problem

You want to have some action taken when your objects are removed from service.

## Solution

Use finalize( )—but don't trust it—or write your own end-of-life method.

## Discussion

Developers coming from a C++ background tend to form a mental map that has a line of equivalency drawn from C++ destructors to Java finalizers. In C++, destructors are called automatically when you delete an object. Java, though, has no such operator as delete; objects are freed automatically by a part of the Java runtime called the *garbage collector*, or GC. GC runs as a background thread in Java processes and looks around every so often to see if any objects are no longer referred to by any reference variable. When it runs, as it frees objects, it calls their finalize( ) methods.

For example, what if you (or some code you called) invoke System.exit( )? In this case, the entire JVM would cease to exist (assuming there isn't a security manager that denies your program permission to do so), and the finalizer is never run. Similarly, a "memory leak," or mistakenly held reference to your object, also prevents finalizers from running.

Can't you just ensure that all finalizers get run simply by calling System.runFinalizersOnExit(true)? Not really! This method is deprecated (see Recipe 1.9); the documentation notes:

> This method is inherently unsafe. It may result in finalizers being called on live objects while other threads are concurrently manipulating those objects, resulting in erratic behavior or deadlock.

So what if you need some kind of cleanup? You must take responsibility for defining a method and invoking it before you let any object of that class go out of reference. You might call such a method cleanUp( ).

JDK 1.3 introduced the runtime method addShutdownHook( ), to which you pass a nonstarted Thread subclass object; if the virtual machine has a chance, it runs your shutdown hook code as part of termination. This normally works, unless the VM was terminated abruptly as by a kill signal on Unix or a KillProcess on Win32, or the VM aborts due to detecting internal corruption of its data structures. Program ShutdownDemo shown in Example 9-1 contains both a finalize( ) method and a shutdown hook. The program normally exits while holding a reference to the object with the finalize method. If run with -f as an argument, it "frees" the object and "forces" a GC run by calling System.gc( ); only in this case does the finalize( ) method run. The shutdown hook is run in every case.

*Example 9-1. Shutdown Demo*

```
/** Demonstrate how finalize() methods and shutdownHooks interact
 *  with calls to System.exit().
 */
public class ShutdownDemo {
    public static void main(String[] args) throws Exception {

        // Create an Object with a finalize() method.
        Object f = new Object() {
```

*Example 9-1. Shutdown Demo (continued)*

```
        public void finalize( ) {
            System.out.println( "Running finalize( )");
        }
    };

    // Add a shutdownHook to the JVM
    Runtime.getRuntime().addShutdownHook(new Thread( ) {
        public void run( ) {
            System.out.println("Running Shutdown Hook");
        }
    });

    // Unless the user puts -f (for "free") on the command line,
    // call System.exit while holding a reference to
    // Object f, which can therefore not be finalized( ).

    if (args.length == 1 && args[0].equals("-f")) {
        f = null;
        System.gc( );
    }

    System.out.println("Calling System.exit( )");
    System.exit(0);
    }
}
```

The bottom line? There's no guarantee, but finalizers and shutdown hooks both have pretty good odds of being run.

# 9.6   Using Inner Classes

## Problem

You need to write a private class, or a class to be used in one other class at the most.

## Solution

Use a nonpublic class or an inner class.

## Discussion

A nonpublic class can be written as part of another class's source file, but it is not included inside that class. An *inner class* is Java terminology for a nonstatic class defined inside another class. Inner classes were first popularized with the advent of JDK 1.1 for use as event handlers for GUI applications (see Recipe 14.4), but they have a much wider application.

Inner classes can, in fact, be constructed in several contexts. An inner class defined as a member of a class can be instantiated anywhere in that class. An inner class defined inside a method can be referred to later only in the same method. Inner classes can also be named or anonymous. A named inner class has a full name that is compiler-dependent; the standard JVM uses a name like MainClass$InnerClass.class for the resulting file. An anonymous inner class, similarly, has a compiler-dependent name; the JVM uses MainClass$1.class, MainClass$2.class, and so on.

These classes cannot be instantiated in any other context; any explicit attempt to refer to, say, OtherMainClass$InnerClass, is caught at compile time:

```java
import java.awt.event.*;
import javax.swing.*;

public class AllClasses {
    /** Inner class can be used anywhere in this file */
    public class Data {
        int x;
        int y;
    }
    public void getResults() {
        JButton b = new JButton("Press me");
        b.addActionListener(new ActionListener() {
            public void actionPerformed(ActionEvent evt) {
                System.out.println("Thanks for pressing me");
            }
        });
    }
}

/** Class contained in same file as AllClasses, but can be used
 * (with a warning) in other contexts.
 */
class AnotherClass {
    // methods and fields here...
}
```

# 9.7    Providing Callbacks via Interfaces

## Problem

You want to provide *callbacks*, that is, have unrelated classes call back into your code.

## Solution

One way is to use a Java interface.

## Discussion

An *interface* is a class-like entity that can contain only abstract methods and final fields. As we've seen, interfaces are used a lot in Java! In the standard API, the following are a few of the commonly used interfaces:

- Runnable, Comparable, and Cloneable (in java.lang)
- List, Set, Map, and Enumeration/Iterator (in the Collections API; see Chapter 7)
- ActionListener, WindowListener, and others (in the AWT GUI; see Recipe 14.4)
- Driver, Connection, Statement, and ResultSet (in JDBC; see Recipe 20.4)

---

## Subclass, Abstract Class, or Interface?

There is usually more than one way to skin a cat. Some problems can be solved by sub-classing, by use of abstract classes, or by interfaces. The following general guidelines may help:

- *Use an abstract class* when you want to provide a template for a series of sub-classes, all of which may inherit some of their functionality from the parent class but are required to implement some of it themselves. (Any subclass of a geometric Shapes class might have to provide a computeArea( ) method; since the top-level Shapes class cannot do this, it would be abstract. This is implemented in Recipe 9.8.)
- *Subclass* whenever you want to extend a class and add some functionality to it, whether the parent class is abstract or not. See the standard Java APIs and the examples in Recipes 1.14, 5.11, 9.12, 10.10, and others throughout this book.
- *Subclass* when you are required to extend a given class. Applets (see Recipe 18.2), servlets, and others use subclassing to ensure "base" functionality in classes that are dynamically loaded (see Recipe 25.3).
- *Define an interface* when there is no common parent class with the desired functionality and when you want only certain unrelated classes to have that functionality (see the PowerSwitchable interface in Recipe 9.7).
- *Use interfaces as "markers"* to indicate something about a class. The standard API uses Cloneable (Recipe 9.4) and Serializable (Recipe 10.18) as markers.

---

- The "remote interface"—the contact between the client and the server—is specified as an Interface (in RMI, CORBA, and EJB)

Suppose we are generating a futuristic building management system. To be energy-efficient, we want to be able to remotely turn off (at night and on weekends) such things as room lights and computer monitors, which use a lot of energy. Assume we have some kind of "remote control" technology. It could be a commercial version of BSR's house-light control technology X10, it could be Bluetooth or 802.11—it doesn't matter. What matters is that we have to be very careful what we turn off. It would cause great ire if we turned off computer processors automatically—people often leave things running overnight. It would be a matter of public safety if we ever turned off the building emergency lighting.[*]

---

[*] Of course these lights wouldn't have remote power-off. But the computers might, for maintenance purposes.

So we've come up with the design shown in Figure 9-1.

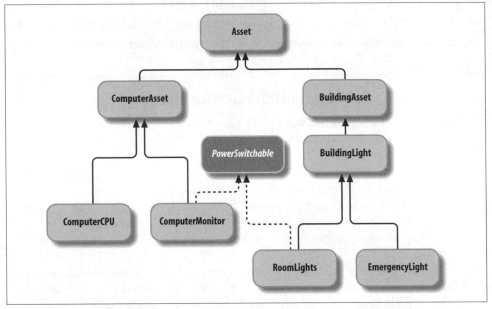

*Figure 9-1. Classes for a building management system*

The code for these classes is not shown (it's pretty trivial) but it's in the online source. The top-level classes—BuildingLight and Asset—are abstract classes. You can't instantiate them, as they don't have any specific functionality. To ensure—both at compile time and at runtime—that we can never switch off the emergency lighting, we need only ensure that the class representing it, EmergencyLight, does not implement the PowerSwitchable interface.

Note that we can't very well use direct inheritance here. No common ancestor class includes both ComputerMonitor and RoomLights that doesn't also include ComputerCPU and EmergencyLight. Use interfaces to define functionality in unrelated classes.

How we use these is demonstrated by the BuildingManagement class; this class is not part of the hierarchy shown in Figure 9-1, but instead uses a collection (actually an array, to make the code simpler for illustrative purposes) of Asset objects from that hierarchy.

Items that can't be switched must nonetheless be in the database, for various purposes (auditing, insurance, and so on). In the method that turns things off, the code is careful to check whether each object in the database is an instance of the PowerSwitchable interface. If so, the object is casted to PowerSwitchable so that its powerDown( ) method can be called. If not, the object is skipped, thus preventing any possibility of turning out the emergency lights or shutting off a machine that is busy running Seti@Home, downloading a big MP3 playlist, or performing system backups.

---

```
/**
 * BuildingManagement - control an energy-saving building.
 * This class shows how we might control the objects in an office
 * that can safely be powered off at nighttime to save energy - lots of
 * it, when applied to a large office!
 */
public class BuildingManagement {

    Asset things[] = new Asset[24];
    int numItems = 0;

    /** goodNight is called from a timer Thread at 2200, or when we
     * get the "shutdown" command from the security guard.
     */
    public void goodNight() {
        for (int i=0; i<things.length; i++)
            if (things[i] instanceof PowerSwitchable)
                ((PowerSwitchable)things[i]).powerDown();
    }

    // goodMorning() would be the same, but call each one's powerUp().

    /** Add an Asset to this building */
    public void add(Asset thing) {
        System.out.println("Adding " + thing);
        things[numItems++] = thing;
    }

    /** The main program */
    public static void main(String[] av) {
        BuildingManagement b1 = new BuildingManagement();
        b1.add(new RoomLights(101));      // control lights in room 101
        b1.add(new EmergencyLight(101));    // and emerg. lights.
        // add the computer on desk#4 in room 101
        b1.add(new ComputerCPU(10104));
        // and its monitor
        b1.add(new ComputerMonitor(10104));

        // time passes, and the sun sets...
        b1.goodNight();
    }
}
```

When you run this program, it shows all the items being added, but only the
PowerSwitchable ones being switched off:

```
> java BuildingManagement
Adding RoomLights@2dc77f32
Adding EmergencyLight@2e3b7f32
Adding ComputerCPU@2e637f32
Adding ComputerMonitor@2f1f7f32
Dousing lights in room 101
Dousing monitor at desk 10104
>
```

## 9.8  Polymorphism/Abstract Methods

### Problem

You want each of a number of subclasses to provide its own version of one or more methods.

### Solution

Make the method abstract in the parent class; this makes the compiler ensure that each subclass implements it.

### Discussion

A hypothetical drawing program uses a Shape subclass for anything that is drawn. Shape has an abstract method called computeArea( ) that computes the exact area of the given shape:

```
public abstract class Shape {
    protected int x, y;
    public abstract double computeArea();
}
```

A Rectangle subclass, for example, has a computeArea( ) that multiplies width times height and returns the result:

```
public class Rectangle extends Shape {
    double width, height;
    public double computeArea() {
        return width * height;
    }
}
```

A Circle subclass returns $\pi r^2$ :

```
public class Circle extends Shape {
    double radius;
    public double computeArea() {
        return Math.PI * radius * radius;
    }
}
```

This system has a very high degree of generality. In the main program, we can pass over a collection of Shape objects and—here's the real beauty—call computeArea( ) on any Shape subclass object without having to worry about what kind of shape it is. Java's polymorphic methods automatically call the correct computeArea( ) method in the class of which the object was originally constructed:

```
/** Part of a main program using Shape objects */
public class Main {

    Collection allShapes;    // created in a Constructor, not shown
```

```
        /** Iterate over all the Shapes, getting their areas */
        public double totalAreas() {
            Iterator it = allShapes.iterator();
            double total = 0.0;
            while (it.hasNext()) {
                Shape s = (Shape)it.next();
                total += s.computeArea();
            }
            return total;
        }
    }
```

Polymorphism is a great boon for software maintenance: if a new subclass is added, the code in the main program does not change. Further, all the code that is specific to, say, polygon handling, is all in one place: in the source file for the Polygon class. This is a big improvement over older languages, where type fields in a structure or record were used with case or switch statements scattered all across the software. Java makes software more reliable and maintainable with the use of polymorphism.

# 9.9   Passing Values

## Problem

You need to pass a number like an int into a routine and get back the routine's updated version of that value in addition to the routine's return value.

This often comes up in working through strings; the routine may need to return a boolean, say, or the number of characters transferred, but also needs to increment an integer array or string index in the calling class.

It is also useful in constructors, which can't return a value but may need to indicate that they have "consumed" or processed a certain number of characters from within a string, such as when the string will be further processed in a subsequent call.

## Solution

Use a specialized class such as the one presented here.

## Discussion

The Integer class is one of Java's predefined Number subclasses, mentioned in the Introduction to Chapter 5. It serves as a wrapper for an int value and also has static methods for parsing and formatting integers.

It's fine as it is, but you may want something simpler.

Here is a class I wrote, called MutableInteger, that is like an Integer but specialized by omitting the overhead of Number and providing only the set, get, and incr operations, the latter overloaded to provide a no-argument version that performs the increment (++) operator on its value, and also a one-integer version that adds that increment into the value (analogous to the += operator). Since Java doesn't support operator overloading, the calling class has to call these methods instead of invoking the operations syntactically, as you would on an int. For applications that need this functionality, the advantages outweigh this minor syntactic restriction. First, let's look at an example of how it might be used. Assume you need to call a scanner function called, say, parse( ) and get back both a Boolean (indicating whether a value was found) and an integer value indicating where it was found:

```
import com.darwinsys.util.*;

/** Show use of MutableInteger to "pass back" a value in addition
 * to a function's return value.
 */
public class StringParse {
    /** This is the function that has a return value of true but
     * also "passes back" the offset into the String where a
     * value was found. Contrived example!
     */
    public static boolean parse(String in,
        char lookFor, MutableInteger whereFound) {
        int i = in.indexOf(lookFor);
        if (i == -1)
            return false;    // not found
        whereFound.setValue(i);     // say where found
        return true;         // say that it was found
    }

    public static void main(String[] args) {
        MutableInteger mi = new MutableInteger( );
        String text = "Hello, World";
        char c = 'W';
        if (parse(text, c, mi)) {
            System.out.println("Character " + c + " found at offset "
                + mi + " in " + text);
        } else {
            System.out.println("Not found");
        }
    }
}
```

Now many OO purists argue—convincingly—that you shouldn't do this, and that you can always rewrite it so there is only one return value. Either return and have the caller interpret a single value (in this case, return the offset in the return statement, and let the user know that -1 indicates not found), or define a trivial wrapper class containing both the integer and the Boolean. However, there is precedent in the standard API: this code is remarkably similar to how the ParsePosition class (see Recipe 6.5) is used. Anyway, this functionality is requested often enough that I feel justified in showing how to do it, accompanied by this disclaimer: try to avoid doing it this way in new code!

Having said all that, here is the MutableInteger class:

```java
package com.darwinsys.lang;

/** A MutableInteger is like an Integer but mutable, to avoid the
 * excess object creation involved in
 * c = new Integer(c.getInt()+1)
 * which can get expensive if done a lot.
 * Not subclassed from Integer, since Integer is final (for performance :-))
 */
public class MutableInteger {
    private int value = 0;

    public MutableInteger() {
    }

    public MutableInteger(int i) {
        value = i;
    }

    public void incr() {
        value++;
    }
    public void incr(int amt) {
        value += amt;
    }

    public void decr() {
        value--;
    }

    public void setValue(int i) {
        value = i;
    }

    public int getValue() {
        return value;
    }

    public String toString() {
        return Integer.toString(value);
    }

    public static String toString(int val) {
        return Integer.toString(val);
    }

    public static int parseInt(String str) {
        return Integer.parseInt(str);
    }
}
```

## See Also

As mentioned, this use of MutableInteger could be replaced with ParsePosition. However, MutableInteger has other uses: it makes a fine in-memory counter in a servlet or other application.

## 9.10   Enforcing the Singleton Pattern

### Problem

You want to be sure there is only one instance of your class in a given Java Virtual Machine.

### Solution

Make your class enforce the Singleton Pattern (see *Design Patterns*, page 127), primarily by having only a private constructor(s).

### Discussion

It is often useful to ensure that only one instance of a class gets created, usually to funnel all requests for some resource through a single point. An example of a Singleton from the standard API is java.lang.Runtime; you cannot create instances of Runtime, you simply ask for a reference by calling the static method Runtime.getRuntime(). Singleton is also a good example of a design pattern because it can be easily implemented.

The easiest implementation consists of a private constructor and a field to hold its result, and a static accessor method with a name like getInstance().

The private field can be assigned from within a static initializer block or, more simply, using an initializer. The getInstance() method (which must be public) then simply returns this instance:

```
// Simple demonstration Singleton instance
public class Singleton {

    private static Singleton singleton = new Singleton();

    /** A private Constructor prevents any other class from instantiating. */
    private Singleton() {
    }

    /** Static 'instance' method */
    public static Singleton getInstance() {
        return singleton;
    }

    // other methods protected by singleton-ness would be here...
}
```

Note that the method advocated in *Design Patterns*, of using "lazy evaluation" in the getInstance() method, is not necessary in Java, since Java already uses "lazy loading." Your Singleton class will probably not get loaded unless its getInstance() is called, so there is no point in trying to defer the singleton construction until it's needed by having getInstance() test the singleton variable for null and creating the singleton there.

Using this class is equally simple: simply get and retain the reference, and invoke methods on it:

```
public class SingletonDemo {
        public static void main(String[] args) {
                Singleton tmp = Singleton.getInstance( );
                tmp.demoMethod( );
        }
}
```

Some commentators believe that a Singleton should also provide a public final clone( ) method (see Recipe 9.4) to avoid subclasses that "cheat" and clone( ) the singleton. However, on inspection, it is clear that a class with only a private constructor cannot be subclassed, so this paranoia does not appear to be necessary.

## Variation

One variation is to make all methods static (as java.lang.Math does), but this works only if methods do not need to share state. You also lose the scalability that is inherent in the Singleton pattern: if you later need, say, 2 or 3 instances, you could easily change the getInstance( ) method to give out references to one of several, but you can't do that if all the methods are static.

## See Also

The Collections class in java.util has methods singletonList( ), singletonMap( ), and singletonSet( ), which give out an immutable List, Map, or Set respectively, containing only the one object that is passed to the method. This does not, of course, convert the object into a Singleton in the sense of preventing that object from being cloned or other instances from being constructed, but it does qualify by providing a single access point that always returns the same instance.

# 9.11  Roll Your Own Exceptions

## Problem

You'd like to use an application-specific exception class or two.

## Solution

Go ahead and subclass Exception or RuntimeException.

## Discussion

In theory, you could subclass Throwable directly, but that's considered rude. You normally subclass Exception (if you want a checked exception) or RuntimeException (if you want an unchecked exception). Checked exceptions are those that an application developer is required to catch or "throw away" by listing them in the throws clause of the invoking method.

When subclassing either of these, it is customary to provide at least a no-argument and a one-string argument constructor:

```
/** A ChessMoveException is thrown when the user makes an illegal move. */
public class ChessMoveException extends RuntimeException {
        public ChessMoveException () {
                super();
        }
        public ChessMoveException (String msg) {
                super(msg);
        }
}
```

### See Also

The Javadoc documentation for Exception lists a very large number of subclasses; you might look there first to see if there is one you can use.

## 9.12  Program: Plotter

Not because it is very sophisticated, but because it is simple, this program serves as an example of some of the things we've covered in this chapter, and also, in its sub-classes, provides a springboard for other discussions. This class describes a series of old-fashioned (i.e., common in the 1970s and 1980s) pen plotters. A pen plotter, in case you've never seen one, is a device that moves a pen around a piece of paper and draws things. It can lift the pen off the paper or lower it, and it can draw lines, letters, and so on. Before the rise of laser printers and ink-jet printers, pen plotters were the dominant means of preparing charts of all sorts, as well as presentation slides (this was, ah, well before the rise of programs like Harvard Presents and Microsoft Power-Point). Today few companies still manufacture pen plotters, but I use them here because they are simple enough to be well understood from this brief description.

I'll present a high-level class that abstracts the key characteristics of a series of such plotters made by different vendors. It would be used, for example, in an analytical or data-exploration program to draw colorful charts showing the relationships found in data. But I don't want my main program to worry about the gory details of any partic-ular brand of plotter, so I'll abstract into a Plotter class, whose source is as follows:

```
/**
 * Plotter abstract class. Must be subclassed
 * for X, DOS, Penman, HP plotter, etc.
 *
 * Coordinate space: X = 0 at left, increases to right.
 *         Y = 0 at top, increases downward (same as AWT).
 */
public abstract class Plotter {
    public final int MAXX = 800;
    public final int MAXY = 600;
    /** Current X co-ordinate (same reference frame as AWT!) */
    protected int curx;
```

```
/** Current Y co-ordinate (same reference frame as AWT!) */
protected int cury;
/** The current state: up or down */
protected boolean penIsUp;
/** The current color */
protected int penColor;

Plotter() {
    penIsUp = true;
    curx = 0; cury = 0;
}
abstract void rmoveTo(int incrx, int incry);
abstract void moveTo(int absx, int absy);
abstract void penUp();
abstract void penDown();
abstract void penColor(int c);

abstract void setFont(String fName, int fSize);
abstract void drawString(String s);

/* Concrete methods */

/** Draw a box of width w and height h */
public void drawBox(int w, int h) {
    penDown();
    rmoveTo(w, 0);
    rmoveTo(0, h);
    rmoveTo(-w, 0);
    rmovelo(0, -h);
    penUp();
}

/** Draw a box given an AWT Dimension for its size */
public void drawBox(java.awt.Dimension d) {
    drawBox(d.width, d.height);
}

/** Draw a box given an AWT Rectangle for its location and size */
public void drawBox(java.awt.Rectangle r) {
    moveTo(r.x, r.y);
    drawBox(r.width, r.height);
}
}
```

Note the variety of abstract methods. Those related to motion, pen control, or drawing are left out, due to the number of different methods for dealing with them. However, the method for drawing a rectangle (drawBox) has a default implementation,
which simply puts the currently selected pen onto the paper at the last-moved-to
location, draws the four sides, and raises the pen. Subclasses for "smarter" plotters
will likely override this method, but subclasses for less-evolved plotters will probably use the default version. This method also has two overloaded convenience methods for cases where the client has an AWT Dimension for the size or an AWT
Rectangle for the location and size.

To demonstrate one of the subclasses of this program, consider the following simple "driver" program. The Class.forName( ) near the beginning of main is discussed in Recipe 25.2; for now you can take my word that it simply creates an instance of the given subclass, which we store in a Plotter reference named "r" and use to draw the plot:

```
/** Main program, driver for Plotter class.
 * This is to simulate a larger graphics application such as GnuPlot.
 */
public class PlotDriver {

    /** Construct a Plotter driver, and try it out. */
    public static void main(String[] argv)
    {
        Plotter r ;
        if (argv.length != 1) {
            System.err.println("Usage: PlotDriver driverclass");
            return;
        }
        try {
            Class c = Class.forName(argv[0]);
            Object o = c.newInstance( );
            if (!(o instanceof Plotter))
                throw new ClassNotFoundException("Not instanceof Plotter");
            r = (Plotter)o;
        } catch (ClassNotFoundException e) {
            System.err.println("Sorry, "+argv[0]+" not a plotter class");
            return;
        } catch (Exception e) {
            e.printStackTrace( );
            return;
        }
        r.penDown( );
        r.penColor(1);
        r.moveTo(200, 200);
        r.penColor(2);
        r.drawBox(123, 200);
        r.rmoveTo(10, 20);
        r.penColor(3);
        r.drawBox(123, 200);
        r.penUp( );
        r.moveTo(300, 100);
        r.penDown( );
        r.setFont("Helvetica", 14);
        r.drawString("Hello World");
        r.penColor(4);
        r.drawBox(10, 10);
    }
}
```

We'll see more examples of this Plotter class and its relatives in several upcoming chapters.

# CHAPTER 10

# Input and Output

## 10.0   Introduction

Most programs need to interact with the outside world, and one common way of doing so is by reading and writing files. Files are normally on some persistent medium such as a disk drive, and, for the most part, we shall happily ignore the differences between a hard disk (and all the operating system-dependent filesystem types), a floppy or zip drive, a CD-ROM, and others. For now, they're just files.

This chapter covers all the normal input/output operations such as opening/closing and reading/writing files. Files are assumed to reside on some kind of file store or permanent storage. I don't discuss how such a filesystem or disk I/O system works—consult a book on operating system design or a platform-specific book on system internals or filesystem design. Network filesystems such as Sun's Network File System (NFS, common on Unix and available for Windows through products such as Hummingbird NFS Maestro), Macintosh Appletalk File System (used for OS 9; available for Unix via the open source Netatalk), and SMB (Windows network filesystem, available for Unix with the open source Samba program) are assumed to work "just like" disk filesystems, except where noted.

JDK 1.5 introduced the Formatter and Scanner classes, which provide substantial new functionality. Formatter allows many formatting tasks to be performed either into a String or to almost any output destination. Scanner parses many kinds of objects, again either from a String or from almost any input source. These are new and very powerful; each is given its own recipe in this chapter.

### Streams and Readers/Writers

Java provides two sets of classes for reading and writing. The Stream section of package java.io (see Figure 10-1) is for reading or writing bytes of data. Older languages tended to assume that a byte (which is a machine-specific collection of bits, usually eight bits on modern computers) is exactly the same thing as a "character"—a letter, digit, or other linguistic element. However, Java is designed to be used internationally, and eight bits is simply not enough to handle the many different character sets used around the world. Script-based languages like Arabic and Indian languages, and pictographic languages like Chinese and Japanese, each have many more than 256 characters, the maximum that can be represented in an eight-bit byte. The unification of these many character code sets is called, not surprisingly, Unicode. Actually, it's not the first such unification, but it's the most widely used standard at this time. Both Java and XML use Unicode as their character sets, allowing you to read and write text in any of these human languages. But you have to use Readers and Writers, not Streams, for textual data.

Unicode itself doesn't solve the entire problem. Many of these human languages were used on computers long before Unicode was invented, and they didn't all pick the same representation as Unicode. And they all have zillions of files *encoded* in a particular representation that isn't Unicode. So conversion routines are needed when reading and writing to convert between Unicode String objects used inside the Java machine and the particular external representation that a user's files are written in. These converters are packaged inside a powerful set of classes called Readers and Writers. Readers and Writers are always used instead of InputStreams and OutputStreams when you want to deal with characters instead of bytes. We'll see more on this conversion, and how to specify which conversion, a little later in this chapter.

## See Also

One topic *not* addressed in depth here is the Java "New IO" package (it was "new" in 1.4). NIO is more complex to use, and the benefits accrue primarily in large-scale server-side processing. Recipe 4.5 provides one example of using NIO. The NIO package is given full coverage in *Java NIO* by Ron Hitchens (O'Reilly).

Another issue not addressed here is hardcopy printing. Java's scheme for printing onto paper uses the same graphics model as is used in AWT, the basic Window System package. For this reason, I defer discussion of printing to Chapter 13.

Another topic not covered here is that of having the read or write occur concurrently with other program activity. This requires the use of threads, or multiple flows of control within a single program. Threaded I/O is a necessity in many programs: those reading from slow devices such as tape drives, those reading from or writing to network connections, and those with a GUI. For this reason the topic is given considerable attention, in the context of multithreaded applications, in Chapter 24.

# 10.1  Reading Standard Input

## Problem

You really do need to read from the standard input, or console. One reason is that simple test programs are often console-driven. Another is that some programs naturally require a lot of interaction with the user and you want something faster than a GUI (consider an interactive mathematics or statistical exploration program). Yet

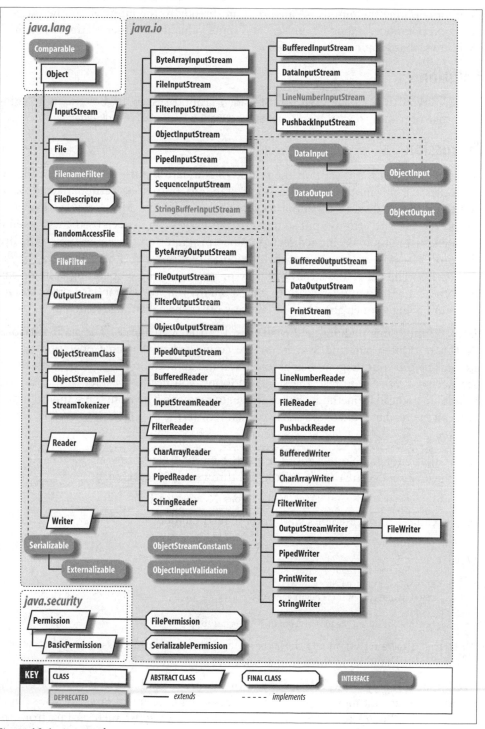

Figure 10-1. java.io classes

another is piping the output of one program directly to the input of another, a very common operation among Unix users and quite valuable on other platforms, such as Windows, that support this operation.

## Solution

To read bytes, wrap a `BufferedInputStream( )` around `System.in`. For the more common case of reading text, use an `InputStreamReader` and a `BufferedReader`.

## Discussion

Most desktop platforms support the notion of standard input—a keyboard, a file, or the output from another program—and standard output—a terminal window, a printer, a file on disk, or the input to yet another program. Most such systems also support a standard error output so that error messages can be seen by the user even if the standard output is being redirected. When programs on these platforms start up, the three streams are preassigned to particular platform-dependent handles, or *file descriptors*. The net result is that ordinary programs on these operating systems can read the standard input or write to the standard output or standard error stream without having to open any files or make any other special arrangements.

Java continues this tradition and enshrines it in the `System` class. The static variables `System.in`, `System.out`, and `System.err` are connected to the three operating system streams before your program begins execution (an application is free to reassign these; see Recipe 10.9). So, to read the standard input, you need only refer to the variable `System.in` and call its methods. For example, to read one byte from the standard input, you call the read method of `System.in`, which returns the byte in an `int` variable:

```
int b = System.in.read( );
```

But is that enough? No, because the `read( )` method can throw an `IOException`. So you must either declare that your program throws an `IOException`, as in:

```
public static void main(String ap[]) throws IOException {
```

or you can put a try/catch block around the read method:

```
int b = 0;
try {
    b = System.in.read( );
} catch (Exception e) {
    System.out.println("Caught " + e);
}
System.out.println("Read this data: " + (char)b);
```

Note that I cavalierly convert the byte to a char for printing, assuming that you've typed a valid character in the terminal window.

Well, that certainly works and gives you the ability to read a byte at a time from the standard input. But most applications are designed in terms of larger units, such as integers, or a line of text. To read a value of a known type, such as `int`, from the standard input, you can use the Scanner class (covered in more detail in Recipe 10.5):

```
// part of ReadStdinInt15.java
Scanner sc = Scanner.create(System.in);      // Requires JDK 1.5
int i = sc.nextInt();
```

For reading characters of text with an input character converter so that your program will work with multiple input encodings around the world, use a Reader class. The particular subclass that allows you to read lines of characters is a BufferedReader. But there's a hitch. Remember I mentioned those two categories of input classes, Streams and Readers? But I also said that System.in is a Stream, and you want a Reader. How do you get from a Stream to a Reader? A "crossover" class called InputStreamReader is tailor-made for this purpose. Just pass your Stream (like System.in) to the InputStreamReader constructor and you get back a Reader, which you in turn pass to the BufferedReader constructor. The usual idiom for writing this in Java is to nest the constructor calls:

```
BufferedReader is = new BufferedReader(new InputStreamReader(System.in));
```

You can then read lines of text from the standard input using the readLine() method. This method takes no argument and returns a String that is made up for you by readLine() containing the characters (converted to Unicode) from the next line of text in the file. If there are no more lines of text, the constant null is returned:

```
import java.io.*;

/**
 * Read and print, using BufferedReader from System.in, onto System.out
 */
public class CatStdin {

    public static void main(String av[]) {
        try {
            BufferedReader is = new BufferedReader(
                new InputStreamReader(System.in));
            String inputLine;

            while ((inputLine = is.readLine()) != null) {
                System.out.println(inputLine);
            }
            is.close();
        } catch (IOException e) {
            System.out.println("IOException: " + e);
        }
    }
}
```

Now that we've covered the InputStreamReader, and because it's something that people have asked me several times, I'll show how to read an Integer from the standard input if you don't have 1.5:

```
import java.io.*;
/**
 * Read an int from Standard Input
 */
```

```
public class ReadStdinInt {
    public static void main(String[] ap) {
        String line = null;
        int val = 0;
        try {
            BufferedReader is = new BufferedReader(
                new InputStreamReader(System.in));
            line = is.readLine();
            val = Integer.parseInt(line);
        } catch (NumberFormatException ex) {
            System.err.println("Not a valid number: " + line);
        } catch (IOException e) {
            System.err.println("Unexpected IO ERROR: " + e);
        }
        System.out.println("I read this number: " + val);
    }
}
```

There are many other things you might want to do with lines of text read from a Reader. In the demo program shown in this recipe, I just printed them. In the demo program in Recipe 10.6, I convert them to integer values using Integer.parseInt() (also see Recipe 5.1) or using a DecimalFormat (Recipe 5.8). You can interpret them as dates (Recipe 6.5), or break them into words with a StringTokenizer (Recipe 3.2). You can also process the lines as you read them; several methods for doing so are listed in Recipe 10.4.

# 10.2   Writing Standard Output

## Problem

You want your program to write to the standard output.

## Solution

Use System.out.

## Discussion

In certain circumstances (such as a server program with no connection back to the user's terminal), System.out can become a very important debugging tool (assuming that you can find out what file the server program has redirected standard output into; see Recipe 10.9).

System.out is a PrintStream, so in every introductory text you see a program containing this line, or one like it:*

```
System.out.println("Hello World of Java");
```

---

* All the examples in this recipe are found in one file, *PrintStandardOutput.java*.

The println method is polymorphic; it has several forms for Object (which obviously calls the given object's toString( ) method), for String, and for each of the primitive types (int, float, boolean, etc.). Each takes only one argument, so it is common to use string concatenation:

```
System.out.println("The answer is " + myAnswer + " at this time.");
```

Remember that string concatenation is also polymorphic: you can "add" anything at all to a string, and the result is a string.

Up to here I have been using a Stream, System.out. What if you want to use a Writer? The PrintWriter class has all the same methods as PrintStream and a constructor that takes a Stream, so you can just say:

```
PrintWriter pw = new PrintWriter(System.out);
pw.println("The answer is " + myAnswer + " at this time.");
```

One caveat with this string concatenation is that if you are appending a bunch of things, and a number and a character come together at the front, they are added before concatenation due to the precedence rules. So don't do this:

```
System.out.println(i + '=' + " the answer.");
```

Assuming that i is an integer, then i + '=' (i added to the equals sign) is a valid *numeric* expression, which will result in a single value of type int. If the variable i has the value 42, and the character = in a Unicode (or ASCII) code chart has the value 61, this prints:

```
103 the answer.
```

The wrong value and no equals sign! Safer methods include using parentheses, using double quotes around the equals sign, and using a StringBuffer (see Recipe 3.3) or a MessageFormat (see Recipe 15.10).

# 10.3  Printing with the 1.5 Formatter

## Problem

You have JDK 1.5 and you want the ease of use that the java.util.Formatter class brings to simple printing tasks.

## Solution

Use Formatter for printing values with fine-grained control over the formatting.

## Discussion

The 1.5 Formatter class is patterned after C's printf routines. In fact, PrintStream and PrintWriter have convenience routines named printf( ), which simply delegate to PrintStream's format( ) method, which uses a default Formatter instance. However, since Java is an object-oriented language, the methods are strongly type-checked, and invalid arguments will throw an exception rather than generating gibberish.

The underlying Formatter class in java.util works on a String containing *format codes*. For each item that you want to format, you put a format code. The format code consists of a percent sign (%), an argument number followed by a dollar sign ($), an optional field width or precision, and a format type (d for decimal integer, that is, an integer with no decimal point, f for floating point, and so on). A simple use might look like the following:

```
System.out.format("%1$04d - the year of %2$f", 1951, Math.PI);
```

As shown in Figure 10-2, the "%1$04d" controls formatting of the year and the "%2$f" controls formatting of the value of PI.

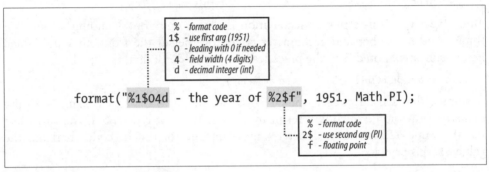

*Figure 10-2. Format codes examined*

Many format codes are available; Table 10-1 lists some of the more common ones. For a complete description, refer to the Javadoc for java.util.Formatter.

*Table 10-1. Formatter format codes*

| Code | Meaning |
| --- | --- |
| c | Character (argument must be char or integral type containing valid character value) |
| d | "decimal int"—integer to be printed as a decimal (radix 10) with no decimal point (argument must be integral type). |
| f | Floating point value with decimal fraction (must be numeric); field width may be followed by decimal point and fractional digit field width; e.g., 7.2f. |
| e | Floating point value in scientific notation. |
| g | Floating point value, as per f or e, depending on magnitude. |
| s | General format; if value is null, prints "null", else if arg implements Formattable, format as per arg.formatTo( ); else format as per arg.toString( ). |
| t | Date codes; follow with secondary code. Common date codes are shown in Table 10-2. Argument must be long, Long, Calendar, or Date. |
| n | Newline; insert the platform-dependent line ending character. |
| % | Insert a literal % character. |

Some examples of using a Formatter are shown in *FormatterDemo.java*, in Example 10-1.

*Example 10-1. FormatterDemo.java*

```java
import java.util.Formatter;

/** Demonstrate some usage patterns and format-code examples
 * of the Formatter class (new in JDK 1.5).
 */
public class FormatterDemo {
    public static void main(String[] args) {

        // The arguments to all these format methods consist of
        // a format code String and 1 or more arguments.
        // Each format code consists of the following:
        // % - code lead-in
        // N$ - which parameter number (1-based) after the code
        // N - field width
        // L - format letter (d: decimal(int); f: float; s: general; many more)
        // For the full(!) story, see javadoc for java.util.Formatter.

        Formatter fmtr = new Formatter();
        Object result = fmtr.format("%1$04d - the year of %2$f", 1951, Math.PI);
        System.out.println(result);

        // A shorter way of doing things. But this
        // way you must provide the newline delimiter
        System.out.format("%1$04d - the year of %2$f%n", 1951, Math.PI);

        // So is this
        System.out.printf("%1$04d - the year of %2$f%n", 1951, Math.PI);

        // Format doubles with more control
        System.out.printf("PI is about %1$4.2f", Math.PI);
    }
}
```

Running FormatterDemo produces this:

```
C:> javac -source 1.5 FormatterDates.java
C:> java FormatterDates
1951 - The year of 3.141593
1951 - The year of 3.141593
1951 - The year of 3.141593
PI is about 3.14
```

For date and time formatting, a large variety of format codes are available.[*] Each must be preceded by a t, so to format the first argument as a year, you would use %1$tY. Table 10-2 lists some of the more common date and time codes.

---

[*] The 1.5 beta 1 documentation lists about 40 conversions plus another 6 "combination" codes; the exact list may change in the final release of 1.5.

*Table 10-2. Formatting codes for dates and times*

| Format code | Meaning |
| --- | --- |
| Y | Year (at least four digits) |
| m | Month as 2-digit (leading zeros) number |
| B | Locale-specific month name (b for abbreviated) |
| d | Day of month (2 digits, leading zeros) |
| e | Day of month (1 or 2 digits) |
| A | Locale-specific day of week (a for abbreviated) |
| H or I | Hour in 24-hour (H) or 12-hour (I) format (2-digits, leading zeros) |
| M | Minute (2 digits) |
| S | Second (2 digits) |
| P or p | Locale-specific AM/PM in uppercase (P) or lowercase (p) |
| R or T | 24-hour time combination: %tH:%tM (R) or %tH:%tM:%tS (T) |
| D | Date formatted as "%tm/%td/%ty" |

In my opinion, using these in applications that you distribute or make available as web applications is a Really Bad Idea because any direct use of them assumes that you know the correct order to print these fields in all locales around the world. Trust me, you don't. Instead of these, I recommend the use of DateFormat, which I show you how to use in Recipe 6.2; I also urge you to read Chapter 15. However, for "quick and dirty" work, as well as for writing log or data files that must be in a given format because some other program reads them, these are hard to beat.

Some date examples are shown in Example 10-2.

*Example 10-2. FormatterDates.java*

```java
import java.util.Formatter;
import java.util.Date;
import java.util.Calendar;

/** Demonstrate some usage patterns and format-code examples
 * of the Formatter class (new in JDK 1.5).
 */
public class FormatterDates {
    public static void main(String[] args) {

        // Format numbers as dates e.g., 2004-06-28
        System.out.printf("%1$4d-%2$02d-%3$2d%n", 2004, 6, 28);

        // Format fields from a Date object: multiple fields from "1$"
        // (hard-coded formatting for Date not advisable; see I18N chapter)
        Date today = Calendar.getInstance().getTime();
        System.out.printf("Today is %1$tB %1$td, %1$tY%n", today);  // e.g., July 4, 2004

    }
}
```

Running this FormatterDates class produces the following output:

```
C:> javac -source 1.5 FormatterDates.java
C:> java FormatterDates
2004-06-28
Today is March 07, 2004
```

The astute reader will notice that this mechanism requires that the Java language now contain a variable arguments mechanism. Var args have been the bane of developers on many platforms and, indeed, they have finally come to Java. However, they are not intended for capricious use, and I do not document them here.* If you really need to use this mechanism, consult the documentation accompanying JDK 1.5.

# 10.4   Scanning a File with StreamTokenizer

## Problem

You need to scan a file with more fine-grained resolution than the readLine( ) method of the BufferedReader class and its subclasses (discussed in Recipe 10.14).

## Solution

Use a StreamTokenizer, readLine( ), and a StringTokenizer; regular expressions (Chapter 4); or one of several scanner generating tools, such as ANTLR or JavaCC. On JDK 1.5, use the Scanner class (see Recipe 10.5).

## Discussion

While you could, in theory, read a file one character at a time and analyze each character, that is a pretty low-level approach. The read( ) method in the Reader class is defined to return int so that it can use the time-honored value -1 (defined as EOF in Unix <stdio.h> for years) to indicate that you have read to the end of the file:

```
void doFile(Reader is) {
    int c;
    while ((c=is.read( )) != -1) {
        System.out.print((char)c);
    }
}
```

The cast to char is interesting. The program compiles fine without it, but does not print correctly because c is declared as int (which it must be, to be able to compare against the end-of-file value -1). For example, the integer value corresponding to capital A treated as an int prints as 65, while (char) prints the character A.

---

* Well, if you insist. But only briefly. The variable argument, which must be the last declaration in the method's header, is declared as Type . . . name, and is treated as Type[ ] in the body of the method. Don't forget to compile with -source 1.5. The invocation must pass a comma-separated list of arguments of the same or compatible types. See lang/VarArgsDemo.java in the online source.

We discussed the StringTokenizer class extensively in Recipe 3.2. The combination of readLine( ) and StringTokenizer provides a simple means of scanning a file. Suppose you need to read a file in which each line consists of a name like *user@host.domain*, and you want to split the lines into users and host addresses. You could use this:

```java
// ScanStringTok.java
protected void process(LineNumberReader is) {
        String s = null;
        try {
            while ((s = is.readLine()) != null) {
                StringTokenizer st = new StringTokenizer(s, "@", true);
                String user = (String)st.nextElement();
                st.nextElement();
                String host = (String)st.nextElement();
                System.out.println("User name: " + user +
                    "; host part: " + host);

                // Presumably you would now do something
                // with the user and host parts...

            }

        } catch (NoSuchElementException ix) {
            System.err.println("Line " + is.getLineNumber() +
                ": Invalid input " + s);
        } catch (IOException e) {
            System.err.println(e);
        }
    }
```

The StreamTokenizer class in java.util provides slightly more capabilities for scanning a file. It reads characters and assembles them into words, or *tokens*. It returns these tokens to you along with a type code describing the kind of token it found. This typecode is one of four predefined types (StringTokenizer.TT_WORD, TT_NUMBER, TT_EOF, or TT_EOL for the end-of-line), or the char value of an ordinary character (such as 40 for the space character). Methods such as ordinaryCharacter( ) allow you to specify how to categorize characters, while others such as slashSlashComment( ) allow you to enable or disable features.

Example 10-3 shows a StreamTokenizer used to implement a simple immediate-mode stack-based calculator:

```
2 2 + =
4
22 7 / =
3.141592857
```

I read tokens as they arrive from the StreamTokenizer. Numbers are put on the stack. The four operators (+, -, *, and /) are immediately performed on the two elements at the top of the stack, and the result is put back on the top of the stack. The = operator causes the top element to be printed, but is left on the stack so that you can say:

```
4 5 * = 2 / =
20.0
10.0
```

*Example 10-3. Simple calculator using StreamTokenizer*

```java
import java.io.*;
import java.io.StreamTokenizer;
import java.util.Stack;

/**
 * SimpleCalc -- simple calculator to show StringTokenizer
 *
 * @author    Ian Darwin, http://www.darwinsys.com/
 * @version   $Id: ch10,v 1.5 2004/05/04 20:12:12 ian Exp $
 */
public class SimpleCalcStreamTok {
    /** The StreamTokenizer Input */
    protected  StreamTokenizer tf;
    /** The Output File */
    protected PrintWriter out = new PrintWriter(System.out, true);
    /** The variable name (not used in this version) */
    protected String variable;
    /** The operand stack */
    protected Stack s;

    /* Driver - main program */
    public static void main(String[] av) throws IOException {
        if (av.length == 0)
            new SimpleCalcStreamTok(
                new InputStreamReader(System.in)).doCalc();
        else
            for (int i=0; i<av.length; i++)
                new SimpleCalcStreamTok(av[i]).doCalc();
    }

    /** Construct by filename */
    public SimpleCalcStreamTok(String fileName) throws IOException {
        this(new FileReader(fileName));
    }

    /** Construct from an existing Reader */
    public SimpleCalcStreamTok(Reader rdr) throws IOException {
        tf = new StreamTokenizer(rdr);
        // Control the input character set:
        tf.slashSlashComments(true);    // treat "//" as comments
        tf.ordinaryChar('-');           // used for subtraction
        tf.ordinaryChar('/');       // used for division

        s = new Stack();
    }

    /** Construct from a Reader and a PrintWriter
     */
```

*Example 10-3. Simple calculator using StreamTokenizer (continued)*

```java
public SimpleCalcStreamTok(Reader in, PrintWriter out) throws IOException {
    this(in);
    setOutput(out);
}

/**
 * Change the output destination.
 */
public void setOutput(PrintWriter out) {
    this.out = out;
}

protected void doCalc( ) throws IOException {
    int iType;
    double tmp;

    while ((iType = tf.nextToken( )) != StreamTokenizer.TT_EOF) {
        switch(iType) {
        case StreamTokenizer.TT_NUMBER: // Found a number, push value to stack
            push(tf.nval);
            break;
        case StreamTokenizer.TT_WORD:
            // Found a variable, save its name. Not used here.
            variable = tf.sval;
            break;
        case '+':
            // + operator is commutative.
            push(pop() + pop());
            break;
        case '-':
            // - operator: order matters.
            tmp = pop();
            push(pop() - tmp);
            break;
        case '*':
            // Multiply is commutative
            push(pop() * pop());
            break;
        case '/':
            // Handle division carefully: order matters!
            tmp = pop();
            push(pop() / tmp);
            break;
        case '=':
            out.println(peek());
            break;
        default:
            out.println("What's this? iType = " + iType);
        }
    }
}
```

*Example 10-3. Simple calculator using StreamTokenizer (continued)*

```
    void push(double val) {
        s.push(new Double(val));
    }
    double pop( ) {
        return ((Double)s.pop()).doubleValue( );
    }
    double peek( ) {
        return ((Double)s.peek()).doubleValue( );
    }
    void clearStack( ) {
        s.removeAllElements( );
    }
}
```

While StreamTokenizer is useful, it knows only a limited number of tokens and has no way of specifying that the tokens must appear in a particular order. To do more advanced scanning, you need some special-purpose scanning tools. Such tools have been used for a long time in the Unix realm. The best-known examples are yacc and lex (discussed in the O'Reilly text *lex & yacc*). These tools let you specify the lexical structure of your input using regular expressions (see Chapter 4). For example, you might say that an email address consists of a series of alphanumerics, followed by an at sign (@), followed by a series of alphanumerics with periods embedded, as:

```
name:    [A-Za-z0-9]ı@[A-Za-z0-0.]
```

The tool then writes code that recognizes the characters you have described. These tools also have a grammatical specification, which says, for example, that the keyword ADDRESS must appear, followed by a colon, followed by a "name" token, as previously defined.

Two widely used scanning tools for Java are ANTLR and *JavaCC*. Terence Parr is the author and maintainer of ANTLR, which can be download from *http://www.antlr.org/*. JavaCC is an open source project on *java.net* (*https://javacc.dev.java.net/*). These "compiler generators" can be used to write grammars for a wide variety of programs, from simple calculators—such as the one earlier in this recipe—through HTML and CORBA/IDL, up to full Java and C/C++ compilers. Examples of these are included with the downloads. Unfortunately, the learning curve for parsers in general precludes providing a simple and comprehensive example here. Please refer to the documentation and the numerous examples provided with the distributions.

Java offers simple line-at-a-time scanners using StringTokenizer, fancier token-based scanners using StreamTokenizer, and grammar-based scanners based on JavaCC and similar tools. In addition to these, JDK 1.5 provides an easier way to scan simple tokens (see Recipe 10.5).

# 10.5    Scanning Input with the 1.5 Scanner Class

## Problem

You have JDK 1.5 and you want the ease of use that the java.util.Scanner class brings to simple reading tasks.

## Solution

Use Scanner's next( ) methods for reading.

## Discussion

The Scanner class lets you read an input source by tokens, somewhat analogous to the StreamTokenizer described in Recipe 10.4. The Scanner is more flexible in some ways—it lets you break tokens based on spaces or regular expressions—but less in others—you need to know the kind of token you are reading. This class bears some resemblance to the C-language scanf( ) function, but in the Scanner you specify the input token types by calling methods like nextInt( ), nextDouble( ), and so on. Here is a simple example of scanning:

```
// From ScannerTest.java
String sampleDate = "25 Dec 1988";

Scanner sDate = Scanner.create(sampleDate);
int dom = sDate.nextInt( );
String mon = sDate.next( );
int year = sDate.nextInt( );
```

The Scanner recognizes Java's eight built-in types, as well as BigInteger and BigDecimal. It can also return input tokens as Strings or by matching regular expressions (see Chapter 4). Table 10-3 lists the "next" methods and corresponding "has" methods; the "has" method returns true if the corresponding "next" method would succeed. There is no nextString( ) method; just use next( ) to get the next token as a String.

*Table 10-3. Scanner methods*

| Returned type | "has" method | "next" method | Comment |
|---|---|---|---|
| String | hasNext( ) | next( ) | The next complete token from this scanner |
| String | hasNext(Pattern) | next(Pattern) | The next string that matches the given regular expression (regex) |
| String | hasNext(String) | next(String) | The next token that matches the regex pattern constructed from the specified string |
| BigDecimal | hasNextBigDecimal( ) | nextBigDecimal( ) | The next token of the input as a BigDecimal |

Table 10-3. Scanner methods (continued)

| Returned type | "has" method | "next" method | Comment |
|---|---|---|---|
| BigInteger | hasNextBigInteger( ) | nextBigInteger( ) | The next token of the input as a BigInteger |
| boolean | hasNextBoolean( ) | nextBoolean( ) | The next token of the input as a boolean |
| byte | hasNextByte( ) | nextByte( ) | The next token of the input as a byte |
| double | hasNextDouble() | nextDouble( ) | The next token of the input as a double |
| float | hasNextFloat( ) | nextFloat( ) | The next token of the input as a float |
| int | hasNextInt( ) | nextInt( ) | The next token of the input as an int |
| String | N/A | nextLine( ) | Reads up to the end-of-line, including the line ending |
| long | hasNextLong( ) | nextLong( ) | The next token of the input as a long |
| short | hasNextShort( ) | nextShort( ) | The next token of the input as a short |

The Scanner class does not provide any public constructors; you must call the static create( ) method with an input source, which can be a File object (Chapter 11), an InputStream, a String, or Readable (new in 1.5, Readable is an interface that Reader and all its subclasses implement).

One way of using the Scanner is based on the Iterator pattern, using while (scanner. hasNext( )) to control the iteration. Example 10-4 shows the simple calculator from Recipe 10.4 rewritten[*] to use the Scanner class.

*Example 10-4. Simple calculator using java.util.Scanner*

```
import java.io.*;
import java.util.Scanner;
import java.util.Stack;

/**
 * SimpleCalc -- simple calculator using 1.5 java.util.Scanner
 * @version    $Id: ch10,v 1.5 2004/05/04 20:12:12 ian Exp $
 */
public class SimpleCalcScanner {
    /** The Scanner */
    protected  Scanner scan;

    /** The output */
    protected PrintWriter out = new PrintWriter(System.out);

    /** The variable name (not used in this version) */
    protected String variable;
```

---

[*] If this were code in a maintained project, I might factor out some of the common code among these two calculators, as well as the one in Recipe 5.19, and divide the code better using interfaces. However, this would detract from the simplicity of self-contained examples.

*Example 10-4. Simple calculator using java.util.Scanner (continued)*

```
/** The operand stack */
protected Stack s = new Stack( );

/* Driver - main program */
public static void main(String[] av) throws IOException {
    if (av.length == 0)
        new SimpleCalcScanner(
            new InputStreamReader(System.in)).doCalc( );
    else
        for (int i=0; i<av.length; i++)
            new SimpleCalcScanner(av[i]).doCalc( );
}

/** Construct a SimpleCalcScanner by name */
public SimpleCalcScanner(String fileName) throws IOException {
    this(new FileReader(fileName));
}

/** Construct a SimpleCalcScanner from an open Reader */
public SimpleCalcScanner(Reader rdr) throws IOException {
    scan = new Scanner(rdr);
    // Control the input character set:
    scan.slashSlashComments(true);    // treat "//" as comments
    scan.ordinaryChar('-');           // used for subtraction
    scan.ordinaryChar('/');      // used for division
}

/** Construct a SimpleCalcScanner from a Reader and a PrintWriter */
public SimpleCalcScanner(Reader rdr, PrintWriter pw) throws IOException {
    this(rdr);
    setWriter(pw);
}

/** Change the output to go to a new PrintWriter */
public void setWriter(PrintWriter pw) {
    out = pw;
}

protected void doCalc( ) throws IOException {
    int iType;
    double tmp;

    while (scan.hasNext( )) {
        if (scan.hasNextDouble( )) {
            push(scan.nextDouble( ));
        } else {
            String token = scan.next().toString();
            if (token.equals("+")) {
                // Found + operator, perform it immediately.
                push(pop() + pop( ));
            } else if (token.equals("-")) {
```

*Example 10-4. Simple calculator using java.util.Scanner (continued)*

```
                  // Found - operator, perform it (order matters).
                  tmp = pop( );
                  push(pop( ) - tmp);
              } else if (token.equals("*")) {
                  // Multiply is commutative
                  push(pop() * pop( ));
              } else if (token.equals("/")) {
                  // Handle division carefully: order matters!
                  tmp = pop( );
                  push(pop( ) / tmp);
              } else if (token.equals("=")) {
                  out.println(peek( ));
              } else {
                  out.println("What's this? " + token);
              }
          }
      }
  }

  void push(double val) {
      s.push(new Double(val));
  }

  double pop( ) {
      return ((Double)s.pop()).doubleValue( );
  }

  double peek( ) {
      return ((Double)s.peek()).doubleValue( );
  }

  void clearStack( ) {
      s.removeAllElements( );
  }
}
```

# 10.6   Opening a File by Name

## Problem

The Java documentation doesn't have methods for opening files. How do I connect a filename on disk with a Reader, Writer, or Stream?

## Solution

Construct a FileReader, FileWriter, FileInputStream, or FileOutputStream.

## Discussion

The action of constructing a `FileReader`, `FileWriter`, `FileInputStream`, or `FileOutputStream` corresponds to the "open" operation in most I/O packages. There is no explicit open operation, perhaps as a kind of rhetorical flourish of the Java API's object-oriented design. So to read a text file, you'd create, in order, a `FileReader` and a `BufferedReader`. To write a file a byte at a time, you'd create a `FileOutputStream` and probably a `BufferedOutputStream` for efficiency:

```
// OpenFileByName.java
BufferedReader is = new BufferedReader(new FileReader("myFile.txt"));
BufferedOutputStream bytesOut = new BufferedOutputStream(
    new FileOutputStream("bytes.dat"));
...
bytesOut.close();
```

Remember that you need to handle `IOExceptions` around these calls.

# 10.7   Copying a File

## Problem

You need to copy a file in its entirety.

## Solution

Use a pair of `Streams` for binary data, or a `Reader` and a `Writer` for text, and a while loop to copy until end-of-file is reached on the input.

## Discussion

This operation is fairly common, so I've packaged it as a set of methods in a class called `FileIO` in my utilities package `com.darwinsys.util`. Here's a simple test program that uses it to copy a source file to a backup file:

```
package regress;   // in javasrc/darwinsys/src
import com.darwinsys.util.FileIO;

import java.io.*;

public class FileIOTest {
    public static void main(String[] av) {
        try {
            FileIO.copyFile("FileIO.java", "FileIO.bak");
            FileIO.copyFile("FileIO.class", "FileIO-class.bak");
        } catch (FileNotFoundException e) {
            System.err.println(e);
        } catch (IOException e) {
            System.err.println(e);
        }
    }
}
```

How does FileIO work? Its copyFile method takes several forms, depending on whether you have two filenames, a filename and a PrintWriter, and so on. The code for FileIO itself is shown in Example 10-5.

*Example 10-5. FileIO.java*

```
package com.darwinsys.io;

import java.io.*;

/**
 * Some simple file IO primitives reimplemented in Java.
 * All methods are static since there is no state.
 */
public class FileIO {

    /** Copy a file from one filename to another */
    public static void copyFile(String inName, String outName)
    throws FileNotFoundException, IOException {
        BufferedInputStream is =
            new BufferedInputStream(new FileInputStream(inName));
        BufferedOutputStream os =
            new BufferedOutputStream(new FileOutputStream(outName));
        copyFile(is, os, true);
    }

    /** Copy a file from an opened InputStream to an opened OutputStream */
    public static void copyFile(InputStream is, OutputStream os, boolean close)
    throws IOException {
        int b;                  // the byte read from the file
        while ((b = is.read()) != -1) {
            os.write(b);
        }
        is.close();
        if (close)
            os.close();
    }

    /** Copy a file from an opened Reader to an opened Writer */
    public static void copyFile(Reader is, Writer os, boolean close)
    throws IOException {
        int b;                  // the byte read from the file
        while ((b = is.read()) != -1) {
            os.write(b);
        }
        is.close();
        if (close)
            os.close();
    }

    /** Copy a file from a filename to a PrintWriter. */
    public static void copyFile(String inName, PrintWriter pw, boolean close)
    throws FileNotFoundException, IOException {
```

*Example 10-5. FileIO.java (continued)*

```
        BufferedReader ir = new BufferedReader(new FileReader(inName));
        copyFile(ir, pw, close);
    }

    /** Open a file and read the first line from it. */
    public static String readLine(String inName)
    throws FileNotFoundException, IOException {
        BufferedReader is = new BufferedReader(new FileReader(inName));
        String line = null;
        line = is.readLine( );
        is.close( );
        return line;
    }

    /** The size of blocking to use */
    protected static final int BLKSIZ = 8192;

    /** Copy a data file from one filename to another, alternate method.
     * As the name suggests, use my own buffer instead of letting
     * the BufferedReader allocate and use the buffer.
     * (just to show how, not necessarily optimal).
     */
    public void copyFileBuffered(String inName, String outName) throws
            FileNotFoundException, IOException {
        InputStream is = new FileInputStream(inName);
        OutputStream os = new FileOutputStream(outName);
        int count = 0;          // the byte count
        byte[] b = new byte[BLKSIZ];    // the bytes read from the file
        while ((count = is.read(b)) != -1) {
            os.write(b, 0, count);
        }
        is.close( );
        os.close( );
    }

    /** Read the entire content of a Reader into a String */
    public static String readerToString(Reader is) throws IOException {
        StringBuffer sb = new StringBuffer( );
        char[] b = new char[BLKSIZ];
        int n;

        // Read a block. If it gets any chars, append them.
        while ((n = is.read(b)) > 0) {
            sb.append(b, 0, n);
        }

        // Only construct the String object once, here.
        return sb.toString( );
    }

    /** Read the content of a Stream into a String */
```

*Example 10-5. FileIO.java (continued)*

```
    public static String inputStreamToString(InputStream is)
    throws IOException {
        return readerToString(new InputStreamReader(is));
    }
}
```

A test main program included in the online source copies the source and class files of this program. When I ran it for testing, I followed up by using *diff* (a text file compare program) on the text file and its backup, and *cmp* (a binary compare program) on the class files. Both of these programs operate on the Unix "no news is good news" principle: if they say nothing, it is because they found nothing of significance to report—i.e., no differences:

```
C:\javasrc\io>java IOUtil
C:\javasrc\io>diff IOUtil.java IOUtil-java.bak
C:\javasrc\io>cmp  IOUtil.class IOUtil-class.bak
C:\javasrc\io>
```

But wait! Did you look closely at the body of copyFile(String inName, PrintWriter pw, boolean close)? If you didn't, have a look. You'll notice that I cheated and just delegated the work to copyFile(Reader is, Writer os, boolean close). If I'm copying a file from one place on disk to another, why go through the overhead of converting it from external form to Unicode and back? Normally, you won't have to. But if you have something like a network filesystem mounted from Windows to Unix, or vice versa, it's better to do it a line at a time.

# 10.8   Reading a File into a String

## Problem

You need to read the entire contents of a file into a string.

## Solution

Use my FileIO.readerToString( ) method.

## Discussion

This is not a common activity in Java, but sometimes you really want to do it. For example, you might want to load a file into a "text area" in a GUI. Or process an entire file looking for multiline regular expressions (as in Recipe 4.11). Even though there's nothing in the standard API to do this, it's still easy to accomplish with the readerToString( ) method in com.darwinsys.util.FileIO, the source for which is included and discussed in Recipe 10.7. You just say something like the following:

```
    Reader is = new FileReader(theFileName);
    String input = FileIO.readerToString(is);
```

## 10.9 Reassigning the Standard Streams

### Problem

You need to reassign one or more of the standard streams System.in, System.out, or System.err.

### Solution

Construct an InputStream or PrintStream as appropriate, and pass it to the appropriate set method in the System class.

### Discussion

The ability to reassign these streams corresponds to what Unix (or DOS command line) users think of as *redirection,* or *piping.* This mechanism is commonly used to make a program read from or write to a file without having to explicitly open it and go through every line of code changing the read, write, print, etc. calls to refer to a different stream object. The *open* operation is performed by the command-line interpreter in Unix or DOS, or by the calling class in Java.

While you could just assign a new PrintStream to the variable System.out, you'd be considered antisocial since there is a defined method to replace it carefully:

```
// Redirect.java
String LOGFILENAME = "error.log";
System.setErr(new PrintStream(new FileOutputStream(LOGFILENAME)));
System.out.println("Please look for errors in " + LOGFILENAME);
// Now assume this is somebody else's code; you'll see it writing to stderr...
int[] a = new int[5];
a[10] = 0;     // here comes an ArrayIndexOutOfBoundsException
```

The stream you use can be one that you've opened, as here, or one you inherited:

```
System.setErr(System.out);     // merge stderr and stdout to same output file.
```

It could also be a stream connected to or from another Process you've started (see Recipe 26.1), a network socket, or URL. Anything that gives you a stream can be used.

### See Also

See Recipe 14.9, which shows how to reassign a file so that it gets "written" to a text window in a GUI application.

## 10.10 Duplicating a Stream as It Is Written

### Problem

You want anything written to a stream, such as the standard output System.out, or the standard error System.err, to appear there but *also* be logged into a file.

## Solution

Subclass `PrintStream` and have its `write()` methods write to two streams. Then use `system.setErr()` or `setOut()`, as in Recipe 10.9, to replace the existing standard stream with this "tee" `PrintStream` subclass.

## Discussion

Classes are meant to be subclassed. Here we're just subclassing `PrintStream` and adding a bit of functionality: a second `PrintStream`! I wrote a class called `TeePrintStream`, named after the ancient Unix command *tee*. That command allowed you to duplicate, or "tee off," a copy of the data being written on a "pipeline" between two programs.

The original Unix *tee* command is used like this: the | character creates a pipeline in which the standard output of one program becomes the standard input to the next. This often-used example of pipes shows how many users are logged into a Unix server:

```
who | wc -l
```

This runs the *who* program (which lists who is logged into the system, one name per line along with the terminal port and login time) and sends its output, not to the terminal, but rather into the standard input of the word count (*wc*) program. Here, *wc* is being asked to count lines, not words; hence the -l option. To *tee* a copy of the intermediate data into a file, you might say:

```
who | tee wholist | wc -l
```

which creates a file *wholist* containing the data. For the curious, the file *wholist* might look something like this:

```
ian      ttyCo     Mar 14 09:59
ben      ttyC3     Mar 14 10:23
ian      Llyp4     Mar 14 13:46  (daroad.darwinsys.com)
```

So both the previous command sequences would print 3 as their output.

`TeePrintStream` is an attempt to capture the spirit of the *tee* command. It can be used like this:

```
System.setErr(new TeePrintStream(System.err, "err.log"));
// ...lots of code that occasionally writes to System.err... Or might.
```

`System.setErr()` is a means of specifying the destination of text printed to `System.err` (there are also `System.setOut()` and `System.setIn()`). This code results in any messages that printed to `System.err` to print to wherever `System.err` was previously directed (normally the terminal, but possibly a text window in an IDE) and into the file `err.log`.

This technique is not limited to the three standard streams. A `TeePrintStream` can be passed to any method that wants a `PrintStream`. Or, for that matter, an `OutputStream`. And you can adapt the technique for `BufferedInputStreams`, `PrintWriters`, `BufferedReaders`, and so on.

Since TeePrintStream is fairly simple, I'll list the main parts of it here (see the online source for the complete version):

```java
import java.io.*;

public class TeePrintStream extends PrintStream {
    protected PrintStream parent;
    protected String fileName;

    /* Construct a TeePrintStream given an existing Stream and a filename.
     */
    public TeePrintStream(PrintStream os, String fn) throws IOException {
        this(os, fn, false);
    }
    /* Construct a TeePrintStream given an existing Stream, a filename,
     * and a boolean to control the flush operation.
     */
    public TeePrintStream(PrintStream orig, String fn,
            boolean flush) throws IOException {
        super(new FileOutputStream(fn), flush);
        fileName = fn;
        parent = orig;
    }

    /** Return true if either stream has an error. */
    public boolean checkError() {
        return parent.checkError() || super.checkError();
    }

    /** override write().    This is the actual "tee" operation! */
    public void write(int x) {
        parent.write(x);              // "write once;
        super.write(x); // write somewhere else"
    }
    /** override write() */
    public void write(byte[] x, int o, int l) {
        parent.write(x, o, l);
        super.write(x, o, l);
    }

    /** Close both streams. */
    public void close() {
        parent.close();
        super.close();
    }
}
```

It's worth mentioning that I do *not* need to override all the polymorphic forms of print( ) and println( ). Since these all ultimately use one of the forms of write( ), if you override the print and println methods to do the *tee*-ing as well, you can get several additional copies of the data written out.

# 10.11 Reading/Writing a Different Character Set

## Problem

You need to read or write a text file using a particular encoding.

## Solution

Convert the text to or from internal Unicode by specifying a converter when you construct an InputStreamReader or PrintWriter.

## Discussion

Classes InputStreamReader and OutputStreamWriter are the bridge from byte-oriented Streams to character-based Readers. These classes read or write bytes and translate them to or from characters according to a specified character encoding. The Unicode character set used inside Java (char and String types) is a 16-bit character set. But most character sets—such as ASCII, Swedish, Spanish, Greek, Turkish, and many others—use only a small subset of that. In fact, many European language character sets fit nicely into 8-bit characters. Even the larger character sets (script-based and pictographic languages) don't all use the same bit values for each particular character. The *encoding*, then, is a mapping between Unicode characters and an external storage format for characters drawn from a particular national or linguistic character set.

To simplify matters, the InputStreamReader and OutputStreamWriter constructors are the only places where you can specify the name of an encoding to be used in this translation. If you do not, the platform's (or user's) default encoding is used. PrintWriters, BufferedReaders, and the like all use whatever encoding the InputStreamReader or OutputStreamWriter class uses. Since these bridge classes only accept Stream arguments in their constructors, the implication is that if you want to specify a nondefault converter to read or write a file on disk, you must start by constructing not a FileReader or FileWriter, but a FileInputStream or FileOutputStream!

```
// UseConverters.java
BufferedReader fromKanji = new BufferedReader(
    new InputStreamReader(new FileInputStream("kanji.txt"), "EUC_JP"));
PrintWriter toSwedish = new PrintWriter(
    new OutputStreamWriter(new FileOutputStream("sverige.txt"), "Cp278"));
```

Not that it would necessarily make sense to read a single file from Kanji and output it in a Swedish encoding; for one thing, most fonts would not have all the characters of both character sets, and, at any rate, the Swedish encoding certainly has far fewer characters in it than the Kanji encoding. Besides, if that were all you wanted, you could use a JDK tool with the ill-fitting name *native2ascii* (see its documentation for details). A list of the supported encodings is also in the JDK documentation, in the file *docs/guide/internat/encoding.doc.html*. A more detailed description is found in Appendix B of O'Reilly's *Java I/O*.

## 10.12 Those Pesky End-of-Line Characters

### Problem

You really want to know about end-of-line characters.

### Solution

Use \r and \n in whatever combination makes sense.

### Discussion

If you are reading text (or bytes containing ASCII characters) in line mode using the readLine( ) method, you'll never see the end-of-line characters, and so you won't be cursed with having to figure out whether \n, \r, or \r\n appears at the end of each line. If you want that level of detail, you have to read the characters or bytes one at a time, using the read( ) methods. The only time I've found this necessary is in networking code, where some of the line-mode protocols assume that the line ending is \r\n. Even here, though, you can still work in line mode. When writing, pass \r\n into the print( ) (not println( )!) method. When reading, use readLine( ) and you won't have to deal with the characters:

```
outputSocket.print("HELO " + myName + "\r\n");
String response = inputSocket.readLine( );
```

For the curious, the strange spelling of "hello" is used in SMTP, the mail sending protocol, where all commands must be four letters.

## 10.13 Beware Platform-Dependent File Code

### Problem

Chastened by the previous recipe, you now wish to write only platform-independent code.

### Solution

Use readLine( ) and println( ). Never use \n by itself; use File.separator if you must.

### Discussion

As mentioned in Recipe 10.12, if you just use readLine( ) and println( ), you won't have to think about the line endings. But a particular problem, especially for recycled C programmers and their relatives, is using the \n character in text strings to mean a newline. What is particularly distressing about this code is that it works—sometimes—usually on the developer's own platform. But it will surely someday fail, on some other system:

```
// BadNewline.java
String myName;
public static void main(String argv[]) {
    BadNewline jack = new BadNewline("Jack Adolphus Schmidt, III");
    System.out.println(jack);
}
/**
 * DON'T DO THIS. THIS IS BAD CODE.
 */
public String toString() {
    return "BadNewlineDemo@" + hashCode() + "\n" + myName;
}

// The obvious Constructor is not shown for brevity; it's in the code
```

The real problem is not that it fails on some platforms, though. What's really wrong is that it mixes formatting and I/O, or tries to. Don't mix line-based display with toString(); avoid "multiline strings"—output from toString() or any other string-returning method. If you need to write multiple strings, then say what you mean:

```
// GoodNewline.java
String myName;
public static void main(String argv[]) {
    GoodNewline jack = new GoodNewline("Jack Adolphus Schmidt, III");
    jack.print(System.out);
}

protected void print(PrintStream out) {
    out.println(toString());    // classname and hashcode
    out.println(myName);        // print name  on next line
}
```

# 10.14 Reading "Continued" Lines

## Problem

You need to read lines that are continued with backslashes (\) or that are continued with leading spaces (such as email or news headers).

## Solution

Use my IndentContLineReader or EscContLineReader classes.

## Discussion

This functionality is likely to be reused, so it should be encapsulated in general-purpose classes. I offer the IndentContLineReader and EscContLineReader classes. EscContLineReader reads lines normally, but if a line ends with the escape character (by default, the backslash), the escape character is deleted and the following line is joined to the preceding line. So if you have lines like this in the input:

```
Here is something I wanted to say:\
Try and Buy in every way.
Go Team!
```

and you read them using EscContLineReader's readLine( ) method, you get the following lines:

```
Here is something I wanted to say: Try and Buy in every way.
Go Team!
```

Note in particular that my reader *does* provide a space character between the abutted parts of the continued line. An IOException is thrown if a file ends with the escape character.

IndentContLineReader reads lines, but if a line begins with a space or tab, that line is joined to the preceding line. This is designed for reading email or Usenet news ("message") header lines. Here is an example input file:

```
From: ian Tuesday, January 1, 2000 8:45 AM EST
To: Book-reviewers List
Received: by darwinsys.com (OpenBSD 2.6)
    from localhost
    at Tuesday, January 1, 2000 8:45 AM EST
Subject: Hey, it's 2000 and MY computer is still up
```

When read using an IndentContLineReader, this text comes out with the continued lines joined together into longer single lines:

```
From: ian Tuesday, January 1, 2000 8:45 AM EST
To: Book-reviewers List
Received: by darwinsys.com (OpenBSD 2.6) from localhost at Tuesday, January 1, 2000
8:45 AM EST
Subject: Hey, it's 2000 and MY computer is still up
```

This class has a setContinueMode(boolean) method that lets you turn continuation mode off. This would normally be used to process the body of a message. Since the header and the body are separated by a null line in the text representation of messages, we can process the entire message correctly as follows:

```
IndentContLineReader is = new IndentContLineReader(
    new StringReader(sampleTxt));
String aLine;
// Print Mail/News Header
System.out.println("----- Message Header -----");
while ((aLine = is.readLine()) != null && aLine.length() > 0) {
    System.out.println(is.getLineNumber() + ": " + aLine);
}
// Make "is" behave like normal BufferedReader
is.setContinuationMode(false);
System.out.println();
// Print Message Body
System.out.println("----- Message Body -----");
while ((aLine = is.readLine()) != null) {
    System.out.println(is.getLineNumber() + ": " + aLine);
}
```

Each of the Reader classes is subclassed from LineNumberReader so that you can use getLineNumber( ). This is a very useful feature when reporting errors back to the user who prepared an input file; it can save them considerable hunting around in the file if you tell them the line number on which the error occurred. The Reader classes are actually subclassed from an abstract ContLineReader subclass, which I'll present first in Example 10-6. This class encapsulates the basic functionality for keeping track of lines that need to be joined together, and for enabling or disabling the continuation processing.

*Example 10-6. ContLineReader.java*

```java
import java.io.*;

/** Subclass of LineNumberReader to allow reading of continued lines
 * using the readLine( ) method. The other Reader methods (readInt( )) etc.)
 * must not be used.  Must subclass to provide the actual implementation
 * of readLine( ).
 */
public abstract class ContLineReader extends LineNumberReader {
    /** Line number of first line in current (possibly continued) line */
    protected int firstLineNumber = 0;
    /** True if handling continuations, false if not; false == "PRE" mode */
    protected boolean doContinue = true;

    /** Set the continuation mode */
    public void setContinuationMode(boolean b) {
        doContinue = b;
    }

    /** Get the continuation mode */
    public boolean getContinuationMode( ) {
        return doContinue;
    }

    /** Read one (possibly continued) line, stripping out the \ that
     * marks the end of each line but the last in a sequence.
     */
    public abstract String readLine( ) throws IOException;

    /** Read one real line. Provided as a convenience for the
     * subclasses, so they don't embarass themselves trying to
     * call "super.readLine( )" which isn't very practical...
     */
    public String readPhysicalLine( ) throws IOException {
        return super.readLine( );
    }

    // Can NOT override getLineNumber in this class to return the #
    // of the beginning of the continued line, since the subclasses
    // all call super.getLineNumber...
```

*Example 10-6. ContLineReader.java (continued)*

```java
    /** Construct a ContLineReader with the default input-buffer size. */
    public ContLineReader(Reader in) {
        super(in);
    }

    /** Construct a ContLineReader using the given input-buffer size. */
    public ContLineReader(Reader in, int sz) {
        super(in, sz);
    }

    // Methods that do NOT work - redirect straight to parent

    /** Read a single character, returned as an int. */
    public int read() throws IOException {
        return super.read();
    }

    /** Read characters into a portion of an array. */
    public int read(char[] cbuf, int off, int len) throws IOException {
        return super.read(cbuf, off, len);
    }

    public boolean markSupported() {
        return false;
    }
}
```

The `ContLineReader` class ends with code for handling the `read()` calls so that the class will work correctly. The `IndentContLineReader` class extends this to allow merging of lines based on indentation. Example 10-7 shows the code for the `IndentContLineReader` class.

*Example 10-7. IndentContLineReader.java*

```java
import java.io.*;

/** Subclass of ContLineReader for lines continued by indentation of
 * following line (like RFC822 mail, Usenet News, etc.).
 */
public class IndentContLineReader extends ContLineReader {
    /** Line number of first line in current (possibly continued) line */
    public int getLineNumber() {
        return firstLineNumber;
    }

    protected String prevLine;

    /** Read one (possibly continued) line, stripping out the '\'s that
     * mark the end of all but the last.
     */
    public String readLine() throws IOException {
        String s;
```

*Example 10-7. IndentContLineReader.java (continued)*

```
        // If we saved a previous line, start with it. Else,
        // read the first line of possible continuation.
        // If non-null, put it into the StringBuffer and its line
        // number in firstLineNumber.
        if (prevLine != null) {
            s = prevLine;
            prevLine = null;
        }
        else {
            s = readPhysicalLine();
        }

        // save the line number of the first line.
        firstLineNumber = super.getLineNumber();

        // Now we have one line. If we are not in continuation
        // mode, or if a previous readPhysicalLine() returned null,
        // we are finished, so return it.
        if (!doContinue || s == null)
            return s;

        // Otherwise, start building a stringbuffer
        StringBuffer sb = new StringBuffer(s);

        // Read as many continued lines as there are, if any.
        while (true) {
            String nextPart = readPhysicalLine();
            if (nextPart == null) {
                // Egad! EOF within continued line.
                // Return what we have so far.
                return sb.toString();
            }
            // If the next line begins with space, it's continuation
            if (nextPart.length() > 0 &&
                Character.isWhitespace(nextPart.charAt(0))) {
                sb.append(nextPart);    // and add line.
            } else {
                // else we just read too far, so put in "pushback" holder
                prevLine = nextPart;
                break;
            }
        }
    }

    return sb.toString();        // return what's left
}

/* Constructors not shown */

// Built-in test case
protected static String sampleTxt =
    "From: ian today now\n" +
    "Received: by foo.bar.com\n" +
    "    at 12:34:56 January 1, 2000\n" +
```

*Example 10-7. IndentContLineReader.java (continued)*

```
            "X-Silly-Headers: Too Many\n" +
            "This line should be line 5.\n" +
            "Test more indented line continues from line 6:\n" +
            "    space indented.\n" +
            "    tab indented;\n" +
            "\n" +
            "This is line 10\n" +
            "the start of a hypothetical mail/news message, \n" +
            "that is, it follows a null line.\n" +
            "    Let us see how it fares if indented.\n" +
            " also space-indented.\n" +
            "\n" +
            "How about text ending without a newline?";

    // A simple main program for testing the class.
    public static void main(String argv[]) throws IOException {
        IndentContLineReader is = new IndentContLineReader(
            new StringReader(sampleTxt));
        String aLine;
        // Print Mail/News Header
        System.out.println("----- Message Header -----");
        while ((aLine = is.readLine()) != null && aLine.length() > 0) {
            System.out.println(is.getLineNumber() + ": " + aLine);
        }
        // Make "is" behave like normal BufferedReader
        is.setContinuationMode(false);
        System.out.println();
        // Print Message Body
        System.out.println("----- Message Body -----");
        while ((aLine = is.readLine()) != null) {
            System.out.println(is.getLineNumber() + ": " + aLine);
        }
        is.close();
    }
}
```

# 10.15 Binary Data

## Problem

You need to read or write binary data, as opposed to text.

## Solution

Use a DataInputStream or DataOutputStream.

## Discussion

The Stream classes have been in Java since the JDK 1.0 release and are optimal for reading and writing bytes rather than characters. The "data" layer over them, comprising DataInputStream and DataOutputStream, is configured for reading and writing binary values, including all of Java's built-in types. Suppose that you want to write a binary integer plus a binary floating-point value into a file and read it back later. This code shows the writing part:

```java
import java.io.*;
/** Write some data in binary. */
public class WriteBinary {
    public static void main(String argv[]) throws IOException {
        int i = 42;
        double d = Math.PI;
        String FILENAME = "binary.dat";
        DataOutputStream os = new DataOutputStream(
            new FileOutputStream(FILENAME));
        os.writeInt(i);
        os.writeDouble(d);
        os.close();
        System.out.println("Wrote " + i + ", " + d + " to file " + FILENAME);
    }
}
```

The reading part is left as an exercise for the reader. Should you need to write all the fields from an object, you should probably use one of the methods described in Recipe 10.18.

# 10.16 Seeking

## Problem

You need to read from or write to a particular location in a file, such as an indexed file.

## Solution

Use a RandomAccessFile.

## Discussion

The class java.io.RandomAccessFile allows you to move the read or write position when writing to any location within a file or past the end. This allows you to create or access "files with holes" on some platforms and lets you read or write indexed or other database-like files in Java. The primary methods of interest are void seek(long where), which moves the position for the next read or write to where; int skipBytes(int howmany), which moves the position forward by howmany bytes; and long getFilePointer( ), which returns the position.

RandomAccessFile class also implements the DataInput and DataOutput interfaces, so everything I said about DataStreams in Recipe 10.15 also applies here. This example reads a binary integer from the beginning of the file, treats that as the position to read from, finds that position, and reads a string from that location within the file:

```
import java.io.*;

/**
 * Read a file containing an offset, and a String at that offset.
 */
public class ReadRandom {
    final static String FILENAME = "random.dat";
    protected String fileName;
    protected RandomAccessFile seeker;

    public static void main(String argv[]) throws IOException {
        ReadRandom r = new ReadRandom(FILENAME);

        System.out.println("Offset is " + r.readOffset());
        System.out.println("Message is \"" + r.readMessage() + "\".");
    }

    /** Constructor: save filename, construct RandomAccessFile */
    public ReadRandom(String fname) throws IOException {
        fileName = fname;
        seeker = new RandomAccessFile(fname, "r");
    }

    /** Read the Offset field, defined to be at location 0 in the file. */
    public int readOffset() throws IOException {
        seeker.seek(0);
        return seeker.readInt();
    }

    /** read the message at the given offset */
    public String readMessage() throws IOException {
        seeker.seek(readOffset());    // move to the offset
        return seeker.readLine();         // and read the String
    }
}
```

# 10.17 Writing Data Streams from C

## Problem

You need to exchange binary data between C and Java.

## Solution

Use the network byte-ordering macros.

## Discussion

The program that created the file *random.dat* read by the program in the previous recipe was not written in Java, but in C. Since the earliest days of the TCP/IP proto-col in the 1980s, and particularly on the 4.2 BSD version of Unix, there was an awareness that not all brands of computers store the bytes within a word in the same order, and there was a means for dealing with it. For this early heterogeneous network to function at all, it was necessary that a 32-bit word be interpreted correctly as a computer's network address, regardless of whether it originated on a PDP-11, a VAX, a Sun workstation, or any other kind of machine then prevalent (no "IBM PC" machines were powerful enough to run TCP/IP at that time). So *network byte order* was established, a standard for which bytes go in which order on the network. And the network byte order macros were written: ntohl for network-to-host order for a long (32 bits), htons for host-to-network order for a short (16 bits), and so on. In most Unix implementations, these C macros live in one of the Internet header files, although in some newer systems, they have been segregated out into a file like *<machine/endian.h>*, as on our OpenBSD system.

The designers of Java, working at Sun, were well aware of these issues and chose to use network byte order in the Java Virtual Machine. Thus, a Java program can read an IP address from a socket using a DataInputStream or write an integer to disk that will be read from C using read( ) and the network byte order macros.

This C program writes the file *random.dat* read in Recipe 10.16. It uses the network byte order macros to make sure that the long integer (32 bits on most C compilers on the IBM PC) is in the correct order to be read as an int in Java:

```
/* Create the random-access file for the RandomAccessFile example
 */

#include <stdio.h>
#include <fcntl.h>
#include <stdlib.h>
#include <unistd.h>
#include <sys/types.h>
#include <machine/endian.h>

const off_t OFFSET = 1234;
const char* FILENAME = "random.dat";
const int MODE = 0644;
const char* MESSAGE = "Ye have sought, and ye have found!\r\n";

int
main(int argc, char **argv) {
    int fd;
    int java_offset;

    if ((fd = creat(FILENAME, MODE)) < 0) {
        perror(FILENAME);
        return 1;
    }

    /* Java's DataStreams etc. are defined to be in network byte order,
     * so convert OFFSET to network byte order.
     */
    java_offset = htonl(OFFSET);
```

```
    if (write(fd, &java_offset, sizeof java_offset) < 0) {
        perror("write");
        return 1;
    }

    if (lseek(fd, OFFSET, SEEK_SET) < 0) {
        perror("seek");
        return 1;
    }

    if (write(fd, MESSAGE, strlen(MESSAGE)) != strlen(MESSAGE)) {
        perror("write2");
        return 1;
    }

    if (close(fd) < 0) {
        perror("close!?");
        return 1;
    }

    return 0;
}
```

The same technique can be used in the other direction, of course, and when exchanging data over a network socket, and anyplace else you need to exchange binary data between Java and C.

# 10.18 Saving and Restoring Java Objects

## Problem

You need to write and (later) read objects.

## Solution

Use the object stream classes, ObjectInputStream and ObjectOutputStream. Or use XMLDecoder and XMLEncoder, or Java Data Objects.

## Discussion

*Object serialization* is the ability to convert in-memory objects to an external form that can be sent serially (a byte at a time) and back again. The "and back again" may happen at a later time, or in another JVM on another computer (even one that has a different byte order); Java handles differences between machines. ObjectInputStream and ObjectOutputStream are specialized stream classes designed to read and write objects. They can be used to save objects to disk, as I'll show here, and are also useful in passing objects across a network connection, as I'll show in Recipe 16.6. This fact was not lost on the designers of remote method invocation, or RMI (see Chapter 22), which uses them for transporting the data involved in remote method calls.

As you might imagine, if we pass an object, such as a MyData object, to the writeObject( ) method, and writeObject( ) notices that one of the fields is itself a reference to an object such as a String, that data will get serialized properly. In other words, writeObject works *recursively*. So, we will give it a List of data objects. The first entry in this list is a java.util.Date, for versioning purposes. All remaining objects are of type MyData, a dummy class made up for this demonstration.

To be serializable, the data class must implement the empty Serializable interface. Also, the keyword transient can be used for any data that should *not* be serialized. You might need to do this for security or to prevent attempts to serialize a reference to an object from a nonserializable class. Here it is used to prevent unencrypted passwords from being saved where they might be readable:

```
/** Simple data class used in Serialization demos. */
public class MyData implements Serializable {
    String userName;
    String passwordCypher;
    transient String passwordClear;

    /** This constructor is required for use by JDO */
    public MyData( ) {
    }

    public MyData(String name, String clear) {
        setUserName(name);
        setPassword(clear);
    }

    public String getUserName( ) {
        return userName;
    }

    public void setUserName(String s) {
        userName = s;
    }

    public String getPasswordCypher( ) {
        return passwordCypher;
    }

    /** Save the clear text p/w in the object, it won't get serialized
     * So we must save the encryption! Encryption not shown here.
     */
    public void setPassword(String s) {
        this.passwordClear = s;
        passwordCypher = encrypt(passwordClear);
    }

    public String toString( ) {
        return "MyData[" + userName + "]";
    }
```

```
    /** In real life this would use Java Cryptography */
    protected String encrypt(String s) {
        return "fjslkjlqj2TOP+SECRETkjlskl";
    }
}
```

Since several methods are available for serializing, I define an abstract base class, called SerialDemoAbstractBase, which creates the data list and whose save( ) method calls the abstract write( ) method to actually save the data:

```
/** Demonstrate use of Serialization. Typical Subclass main will be:
 *     public static void main(String[] s) throws Exception {
 *         new SerialDemoZZZ().save( );        // in parent class; calls write
 *         new SerialDemoZZZ().dump( );
 *     }
 */
public abstract class SerialDemoAbstractBase {

    /** The save method in an application */
    public void save( ) throws IOException {
        List l = new ArrayList( );
        // Gather the data
        l.add(new Date( ));
        l.add(new MyData("Ian Darwin", "secret_java_cook"));
        l.add(new MyData("Abby Brant Charles", "dujordian"));
        write(l);
    }

    /** Does the actual serialization */
    public abstract void write(Object theGraph) throws IOException;

    /** Reads the file and displays it. */
    public abstract void dump( ) throws IOException, ClassNotFoundException;
}
```

The implementation for Object Stream serialization is shown here:

```
/** Demonstrate use of standard Object Serialization. */
public class SerialDemoObjectStream extends SerialDemoAbstractBase {
    protected static final String FILENAME = "serial.dat";

    public static void main(String[] s) throws Exception {
        new SerialDemoObjectStream().save( );        // in parent class; calls write
        new SerialDemoObjectStream().dump( );
    }

    /** Does the actual serialization */
    public void write(Object theGraph) throws IOException {
        // Save the data to disk.
        ObjectOutputStream os = new ObjectOutputStream(
            new BufferedOutputStream(
                new FileOutputStream(FILENAME)));
        os.writeObject(theGraph);
        os.close( );
    }
```

```
    public void dump( ) throws IOException, ClassNotFoundException {
        ObjectInputStream is = new ObjectInputStream(
            new FileInputStream(FILENAME));
        System.out.println(is.readObject( ));
        is.close( );
    }
}
```

## See Also

There are other ways to serialize objects, depending upon your storage/interchange goals. One way is to serialize using Java Data Objects (JDO), as discussed in Recipe 20.1. Another is to write the individual data members into an XML file, discussed in Recipe 21.1. The implementation classes for this demonstration are SerialDemoJDO and SerialDemoXML respectively.

# 10.19 Preventing ClassCastExceptions with SerialVersionUID

## Problem

Your classes were recompiled, and you're getting ClassCastExceptions that you shouldn't.

## Solution

Run serialver and paste its output into your classes before you start.

## Discussion

When a class is undergoing a period of evolution, particularly a class being used in a networking context such as RMI or servlets, it may be useful to provide a serialVersionUID value in this class. This is a long integer that is basically a hash of the methods and fields in the class. Both the object serialization API (see Recipe 10. 18) and the JVM, when asked to cast one object to another (common when using collections, as in Chapter 7), either look up or, if not found, compute this value. If the value on the source and destination do not match, a ClassCastException is thrown. Most of the time, this is the correct thing for Java to do.

However, sometimes you may want to allow a class to evolve in a compatible way, but you can't immediately replace all instances in circulation. You must be willing to write code to account for the additional fields being discarded if restoring from the longer format to the shorter and having the default value (null for objects, 0 for numbers and false for Boolean) if you're restoring from the shorter format to the longer. If you are only adding fields and methods in a reasonably compatible way, you can control the compatibility by providing a long int named serialVersionUID. The initial value should be obtained from a JDK tool called serialver, which takes just the class name. Consider a simple class called SerializableUser:

```
/** Demo of a data class that will be used as a JavaBean or as a data
 * class in a Servlet container; making it Serializable allows
 * it to be saved ("serialized") to disk or over a network connection.
 */
public class SerializableUser implements java.io.Serializable {
    public String name;
    public String address;
    public String country;

    // other fields, and methods, here...
}
```

I first compiled it with two different compilers to ensure that the value is a product of the class structure, not of some minor differences in class file format that different compilers might emit:

```
$ jikes +E SerializableUser.java
$ serialver SerializableUser
SerializableUser:    static final long serialVersionUID = -7978489268769667877L;
$ javac SerializableUser.java
$ serialver SerializableUser
SerializableUser:    static final long serialVersionUID = -7978489268769667877L;
```

Sure enough, the class file from both compilers has the same hash. Now let's change the file. I go in with an editor and add a new field, phoneNum, right after country:

```
        public String country;
        public String phoneNum;        // Added this line.

ian:145$ jikes +E SerializableUser.java
ian:146$ serialver SerializableUser
SerializableUser:    static final long serialVersionUID = -8339341455288589756L;
```

Notice how the addition of the field changed the serialVersionUID! Now, if I had wanted this class to evolve in a compatible fashion, here's what I should have done before I started expanding it. I copy and paste the original serialver output into the source file (again using an editor to insert a line before the last line):

```
// SerializableUser.java
    static final long serialVersionUID = -7978489268769667877L;   // Added this line
$ jikes +E SerializableUser.java
$ serialver SerializableUser
SerializableUser:    static final long serialVersionUID = -7978489268769667877L;
$
```

Now all is well: I can interchange serialized versions of this file.

Note that serialver is part of the "object serialization" mechanism, and, therefore, it works only on classes that implement the Serializable interface described in Recipe 10.18.

# 10.20 Reading and Writing JAR or Zip Archives

## Problem

You need to create and/or extract from a JAR archive or a file in the well-known Zip Archive format, as established by PkZip and used by Unix zip/unzip and WinZip.

## Solution

You could use the *jar* program in the Java Development Kit since its file format is identical to the zip format with the addition of the META-INF directory to contain additional structural information. But since this is a book about programming, you are probably more interested in the ZipFile and ZipEntry classes and the stream classes that they provide access to.

## Discussion

The class java.util.zip.ZipFile is not an I/O class *per se*, but a utility class that allows you to read or write the contents of a JAR or zip-format file.* When constructed, it creates a series of ZipEntry objects, one to represent each entry in the archive. In other words, the ZipFile represents the entire archive, and the ZipEntry represents one entry, or one file that has been stored (and compressed) in the archive. The ZipEntry has methods like getName( ), which returns the name that the file had before it was put into the archive, and getInputStream( ), which gives you an InputStream that will transparently uncompress the archive entry by filtering it as you read it. To create a ZipFile object, you need either the name of the archive file or a File object representing it:

```
ZipFile zippy = new ZipFile(fileName);
```

If you want to see whether a given file is present in the archive, you can call the getEntry( ) method with a filename. More commonly, you'll want to process all the entries; for this, use the ZipFile object to get a list of the entries in the archive, in the form of an Enumeration (see Recipe 7.4):

```
Enumeration all = zippy.entries( );
while (all.hasMoreElements( )) {
    ZipEntry entry = (ZipEntry)all.nextElement( );
```

We can then process each entry as we wish. A simple listing program could be:

```
if (entry.isDirectory( ))
    println("Directory: " + e.getName( ));
else
    println("File: " + e.getName( ));
```

---

* There is no support for adding files to an existing archive, so make sure you put all the files in at once or be prepared to recreate the archive from scratch.

A fancier version would extract the files. The program in Example 10-8 does both: it lists by default, but with the -x (extract) switch, it actually extracts the files from the archive.

*Example 10-8. UnZip.java*

```java
import java.io.*;
import java.util.*;
import java.util.zip.*;

/**
 * UnZip -- print or unzip a JAR or PKZIP file using java.util.zip.
 * Final command-line version: extracts files.
 */
public class UnZip {
    /** Constants for mode listing or mode extracting. */
    public static final int LIST = 0, EXTRACT = 1;
    /** Whether we are extracting or just printing TOC */
    protected int mode = LIST;

    /** The ZipFile that is used to read an archive */
    protected ZipFile zippy;

    /** The buffer for reading/writing the ZipFile data */
    protected byte[] b;

    /** Simple main program, construct an UnZipper, process each
     * .ZIP file from argv[] through that object.
     */
    public static void main(String[] argv) {
        UnZip u = new UnZip( );

        for (int i=0; i<argv.length; i++) {
            if ("-x".equals(argv[i])) {
                u.setMode(EXTRACT);
                continue;
            }
            String candidate = argv[i];
            // System.err.println("Trying path " + candidate);
            if (candidate.endsWith(".zip") ||
                candidate.endsWith(".jar"))
                    u.unZip(candidate);
            else System.err.println("Not a zip file? " + candidate);
        }
        System.err.println("All done!");
    }

    /** Construct an UnZip object. Just allocate the buffer */
    UnZip( ) {
        b = new byte[8092];
    }
```

*Example 10-8. UnZip.java (continued)*

```java
    /** Set the Mode (list, extract). */
    protected void setMode(int m) {
        if (m == LIST ||
            m == EXTRACT)
            mode = m;
    }

    /** For a given Zip file, process each entry. */
    public void unZip(String fileName) {
        try {
            zippy = new ZipFile(fileName);
            Enumeration all = zippy.entries();
            while (all.hasMoreElements()) {
                getFile((ZipEntry)all.nextElement());
            }
        } catch (IOException err) {
            System.err.println("IO Error: " + err);
            return;
        }
    }

    /** Process one file from the zip, given its name.
     * Either print the name, or create the file on disk.
     */
    protected void getFile(ZipEntry e) throws IOException {
        String zipName = e.getName();
        if (mode == EXTRACT) {
            // double-check that the file is in the zip
            // if a directory, mkdir it (remember to
            // create intervening subdirectories if needed!)
            if (zipName.endsWith("/")) {
                new File(zipName).mkdirs();
                return;
            }
            // Else must be a file; open the file for output
            System.err.println("Creating " + zipName);
            FileOutputStream os = new FileOutputStream(zipName);
            InputStream  is = zippy.getInputStream(e);
            int n = 0;
            while ((n = is.read(b)) >0)
                os.write(b, 0, n);
            is.close();
            os.close();
        } else
            // Not extracting, just list
            if (e.isDirectory()) {
                System.out.println("Directory " + zipName);
            } else {
                System.out.println("File " + zipName);
            }
    }
}
```

## See Also

JDK 1.5 introduces a new format, called *Pack200*, that is specified as the JSR 200 Network File Transfer Format. See *http://jcp.org/en/jsr/detail?id=200* for details. The new class `javax.pack.Pack200` converts between JAR and Pack200 formats.

# 10.21 Reading and Writing Compressed Files

## Problem

You need to read or write files that have been compressed using GNU zip, or *gzip*. These files are usually saved with the extension *.gz*.

## Solution

Use a `GZipInputStream` or `GZipOutputStream` as appropriate.

## Discussion

The GNU *gzip/gunzip* utilities originated on Unix and are commonly used to compress files. Unlike the Zip format discussed in Recipe 10.20, these programs do not combine the functionality of archiving and compressing, and, therefore, they are easier to work with. However, because they are not archives, people often use them in conjunction with an archiver. On Unix, *tar* and *cpio* are common, with *tar* and *gzip* being the *de facto* standard combination. Many web sites and FTP sites make files available with the extension *.tar.gz*; such files originally had to be first decompressed with *gunzip* and then extracted with *tar*. As this became a common operation, modern versions of *tar* have been extended to support a -z option, which means to *gunzip* before extracting, or to *gzip* before writing, as appropriate.

You may find archived files in *gzip* format on any platform. If you do, they're quite easy to read, again using classes from the `java.util.zip` package. This program assumes that the gzipped file originally contained text (Unicode characters). If not, you would treat it as a stream of bytes, that is, use a `BufferedInputStream` instead of a `BufferedReader`:

```
import java.io.*;
import java.util.zip.*;

public class ReadGZIP {
    public static void main(String argv[]) throws IOException {
        String FILENAME = "file.txt.gz";

        // Since there are 4 constructors here, I wrote them all out in full.
        // In real life you would probably nest these constructor calls.
        FileInputStream fin = new FileInputStream(FILENAME);
        GZIPInputStream gzis = new GZIPInputStream(fin);
        InputStreamReader xover = new InputStreamReader(gzis);
        BufferedReader is = new BufferedReader(xover);
```

```
        String line;
        // Now read lines of text: the BufferedReader puts them in lines,
        // the InputStreamReader does Unicode conversion, and the
        // GZipInputStream "gunzip"s the data from the FileInputStream.
        while ((line = is.readLine()) != null)
            System.out.println("Read: " + line);
    }
}
```

If you need to write files in this format, everything works as you'd expect: you create a GZipOutputStream and write on it, usually using it through a DataOutputStream, BufferedWriter, or PrintWriter.

## See Also

The Inflater and Deflater classes provide access to general-purpose compression and decompression. The InflaterStream and DeflaterStream stream classes provide an I/O-based implementation of Inflater and Deflater.

# 10.22 Program: Text to PostScript

There are several approaches to printing in Java. In a GUI application, or if you want to use the graphical facilities that Java offers (fonts, colors, drawing primitives, and the like), you should refer to Recipe 13.11. However, sometimes you simply want to convert text into a form that prints nicely on a printer that isn't capable of handling raw text on its own (such as most of the PostScript devices on the market). The program in Example 10-9 shows code for reading one or more text files and outputting each of them in a plain font with PostScript around it. Because of the nature of Post-Script, certain characters must be escaped; this is handled in toPsString( ), which in turn is called from doLine( ). There is also code for keeping track of the current position on the page. The output of this program can be sent directly to a PostScript printer.

*Example 10-9. PSFormatter.java*

```
import java.io.*;

/** Text to PS */
public class PSFormatter {
    /** The current input source */
    protected BufferedReader br;
    /** The current page number */
    protected int pageNum;
    /** The current X and Y on the page */
    protected int curX, curY;
    /** The current line number on page */
    protected int lineNum;
    /** The current tab setting */
    protected int tabPos = 0;
    public static final int INCH = 72;     // PS constant: 72 pts/inch
```

*Example 10-9. PSFormatter.java (continued)*

```
// Page parameters
/** The left margin indent */
protected int leftMargin = 50;
/** The top of page indent */
protected int topMargin = 750;
/** The bottom of page indent */
protected int botMargin = 50;

// FORMATTING PARAMETERS
protected int points = 12;
protected int leading = 14;

public static void main(String[] av) throws IOException {
    if (av.length == 0)
        new PSFormatter(
            new InputStreamReader(System.in)).process();
    else for (int i = 0; i < av.length; i++) {
        new PSFormatter(av[i]).process();
    }
}

public PSFormatter(String fileName) throws IOException {
    br = new BufferedReader(new FileReader(fileName));
}

public PSFormatter(Reader in) throws IOException {
    if (in instanceof BufferedReader)
        br = (BufferedReader)in;
    else
        br = new BufferedReader(in);
}

/** Main processing of the current input source. */
protected void process() throws IOException {

    String line;

    prologue();             // emit PostScript prologue, once.

    startPage();          // emit top-of-page (ending previous)

    while ((line = br.readLine()) != null) {
        if (line.startsWith("\f") || line.trim().equals(".bp")) {
            startPage();
            continue;
        }
        doLine(line);
    }

    // finish last page, if not already done.
    if (lineNum != 0)
        println("showpage");
}
```

*Example 10-9. PSFormatter.java (continued)*

```java
    /** Handle start of page details. */
    protected void startPage() {
        if (pageNum++ > 0)
            println("showpage");
        lineNum = 0;
        moveTo(leftMargin, topMargin);
    }

    /** Process one line from the current input */
    protected void doLine(String line) {
        tabPos = 0;
        // count leading (not imbedded) tabs.
        for (int i=0; i<line.length(); i++) {
            if (line.charAt(i)=='\t')
                tabPos++;
            else
                break;
        }
        String l = line.trim(); // removes spaces AND tabs
        if (l.length() == 0) {
            ++lineNum;
            return;
        }
        moveTo(leftMargin + (tabPos * INCH),
            topMargin-(lineNum++ * leading));
        println('(' + toPSString(l)+ ") show");

        // If we just hit the bottom, start a new page
        if (curY <= botMargin)
            startPage();
    }

    /** Overly-simplistic conversion to PS, e.g., breaks on "foo\)bar" */
    protected String toPSString(String o) {
        StringBuffer sb = new StringBuffer();
        for (int i=0; i<o.length(); i++) {
            char c = o.charAt(i);
            switch(c) {
                case '(':   sb.append("\\("); break;
                case ')':   sb.append("\\)"); break;
                default:    sb.append(c); break;
            }
        }
        return sb.toString();
    }

    protected void println(String s) {
        System.out.println(s);
    }
```

*Example 10-9. PSFormatter.java (continued)*

```
    protected void moveTo(int x, int y) {
        curX = x;
        curY = y;
        println(x + " " + y + " " + "moveto");
    }

    void prologue( ) {
        println("%!PS-Adobe");
        println("/Courier findfont " + points + " scalefont setfont ");
    }
}
```

The program could certainly be generalized more, and certain features (such as wrapping long lines) could be handled. I could also wade into the debate among Post-Script experts as to how much of the formatting should be done on the main computer and how much should be done by the PostScript program interpreter running in the printer. But perhaps I won't get into that discussion. At least, not today.

## See Also

As mentioned, Recipe 13.11 contains "better" recipes for printing under Java.

For all topics in this chapter, Elliotte Rusty Harold's book *Java I/O* should be considered the antepenultimate documentation. The penultimate reference is the Javadoc documentation, while the ultimate reference is, if you really need it, the source code for the Java API, to which I have not needed to make a single reference in writing this chapter.

# CHAPTER 11

# Directory and Filesystem Operations

## 11.0 Introduction

This chapter is largely devoted to one class: java.io.File. The File class gives you the ability to list directories, obtain file status, rename and delete files on disk, create directories, and perform other filesystem operations. Many of these would be considered "system programming" functions on some operating systems; Java makes them all as portable as possible.

Note that many of the methods of this class attempt to modify the permanent file store, or disk filesystem, of the computer you run them on. Naturally, you might not have permission to change certain files in certain ways. This can be detected by the Java Virtual Machine's (or the browser's, in an applet) SecurityManager, which will throw an instance of the unchecked exception SecurityException. But failure can also be detected by the underlying operating system: if the security manager approves it, but the user running your program lacks permissions on the directory, for example, you will either get back an indication (such as false) or an instance of the checked exception IOException. This must be caught (or declared in the throws clause) in any code that calls any method that tries to change the filesystem.

## 11.1 Getting File Information

### Problem

You need to know all you can about a given file on disk.

### Solution

Use a java.io.File object.

## Discussion

The File class has a number of "informational" methods. To use any of these, you must construct a File object containing the name of the file it is to operate upon. It should be noted up front that creating a File object has no effect on the permanent filesystem; it is only an object in Java's memory. You must call methods on the File object in order to change the filesystem; as we'll see, there are numerous "change" methods, such as one for creating a new (but empty) file, one for renaming a file, etc., as well as many informational methods. Table 11-1 lists some of the informational methods.

*Table 11-1. java.io.File methods*

| Return type | Method name | Meaning |
|---|---|---|
| boolean | exists() | True if something of that name exists |
| String | getCanonicalPath() | Full name |
| String | getName() | Relative filename |
| String | getParent() | Parent directory |
| boolean | canRead() | True if file is readable |
| boolean | canWrite() | True if file is writable |
| long | lastModified() | File modification time |
| long | length() | File size |
| boolean | isFile() | True if it's a file |
| boolean | isDirectory() | True if it's a directory (note: it might be neither) |

You can't change the name stored in a File object; you simply create a new File object each time you need to refer to a different file:

```
import java.io.*;
import java.util.*;

/**
 * Report on a file's status in Java
 */
public class FileStatus {
    public static void main(String[] argv) throws IOException {

        // Ensure that a filename (or something) was given in argv[0]
        if (argv.length == 0) {
            System.err.println("Usage: FileStatus filename");
            System.exit(1);
        }
        for (int i = 0; i< argv.length; i++) {
            status(argv[i]);
        }
    }
```

```
    public static void status(String fileName) throws IOException {
        System.out.println("---" + fileName + "---");

        // Construct a File object for the given file.
        File f = new File(fileName);

        // See if it actually exists
        if (!f.exists()) {
            System.out.println("file not found");
            System.out.println();      // Blank line
            return;
        }
        // Print full name
        System.out.println("Canonical name " + f.getCanonicalPath());
        // Print parent directory if possible
        String p = f.getParent();
        if (p != null) {
            System.out.println("Parent directory: " + p);
        }
        // Check if the file is readable
        if (f.canRead()) {
            System.out.println("File is readable.");
        }
        // Check if the file is writable
        if (f.canWrite()) {
            System.out.println("File is writable.");
        }
        // Report on the modification time.
        Date d = new Date();
        d.setTime(f.lastModified());
        System.out.println("Last modified " + d);

        // See if file, directory, or other. If file, print size.
        if (f.isFile()) {
            // Report on the file's size
            System.out.println("File size is " + f.length() + " bytes.");
        } else if (f.isDirectory()) {
            System.out.println("It's a directory");
        } else {
            System.out.println("I dunno! Neither a file nor a directory!");
        }

        System.out.println();      // blank line between entries
    }
}
```

When run with the three arguments shown, it produces this output:

```
C:\javasrc\dir_file>java FileStatus  / /tmp/id /autoexec.bat
---/---
Canonical name C:\
File is readable.
File is writable.
Last modified Thu Jan 01 00:00:00 GMT 1970
It's a directory
```

```
---/tmp/id---
file not found

---/autoexec.bat---
Canonical name C:\AUTOEXEC.BAT
Parent directory: \
File is readable.
File is writable.
Last modified Fri Sep 10 15:40:32 GMT 1999
File size is 308 bytes.
```

As you can see, the so-called "canonical name" not only includes a leading directory root of C:\, but also has had the name converted to uppercase. You can tell I ran that on Windows. On Unix, it behaves differently:

```
$ java FileStatus / /tmp/id /autoexec.bat
---/---
Canonical name /
File is readable.
Last modified October 4, 1999 6:29:14 AM PDT
It's a directory

---/tmp/id---
Canonical name /tmp/id
Parent directory: /tmp
File is readable.
File is writable.
Last modified October 8, 1999 1:01:54 PM PDT
File size is 0 bytes.

---/autoexec.bat---
file not found

$
```

A typical Unix system has no *autoexec.bat* file. And Unix filenames (like those on a Mac) can consist of upper- and lowercase characters: what you type is what you get.

## 11.2  Creating a File

### Problem

You need to create a new file on disk, but you don't want to write into it.

### Solution

Use a java.io.File object's createNewFile( ) method.

### Discussion

You could easily create a new file by constructing a FileOutputStream or FileWriter (see Recipe 10.6). But then you'd have to remember to close it as well. Sometimes you want a file to exist, but you don't want to bother putting anything into it. This might be used, for example, as a simple form of interprogram communication: one program could test for the presence of a file and interpret that to mean that the other program has reached a certain state. Here is code that simply creates an empty file for each name you give:

```java
import java.io.*;

/**
 * Create one or more files by name.
 * The final "e" is omitted in homage to the underlying UNIX system call.
 */
public class Creat {
    public static void main(String[] argv) throws IOException {

        // Ensure that a filename (or something) was given in argv[0]
        if (argv.length == 0) {
            System.err.println("Usage: Creat filename");
            System.exit(1);
        }

        for (int i = 0; i< argv.length; i++) {
            // Constructing a File object doesn't affect the disk, but
            // the createNewFile() method does.
            new File(argv[i]).createNewFile();
        }
    }
}
```

# 11.3   Renaming a File

## Problem

You need to change a file's name on disk.

## Solution

Use a java.io.File object's renameTo( ) method.

## Discussion

For reasons best left to the gods of Java, the renameTo( ) method requires not the name you want the file renamed to, but another File object referring to the new name. So to rename a file you must create two File objects, one for the existing name and another for the new name. Then call the renameTo method of the existing name's File object, passing in the second File object. This is easier to see than to explain, so here goes:

```java
import java.io.*;

/**
 * Rename a file in Java
 */
```

```
public class Rename {
    public static void main(String[] argv) throws IOException {

        // Construct the file object. Does NOT create a file on disk!
        File f = new File("Rename.java~"); // backup of this source file.

        // Rename the backup file to "junk.dat"
        // Renaming requires a File object for the target.
        f.renameTo(new File("junk.dat"));
    }
}
```

# 11.4   Deleting a File

## Problem

You need to delete one or more files from the disk.

## Solution

Use a java.io.File object's delete( ) method; it deletes files (subject to permissions) and directories (subject to permissions and to the directory being empty).

## Discussion

This is not very complicated. Simply construct a File object for the file you wish to delete, and call its delete( ) method:

```
import java.io.*;

/**
 * Delete a file from within Java
 */
public class Delete {
    public static void main(String[] argv) throws IOException {

        // Construct a File object for the backup created by editing
        // this source file. The file probably already exists.
        // My editor creates backups by putting ~ at the end of the name.
        File target = new File("Delete.java~");
        // Now delete the file from disk.
        target.delete( );
    }
}
```

Just recall the caveat about permissions in the Introduction to this chapter: if you don't have permission, you can get a return value of false or, possibly, a SecurityException. Note also that there are some differences between platforms. Some versions of Windows allow Java to remove a file that has the read-only bit, but Unix does not allow you to remove a file that you don't have permission on or to remove a directory that isn't empty. Here is a version of Delete with error checking (and reporting of success, too):

---

```
import java.io.*;

/**
 * Delete a file from within Java, with error handling.
 */
public class Delete2 {

    public static void main(String argv[]) {
        for (int i=0; i<argv.length; i++)
            delete(argv[i]);
    }

    public static void delete(String fileName) {
        try {
            // Construct a File object for the file to be deleted.
            File target = new File(fileName);
            // Now delete the file from disk.
            if (target.delete())
                System.out.println("** Deleted " + fileName);
            else
                System.err.println("Failed to delete " + fileName);
        } catch (SecurityException e) {
            System.err.println("Unable to delete " + fileName +
                "(" + e.getMessage() + ")");
        }
    }
}
```

Running it, we get this:

```
$ ls -ld ?
-rw-r--r--  1 ian   ian     0 Oct  8 16:50 a
drwxr-xr-x  2 ian   ian   512 Oct  8 16:50 b
drwxr-xr-x  3 ian   ian   512 Oct  8 16:50 c
$ java Delete2 ?
**Deleted** a
**Deleted** b
Failed to delete c
$ ls -l  c
total 2
drwxr-xr-x  2 ian   ian   512 Oct  8 16:50 d
$ java Delete2 c/d c
**Deleted** c/d
**Deleted** c
$
```

# 11.5   Creating a Transient File

## Problem

You need to create a file with a unique temporary filename, or arrange for a file to be deleted when your program is finished.

## Solution

Use a java.io.File object's createTempFile() or deleteOnExit() method.

## Discussion

The File object has a createTempFile method and a deleteOnExit method. The former creates a file with a unique name (in case several users run the same program at the same time on a server) and the latter arranges for any file (no matter how it was created) to be deleted when the program exits. Here we arrange for a backup copy of a program to be deleted on exit, and we also create a temporary file and arrange for it to be removed on exit. Both files are gone after the program runs:

```java
import java.io.*;

/**
 * Work with temporary files in Java.
 */
public class TempFiles {
    public static void main(String[] argv) throws IOException {

        // 1. Make an existing file temporary

        // Construct a File object for the backup created by editing
        // this source file. The file probably already exists.
        // My editor creates backups by putting ~ at the end of the name.
        File bkup = new File("Rename.java~");
        // Arrange to have it deleted when the program ends.
        bkup.deleteOnExit();

        // 2. Create a new temporary file.

        // Make a file object for foo.tmp, in the default temp directory
        File tmp = File.createTempFile("foo", "tmp");
        // Report on the filename that it made up for us.
        System.out.println("Your temp file is " + tmp.getCanonicalPath());
        // Arrange for it to be deleted at exit.
        tmp.deleteOnExit();
        // Now do something with the temporary file, without having to
        // worry about deleting it later.
        writeDataInTemp(tmp.getCanonicalPath());
    }

    public static void writeDataInTemp(String tempnam) {
        // This version is dummy. Use your imagination.
    }
}
```

Notice that the createTempFile method is like createNewFile (see Recipe 11.2) in that it does create the file. Also be aware that, should the Java Virtual Machine terminate abnormally, the deletion probably does not occur. Finally, there is no way to undo the setting of deleteOnExit() short of something drastic like powering off the computer before the program exits.

# 11.6  Changing File Attributes

## Problem

You want to change attributes of a file other than its name.

## Solution

Use setReadOnly( ) or setLastModified( ).

## Discussion

As we saw in Recipe 11.1, many methods report on a file. By contrast, only a few change the file.

setReadOnly( ) turns on read-only for a given file or directory. It returns true if it succeeds, otherwise false. There is no corresponding method setReadWrite( ). Since you can't undo a setReadOnly( ), use this method with care!

setLastModified( ) allows you to play games with the modification time of a file. This is normally not a good game to play, but it is useful in some types of backup/ restore programs. This method takes an argument that is the number of milliseconds (not seconds) since the beginning of time (January 1, 1970). You can get the original value for the file by calling getLastModified( ) (see Recipe 11.1), or you can get the value for a given date by calling the Date class's getTime( ) method (see Recipe 6.1). setLastModified( ) returns true if it succeeded and false otherwise.

The interesting thing is that the documentation claims that "File objects are immutable," meaning that their state doesn't change. But does calling setReadOnly( ) affect the return value of canRead( )? Let's find out:

```
import java.io.*;

public class ReadOnly {
    public static void main(String[] a) throws IOException {

        File f = new File("f");

        if (!f.createNewFile( )) {
            System.out.println("Can't create new file.");
            return;
        }

        if (!f.canWrite( )) {
            System.out.println("Can't write new file!");
            return;
        }

        if (!f.setReadOnly( )) {
            System.out.println("Grrr! Can't set file read-only.");
            return;
        }
```

```
        if (f.canWrite()) {
            System.out.println("Most immutable, captain!");
            System.out.println("But it still says canWrite() after setReadOnly");
            return;
        } else {
            System.out.println("Logical, captain!");
            System.out.println
                ("canWrite() correctly returns false after setReadOnly");
        }
    }
}
```

When I run it, this program reports what I (and I hope you) would expect:

```
$ jr ReadOnly
+ jikes +E -d . ReadOnly.java
+ java ReadOnly
Logical, captain!
canWrite() correctly returns false after setReadOnly
$
```

So the immutability of a File object refers only to the pathname it contains, not to its read-only-ness.

# 11.7  Listing a Directory

## Problem

You need to list the filesystem entries named in a directory.

## Solution

Use a java.io.File object's list() or listFiles() method.

## Discussion

The java.io.File class contains several methods for working with directories. For example, to list the filesystem entities named in the current directory, just write:

```
String[] list = new File(".").list()
```

To get an array of already constructed File objects rather than Strings, use:

```
File[] list = new File(".").listFiles();
```

This can become a complete program with as little as the following:

```
/** Simple directory lister.
 */
public class Ls {
    public static void main(String argh_my_aching_fingers[]) {
        String[] dir = new java.io.File(".").list(); // Get list of names
        java.util.Arrays.sort(dir);        // Sort it (see  Recipe 7.8)
```

```
        for (int i=0; i<dir.length; i++)
            System.out.println(dir[i]);      // Print the list
    }
}
```

Of course, there's lots of room for elaboration. You could print the names in multiple columns across the page. Or even down the page since you know the number of items in the list before you print. You could omit filenames with leading periods, as does the Unix *ls* program. Or print the directory names first; I once used a directory lister called *lc* that did this, and I found it quite useful. By using listFiles( ), which constructs a new File object for each name, you could print the size of each, as per the DOS *dir* command or the Unix *ls –l* command (see Recipe 11.1). Or you could figure out whether each is a file, a directory, or neither. Having done that, you could pass each directory to your top-level function, and you'd have directory recursion (the Unix *find* command, or *ls –R*, or the DOS *DIR /S* command).

A more flexible way to list filesystem entries is with list(FilenameFilter ff). FilenameFilter is a tiny little interface with only one method: boolean accept(File inDir, String fileName). Suppose you want a listing of only Java-related files (*.java*, *.class*, *.jar*, etc.). Just write the accept( ) method so that it returns true for these files and false for any others. Here is the Ls class warmed over to use a FilenameFilter instance (my OnlyJava class implements this interface) to restrict the listing:

```
import java.io.*;

/**
 * FNFilter - Ls directory lister modified to use FilenameFilter
 */
public class FNFilter {
    public static void main(String argh_my_aching_fingers[]) {
        // Generate the selective list, with a one-use File object.
        String[] dir = new java.io.File(".").list(new OnlyJava());
        java.util.Arrays.sort(dir);        // Sort it (Data Structuring chapter))
        for (int i=0; i<dir.length; i++)
            System.out.println(dir[i]);      // Print the list
    }
}

/** This class implements the FilenameFilter interface.
 * The Accept method only returns true for .java , .jar and .class files.
 */
class OnlyJava implements FilenameFilter {
    public boolean accept(File dir, String s) {
        if (s.endsWith(".java") || s.endsWith(".class") || s.endsWith(".jar"))
            return true;
        // others: projects, ... ?
        return false;
    }
}
```

The `FilenameFilter` need not be a separate class; the online code example `FNFilter2` implements the interface directly in the main class, resulting in a slightly shorter file. In a full-scale application, the list of files returned by the `FilenameFilter` would be chosen dynamically, possibly automatically, based on what you were working on. As we'll see in Recipe 14.11, the file chooser dialogs implement a superset of this functionality, allowing the user to select interactively from one of several sets of files to be listed. This is a great convenience in finding files, just as it is here in reducing the number of files that must be examined.

# 11.8  Getting the Directory Roots

## Problem

You want to know about the top-level directories, such as C:\ and D:\ on Windows.

## Solution

Use the static method `File.listRoots( )`.

## Discussion

Speaking of directory listings, you surely know that all modern desktop computing systems arrange files into hierarchies of directories. But you might not know that on Unix all filenames are somehow "under" the single root directory named /, while on Microsoft platforms, each disk drive has a root directory named \ (A:\ for the first floppy, C:\ for the first hard drive, and other letters for CD-ROM and network drives). If you need to know about all the files on all the disks, you should find out what "directory root" names exist on the particular platform. The static method `listRoots( )` returns (in an array of `File` objects) the available filesystem roots on whatever platform you are running on. Here is a short program to list these, along with its output:

```
C:> type DirRoots.java
import java.io.*;

public class  ListRoots {
    public static void main(String argh_my_aching_fingers[]) {
        File[] drives = File.listRoots(); // Get list of names
        for (int i=0; i<drives.length; i++)
            System.out.println(drives[i]);    // Print the list
    }
}
C:> java DirRoots
A:\
C:\
D:\
C:>
```

As you can see, the program listed my floppy drive (even though the floppy drive was not only empty, but left at home while I wrote this recipe on my notebook computer in a parking lot), the hard disk drive, and the CD-ROM drive.

On Unix there is only one:

```
$ java DirRoots
/
$
```

One thing that is "left out" of the list of roots is the so-called UNC filename. UNC filenames are used on Microsoft platforms to refer to a network-available resource that hasn't been mounted locally on a particular drive letter. For example, my server (running Unix with the Samba SMB file server software) is named darian (made from my surname and first name), and my home directory on that machine is exported or shared with the name ian, so I could refer to a directory named *book* in my home directory under the UNC name \\*darian*\*ian*\*book*. Such a filename would be valid in any Java filename context (assuming you're running on Windows), but you would not learn about it from the File.listRoots( ) method.

# 11.9  Creating New Directories

## Problem

You need to create a directory.

## Solution

Use java.io.File's mkdir( ) or mkdirs( ) method.

## Discussion

Of the two methods used for creating directories, mkdir( ) creates just one directory, while mkdirs( ) creates any parent directories that are needed. For example, if */home/ian* exists and is a directory, the calls:

```
new File("/home/ian/bin").mkdir();
new File("/home/ian/src").mkdir();
```

succeed, whereas:

```
new File("/home/ian/once/twice/again").mkdir();
```

fails, assuming that the directory *once* does not exist. If you wish to create a whole path of directories, you would tell File to make all the directories at once by using mkdirs( ):

```
new File("/home/ian/once/twice/again").mkdirs();
```

Both variants of this command return true if they succeed and false if they fail. Notice that it is possible (but not likely) for mkdirs( ) to create some of the directories and then fail; in this case, the newly created directories are left in the filesystem.

Notice that the spelling `mkdir( )` is all lowercase. While this might be said to violate the normal Java naming conventions (which would suggest `mkDir( )` as the name), it is the name of the underlying operating system call and command on both Unix and DOS (though DOS allows *md* as an alias on the command-line).

## 11.10 Program: Find

This program implements a small subset of the Windows Find Files dialog or the Unix *find* command. However, it has much of the structure needed to build a more complete version of either of these. It uses a custom filename filter controlled by the -n command-line option, which is parsed using my `GetOpt` (see Recipe 2.6). It has a hook for filtering by file size, whose implementation is left as an exercise for the reader:

```java
import com.darwinsys.util.*;
import java.io.*;
import java.io.*;

/**
 * Find - find files by name, size, or other criteria. Non-GUI version.
 */
public class Find {
    /** Main program */
    public static void main(String[] args) {
        Find finder = new Find();
        GetOpt argHandler = new GetOpt("n:s:");
        int c;
        while ((c = argHandler.getopt(args)) != GetOpt.DONE) {
            switch(c) {
            case 'n': finder.filter.setNameFilter(argHandler.optarg( )); break;
            case 's': finder.filter.setSizeFilter(argHandler.optarg( )); break;
            default:
                System.out.println("Got: " + c);
                usage( );
            }
        }
        if (args.length == 0 || argHandler.getOptInd( )-1 == args.length) {
            finder.doName(".");
        } else {
            for (int i = argHandler.getOptInd( )-1; i<args.length; i++)
                finder.doName(args[i]);
        }
    }

    protected FindFilter filter = new FindFilter( );

    public static void usage( ) {
        System.err.println(
            "Usage: Find [-n namefilter][-s sizefilter][dir...]");
        System.exit(1);
    }
```

```
    /** doName - handle one filesystem object by name */
    private void doName(String s) {
        Debug.println("flow", "doName(" + s + ")");
        File f = new File(s);
        if (!f.exists()) {
            System.out.println(s + " does not exist");
            return;
        }
        if (f.isFile())
            doFile(f);
        else if (f.isDirectory()) {
            // System.out.println("d " + f.getPath());
            String objects[] = f.list(filter);

            for (int i=0; i<objects.length; i++)
                doName(s + f.separator + objects[i]);
        } else
            System.err.println("Unknown type: " + s);
    }

    /** doFile - process one regular file. */
    private static void doFile(File f) {
        System.out.println("f " + f.getPath());
    }
}
```

The program uses a class called FindFilter to implement matching:

```
import java.io.*;
import java.util.regex.*;
import com.darwinsys.util.Debug;

/** Class to encapsulate the filtration for Find.
 * For now just setTTTFilter() methods. Really needs to be a real
 * data structure to allow complex things like
 *          -n "*.html" -a \( -size < 0 -o mtime < 5 \).
 * @version $Id: ch11,v 1.5 2004/05/04 20:12:20 ian Exp $
 */
public class FindFilter implements FilenameFilter {
    boolean sizeSet;
    int size;
    String name;
    Pattern nameRE;

    public FindFilter() {
    }

    void setSizeFilter(String sizeFilter) {
        size = Integer.parseInt(sizeFilter);
        sizeSet = true;
    }
```

```
/** Convert the given shell wildcard pattern into internal form (a regex) */
void setNameFilter(String nameFilter) {
    name = nameFilter;
    StringBuffer sb = new StringBuffer('^');
    for (int i = 0; i < nameFilter.length(); i++) {
        char c = nameFilter.charAt(i);
        switch(c) {
            case '.':    sb.append("\\."); break;
            case '*':    sb.append(".*"); break;
            case '?':    sb.append('.'); break;
            default:     sb.append(c); break;
        }
    }
    sb.append('$');
    Debug.println("name", "RE=\"" + sb + "\".");
    try {
        nameRE = Pattern.compile(sb.toString());
    } catch (PatternSyntaxException ex) {
        System.err.println("Error: RE " + sb.toString() +
            " didn't compile: " + ex);
    }
}

/** Do the filtering. For now, only filter on name */
public boolean accept(File dir, String fileName) {
    File f = new File(dir, fileName);
    if (f.isDirectory()) {
        return true;      // allow recursion
    }

    if (nameRE != null) {
        return nameRE.matcher(fileName).matches();
    }

    // TODO size handling.

    // Catchall
    return false;
}
}
```

Exercise for the reader: in the online source directory, you'll find a class called FindNumFilter, which is meant to (someday) allow relational comparison of sizes, modification times, and the like, as most find services already offer. Make this work from the command line, and write a GUI frontend to this program.

---

# CHAPTER 12

# Programming External Devices: Serial and Parallel Ports

## 12.0  Introduction

Peripheral devices are usually external to the computer.* Printers, mice, video cameras, scanners, data/fax modems, plotters, robots, telephones, light switches, weather gauges, Personal Digital Assistants (PDAs), and many others exist "out there," beyond the confines of your desktop or server machine. We need a way to reach out to them.

The Java Communications API not only gives us that but cleverly unifies the programming model for dealing with a range of external devices. It supports both serial (RS232/434, COM, or tty) and parallel (printer, LPT) ports. We'll cover this in more detail later, but briefly, serial ports are used for modems and occasionally printers, and parallel ports are used for printers and sometimes (in the PC world) for Zip drives and other peripherals.

Before USB (Universal Serial Bus) came along, it seemed that parallel ports would dominate for such peripherals, as manufacturers were starting to make video cameras, scanners, and the like. Now, however, USB has become the main attachment mode for such devices. A Java Standards Request (JSR) is in the works to build a standard API for accessing USB devices under Java, but it has not progressed to the release stage. A reference implementation can be downloaded from *http://sourceforge.net/projects/javax-usb*. A competing Java API for USB can be found at *http://jusb.sourceforge.net*. Since the JSR is not completed, I do not document its use here in this edition.

This chapter aims to teach you the principles of controlling many kinds of devices in a machine-independent way using the Java Communications API, which is in package `javax.comm`.

---

* Conveniently ignoring things like "internal modem cards" on desktop machines!

---

I'll start this chapter by showing you how to get a list of available ports and how to control simple serial devices like modems. Such details as baud rate, parity, and word size are attended to before we can write commands to the modem, read the results, and establish communications. We'll move on to parallel (printer) ports and then look at how to transfer data synchronously (using read/write calls directly) and asynchronously (using Java listeners). Then we build a simple phone dialer that can call a friend's voice phone for you—a simple phone controller, if you will. The discussion ends with a serial-port printer/plotter driver.

## The Communications API

The Communications API is centered around the abstract class `CommPort` and its two subclasses, `SerialPort` and `ParallelPort`, which describe two types of ports found on desktop computers. `CommPort` represents a general model of communications and has general methods like `getInputStream( )` and `getOutputStream( )` that allow you to use the information from Chapter 10 to communicate with the device on that port.

However, the constructors for these classes are intentionally nonpublic. Rather than constructing them, you instead use the static factory method `CommPortIdentifier.getPortIdentifiers( )` to get a list of ports, let the user choose a port from this list, and call this `CommPortIdentifier`'s open( ) method to receive a `CommPort` object. You cast the `CommPort` reference to a nonabstract subclass representing a particular type of communications device. At present, the subclass must be either `SerialPort` or `ParallelPort`.

Each of these subclasses has some methods that apply only to that type. For example, the `SerialPort` class has a method to set baud rate, parity, and the like, while the `ParallelPort` class has methods for setting the "port mode" to original PC mode, bidirectional mode, etc.

Both subclasses also have methods that allow you to use the standard Java event model to receive notification of events such as data available for reading and output buffer empty. You can also receive notification of type-specific events such as ring indicator for a serial port and out-of-paper for a parallel port. (Parallel ports were originally for printers and still use their terminology in a few places.)

## About the Code Examples in This Chapter

Java Communication is a standard extension, so it is not a required part of the Java API, which in turn means that your vendor probably didn't ship it. You may need to download the Java Communications API from Sun's Java web site, *http://java.sun.com*, or from your system vendor's web site, and install it. If your platform or vendor doesn't ship it, you may need to find, modify, compile, and install some C code. And, naturally enough, to run some of the examples, you will need additional peripheral devices beyond those normally provided with a desktop computer. Batteries—and peripheral devices—are not included with the purchase of this book.

---

## See Also

Elliotte Rusty Harold's book *Java I/O* contains a chapter that discusses the Communications API in considerable detail, as well as some background issues such as baud rate that we take for granted here. Rusty also discusses some details that I have glossed over, such as the ability to set receive timeouts and buffer sizes.

This book is about portable Java. If you want the gory, low-level details of setting device registers on a 16451 UART on an ISA or PCI PC, you'll have to look elsewhere; several books cover these topics. If you really need the hardware details for I/O ports on other platforms such as Sun Workstations and the Palm Computing Platform, consult either the vendor's documentation and/or the available open source operating systems that run on that platform.

# 12.1  Choosing a Port

## Problem

You need to know what ports are available on a given computer.

## Solution

Use `CommPortIdentifier.getPortIdentifiers()` to return the list of ports.

## Discussion

Many kinds of computers are out there. It's unlikely that you'd find yourself running on a desktop computer with no serial ports, but you might find that there is only one and it's already in use by another program. Or you might want a parallel port and find that the computer has only serial ports. This program shows you how to use the static `CommPortIdentifier` method `getPortIdentifiers()`. This gives you an `Enumeration` (Recipe 7.4) of the serial and parallel ports available on your system. My routine `populate()` processes this list and loads it into a pair of `JComboBoxes` (graphical choosers; see Recipe 14.1), one for serial ports and one for parallel (a third, unknown, covers future expansion of the API). The routine `makeGUI` creates the `JComboBoxes` and arranges to notify us when the user picks one from either of the lists. The name of the selected port is displayed at the bottom of the window. So that you won't have to know much about it to use it, there are public methods. `getSelectedName()` returns the name of the last port chosen by either `JComboBox`; `getSelectedIdentifier()` returns an object called a `CommPortIdentifier` corresponding to the selected port name. Figure 12-1 shows the Port Chooser in action.

Example 12-1 shows the code.

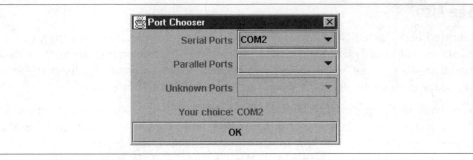

*Figure 12-1. The Communications Port Chooser in action*

*Example 12-1. PortChooser.java*

```java
import java.io.*;
import javax.comm.*;
import java.awt.*;
import java.awt.event.*;
import javax.swing.*;
import java.util.*;

/**
 * Choose a port, any port!
 *
 * Java Communications is a "standard extension" and must be downloaded
 * and installed separately from the JDK before you can even compile this
 * program.
 */
public class PortChooser extends JDialog implements ItemListener {
    /** A mapping from names to CommPortIdentifiers. */
    protected HashMap map = new HashMap( );
    /** The name of the choice the user made. */
    protected String selectedPortName;
    /** The CommPortIdentifier the user chose. */
    protected CommPortIdentifier selectedPortIdentifier;
    /** The JComboBox for serial ports */
    protected JComboBox serialPortsChoice;
    /** The JComboBox for parallel ports */
    protected JComboBox parallelPortsChoice;
    /** The JComboBox for anything else */
    protected JComboBox other;
    /** The SerialPort object */
    protected SerialPort ttya;
    /** To display the chosen */
    protected JLabel choice;
    /** Padding in the GUI */
    protected final int PAD = 5;

    /** This will be called from either of the JComboBoxes when the
     * user selects any given item.
     */
```

*Example 12-1. PortChooser.java (continued)*

```
public void itemStateChanged(ItemEvent e) {
    // Get the name
    selectedPortName = (String)((JComboBox)e.getSource()).getSelectedItem();
    // Get the given CommPortIdentifier
    selectedPortIdentifier = (CommPortIdentifier)map.get(selectedPortName);
    // Display the name.
    choice.setText(selectedPortName);
}

/* The public "getter" to retrieve the chosen port by name. */
public String getSelectedName() {
    return selectedPortName;
}

/* The public "getter" to retrieve the selection by CommPortIdentifier. */
public CommPortIdentifier getSelectedIdentifier() {
    return selectedPortIdentifier;
}

/** A test program to show up this chooser. */
public static void main(String[] ap) {
    PortChooser c = new PortChooser(null);
    c.setVisible(true);      // blocking wait
    System.out.println("You chose " + c.getSelectedName() +
        " (known by " + c.getSelectedIdentifier() + ").");
    System.exit(0);
}

/** Construct a PortChooser --make the GUI and populate the ComboBoxes.
 */
public PortChooser(JFrame parent) {
    super(parent, "Port Chooser", true);

    makeGUI();
    populate();
    finishGUI();
}

/** Build the GUI. You can ignore this for now if you have not
 * yet worked through the GUI chapter. Your mileage may vary.
 */
protected void makeGUI() {
    // CONTENTS OF THIS METHOD OMITTED -- SEE ONLINE SOURCE VERSION
}

/** Populate the ComboBoxes by asking the Java Communications API
 * what ports it has.  Since the initial information comes from
 * a Properties file, it may not exactly reflect your hardware.
 */
protected void populate() {
    // get list of ports available on this particular computer,
    // by calling static method in CommPortIdentifier.
    Enumeration pList = CommPortIdentifier.getPortIdentifiers();
```

*Example 12-1. PortChooser.java (continued)*

```
        // Process the list, putting serial and parallel into ComboBoxes
        while (pList.hasMoreElements( )) {
            CommPortIdentifier cpi = (CommPortIdentifier)pList.nextElement( );
            // System.out.println("Port " + cpi.getName( ));
            map.put(cpi.getName( ), cpi);
            if (cpi.getPortType( ) == CommPortIdentifier.PORT_SERIAL) {
                serialPortsChoice.setEnabled(true);
                serialPortsChoice.addItem(cpi.getName( ));
            } else if (cpi.getPortType( ) == CommPortIdentifier.PORT_PARALLEL) {
                parallelPortsChoice.setEnabled(true);
                parallelPortsChoice.addItem(cpi.getName( ));
            } else {
                other.setEnabled(true);
                other.addItem(cpi.getName( ));
            }
        }
        serialPortsChoice.setSelectedIndex(-1);
        parallelPortsChoice.setSelectedIndex(-1);
    }

    protected void finishGUI( ) {
        serialPortsChoice.addItemListener(this);
        parallelPortsChoice.addItemListener(this);
        other.addItemListener(this);
        pack( );
        addWindowListener(new WindowCloser(this, true));
    }
}
```

# 12.2   Opening a Serial Port

## Problem

You want to set up a serial port and open it for input/output.

## Solution

Use a CommPortIdentifier's open( ) method to get a SerialPort object.

## Discussion

Now you've picked your serial port, but it's not yet ready to go. Baud rate. Parity. Stop bits. These things have been the bane of many a programmer's life. Having needed to work out the details of setting them on many platforms over the years, including CP/M systems, IBM PCs, and IBM System/370 mainframes, I can report that it's no fun. Finally, Java has provided a portable interface for setting all these parameters.

The steps in setting up and opening a serial port are as follows:

1. Get the name and `CommPortIdentifier` (which you can do using my `PortChooser` class).

2. Call the `CommPortIdentifier`'s open( ) method; cast the resulting `CommPort` object to a `SerialPort` object (this cast fails if the user chooses a parallel port!).

3. Set the serial communications parameters, such as baud rate, parity, stop bits, and the like, either individually or all at once, using the convenience routine `setSerialPortParams( )`.

4. Call the `getInputStream` and `getOutputStream` methods of the `SerialPort` object, and construct any additional `Stream` or `Writer` objects (see Chapter 10).

You are then ready to read and write on the serial port. Example 12-2 is code that implements all these steps for a serial port. Some of this code is for parallel ports, which we'll discuss in Recipe 12.3.

*Example 12-2. CommPortOpen.java*

```java
import java.awt.*;
import java.io.*;
import javax.comm.*;
import java.util.*;

/**
 * Open a serial port using Java Communications.
 *
 */
public class CommPortOpen {
    /** How long to wait for the open to finish up. */
    public static final int TIMEOUTSECONDS = 30;
    /** The baud rate to use. */
    public static final int BAUD = 9600;
    /** The parent Frame, for the chooser. */
    protected Frame parent;
    /** The input stream */
    protected DataInputStream is;
    /** The output stream */
    protected PrintStream os;
    /** The chosen Port Identifier */
    CommPortIdentifier thePortID;
    /** The chosen Port itself */
    CommPort thePort;

    public static void main(String[] argv)
        throws IOException, NoSuchPortException, PortInUseException,
            UnsupportedCommOperationException {

        new CommPortOpen(null).converse( );

        System.exit(0);
    }
```

*Example 12-2. CommPortOpen.java (continued)*

```java
/* Constructor */
public CommPortOpen(Frame f)
    throws IOException, NoSuchPortException, PortInUseException,
        UnsupportedCommOperationException {

    // Use the PortChooser from before. Pop up the JDialog.
    PortChooser chooser = new PortChooser(null);

    String portName = null;
    do {
        chooser.setVisible(true);

        // Dialog done. Get the port name.
        portName = chooser.getSelectedName( );

        if (portName == null)
            System.out.println("No port selected. Try again.\n");
    } while (portName == null);

    // Get the CommPortIdentifier.
    thePortID = chooser.getSelectedIdentifier( );

    // Now actually open the port.
    // This form of openPort takes an Application Name and a timeout.
    //
    System.out.println("Trying to open " + thePortID.getName( ) + "...");

    switch (thePortID.getPortType( )) {
    case CommPortIdentifier.PORT_SERIAL:
        thePort = thePortID.open("DarwinSys DataComm",
            TIMEOUTSECONDS * 1000);
        SerialPort myPort = (SerialPort) thePort;

        // set up the serial port
        myPort.setSerialPortParams(BAUD, SerialPort.DATABITS_8,
            SerialPort.STOPBITS_1, SerialPort.PARITY_NONE);
        break;

    case CommPortIdentifier.PORT_PARALLEL:
        thePort = thePortID.open("DarwinSys Printing",
            TIMEOUTSECONDS * 1000);
        ParallelPort pPort = (ParallelPort)thePort;

        // Tell API to pick "best available mode" - can fail!
        // myPort.setMode(ParallelPort.LPT_MODE_ANY);

        // Print what the mode is
        int mode = pPort.getMode( );
        switch (mode) {
            case ParallelPort.LPT_MODE_ECP:
                System.out.println("Mode is: ECP");
                break;
```

*Example 12-2. CommPortOpen.java (continued)*

```
                    case ParallelPort.LPT_MODE_EPP:
                        System.out.println("Mode is: EPP");
                        break;
                    case ParallelPort.LPT_MODE_NIBBLE:
                        System.out.println("Mode is: Nibble Mode.");
                        break;
                    case ParallelPort.LPT_MODE_PS2:
                        System.out.println("Mode is: Byte mode.");
                        break;
                    case ParallelPort.LPT_MODE_SPP:
                        System.out.println("Mode is: Compatibility mode.");
                        break;
                    // ParallelPort.LPT_MODE_ANY is a "set only" mode;
                    // tells the API to pick "best mode"; will report the
                    // actual mode it selected.
                    default:
                        throw new IllegalStateException
                            ("Parallel mode " + mode + " invalid.");
                }
                break;
        default:    // Neither parallel nor serial??
            throw new IllegalStateException("Unknown port type " + thePortID);
        }

        // Get the input and output streams
        // Printers can be write-only
        try {
            is = new DataInputStream(thePort.getInputStream());
        } catch (IOException e) {
            System.err.println("Can't open input stream: write-only");
            is = null;
        }
        os = new PrintStream(thePort.getOutputStream(), true);
    }

    /** This method will be overridden by nontrivial subclasses
     * to hold a conversation.
     */
    protected void converse() throws IOException {

        System.out.println("Ready to read and write port.");

        // Input/Output code not written -- must subclass.

        // Finally, clean up.
        if (is != null)
            is.close();
        os.close();
    }
}
```

As noted in the comments, this class contains a dummy version of the converse method. In following sections we'll expand on the input/output processing by subclassing and overriding this method.

# 12.3   Opening a Parallel Port

## Problem

You want to open a parallel port.

## Solution

Use a `CommPortIdentifier`'s open( ) method to get a `ParallelPort` object.

## Discussion

Enough of serial ports! Parallel ports as we know 'em are an outgrowth of the "dot matrix" printer industry. Before the IBM PC, Tandy and other "pre-PC" PC makers needed a way to hook printers to their computers. Centronics, a company that made a variety of dot matrix printers, had a standard connector mechanism that caught on, changing only when IBM got into the act. Along the way, PC makers found they needed more speed, so they built faster printer ports. And peripheral makers took advantage of this by using the faster (and by now bidirectional) printer ports to hook up all manner of weird devices—like scanners, SCSI and Ethernet controllers, and others—via parallel ports. You can, in theory, open any of these devices and control them; the logic of controlling such devices is left as an exercise for the reader. For now we'll just open a parallel port.

Just as the `SerialPortOpen` program sets the port's parameters, the `ParallelPortOpen` program sets the parallel port access type or "mode." Like baud rate and parity, this requires some knowledge of the particular desktop computer's hardware. There are several common modes, or types of printer interface and interaction. The oldest is "simple parallel port," which the API calls `MODE_SPP`. This is an output-only parallel port. Other common modes include EPP (extended parallel port, `MODE_EPP`) and ECP (extended communication port, `MODE_ECP`). The API defines a few rare ones—as well as `MODE_ANY`, the default—and allows the API to pick the best mode. In my experience, the API doesn't always do a very good job of picking, either with `MODE_ANY` or with explicit settings. And indeed, there may be interactions with the BIOS (at least on a PC) and on device drivers (Windows, Unix). What follows is a simple example that opens a parallel port (although it works on a serial port also), opens a file, and sends it; in other words, a very trivial printer driver. Now this is obviously *not* the way to drive printers. Most operating systems provide support for a wide variety of printers (Mac OS and Windows both do, at least; Unix systems tend to assume a PostScript or HP printer). This example, just to make life simple by allowing us to work with ASCII files, copies a short file of PostScript. The intent of the PostScript job is just to print the little logo in Figure 12-2.

*Figure 12-2. PostScript printer output*

The PostScript code used in this particular example is fairly short:

```
%!PS-Adobe

% Draw a circle of "Java Cookbook"
% simplified from Chapter 9 of the Adobe Systems "Blue Book",
% PostScript Language Tutorial and Cookbook

% center the origin
250 350 translate

/Helvetica-BoldOblique findfont
    30 scalefont
    setfont

% print circle of Java
0.4 setlinewidth     % make outlines not too heavy
20 20 340 {
    gsave
    rotate 0 0 moveto
    (Java) true charpath stroke
    grestore
} for

% print "Java Cookbook" in darker outline
% fill w/ light gray to contrast w/ spiral
1.5 setlinewidth
0 0 moveto
(Java Cookbook) true charpath
gsave 1 setgray fill grestore
stroke

% now send it all to the printed page
showpage
```

It doesn't matter if you know PostScript; it's just the printer control language that some printers accept. What matters to us is that we can open the parallel port, and, if an appropriate printer is connected (I used an HP6MP, which supports Post-Script), the logo prints, appearing near the middle of the page. Example 12-3 is a short program that again subclasses CommPortOpen, opens a file that is named on the command line, and copies it to the given port. Using it looks like this:

```
C:\javasrc\io\javacomm>java ParallelPrint javacook.ps
Mode is: Compatibility mode.
Can't open input stream: write-only

C:\javasrc\io\javacomm>
```

The message "Can't open input stream" appears because my notebook's printer port is (according to the Java Comm API) unable to do bidirectional I/O. This is, in fact, incorrect, as I have used various printer-port devices that require bidirectional I/O, such as the Logitech (formerly Connectix) QuickCam, on this same hardware platform (but under Unix and Windows, not using Java). This message is just a warning; the program works correctly despite it.

*Example 12-3. ParallelPrint.com*

```java
import java.awt.*;
import java.io.*;
import javax.comm.*;

/**
 * Print to a serial port using Java Communications.
 *
 */
public class ParallelPrint extends CommPortOpen {

    protected static String inputFileName;

    public static void main(String[] argv)
        throws IOException, NoSuchPortException, PortInUseException,
            UnsupportedCommOperationException {

        if (argv.length != 1) {
            System.err.println("Usage: ParallelPrint filename");
            System.exit(1);
        }
        inputFileName = argv[0];

        new ParallelPrint(null).converse();

        System.exit(0);
    }

    /* Constructor */
    public ParallelPrint(Frame f)
        throws IOException, NoSuchPortException, PortInUseException,
            UnsupportedCommOperationException {

        super(f);
    }

    /**
     * Hold the (one-way) conversation.
     */
    protected void converse() throws IOException {
```

*Example 12-3. ParallelPrint.com (continued)*

```
        // Make a reader for the input file.
        BufferedReader file = new BufferedReader(
            new FileReader(inputFileName));

        String line;
        while ((line = file.readLine()) != null)
            os.println(line);

        // Finally, clean up.
        file.close();
        os.close();
    }
}
```

# 12.4  Resolving Port Conflicts

## Problem

Somebody else is using the port you want, and they won't let go!

## Solution

Use a PortOwnershipListener.

## Discussion

If you run the CommPortOpen program and select a port that is opened by a native program such as HyperTerminal on Windows, you get a PortInUseException after the timeout period is up:

```
C:\javasrc\commport>java CommPortOpen
Exception in thread "main" javax.comm.PortInUseException: Port currently owned by
Unknown Windows Application
        at javax.comm.CommPortIdentifier.open(CommPortIdentifier.java:337)
        at CommPortOpen.main(CommPortOpen.java:41)
```

If, on the other hand, you run two copies of CommPortOpen at the same time for the same port, you will see something like the following:

```
C:\javasrc\commport>java CommPortOpen
Exception in thread "main" javax.comm.PortInUseException: Port currently owned by
DarwinSys DataComm
        at javax.comm.CommPortIdentifier.open(CommPortIdentifier.java:337)
        at CommPortOpen.main(CommPortOpen.java:41)

C:\javasrc\commport>
```

To resolve conflicts over port ownership, you can register a PortOwnershipListener so that you are told if another (Java) application wants to use the port. Then you can either close the port and the other application will get it, or ignore the request and the other program will get a PortInUseException, as we did here.

What is this "listener"? The Event Listener model is used in many places in Java. It may be best known for its uses in GUIs (see Recipe 14.4). The basic form is that you have to *register* an object as a *listener* with an *event source*. The event source then calls a well-known method to notify you that a particular event has occurred. In the GUI, for example, an event occurs when the user presses a button with the mouse; if you wish to monitor these events, you need to call the button object's `addActionListener( )` method, passing an instance of the `ActionListener` interface (which can be your main class, an inner class, or some other class).

How does a listener work in practice? To simplify matters, we've again subclassed from our command-line program `CommPortOpen` to pop up a dialog if one copy of the program tries to open a port that another copy already has open. If you run two copies of the new program `PortOwner` at the same time, and select the same port in each, you'll see the dialog shown in Figure 12-3.

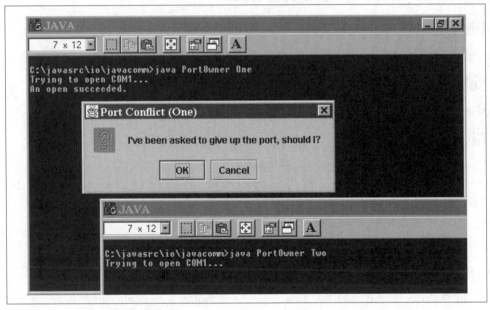

*Figure 12-3. Port conflict resolution*

The trick to make this happen is simply to add a `CommPortOwnershipListener` to the `CommPortIdentifier` object. You are then called when any program gets ownership, gives up ownership, or if there is a conflict. Example 12-4 shows the program with this addition.

*Example 12-4. PortOwner.java*

```
import javax.comm.*;
import java.io.*;
import javax.swing.*;
```

*Example 12-4. PortOwner.java (continued)*

```java
/** Demonstrate the port conflict resolution mechanism.
 * Run two copies of this program and choose the same port in each.
 */
public class PortOwner extends CommPortOpen {
    /** A name for showing which of several instances of this program */
    String myName;

    public PortOwner(String name)
        throws IOException, NoSuchPortException, PortInUseException,
            UnsupportedCommOperationException {

        super(null);
        myName = name;
        thePortID.addPortOwnershipListener(new MyResolver());
    }

    public void converse() {
        // lah de dah...
        // To simulate a long conversation on the port...

        try {
            Thread.sleep(1000 * 1000);
        } catch (InterruptedException cantHappen) {
            //
        }
    }

    /** An inner class that handles the ports conflict resolution. */
    class MyResolver implements CommPortOwnershipListener {
        protected boolean owned = false;
        public void ownershipChange(int whaHoppen) {
            switch (whaHoppen) {
            case PORT_OWNED:
                System.out.println("An open succeeded.");
                owned = true;
                break;
            case PORT_UNOWNED:
                System.out.println("A close succeeded.");
                owned = false;
                break;
            case PORT_OWNERSHIP_REQUESTED:
                if (owned) {
                    if (JOptionPane.showConfirmDialog(null,
                        "I've been asked to give up the port, should I?",
                        "Port Conflict (" + myName + ")",
                        JOptionPane.OK_CANCEL_OPTION) == 0)
                    thePort.close();
                } else {
                    System.out.println("Somebody else has the port");
                }
            }
        }
    }
}
```

*Example 12-4. PortOwner.java (continued)*

```
public static void main(String[] argv)
    throws IOException, NoSuchPortException, PortInUseException,
        UnsupportedCommOperationException {

    if (argv.length != 1) {
        System.err.println("Usage: PortOwner aname");
        System.exit(1);
    }

    new PortOwner(argv[0]).converse();

    System.exit(0);
    }
}
```

Note the single argument to ownershipChange( ). Do not assume that only your listener will be told when an event occurs; it will be called whether you are the affected
program or simply a bystander. To see if you are the program being requested to give
up ownership, you have to check to see if you already have the port that is being
requested (for example, by opening it successfully!).

# 12.5  Reading and Writing: Lock-Step

## Problem

You want to read and write on a port, and your communications needs are simple.

## Solution

Just use read and write calls.

## Discussion

Suppose you need to send a command to a device and get a response back, and then
send another, and get another. This has been called a "lock-step" protocol, since
both ends of the communication are locked into step with one another, like soldiers
on parade. There is no requirement that both ends be able to write at the same time
since you know what the response to your command should be and don't proceed
until you have received that response. A well-known example is using a standard
Hayes-command-set modem to just dial a phone number. In its simplest form, you
send the command string ATZ and expect the response OK; then send ATD with the
number, and expect CONNECT. To implement this, we first subclass from
CommPortOpen to add two functions, send and expect, which perform reasonably obvious functions for dealing with such devices. See Example 12-5.

---

*Example 12-5. CommPortModem.java*

```java
import java.awt.*;
import java.io.*;
import javax.comm.*;
import java.util.*;

/**
 * Subclasses CommPortOpen and adds send/expect handling for dealing
 * with Hayes-type modems.
 *
 */
public class CommPortModem extends CommPortOpen {
    /** The last line read from the serial port. */
    protected String response;
    /** A flag to control debugging output. */
    protected boolean debug = true;

    public CommPortModem(Frame f)
        throws IOException, NoSuchPortException,PortInUseException,
            UnsupportedCommOperationException {
        super(f);
    }

    /** Send a line to a PC-style modem. Send \r\n, regardless of
     * what platform we're on, instead of using println().
     */
    protected void send(String s) throws IOException {
        if (debug) {
            System.out.print(">>> ");
            System.out.print(s);
            System.out.println();
        }
        os.print(s);
        os.print("\r\n");

        // Expect the modem to echo the command.
        if (!expect(s)) {
            System.err.println("WARNING: Modem did not echo command.");
        }

        // The modem sends an extra blank line by way of a prompt.
        // Here we read and discard it.
        String junk = is.readLine();
        if (junk.length() != 0) {
            System.err.print("Warning: unexpected response: ");
            System.err.println(junk);
        }
    }

    /** Read a line, saving it in "response".
     * @return true if the expected String is contained in the response, false if not.
     */
```

*Example 12-5. CommPortModem.java (continued)*

```java
    protected boolean expect(String exp) throws IOException {
        response = is.readLine( );
        if (debug) {
            System.out.print("<<< ");
            System.out.print(response);
            System.out.println( );
        }
        return response.indexOf(exp) >= 0;
    }
}
```

Finally, Example 12-6 extends our `CommPortModem` program to initialize the modem and dial a telephone number.

*Example 12-6. CommPortDial.java*

```java
import java.io.*;
import javax.comm.*;
import java.util.*;

/**
 * Dial a phone using the Java Communications Package.
 *
 */
public class CommPortDial extends CommPortModem {

    protected static String number = "000-0000";

    public static void main(String[] ap)
        throws IOException, NoSuchPortException,PortInUseException,
            UnsupportedCommOperationException {
        if (ap.length == 1)
            number = ap[0];
        new CommPortDial( ).converse( );
        System.exit(0);
    }

    public CommPortDial( )
        throws IOException, NoSuchPortException, PortInUseException,
            UnsupportedCommOperationException {
        super(null);
    }

    protected void converse( ) throws IOException {

        String resp;          // the modem response.

        // Send the reset command
        send("ATZ");

        expect("OK");

        send("ATDT" + number);
```

*Example 12-6. CommPortDial.java (continued)*

```
        expect("OK");

        try {
            Thread.sleep(5000);
        } catch (InterruptedException e) {
            // nothing to do
        }
        is.close();
        os.close();
    }
}
```

# 12.6  Reading and Writing: Event-Driven

## Problem

After the connection is made, you don't know what order to read or write in.

## Solution

Use Java Communication Events to notify you when data becomes available. Or use threads (see Recipe 12.7).

## Discussion

While lock-step mode is acceptable for dialing a modem, it breaks down when you have two independent agents communicating over a port. Either end may be a person or a program, so you cannot predict who will need to read and who will need to write. Consider the simplest case: the programs at both ends try to read at the same time! Using the lock-step model, each end will wait forever for the other end to write something. This error condition is known as a *deadlock*, since both ends are locked up, dead, until a person intervenes, or the communication line drops, or the world ends, or somebody making tea blows a fuse and causes one of the machines to halt.

There are two general approaches to this problem: event-driven activity, wherein the Communications API notifies you when the port is ready to be read or written; and threads-based activity, wherein each "direction" (from the user to the remote, and from the remote to the user) has its own little flow of control, causing only the reads in that direction to wait. We'll discuss each of these.

First, Example 12-7 reads from a serial port using the event-driven approach.

*Example 12-7. SerialReadByEvents.java*

```
import java.awt.*;
import java.io.*;
import javax.comm.*;
import java.util.*;
```

*Example 12-7. SerialReadByEvents.java (continued)*

```java
/**
 * Read from a Serial port, notifying when data arrives.
 * Simulation of part of an event-logging service.
 */
public class SerialReadByEvents extends CommPortOpen
    implements SerialPortEventListener {

    public static void main(String[] argv)
        throws IOException, NoSuchPortException, PortInUseException,
            UnsupportedCommOperationException {

        new SerialReadByEvents(null).converse( );
    }

    /* Constructor */
    public SerialReadByEvents(Frame f)
        throws IOException, NoSuchPortException, PortInUseException,
            UnsupportedCommOperationException {

        super(f);
    }

    protected BufferedReader ifile;

    /**
     * Hold the conversation.
     */
    protected void converse( ) throws IOException {

        if (!(thePort instanceof SerialPort)) {
            System.err.println("But I wanted a SERIAL port!");
            System.exit(1);
        }
        // Tell the Comm API that we want serial events.
        ((SerialPort)thePort).notifyOnDataAvailable(true);
        try {
            ((SerialPort)thePort).addEventListener(this);
        } catch (TooManyListenersException ev) {
            // "CantHappen" error
            System.err.println("Too many listeners(!) " + ev);
            System.exit(0);
        }

        // Make a reader for the input file.
        ifile = new BufferedReader(new InputStreamReader(is));

        //
    }
    public void serialEvent(SerialPortEvent ev) {
        String line;
        try {
            line = ifile.readLine( );
```

*Example 12-7. SerialReadByEvents.java (continued)*

```
            if (line == null) {
                System.out.println("EOF on serial port.");
                System.exit(0);
            }
            os.println(line);
        } catch (IOException ex) {
            System.err.println("IO Error " + ex);
        }
    }
}
```

As you can see, the serialEvent( ) method does the readLine( ) calls. "But wait!" I hear you say. "This program is not a very meaningful example. It could just as easily be implemented using the lock-step method of Recipe 12.5." True enough, gentle reader. Have patience with your humble and obedient servant. Here is a program that reads from any of the serial ports, whenever data arrives. The program is representative of a class of programs called "data loggers," which receive data from a number (possibly a large number) of remote locations, and log them centrally. One example is a burglar alarm monitoring station, which needs to log activities such as the alarm being turned off at the close of the day, entry by the cleaners later, what time they left, and so on. And then, of course, it needs to notify the operator of the monitoring station when an unexpected event occurs. This last step is left as an exercise for the reader.

Example 12-8 makes use of the EventListener model and uses a unique instance of the inner class Logger for each serial port it's able to open.

*Example 12-8. SerialLogger.java*

```
import java.io.*;
import javax.comm.*;
import java.util.*;

/**
 * Read from multiple Serial ports, notifying when data arrives on any.
 */
public class SerialLogger {

    public static void main(String[] argv)
        throws IOException, NoSuchPortException, PortInUseException,
            UnsupportedCommOperationException {

        new SerialLogger();
    }

    /* Constructor */
    public SerialLogger()
        throws IOException, NoSuchPortException, PortInUseException,
            UnsupportedCommOperationException {
```

*Example 12-8. SerialLogger.java (continued)*

```java
        // get list of ports available on this particular computer,
        // by calling static method in CommPortIdentifier.
        Enumeration pList = CommPortIdentifier.getPortIdentifiers();

        // Process the list, saving Serial Ports in ComboBoxes
        while (pList.hasMoreElements()) {
            CommPortIdentifier cpi = (CommPortIdentifier)pList.nextElement();
            String name = cpi.getName();
            System.out.print("Port " + name + " ");
            if (cpi.getPortType() == CommPortIdentifier.PORT_SERIAL) {
                System.out.println("is a Serial Port: " + cpi);

                SerialPort thePort;
                try {
                    thePort = (SerialPort)cpi.open("Logger", 1000);
                } catch (PortInUseException ev) {
                    System.err.println("Port in use: " + name);
                    continue;
                }

                // Tell the Comm API that we want serial events.
                thePort.notifyOnDataAvailable(true);
                try {
                    thePort.addEventListener(new Logger(cpi.getName(), thePort));
                } catch (TooManyListenersException ev) {
                    // "CantHappen" error
                    System.err.println("Too many listeners(!) " + ev);
                    System.exit(0);
                }
            }
        }
    }

    /** Handle one port. */
    public class Logger implements SerialPortEventListener {
        String portName;
        SerialPort thePort;
        BufferedReader ifile;
        public Logger(String name, SerialPort port) throws IOException {
            portName = name;
            thePort = port;
            // Make a reader for the input file.
            ifile = new BufferedReader(
                new InputStreamReader(thePort.getInputStream()));
        }
        public void serialEvent(SerialPortEvent ev) {
            String line;
            try {
                line = ifile.readLine();
                if (line == null) {
                    System.out.println("EOF on serial port.");
                    System.exit(0);
```

*Example 12-8. SerialLogger.java (continued)*

```
            }
            System.out.println(portName + ": " + line);
        } catch (IOException ex) {
            System.err.println("IO Error " + ex);
        }
    }
  }
}
```

# 12.7   Reading and Writing: Threads

## Problem

After the connection is made, you don't know what order to read or write in.

## Solution

Use a *thread* to handle each direction.

## Discussion

When you have two things that must happen at the same time or unpredictably, the normal Java paradigm is to use a thread for each. We discuss threads in detail in Chapter 24, but for now, think of a thread as a small, semi-independent flow of control within a program, just as a program is a small, self-contained flow of control within an operating system. The Thread API requires you to construct a method whose signature is public void run( ) to do the body of work for the thread and call the start( ) method of the thread to "ignite" it and start it running independently. This example creates a Thread subclass called DataThread, which reads from one file and writes to another. DataThread works a byte at a time so that it works correctly with interactive prompts, which don't end at a line ending. My now-familiar converse( ) method creates two of these DataThreads, one to handle data "traffic" from the keyboard to the remote, and one to handle bytes arriving from the remote and copy them to the standard output. For each of these, the start( ) method is called. Example 12-9 shows the entire program.

*Example 12-9. CommPortThreaded.java*

```
import java.io.*;
import javax.comm.*;
import java.util.*;

/**
 * This program tries to do I/O in each direction using a separate Thread.
 */
public class CommPortThreaded extends CommPortOpen {
```

*Example 12-9. CommPortThreaded.java (continued)*

```java
    public static void main(String[] ap)
        throws IOException, NoSuchPortException,PortInUseException,
            UnsupportedCommOperationException {
        CommPortThreaded cp;
        try {
            cp = new CommPortThreaded( );
            cp.converse( );
        } catch(Exception e) {
            System.err.println("You lose!");
            System.err.println(e);
        }
    }

    public CommPortThreaded( )
        throws IOException, NoSuchPortException, PortInUseException,
            UnsupportedCommOperationException {
        super(null);
    }

    /** This version of converse( ) just starts a Thread in each direction.
     */
    protected void converse( ) throws IOException {

        String resp;        // the modem response.

        new DataThread(is, System.out).start( );
        new DataThread(new DataInputStream(System.in), os).start( );

    }

    /** This inner class handles one side of a conversation. */
    class DataThread extends Thread {
        DataInputStream inStream;
        PrintStream pStream;

        /** Construct this object */
        DataThread(DataInputStream is, PrintStream os) {
            inStream = is;
            pStream = os;
        }

        /** A Thread's run method does the work. */
        public void run( ) {
            byte ch = 0;
            try {
                while ((ch = (byte)inStream.read( )) != -1)
                    pStream.print((char)ch);
            } catch (IOException e) {
                System.err.println("Input or output error: " + e);
                return;
            }
        }
    }
}
```

# 12.8  Program: Penman Plotter

The program in Example 12-10 is an outgrowth of the Plotter class from Recipe 9.12. It connects to a *Penman* plotter. These serial-port plotters were made in the United Kingdom in the 1980s, so it is unlikely that you will meet one. However, several companies still make pen plotters. See Figure 12-4 for a photograph of the plotter in action.

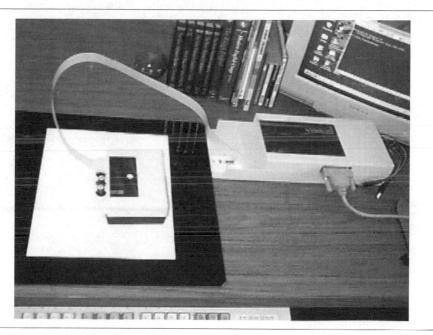

*Figure 12-4. Penman plotter in action*

*Example 12-10. Penman.java*

```java
import java.io.*;
import javax.comm.*;
import java.util.*;

/**
 * A Plotter subclass for drawing on a Penman plotter.
 * These were made in the UK and sold into North American markets.
 * It is a little "turtle" style robot plotter that communicates
 * over a serial port. For this, we use the "Java Communications" API.
 *
 */
public class Penman  extends Plotter {
    private final String OK_PROMPT = "\r\n!";
    private final int MAX_REPLY_BYTES = 50;    // paranoid upper bound
    private SerialPort tty;
    private DataInputStream is;
    private DataOutputStream os;
```

*Example 12-10. Penman.java (continued)*

```java
/** Construct a Penman plotter object */
public Penman( ) throws NoSuchPortException,PortInUseException,
        IOException,UnsupportedCommOperationException {
    super( );
    init_comm("COM2");          // setup serial commx
    init_plotter( );            // set plotter to good state
}

private void init_plotter( ) {
    send("I"); expect('!');     // eat VERSION etc., up to !
    send("I"); expect('!');     // wait for it!
    send("H");          // find home position
    expect('!');    // wait for it!
    send("A");          // Set to use absolute coordinates
    expect('!');
    curx = cury = 0;
    penUp( );
}


//
// PUBLIC DRAWING ROUTINES
//

public void setFont(String fName, int fSize) {
    // Font name is ignored for now...

    // Penman's size is in mm, fsize in points (inch/72).
    int size = (int)(fSize*25.4f/72);
    send("S"+size + ","); expect(OK_PROMPT);
    System.err.println("Font set request: " + fName + "/" + fSize);
}

public void drawString(String mesg) {
    send("L" + mesg + "\r"); expect(OK_PROMPT);
}

/** Move to a relative location */
public void rmoveTo(int incrx, int incry){
    moveTo(curx + incrx, cury + incry);
}

/** move to absolute location */
public void moveTo(int absx, int absy) {
    System.err.println("moveTo ["+absx+","+absy+"]");
    curx = absx;
    cury = absy;
    send("M" + curx + "," + cury + ","); expect(OK_PROMPT);
}

private void setPenState(boolean up) {
    penIsUp = up;
    System.err.println("Pen Up is ["+penIsUp+"]");
}
```

*Example 12-10. Penman.java (continued)*

```java
public void penUp( ) {
    setPenState(true);
    send("U"); expect(OK_PROMPT);
}
public void penDown( ) {
    setPenState(false);
    send("D"); expect(OK_PROMPT);
}
public void penColor(int c) {
    penColor = (c%3)+1;          // only has 3 pens, 4->1
    System.err.println("PenColor is ["+penColor+"]");
    send("P" + c + ","); expect(OK_PROMPT);
}


//
// PRIVATE COMMUNICATION ROUTINES
// (XXX Should re-use CommPortOpen here).

private void init_comm(String portName) throws
            NoSuchPortException, PortInUseException,
        IOException, UnsupportedCommOperationException {

    // get list of ports available on this particular computer.
    // Enumeration pList = CommPortIdentifier.getPortIdentifiers( );

    // Print the list. A GUI program would put these in a chooser!
    // while (pList.hasMoreElements( )) {
    //     CommPortIdentifier cpi = (CommPortIdentifier)pList.nextElement( );
    //     System.err.println("Port " + cpi.getName( ));
    // }

    // Open a port.
    CommPortIdentifier port =
        CommPortIdentifier.getPortIdentifier(portName);

    // This form of openPort takes an Application Name and a timeout.
    tty = (SerialPort) port.openPort("Penman Driver", 1000);

    // set up the serial port
    tty.setSerialPortParams(9600, SerialPort.DATABITS_8,
        SerialPort.STOPBITS_1, SerialPort.PARITY_NONE);
    tty.setFlowControlMode(SerialPort.FLOWCONTROL_RTSCTS_OUT|
        SerialPort.FLOWCONTROL_RTSCTS_OUT);

    // Get the input and output streams
    is = new DataInputStream(tty.getInputStream( ));
    os = new DataOutputStream(tty.getOutputStream( ));
}

/** Send a command to the plotter. Although the argument is a String,
 * we send each char as a *byte*, so avoid 16-bit characters!
 * Not that it matters: the Penman only knows about 8-bit chars.
 */
```

*Example 12-10. Penman.java (continued)*

```java
    private    void send(String s) {
        System.err.println("sending " + s + "...");
        try {
            for (int i=0; i<s.length(); i++)
                os.writeByte(s.charAt(i));
        } catch(IOException e) {
            e.printStackTrace( );
        }
    }

    /** Expect a given CHAR for a result */
    private    void expect(char s) {
        byte b;
        try {
            for (int i=0; i<MAX_REPLY_BYTES; i++){
                if ((b = is.readByte()) == s) {
                        return;
                }
                System.err.print((char)b);
            }
        } catch (IOException e) {
            System.err.println("Penman:expect(char "+s+"): Read failed");
            System.exit(1);
        }
        System.err.println("ARGHH!");
    }

    /** Expect a given String for a result */
    private    void expect(String s) {
        byte ans[] = new byte[s.length()];

        System.err.println("expect " + s + " ...");
        try {
            is.read(ans);
        } catch (IOException e) {
            System.err.println("Penman:expect(String "+s+"): Read failed");
            System.exit(1);
        };
        for (int i=0; i<s.length() && i<ans.length; i++)
            if (ans[i] != s.charAt(i)) {
                System.err.println("MISMATCH");
                break;
            }
        System.err.println("GOT: " + new String(ans));

    }
}
```

## See Also

The online source includes a program called JModem that implements remote connections (like *tip* or *cu* on Unix, or HyperTerminal on Windows). It is usable but too long to include in this book.

As mentioned, a USB standard for Java is in progress; check on *http://www.jcp.org/jsr/detail/80.jsp* to see if it has been released by the time you read this. The JSR reference implementation can be downloaded from *http://sourceforge.net/projects/javax-usb/*.

There are other specialized APIs for dealing with particular devices. For communicating with Palm Computing Platform devices, you can either use the Palm SDK for Java from Palm Computing, or one of various third-party APIs such as jSyncManager by Brad Barclay, now available from *http://www.jsyncmanager.org/*. Consult your favorite search engine to find others. There is also an XML-based synchronization interface for mobile devices, called SyncML. Information about SyncML can be found at *http://www.openmobilealliance.org/syncml/*.

# CHAPTER 13

# Graphics and Sound

## 13.0 Introduction

The Graphics class and the Component method paint() have survived virtually unchanged since the early days of Java. Together they provide a basic but quite functional graphics capability. The first printing API was put forward in 1.1, and it was promptly replaced in 1.2. Both printing APIs, fortunately, are based on use of Graphics objects, so drawing code did not have to change; only the details of getting the right kind of Graphics object changed in moving from 1.1 to 1.2. The 2D (two-dimensional graphics) package is also based on Graphics; Graphics2D is a subclass of Graphics. To put the 2D graphics in perspective, think about the tremendous boost that the Adobe PostScript language gave to desktop publishing and printing. PostScript is both a scripting language and a *marking engine*: it has the ability to make a terrific variety of marks on paper. Since Java is already a comprehensive programming language, the 2D API needed only to add the marking engine. This it did very well, using several ideas imported from PostScript via Adobe's participation in the early design.

Also present from the beginning was the AudioClip class, which represents a playable sound file. In JDK 1.2, this was extended to support additional formats (including MIDI) and to be usable from within an application as well. Meanwhile, the Java Media Framework—standard extension javax.media—provides for playing (and eventually recording) audio, video, and possibly other media with much greater control over the presentation. You'll see examples in this chapter.

But first let's look at the Graphics class. Many of the code examples in this chapter can be used either in applications (which we'll see in Recipe 13.2) or in applets (discussed more in Chapter 18).

## 13.1 Painting with a Graphics Object

### Problem

You want to draw something on the screen.

## Solution

In your paint( ) method, use the provided Graphics object's drawing methods:

```java
// graphics/PaintDemo.java
import java.awt.*;

public class PaintDemo extends Component {
    int rectX = 20, rectY = 30;
    int rectWidth = 50, rectHeight = 50;

    public void paint(Graphics g) {
        g.setColor(Color.red);
        g.fillRect(rectX, rectY, rectWidth, rectHeight);
    }
    public Dimension getPreferredSize() {
        return new Dimension(100, 100);
    }
}
```

## Discussion

The Graphics class has a large set of drawing primitives. Each shape—Rect(angle), Arc, Ellipse, and Polygon—has a draw method (draws just the outline) and a fill method (fills inside the outline). You don't need both, unless you want the outline and the interior (fill) of a shape to be different colors. The method drawString( ) and its relatives let you print text on the screen (see Recipe 13.3). There are also drawLine( )—which draws straight line segments—setColor/getColor, setFont/getFont, and many other methods. Too many to list here, in fact; see Sun's online documentation for java.awt.Graphics.

### When to draw?

A common beginner's mistake used to be to call getGraphics( ) and call the Graphics object's drawing methods from within a main program or the constructor of a Component subclass. Fortunately we now have any number of books to tell us that the correct way to draw anything is with your component's paint method. Why? Because you can't draw in a window until it's actually been created and (on most window systems) mapped to the screen, which takes much more time than your main program or constructor has. The drawing code needs to wait patiently until the window system notifies the Java runtime that it's time to paint the window.

Where do you put your drawing code? This is one situation where you need to think about AWT versus Swing. AWT, the basic windowing system (and the only one in JDK 1.1) uses a method called paint( ). This method is still available in Swing, but due to interaction with borders and the like, it is recommended that you override paintComponent( ) instead. Both are called with a single argument of type Graphics. Your paintComponent( ) should start by calling super.paintComponent( ) with the same argument to ensure that components are painted in proper back-to-front order, while paint( ) should not call its parent. Some examples in this chapter use paint( ) and others use paintComponent( ); the latter also usually extend JPanel. This allows better interaction with Swing, and also allows you to place these as the main component in a JFrame by calling setContentPane( ), which eliminates an extra layer of container. (JFrame's ContentPane is discussed in Recipe 14.1.)

## 13.2   Testing Graphical Components

### Problem

You don't want to have to write a little main program with a frame each time you write a subclass of Component.

### Solution

Use my CompTest class, which has a main method that builds a frame and installs your component into it.

### Discussion

CompTest is a small main program that takes a class name from the command line, instantiates it (see Recipe 25.3), and puts it in a JFrame, along with an Exit button and its action handler. It also worries a bit over making sure the window comes out the right size. Many of these issues relate to the GUI rather than graphics and are discussed in Chapter 14.

The class to be tested must be a subclass of Component, or an error message is printed. This is very convenient for running small component classes, and I show a lot of these in this chapter and the next. Using it is simplicity itself; for example, to instantiate the DrawStringDemo2 class from Recipe 13.3, you just say:

```
java CompTest DrawStringDemo2
```

The result is shown on the left side of Figure 13-1. It's interesting to try running it on some of the predefined classes. A JTree (Java's tree view widget, used in Recipe 19.9) no-argument constructor creates a JTree that comes up with a demonstration set of data, as in Figure 13-1, right.

Since little of this relates to the material in this chapter, I don't show the source for CompTest; however, it's included in the online code examples for the book.

## 13.3   Drawing Text

### Problem

You need to draw text in a component.

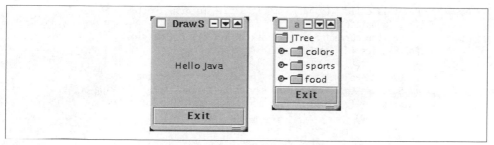

*Figure 13-1. CompTest showing DrawStringDemo2 (left) and javax.swing.JTree (right)*

## Solution

Simply call the `drawString()` method in the Graphics class:

```
// graphics/DrawStringDemo.java
import java.awt.*;

public class DrawStringDemo extends Component {
    int textX = 10, textY = 20;
    public void paint(Graphics g) {
        g.drawString("Hello Java", textX, textY);
    }
    public Dimension getPreferredSize() {
        return new Dimension(100, 100);
    }
}
```

# 13.4 Drawing Centered Text in a Component

## Problem

You want to draw text neatly centered in a component.

## Solution

Measure the width and height of the string in the given font, and subtract it from the width and height of the component. Divide by two, and use this as your drawing location.

## Discussion

The program DrawStringDemo2 measures the width and height of a string (see Figure 13-2 for some attributes of the text). The program then subtracts the size of the text from the size of the component, divides this by two, and thereby centers the text in the given component.

```
public class DrawStringDemo2 extends Component {
    String message = "Hello Java";
```

```
/** Paint is called (by AWT) when it's time to draw the text. */
public void paint(Graphics g) {
    // Get the current Font, and ask it for its FontMetrics.
    FontMetrics fm = getFontMetrics(getFont());

    // Use the FontMetrics to get the width of the String.
    // Subtract this from width, divide by 2, that's our starting point.
    int textX = (getSize().width - fm.stringWidth(message))/2;
    if (textX<0)          // If string too long, start at 0
        textX = 0;

    // Same as above but for the height
    int textY = (getSize().height + fm.getAscent())/2 - fm.getDescent();
    if (textY<0)
        textY = 0;

    // Now draw the text at the computed spot.
    g.drawString(message, textX, textY);
}

public Dimension getPreferredSize() {
    return new Dimension(100, 100);
}
}
```

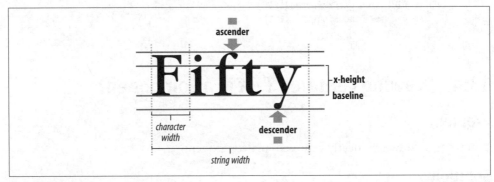

*Figure 13-2. Font metrics*

This is so common that you'd expect Java to have encapsulated the whole thing as a service, and in fact, Java does do this. What we have here is what most GUI component architectures call a *label*. As we'll see in Chapter 14, Java provides a Label component that allows for centered (or left- or right-aligned) text and supports the setting of fonts and colors. It also offers JLabel, which provides image icons in addition to or instead of text.

## See Also

To draw formatted text—as in a word processor—requires considerably more complexity. You'll find an example in the online source under the JabberPoint program (see *ShowView.java*). This program also implements the Model-View-Controller pattern.

# 13.5  Drawing a Drop Shadow

## Problem

You want to draw text or graphical objects with a "drop shadow" effect, as in Figure 13-3.

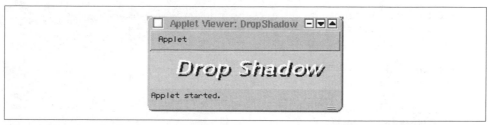

*Figure 13-3. Drop shadow text*

## Solution

Draw the component twice, with the darker shadow behind and the "real" color, slightly offset, in front.

## Discussion

Program DropShadow does just this. It also uses a Font object from *java.awt* to exercise some control over the typeface.

The program in Example 13-1 is unabashedly an applet; to run it, you should invoke it as **appletviewer DropShadow.htm** (the details of such HTML files* are in Recipe 18.1).

*Example 13-1. DropShadow.java*

```
import java.applet.*;
import java.awt.*;

/**
 * DropShadow -- show overlapped painting.
 */
public class DropShadow extends Applet {
    /** The label that is to appear in the window */
    protected String theLabel = null;
    /** The width and height */
    protected int width, height;
    /** The name of the font */
    protected String fontName;
    /** The font */
    protected Font theFont;
```

---

\* In all my applet examples I use a filename ending in *htm* instead of the more traditional *html* because the Javadoc program (see Recipe 23.2) overwrites the *html* file without notice. AppletViewer doesn't care either way.

*Example 13-1. DropShadow.java (continued)*

```java
/** The size of the font */
protected int fontSize = 18;
/** The offset for the drop shadow */
protected int theOffset = 3;
/** True if we got all required parameters */
protected boolean inittedOK = false;

/** Called from the browser to set up. We want to throw various
 * kinds of exceptions but the API predefines that we don't, so we
 * limit ourselves to the ubiquitous IllegalArgumentException.
 */
public void init( ) {
    // System.out.println("In DropShadow init( )");

    theLabel = getParameter("label");
    if (theLabel == null)
            throw new IllegalArgumentException("LABEL is REQUIRED");
    // Now handle font stuff.
    fontName = getParameter("fontname");
    if (fontName == null)
            throw new IllegalArgumentException("FONTNAME is REQUIRED");
    String s;
    if ((s = getParameter("fontsize")) != null)
        fontSize = Integer.parseInt(s);
    if (fontName != null || fontSize != 0) {
        theFont = new Font(fontName, Font.BOLD + Font.ITALIC, fontSize);
        System.out.println("Name " + fontName + ", font " + theFont);
    }
    if ((s = getParameter("offset")) != null)
        theOffset = Integer.parseInt(s);
    setBackground(Color.green);
    inittedOK = true;
}

/** Paint method showing drop shadow effect */
public void paint(Graphics g) {
    if (!inittedOK)
        return;
    g.setFont(theFont);
    g.setColor(Color.black);
    g.drawString(theLabel, theOffset+30, theOffset+50);
    g.setColor(Color.white);
    g.drawString(theLabel, 30, 50);
}

/** Give Parameter info to the AppletViewer, just for those
 * writing HTML without hardcopy documentation :-)
 */
public String[][] getParameterInfo( ) {
    String info[][] = {
        { "label",      "string",   "Text to display" },
        { "fontname",   "name",      "Font to display it in" },
        { "fontsize",    "10-30?",   "Size to display it at" },
```

*Example 13-1. DropShadow.java (continued)*

```
    };
    return info;
  }
}
```

Standard AWT uses a very simple paint model for drawing. I guess that's why the method you have to write is called paint( ). Let's go back to the paper age for a moment. If you paint something on a piece of paper and then paint over it with a different color, what happens? If you're old enough to remember paper, you'll know that the second color covers up the first color. Well, AWT works in pretty much the same way. No fair asking about water-based paints that run together; Java's painting is more like fast-drying oil paints. The fact that AWT retains all the bits (pixels, or picture elements) that you don't draw, plus the fact that methods like drawString( ) have extremely good aim, make it very easy to create a drop shadow and to combine graphics drawings in interesting ways.

Remember to draw from the back to the front, though. To see why, try interchanging the two calls to drawString( ) in the previous code.

A word of warning: don't mix drawing with added GUI components (see Chapter 14). For example, say you had a paint method in an applet or other container and had add( )ed a button to it. This works on some implementations of Java, but not on others: only the painting or the button appears, not both. It's not portable, so don't do it—you've been warned! Instead, you should probably use multiple components; see the JFrame's getContentPane( ) and getGlassPane( ), discussed in Chapter 8 of *Java Swing*, for details.

An alternative method of obtaining a drop shadow effect is covered in Recipe 13.6.

# 13.6   Drawing Text with 2D

## Problem

You want fancier drawing abilities.

## Solution

Use a Graphics2D object.

## Discussion

The 2D graphics added in JDK 1.2 could be the subject of an entire book, and in fact, it is. *Java 2D Graphics* by Jonathan Knudsen (O'Reilly) covers every imaginable aspect of this comprehensive graphics package. Here I'll just show one example: drawing text with a textured background.

The `Graphics2D` class is a direct subclass of the original Java `Graphics` object. In fact, your paint() method is always called with an instance of `Graphics2D`. So begin your paint method by casting appropriately:

```
public void paint(Graphics g) {
    Graphics2D g2 = (Graphics2D) g;
```

You can then use any `Graphics2D` methods or any regular `Graphics` methods, getting to them with the object reference g2. One of the additional methods in `Graphics2D` is setPaint(), which can take the place of setColor() to draw with a solid color. However, it can also be called with several other types, and in this case we pass in an object called a `TexturePaint`, which refers to a pattern. Our pattern is a simple set of diagonal lines, but any pattern or even a bitmap from a file (see Recipe 13.8) can be used. Figure 13-4 shows the resulting screen (it looks even better in color); the program itself is shown in Example 13-2.

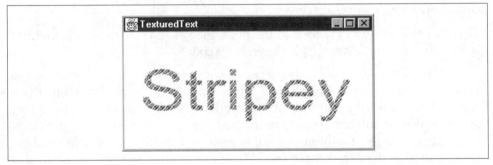

*Figure 13-4. TexturedText in action*

*Example 13-2. TexturedText.java*

```java
import java.awt.*;
import java.awt.event.*;
import java.awt.image.*;

/** Text with a Texture
 */
public class TexturedText extends Component {
    /** The image we draw in the texture */
    protected BufferedImage bim;
    /** The texture for painting. */
    TexturePaint tp;
    /** The string to draw. */
    String mesg = "Stripey";
    /** The font */
    Font myFont = new Font("Lucida Regular", Font.BOLD, 72);

    /** "main program" method - construct and show */
    public static void main(String av[]) {
        // create a TexturedText object, tell it to show up
        final Frame f = new Frame("TexturedText");
```

*Example 13-2. TexturedText.java (continued)*

```java
        TexturedText comp = new TexturedText( );
        f.add(comp);
        f.addWindowListener(new WindowAdapter( ) {
            public void windowClosing(WindowEvent e) {
                f.setVisible(false);
                f.dispose( );
                System.exit(0);
            }
        });
        f.pack( );
        f.setLocation(200, 200);
        f.setVisible(true);
    }

    protected static Color[] colors = {
        Color.green, Color.red, Color.blue, Color.yellow,
    };

    /** Construct the object */
    public TexturedText( ) {
        super( );
        setBackground(Color.white);
        int width = 8, height = 8;
        bim = new BufferedImage(width, height, BufferedImage.TYPE_INT_ARGB);
        Graphics2D g2 = bim.createGraphics( );
        for (int i=0; i<width; i++) {
            g2.setPaint(colors[(i/2)%colors.length]);
            g2.drawLine(0, i, i, 0);
            g2.drawLine(width-i, height, width, height-i);
        }
        Rectangle r = new Rectangle(0, 0, bim.getWidth( ), bim.getHeight( ));
        tp = new TexturePaint(bim, r);
    }

    public void paint(Graphics g) {
        Graphics2D g2 = (Graphics2D)g;
        g2.setRenderingHint(RenderingHints.KEY_ANTIALIASING,
            RenderingHints.VALUE_ANTIALIAS_ON);
        g2.setPaint(tp);
        g2.setFont(myFont);
        g2.drawString(mesg, 20, 100);
    }

    public Dimension getMinimumSize( ) {
        return new Dimension(250, 100);
    }

    public Dimension getPreferredSize( ) {
        return new Dimension(320, 150);
    }
}
```

## See Also

I have not discussed how to scale, rotate, or otherwise transmogrify an image using the AffineTransform class in Java 2D graphics, as such topics are beyond the scope of this book. Consult the previously mentioned *Java 2D Graphics*.

# 13.7   Drawing Text with an Application Font

## Problem

You want to provide a font with your application but not require users to install it as a "system font" on all platforms.

## Solution

Use Font.createFont(...), which returns a scalable Font object, and scale it with deriveFont(int nPoints).

## Discussion

JDK 1.3 introduced the static method Font.createFont( ), which allows you to have a "private" font that can be used in your application without having it installed using the operating system's font mechanism. Users can then use your application and its custom font without having to have "root" or "administration" privileges on systems that require this in order to install fonts.

The createFont( ) method requires two arguments. The first is an int, which must be the public static field Font.TRUETYPE_FONT, and the second is an InputStream (see Recipe 10.15) that is open for reading the binary file. As you can infer from the requirement that the first argument be Font.TRUETYPE_FONT, only TrueType fonts are supported at present. The Font class documentation, ever the optimist, states that this field is to allow possible future addition of other font formats, though none is promised. Given the availability of free PostScript font renderers, such as the one in the X Window System XFree86, it should be possible to add PostScript font support in the future. Example 13-3 is a listing of a small standalone application that creates the window shown in Figure 13-5.

*Figure 13-5. TTFontDemo in action*

*Example 13-3. Demo of an application font*

```
/** Demo of making TrueType font usable in Java. This is a way cool facility
 * because it means you can have "application-specific" fonts in Java;
 * your application can have its own distinctive font that the user does
 * NOT have to install into the JRE before you can use it.
 * (of course they can install it if they have privileges and want to).
 * <p>
 * Must remain Swing-based despite problems on older systems, since
 * apparently only Swing components can use TTF fonts in this implementation.
 * <p>
 * Did  NOT work for me in Applet  nor  JApplet due to
 * security problems (requires to create a temp file). Could be made
 * to work by providing a policy file.
 * @author     Ian Darwin
 * @since 1.3
 */
public class TTFontDemo extends JLabel {

    /** Construct a TTFontDemo -- Create a Font from ttf.
     */
    public TTFontDemo(String fontFileName, String text)
    throws IOException, FontFormatException {
        super(text, JLabel.CENTER);

        setBackground(Color.white);

        // First, see if we can load the font file.
        InputStream is = this.getClass().getResourceAsStream(fontFileName);
        if (is == null) {
            throw new IOException("Cannot open " + fontFileName);
        }

        // createFont makes a 1-point font, bit hard to read :-)
        Font ttfBase = Font.createFont(Font.TRUETYPE_FONT, is);

        // So scale it to 24 pt.
        Font ttfReal = ttfBase.deriveFont(Font.PLAIN, 24);

        setFont(ttfReal);
    }

    /** Simple main program for TTFontDemo */
    public static void main(String[] args) throws Exception {

        String DEFAULT_MESSAGE =
            "What hath man wrought? Or at least rendered?";
        String DEFAULT_FONTFILE =
            "Kellyag_.ttf";
        String message = args.length == 1 ? args[0] : DEFAULT_MESSAGE;
        JFrame f = new JFrame("TrueType Font Demo");

        TTFontDemo ttfd = new TTFontDemo(DEFAULT_FONTFILE, message);
        f.getContentPane().add(ttfd);
```

*Example 13-3. Demo of an application font (continued)*

```
        f.setBounds(100, 100, 700, 250);
        f.setVisible(true);
        f.setDefaultCloseOperation(JFrame.EXIT_ON_CLOSE);
    }
}
```

This font technology has some restrictions. First, as noted in the comments, you can use this font only on a Swing JComponent, not on an AWT Component (see Chapter 14).

Also, this technique cannot easily be used in an applet. The createFont( ) method obviously requires some very clever code and, for this reason, is apparently unable to do its work from an opened InputStream; it copies the TrueType font file to the local disk to work on it. This may cause a security exception to be thrown. The program in TTFontApplet in the online source shows an applet that attempts to reuse the code from the TTFontDemo program. Invoking this as an applet fails when used with Netscape 4 due to lack of a complete Swing implementation; it throws a SecurityException when used with the Java Plug-in under older Netscape versions, but works fine when invoked under Apple's browser, Safari, which uses the latest installed JRE (in my case, Java 1.4.1_03). And it should also work in an application downloaded using Java WebStart (see Recipe 23.13).

## 13.8   Drawing an Image

### Problem

You want to display an image, a preformatted bitmap, or raster file.

### Solution

Use the Graphics drawImage( ) method in your paint routine. Image objects represent bitmaps. They are normally loaded from a file via getImage( ) but can also be synthesized using createImage( ). You can't construct them yourself, however: the Image class is abstract. Once you have an image, displaying it is trivial:

```
// File graphics/DrawImageDemo.java
public void paint(Graphics g) {
    g.drawImage(myImage, 0, 0, this);
}
```

### Discussion

You can get an image by using a routine named, naturally, getImage( ). If your code is used only in an applet, you can use the Applet method getImage( ), but if you want it to run in an application as well, you need to use the Toolkit version, which takes either a filename or a URL. The filename, of course, when it turns up in an applet, fails with a security exception unless the user installs a policy file. Program GetImage shows the code for doing this both ways:

```
/*
 * For Applet, invoke as:
 * <applet code="GetImage" width="100" height="100">
 * </applet>
 * For Application, just run it (has own main).
 */

import java.awt.Graphics;
import java.awt.Image;
import java.net.URL;

import javax.swing.JApplet;
import javax.swing.JFrame;

/** This program, which can be an Applet or an Application,
 * shows a form of Toolkit.getImage() which works the same
 * in either Applet or Application!
 */
public class GetImage extends JApplet {

    Image image;

    public void init() {
        loadImage();
    }

    public void loadImage() {
        // Applet-only version:
        // image = getImage(getCodeBase(), "Duke.gif");

        // Portable version: getClass().getResource() works in either
        // applet or application, 1.1 or 1.3, returns URL for file name.
        URL url = getClass().getResource("Duke.gif");
        image = getToolkit().getImage(url);
        // Shorter portable version: same but avoids temporary variables
        // image = getToolkit().getImage(getClass().getResource("Duke.gif"));
    }

    public void paint(Graphics g) {
        g.drawImage(image, 20, 20, this);
    }

    public static void main(String[] args) {
        JFrame f = new JFrame("GetImage");
        f.setDefaultCloseOperation(JFrame.EXIT_ON_CLOSE);
        GetImage myApplet = new GetImage();
        f.getContentPane().add(myApplet);
        myApplet.init();
        f.setSize(100, 100);
        f.setVisible(true);
        myApplet.start();
    }
}
```

You may sometimes want to display an image more than once in the same panel. Example 13-4 is a program that paints its background with the same image over and over. We use the image's getWidth( ) and getHeight( ) methods to find the image's size and the more regular getSize( ) method on the component itself. As usual, we don't hardcode the window size in the paint( ) method, since the user has the option of resizing with the mouse.

*Example 13-4. TiledImageComponent.java*

```java
import com.darwinsys.util.WindowCloser;

import java.awt.*;
import java.awt.event.*;
import java.net.*;

/**
 * Demo of Tiled Image
 */
public class TiledImageComponent extends Container {
    TextField nameTF, passTF, domainTF;
    Image im;
    String IMAGE_NAME = "background.gif";

    /** Set things up nicely. */
    public TiledImageComponent() {
        Label l;

        setLayout(new FlowLayout());
        add(l = new Label("Name:", Label.CENTER));
        add(nameTF=new TextField(10));

        add(l = new Label("Password:", Label.CENTER));
        add(passTF=new TextField(10));
        passTF.setEchoChar('*');

        add(l = new Label("Domain:", Label.CENTER));
        add(domainTF=new TextField(10));

        im = getToolkit().getImage(IMAGE_NAME);
    }

    /** paint()  - just tile the background.   */
    public void paint(Graphics g) {
        // System.out.println("In paint()");
        if (im == null)
            return;
        int iw = im.getWidth(this), ih=im.getHeight(this);
        if (iw < 0 || ih < 0)    // image not ready
            return;                     // live to try again later.
        int w = getSize().width, h = getSize().height;
        // System.out.println(iw + "," + ih + "; " + w + ", " + h);
        for (int i = 0; i<=w; i+=iw) {
```

*Example 13-4. TiledImageComponent.java (continued)*

```
        for (int j = 0; j<=h; j+=ih) {
            // System.out.println("drawImage(im,"+i+","+j+")");
            g.drawImage(im, i, j, this);
        }
    }
}

public static void main(String[] av) {
    Frame f = new Frame("TiledImageComponent Demo");
    f.add(new TiledImageComponent( ));
    f.setSize(200, 200);
    f.setVisible(true);
    f.addWindowListener(new WindowCloser(f, true));
}
}
```

In the paint( ) method, we must check that the image is not null and has a nonnegative width and height—we are more careful than we were in the previous, somewhat cavalier, example. The image is null only if something went very wrong in the constructor, but it can have a negative size. How? In certain creation myths, time ran backward before the beginning of time; therefore, before an image is fully created, its size is backward, that is, it has a width and height of –1. The getImage( ) method doesn't actually get the image, you see. It creates the Image object, true, but it doesn't necessarily load all the bits: it starts a background thread to do the reading and returns. This dates from the days when the Web was slower and took a long time to fully load an image. In particular, with some image file formats (some kinds of TIFF files, perhaps), you don't know the actual image size until you've read the entire file. Thus, when getImage( ) returns, the Image object is created, but its size is set to –1, –1. Since two threads are now running (see Chapter 24), two outcomes are possible. Either the image-reading thread reads enough to know the width and height before you need them, or you need them before the thread reads enough to know them. The curious-looking code in paint( ) is defensive about this. You should be, too.

But what if you really need the size of the image, for example to lay out a larger panel? If you read a bit of the Image documentation, you might think you can use the prepareImage( ) method to ensure that the object has been loaded. Unfortunately, this method can get you stuck in a loop if the image file is missing because prepareImage never returns true! If you need to be sure, you must construct a MediaTracker object to ensure that the image has been loaded successfully. That looks something like this:

```
/**
 * This CODE FRAGMENT shows using a MediaTracker to ensure
 * that an Image has been loaded successfully, then obtaining
 * its Width and Height. The MediaTracker can track an arbitrary
 * number of Images; the "0" is an arbitrary number used to track
 * this particular image.
 */
```

```
    Image im;
    int imWidth, imHeight;
    public void setImage(Image i) {
        im = i;
        MediaTracker mt = new MediaTracker(this);
        // use of "this" assumes we're in a Component subclass.
        mt.addImage(im, 0);
        try {
            mt.waitForID(0);
        } catch(InterruptedException e) {
            throw new IllegalArgumentException(
                "InterruptedException while loading Image");
        }
        if (mt.isErrorID(0)) {
            throw new IllegalArgumentException(
                              "Couldn't load image");
        }
        imWidth  = im.getWidth(this);
        imHeight = im.getHeight(this);
    }
```

You can ask the MediaTracker for its status at any time using the method status(int ID, boolean load), which returns an integer made by or-ing together the values shown in Table 13-1. The Boolean load flag, if true, tells the MediaTracker to start loading any images that haven't yet been started. A related method, statusAll( ), returns the inclusive or of any flags applying to images that have started loading.

*Table 13-1. MediaTracker status values*

| Flag | Meaning |
| --- | --- |
| ABORTED | Downloading of at least one item was aborted. |
| COMPLETE | Downloading of all items completed without error. |
| ERRORED | Something went wrong while downloading at least one item. |
| LOADING | Downloading is ongoing. |

You can shorten the previous code by using the Swing ImageIcon class, which includes this functionality. The ImageIcon class has several constructor forms, one of which takes just a filename argument. ImageIcon uses a MediaTracker internally; you can ask for its status using the ImageIcon's getImageLoadStatus( ) method, which returns the same values as MediaTracker's statusAll( )/statusID( ).

# 13.9   Playing a Sound File

## Problem

You want a quick and easy way to "make noise" or play an existing sound file.

---

## Solution

Get an AudioClip object and use its play( ) method.

## Discussion

This might seem out of place in the midst of all this Graphics code, but there's a pattern. We're moving from the simpler graphical forms to more dynamic multimedia. You can play a sound file using an AudioClip to represent it. Back in the days of 1.0 and 1.1, you could do this only in an applet (or using unsupported sun.java classes). But starting with JDK 1.2, this capability was extended to applications. Here is a program that plays either two demonstration files from a precompiled list or the list of files you give. Due to the applet legacy, each file must be given as a URL:

```
import java.applet.*;
import java.net.*;

/** Simple program to try out the "new Sound" stuff in JDK1.2 --
 * allows Applications, not just Applets, to play Sound.
 */
public class SoundPlay {
    static String defSounds[] = {
        "file:///javasrc/graphics/test.wav",
        "file:///music/midi/Beet5th.mid",
    };
    public static void main(String[] av) {
        if (av.length == 0)
            main(defSounds);
        else for (int i=0;i<av.length; i++) {
            System.out.println("Starting " + av[i]);
            try {
                URL snd = new URL(av[i]);
                // open to see if works or throws exception, close to free fd's
                // snd.openConnection().getInputStream( ).close( );
                Applet.newAudioClip(snd).play( );
            } catch (Exception e) {
                System.err.println(e);
            }
        }
        // With this call, program exits before/during play.
        // Without it, on some versions, program hangs forever after play.
        // System.exit(0);
    }
}
```

As the code comment reports, you can open the URL to see if it succeeds; if it throws an IOException, there is not much point in trying the newAudioClip( ) call, and catching it this way might allow you to print a better error message.

## See Also

There are several limitations on the applet sound API. The JMFPlayer interface discussed in Recipe 13.10 plays sound files with a volume control panel.

# 13.10 Playing a Video Clip

## Problem

You want to display a video file within a Java program.

## Solution

Use the Java Media Framework (JMF), a standard extension.

## Discussion

Example 13-5 shows a program that displays a movie or other media file named on the command line. JMF is very flexible; this program plays an audio file, supplying a volume control if the media object that you name contains a sound clip instead of a movie. Figure 13-6 shows JMFPlayer displaying a sound file and a movie.

*Figure 13-6. JMFPlayer in action: audio (left), video (right)*

*Example 13-5. JMFPlayer.java*

```
import com.darwinsys.util.WindowCloser;

import java.applet.*;
import java.awt.*;
import javax.swing.*;
import java.net.*;
import java.io.*;
import java.util.*;
import javax.media.*;

/**
 * Demonstrate simple code to play a movie with Java Media Framework.
 */
public class JMFPlayer extends JPanel implements ControllerListener {

    /** The player object */
    Player thePlayer = null;
    /** The parent Frame we are in. */
    JFrame parentFrame = null;
```

*Example 13-5. JMFPlayer.java (continued)*

```java
/** Our contentpane */
Container cp;
/** The visual component (if any) */
Component visualComponent = null;
/** The default control component (if any) */
Component controlComponent = null;
/** The name of this instance's media file. */
String mediaName;
/** The URL representing this media file. */
URL theURL;

/** Construct the player object and the GUI. */
public JMFPlayer(JFrame pf, String media) {
    parentFrame = pf;
    mediaName = media;
    // cp = getContentPane();
    cp = this;
    cp.setLayout(new BorderLayout());
    try {
        theURL = new URL(getClass().getResource("."), mediaName);
        thePlayer = Manager.createPlayer(theURL);
        thePlayer.addControllerListener(this);
    } catch (MalformedURLException e) {
        System.err.println("JMF URL creation error: " + e);
    } catch (Exception e) {
        System.err.println("JMF Player creation error: " + e);
        return;
    }
    System.out.println("theURL = " + theURL);

    // Start the player: this will notify our ControllerListener.
    thePlayer.start();          // start playing
}

/** Called to stop the audio, as from a Stop button or menuitem */
public void stop() {
    if (thePlayer == null)
        return;
    thePlayer.stop();           // stop playing!
    thePlayer.deallocate();     // free system resources
}

/** Called when we are really finished (as from an Exit button). */
public void destroy() {
    if (thePlayer == null)
        return;
    thePlayer.close();
}

/** Called by JMF when the Player has something to tell us about. */
public synchronized void controllerUpdate(ControllerEvent event) {
    // System.out.println("controllerUpdate(" + event + ")");
    if (event instanceof RealizeCompleteEvent) {
```

*Example 13-5. JMFPlayer.java (continued)*

```
            if ((visualComponent = thePlayer.getVisualComponent( )) != null)
                    cp.add(BorderLayout.CENTER, visualComponent);
            if ((controlComponent =
                thePlayer.getControlPanelComponent( )) != null)
                    cp.add(BorderLayout.SOUTH, controlComponent);
            // re-size the main window
            if (parentFrame != null) {
                parentFrame.pack( );
                parentFrame.setTitle(mediaName);
            }
        }
    }

    public static void main(String[] argv) {
        JFrame f = new JFrame("JMF Player Demo");
        Container frameCP = f.getContentPane( );
        JMFPlayer p = new JMFPlayer(f, argv.length == 0 ?
            "file:///C:/music/midi/beet5th.mid" : argv[0]);
        frameCP.add(BorderLayout.CENTER, p);
        f.setSize(200, 200);
        f.setVisible(true);
        f.addWindowListener(new WindowCloser(f, true));
    }
}
```

The optional Java Media Framework includes much more functionality than this example shows. However, the ability to display a QuickTime or MPEG movie with only a few lines of code is one of JMF's most endearing young charms. We load the media file from a URL and create a Player object to manage it. If it makes sense for the given player to have a controller, it will have one, and we add it to the bottom of the applet. Controllers may include volume controls, forward/backward buttons, position sliders, etc. However, we don't have to care: we get a component that contains all the appropriate controls for the kind of media clip for which we've created the player. If the given player represents a medium with a visual component (like a movie or a bitmap image), we add this to the center of the applet.

## See Also

Of course, there is much more to the JMF API than this. You can, for example, coordinate playing of audio and video with each other or with other events.

# 13.11  Printing in Java

## Problem

You need to generate hardcopy.

## Solution

Use `java.awt.print.PrinterJob`.

## Discussion

The JDK 1.2 Printing API makes you divide the data into pages. Again, you start by getting a `PrinterJob` object to control your printing. You'll usually want to let the user pick a printer, which you do by calling the `PrinterJob`'s method `printerDialog()`. This pops up a platform-specific print chooser dialog, and if the user picks a printer, you get back a `PrinterJob` object (otherwise, again, you get back null). If you don't call `printerDialog()` and there is a default printer, your job is sent to that printer (if there isn't a default printer, I don't know what happens). Unlike the 1.1 Printing API, however, Java is in charge of what to print and in what order, although your program is still responsible for pagination and drawing each page onto a print buffer. You need to provide an object that implements the `Printable` interface (see Recipe 9.7). In this example, we pass an anonymous inner class (see Recipe 9.6); this is not required, but as usual, it makes the code more succinct by eliminating having to write another class in another file and by keeping the action and the result together. Java calls this object's `print()` method once for each page the user has requested. This is efficient because if the user wants to print only page 57, you get called only once to print that page. Note that the official documentation calls the third argument a `pageIndex`, but it's really a page number. Trust me. Presumably it's called a `pageIndex` to remind you that in some printing jobs (such as this book), there are unnumbered pages and pages with those funny little roman numerals at the front (see Recipe 5.11).

The source code is shown in Example 13-6. The screenshots in Figure 13-7 show this program in action.

*Example 13-6. PrintDemoGfx*

```
import java.awt.*;
import java.awt.event.*;
import java.awt.print.*;
import javax.swing.*;

/** PrintDemoGfx -- Construct and print a GfxDemoCanvas. */
public class PrintDemoGfx {

    /** Simple demo main program. */
    public static void main(String[] av) throws PrinterException {
        final JFrame f = new JFrame("Printing Test Dummy Frame");

        // Construct the object we want to print. Contrived:
        // this object would already exist in a real program.
        final GfxDemoCanvas thing - new GfxDemoCanvas(400, 300);

        f.getContentPane().add(thing, BorderLayout.CENTER);
```

*Example 13-6. PrintDemoGfx (continued)*

```java
        JButton printButton = new JButton("Print");
        f.getContentPane( ).add(printButton, BorderLayout.SOUTH);

        printButton.addActionListener(new ActionListener( ) {
            public void actionPerformed(ActionEvent e) {
                try {
                    PrinterJob pjob = PrinterJob.getPrinterJob( );
                    pjob.setJobName("DemoGfx - Graphics Demo Printout");
                    pjob.setCopies(1);
                    // Tell the print system how to print our pages.
                    pjob.setPrintable(new Printable( ) {
                        /** called from the printer system to print each page */
                        public int print(Graphics pg, PageFormat pf, int pageNum) {
                            if (pageNum>0)          // we only print one page
                                return Printable.NO_SUCH_PAGE;    // ie., end of job

                            // Now (drum roll please), ask "thing" to paint itself
                            // on the printer, by calling its paint( ) method with
                            // a Printjob Graphics instead of a Window Graphics.
                            thing.paint(pg);

                            // Tell print system that the page is ready to print
                            return Printable.PAGE_EXISTS;
                        }
                    });

                    if (pjob.printDialog( ) == false)    // choose printer
                        return;                  // user cancelled

                    pjob.print( );              // Finally, do the printing.
                } catch (PrinterException pe) {
                    JOptionPane.showMessageDialog(f,
                        "Printer error" + pe, "Printing error",
                        JOptionPane.ERROR_MESSAGE);
                }
            }
        });

        f.pack( );
        f.setVisible(true);
    }
}
```

# See Also

The Printing API has other useful methods in the `PrinterJob` class; see the documentation. `Paper`, `PageFormat`, and `Book` classes describe a physical page, a page by size and orientation, and a collection of pages, respectively.

Both Java printing APIs require you to think in "page mode." That is, you must know where the page breaks are and request the start of each new page. This is optimal for graphically oriented programs, and less optimal for "report writing" applications; handling pagination for yourself can become quite a tedium. See the HardCopyWriter class in O'Reilly's *Java Examples in a Nutshell* for code that neatly paginates and prints plain text.

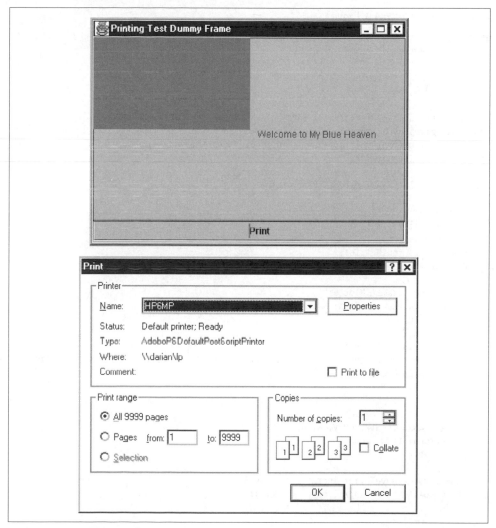

*Figure 13-7. PrintDemoGfx program in action*

# 13.12 Program: PlotterAWT

In Recipe 9.12, we discussed a series of Plotter classes. The PlotterAWT class shown in Example 13-7 extends that to provide a "plot preview" service: before being plotted on a (probably slow) plotter, the plot is displayed in an AWT window using the Graphics drawing primitives.

*Example 13-7. PlotterAWT.java*

```java
import java.awt.*;
import java.awt.event.*;

import com.darwinsys.swingui.WindowCloser;

/**
 * A Plotter subclass for drawing into an AWT Window. Reflecting back
 * to AWT gives us a "known working" plotter to test on.
 * You can also steal this as a basis for your own plotter driver.
 * @author    Ian Darwin
 */
public class PlotterAWT extends Plotter {
    Frame f;
    PCanvas p;
    Graphics g;
    Font font;
    FontMetrics fontMetrics;
    PlotterAWT() {
        super();
        f = new Frame("Plotter");
        p = new PCanvas(MAXX, MAXY);
        f.add(p);
        f.pack();
        f.setVisible(true);
        f.addWindowListener(new WindowCloser(f, true));  // ignore deprecation warning
        g = p.getOsGraphics();
    }

    public void drawBox(int w, int h) {
        g.drawRect(curx, cury, w, h);
        p.repaint();
    }

    public void rmoveTo(int incrx, int incry){
        moveTo(curx += incrx, cury += incry);
    }

    public void moveTo(int absx, int absy){
        if (!penIsUp)
            g.drawLine(curx, cury, absx, absy);
        curx = absx;
        cury = absy;
    }
```

*Example 13-7. PlotterAWT.java (continued)*

```
public void setdir(float deg){}
void penUp( ){ penIsUp = true; }
void penDown( ){ penIsUp = false; }
void penColor(int c){
    switch(c) {
    case 0: g.setColor(Color.white); break;
    case 1: g.setColor(Color.black); break;
    case 2: g.setColor(Color.red); break;
    case 3: g.setColor(Color.green); break;
    case 4: g.setColor(Color.blue); break;
    default: g.setColor(new Color(c)); break;
    }
}
void setFont(String fName, int fSize) {
    font = new Font(fName, Font.BOLD, fSize);
    fontMetrics = p.getFontMetrics(font);
}
void drawString(String s) {
    g.drawString(s, curx, cury);
    curx += fontMetrics.stringWidth(s);
}


/** A Member Class that contains an off-screen Image that is
 * drawn into; this component's paint( ) copies from there to
 * the screen. This avoids having to keep a list of all the
 * things that have been drawn.
 */
class PCanvas extends Canvas {
    Image offScreenImage;
    int width;
    int height;
    Graphics pg;

    PCanvas(int w, int h) {
        width = w;
        height = h;
        setBackground(Color.white);
        setForeground(Color.red);
    }

    public Graphics getOsGraphics( ) {
        return pg;
    }

    /** This is called by AWT after the native window peer is created,
     * and before paint( ) is called for the first time, so
     * is a good time to create images and the like.
     */
    public void addNotify( ) {
        super.addNotify( );
        offScreenImage = createImage(width, height);
        // assert (offScreenImage != null);
```

*Example 13-7. PlotterAWT.java (continued)*

```
        pg = offScreenImage.getGraphics( );
    }

    public void paint(Graphics pg) {
        pg.drawImage(offScreenImage, 0, 0, null);
    }
    public Dimension getPreferredSize( ) {
        return new Dimension(width, height);
    }
  }
}
```

# 13.13 Program: Grapher

Grapher is a simple program that reads a table of numbers and graphs them. The input format is two or more lines that each contain an X and a Y value. The output is an onscreen display that can also be printed. Figure 13-8 shows the results of running it with the following simple data; the first column is the X coordinate and the second is the Y coordinate of each point. The program scales the data to fit the window:

```
1.5  5
1.7  6
1.8  8
2.2  7
```

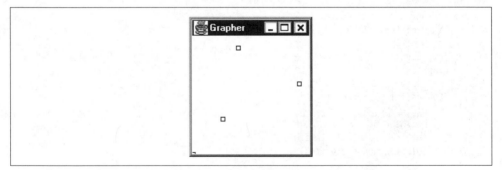

*Figure 13-8. Grapher in action*

Example 13-8 shows the code.

*Example 13-8. Grapher.java*

```
import com.darwinsys.util.Debug;
import java.awt.*;
import java.awt.event.*;
import javax.swing.*;
import java.io.*;
import java.util.*;
```

*Example 13-8. Grapher.java (continued)*

```java
/** Simple Graphing program.
 */
public class Grapher extends JPanel {
    /** Multiplier for range to allow room for a border */
    public final static float BORDERFACTOR = 1.1f;

    /* Small inner class to hold x, y. Called Apoint to differentiate
     * from java.awt.Point.
     */
    class Apoint {
        float x;
        float y;
        public String toString() {
            return "Apoint("+x+","+y+")";
        }
    }

    /** The list of Apoint points. */
    protected Vector data;

    /** The minimum and maximum X values */
    protected float minx = Integer.MAX_VALUE, maxx = Integer.MIN_VALUE;
    /** The minimum and maximum Y values */
    protected float miny = Integer.MAX_VALUE, maxy = Integer.MIN_VALUE;
    /** The number of data points */
    protected int n;
    /** The range of X and Y values */
    protected float xrange, yrange;

    public Grapher() {
        data = new Vector();
    }

    /** Read the data file named. Each line has an x and a y coordinate. */
    public void read(String fname) {
        LineNumberReader is = null;
        try {
            is = new LineNumberReader(new FileReader(fname));

            String txt;
            // Read the file a line at a time, parse it, save the data.
            while ((txt = is.readLine()) != null) {
                StringTokenizer st = new StringTokenizer(txt);
                try {
                    Apoint d = new Apoint();
                    d.x = Float.parseFloat(st.nextToken());
                    d.y = Float.parseFloat(st.nextToken());
                    data.add(d);
                } catch(NumberFormatException nfe) {
                    System.err.println("Invalid number on line " +
                        is.getLineNumber());
                }
            }
```

*Example 13-8. Grapher.java (continued)*

```
        } catch (FileNotFoundException e) {
            System.err.println("File " + fname + " unreadable: " + e);
        } catch (IOException e) {
            System.err.println("I/O error on line " + is.getLineNumber());
        }
        n = data.size();
        if (n < 2) {
            System.err.println("Not enough data points!");
            return;
        }

        // find min & max
        for (int i=0 ; i < n; i++) {
            Apoint d = (Apoint)data.elementAt(i);
            if (d.x < minx) minx = d.x;
            if (d.x > maxx) maxx = d.x;
            if (d.y < miny) miny = d.y;
            if (d.y > maxy) maxy = d.y;
        }

        // Compute ranges
        xrange = (maxx - minx) * BORDERFACTOR;
        yrange = (maxy - miny) * BORDERFACTOR;
        Debug.println("range", "minx,x,r = " + minx +' '+ maxx +' '+ xrange);
        Debug.println("range", "miny,y,r = " + miny +' '+ maxy +' '+ yrange);
    }

    /** Called when the window needs painting.
     * Computes X and Y range, scales.
     */
    public void paintComponent(Graphics g) {
        super.paintComponent(g);
        Dimension s = getSize();
        if (n < 2) {
            g.drawString("Insufficient data", 10, 40);
            return;
        }

        // Compute scale factors
        float xfact =  s.width  / xrange;
        float yfact =  s.height / yrange;

        // Scale and plot the data
        for (int i=0 ; i < n; i++) {
            Apoint d = (Apoint)data.elementAt(i);
            float x = (d.x-minx) * xfact;
            float y = (d.y-miny) * yfact;
            Debug.println("point", "AT " + i + " " + d + "; " +
                "x = " + x + "; y = " + y);
            // Draw a 5-pixel rectangle centered, so -2 both x and y.
            // AWT numbers Y from 0 down, so invert:
            g.drawRect(((int)x)-2, s.height-2-(int)y, 5, 5);
```

*Example 13-8. Grapher.java (continued)*

```
        }
    }

    public Dimension getPreferredSize() {
        return new Dimension(150, 150);
    }

    public static void main(String[] rgs) {
        final JFrame f = new JFrame("Grapher");
        f.addWindowListener(new WindowAdapter() {
            public void windowClosing(WindowEvent e) {
                f.setVisible(false);
                f.dispose();
                System.exit(0);
            }
        });
        Grapher g = new Grapher();
        f.setContentPane(g);
        f.setLocation(100, 100);
        f.pack();
        if (rgs.length == 0)
            g.read("Grapher.dat");
        else
            g.read(rgs[0]);
        f.setVisible(true);
    }
}
```

Most of the complexity of Grapher lies in determining the range and scaling. You could obviously extend this to draw fancier drawings such as bar charts and the like. If pie charts interest you, see ChartBean in the online source.

# CHAPTER 14

# Graphical User Interfaces

## 14.0 Introduction

Java has had windowing capabilities since its earliest days. The first version made public was the Abstract Windowing Toolkit, or AWT. AWT used the native toolkit components, so it was relatively small and simple. AWT suffered somewhat from being a "least common denominator"; a feature could not be added unless it could be implemented on all major platforms that Java supported. The second major implementation was the Swing classes, released in 1998 as part of the Java Foundation Classes. Swing is a full-function, professional-quality GUI toolkit designed to enable almost any kind of client-side GUI-based interaction. AWT lives inside, or rather underneath, Swing, and, for this reason, many programs begin by importing both java.awt and javax.swing. An alternate approach is exemplified by IBM's SWT (Standard Windowing Toolkit), which is a thin wrapper for direct access to the underlying toolkit. SWT is used in building the Eclipse IDE discussed in Recipe 1.3. It's possible to build new applications using SWT, but Swing is more portable and more widely used.

This chapter presents a few elements of Java windowing for the developer whose main exposure to Java has been on the server side. Most of the examples are shown using Swing, rather than the obsolescent AWT components; SWT is not covered at all. I assume that you have at least a basic understanding of what GUI components are, which ones should be used where, and so on. I will refer to JButton, JList, and JFrame, to name a few, without saying much more about their basics or functionality. This is not intended to be a complete tutorial; the reader needing more background should refer to *Java in a Nutshell* or *Head First Java*. For a very thorough presentation on all aspects of Swing, I recommend *Java Swing* by Marc Loy, Bob Eckstein, Dave Wood, Jim Elliott, and Brian Cole (O'Reilly). At around 1,250 pages, it's not an overnight read. But it *is* comprehensive.

Java's event model has evolved over time, too. In JDK 1.0, the writer of a windowed application had to write a single large event-handling method to deal with button presses from all the GUI controls in the window. This was simple for small programs, but it did not scale well. My JabaDex application had one large event handler method that tried to figure out which of 50 or 60 GUI controls had caused an event, which was tedious and error prone. In JDK 1.1, a new delegation event model was introduced. In this model, events are given only to classes that request them, which is done by *registering* a *listener*. This is discussed in Recipe 14.4 and shown in Example 14-1. At the same time, the language was extended ever so slightly to include the notion of *inner classes*. An inner class is simply a class whose definition is contained inside the body of another class. We use examples of two types of inner classes here; for details on the half-dozen different categories of inner classes, the reader is referred to *Java in a Nutshell*.

Most of the GUI construction techniques in this chapter can be done for you, in some cases more quickly, by an integrated development environment (IDE). I have always believed, however, that understanding what goes on inside the code should be a prerequisite for being allowed to use an IDE. Those who disagree may be inclined to skip this chapter, go press a few buttons, and have the computer do the work for them. But you should at least skim this chapter to see what's going on so that you'll know where to look when you need it later.

## See Also

Please do not unleash your GUI application upon the world until you have read Sun's official *Java Look and Feel Design Guidelines* (Addison Wesley). This work presents the views of a large group of human factors and user-interface experts at Sun who have worked with the Swing GUI package since its inception; they tell you how to make it work well.

# 14.1  Displaying GUI Components

## Problem

You want to create some GUI components and have them appear in a window.

## Solution

Create a JFrame and add the components to its ContentPane.

## Discussion

The older Abstract Windowing Toolkit (AWT) had a simple Frame component for making main windows; this allowed you to add components directly to it. "Good" programs usually created a panel to fit inside and populate the frame. But some less-educated heathens, and those in a hurry, often added components directly to the frame. The Swing JFrame is more complex—it comes with not one but two containers already constructed inside it. The ContentPane is the main container; you should normally use it as your JFrame's main container. The GlassPane has a clear background and sits over the top of the ContentPane; its primary use is in temporarily painting something over the top of the main ContentPane. Because of this, you need to use the JFrame's getContentPane( ) method:

```java
import java.awt.*;
import javax.swing.*;

public class ContentPane extends JFrame {
    public ContentPane() {
        Container cp = getContentPane();
        // now add Components to "cp"...
    }
}
```

You can add any number of components (including containers) into this existing container, using the ContentPane add( ) method:

```java
import java.awt.*;
import java.awt.event.*;
import javax.swing.*;

/** Just a Frame
 * @version $Id: ch14,v 1.6 2004/05/07 15:20:56 ian Exp $
 */
public class JFrameDemo extends JFrame {
    JButton quitButton;

    /** Construct the object including its GUI */
    public JFrameDemo() {
        super("JFrameDemo");
        Container cp = getContentPane();
        cp.add(quitButton = new JButton("Exit"));

        // Set up so that "Close" will exit the program,
        // not just close the JFrame.
        setDefaultCloseOperation(JFrame.EXIT_ON_CLOSE);

        // This "action handler" will be explained later in the chapter.
        quitButton.addActionListener(new ActionListener() {
            public void actionPerformed(ActionEvent e) {
                setVisible(false);
                dispose();
                System.exit(0);
            }
        });

        pack();
    }
    public static void main(String[] args) {
        new JFrameDemo().setVisible(true);
    }
}
```

This code compiles fine. But when we try to run it, of course, there is no main method. We need to create one, either inside the JFrameDemo class or on its own:

```
public class JFrameDemoMain {
    // We need a main program to instantiate and show.
    public static void main(String[] args) {
        new JFrameDemo( ).setVisible(true);
    }
}
```

Now we can run it and have it display. But it has two obvious problems: it starts off tiny (on Windows) or huge (on X Windows). And, when we do resize it, only the buttons show, and it always takes up the full size of the window. To solve these problems, we need to discuss layout management, to which we now turn our attention.

A less obvious problem has to do with thread safety (see Chapter 24). The basic idea is that the first component that gets created starts a Thread of control running, and both this thread and your main thread can be doing things to the GUI at the same time. The solution is to do the setVisible(true) on the window system's event thread, using the static EventQueue.invokeLater( ) method. The code to start the GUI in a thread-safe way is only a few lines longer. This code uses an "anonymous inner class"; see Recipe 9.6 for details on this technique:

```
public class JFrameDemoSafe {
    // We need a main program to instantiate and show.
    public static void main(String[] args) {

        // Create the GUI (variable is final because used by inner class).
        final JFrame demo = new JFrameDemo( );

        // Create a Runnable to set the main visible, and get Swing to invoke.
        EventQueue.invokeLater(new Runnable( ) {
            public void run( ) {
                demo.setVisible(true);
            }
        });
    }
}
```

Most books and articles on Swing GUIs do not mention Swing's thread-safety issues, but you can read about it on Sun's web site, at *http://java.sun.com/developer/ JDCTechTips/2003/tt1208.html*. We will omit this code for brevity from the simple demos herein, but production code should use it.

# 14.2  Designing a Window Layout

## Problem

The default layout isn't good enough.

## Solution

Learn to deal with a layout manager.

# Discussion

The container classes such as `Panel` have the ability to contain a series of components, but you can arrange components in a window in many ways. Rather than clutter up each container with a variety of different layout computations, the designers of the Java API used a sensible design pattern to divide the labor. A *layout manager* is an object that performs the layout computations for a container.[*] The AWT package has five common layout manager classes (see Table 14-1), and Swing has a few more. Plus, as we'll see in Recipe 14.18, it's not that big a deal to write your own!

*Table 14-1. Layout managers*

| Name | Notes | Default on |
|------|-------|-----------|
| FlowLayout | Flows across the container | (J)Panel, (J)Applet |
| BorderLayout | Five "geographic" regions | (J)Frame, (J)Window |
| GridLayout | Regular grid (all items same size) | None |
| CardLayout | Display one of many components at a time; useful for wizard-style layouts | None |
| GridBagLayout | Very flexible but maximally complex | None |
| BoxLayout (Swing) | Single row or column of components | None |

Since we've broached the subject of layout management, I should mention that each component has a method called `getPreferredSize( )`, which the layout managers use in deciding how and where to place components. A well-behaved component overrides this method to return something meaningful. A button or label, for example, will indicate that it wishes to be large enough to contain its text and/or icon, plus a bit of space for padding. And, if your `JFrame` is full of well-behaved components, you can set its size to be "just the size of all included components, plus a bit for padding," just by calling the `pack( )` method, which takes no arguments. The `pack( )` method goes around and asks each embedded component for its preferred size (and any nested container's `getPreferredSize( )` will ask each of its components, and so on). The `JFrame` is then set to the best size to give the components their preferred sizes as much as is possible. If not using `pack( )`, you need to call the `setSize( )` method, which requires either a width and a height, or a `Dimension` object containing this information.

A `FlowLayout` is the default in `JPanel` and `Applet/JApplet`. It simply lays the components out along the "normal" axis (left to right in European and English-speaking locales, right to left in Hebrew or Arabic locales, and so on, as set by the user's `Locale` settings). The overall collection of them is centered within the window.

---

[*] The `LayoutManager` specification is actually a Java interface rather than a class. In fact, it's two interfaces: quoting the code, interface `LayoutManager2` extends `LayoutManager`. The differences between these two interfaces don't concern us here; we want to concentrate on using the layout managers.

The default for JFrame and JWindow is BorderLayout. This explains the problem of the single button appearing in the JFrameDemo class at the end of the previous recipe. BorderLayout divides the screen into the five areas shown in Figure 14-1. If you don't specify where to place a component, it goes into the Center. And if you place multiple components in the same region (perhaps by adding several components without specifying where to place them!), only the last one appears.

*Figure 14-1. BorderLayout's five regions*

So we can fix the previous version of the JFrameDemo in one of two ways: either we can use a FlowLayout or specify BorderLayout regions for the label and the button. The former being simpler, we'll try it out:

```java
import java.awt.*;
import javax.swing.*;

public class JFrameFlowLayout extends JFrame {
    public JFrameFlowLayout( ) {
        Container cp = getContentPane( );

        // Make sure it has a FlowLayout layoutmanager.
        cp.setLayout(new FlowLayout( ));

        // now add Components to "cp"...
        cp.add(new JLabel("Wonderful?"));
        cp.add(new JButton("Yes!"));
        pack( );
    }

    // We need a main program to instantiate and show.
    public static void main(String[] args) {
        new JFrameFlowLayout( ).setVisible(true);
    }
}
```

## See Also

I have not discussed the details of the advanced layouts. For an example of a dialog layout using nested panels, see the Font Chooser in Recipe 14.17. For an example of a GridBagLayout, see the GUI network client in Recipe 18.3. For more details, see the AWT and Swing books.

## 14.3   A Tabbed View of Life

### Problem

These layouts don't include a tab layout, and you need one.

### Solution

Use a JTabbedPane.

### Discussion

The JTabbedPane class acts as a combined container and layout manager. It implements a conventional tab layout, which looks like Figure 14-2.

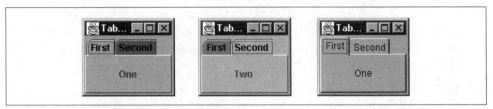

*Figure 14-2. JTabbedPane: two views in Java Look and one in Windows Look*

To add a tab to the layout, you do not use setLayout( ). You simply create the JTabbedPane and call its addTab( ) method, passing in a String and a Component; you usually need to add JPanels or some similar Container to make a sophisticated layout. Example 14-1 is the code for our simple program.

*Example 14-1. TabPaneDemo.java*

```
import javax.swing.*;

public class TabPaneDemo {
    protected JTabbedPane tabPane;
    public TabPaneDemo( ) {
        tabPane = new JTabbedPane( );
        tabPane.add(new JLabel("One", JLabel.CENTER), "First");
        tabPane.add(new JLabel("Two", JLabel.CENTER), "Second");
    }

    public static void main(String[] a) {
        JFrame f = new JFrame("Tab Demo");
        f.getContentPane( ).add(new TabPaneDemo( ).tabPane);
        f.setSize(120, 100);
        f.setVisible(true);
    }
}
```

## See Also

The third screenshot in Figure 14-2 shows the program with a Windows look and feel, instead of the default Java look and feel. See Recipe 14.15 for how to change the look and feel of a Swing-based GUI application.

# 14.4   Action Handling: Making Buttons Work

## Problem

Your button doesn't do anything when the user presses it.

## Solution

Add an ActionListener to do the work.

## Discussion

Event listeners come in about half a dozen different types. The most common is the ActionListener, used by push buttons, text fields, and certain other components to indicate that the user has performed a high-level action, such as activating a push button or pressing Enter in a text field. The paradigm (shown in Figure 14-3) is that you create a Listener object, register it with the event source (such as the push button), and wait. Later, when and if the user pushes the button, the button will call your Listener.

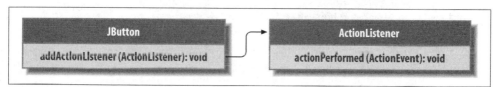

| JButton | ActionListener |
|---|---|
| addActionListener (ActionListener): void | actionPerformed (ActionEvent): void |

Figure 14-3. AWT listener relationships

Here's some simple code in which pushing a button causes the program to print a friendly message. This program is an applet (see Recipe 18.2), so it can use the showStatus( ) method to print its text:

```
import java.applet.*;
import java.awt.*;
import java.awt.event.*;

/** Demonstrate use of Button */
public class ButtonDemo extends Applet implements ActionListener {
    Button b1;

    public ButtonDemo( ) {
        add(b1 = new Button("A button"));
        b1.addActionListener(this);
    }
```

```
        public void actionPerformed(ActionEvent event) {
            showStatus("Thanks for pushing my button!");
        }
    }
```

This version does not use an inner class to handle the events but does so itself by directly implementing the ActionListener interface. This works for small programs, but as an application grows, it quickly becomes unserviceable; how do you sort out which button was pressed? To solve this problem, we normally use an inner class as the action handler and have a different class for each button. First, let's write the previous code with two buttons so that you can see what I mean:

```
import java.applet.*;
import java.awt.*;
import java.awt.event.*;

/** Demonstrate use of two buttons, using a single ActionListener,
 * being the class itself.
 */
public class ButtonDemo2a extends Applet implements ActionListener {
    Button b1, b2;

    public void init() {
        add(b1 = new Button("A button"));
        b1.addActionListener(this);

        add(b2 = new Button("Another button"));
        b2.addActionListener(this);
    }

    public void actionPerformed(ActionEvent e) {
        if (e.getSource() == b1)
            showStatus("Thanks for pushing my first button!");
        else
            showStatus("Thanks for pushing my second button!");
    }
}
```

Now here it is using a *member inner class*, that is, a class that is a named part of another class:

```
import java.applet.*;
import java.awt.*;
import java.awt.event.*;

/** Demonstrate use of two buttons, using a single ActionListener
 * made of a named inner class
 */
public class ButtonDemo2b extends Applet {
    Button b1, b2;
    ActionListener handler = new ButtonHandler();

    public void init() {
        add(b1 = new Button("A button"));
        b1.addActionListener(handler);
```

```
        add(b2 = new Button("Another button"));
        b2.addActionListener(handler);
    }

    class ButtonHandler implements ActionListener {
        public void actionPerformed(ActionEvent e) {
            if (e.getSource( ) == b1)
                showStatus("Thanks for pushing my first button!");
            else
                showStatus("Thanks for pushing my second button!");
        }
    }
}
```

Note that merely breaking the action handling code into its own class doesn't really contribute much to readability. But there is a way to use inner classes that does promote readability and maintainability. We create an inner class (see Recipe 9.6) for each event source—each button, each menu item, and so on. Sounds like a lot of work, and it would be, if you used the previous method. But there is a shorter way, using anonymous inner classes, described next.

# 14.5  Action Handling Using Anonymous Inner Classes

## Problem

You want action handling with less creation of special classes.

## Solution

Use anonymous inner classes.

## Discussion

*Anonymous inner classes* are declared and instantiated at the same time, using the new operator with the name of an existing class or interface. If you name a class, it will be subclassed; if you name an interface, the anonymous class will extend java. lang.Object and implement the named interface. The paradigm is:

```
    b.addActionListener(new ActionListener( ) {
        public void actionPerformed(ActionEvent e) {
            showStatus("Thanks for pushing my second button!");
        }
    });
```

Did you notice the }); by itself on the last line? Good, because it's important. The } terminates the definition of the inner class, while the ) ends the argument list to the addActionListener method; the single argument inside the parenthesis is an argument of type ActionListener that refers to the one and only instance created of your anonymous class. Example 14-2 contains a complete example.

*Example 14-2. ButtonDemo2c.java*

```java
import java.applet.*;
import java.awt.*;
import java.awt.event.*;

/** Demonstrate use of Button */
public class ButtonDemo2c extends Applet {
    Button    b;

    public void init( ) {
        add(b = new Button("A button"));
        b.addActionListener(new ActionListener( ) {
            public void actionPerformed(ActionEvent e) {
                showStatus("Thanks for pushing my first button!");
            }
        });
        add(b = new Button("Another button"));
        b.addActionListener(new ActionListener( ) {
            public void actionPerformed(ActionEvent e) {
                showStatus("Thanks for pushing my second button!");
            }
        });
    }
}
```

The real benefit of these anonymous inner classes, by the way, is that they keep the action handling code in the same place that the GUI control is being instantiated. This saves a lot of looking back and forth to see what a GUI control really does.

Those `ActionListener` objects have no instance name and appear to have no class name: is that possible? The former yes, but not the latter. In fact, class names are assigned to anonymous inner classes by the compiler. After compiling and testing ButtonDemo2c, I list the directory in which I ran the program:

```
C:\javasrc\gui>ls -1 ButtonDemo2c*
ButtonDemo2c$1.class
ButtonDemo2c$2.class
ButtonDemo2c.class
ButtonDemo2c.htm
ButtonDemo2c.java
C:\javasrc\gui>
```

Those first two are the anonymous inner classes. Note that a different compiler might assign different names to them; it doesn't matter to us. A word to the wise: don't depend on those names!

## See Also

Most IDEs (see Recipe 1.1) have drag-and-drop GUI builder tools that make this task easier, at least for simpler projects.

# 14.6  Terminating a Program with "Window Close"

## Problem

Nothing happens when you click on the close button on the titlebar of an AWT Frame. When you do this on a Swing JFrame, the window disappears but the application does not exit.

## Solution

Use JFrame's setDefaultCloseOperation( ) method or add a WindowListener and have it exit the application.

## Discussion

Main windows—subclasses of java.awt.Window, such as (J)Frames and (J)Dialogs—are treated specially. Unlike all other Component subclasses, Window and its subclasses are not initially visible. This is sensible, as they have to be packed or resized, and you don't want the user to watch the components getting rearranged. Once you call a Window's setVisible(true) method, all components inside it become visible. You can listen for WindowEvents on a Window.

The WindowListener interface contains a plenitude of methods to notify a listener when anything happens to the window. You can be told when the window is activated (gets keyboard and mouse events) or deactivated. Or you can find out when the window is iconified or deiconified: these are good times to suspend and resume processing, respectively. You can be notified the first time the window is opened. And, most importantly for us, you can be notified when the user requests that the window be closed. (Some sample close buttons are shown in Figure 14-4.) You can respond in two ways. With Swing's JFrame, you can set the "default close operation." Alternatively, with any Window subclass, you can provide a WindowListener to be notified of window events.

In some cases, you may not need a window closer. The Swing JFrame has a setDefaultCloseOperation( ) method, which controls the default behavior. You can pass it one of the values defined in the Swing WindowConstants class:

WindowConstants.DO_NOTHING_ON_CLOSE
> Ignore the request. The window stays open. Useful for critical dialogs; probably antisocial for most "main application"-type windows.

WindowConstants.HIDE_ON_CLOSE
> Hide the window (default).

WindowConstants.DISPOSE_ON_CLOSE
> Hide and dispose the window.

`WindowConstants.EXIT_ON_CLOSE`

JDK 1.3 (and later). Exit the application on close, obviating the need for a `WindowListener`! Does not give you a chance to save data; for that, you need a `WindowListener`.

The action set by `setDefaultCloseOperation()` will be performed after the last `windowClosing()` method on the `Window` (if you have one) returns.

The `windowClosing()` method of your `WindowListener` is called when the user clicks on the close button (this depends on the window system and, on X Windows, on the window manager) or sends the close message from the keyboard (normally Alt-F4).

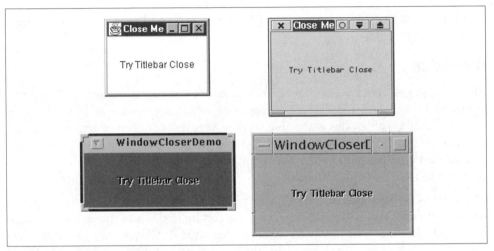

*Figure 14-4. Some close buttons*

The method signature is:

```
public void windowClosing(WindowEvent);
```

But this method comes from the interface `WindowListener`, which has half a dozen other methods. If you define a `WindowListener` and implement only this one method, the compiler declares your class abstract and refuses to instantiate it. You might start by writing stub or dummy versions (methods whose body is just the two characters `{}`), but you'd then be doing more work than necessary; an "adapter" class already does this for all methods in the `Listener` interface. So you really need only to subclass from `WindowAdapter` and override the one method, `windowClosing`, that you care about. Figure 14-5 shows this model.

Let's put this all together in some code examples. Class `WindowDemo` puts up a frame and closes when you ask it to. The online source includes class `WindowDemo2`, which is the same, but implemented as a Swing `JFrame`.

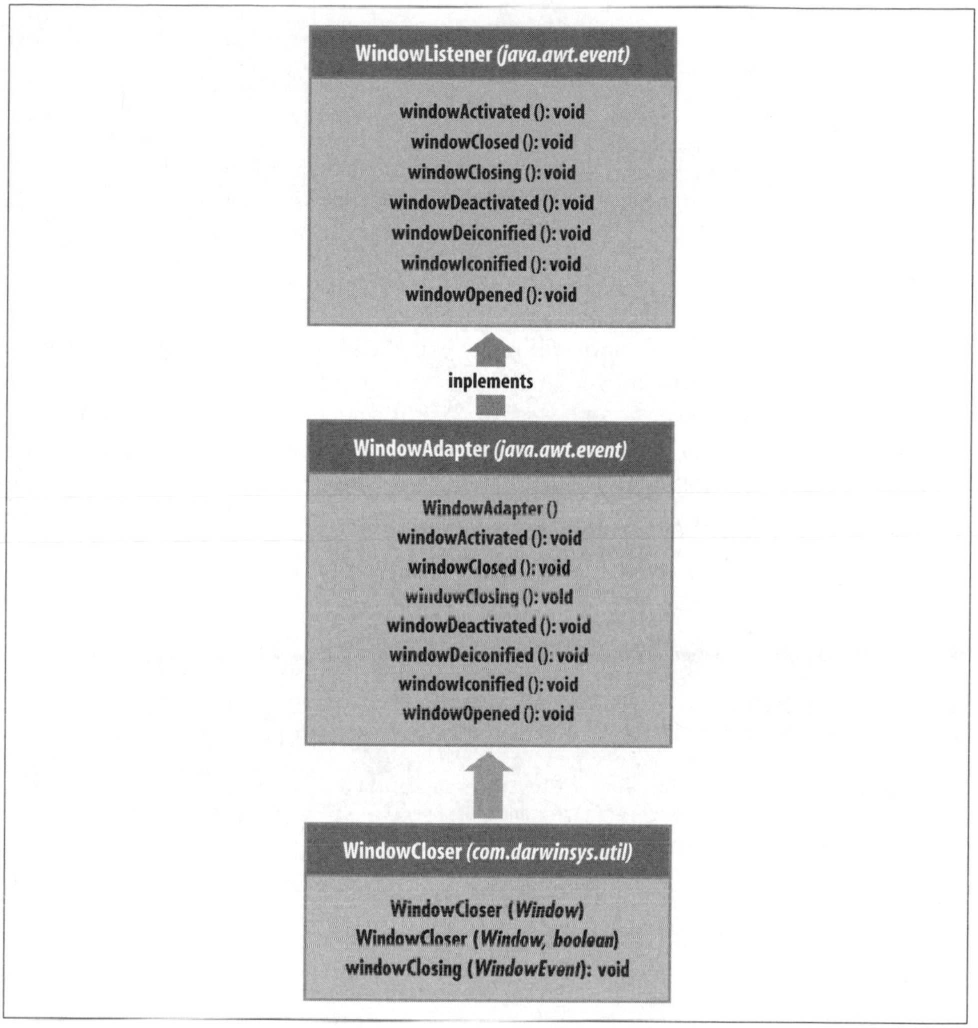

```
WindowListener (java.awt.event)

windowActivated (): void
windowClosed (): void
windowClosing (): void
windowDeactivated (): void
windowDeiconified (): void
windowIconified (): void
windowOpened (): void
```

**inplements**

```
WindowAdapter (java.awt.event)

WindowAdapter ()
windowActivated (): void
windowClosed (): void
windowClosing (): void
windowDeactivated (): void
windowDeiconified (): void
windowIconified (): void
windowOpened (): void
```

```
WindowCloser (com.darwinsys.util)

WindowCloser (Window)
WindowCloser (Window, boolean)
windowClosing (WindowEvent): void
```

*Figure 14-5. WindowListener, WindowAdapter, and my WindowCloser*

```java
import java.awt.*;
import java.awt.event.*;

/* Show an example of closing a Window.
 */
public class WindowDemo extends Frame {

    public static void main(String[] argv) {
        Frame f = new WindowDemo( );
        f.setVisible(true);
    }
    public WindowDemo( ) {
        setSize(200, 100);
        addWindowListener(new WindowDemoAdapter( ));
```

```
        }

        /** Named Inner class that closes a Window. */
        class WindowDemoAdapter extends WindowAdapter {
            public void windowClosing(WindowEvent e) {
                    System.out.println("Goodbye!");
                    WindowDemo.this.setVisible(false);    // window will close
                    WindowDemo.this.dispose();         // and be freed up.
                    System.exit(0);
            }
        }
    }
```

Since making a `Window` close—and optionally exit the program—is a common operation, I've encapsulated this into a small class called `WindowCloser`, which is in my public package com.darwinsys.util. Most AWT and Swing books have similar classes. Example 14-3 contains my `WindowCloser` class. Note that the class is marked deprecated; this is to remind you that, on Swing, you should just use setDefaultCloseOperation( ). If you're writing an AWT-only application, you'll have to live with the deprecation warning.

*Example 14-3. WindowCloser.java*

```
package com.darwinsys.swingui;

import java.awt.Window;
import java.awt.event.*;

/** A WindowCloser - watch for Window Closing events, and
 * follow them up with setVisible(false) and dispose().
 * @deprecated Use setDefaultCloseOperation( ) instead.
 */
public class WindowCloser extends WindowAdapter {
    /** True if we are to exit as well. */
    boolean doExit = false;
    public WindowCloser( ) {
    }
    public WindowCloser(Window w) {
        // nothing to do
    }
    public WindowCloser(Window w, boolean exit) {
        doExit = exit;
    }

    public void windowClosing(WindowEvent e) {
        Window win = e.getWindow();
        win.setVisible(false);
        win.dispose();
        if (doExit)
            System.exit(0);
    }
}
```

Using it is straightforward:

```
import java.awt.Frame;
import java.awt.Label;
import com.darwinsys.swingui.WindowCloser;

/* Show an example of closing a Window.
 */
public class WindowCloserTest {

    /* Main method */
    public static void main(String[] argv) {
        Frame f = new Frame("Close Me");
        f.add(new Label("Try Titlebar Close", Label.CENTER));
        f.setSize(100, 100);
        f.setVisible(true);
        f.addWindowListener(new WindowCloser(f, true));
    }
}
```

Notice that some of this "quick and dirty" class extends Frame or JFrame directly. It is generally better to have a main program that creates a JFrame and installs the "main" GUI component into that. This scheme promotes greater reusability. For example, if your graphing program's main component extends JComponent, it can be added to a JPanel in another application; whereas if it extends JFrame, it cannot.

## See Also

I've mentioned dispose( ) several times without saying much about it. The dispose( ) method (inherited from Window) causes the underlying (operating system-specific) window system resources to be released without totally destroying the Window. If you later call pack( ) or setVisible(true) on the Window, the native resources are recreated. It's a good idea to dispose( ) a window if you won't be using it for a while, but not if there's a good chance you'll need it again soon.

In addition to WindowListener, Swing has several other multimethod interfaces, including MouseListener and ComponentListener, and an Adapter class for each of these.

# 14.7   Dialogs: When Later Just Won't Do

## Problem

You need a bit of feedback from the user *right now*.

## Solution

Use a JOptionPane method to show a prebuilt dialog. Or subclass JDialog.

## Discussion

It's fairly common to want to confirm an action with the user or to bring some problem to her attention right away, rather than waiting for her to read a log file that she might or might not get around to. These popup windows are called *Dialogs*. The JOptionPane class has a number of show...Dialog() methods that let you display most prebuilt dialogs, including those shown in Figure 14-6.

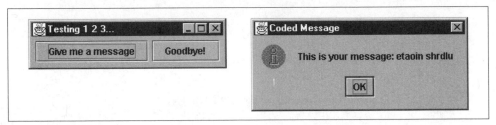

*Figure 14-6. JOptionPane in action*

The simplest form is showMessageDialog(), and its first argument is the owning Frame or JFrame. If you don't know it, pass null, but Java doesn't guarantee to give input focus back to your main window when the dialog is dismissed. The second argument is the message text, and the third is the titlebar title. Last but not least is code telling which of several prebuilt bitmaps should be displayed. This program produces the "Coded Message" dialog in the figure:

```
import java.awt.*;
import java.awt.event.*;
import javax.swing.*;

/**
 * Demonstrate JOptionPane
 */
public class JOptionDemo extends JFrame {

    // Constructor
    JOptionDemo(String s) {
        super(s);

        Container cp = getContentPane();
        cp.setLayout(new FlowLayout());

        JButton b = new JButton("Give me a message");
        b.addActionListener(new ActionListener() {
            public void actionPerformed(ActionEvent e) {
                JOptionPane.showMessageDialog(
                    JOptionDemo.this,
                    "This is your message: etaoin shrdlu", "Coded Message",
                    JOptionPane.INFORMATION_MESSAGE);
            }
        });
        cp.add(b);
```

```
        b = new JButton("Goodbye!");
        b.addActionListener(new ActionListener( ) {
            public void actionPerformed(ActionEvent e) {
                System.exit(0);
            }
        });
        cp.add(b);

        // the main window
        setSize(200, 150);
        pack( );
    }

    public static void main(String[] arg) {
        JOptionDemo x = new JOptionDemo("Testing 1 2 3...");
        x.setVisible(true);
    }
}
```

You can use the JOptionPane class in several other ways. For example, you can call its showDialog( ) method with a list of strings; each is displayed on a push button in the dialog. This method blocks until the user selects one of the buttons; the return value of the method is an int telling which button the user clicked on (it returns the array index of the string whose button was pressed). Another method, showInputDialog( ), lets you prompt the user for a data value. Very, very convenient!

## See Also

JDialog lets you write arbitrarily complicated dialogs. You subclass them in a manner similar to JFrame, specifying whether you want an application-modal or non-modal dialog (a modal dialog locks out the rest of the application, which is less convenient for the user but much easier for the programmer). See *Java Swing* (O'Reilly) for information on JDialog.

# 14.8   Catching and Formatting GUI Exceptions

## Problem

Your application code is throwing an exception, and you want to catch it, but the GUI runs in a different Thread (see Chapter 24), so you can't.

## Solution

There is an "undocumented feature" for doing this; you can use it for now, but expect the interface to change someday.

# Discussion

This is one of the few cases in the book where I venture to document an unsupported feature, and only because Sun's unwillingness to formally document it has generated so much frustration for developers.

You can find out about this by reading the source code for AWT.

To specify an error handler, you must set the System Property (see Recipe 2.2) sun. awt.exception.handler to the full class name of your exception handler *before* you create any GUI components (the fact that this name begins with sun. rather than java. is your assurance that it is unsupported). The class you name must be on your CLASSPATH at runtime, must have a public, no-argument constructor, and must contain a method exactly matching the signature public void handle(Throwable t). If the named class can be found and loaded, the GUI exception dispatching mechanism calls the handle( ) method whenever an uncaught exception is received.

To display the caught exceptions, show each one in a dialog. My API class com. darwinsys.swingui.ErrorUtil contains both a handle( ) method as described and a more general method public static void showExceptions(Component parent, Throwable t). This method displays the Throwable (and, on 1.4 and later, any nested exceptions) in an error dialog. See the program ErrorUtilTest in the *darwinsys/src/ regress* directory for an example of running this program directly, and see ErrorUtilCatchTest in the same directory for an example of using it with uncaught exceptions from the GUI thread as described. The command ant regress.gui in the *darwinsys* directory runs both.

In JDK 1.5, an easier method may be to use the new Thread method setDefaultUncaughtExceptionHandler( ), whose signature is:

```
public static void setDefaultUncaughtExceptionHandler(Thread.
UncaughtExceptionHandler eh);
```

The code in Example 14-4 shows a tiny demonstration of this technique.

*Example 14-4. ThreadBasedCatcher.java*

```
/**
 * ThreadBasedCatcher - Demonstrate catching uncaught exceptions
 * thrown in an unrelated Thread.
 * @version $Id: ch14,v 1.6 2004/05/07 15:20:56 ian Exp $
 */
public class ThreadBasedCatcher extends JFrame{

    public static void main(String[] args) {
        new ThreadBasedCatcher( ).setVisible(true);
    }
    public ThreadBasedCatcher( ){
        Container cp = getContentPane( );
        JButton crasher = new JButton("Crash");
        cp.add(crasher);
```

*Example 14-4. ThreadBasedCatcher.java (continued)*

```
        crasher.addActionListener(new ActionListener(){
            public void actionPerformed(ActionEvent e){
                throw new RuntimeException("You asked for it");
            }
        });
        Thread.setDefaultUncaughtExceptionHandler(
                new Thread.UncaughtExceptionHandler(){
                    public void uncaughtException(Thread t, Throwable ex){
                        System.out.println(
                            "You crashed thread " + t.getName());
                        System.out.println(
                            "Exception was: " + ex.toString());
                    }
                });
        pack();
    }
}
```

Figure 14-7 shows the program running; pushing the button produced this output.

*Figure 14-7. ThreadBasedCatcher running*

```
You crashed thread AWT-EventQueue-0
Exception was: java..lang.RuntimeException: You asked for it.
```

# 14.9   Getting Program Output into a Window

## Problem

You want to capture an input/output stream and display it in a text field.

## Solution

Use an interconnected pair of piped streams and a Thread to read from the input half, and write it to the text area. You may also want to redirect System.out and System.err to the stream; see Recipe 10.9.

## Discussion

PipedInputStream and PipedOutputStream provide two streams (see "Streams and Readers/Writers" at the beginning of Chapter 10) that are connected together by a buffer and are designed to provide communication between multiple threads (see the Introduction to Chapter 24).

As you'll see in Chapter 19, I am fairly aggressive in the pursuit of SPAM perpetrators. I have a program called TestOpenMailRelay, derived from the mail sender in Recipe 19.2, that I use to test whether remote servers are willing to accept mail from unknown third parties and forward it as their own. Example 14-5 is the GUI for that program; both this and the main program are online in the email directory.

In the constructor, I arrange for the main class to write to the PipedOutputStream; the call to TestOpenMailRelay.process() passing the *ps* argument arranges this. That method writes its own output to the stream in addition to assigning standard output and standard error, so we should see anything it tries to print. To avoid long (possibly infinitely long!) delays, I start an additional thread to read from the pipe buffer. Figure 14-8 shows three windows: the program output window (the goal of this whole exercise), a terminal window from which I copied the IP address (some parts of the text in this window have been deliberately obfuscated), and another command window in which I started the GUI program running.

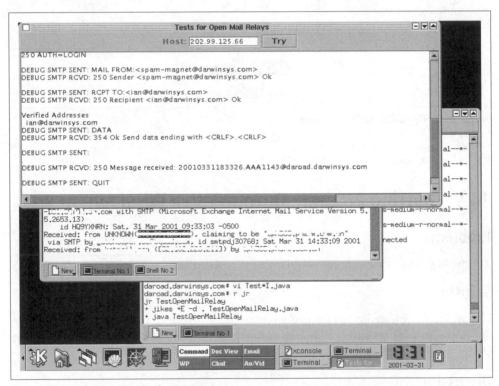

*Figure 14-8. TestOpenMailRelayGUI in action*

The code is shown in Example 14-5.

*Example 14-5. TestOpenMailRelayGUI.java*

```java
import java.awt.*;
import java.awt.event.*;
import javax.swing.*;
import java.io.*;

/** GUI for TestOpenMailRelay, lets you run it multiple times in one JVM
 * to avoid startup delay.
 *
 * Starts each in its own Thread for faster return to ready state.
 *
 * Uses PipedI/OStreams to capture system.out/err into a window.
 */
public class TestOpenMailRelayGUI extends JFrame {

    public static void main(String unused[]) throws IOException {
        new TestOpenMailRelayGUI().setVisible(true);
    }


    /** The one-line textfield for the user to type Host name/IP */
    protected JTextField hostTextField;
    /** The push button to start a test; a field so can disable/enable it. */
    protected JButton goButton;
    /** Multi-line text area for results. */
    protected JTextArea results;
    /** The piped stream for the main class to write into ""results" */
    protected PrintStream ps;
    /** The piped stream to read from "ps" into "results" */
    protected BufferedReader iis;

    /** This inner class is the action handler both for pressing
     * the "Try" button and also for pressing <ENTER> in the text
     * field. It gets the IP name/address from the text field
     * and passes it to process() in the main class. Run in the
     * GUI Dispatch thread to avoid messing the GUI. -- tmurtagh.
     */
    ActionListener runner = new ActionListener() {
        public void actionPerformed(ActionEvent evt) {
            goButton.setEnabled(false);
            SwingUtilities.invokeLater(
                new Thread() {
                    public void run() {
                        String host = hostTextField.getText().trim();
                        ps.println("Trying " + host);
                        TestOpenMailRelay.process(host, ps);
                        goButton.setEnabled(true);
                    }
                });
        }
    };

    /** Construct a GUI and some I/O plumbing to get the output
     * of "TestOpenMailRelay" into the "results" textfield.
     */
```

*Example 14-5. TestOpenMailRelayGUI.java (continued)*

```java
public TestOpenMailRelayGUI( ) throws IOException {
    super("Tests for Open Mail Relays");
    PipedInputStream is;
    PipedOutputStream os;
    JPanel p;
    Container cp = getContentPane( );
    cp.add(BorderLayout.NORTH, p = new JPanel( ));

    // The entry label and text field.
    p.add(new JLabel("Host:"));
    p.add(hostTextField = new JTextField(10));
    hostTextField.addActionListener(runner);

    p.add(goButton = new JButton("Try"));
    goButton.addActionListener(runner);

    JButton cb;
    p.add(cb = new JButton("Clear Log"));
    cb.addActionListener(new ActionListener( ) {
        public void actionPerformed(ActionEvent evt) {
            results.setText("");
        }
    });
    JButton sb;
    p.add(sb = new JButton("Save Log"));
    sb.setEnabled(false);

    results = new JTextArea(20, 60);
    // Add the text area to the main part of the window (CENTER).
    // Wrap it in a JScrollPane to make it scroll automatically.
    cp.add(BorderLayout.CENTER, new JScrollPane(results));

    setDefaultCloseOperation(JFrame.EXIT_ON_CLOSE);

    pack( );              // end of GUI portion

    // Create a pair of Piped Streams.
    is = new PipedInputStream( );
    os = new PipedOutputStream(is);

    iis = new BufferedReader(new InputStreamReader(is, "ISO8859_1"));
    ps = new PrintStream(os);

    // Construct and start a Thread to copy data from "is" to "os".
    new Thread( ) {
        public void run( ) {
            try {
                String line;
                while ((line = iis.readLine( )) != null) {
                    results.append(line);
                    results.append("\n");
                }
```

*Example 14-5. TestOpenMailRelayGUI.java (continued)*

```
                } catch(IOException ex) {
                    JOptionPane.showMessageDialog(null,
                        "*** Input or Output error ***\n" + ex,
                        "Error",
                        JOptionPane.ERROR_MESSAGE);
                }
            }
        }.start();
    }
}
```

# 14.10 Choosing a Value with JSpinner

## Problem

You want to let the user choose from a fixed set of values, but do not want to use a JList or JComboBox because they take up too much "screen real estate."

## Solution

Use a JSpinner.

## Discussion

The JSpinner class introduced in JDK 1.4 lets the user click up or down to cycle through a set of values. The values can be of any type, as they are managed by a helper of type SpinnerModel and displayed by another helper of type SpinnerEditor. A series of predefined SpinnerModels handle Numbers, Dates, and Lists (which can be arrays or Collections). A demonstration program is listed in Example 14-6; its output is shown in Figure 14-9.

*Example 14-6. SpinnerDemo.java*

```java
import java.awt.Container;
import java.awt.GridLayout;
import javax.swing.*;

/**
 * Demonstrate the Swing "Spinner" control.
 * @author ian
 */
public class SpinnerDemo {

    public static void main(String[] args) {
        JFrame jf = new JFrame("It Spins");
        Container cp = jf.getContentPane();
        cp.setLayout(new GridLayout(0,1));
```

*Example 14-6. SpinnerDemo.java (continued)*

```
        // Create a JSpinner using one of the pre-defined SpinnerModels
        JSpinner dates = new JSpinner(new SpinnerDateModel( ));
        cp.add(dates);

        // Create a JSPinner using a SpinnerListModel.
        String[] data = { "One", "Two", "Three" };
        JSpinner js = new JSpinner(new SpinnerListModel(data));
        cp.add(js);

        jf.setSize(100, 80);
        jf.setVisible(true);
    }
}
```

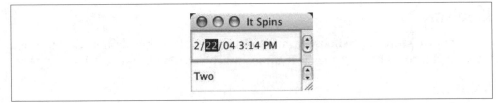

*Figure 14-9. SpinnerDemo output*

JSpinner's editors are reasonably clever. For example, if you select the leading zero of a number (such as the 04 in 2004), and try to increment it, the editor updates the entire number (04 to 05) rather than producing something silly like 15.

## See Also

The earlier Swing classes JList and JComboBox also let you choose among values.

# 14.11 Choosing a File with JFileChooser

## Problem

You want to allow the user to select a file by name using a traditional windowed file dialog.

## Solution

Use a JFileChooser.

## Discussion

The JFileChooser dialog provides a fairly standard file chooser. It has elements of both a Windows chooser and a Mac chooser, with more resemblance to the former than the latter. If you want to have control over which files appear, you need to provide one or more FileFilter subclasses. Each FileFilter subclass instance passed into the JFileChooser's addChoosableFileFilter( ) method becomes a selection in the chooser's Files of Type: choice. The default is All Files (*.*). Figure 14-10 shows my demo program in action.

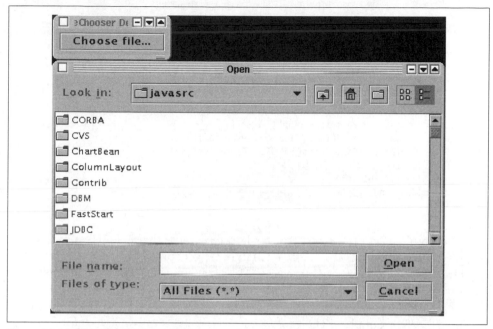

*Figure 14-10. JFileChooserDemo in action*

Let's look at the code for using JFileChooser:

```
import com.darwinsys.util.*;

import javax.swing.*;
import java.awt.event.*;
import java.io.*;
import java.util.*;

/** A simple demo of a JFileChooser in action. */
public class JFileChooserDemo extends JPanel {

    /** Constructor */
    public JFileChooserDemo(JFrame f) {
        final JFrame frame = f;
        final JFileChooser chooser = new JFileChooser();
        JFileFilter filter = new JFileFilter();
        filter.addType("java");
        filter.addType("class");
        filter.addType("jar");
        filter.setDescription("Java-related files");
        chooser.addChoosableFileFilter(filter);
        JButton b = new JButton("Choose file...");
        add(b);
```

```
            b.addActionListener(new ActionListener( ) {
                public void actionPerformed(ActionEvent e) {
                int returnVal = chooser.showOpenDialog(frame);
                if (returnVal == JFileChooser.APPROVE_OPTION) {
                    System.out.println("You chose a file named: " +
                        chooser.getSelectedFile( ).getPath( ));
                } else {
                    System.out.println("You did not choose a file.");
                }
                }
            });
        }

        public static void main(String[] args) {
            JFrame f = new JFrame("JFileChooser Demo");
            f.getContentPane( ).add(new JFileChooserDemo(f));
            f.pack( );
            f.setVisible(true);
            f.addWindowListener(new WindowCloser(f, true));
        }
    }
```

In this example, I set up a FileFilter for Java files. Note that FileFilter exists both in javax.swing.filechooser and java.io (an older version, not for use here; see Recipe 11.7). The javax.swing.filechooser.FileFilter interface has only two methods: boolean accept(File) and String getDescription( ). This is enough for a totally fixed-function file filter: you could hardcode the list of extensions that should be accepted, for example. The following class is similar in spirit to the ExampleFileFilter included in the JDK demo directory; Sun claims that its version will be moved into javax.swing.filechooser in a subsequent release of Swing.

```
/** A simple FileFilter class that works by filename extension,
 * like the one in the JDK demo called ExampleFileFilter, which
 * has been announced to be supported in a future Swing release.
 */
class JFileFilter extends javax.swing.filechooser.FileFilter {
    protected String description;
    protected ArrayList exts = new ArrayList( );

    public void addType(String s) {
        exts.add(s);
    }

    /** Return true if the given file is accepted by this filter. */
    public boolean accept(File f) {
        // Little trick: if you don't do this, only directory names
        // ending in one of the extensions appear in the window.
        if (f.isDirectory( )) {
            return true;

        } else if (f.isFile( )) {
            Iterator it = exts.iterator( );
            while (it.hasNext( )) {
```

```
            if (f.getName( ).endsWith((String)it.next( )))
                return true;
        }
    }

    // A file that didn't match, or a weirdo (e.g., Unix device file?).
    return false;
}

/** Set the printable description of this filter. */
public void setDescription(String s) {
    description = s;
}
/** Return the printable description of this filter. */
public String getDescription( ) {
    return description;
}
}
```

# 14.12 Choosing a Color

## Problem

You want to allow the user to select a color from all the colors available on your computer.

## Solution

Use Swing's JColorChooser.

## Discussion

OK, so it may be just glitz or a passing fad, but with today's displays, the 13 original AWT colors are too limiting. Swing's JColorChooser lets you choose from zillions of colors. From a program's view, it can be used in three ways:

- Construct it and place it in a panel
- Call its createDialog( ) and get a JDialog back
- Call its showDialog( ) and get back the chosen color

We use the last method since it's the simplest and the most likely to be used in a real application. The user has several methods of operating the chooser, too:

*Swatches mode*
 The user can pick from one of a few hundred color variants.

*HSB mode*
 This one's my favorite. The user picks one of Hue, Saturation, or Brightness, a standard way of representing color value. The user can adjust each value by slider. There is a huge range of different pixel values to choose from, by clicking (or, more fun, *dragging*) in the central area. See Figure 14-11.

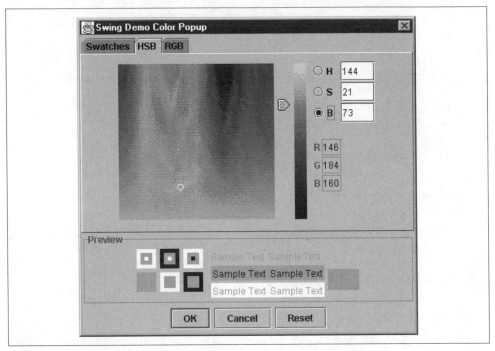

*Figure 14-11. JColorChooser: HSB view in action*

*RGB mode*

The user picks Red, Green, and Blue components by sliders.

Example 14-7 contains a short program that makes it happen.

*Example 14-7. JColorDemo.java*

```
import com.darwinsys.util.*;

import javax.swing.*;
import java.awt.*;
import java.awt.event.*;

/*
 * Colors - demo of Swing JColorChooser.
 * Swing's JColorChooser can be used in three ways:
 * <UL><LI>Construct it and place it in a panel;
 * <LI>Call its createDialog() and get a JDialog back
 * <LI>Call its showDialog() and get back the chosen color
 * </UL>
 * <P>We use the last method, as it's the simplest, and is how
 * you'd most likely use it in a real application.
 *
 * Originally appeared in the Linux Journal, 1999.
 */
```

*Example 14-7. JColorDemo.java (continued)*

```java
public class JColorDemo extends JFrame
{
    /** A canvas to display the color in. */
    JLabel demo;
    /** The latest chosen Color */
    Color lastChosen;

    /** Constructor - set up the entire GUI for this program */
    public JColorDemo() {
        super("Swing Color Demo");
        Container cp = getContentPane();
        JButton jButton;
        cp.add(jButton = new JButton("Change Color..."), BorderLayout.NORTH);
        jButton.setToolTipText("Click here to see the Color Chooser");
        jButton.addActionListener(new ActionListener() {
            public void actionPerformed(ActionEvent actionEvent)
            {
                Color ch = JColorChooser.showDialog(
                    JColorDemo.this,              // parent
                    "Swing Demo Color Popup",     // title
                    demo.getForeground());            // default
                if (ch != null)
                    demo.setForeground(ch);
            }
        });
        cp.add(BorderLayout.CENTER, demo =
            new MyLabel("Your One True Color", 200, 100));
        demo.setToolTipText("This is the last color you chose");
        pack();
        addWindowListener(new WindowCloser(this, true));
    }

    /** good old main */
    public static void main(String[] argv)
    {
        new JColorDemo().setVisible(true);
    }
}
```

## See Also

This program introduces setToolTipText( ), a method to set the text for pop-up "tooltips" that appear when you position the mouse pointer over a component and don't do anything for a given time (initially half a second). Tooltips originated with Macintosh Balloon Help and were refined into ToolTips under Microsoft Windows.[*] Tooltips are easy to use; the simplest form is shown here. For more documentation, see Chapter 3 of *Java Swing*.

---

[*] See? I even said something nice about Microsoft. I do believe in credit where credit's due.

## 14.13 Formatting JComponents with HTML

### Problem

You want more control over the formatting of text in JLabel and friends.

### Solution

Use HTML in the text of the component.

### Discussion

The Swing components that display text, such as JLabel, format the text as HTML—instead of as plain text—if the first six characters are the obvious tag <html>. The program JLabelHTMLDemo just puts up a JLabel formatted using this Java code:

```
// Part of JLabelHTMLDemo.java
  JButton component = new JButton(
          "<html>" +
          "<body bgcolor='white'>" +
          "<h1><font color='red'>Welcome</font></h1>" +
          "<p>This button will be formatted according to the usual " +
          "HTML rules for formatting of paragraphs.</p>" +
          "</body></html>");
```

Figure 14-12 shows the program in operation.

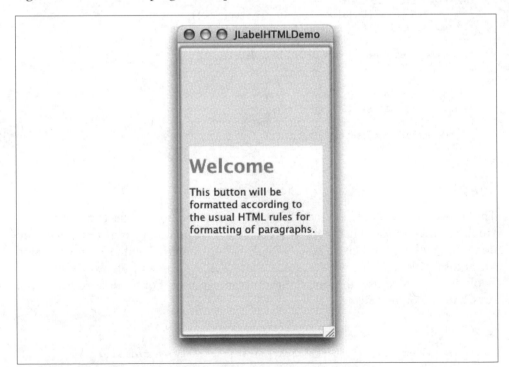

*Figure 14-12. JLabel with HTML text*

# 14.14 Centering a Main Window

## Problem

You want your main window to be centered on the screen.

## Solution

First, be aware that some users on some platforms would rather that you didn't do this, as they have existing "placement" schemes. However, at least on Windows, this technique is useful.

Subtract the width and height of the window from the width and height of the screen, divide by two, and go there. Be aware that some platforms (Mac, Unix) make it pretty easy for the power user to have multiple monitors active, so you don't always want to do this.

## Discussion

The code for this is pretty simple. The part that might take a while to figure out is the Dimension of the screen. Two methods can help: getScreenSize( ) in the Toolkit class and the static method getDefaultToolkit( ). (The Toolkit class relates to the underlying windowing toolkit; it has several subclasses, including two different ones for X Windows on Unix (Motif and non-Motif), another for Macintosh, etc.) Put these together and you have the Dimension you need.

Centering a Window is such a common need that I have packaged it in its own little class: UtilGUI. Here is the complete source for UtilGUI, which I'll use without comment from now on:

```
package com.darwinsys.util;

import java.awt.*;

/** Utilities for GUI work.
 */
public class UtilGUI {
    /** Centre a Window, Frame, JFrame, Dialog, etc. */
    public static void centre(Window w) {
        // After packing a Frame or Dialog, centre it on the screen.
        Dimension us = w.getSize( ),
            them = Toolkit.getDefaultToolkit( ).getScreenSize( );
        int newX = (them.width - us.width) / 2;
        int newY = (them.height- us.height)/ 2;
        w.setLocation(newX, newY);
    }
    /** Center a Window, Frame, JFrame, Dialog, etc.,
     * but do it the American Spelling Way :-)
     */
```

```
        public static void center(Window w) {
            UtilGUI.centre(w);
        }
    }
```

To use it after the relevant import, you can simply say, for example:

```
    myFrame.pack();
    UtilGUI.centre(myFrame);
    myFrame.setVisible(true);
```

# 14.15 Changing a Swing Program's Look and Feel

## Problem

You want to change the look and feel of an application.

## Solution

Use the static UIManager.setLookAndFeel() method. Maybe.

## Discussion

If you wish to specify the entire look and feel for a program, set it with the static UIManager.setLookAndFeel() method; the name you pass in must be the full name (as a string) of a class that implements a Java look and feel. The details of writing a look and feel class are beyond the scope of this book; refer to the book *Java Swing* or the Sun documentation. But using these classes is easy. For example:

```
    UIManager.setLookAndFeel("javax.swing.plaf.metal.MetalLookAndFeel");
```

This must appear before you create the GUI of the program, and it can throw an exception if the class name is invalid.

People sometimes like to show off the fact that you can change the look and feel on the fly. You call setLookAndFeel() as previously, and then call the static SwingUtilities.updateComponentTree() for your JFrame and all detached trees, such as dialog classes. But before you rush out to do it, please be advised that the official Sun position is that you shouldn't! The official *Java Look and Feel Design Guideline* book says, on page 23 (first edition):

> Because there is far more to the design of an application than the look and feel of components, it is unwise to give end users the ability to swap look and feel while [running] your application. Switching look and feel designs in this way only swaps the look and feel designs from one platform to another. The layout and vocabulary used are platform-specific and do not change. For instance, swapping look and feel designs does not change the titles of the menus.

The book does recommend that you let users specify an alternate look and feel, presumably in your properties file, at program startup time. Even so, the capability to switch while an application is running is too tempting to ignore; even Sun's own Swing Demonstration (included with the JDK) offers a menu item to change its look and feel. Figure 14-13 is my nice little program in the Java style; see Example 14-8 for the source code.

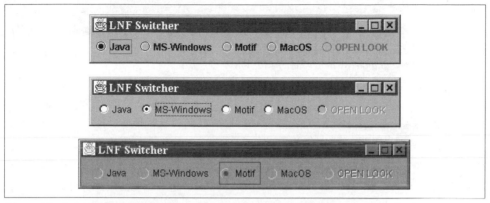

Figure 14-13. Java, Windows, and Motif look and feel under Windows

Of course, not all looks work on all platforms. If I try the Mac OS look and feel under Windows, I get the error dialog shown in Figure 14-14, which shows what happens when you request any look and feel that is unavailable on the current platform.

Figure 14-14. Look and feel request refused on Windows

The OPEN LOOK design alluded to in the code is, well, not written yet. Vaporware. That's why it's grayed out.

Under Mac OS X, the default look and feel is, of course, the Mac OS look and feel. You can also select the Java or Motif look, but not the Windows look. See Figure 14-15.

Example 14-8 shows the code that implements the look and feel switcher. It's pretty straightforward based on what we've seen already. The only neat trick is that I've set the selected button back to what it was if the look and feel that the user selects is not available.

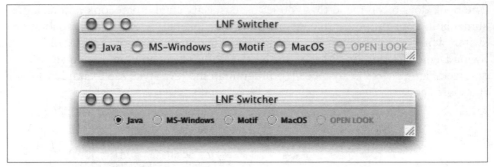

*Figure 14-15. Look and feel switcher under Mac OS X*

*Example 14-8. LNFSwitcher.java*

```java
/**
 * A Look-and-feel switcher.
 * @author    Ian Darwin, http://www.darwinsys.com/
 * @version    $Id: ch14,v 1.6 2004/05/07 15:20:56 ian Exp $
 */
public class LNFSwitcher {
    /** The frame. */
    protected JFrame theFrame;
    /** Its content pane */
    protected Container cp;

    /** Start with the Java look-and-feel, if possible */
    final static String PREFERREDLOOKANDFEELNAME =
        "javax.swing.plaf.metal.MetalLookAndFeel";
    protected String curLF = PREFERREDLOOKANDFEELNAME;
    protected JRadioButton previousButton;

    /** Construct a program... */
    public LNFSwitcher( ) {
        super( );
        theFrame = new JFrame("LNF Switcher");
        theFrame.setDefaultCloseOperation(JFrame.EXIT_ON_CLOSE);
        cp = theFrame.getContentPane( );
        cp.setLayout(new FlowLayout( ));

        ButtonGroup bg = new ButtonGroup( );

        JRadioButton bJava = new JRadioButton("Java");
        bJava.addActionListener(new LNFSetter(
            "javax.swing.plaf.metal.MetalLookAndFeel", bJava));
        bg.add(bJava);
        cp.add(bJava);

        JRadioButton bMSW  = new JRadioButton("MS-Windows");
        bMSW.addActionListener(new LNFSetter(
            "com.sun.java.swing.plaf.windows.WindowsLookAndFeel", bMSW));
        bg.add(bMSW);
        cp.add(bMSW);
```

*Example 14-8. LNFSwitcher.java (continued)*

```java
        JRadioButton bMotif = new JRadioButton("Motif");
        bMotif.addActionListener(new LNFSetter(
            "com.sun.java.swing.plaf.motif.MotifLookAndFeel", bMotif));
        bg.add(bMotif);
        cp.add(bMotif);

        JRadioButton bMac = new JRadioButton("Sun-MacOS");
        bMac.addActionListener(new LNFSetter(
            "com.sun.java.swing.plaf.mac.MacLookAndFeel", bMac));
        bg.add(bMac);
        cp.add(bMac);

        String defaultLookAndFeel = UIManager.getSystemLookAndFeelClassName();
        // System.out.println(defaultLookAndFeel);
        JRadioButton bDefault = new JRadioButton("Default");
        bDefault.addActionListener(new LNFSetter(
            defaultLookAndFeel, bDefault));
        bg.add(bDefault);
        cp.add(bDefault);

        previousButton - bDefault;
        bDefault.setSelected(true);

        theFrame.pack();
        theFrame.setVisible(true);
    }

    /* Class to set the Look and Feel on a frame */
    class LNFSetter implements ActionListener {
        String theLNFName;
        JRadioButton thisButton;

        /** Called to setup for button handling */
        LNFSetter(String lnfName, JRadioButton me) {
            theLNFName = lnfName;
            thisButton = me;
        }

        /** Called when the button actually gets pressed. */
        public void actionPerformed(ActionEvent e) {
            try {
                UIManager.setLookAndFeel(theLNFName);
                SwingUtilities.updateComponentTreeUI(theFrame);
                theFrame.pack();
            } catch (Exception evt) {
                JOptionPane.showMessageDialog(null,
                    "setLookAndFeel didn't work: " + evt,
                    "UI Failure", JOptionPane.INFORMATION_MESSAGE);
                previousButton.setSelected(true);      // reset the GUI to agree
            }
            previousButton = thisButton;
        }
    }
}
```

*Example 14-8. LNFSwitcher.java (continued)*

```
    public static void main(String[] argv) {
        new LNFSwitcher( );
    }
}
```

## See Also

Some alternate look-and-feel implementations can be found on the Web. If you'd like to build your own look and feel, perhaps for corporate identity reasons, some of these, in conjunction with O'Reilly's *Java Swing*, would be a good starting point.

# 14.16 Enhancing Your GUI for Mac OS X

## Problem

You tried running your Swing GUI application on Mac OS X, and it didn't look right.

## Solution

There are a variety of small steps you can take to improve your GUI's appearance and behavior under Mac OS X.

## Discussion

While Swing aims to be a portable GUI, Apple's implementation for Mac OS X does not automatically do "the right thing" for everyone. For example, a JMenuBar menu container appears by default at the top of the application window. This is the norm on Windows and on most Unix platforms, but Mac users expect the menu bar for the active application to appear at the top of the screen. To enable "normal" behavior, you have to set the System property apple.laf.useScreenMenuBar to the value true, as in **java -Dapple.laf.useScreenMenuBar=true SomeClassName**. You might want to set some other properties too, such as a short name for your application to appear in the menu bar (the default is the full class name of your main application class).

But there is no point setting these properties unless you are, in fact, running on Mac OS X. How do you tell? Apple's recommended way is to check for the system property mrj.runtime and, if so, assume you are on Mac OS X.* So the code might be something like this:

```
    boolean isMacOS = System.getProperty("mrj.version") != null;
    if (isMacOS) {
      System.setProperty("apple.laf.useScreenMenuBar", "true");
      System.setProperty("com.apple.mrj.application.apple.menu.about.name", "JabaDex");
    }
```

---

* In fact, you could be running on the ancient (JDK 1.1.8) MRJ under Mac OS 8 or 9, but that's statistically very unlikely.

But there's more! You still don't get to handle "normal" Mac-style Quit, Preferences, Print or About requests (Command-Q, Command-comma, Command-P, or Application → About, respectively). For these you may need to use some classes in the com. apple.eawt package. You can read about this in the Apple Developer Documentation that comes with Mac OS X. Or you can just use my adapter class, com. darwinsys.macosui.MacOSAppAdapter. You need to implement some of my four interfaces (in the same package): AboutBoxHandler, PrefsHandler, PrintHandler, and ShutdownHandler. Each of these has one method that is invoked when the Mac user invokes the relevant request. Sample code that implements this is in Example 14-9; this program doubles as a primitive interactive test, and it can be invoked by **ant regress.macosui** in the *darwinsys* directory of the online source code.

As of build 1.4.2, the Print dialog is not invoked. Also, you (obviously) can neither compile nor run any program using this package against a copy of the *darwinsys.jar* file that was compiled on a non-Mac OS X platform, such as Windows or Unix.

*Example 14-9. MacOSUITest.java*

```
/**
 * Interactive test for "macosui" package.
 * Class can not extend JFrame; must invoke setMacOS() before first
 * call to any Swing constructor.
 */
public class MacOSUITest {

    public static void main(String[] args) {
        // Tester: check that this string appears in the Application Menu.
        MacOSUtil.setMacOS("MacOSUITest");
        new MacOSUITest();

    }

    public MacOSUITest() {
        JFrame jf = new JFrame("MacOSUITest");
        JButton button = new JButton("Exit");
        button.addActionListener(new ActionListener() {
            public void actionPerformed(ActionEvent arg0) {
                System.exit(0);
            }
        });
        jf.getContentPane().add(button);
        // Tester: see that Application->About produces our popup
        // Ditto for Preferences and Shutdown.
        MacOSAppAdapter adapter =
            new MacOSAppAdapter(jf, abouter, prefser, printer, shutter);
        adapter.register();
        jf.setSize(300, 200);
        jf.setVisible(true);
    }

        // Definitions of individual action handlers omitted.
}
```

## See Also

See the O'Reilly book *Mac OS X for Java Geeks* by Will Iverson for more information on Mac OS X. Apple's web site includes several Technical Notes at *http://developer.apple.com/qa/indexes/java-a.html*.

# 14.17 Program: Custom Font Chooser

## Problem

You want to allow the user to select a font, but standard Java doesn't yet include a Font Chooser dialog.

## Solution

Use my FontChooser dialog class.

## Discussion

As we saw in Recipe 13.3, you can manually select a font by calling the java.awt. Font class constructor, passing in the name of the font, the type you want (plain, bold, italic, or bold+italic), and the point size:

```
Font f = new Font("Helvetica", Font.BOLD, 14);
setfont(f);
```

This is not very flexible for interactive applications. You normally want the user to be able to choose fonts with the same ease as using a File Chooser dialog. Until the Java API catches up with this, you are more than welcome to use the Font Chooser that I wrote when faced with a similar need.

The source code is shown in Example 14-10; it ends, as many of my classes do, with a short main method that is both a test case and an example of using the class in action. The display is shown in Figure 14-16.

*Example 14-10. FontChooser.java*

```
import java.awt.*;
import java.awt.event.*;
import javax.swing.*;

/** A font selection dialog. .
 * <p>Note: can take a LONG time to start up on systems
 * with (literally) hundreds of fonts.
 */
public class FontChooser extends JDialog {
    /** The font the user has chosen */
    protected Font resultFont;
    /** The resulting font name */
    protected String resultName;
```

*Example 14-10. FontChooser.java (continued)*

```java
/** The resulting font size */
protected int resultSize;
/** The resulting boldness */
protected boolean isBold;
/** The resulting italicness */
protected boolean isItalic;

/** The list of Fonts */
protected String fontList[];
/** The font name chooser */
protected List fontNameChoice;
/** The font size chooser */
protected List fontSizeChoice;
/** The bold and italic choosers */
Checkbox bold, italic;
/** The list of font sizes */
protected String fontSizes[] = {
    "8", "10", "11", "12", "14", "16", "18", "20", "24",
    "30", "36", "40", "48", "60", "72"
    };
/** The display area. Use a JLabel as the AWT label doesn't always
 * honor setFont() in a timely fashion :-)
 */
protected JLabel previewArea;

/** Construct a FontChooser -- Sets title and gets
 * array of fonts on the system. Builds a GUI to let
 * the user choose one font at one size.
 */
public FontChooser(Frame f) {
    super(f, "Font Chooser", true);

    Container cp = this;    // or getContentPane() in Swing

    Panel top = new Panel();
    top.setLayout(new FlowLayout());

    fontNameChoice = new List(8);
    top.add(fontNameChoice);

    Toolkit toolkit = Toolkit.getDefaultToolkit();
    // For JDK 1.1: returns about 10 names (Serif, SansSerif, etc.)
    // fontlist = toolkit.getFontList();
    // For JDK 1.2: a much longer list; most of the names that come
    // with your OS (e.g., Arial), plus the Sun/Java ones (Lucida,
    // Lucida Bright, Lucida Sans...)
    fontList = GraphicsEnvironment.getLocalGraphicsEnvironment().
        getAvailableFontFamilyNames();

    for (int i=0; i<fontList.length; i++)
        fontNameChoice.add(fontList[i]);
    fontNameChoice.select(0);
```

*Example 14-10. FontChooser.java (continued)*

```
fontSizeChoice = new List(8);
top.add(fontSizeChoice);

for (int i=0; i<fontSizes.length; i++)
    fontSizeChoice.add(fontSizes[i]);
fontSizeChoice.select(5);

cp.add(top, BorderLayout.NORTH);

Panel attrs = new Panel( );
top.add(attrs);
attrs.setLayout(new GridLayout(0,1));
attrs.add(bold  =new Checkbox("Bold", false));
attrs.add(italic=new Checkbox("Italic", false));

previewArea = new JLabel("Qwerty Yuiop", JLabel.CENTER);
previewArea.setSize(200, 50);
cp.add(BorderLayout.CENTER, previewArea);

Panel bot = new Panel( );

Button okButton = new Button("Apply");
bot.add(okButton);
okButton.addActionListener(new ActionListener( ) {
    public void actionPerformed(ActionEvent e) {
        previewFont( );
        dispose( );
        setVisible(false);
    }
});

Button pvButton = new Button("Preview");
bot.add(pvButton);
pvButton.addActionListener(new ActionListener( ) {
    public void actionPerformed(ActionEvent e) {
        previewFont( );
    }
});

Button canButton = new Button("Cancel");
bot.add(canButton);
canButton.addActionListener(new ActionListener( ) {
    public void actionPerformed(ActionEvent e) {
        // Set all values to null. Better: restore previous.
        resultFont = null;
        resultName = null;
        resultSize = 0;
        isBold = false;
        isItalic = false;

        dispose( );
        setVisible(false);
```

*Example 14-10. FontChooser.java (continued)*

```
        }
    });

    cp.add(BorderLayout.SOUTH, bot);

    previewFont(); // ensure view is up to date!

    pack();
    setLocation(100, 100);
}

/** Called from the action handlers to get the font info,
 * build a font, and set it.
 */
protected void previewFont() {
    resultName = fontNameChoice.getSelectedItem();
    String resultSizeName = fontSizeChoice.getSelectedItem();
    int resultSize = Integer.parseInt(resultSizeName);
    isBold = bold.getState();
    isItalic = italic.getState();
    int attrs = Font.PLAIN;
    if (isBold) attrs = Font.BOLD;
    if (isItalic) attrs |= Font.ITALIC;
    resultFont = new Font(resultName, attrs, resultSize);
    // System.out.println("resultName = " + resultName + "; " +
    //           "resultFont = " + resultFont);
    previewArea.setFont(resultFont);
    pack();                   // ensure Dialog is big enough.
}

/** Retrieve the selected font name. */
public String getSelectedName() {
    return resultName;
}
/** Retrieve the selected size */
public int getSelectedSize() {
    return resultSize;
}

/** Retrieve the selected font, or null */
public Font getSelectedFont() {
    return resultFont;
}

/** Simple main program to start it running */
public static void main(String[] args) {
    final JFrame f = new JFrame("Dummy");
    final FontChooser fc = new FontChooser(f);
    final Container cp = f.getContentPane();
    cp.setLayout(new GridLayout(0, 1));    // one vertical column
```

*Example 14-10. FontChooser.java (continued)*

```
    JButton theButton = new JButton("Change font");
    cp.add(theButton);

    final JLabel theLabel = new JLabel("Java is great!");
    cp.add(theLabel);

    // Now that theButton and theLabel are ready, make the action listener
    theButton.addActionListener(new ActionListener() {
        public void actionPerformed(ActionEvent e) {
            fc.setVisible(true);
            Font myNewFont = fc.getSelectedFont();
            System.out.println("You chose " + myNewFont);
            theLabel.setFont(myNewFont);
            f.pack();      // again
            fc.dispose();
        }
    });

    f.pack();
    f.setVisible(true);
    f.addWindowListener(new WindowCloser(f, true));
  }
}
```

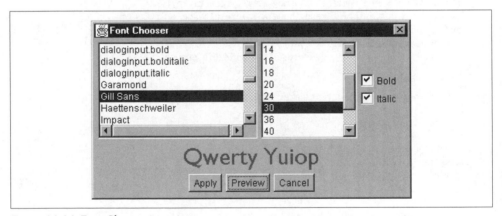

*Figure 14-16. Font Chooser in action*

# 14.18 Program: Custom Layout Manager

## Problem

None of the standard layout managers do quite what you need.

## Solution

Roll your own. All you need to do is implement the methods of the java.awt. LayoutManager interface.

---

# Discussion

While many people are intimidated by the thought of writing their own layout manager, it beats the alternative of using only "the big five" layouts (BorderLayout, CondLayout, FlowLayout, GridBagLayout, and GridLayout). BorderLayout isn't quite flexible enough, and GridBaglayout is too complex for many applications. Suppose, for instance, that you wanted to lay out an arbitrary number of components in a circle. In a typical X Windows or Windows application, you would write the geometry calculations within the code for creating the components to be drawn. This would work, but the code for the geometry calculations would be unavailable to anybody who needed it later. The LayoutManager interface is another great example of how the Java API's design promotes code reuse: if you write the geometry calculations as a layout manager, then anybody needing this type of layout could simply instantiate your CircleLayout class to get circular layouts.

As another example, consider the layout shown in Figure 14-17, where the labels column and the textfield column have different widths. Using the big five layouts, there's no good way to ensure that the columns line up and that you have control over their relative widths. Suppose you wanted the label field to take up 40% of the panel and the entry field to take up 60%. I'll implement a simple layout manager here, both to show you how easy it is and to give you a useful class for making panels like the one shown.

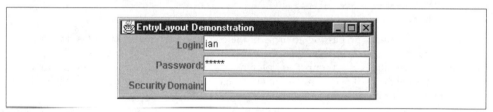

*Figure 14-17. EntryLayout in action*

The methods for the LayoutManager interface are shown in Table 14-2.

*Table 14-2. LayoutManager methods*

| Method name | Description |
| --- | --- |
| preferredLayoutSize(Container ) | Like getPreferredSize( ) for a component: the "best" size for the container |
| minimumLayoutSize(Container ) | Same, but for the minimum workable size |
| layoutContainer(Container ) | Perform the layout calculations, and resize and reposition all the components at the current size of the container |
| addLayoutComponent(String, Component) | Associate a constraint with a given component (you normally store these mappings in a java.util.HashMap( )) |
| removeLayoutComponent( Component) | Remove a component from the HashMap |

If you don't need Constraint objects (like BorderLayout.NORTH or a GridBagConstraint object), you can ignore the last two methods. Well, you can't ignore them completely. Since this is an interface, you must implement them. But they can be as simple as {}, that is, a null-bodied method.

That leaves only three serious methods. The first, preferredLayoutSize( ), normally loops through all the components—either in the HashMap if using constraints, or in an array returned by the container's getComponents( ) method—asking each for its preferred size and adding them up, while partly doing the layout calculations. And minimumLayoutSize( ) is the same for the smallest possible layout that will work. It may be possible for these methods to delegate either to a common submethod or to invoke layoutContainer( ), depending upon how the given layout policy works.

The most important method is layoutContainer( ). This method needs to examine all the components and decide where to put them and how big to make each one. Having made the decision, it can use setBounds( ) to set each one's position and size.

Other than a bit of error checking, that's all that's involved. Here's an example, EntryLayout, that implements the multicolumn layout shown in Figure 14-17. Quoting its Javadoc documentation:

> A simple layout manager, for Entry areas like:
>
> Login: _____
>
> Password: _____
>
> Basically two (or more) columns of different, but constant, widths.
>
> Construct instances by passing an array of the column width percentages (as doubles, fractions from 0.1 to 0.9, so 40%, 60% would be {0.4, 0.6}). The length of this array uniquely determines the number of columns. Columns are forced to be the relevant widths. As with GridLayout, the number of items added must be an even multiple of the number of columns. If not, exceptions may be thrown!

First, let's look at the program that uses this layout to produce Figure 14-17. This program simply creates a JFrame, gets the contentPane container, and sets its layout to an instance of EntryLayout, passing an array of two doubles representing the relative widths (decimal fractions, not percentages) into the EntryLayout constructor. Then we add an even number of components, and call pack( )—which in turn calls our preferredLayoutSize( )—and setVisible(true):

```
import java.awt.*;
import java.awt.event.*;
import javax.swing.*;

/** Testbed for EntryLayout layout manager.
 */
public class EntryLayoutTest {

    /** "main program" method - construct and show */
    public static void main(String[] av) {
```

```
                final JFrame f = new JFrame("EntryLayout Demonstration");
                Container cp = f.getContentPane();
                double widths[] = { .33, .66 };
                cp.setLayout(new EntryLayout(widths));
                cp.add(new JLabel("Login:", SwingConstants.RIGHT));
                cp.add(new JTextField(10));
                cp.add(new JLabel("Password:", SwingConstants.RIGHT));
                cp.add(new JPasswordField(20));
                cp.add(new JLabel("Security Domain:", SwingConstants.RIGHT));
                cp.add(new JTextField(20));
                // cp.add(new JLabel("Monkey wrench in works"));
                f.pack();
                f.addWindowListener(new WindowCloser(f, true));
                f.setLocation(200, 200);
                f.setVisible(true);
        }
    }
```

Nothing complicated about it. The last JLabel ("Monkey wrench in works") is commented out since, as noted, the LayoutManager throws an exception if the number of components is not evenly divisible by the number of columns. It was put in during testing and then commented out, but was left in place for further consideration. Note that this layout operates correctly with more than two columns, but it does assume that all columns are approximately the same height (relaxing this requirement has been left as an exercise for the reader).

Finally, let's look at the code for the layout manager itself, shown in Example 14-11. After some constants and fields and two constructors, the methods are listed in about the same order as the discussion earlier in this recipe: the dummy add/remove component methods; then the preferredSize() and minimumLayoutSize() methods (which delegate to computeLayoutSize); and, finally, layoutContainer, which does the actual laying out of the components within the container. As you can see, the entire EntryLayout layout manager class is only about 140 lines, including a lot of comments.

*Example 14-11. EntryLayout.java*

```
// package com.darwinsys.entrylayout;

import java.awt.*;
import java.util.*;

/** A simple layout manager, for Entry areas like:
 * <pre>
 *    Login: _____
 * Password: _____
 * </pre>
 * <b>Note: all columns must be approximately the same height!</b>
 */
public class EntryLayout implements LayoutManager {
    /** The array of widths, as decimal fractions (0.4 == 40%, etc.). */
    protected final double[] widthPercentages;
```

*Example 14-11. EntryLayout.java (continued)*

```java
/** The number of columns. */
protected final int COLUMNS;

/** The default padding */
protected final static int HPAD = 5, VPAD = 5;
/** The actual padding */
protected final int hpad, vpad;

/** True if the list of widths was valid. */
protected boolean validWidths = false;

/** Construct an EntryLayout with widths and padding specified.
 * @param widths    Array of doubles specifying column widths.
 * @param h             Horizontal padding between items
 * @param v             Vertical padding between items
 */
public EntryLayout(double[] widths, int h, int v) {
    COLUMNS = widths.length;
    widthPercentages = new double[COLUMNS];
    for (int i=0; i<widths.length; i++) {
        if (widths[i] >= 1.0)
            throw new IllegalArgumentException(
                "EntryLayout: widths must be fractions < 1");
        widthPercentages[i] = widths[i];
    }
    validWidths = true;
    hpad = h;
    vpad = v;
}
/** Construct an EntryLayout with widths and with default padding amounts.
 * @param widths    Array of doubles specifying column widths.
 */
public EntryLayout(double[] widths) {
    this(widths, HPAD, VPAD);
}

/** Adds the specified component with the specified constraint
 * to the layout; required by LayoutManager but not used.
 */
public void addLayoutComponent(String name, Component comp) {
    // nothing to do
}

/** Removes the specified component from the layout;
 * required by LayoutManager, but does nothing.
 */
public void removeLayoutComponent(Component comp)  {
    // nothing to do
}

/** Calculates the preferred size dimensions for the specified panel
 * given the components in the specified parent container. */
```

*Example 14-11. EntryLayout.java (continued)*

```
public Dimension preferredLayoutSize(Container parent) {
    // System.out.println("preferredLayoutSize");
    return computeLayoutSize(parent, hpad, vpad);
}

/** Find the minimum Dimension for the
 * specified container given the components therein.
 */
public Dimension minimumLayoutSize(Container parent) {
    // System.out.println("minimumLayoutSize");
    return computeLayoutSize(parent, 0, 0);
}

/** The width of each column, as found by computLayoutSize(). */
int[] widths;
/** The height of each row, as found by computLayoutSize(). */
int[] heights;

/** Compute the size of the whole mess. Serves as the guts of
 * preferredLayoutSize() and minimumLayoutSize().
 */
protected Dimension computeLayoutSize(Container parent, int hpad, int vpad) {
    if (!validWidths)
        return null;
    Component[] components = parent.getComponents();
    Dimension contSize = parent.getSize();
    int preferredWidth = 0, preferredHeight = 0;
    widths = new int[COLUMNS];
    heights = new int[components.length / COLUMNS];
    // System.out.println("Grid: " + widths.length + ", " + heights.length);

    int i;
    // Pass One: Compute largest widths and heights.
    for (i=0; i<components.length; i++) {
        int row = i / widthPercentages.length;
        int col = i % widthPercentages.length;
        Component c = components[i];
        Dimension d = c.getPreferredSize();
        widths[col] = Math.max(widths[col], d.width);
        heights[row] = Math.max(heights[row], d.height);
    }

    // Pass two: aggregate them.
    for (i=0; i<widths.length; i++)
        preferredWidth += widths[i] + hpad;
    for (i=0; i<heights.length; i++)
        preferredHeight += heights[i] + vpad;

    // Finally, pass the sums back as the actual size.
    return new Dimension(preferredWidth, preferredHeight);
}
```

*Example 14-11. EntryLayout.java (continued)*

```
/** Lays out the container in the specified panel. */
public void layoutContainer(Container parent) {
    // System.out.println("layoutContainer:");
    if (!validWidths)
        return;
    Component[] components = parent.getComponents();
    Dimension contSize = parent.getSize();
    int x = 0;
    for (int i=0; i<components.length; i++) {
        int row = i / COLUMNS;
        int col = i % COLUMNS;
        Component c = components[i];
        Dimension d = c.getPreferredSize();
        int colWidth = (int)(contSize.width * widthPercentages[col]);
        if (col == 0) {
            x = hpad;
        } else {
            x += hpad * (col-1) + (int)(contSize.width * widthPercentages[col-1]);
        }
        int y = vpad * (row) + (row * heights[row]) + (heights[row]-d.height);
        Rectangle r = new Rectangle(x, y,
            colWidth, d.height);
        c.setBounds(r);
    }
}

}
```

## See Also

For more on layouts, see Jim Elliott's RelativeLayout, described in *http://www.onjava.com/pub/a/onjava/2002/09/18/relativelayout.html*. This is not to be confused with the like-named but much simpler RelativeLayout in the source distribution accompanying the book; Jim's is more complete.

As mentioned in the Introduction, there are many good books on windowed application programming with Java. O'Reilly's *Java Swing* discusses the many Swing components not covered here, such as JTable, JScrollPane, JList, and JTree, and many more. My JabaDex application contains examples of many of these, and some are used in later recipes in this book (for example, JTree is discussed in Recipe 19.9).

# CHAPTER 15

# Internationalization and Localization

## 15.0 Introduction

"All the world's a stage," wrote William Shakespeare. But not all the players upon that great and turbulent stage speak the great Bard's native tongue. To be usable on a global scale, your software needs to communicate in many different languages. The menu labels, button strings, dialog messages, titlebar titles, and even command-line error messages must be settable to the user's choice of language. This is the topic of *internationalization* and *localization*. Because these words take a long time to say and write, they are often abbreviated by their first and last letters and the count of omitted letters, that is, I18N and L10N.

Java provides a Locale class to discover/control the internationalization settings. A default Locale is inherited from operating system runtime settings when Java starts up and can be used most of the time!

---

### Ian's Basic Steps: Internationalization

Internationalization and localization consist of:

- Sensitivity training (Internationalization or I18N): making your software sensitive to these issues
- Language lessons (Localization or L10N): writing configuration files for each language
- Culture lessons (optional): customizing the presentation of numbers, fractions, dates, and message-formatting

---

See also *Java Internationalization* by Andy Deitsch and David Czarnecki (O'Reilly).

# 15.1 Creating a Button with I18N Resources

## Problem

You want your program to take "sensitivity lessons" so that it can communicate well internationally.

## Solution

Your program must obtain all control and message strings via the internationalization software. Here's how:

1. Get a ResourceBundle.

    ```
    ResourceBundle rb = ResourceBundle.getBundle("Menus");
    ```

    I'll talk about ResourceBundle in Recipe 15.6, but briefly, a ResourceBundle represents a collection of name-value pairs (resources). The names are names you assign to each GUI control or other user interface text, and the values are the text to assign to each control in a given language.

2. Use this ResourceBundle to fetch the localized version of each control name.

    Old way:

    ```
    somePanel.add(new JButton("Exit"));
    ```

    New way:

    ```
    try { label = rb.getString("exit.label"); }
    catch (MissingResourceException e) { label="Exit"; } // fallback
    somePanel.add(new JButton(label));
    ```

    This is quite a bit of code for one button but distributed over all the widgets (buttons, menus, etc.) in a program, it can be as little as one line with the use of *convenience routines*, which I'll show in Recipe 15.4.

### What happens at runtime?

The default locale is used, since we didn't specify one. The default locale is platform-dependent:

- Unix/POSIX: LANG environment variable (per user)
- Windows: Control Panel → Regional Settings
- Mac OS X: System Preferences → International
- Others: see platform documentation

ResourceBundle.getBundle( ) locates a file with the named resource bundle name (Menus in the previous example), plus an underscore and the locale name (if any locale is set), plus another underscore and the locale variation (if any variation is set), plus the extension *.properties*. If a variation is set but the file can't be found, it falls back to just the country code. If that can't be found, it falls back to the original default. Table 15-1 shows some examples for various locales.

---

*Table 15-1. Property filenames for different locales*

| Locale | Filename |
|---|---|
| Default locale | Menus.Properties |
| Swedish | Menus_sv.properties |
| Spanish | Menus_es.properties |
| French | Menus_fr.properties |
| French-Canadian | Menus_fr_CA.properties |

Locale names are two-letter ISO language codes (lowercase); locale variations are two-letter ISO country codes (uppercase).

### Setting the locale

On Windows, go into Regional Settings in the Control Panel. Changing this setting may entail a reboot, so exit any editor windows.

On Unix, set your LANG environment variable. For example, a Korn shell user in Mexico might have this line in his or her *.profile*:

```
export LANG-es_MX
```

On either system, for testing a different locale, you need only define the locale in the System Properties at runtime using the command-line option -D, as in:

```
java -Duser.language=es Browser
```

to run the program named Browser in the Spanish locale.

# 15.2   Listing Available Locales

## Problem

You want to see what locales are available.

## Solution

Call Locale.getAvailableLocales().

## Discussion

A typical runtime may have dozens of locales available. The program ListLocales uses the method getAvailableLocales() and prints the list:

```
// File ListLocales.java
Locale[] list = Locale.getAvailableLocales();
      for (int i=0; i<list.length; i++)
            System.out.println(list[i]);
    }
}
```

The list is far too long to show here, as you can judge by the first few entries:

```
> java ListLocales
en
en_US
ar
ar_AE
ar_BH
ar_DZ
ar_EG
ar_IQ
ar_JO
ar_KW
ar_LB
ar_LY
ar_MA
ar_OM
ar_QA
ar_SA
ar_SD
ar_SY
ar_TN
ar_YE
be
be_BY
```

On my system, the complete list has an even dozen dozen (144) locales, as listed by the command `java ListLocales | wc -l`.

# 15.3  Creating a Menu with I18N Resources

## Problem

You want to internationalize an entire `Menu`.

## Solution

Get the `Menu`'s label, and each `MenuItem`'s label, from a `ResourceBundle`.

## Discussion

Fetching a single menu item is the same as fetching a button:

```
rb = getResourceBundle("Widgets");
try { label = rb.getString("exitMenu.label"); }
catch (MissingResourceException e) { label="Exit"; } // fallback
someMenu.add(new JMenuItem(label));
```

This is a lot of code, so we typically consolidate it in *convenience routines* (see Recipe 15.4). Here is sample code, using our convenience routines:

```
JMenu fm = mkMenu(rb, "file");
fm.add(mkMenuItem(rb, "file", "open"));
fm.add(mkMenuItem(rb, "file", "new"));
```

```
fm.add(mkMenuItem(rb, "file", "save"));
fm.add(mkMenuItem(rb, "file", "exit"));
mb.add(fm);
Menu um = mkMenu(rb, "edit");
um.add(mkMenuItem(rb, "edit", "copy"));
um.add(mkMenuItem(rb, "edit", "paste"));
mb.add(um);
```

# 15.4  Writing Internationalization Convenience Routines

## Problem

You want convenience.

## Solution

I've got it.

## Discussion

Convenience routines are mini-implementations that can be more convenient and effective than the general-purpose routines. Here I present the convenience routines to create buttons, menus, etc. First, a simple one, mkMenu( ):

```
/** Convenience routine to make up a Menu with its name L10N'd */
Menu mkMenu(ResourceBundle b, String menuName) {
    String label;
    try { label = b.getString(menuName+".label"); }
    catch (MissingResourceException e) { label=menuName; }
    return new Menu(label);
}
```

There are many such routines that you might need; I have consolidated several of them into my class *I18N.java*, which is part of the com.darwinsys.swingui package. All methods are static, and can be used without having to instantiate an I18N object because they do not maintain any state across calls. The method mkButton( ) creates and returns a localized Button, and so on. The method mkDialog is slightly misnamed since the JOptionPane method showMessageDialog( ) doesn't create and return a Dialog object, but it seemed more consistent to write it as shown here:

```
package com.darwinsys.util;

import java.util.*;
import javax.swing.*;

/** Set of convenience routines for internationalized code.
 * All convenience methods are static, for ease of use.
 */
public class I18N {
```

```
/** Convenience routine to make a JButton */
public static JButton mkButton(ResourceBundle b, String name) {
    String label;
    try { label = b.getString(name+".label"); }
    catch (MissingResourceException e) { label=name; }
    return new JButton(label);
}

/** Convenience routine to make a JMenu */
public static JMenu mkMenu(ResourceBundle b, String name) {
    String menuLabel;
    try { menuLabel = b.getString(name+".label"); }
    catch (MissingResourceException e) { menuLabel=name; }
    return new JMenu(menuLabel);
}

/** Convenience routine to make a JMenuItem */
public static JMenuItem mkMenuItem(ResourceBundle b,
        String menu, String name) {

    String miLabel;
    try { miLabel = b.getString(menu + "." + name + ".label"); }
    catch (MissingResourceException e) { miLabel=name; }
    String key = null;
    try { key = b.getString(menu + "." + name + ".key"); }
    catch (MissingResourceException e) { key=null; }

    if (key == null)
        return new JMenuItem(miLabel);
    else
        return new JMenuItem(miLabel, key.charAt(0));
}

/** Show a JOptionPane message dialog */
public static void mkDialog(ResourceBundle b,JFrame parent,
    String dialogTag, String titleTag, int messageType) {
        JOptionPane.showMessageDialog(
            parent,
            getString(b, dialogTag, "DIALOG TEXT MISSING " + dialogTag),
            getString(b, titleTag, "DIALOG TITLE MISSING" + titleTag),
            messageType);
}

/** Just get a String (for dialogs, labels, etc.) */
public static String getString(ResourceBundle b, String name, String dflt) {
    String result;
    try {
        result = b.getString(name);
    } catch (MissingResourceException e) {
        result = dflt;
    }
    return result;
}
}
```

## 15.5   Creating a Dialog with I18N Resources

### Problem

You want to internationalize a dialog.

### Solution

Use a ResourceBundle.

### Discussion

This is similar to the use of ResourceBundle in the previous recipes and shows the code for an internationalized version of the JOptionDemo program from Recipe 14.7:

```java
package com.darwinsys.util;

import java.awt.*;
import java.awt.event.*;
import javax.swing.*;
import java.util.*;

/**
 * I18N'd JOptionPane
 */
public class JOptionDemo extends JFrame {

    ResourceBundle rb;

    // Constructor
    JOptionDemo(String s) {
        super(s);

        Container cp = getContentPane( );
        cp.setLayout(new FlowLayout( ));

        rb = ResourceBundle.getBundle("Widgets");

        JButton b = I18N.mkButton(rb, "getButton");
        b.addActionListener(new ActionListener( ) {
            public void actionPerformed(ActionEvent e) {
                JOptionPane.showMessageDialog(
                    JOptionDemo.this,
                    rb.getString("dialog1.text"),
                    rb.getString("dialog1.title"),
                    JOptionPane.INFORMATION_MESSAGE);
            }
        });
        cp.add(b);

        b = I18N.mkButton(rb, "goodbye");
        b.addActionListener(new ActionListener( ) {
```

```
        public void actionPerformed(ActionEvent e) {
            System.exit(0);
        }
    });
    cp.add(b);

    // the main window
    setSize(200, 150);
    pack();
}

public static void main(String[] arg) {
    JOptionDemo x = new JOptionDemo("Testing 1 2 3...");
    x.setVisible(true);
}
}
```

# 15.6   Creating a Resource Bundle

## Problem

You need to create a resource bundle for use by I18N.

## Solution

A resource bundle is just a collection of names and values. You can write a java.
util.ResourceBundle subclass, but it is easier to create textual Properties files (see
Recipe 7.7) that you then load with ResourceBundle.getBundle( ). The files can be
created using any text editor. Leaving it in a text file format also allows user customization; a user whose language is not provided for, or who wishes to change the word-
ing somewhat due to local variations in dialect, will have no trouble editing the file.

Note that the resource bundle text file should not have the same name as any of your
Java classes. The reason is that the ResourceBundle constructs a class dynamically
with the same name as the resource files. You can confirm this by running **java –verbose**
on any of the programs that use the I18N class from this chapter.

## Discussion

Here is a sample properties file for a simple browser (see the MenuIntl program in
Recipe 15.11):

```
# Default Menu properties
# The File Menu
file.label=File Menu
file.new.label=New File
file.new.key=N
```

Creating the default properties file is usually not a problem, but creating properties
files for other languages might be. Unless you are a large multinational corporation,
you will probably not have the resources (pardon the pun) to create resource files

in-house. If you are shipping commercial software, you need to identify your target markets and understand which of these are most sensitive to wanting menus and the like in their own languages. Then, hire a professional translation service that has expertise in the required languages to prepare the files. Test them well before you ship, as you would any other part of your software.

If you need special characters, multiline text, or other complex entry, remember that a ResourceBundle is also a Properties file.

As an alternate approach, the next recipe describes a program that automates some of the work of isolating strings, creating resource files, and translating them to other languages.

# 15.7   Extracting Strings from Your Code

## Problem

You have existing code that contains hardcoded strings.

## Solution

Use JILT, Eclipse, or your favorite IDE.

## Discussion

Many tools extract Strings into resource bundles. This process is also known as *externalization*. Nothing to do with jilting your lover, JILT is Sun's Java Internationalization and Localization Toolkit, Version 2.0.* JILTing your code means processing it with JILT, which facilitates I18N and L10N'ing the Java classes. JILT has four GUI-based tools, which can be used independently, started from a GUI frontend called JILKIT. Figure 15-1 shows JILT in action.

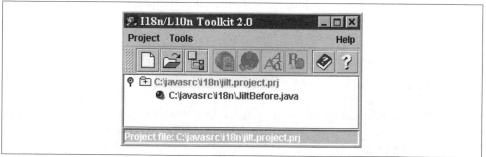

*Figure 15-1. JILT in action*

---

\* Ironically, though, Sun appears to be jilting JILT; it's nearing the end of its lifecycle, so you may want to look at the externalization support offered by your IDE instead.

The tools are listed in Table 15-2.

*Table 15-2. JILT programs*

| Tool | Function |
|------|----------|
| I18N Verifier | Tests program for international use and suggests improvements. |
| Message Tool | Finds and allows you to edit hardcoded or inconsistent messages. |
| Translator | Translates messages in a resource bundle file into a given locale/language. |
| Resource Tool | Merges multiple resource files into a new resource bundle. Can also find differences between resource files. |

It's worth noting that the time it takes to learn these tools may overshadow their benefits on small projects, but on large projects they will likely prove worthwhile.

Version 2 of the Translator ships with a Chinese dictionary, but you can provide your own dictionaries as well.

The Java Internationalization and Localization Toolkit is nearing its end-of-life support from Sun but can, as of this writing, still be downloaded for free from Sun's Java page, *http://java.sun.com/products/jilkit/*.

Many IDEs provide an externalization mechanism. Under Eclipse, for example, select a Java source file, then select Externalize Strings from the Source menu. Eclipse generates a Properties file and a class with static methods to retrieve the values of the Strings and replace the strings in your code with calls to those methods. Other IDEs provide similar mechanisms.

# 15.8   Using a Particular Locale

## Problem

You want to use a locale other than the default in a particular operation.

## Solution

Use `Locale.getInstance(Locale)`.

## Discussion

Classes that provide formatting services, such as `DateFormat` and `NumberFormat`, provide an overloaded `getInstance( )` method that can be called either with no arguments or with a `Locale` argument.

To use these, you can use one of the predefined locale variables provided by the `Locale` class, or you can construct your own `Locale` object giving a language code and a country code:

```
Locale locale1 = Locale.FRANCE;    // predefined
Locale locale2 = new Locale("en", "UK");    // English, UK version
```

Either of these can be used to format a date or a number, as shown in class UseLocales:

```java
import java.text.*;
import java.util.*;

/** Use some locales
 * choices or -Duser.lang= or -Duser.region=.
 */
public class UseLocales {
    public static void main(String[] args) {

        Locale frLocale = Locale.FRANCE;    // predefined
        Locale ukLocale = new Locale("en", "UK");    // English, UK version

        DateFormat defaultDateFormatter = DateFormat.getDateInstance(
            DateFormat.MEDIUM);
        DateFormat frDateFormatter = DateFormat.getDateInstance(
            DateFormat.MEDIUM, frLocale);
        DateFormat ukDateFormatter = DateFormat.getDateInstance(
            DateFormat.MEDIUM, ukLocale);

        Date now = new Date();
        System.out.println("Default: " + ' ' +
            defaultDateFormatter.format(now));
        System.out.println(frLocale.getDisplayName() + ' ' +
            frDateFormatter.format(now));
        System.out.println(ukLocale.getDisplayName() + ' ' +
            ukDateFormatter.format(now));
    }
}
```

The program prints the locale name and formats the date in each of the locales:

```
$ java UseLocales
Default:  Nov 30, 2000
French (France) 30 nov. 00
English (UK) Nov 30, 2000
$
```

# 15.9  Setting the Default Locale

## Problem

You want to change the default Locale for all operations within a given Java runtime.

## Solution

Set the system property user.language or call Locale.setDefault( ).

## Discussion

Here is a program called SetLocale, which takes the language and country codes from the command line, constructs a Locale object, and passes it to Locale.setDefault( ). When run with different arguments, it prints the date and a number in the appropriate locale:

```
C:\javasrc\i18n>java SetLocale en US
6/30/00 1:45 AM
123.457

C:\javasrc\i18n>java SetLocale fr FR
30/06/00 01:45
123,457
```

The code is similar to the previous recipe in how it constructs the locale:

```java
import java.text.*;
import java.util.*;

/** Change the default locale */
public class SetLocale {
    public static void main(String[] args) {

        switch (args.length) {
        case 0:
            Locale.setDefault(Locale.FRANCE);
            break;
        case 1:
            throw new IllegalArgumentException( );
        case 2:
            Locale.setDefault(new Locale(args[0], args[1]));
            break;
        default:
            System.out.println("Usage: SetLocale [language [country]]");
            // FALLTHROUGH
        }

        DateFormat df = DateFormat.getInstance( );
        NumberFormat nf = NumberFormat.getInstance( );

        System.out.println(df.format(new Date( )));
        System.out.println(nf.format(123.4567));
    }
}
```

# 15.10 Formatting Messages

## Problem

Messages may need to be formatted differently in different languages.

---

## Solution

Use a `MessageFormat` object.

## Discussion

In English, for example, we say "file not found." But in other languages the word order is different: the word for "not found" might need to precede the word for "file." Java provides for this using the `MessageFormat` class. Suppose we want to format a message as follows:

```
$ java MessageFormatDemoIntl
At 3:33:02 PM on 01-Jul-00, myfile.txt could not be opened.
$ java -Duser.language=es MessageFormatDemoIntl
A 3:34:49 PM sobre 01-Jul-00, no se puede abrir la fila myfile.txt.
$
```

The `MessageFormat` in its simplest form takes a format string with a series of numeric indexes and an array of objects to be formatted. The objects are inserted into the resulting string, where the given array index appears. Here is a simple example of a `MessageFormat` in action:

```java
import java.text.*;

public class MessageFormatDemo {

    static Object[] data = {
            new java.util.Date(),
            "myfile.txt",
            "could not be opened"
    };

    public static void main(String[] args) {
        String result = MessageFormat.format(
            "At {0,time} on {0,date}, {1} {2}.", data);
        System.out.println(result);
    }
}
```

But we still need to internationalize this, so we'll add some lines to our widget's properties files. In the default (English) version:

```
# These are for MessageFormatDemo
#
filedialogs.cantopen.string=could not be opened
filedialogs.cantopen.format=At {0,time} on {0,date}, {1} {2}.
```

In the Spanish version, we'll add these lines:

```
# These are for MessageFormatDemo
#
filedialogs.cantopen.string=no se puede abrir la fila
filedialogs.cantopen.format=A {0,time} sobre {0,date}, {2} {1}.
```

Then `MessageFormatDemo` still needs to have a `ResourceBundle` and get both the format string and the message from the bundle. Here is `MessageFormatDemoIntl`:

```java
import java.text.*;
import java.util.*;

public class MessageFormatDemoIntl {

    static Object[] data = {
            new Date( ),
            "myfile.txt",
            null
    };

    public static void main(String[] args) {
        ResourceBundle rb = ResourceBundle.getBundle("Widgets");
        data[2] = rb.getString("filedialogs.cantopen.string");
        String result = MessageFormat.format(
            rb.getString("filedialogs.cantopen.format"), data);
        System.out.println(result);
    }
}
```

`MessageFormat` is more complex than this; see the Javadoc page for more details and examples.

## 15.11 Program: MenuIntl

`MenuIntl` (shown in Example 15-1) is a complete version of the menu code presented in Recipe 15.3.

*Example 15-1. MenuIntl.java*

```java
import java.awt.*;
import java.awt.event.*;
import javax.swing.*;
import java.util.*;

/** This is a partly-internationalized version of MenuDemo.
 * To try it out, use
 *       java MenuIntl
 *       java -Duser.language=es MenuIntl
 */
public class MenuIntl extends JFrame {

    /** "main program" method - construct and show */
    public static void main(String[] av) {
        // create an MenuIntl object, tell it to show up
        new MenuIntl( ).setVisible(true);
    }
```

*Example 15-1. MenuIntl.java (continued)*

```
    /** Construct the object including its GUI */
    public MenuIntl( ) {
        super("MenuIntlTest");
        JMenuItem mi;          // used in various spots

        Container cp = getContentPane( );
        cp.setLayout(new FlowLayout( ));
        JLabel lab;
        cp.add(lab = new JLabel( ));

        addWindowListener(new WindowAdapter( ) {
            public void windowClosing(WindowEvent e) {
                setVisible(false);
                dispose( );
                System.exit(0);
            }
        });
        JMenuBar mb = new JMenuBar( );
        setJMenuBar(mb);

        ResourceBundle b = ResourceBundle.getBundle("Menus");

        String titlebar;
        try { titlebar = b.getString("program"+".title"); }
        catch (MissingResourceException e) { titlebar="MenuIntl Demo"; }
        setTitle(titlebar);

        String message;
        try { message = b.getString("program"+".message"); }
        catch (MissingResourceException e) {
            message="Welcome to the world of Java";
        }
        lab.setText(message);

        JMenu fm = mkMenu(b, "file");
        fm.add(mi = mkMenuItem(b, "file", "open"));
        // In finished code there would be a call to
        // mi.addActionListener(...) after *each* of
        // these mkMenuItem calls!
        fm.add(mi = mkMenuItem(b, "file", "new"));
        fm.add(mi = mkMenuItem(b, "file", "save"));
        fm.add(mi = mkMenuItem(b, "file", "exit"));
        mi.addActionListener(new ActionListener( ) {
            public void actionPerformed(ActionEvent e) {
                MenuIntl.this.setVisible(false);
                MenuIntl.this.dispose( );
                System.exit(0);
            }
        });
        mb.add(fm);
```

*Example 15-1. MenuIntl.java (continued)*

```
        JMenu vm = mkMenu(b,  "view");
        vm.add(mi = mkMenuItem(b, "view", "tree"));
        vm.add(mi = mkMenuItem(b, "view", "list"));
        vm.add(mi = mkMenuItem(b, "view", "longlist"));
        mb.add(vm);

        JMenu hm = mkMenu(b,  "help");
        hm.add(mi = mkMenuItem(b, "help", "about"));
        // mb.setHelpMenu(hm);    // needed for portability (Motif, etc.).

        // the main window
        JLabel jl = new JLabel("Menu Demo Window");
        jl.setSize(200, 150);
        cp.add(jl);
        pack();
    }

    /** Convenience routine to make a JMenu */
    public JMenu mkMenu(ResourceBundle b, String name) {
        String menuLabel;
        try { menuLabel = b.getString(name+".label"); }
        catch (MissingResourceException e) { menuLabel=name; }
        return new JMenu(menuLabel);
    }

    /** Convenience routine to make a JMenuItem */
    public JMenuItem mkMenuItem(ResourceBundle b, String menu, String name) {
        String miLabel;
        try { miLabel = b.getString(menu + "." + name + ".label"); }
        catch (MissingResourceException e) { miLabel=name; }
        String key = null;
        try { key = b.getString(menu + "." + name + ".key"); }
        catch (MissingResourceException e) { key=null; }

        if (key == null)
            return new JMenuItem(miLabel);
        else
            return new JMenuItem(miLabel, key.charAt(0));
    }
}
```

# 15.12 Program: BusCard

This program may seem a bit silly, but it's a good example of configuring a variety of user interface controls from a resource bundle. The BusCard program allows you to create a digital business card ("interactive business card") onscreen (see Figure 15-2). The labels for all the GUI controls, and even the pull-down menu options, are loaded from a ResourceBundle.

Example 15-2 shows the code for the BusCard program.

---

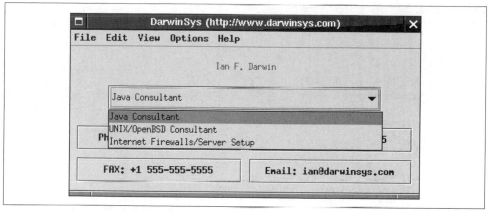

Figure 15-2. BusCard program in action

*Example 15-2. BusCard.java*

```java
import java.awt.*;
import java.awt.event.*;
import java.util.*;
import javax.swing.*;

/** Display your business-card information in a Java window.
 *
 * This is a first attempt. The next version should use a GridBagLayout.
 */
public class BusCard extends JFrame {

    JLabel nameTF;
    JComboBox jobChoice;
    JButton B1, B2, B3, B4;

    /** "main program" method - construct and show */
    public static void main(String[] av) {

        // create a BusCard object, tell it to show up
        new BusCard().setVisible(true);
    }

    /** Construct the object including its GUI */
    public BusCard() {
        super();

        Container cp = getContentPane();

        cp.setLayout(new GridLayout(0, 1));

        addWindowListener(new WindowAdapter() {
            public void windowClosing(WindowEvent e) {
                setVisible(false);
                dispose();
```

*Example 15-2. BusCard.java (continued)*

```
                    System.exit(0);
            }
    });

    JMenuBar mb = new JMenuBar( );
    setJMenuBar(mb);

    ResourceBundle b = ResourceBundle.getBundle("BusCard");

    JMenu aMenu;
    aMenu = I18N.mkMenu(b, "filemenu");
    mb.add(aMenu);
    JMenuItem mi = I18N.mkMenuItem(b, "filemenu", "exit");
    aMenu.add(mi);
    mi.addActionListener(new ActionListener( ) {
        public void actionPerformed(ActionEvent e) {
            System.exit(0);
        }
    });
    aMenu = I18N.mkMenu(b, "editmenu");
    mb.add(aMenu);
    aMenu = I18N.mkMenu(b, "viewmenu");
    mb.add(aMenu);
    aMenu = I18N.mkMenu(b, "optionsmenu");
    mb.add(aMenu);
    aMenu = I18N.mkMenu(b, "helpmenu");
    mb.add(aMenu);
    //mb.setHelpMenu(aMenu);         // needed for portability (Motif, etc.).

    setTitle(I18N.getString(b, "card"+".company", "TITLE"));

    JPanel p1 = new JPanel( );
    p1.setLayout(new GridLayout(0, 1, 50, 10));

    nameTF = new JLabel("My Name", JLabel.CENTER);
    nameTF.setFont(new Font("helvetica", Font.BOLD, 18));
    nameTF.setText(I18N.getString(b, "card"+".myname", "MYNAME"));
    p1.add(nameTF);

    jobChoice = new JComboBox( );
    jobChoice.setFont(new Font("helvetica", Font.BOLD, 14));

    // Get Job Titles ofrom the Properties file loaded into "b"!
    String next;
    int i=1;
    do {
        next = I18N.getString(b, "job_title" + i++, null);
        if (next != null)
            jobChoice.addItem(next);
    } while (next != null);
    p1.add(jobChoice);
```

*Example 15-2. BusCard.java (continued)*

```
        cp.add(p1);

        JPanel p2 = new JPanel( );
        p2.setLayout(new GridLayout(2, 2, 10, 10));

        B1 = new JButton( );
        B1.setLabel(I18N.getString(b, "button1.label", "BUTTON LABEL"));
        p2.add(B1);

        B2 = new JButton( );
        B2.setLabel(I18N.getString(b, "button2.label", "BUTTON LABEL"));
        p2.add(B2);

        B3 = new JButton( );
        B3.setLabel(I18N.getString(b, "button3.label", "BUTTON LABEL"));
        p2.add(B3);

        B4 = new JButton( );
        B4.setLabel(I18N.getString(b, "button4.label", "BUTTON LABEL"));
        p2.add(B4);
        cp.add(p2);

        pack( );
    }
}
```

# See Also

Other things may need to be internationalized as well:

*Character comparisons*
    These are set separately on Unix/POSIX; on other operating systems, they depend on the default `Locale`.

*Date and time formats*
    See `GregorianCalendar` and `DateFormat` in the Introduction to Chapter 6.

*Number formats*
    See `java.util.NumberFormat` in Recipe 5.8.

*Message insertions*
    These appear in different orders in different languages (something the C-language `printf( )` could never handle). See `java.util.MessageFormat` in Recipe 14.10.

Sun maintains an Internationalization Home Page at *http://java.sun.com/j2se/corejava/intl/*.

## Internationalization Caveats

Internationalizing your menus and push buttons is only one step. You also need to internationalize message text in dialogs as well as help files (see the JavaHelp API at *http://java.sun.com/products/javahelp/*).

Some items such as AWT `FileDialog` use native components; their appearance depends on the native operating system (your application can change its own default locale, but not the system's. If your customer has a differently internationalized copy of the same OS, the file dialogs will appear differently).

## Documentation

A short, readable, non-Java-specific introduction to the overall topic of internationalization is *The Guide to Translation and Localization*, written by the staff of Lingo Systems and published by the IEEE Computer Society. For more on Java I18N, see the online documentation that ships with the JDK; start at *docs/guide/intl/index.html*. See also *Java Internationalization* (O'Reilly).

## The Last Word

Good luck. Bonne chance. Buena suerte....

# CHAPTER 16

# Network Clients

## 16.0 Introduction

Java can be used to write many types of networked programs. In traditional socket-based code, the programmer is responsible for the entire interaction between the client and server. In higher-level types, such as RMI, CORBA, and EJB, the software takes over increasing degrees of control. Sockets are often used for connecting to "legacy" servers; if you were writing a new application from scratch, you'd be better off using a higher-level service.

It may be helpful to compare sockets with the telephone system. Telephones were originally used for analog voice traffic, which is pretty unstructured. Then it began to be used for some "layered" applications; the first widely popular one was facsimile transmission, or fax. Where would fax be without the widespread availability of voice telephony? The second wildly popular layered application is dialup TCP/IP. This coexisted with the Web to become popular as a mass-market service. Where would dialup IP be without widely deployed voice lines? And where would the Internet be without dialup IP?

Sockets are like that too. The Web, RMI, JDBC, CORBA, and EJB are all layered on top of sockets.

Ever since the alpha release of Java (originally as a sideline to the HotJava browser) in May 1995, Java has been popular as a programming language for building network applications. It's easy to see why, particularly if you've ever built a networked application in C. First, C programmers have to worry about the platform they are on. Unix uses synchronous sockets, which work rather like normal disk files vis-a-vis reading and writing, while Microsoft OSes use asynchronous sockets, which use callbacks to notify when a read or write has completed. Java glosses over this distinction. Further, the amount of code needed to set up a socket in C is intimidating. Just for fun, Example 16-1 shows the "typical" C code for setting up a client socket. And remember, this is only the Unix part. And only the part that makes the connection.

To be portable to Windows, it would need additional conditional code (using C's #ifdef mechanism). And C's #include mechanism requires that exactly the right files be included in exactly the right order; Java's import mechanism lets you use * to import a whole section of the API, and the imports can be listed in any order you like.

*Example 16-1. C client setup*

```
/*
 * Simple demonstration of code to setup a client connection in C.
 */

#include <sys/types.h>
#include <sys/socket.h>
#include <netinet/in.h>
#include <netdb.h>
#include <stdio.h>
#include <string.h>
#include <fcntl.h>

int
main(int argc, char *argv[])
{
    char* server_name = "localhost";
    struct hostent *host_info;
    int sock;
    struct sockaddr_in server;

    /* Look up the remote host's IP address */
    host_info = gethostbyname(server_name);
    if (host_info == NULL) {
        fprintf(stderr, "%s: unknown host: %s\n", argv[0], server_name);
        exit(1);
    }

    /* Create the socket */
    if ((sock = socket(AF_INET, SOCK_STREAM, 0)) < 0) {
        perror("creating client socket");
        exit(2);
    }

    /* Set up the server's socket address */
    server.sin_family = AF_INET;
    memcpy((char *)&server.sin_addr, host_info->h_addr,
                   host_info->h_length);
    server.sin_port = htons(80);

    /* Connect to the server */
    if (connect(sock,(struct sockaddr *)&server,sizeof server) < 0) {
        perror("connecting to server");
        exit(4);
    }
```

*Example 16-1. C client setup (continued)*

```
    /* Finally, we can read and write on the socket. */
    /* ... */

    (void) close(sock);
}
```

In the first recipe, we'll see how to do the connect in essentially one line of Java (plus a bit of error handling). We'll then cover error handling and transferring data over a socket. Next, we'll take a quick look at a datagram or UDP client that implements most of the TFTP (trivial file transfer protocol) that has been used for two decades to boot diskless workstations. We'll end with a program that connects interactively to a text-based server such as Telnet or email.

A common theme through most of these client examples is to use existing servers so that we don't have to generate both the client and the server at the same time. With one exception, all of these are services that exist on any standard Unix platform. If you can't find a Unix server near you to try them on, let me suggest that you take an old PC, maybe one that's underpowered for running the latest Microsoft software, and put up a free, open source Unix system on it. My personal favorite is OpenBSD, and the market's overall favorite is Linux. Both are readily available on CD-ROM, can be installed for free over the Internet, and offer all the standard services used in the client examples, including the time servers and TFTP. Both have free Java implementations available.

# 16.1 Contacting a Server

## Problem

You need to contact a server using TCP/IP.

## Solution

Just create a Socket, passing the hostname and port number into the constructor.

## Discussion

There isn't much to this in Java, in fact. When creating a socket, you pass in the hostname and the port number. The java.net.Socket constructor does the gethostbyname( ) and the socket( ) system call, sets up the server's sockaddr_in structure, and executes the connect( ) call. All you have to do is catch the errors, which are subclassed from the familiar IOException. Example 16-2 sets up a Java network client, using IOException to catch errors.

*Example 16-2. Connect.java (simple client connection)*

```java
import java.net.*;

/*
 * A simple demonstration of setting up a Java network client.
 */
public class Connect {
    public static void main(String[] argv) {
        String server_name = "localhost";

        try {
            Socket sock = new Socket(server_name, 80);

            /* Finally, we can read and write on the socket. */
            System.out.println(" *** Connected to " + server_name  + " ***");

            /* . do the I/O here .. */

            sock.close( );

        } catch (java.io.IOException e) {
            System.err.println("error connecting to " +
                server_name + ": " + e);
            return;
        }

    }
}
```

## See Also

Java supports other ways of using network applications. You can also open a URL and read from it (see Recipe 18.7). You can write code so that it will run from a URL, when opened in a web browser, or from an application.

# 16.2   Finding and Reporting Network Addresses

## Problem

You want to look up a host's address name or number or get the address at the other end of a network connection.

## Solution

Get an InetAddress object.

## Discussion

The InetAddress object represents the Internet address of a given computer or host. It has no public constructors; you obtain an InetAddress by calling the static getByName( ) method, passing in either a hostname like *www.darwinsys.com* or a network address as a string, like 1.23.45.67. All the "lookup" methods in this class can throw the checked UnknownHostException (a subclass of java.ioIOException), which must be caught or declared on the calling method's header. None of these methods actually contacts the remote host, so they do not throw the other exceptions related to network connections.

The method getHostAddress( ) gives you the numeric IP address (as a string) corresponding to the InetAddress. The inverse is getHostName( ), which reports the name of the InetAddress. This can be used to print the address of a host given its name, or vice versa:

```
// From InetAddrDemo.java
String ipNumber = "123.45.67.89";
String hostName = "www.darwinsys.com";
System.out.println(hostName + "'s address is " +
    InetAddress.getByName(hostName).getHostAddress( ));
System.out.println(ipNumber + "'s name is " +
    InetAddress.getByName(ipNumber).getHostName( ));
```

You can also get an InetAddress from a Socket by calling its getInetAddress( ) method. You can construct a Socket using an InetAddress instead of a hostname string. So, to connect to port number myPortNumber on the same host as an existing socket, you'd use:

```
InetAddress remote = theSocket.getInetAddress( );
Socket anotherSocket = new Socket(remote, myPortNumber);
```

Finally, to look up all the addresses associated with a host—a server may be on more than one network—use the static method getAllByName(host), which returns an array of InetAddress objects, one for each IP address associated with the given name.

A static method getLocalHost( ) returns an InetAddress equivalent to "localhost" or 127.0.0.1. This can be used to connect to a server program running on the same machine as the client.

If you are using IPV6, you can use Inet6Address instead.

## See Also

See NetworkInterface in Recipe 17.10 which lets you find out more about the networking of the machine you are running on.

There is not yet a way to look up services—i.e., to find out that the HTTP service is on port 80. Full implementations of TCP/IP have always included an additional set of resolvers; in C, the call getservbyname("http", "tcp"); would look up the given service[*] and return a servent (service entry) structure whose s_port member would contain the value 80. The numbers of established services do not change, but when

---

[*] The location where it is looked up varies. It might be in a file named /etc/services on Unix or the services file in a subdirectory of \windows or \winnt under Windows; in a centralized registry such as Sun's Network Information Services (NIS, formerly YP); or in some other platform- or network-dependent location.

services are new or installed in nonroutine ways, it is convenient to be able to change the service number for all programs on a machine or network (regardless of programming language) just by changing the services definitions. Java should provide this capability in a future release.

# 16.3 Handling Network Errors

## Problem

You want more detailed reporting than just IOException if something goes wrong.

## Solution

Catch a greater variety of exception classes. SocketException has several subclasses; the most notable are ConnectException and NoRouteToHostException. The names are self-explanatory: the first means that the connection was refused by the machine at the other end (the server machine), and the second completely explains the failure. Example 16-3 is an excerpt from the Connect program, enhanced to handle these conditions.

*Example 16-3. ConnectFriendly.java*

```
/* Client with error handling */
public class ConnectFriendly {
    public static void main(String[] argv) {
        String server_name = argv.length == 1 ? argv[0] : "localhost";
        int tcp_port = 80;
        try {
            Socket sock = new Socket(server_name, tcp_port);

            /* Finally, we can read and write on the socket. */
            System.out.println(" *** Connected to " + server_name  + " ***");
            /* ... */

            sock.close( );

        } catch (UnknownHostException e) {
            System.err.println(server_name + " Unknown host");
            return;
        } catch (NoRouteToHostException e) {
            System.err.println(server_name + " Unreachable" );
            return;
        } catch (ConnectException e) {
            System.err.println(server_name + " connect refused");
            return;
        } catch (java.io.IOException e) {
            System.err.println(server_name + ' ' + e.getMessage( ));
            return;
        }
    }
}
```

# 16.4  Reading and Writing Textual Data

## Problem

Having connected, you wish to transfer textual data.

## Solution

Construct a `BufferedReader` or `PrintWriter` from the socket's `getInputStream( )` or `getOutputStream( )`.

## Discussion

The Socket class has methods that allow you to get an `InputStream` or `OutputStream` to read from or write to the socket. It has no method to fetch a `Reader` or `Writer`, partly because some network services are limited to ASCII, but mainly because the Socket class was decided on before there were `Reader` and `Writer` classes. You can always create a `Reader` from an `InputStream` or a `Writer` from an `OutputStream` using the conversion classes. The paradigm for the two most common forms is:

```
BufferedReader is = new BufferedReader(
    new InputStreamReader(sock.getInputStream( )));
PrintWriter os = new PrintWriter(sock.getOutputStream( ), true);
```

Here is code that reads a line of text from the "daytime" service, which is offered by full-fledged TCP/IP suites (such as those included with most Unixes). You don't have to send anything to the Daytime server; you simply connect and read one line. The server writes one line containing the date and time and then closes the connection.

Running it looks like this. I started by getting the current date and time on the local host, then ran the DaytimeText program to see the date and time on the server (machine *darian* is my local server):

```
C:\javasrc\network>date
Current date is Sun 01-23-2000
Enter new date (mm-dd-yy):
C:\javasrc\network>time
Current time is  1:13:18.70p
Enter new time:
C:\javasrc\network>java DaytimeText darian
Time on darian is Sun Jan 23 13:14:34 2000
```

The code is in class DaytimeText, shown in Example 16-4.

*Example 16-4. DaytimeText.java*

```
/**
 * DaytimeText - connect to the Daytime (ascii) service.
 */
public class DaytimeText {
    public static final short TIME_PORT = 13;
```

*Example 16-4. DaytimeText.java (continued)*

```java
    public static void main(String[] argv) {
        String hostName;
        if (argv.length == 0)
            hostName = "localhost";
        else
            hostName = argv[0];

        try {
            Socket sock = new Socket(hostName, TIME_PORT);
            BufferedReader is = new BufferedReader(new
                InputStreamReader(sock.getInputStream( )));
            String remoteTime = is.readLine( );
            System.out.println("Time on " + hostName + " is " + remoteTime);
        } catch (IOException e) {
            System.err.println(e);
        }
    }
}
```

The second example, shown in Example 16-5, shows both reading and writing on the same socket. The Echo server simply echoes back whatever lines of text you send it. It's not a very clever server, but it is a useful one. It helps in network testing and also in testing clients of this type!

The converse( ) method holds a short conversation with the Echo server on the named host; if no host is named, it tries to contact localhost, a universal alias[*] for "the machine the program is running on."

*Example 16-5. EchoClientOneLine.java*

```java
/**
 * EchoClientOneLine - create client socket, send one line,
 * read it back. See also EchoClient.java, slightly fancier.
 */
public class EchoClientOneLine {
    /** What we send across the net */
    String mesg = "Hello across the net";

    public static void main(String[] argv) {
        if (argv.length == 0)
            new EchoClientOneLine( ).converse("localhost");
        else
            new EchoClientOneLine( ).converse(argv[0]);
    }

    /** Hold one conversation across the net */
    protected void converse(String hostName) {
        try {
```

---

[*] It used to be universal, when most networked systems were administered by full-time systems people who had been trained or served an apprenticeship. Today many machines on the Internet don't have localhost configured properly.

*Example 16-5. EchoClientOneLine.java (continued)*

```
            Socket sock = new Socket(hostName, 7); // echo server.
            BufferedReader is = new BufferedReader(new
                InputStreamReader(sock.getInputStream( )));
            PrintWriter os = new PrintWriter(sock.getOutputStream( ), true);
            // Do the CRLF ourself since println appends only a \r on
            // platforms where that is the native line ending.
            os.print(mesg + "\r\n"); os.flush( );
            String reply = is.readLine( );
            System.out.println("Sent \"" + mesg  + "\"");
            System.out.println("Got  \"" + reply + "\"");
        } catch (IOException e) {
            System.err.println(e);
        }
    }
}
```

It might be a good exercise to isolate the reading and writing code from this method into a `NetWriter` class, possibly subclassing `PrintWriter` and adding the \r\n and the flushing.

# 16.5   Reading and Writing Binary Data

## Problem

Having connected, you wish to transfer binary data.

## Solution

Construct a `DataInputStream` or `DataOutputStream` from the socket's `getInputStream( )` or `getOutputStream( )`.

## Discussion

The simplest paradigm is:

```
DataInputStream is = new DataInputStream(sock.getInputStream( ));
DataOutputStream is = new DataOutputStream(sock.getOutputStream( ));
```

If the volume of data might be large, insert a buffered stream for efficiency. The paradigm is:

```
DataInputStream is = new DataInputStream(
    new BufferedInputStream(sock.getInputStream( )));
DataOutputStream is = new DataOutputStream(
    new BufferedOutputStream(sock.getOutputStream( )));
```

This program uses another standard service that gives out the time as a binary integer representing the number of seconds since 1900. Since the Java Date class base is 1970, we convert the time base by subtracting the difference between 1970 and 1900.

When I used this exercise in a course, most of the students wanted to *add* this time difference, reasoning that 1970 is later. But if you think clearly, you'll see that there are fewer seconds between 1999 and 1970 than there are between 1999 and 1900, so subtraction gives the correct number of seconds. And since the Date constructor needs milliseconds, we multiply the number of seconds by 1,000.

The time difference is the number of years multiplied by 365, plus the number of leap days between the two dates (in the years 1904, 1908, ..., 1968)—i.e., 19 days.

The integer that we read from the server is a C-language unsigned int. But Java doesn't provide an unsigned integer type; normally when you need an unsigned number, you use the next-larger integer type, which would be long. But Java also doesn't give us a method to read an unsigned integer from a data stream. The DataInputStream method readInt( ) reads Java-style signed integers. There are readUnsignedByte( ) methods and readUnsignedShort( ) methods, but no readUnsignedInt( ) method. Accordingly, we synthesize the ability to read an unsigned int (which must be stored in a long, or else you'd lose the signed bit and be back where you started from) by reading unsigned bytes and reassembling them using Java's bit-shifting operators:

```
$ date
Fri Mar 30 10:02:28 EST 2001
$ java DaytimeBinary darian
Remote time is 3194953367
BASE_DIFF is 2208988800
Time diff == 985964567
Time on darian is Fri Mar 30 10:02:47 EST 2001
$
```

Looking at the output, you can see that the server agrees within a few seconds. So the date calculation code in Example 16-6 is probably correct.

*Example 16-6. DaytimeBinary.java*

```
/**
 * DaytimeBinary - connect to the Time (binary) service.
 */
public class DaytimeBinary {
    /** The TCP port for the binary time service. */
    public static final short TIME_PORT = 37;
    /** Seconds between 1970, the time base for Date(long) and Time.
     * Factors in leap years (up to 2100), hours, minutes, and seconds.
     * Subtract 1 day for 1900, add in 1/2 day for 1969/1970.
     */
    protected static final long BASE_DAYS =
        (long)((1970-1900)*365 + (1970-1900-1)/4);
    /* Seconds since 1970 */
    public static final long BASE_DIFF = (BASE_DAYS * 24 * 60 * 60);
    /** Convert from seconds to milliseconds */
    public static final int MSEC = 1000;
```

*Example 16-6. DaytimeBinary.java (continued)*

```java
public static void main(String[] argv) {
    String hostName;
    if (argv.length == 0)
        hostName = "localhost";
    else
        hostName = argv[0];

    try {
        Socket sock = new Socket(hostName, TIME_PORT);
        DataInputStream is = new DataInputStream(new
            BufferedInputStream(sock.getInputStream( )));
        // Need to read 4 bytes from the network, unsigned.
        // Do it yourself; there is no readUnsignedInt( ).
        // Long is 8 bytes on Java, but we are using the
        // existing time protocol, which uses 4-byte ints.
        long remoteTime = (
            ((long)(is.readUnsignedByte( ) ) << 24) |
            ((long)(is.readUnsignedByte( )) << 16) |
            ((long)(is.readUnsignedByte( )) <<  8) |
            ((long)(is.readUnsignedByte( )) <<  0));
        System.out.println("Remote time is " + remoteTime);
        System.out.println("BASE_DIFF is " + BASE_DIFF);
        System.out.println("Time diff == " + (remoteTime - BASE_DIFF));
        Date d = new Date((remoteTime - BASE_DIFF) * MSEC);
        System.out.println("Time on " + hostName + " is " + d.toString( ));
    } catch (IOException e) {
        System.err.println(e);
    }
}
}
```

# 16.6   Reading and Writing Serialized Data

## Problem

Having connected, you wish to transfer serialized object data.

## Solution

Construct an `ObjectInputStream` or `ObjectOutputStream` from the socket's `getInputStream( )` or `getOutputStream( )`.

## Discussion

*Object serialization* is the ability to convert in-memory objects to an external form that can be sent *serially* (a byte at a time). This is discussed in Recipe 10.18.

This program (and its server) operate one service that isn't normally provided by TCP/IP, as it is Java-specific. It looks rather like the DaytimeBinary program in the previous recipe, but the server sends us a Date object already constructed. You can find the server for this program in Recipe 17.2; Example 16-7 shows the client code.

*Example 16-7. DaytimeObject.java*

```java
/**
 * DaytimeObject - connect to the non-standard Time (object)  service.
 */
public class DaytimeObject {
    /** The TCP port for the object time service. */
    public static final short TIME_PORT = 1951;

    public static void main(String[] argv) {
        String hostName;
        if (argv.length == 0)
            hostName = "localhost";
        else
            hostName = argv[0];

        try {
            Socket sock = new Socket(hostName, TIME_PORT);
            ObjectInputStream is = new ObjectInputStream(new
                BufferedInputStream(sock.getInputStream( )));

            // Read and validate the Object
            Object o = is.readObject( );
            if (!(o instanceof Date))
                throw new IllegalArgumentException("Wanted Date, got " + o);

            // Valid, so cast to Date, and print
            Date d = (Date) o;
            System.out.println("Time on " + hostName + " is " + d.toString( ));
        } catch (ClassNotFoundException e) {
            System.err.println("Wanted date, got INVALID CLASS (" + e + ")");
        } catch (IOException e) {
            System.err.println(e);
        }
    }
}
```

I ask the operating system for the date and time, and then run the program, which prints the date and time on a remote machine.

```
C:\javasrc\network>date /t
Current date is Sun 01-23-2000
C:\javasrc\network>time /t
Current time is  2:52:35.43p
C:\javasrc\network>java DaytimeObject aragorn
Time on aragorn is Sun Jan 23 14:52:25 GMT 2000
C:\javasrc\network>
```

# 16.7 UDP Datagrams

## Problem

You need to use a datagram connection (UDP) instead of a stream connection (TCP).

## Solution

Use DatagramSocket and DatagramPacket.

## Discussion

Datagram network traffic is a kindred spirit to the underlying packet-based Ethernet and IP (Internet protocol) layers. Unlike a stream-based connection such as TCP, datagram transports such as UDP transmit each "packet," or chunk of data, as a single entity with no necessary relation to any other. A common analogy is that TCP is like talking on the telephone, while UDP is like sending postcards or maybe fax messages.

The differences show up most in error handling. Packets can, like postcards, go astray. When was the last time the postman rang your bell to tell you that the post office had lost one of several postcards it was supposed to deliver to you? It doesn't happen, right? Because they don't keep track of them. On the other hand, when you're talking on the phone and there's a noise burst—like somebody yelling in the room, or even a bad connection—you can ask the person at the other end to repeat what they just said.

With a stream-based connection like a TCP socket, the network transport layer handles errors for you: it asks the other end to retransmit. With a datagram transport such as UDP, you have to handle retransmission yourself. It's kind of like numbering the postcards you send so that you can go back and resend any that don't arrive—a good excuse to return to your vacation spot, perhaps.

Another difference is that datagram transmission preserves message boundaries. That is, if you write 20 bytes and then write 10 bytes when using TCP, the program reading from the other end will not know if you wrote one chunk of 30 bytes, two chunks of 15, or even 30 individual characters. With a DatagramSocket, you construct a DatagramPacket object for each buffer, and its contents are sent as a *single* entity over the network; its contents will not be mixed together with the contents of any other buffer. The DatagramPacket object has methods like getLength( ), setPort( ), and so on.

Example 16-8 is a short program that connects via UDP to the Daytime date and time server used in Recipe 16.4. Since UDP has no real notion of "connection," even services that only send you data must be contacted by sending an empty packet, which the UDP server uses to return its response.

*Example 16-8. DaytimeUDP.java*

```java
public class DaytimeUDP {
    /** The UDP port number */
    public final static int DAYTIME_PORT = 13;

    /** A buffer plenty big enough for the date string */
    protected final static int PACKET_SIZE = 100;

    // main program
    public static void main(String[] argv) throws IOException {
        if (argv.length < 1) {
            System.err.println("usage: java DaytimeUDP host");
            System.exit(1);
        }
        String host = argv[0];
        InetAddress servAddr = InetAddress.getByName(host);
        DatagramSocket sock = new DatagramSocket();

        // Allocate the data buffer
        byte[] buffer = new byte[PACKET_SIZE];

        // The udp packet we will send and receive
        DatagramPacket packet = new DatagramPacket(
            buffer, PACKET_SIZE, servAddr, DAYTIME_PORT);

        /* Send empty max-length (-1 for null byte) packet to server */
        packet.setLength(PACKET_SIZE-1);
        sock.send(packet);
        Debug.println("net", "Sent request");

        // Receive a packet and print it.
        sock.receive(packet);
        Debug.println("net", "Got packet of size " + packet.getLength());
```

*Example 16-8. DaytimeUDP.java (continued)*

```
        System.out.print("Date on " + host + " is " +
            new String(buffer, 0, packet.getLength( )));
    }
}
```

I'll run it to my server just to be sure that it works:

```
$ javac DaytimeUDP.java
$ java DaytimeUDP  darian
Date on darian is Sat Jan 27 12:42:41 2001
$
```

# 16.8  Program: TFTP UDP Client

This program implements the client half of the TFTP application protocol, a well-known service that has been used in the Unix world for network booting of workstations since before Windows 3.1. I chose this protocol because it's widely implemented on the server side, so it's easy to find a test server for it.

The TFTP protocol is a bit odd. The client contacts the server on the well-known UDP port number 69, from a generated port number,* and the server responds to the client from a generated port number. Further communication is on the two generated port numbers.

Getting into more detail, as shown in Figure 16-1, the client initially sends a read request with the filename and reads the first packet of data. The read request consists of two bytes (a short) with the read request code (short integer with a value of 1, defined as OP_RRQ), two bytes for the sequence number, then the ASCII filename, null terminated, and the string octet, also null terminated. The server reads the read request from the client, verifies that it can open the file and, if so, sends the first data packet (OP_DATA), and then reads again. This read-acknowledge cycle is repeated until all the data is read. Note that each packet is 516 bytes (512 bytes of data, plus 2 bytes for the packet type and 2 more for the packet number) except the last, which can be any length from 4 (zero bytes of data) to 515 (511 bytes of data). If a network I/O error occurs, the packet is resent. If a given packet goes astray, both client and server are supposed to perform a timeout cycle. This client does not, but the server does. You could add timeouts using a thread; see Recipe 24.4. The client code is shown in Example 16-9.

---

* When the application doesn't care, these port numbers are usually made up by the operating system. For example, when you call a company from a pay phone or cell phone, the company doesn't usually care what number you are calling from, and if it does, there are ways to find out. Generated port numbers generally range from 1024 (the first nonprivileged port; see Chapter 17) to 65535 (the largest value that can be held in a 16-bit port number).

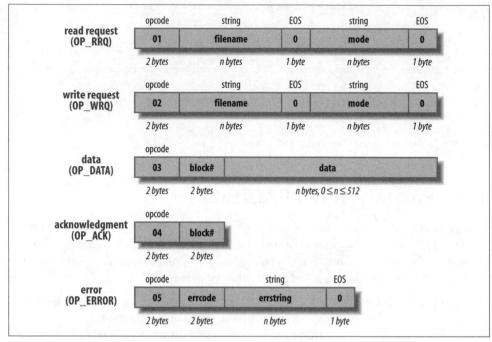

*Figure 16-1. The TFTP protocol packet formats*

*Example 16-9. RemCat.java*

```java
import java.io.*;
import java.net.*;

/**
 * RemCat - remotely cat (DOS type) a file, using the TFTP protocol.
 * Inspired by the "rcat" exercise in Learning Tree Course 363,
 * <I>UNIX Network Programming</I>, by Dr. Chris Brown.
 *
 * Note that the TFTP server is NOT "internationalized"; the name and
 * mode in the protocol are defined in terms of ASCII, not UniCode.
 */
public class RemCat {
    /** The UDP port number */
    public final static int TFTP_PORT = 69;
    /** The mode we will use - octet for everything. */
    protected final String MODE = "octet";

    /** The offset for the code/response as a byte */
    protected final int OFFSET_REQUEST = 1;
    /** The offset for the packet number as a byte */
    protected final int OFFSET_PACKETNUM = 3;

    /** Debugging flag */
    protected static boolean debug = false;
```

*Example 16-9. RemCat.java (continued)*

```java
/** TFTP op-code for a read request */
public final int OP_RRQ = 1;
/** TFTP op-code for a write request */
public final int OP_WRQ = 2;
/** TFTP op-code for a data packet */
public final int OP_DATA    = 3;
/** TFTP op-code for an acknowledgement */
public final int OP_ACK     = 4;
/** TFTP op-code for an error packet */
public final int OP_ERROR = 5;
protected final static int PACKET_SIZE = 516;    // == 2 + 2 + 512
protected String host;
protected InetAddress servAddr;
protected DatagramSocket sock;
protected byte buffer[];
protected DatagramPacket inp, outp;

/** The main program that drives this network client.
 * @param argv[0] hostname, running TFTP server
 * @param argv[1..n] filename(s), must be at least one
 */
public static void main(String[] argv) throws IOException {
    if (argv.length < 2) {
        System.err.println("usage: java RemCat host filename[...]");
        System.exit(1);
    }
    if (debug)
        System.err.println("Java RemCat starting");
    RemCat rc = new RemCat(argv[0]);
    for (int i = 1; i<argv.length; i++) {
        if (debug)
            System.err.println("-- Starting file " +
                argv[0] + ":" + argv[i] + "---");
        rc.readFile(argv[i]);
    }
}

RemCat(String host) throws IOException {
    super();
    this.host = host;
    servAddr = InetAddress.getByName(host);
    sock = new DatagramSocket();
    buffer = new byte[PACKET_SIZE];
    inp = new DatagramPacket(buffer, PACKET_SIZE);
    outp = new DatagramPacket(buffer, PACKET_SIZE, servAddr, TFTP_PORT);
}

void readFile(String path) throws IOException {
    /* Build a tftp Read Request packet. This is messy because the
     * fields have variable length. Numbers must be in
     * network order, too; fortunately Java just seems
     * naturally smart enough :-) to use network byte order.
     */
```

*Example 16-9. RemCat.java (continued)*

```
buffer[0] = 0;
buffer[OFFSET_REQUEST] = OP_RRQ;        // read request
int p = 2;              // number of chars into buffer

// Convert filename String to bytes in buffer , using "p" as an
// offset indicator to get all the bits of this request
// in exactly the right spot.
byte[] bTemp = path.getBytes(); // i.e., ASCII
 System.arraycopy(bTemp, 0, buffer, p, path.length());
p += path.length();
buffer[p++] = 0;        // null byte terminates string

// Similarly, convert MODE ("octet") to bytes in buffer
MODE.getBytes(0, MODE.length(), buffer, p);
p += MODE.length();
buffer[p++] = 0;        // null terminate

/* Send Read Request to tftp server */
outp.setLength(p);
sock.send(outp);

/* Loop reading data packets from the server until a short
 * packet arrives; this indicates the end of the file.
 */
int len = 0;
do {
    sock.receive(inp);
    if (debug)
        System.err.println(
            "Packet # " + Byte.toString(buffer[OFFSET_PACKETNUM])+
            "RESPONSE CODE " + Byte.toString(buffer[OFFSET_REQUEST]));
    if (buffer[OFFSET_REQUEST] == OP_ERROR) {
        System.err.println("remcat ERROR: " +
            new String(buffer, 4, inp.getLength()-4));
        return;
    }
    if (debug)
        System.err.println("Got packet of size " +
            inp.getLength());

    /* Print the data from the packet */
    System.out.write(buffer, 4, inp.getLength()-4);

    /* Ack the packet. The block number we
     * want to ack is already in buffer so
     * we just change the opcode. The ACK is
     * sent to the port number which the server
     * just sent the data from, NOT to port
     * TFTP_PORT.
     */
    buffer[OFFSET_REQUEST] = OP_ACK;
    outp.setLength(4);
```

*Example 16-9. RemCat.java (continued)*

```
            outp.setPort(inp.getPort( ));
            sock.send(outp);
        } while (inp.getLength( ) == PACKET_SIZE);

        if (debug)
            System.err.println("** ALL DONE** Leaving loop, last size " +
                inp.getLength( ));
    }
}
```

To test this client, you would need a TFTP server. If you are on a Unix system that you administer, you can enable the TFTP server to test this client just by editing the file */etc/inetd.conf* and restarting (or just reloading, with **kill -HUP**) the inetd server. inetd is a program that listens for a wide range of connections and starts the servers only when a connection from a client comes along (a kind of lazy evaluation). Beware of security holes; don't turn a TFTP server loose on the Internet without first reading a good security book, such as O'Reilly's *Building Internet Firewalls*. I set up the traditional */tftpboot* directory, put this line in my *inetd.conf*, and reloaded inetd:

```
tftp  dgram udp wait root /usr/libexec/tftpd tftpd -s /tftpboot
```

Then I put a few test files, one named *foo*, into the */tftpboot* directory. Running:

```
$ java RemCat localhost foo
```

produced what looked like the file. But just to be safe, I tested the output of RemCat against the original file, using the Unix *diff* comparison program. No news is good news:

```
$ java RemCat localhost foo | diff - /tftpboot/foo
```

So far so good. Let's not slip this program on an unsuspecting network without exercising the error handling at least briefly:

```
$ java RemCat localhost nosuchfile
remcat ERROR: File not found
$
```

# 16.9  Program: Telnet Client

This program is a simple Telnet client. Telnet, as you probably know, is the oldest surviving remote login program in use on the Internet. It began on the original ARPAnet and was later translated for the Internet. A Unix command-line client lives on, and several windowed clients are in circulation. For security reasons, the use of Telnet as a means of logging in remotely over the Internet has largely been superseded by SSH (see *http://www.openssh.com*). However, a Telnet client remains a necessity for such purposes as connecting locally, as well as debugging textual socket servers and understanding their protocols. For example, it is common to connect from a Telnet client to an SMTP (email) server; you can often intuit quite a bit about the SMTP server, even if you wouldn't normally type an entire mail session interactively.

When you need to have data copied in both directions at more or less the same time—from the keyboard to the remote program, and from the remote program to the screen—there are two approaches. Some I/O libraries in C have a function called poll( ) or select( ) that allows you to examine a number of files to see which ones are ready for reading or writing. Java does not support this model. The other model, which works on most platforms and is the norm in Java, is to use two threads,* one to handle the data transfer in each direction. That is our plan here; the class Pipe encapsulates one thread and the code for copying data in one direction; two instances are used, one to drive each direction of transfer independently of the other.

This program allows you to connect to any text-based network service. For example, you can talk to your system's SMTP (simple mail transport protocol) server, or the Daytime server (port 13) used in several earlier recipes in this chapter:

```
$ java Telnet darian 13
Host darian; port 13
Connected OK
Sat Apr 28 14:07:41 2001
^C
$
```

The source code is shown in Example 16-10.

*Example 16-10. Telnet.java*

```java
import java.net.*;
import java.io.*;

/**
 * Telnet - very minimal (no options); connect to given host and service
 */
public class Telnet {
    String host;
    int portNum;
    public static void main(String[] argv) {
        new Telnet( ).talkTo(argv);
    }
    private void talkTo(String av[]) {
        if (av.length >= 1)
            host = av[0];
        else
            host = "localhost";
        if (av.length >= 2)
            portNum = Integer.parseInt(av[1]);
        else portNum = 23;
        System.out.println("Host " + host + "; port " + portNum);
        try {
            Socket s = new Socket(host, portNum);
```

---

* A thread is one of (possibly) many separate flows of control within a single process; see Recipe 24.1.

*Example 16-10. Telnet.java (continued)*

```
            // Connect the remote to our stdout
            new Pipe(s.getInputStream( ), System.out).start( );

            // Connect our stdin to the remote
            new Pipe(System.in, s.getOutputStream( )).start( );

        } catch(IOException e) {
            System.out.println(e);
            return;
        }
        System.out.println("Connected OK");
    }
}

/* This class handles one half of a full-duplex connection.
 * Line-at-a-time mode.
 */
class Pipe extends Thread {
    BufferedReader is;
    PrintStream os;

    /** Construct a Pipe to read from "is" and write to "os" */
    Pipe(InputStream is, OutputStream os) {
        this.is = new BufferedReader(new InputStreamReader(is));
        this.os = new PrintStream(os);
    }

    /** Do the reading and writing. */
    public void run( ) {
        String line;
        try {
            while ((line = is.readLine( )) != null) {
                os.print(line);
                os.print("\r\n");
                os.flush( );
            }
        } catch(IOException e) {
            throw new RuntimeException(e.getMessage( ));
        }
    }
}
```

# 16.10 Program: Chat Client

This program is a simple chat program. You can't break in on ICQ or AIM with it, because they each use their own protocol;* this one simply writes to and reads from a server, locating the server with the applet method getCodeBase( ). The server for this

---

\* For an open source program that "AIMs" to let you talk to both from the same program, check out *Jabber* at *http://www.jabber.org*.

will be presented in Chapter 17. How does it look when you run it? Figure 16-2 shows me chatting all by myself one day.

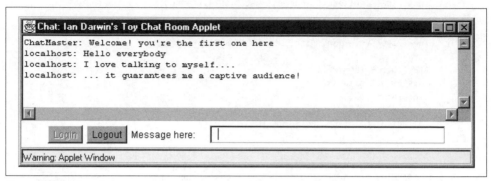

*Figure 16-2. Chat client in action*

The code is reasonably self-explanatory. We read from the remote server in a thread to make the input and the output run without blocking each other; this is discussed in Chapter 24. The reading and writing are discussed in this chapter. The program is an applet (see Recipe 18.2) and is shown in Example 16-11.

*Example 16-11. ChatRoom.java (chat client)*

```java
import java.applet.*;
import java.awt.*;
import java.awt.event.*;
import java.io.*;
import java.net.*;

/** Simple Chat Room Applet.
 * Writing a Chat Room seems to be one of many obligatory rites (or wrongs)
 * of passage for Java experts these days.
 * <P>
 * This one is a toy because it doesn't implement much of a command protocol, which
 * means we can't query the server as to * who's logged in,
 *  or anything fancy like that. However, it works OK for small groups.
 * <P>
 * Uses client socket w/ two Threads (main and one constructed),
 * one for reading and one for writing.
 * <P>
 * Server multiplexes messages back to all clients.
 */
public class ChatRoom extends Applet {
    /** The state */
    protected boolean loggedIn;
    /* The Frame, for a pop-up, durable Chat Room. */
    protected Frame cp;
    /** The default port number */
    protected static int PORTNUM = 7777;
    /** The actual port number */
    protected int port;
```

*Example 16-11. ChatRoom.java (chat client) (continued)*

```java
/** The network socket */
protected Socket sock;
/** BufferedReader for reading from socket */
protected BufferedReader is;
/** PrintWriter for sending lines on socket */
protected PrintWriter pw;
/** TextField for input */
protected TextField tf;
/** TextArea to display conversations */
protected TextArea ta;
/** The Login button */
protected Button lib;
/** The LogOUT button */
protected Button lob;
/** The TitleBar title */
final static String TITLE = "Chat: Ian Darwin's Toy Chat Room Applet";
/** The message that we paint */
protected String paintMessage;

/** Init, overrides method in Applet */
public void init() {
    paintMessage = "Creating Window for Chat";
    repaint();
    cp = new Frame(TITLE);
    cp.setLayout(new BorderLayout());
    String portNum = getParameter("port");
    port = PORTNUM;
    if (portNum == null)
        port = Integer.parseInt(portNum);

    // The GUI
    ta = new TextArea(14, 80);
    ta.setEditable(false);          // readonly
    ta.setFont(new Font("Monospaced", Font.PLAIN, 11));
    cp.add(BorderLayout.NORTH, ta);

    Panel p = new Panel();
    Button b;

    // The login button
    p.add(lib = new Button("Login"));
    lib.setEnabled(true);
    lib.requestFocus();
    lib.addActionListener(new ActionListener() {
        public void actionPerformed(ActionEvent e) {
            login();
            lib.setEnabled(false);
            lob.setEnabled(true);
            tf.requestFocus();      // set keyboard focus in right place!
        }
    });
```

*Example 16-11. ChatRoom.java (chat client) (continued)*

```
    // The logout button
    p.add(lob = new Button("Logout"));
    lob.setEnabled(false);
    lob.addActionListener(new ActionListener() {
        public void actionPerformed(ActionEvent e) {
            logout();
            lib.setEnabled(true);
            lob.setEnabled(false);
            lib.requestFocus();
        }
    });

    p.add(new Label("Message here:"));
    tf = new TextField(40);
    tf.addActionListener(new ActionListener() {
        public void actionPerformed(ActionEvent e) {
            if (loggedIn) {
                pw.println(Chat.CMD_BCAST+tf.getText());
                tf.setText("");
            }
        }
    });
    p.add(tf);

    cp.add(BorderLayout.SOUTH, p);

    cp.addWindowListener(new WindowAdapter() {
        public void windowClosing(WindowEvent e) {
            // If we do setVisible and dispose, then the Close completes
            ChatRoom.this.cp.setVisible(false);
            ChatRoom.this.cp.dispose();
            logout();
        }
    });
    cp.pack();
    // After packing the Frame, centre it on the screen.
    Dimension us = cp.getSize(),
        them = Toolkit.getDefaultToolkit().getScreenSize();
    int newX = (them.width - us.width) / 2;
    int newY = (them.height- us.height)/ 2;
    cp.setLocation(newX, newY);
    cp.setVisible(true);
    paintMessage = "Window should now be visible";
    repaint();
}

/** LOG ME IN TO THE CHAT */
public void login() {
    if (loggedIn)
        return;
    try {
```

*Example 16-11. ChatRoom.java (chat client) (continued)*

```
        sock = new Socket(getCodeBase( ).getHost( ), port);
        is = new BufferedReader(new InputStreamReader(sock.getInputStream( )));
        pw = new PrintWriter(sock.getOutputStream( ), true);
    } catch(IOException e) {
        showStatus("Can't get socket: " + e);
        cp.add(new Label("Can't get socket: " + e));
        return;
    }

    // construct and start the reader: from server to textarea
    // make a Thread to avoid lockups.
    new Thread(new Runnable( ) {
        public void run( ) {
            String line;
            try {
                while (loggedIn && ((line = is.readLine( )) != null))
                    ta.append(line + "\n");
            } catch(IOException e) {
                showStatus("GAA! LOST THE LINK!!");
                return;
            }
        }
    }).start( );

    // FAKE LOGIN FOR NOW
    pw.println(Chat.CMD_LOGIN + "AppletUser");
    loggedIn = true;
}

/** Log me out, Scotty, there's no intelligent life here! */
public void logout( ) {
    if (!loggedIn)
        return;
    loggedIn = false;
    try {
        if (sock != null)
            sock.close( );
    } catch (IOException ign) {
        // so what?
    }
}

// It is deliberate that there is no STOP method - we want to keep
// going even if the user moves the browser to another page.
// Anti-social? Maybe, but you can use the CLOSE button to kill
// the Frame, or you can exit the Browser.

/** Paint paints the small window that appears in the HTML,
 * telling the user to look elsewhere!
 */
```

*Example 16-11. ChatRoom.java (chat client) (continued)*

```
    public void paint(Graphics g) {
        Dimension d = getSize( );
        int h = d.height;
        int w = d.width;
        g.fillRect(0, 0, w, 0);
        g.setColor(Color.black);
        g.drawString(paintMessage, 10, (h/2)-5);
    }
}
```

## See Also

This chat applet might not work on all browser flavors; you might need the Java Plug-in. See Recipe 23.6.

There are many better-structured ways to write a chat client, including RMI, Java's RPC interface (see the Introduction to Chapter 22) and the Java Messaging Services, part of the Java 2 Enterprise Edition.

If you need to encrypt your socket connection, check out Sun's JSSE (Java Secure Socket Extension).

For a good overview of network programming from the C programmer's point of view, see the late W. Richard Stevens's *Unix Network Programming* (Prentice Hall). Despite the book's name, it's really about socket and TCP/IP/UDP programming and covers all parts of the (Unix) networking API and protocols such as TFTP in amazing detail.

# CHAPTER 17

# Server-Side Java: Sockets

## 17.0 Introduction

Sockets form the underpinnings of almost all networking protocols. JDBC, RMI, CORBA, EJB, and the non-Java RPC (Remote Procedure Call) and NFS (Network File System) are all implemented by connecting various types of sockets together. Socket connections can be implemented in many languages, not just Java: C, C++, Perl, and Python are also popular, and many others are possible. A client or server written in any one of these languages can communicate with its opposite written in any of the other languages. Therefore, it's worth taking a quick look at how the ServerSocket behaves, even if you wind up utilizing the higher-level services such as RMI, JDBC, CORBA, or EJB.

The discussion looks first at the ServerSocket itself, then at writing data over a socket in various ways. Finally, we show a complete implementation of a usable network server written in Java: the chat server from the client in the previous chapter.

## 17.1 Opening a Server for Business

### Problem

You need to write a socket-based server.

### Solution

Create a ServerSocket for the given port number.

### Discussion

The ServerSocket represents the "other end" of a connection, the server that waits patiently for clients to come along and connect to it. You construct a ServerSocket with just the port number.* Since it doesn't need to connect to another host, it doesn't need a particular host's address as the client socket constructor does.

Assuming the ServerSocket constructor doesn't throw an exception, you're in business. Your next step is to await client activity, which you do by calling accept( ). This call blocks until a client connects to your server; at that point, the accept( ) returns to you a Socket object (not a ServerSocket) that is connected in both directions to the Socket object on the client (or its equivalent, if written in another language). Example 17-1 shows the code for a socket-based server.

*Example 17-1. Listen.java*

```
/**
 * Listen -- make a ServerSocket and wait for connections.
 */
public class Listen {
    /** The TCP port for the service. */
    public static final short PORT = 9999;

    public static void main(String[] argv) throws IOException {
        ServerSocket sock;
        Socket  clientSock;
        try {
            sock = new ServerSocket(PORT);
            while ((clientSock = sock.accept()) != null) {

                // Process it.
                process(clientSock);
            }

        } catch (IOException e) {
            System.err.println(e);
        }
    }

    /** This would do something with one client. */
    static void process(Socket s) throws IOException {
        System.out.println("Accept from client " + s.getInetAddress());
        // The conversation would be here.
        s.close();
    }
}
```

You would normally use the socket for reading and writing, as shown in the next few recipes.

---

* You may not be able to pick just any port number for your own service, of course. Certain well-known port numbers are reserved for specific services and listed in your *services* file, such as 22 for Secure Shell, 25 for SMTP, and hundreds more. Also, on server-based operating systems, ports below 1024 are considered "privileged" ports and require root or administrator privilege to create. This was an early security mechanism; today, with zillions of single-user desktops connected to the Internet, it provides little real security, but the restriction remains.

You may want to listen only on a particular *network interface*. While we tend to think of network addresses as computer addresses, the two are not the same. A network address is actually the address of a particular network card, or network interface connection, on a given computing device. A desktop computer, laptop, Palm handheld, or cellular phone might have only a single interface, hence a single network address. But a large server machine might have two or more interfaces, usually when it is connected to several networks. A network *router* is a box (either special-purpose, e.g., a Cisco router, or general-purpose, e.g., a Unix host) that has interfaces on multiple networks *and* has both the capability and the administrative permission to forward packets from one network to another. A program running on such a server machine might want to provide services only to its inside network or its outside network. One way to accomplish this is by specifying the network interface to be listened on. Suppose you want to provide a different view of web pages for your intranet than you provide to outside customers. For security reasons, you probably wouldn't run both these services on the same machine. But if you wanted to, you could do this by providing the network interface addresses as arguments to the ServerSocket constructor.

However, to use this form of the constructor, you don't have the option of using a string for the network address's name, as you did with the client socket; you must convert it to an InetAddress object. You also have to provide a *backlog* argument, which is the number of connections that can queue up to be accepted before clients are told that your server is too busy. The complete setup is shown in Example 17-2.

*Example 17-2. ListenInside.java*

```
/**
 * ListenInside -- make a server socket that listens only on
 * a particular interface, in this case, one named by INSIDE_HOST.
 */
public class ListenInside {
    /** The TCP port for the service. */
    public static final short PORT = 9999;
    /** The name of the network interface. */
    public static final String INSIDE_HOST = "acmewidgets-inside";
    /** The number of clients allowed to queue */
    public static final int BACKLOG = 10;

    public static void main(String[] argv) throws IOException {
        ServerSocket sock;
        Socket  clientSock;
        try {
            sock = new ServerSocket(PORT, BACKLOG,
                InetAddress.getByName(INSIDE_HOST));
            while ((clientSock = sock.accept()) != null) {

                // Process it.
                process(clientSock);
            }
```

*Example 17-2. ListenInside.java (continued)*

```
        } catch (IOException e) {
            System.err.println(e);
        }
    }

    /** Hold server's conversation with one client. . */
    static void process(Socket s) throws IOException {
        System.out.println("Connected from  " + INSIDE_HOST + "": " + s.getInetAddress());
        // The conversation would be here.
        s.close();
    }
}
```

The `InetAddress.getByName( )` looks up the given hostname in a system-dependent way, referring to a configuration file in the */etc* or *\windows* directory, or to some kind of resolver such as the Domain Name System. Consult a good book on networking and system administration if you need to modify this data.

# 17.2   Returning a Response (String or Binary)

## Problem

You need to write a string or binary data to the client.

## Solution

The socket gives you an `InputStream` and an `OutputStream`. Use them.

## Discussion

The client socket examples in the previous chapter called the `getInputStream( )` and `getOutputStream( )` methods. These examples do the same. The main difference is that these ones get the socket from a `ServerSocket`'s `accept( )` method. Another distinction is, by definition, that normally the server creates or modifies the data and sends it to the client. Example 17-3 is a simple `Echo` server, which the `Echo` client of Recipe 16.4 can connect to. This server handles one complete connection with a client, then goes back and does the `accept( )` to wait for the next client.

*Example 17-3. EchoServer.java*

```
/**
 * EchoServer - create server socket, do I-O on it.
 */
public class EchoServer {
    /** Our server-side rendezvous socket */
    protected ServerSocket sock;
    /** The port number to use by default */
    public final static int ECHOPORT = 7;
```

---

*Example 17-3. EchoServer.java (continued)*

```
/** Flag to control debugging */
protected boolean debug = true;

/** main: construct and run */
public static void main(String[] argv) {
    new EchoServer(ECHOPORT).handle();
}

/** Construct an EchoServer on the given port number */
public EchoServer(int port) {
    try {
        sock = new ServerSocket(port);
    } catch (IOException e) {
        System.err.println("I/O error in setup");
        System.err.println(e);
        System.exit(1);
    }
}

/** This handles the connections */
protected void handle() {
    Socket ios = null;
    BufferedReader is = null;
    PrintWriter os = null;
    while (true) {
        try {
            ios = sock.accept();
            System.err.println("Accepted from " +
                ios.getInetAddress().getHostName());
            is = new BufferedReader(
                new InputStreamReader(ios.getInputStream(), "8859_1"));
            os = new PrintWriter(
                    new OutputStreamWriter(
                        ios.getOutputStream(), "8859_1"), true);
            String echoLine;
            while ((echoLine = is.readLine()) != null) {
                System.err.println("Read " + echoLine);
                os.print(echoLine + "\r\n"); os.flush();
                System.err.println("Wrote " + echoLine);
            }
            System.err.println("All done!");
        } catch (IOException e) {
            System.err.println(e);
        } finally {
            try {
                if (is != null)
                    is.close();
                if (os != null)
                    os.close();
                if (ios != null)
                    ios.close();
            } catch (IOException e) {
```

*Example 17-3. EchoServer.java (continued)*

```
                    // These are unlikely, but might indicate that
                    // the other end shut down early, a disk filled up
                    // but wasn't detected until close, etc.
                    System.err.println("IO Error in close");
                }
            }
        }
        /*NOTREACHED*/
    }
}
```

To send a string across an arbitrary network connection, some authorities recommend sending both the carriage return and the newline character. This explains the \r\n in the code. If the other end is a DOS program or a Telnet-like program, it may be expecting both characters. On the other hand, if you are writing both ends, you can simply use println( )—followed always by an explicit flush( ) before you read— to prevent the deadlock of having both ends trying to read with one end's data still in the PrintWriter's buffer!

If you need to process binary data, use the data streams from java.io instead of the readers/writers. I need a server for the DaytimeBinary program of Recipe 16.5. In operation, it should look like the following.

```
C:\javasrc\network>java DaytimeBinary
Remote time is 3161316799
BASE_DIFF is 2208988800
Time diff == 952284799
Time on localhost is Sun Mar 05 19:33:19 GMT 2000

C:\javasrc\network>time/t
Current time is  7:33:23.84p

C:\javasrc\network>date/t
Current date is Sun 03-05-2000

C:\javasrc\network>
```

Well, it happens that I have such a program in my arsenal, so I present it in Example 17-4. Note that it directly uses certain public constants defined in the client class. Normally these are defined in the server class and used by the client, but I wanted to present the client code first.

*Example 17-4. DaytimeServer.java*

```
/**
 * DaytimeServer - send the binary time.
 */
public class DaytimeServer {
    /** Our server-side rendezvous socket */
    ServerSocket sock;
```

*Example 17-4. DaytimeServer.java (continued)*

```java
/** The port number to use by default */
public final static int PORT = 37;

/** main: construct and run */
public static void main(String[] argv) {
    new DaytimeServer(PORT).runService();
}

/** Construct a DaytimeServer on the given port number */
public DaytimeServer(int port) {
    try {
        sock = new ServerSocket(port);
    } catch (IOException e) {
        System.err.println("I/O error in setup\n" + e);
        System.exit(1);
    }
}

/** This handles the connections */
protected void runService() {
    Socket ios = null;
    DataOutputStream os = null;
    while (true) {
        try {
            System.out.println("Waiting for connection on port " + PORT);
            ios = sock.accept();
            System.err.println("Accepted from " +
                ios.getInetAddress().getHostName());
            os = new DataOutputStream(ios.getOutputStream());
            long time = System.currentTimeMillis();

            time /= DaytimeBinary.MSEC;     // Daytime Protocol is in seconds

            // Convert to Java time base.
            time += DaytimeBinary.BASE_DIFF;

            // Write it, truncating cast to int since it is using
            // the Internet Daytime protocol which uses 4 bytes.
            // This will fail in the year 2038, along with all
            // 32-bit timekeeping systems based from 1970.
            // Remember, you read about the Y2038 crisis here first!
            os.writeInt((int)time);
            os.close();
        } catch (IOException e) {
            System.err.println(e);
        }
    }
}
```

## 17.3  Returning Object Information

### Problem

You need to return an object.

### Solution

Create the object you need, and write it using an `ObjectOutputStream` created on top of the socket's output stream.

### Discussion

The program in Example 16-7 in the previous chapter reads a `Date` object over an `ObjectInputStream`. Example 17-5, the `DaytimeObjectServer`—the other end of that process—is a program that constructs a `Date` object each time it's connected to and returns it to the client.

*Example 17-5. DaytimeObjectServer.java*

```
/*
 * DaytimeObjectServer - server for the non-standard Time (object) service.
 */
public class DaytimeObjectServer {
    /** The TCP port for the object time service. */
    public static final short TIME_PORT = 1951;

    public static void main(String[] argv) {
        ServerSocket sock;
        Socket  clientSock;
        try {
            sock = new ServerSocket(TIME_PORT);
            while ((clientSock = sock.accept()) != null) {
                System.out.println("Accept from " +
                    clientSock.getInetAddress());
                ObjectOutputStream os = new ObjectOutputStream(
                    clientSock.getOutputStream());

                // Construct and write the Object
                os.writeObject(new Date());

                os.close();
            }

        } catch (IOException e) {
            System.err.println(e);
        }
    }
}
```

# 17.4  Handling Multiple Clients

## Problem

Your server needs to handle multiple clients.

## Solution

Use a thread for each.

## Discussion

In the C world, several mechanisms allow a server to handle multiple clients. One is to use a special "system call" select( ) or poll( ), which notifies the server when any of a set of file/socket descriptors is ready to read, ready to write, or has an error. By including its *rendezvous socket* (equivalent to our ServerSocket) in this list, the C-based server can read from any of a number of clients in any order. Java does not provide this call, as it is not readily implementable on some Java platforms. Instead, Java uses the general-purpose Thread mechanism, as described in Recipe 24.10. Threads are, in fact, one of the other mechanisms available to the C programmer on most platforms. Each time the code accepts a new connection from the ServerSocket, it immediately constructs and starts a new thread object to process that client.*

The code to implement accepting on a socket is pretty simple, apart from having to catch IOExceptions:

```
/** Run the main loop of the Server. */
void runServer( ) {
    while (true) {
        try {
            Socket clntSock = sock.accept( );
            new Handler(clntSock).start( );
        } catch(IOException e) {
            System.err.println(e);
        }
    }
}
```

To use a thread, you must either subclass Thread or implement Runnable. The Handler class must be a subclass of Thread for this code to work as written; if Handler instead implemented the Runnable interface, the code would pass an instance of the Runnable into the constructor for Thread, as in:

```
Thread t = new Thread(new Handler(clntSock));
t.start( );
```

---

* There are some limits to how many threads you can have, which affect only very large, enterprise-scale servers. You can't expect to have thousands of threads running in the standard Java runtime. For large, high-performance servers, you may wish to resort to native code (see Recipe 26.5) using select( ) or poll( ).

But as written, `Handler` is constructed using the normal socket returned by the accept( ) call, and normally calls the socket's getInputStream( ) and getOutputStream( ) methods and holds its conversation in the usual way. I'll present a full implementation, a threaded echo client. First, a session showing it in use:

```
$ java  EchoServerThreaded
EchoServerThreaded ready for connections.
Socket starting: Socket[addr=localhost/127.0.0.1,port=2117,localport=7]
Socket starting: Socket[addr=darian/192.168.1.50,port=13386,localport=7]
Socket starting: Socket[addr=darian/192.168.1.50,port=22162,localport=7]
Socket ENDED: Socket[addr=darian/192.168.1.50,port=22162,localport=7]
Socket ENDED: Socket[addr=darian/192.168.1.50,port=13386,localport=7]
Socket ENDED: Socket[addr=localhost/127.0.0.1,port=2117,localport=7]
```

Here, I connected to the server once with my `EchoClient` program and, while still connected, called it up again (and again) with an operating system-provided Telnet client. The server communicated with all the clients concurrently, sending the answers from the first client back to the first client, and the data from the second client back to the second client. In short, it works. I ended the sessions with the end-of-file character in the program and used the normal disconnect mechanism from the Telnet client. Example 17-6 is the code for the server.

*Example 17-6. EchoServerThreaded.java*

```
/**
 * Threaded Echo Server, sequential allocation scheme.
 */
public class EchoServerThreaded {

    public static final int ECHOPORT = 7;

    public static void main(String[] av)
    {
        new EchoServerThreaded( ).runServer( );
    }

    public void runServer( )
    {
        ServerSocket sock;
        Socket clientSocket;

        try {
            sock = new ServerSocket(ECHOPORT);

            System.out.println("EchoServerThreaded ready for connections.");

            /* Wait for a connection */
            while(true){
                clientSocket = sock.accept( );
                /* Create a thread to do the communication, and start it */
                new Handler(clientSocket).start( );
            }
```

*Example 17-6. EchoServerThreaded.java (continued)*

```java
        } catch(IOException e) {
            /* Crash the server if IO fails. Something bad has happened */
            System.err.println("Could not accept " + e);
            System.exit(1);
        }
    }

    /** A Thread subclass to handle one client conversation. */
    class Handler extends Thread {
        Socket sock;

        Handler(Socket s) {
            sock = s;
        }

        public void run()
        {
            System.out.println("Socket starting: " + sock);
            try {
                DataInputStream is = new DataInputStream(
                    sock.getInputStream());
                PrintStream os = new PrintStream(
                    sock.getOutputStream(), true);
                String line;
                while ((line = is.readLine()) != null) {
                    os.print(line + "\r\n");
                    os.flush();
                }
                sock.close();
            } catch (IOException e) {
                System.out.println("IO Error on socket " + e);
                return;
            }
            System.out.println("Socket ENDED: " + sock);
        }
    }
}
```

A lot of short transactions can degrade performance since each client causes the creation of a new threaded object. If you know or can reliably predict the degree of concurrency that is needed, an alternative paradigm involves the precreation of a fixed number of threads. But then how do you control their access to the ServerSocket? A look at the ServerSocket class documentation reveals that the accept() method is not synchronized, meaning that any number of threads can call the method concurrently. This could cause bad things to happen. So I use the synchronized keyword around this call to ensure that only one client runs in it at a time, because it updates global data. When no clients are connected, you will have one (randomly selected) thread running in the ServerSocket object's accept() method, waiting for a connection, plus *n–1* threads waiting for the first thread to return from the method. As soon as the first thread manages to accept a connection, it goes off and holds its conversation, releasing its lock in the process so that another randomly chosen thread is allowed into the accept( ) method. Each thread's run( ) method has an indefinite loop beginning with an accept( ) and then holding the conversation. The result is that client connections can get started more quickly, at a cost of slightly greater server startup time. Doing it this way also avoids the overhead of constructing a new Handler or Thread object each time a request comes along. This general approach is similar to what the popular Apache web server does, although it normally creates a number or *pool* of identical processes (instead of threads) to handle client connections. Accordingly, I have modified the EchoServerThreaded class shown in Example 17-6 to work this way, as you can see in Example 17-7.

*Example 17-7. EchoServerThreaded2.java*

```
/**
 * Threaded Echo Server, pre-allocation scheme.
 */
public class EchoServerThreaded2 {

    public static final int ECHOPORT = 7;

    public static final int NUM_THREADS = 4;

    /** Main method, to start the servers. */
    public static void main(String[] av)
    {
        new EchoServerThreaded2(ECHOPORT, NUM_THREADS);
    }

    /** Constructor */
    public EchoServerThreaded2(int port, int numThreads)
    {
        ServerSocket servSock;
        Socket clientSocket;

        try {
            servSock = new ServerSocket(ECHOPORT);

        } catch(IOException e) {
            /* Crash the server if IO fails. Something bad has happened */
            throw new RuntimeException("Could not create ServerSocket " + e);
        }

        // Create a series of threads and start them.
        for (int i=0; i<numThreads; i++) {
            new Handler(servSock, i).start();
        }
    }
```

*Example 17-7. EchoServerThreaded2.java (continued)*

```java
/** A Thread subclass to handle one client conversation. */
class Handler extends Thread {
    ServerSocket servSock;
    int threadNumber;

    /** Construct a Handler. */
    Handler(ServerSocket s, int i) {
        super( );
        servSock = s;
        threadNumber = i;
        setName("Thread " + threadNumber);
    }

    public void run( )
    {
        /* Wait for a connection */
        while (true){
            try {
                System.out.println( getName( ) + " waiting");

                Socket clientSocket;
                // Wait here for the next connection.
                synchronized(servSock) {
                    clientSocket = servSock.accept( );
                }
                System.out.println(getName( ) + " starting, IP=" +
                    clientSocket.getInetAddress( ));
                BufferedReader is = new BufferedReader(new InputStreamReader(
                    clientSocket.getInputStream( ));
                PrintStream os = new PrintStream(
                    clientSocket.getOutputStream( ), true);
                String line;
                while ((line = is.readLine( )) != null) {
                    os.print(line + "\r\n");
                    os.flush( );
                }
                System.out.println(getName( ) + " ENDED ");
                clientSocket.close( );
            } catch (IOException ex) {
                System.out.println(getName( ) + ": IO Error on socket " + ex);
                return;
            }
        }
    }
}
```

# 17.5  Serving the HTTP Protocol

## Problem

You want to serve up a protocol such as HTTP.

## Solution

Create a ServerSocket and write some code that "speaks" the particular protocol.

## Discussion

This example just constructs a ServerSocket and listens on it. When connections come in, they are replied to using the HTTP protocol. So it is somewhat more involved than the simple Echo server presented in Recipe 17.2. However, it's not a complete web server; the filename in the request is ignored, and a standard message is always returned. This is thus a *very* simple web server; it follows only the bare minimum of the HTTP protocol needed to send its response back. A somewhat more complete example is presented in Recipe 24.8, after the issues of multithreading have been covered. For a real web server written in Java, get Tomcat from *http://jakarta. apache.org/tomcat/*. The code shown in Example 17-8, however, is enough to understand how to structure a simple server that communicates using a protocol.

*Example 17-8. WebServer0.java*

```java
import java.net.*;
import java.util.StringTokenizer;
import java.io.*;

/**
 * A very very very simple Web server.
 *
 * There is only one response to all requests, and it's hard-coded.
 * This version is not threaded and doesn't do very much.
 * Really just a proof of concept.
 * However, it is still useful on notebooks in case somebody connects
 * to you on the Web port by accident (or otherwise).
 *
 * Can't claim to be fully standards-conforming, but has been
 * tested with Netscape Communicator and with the Lynx text browser.
 *
 * @author    Ian Darwin, http://www.darwinsys.com/
 * @version   $Id: ch17,v 1.4 2004/05/04 18:04:54 ian Exp $
 * @see       webserver/* for more fully-fleshed-out version(s).
 */
public class WebServer0 {
    public static final int HTTP = 80;
    ServerSocket s;
```

*Example 17-8. WebServer0.java (continued)*

```java
/**
 * Main method, just creates a server and call its runServer().
 */
public static void main(String[] argv) throws Exception {
    System.out.println("DarwinSys JavaWeb Server 0.0 starting...");
    WebServer0 w = new WebServer0();
    w.runServer(HTTP);          // never returns!!
}

/** Get the actual ServerSocket; deferred until after Constructor
 * so subclass can mess with ServerSocketFactory (e.g., to do SSL).
 * @param port The port number to listen on
 */
protected ServerSocket getServerSocket(int port) throws Exception {
    return new ServerSocket(port);
}

/** RunServer accepts connections and passes each one to handler. */
public void runServer(int port) throws Exception {
    s = getServerSocket(port);
    while (true) {
        try {
            Socket us = s.accept();
            Handler(us);
        } catch(IOException e) {
            System.err.println(e);
            System.exit(0);
            return;
        }

    }
}

/** Handler() handles one conversation with a Web client.
 * This is the only part of the program that "knows" HTTP.
 */
public void Handler(Socket s) {
    BufferedReader is;    // inputStream, from Viewer
    PrintWriter os;       // outputStream, to Viewer
    String request;       // what Viewer sends us.
    try {
        String from = s.getInetAddress().toString();
        System.out.println("Accepted connection from " + from);
        is = new BufferedReader(new InputStreamReader(s.getInputStream()));
        request = is.readLine();
        StringTokenizer st = new StringTokenizer(request);
        System.out.println(""Request: " + request);
        String nullLine = is.readLine();
        os = new PrintWriter(s.getOutputStream(), true);
        os.println("HTTP/1.0 200 Here is your data");
        os.println("Content-type: text/html");
        os.println("Server-name: DarwinSys NULL Java WebServer 0");
```

*Example 17-8. WebServer0.java (continued)*

```
        String reply = "<html><head>" +
            "<title>Wrong System Reached</title></head>\n" +
            "<h1>Welcome, " + from + ", but...</h1>\n" +
            "<p>You have reached a desktop machine " +
            "that does not run a real Web service.\n" +
            "<p>Please pick another system!</p>\n" +
            "<p>Or view <A HREF=\"http://www.darwinsys.com/java/server.html\">" +
            "the WebServer0 source (at the Authors Web Site)</A>.</p>\n" +
            "<hr/><em>Java-based WebServer0</em><hr/>\n" +
            "</html>\n";
        os.println("Content-length: " + reply.length());
        os.println("");
        os.println(reply);
        os.flush();
        s.close();
    } catch (IOException e) {
        System.out.println("IOException " + e);
    }
    return;
    }
}
```

# 17.6   Securing a Web Server with SSL and JSSE

## Problem

You want to protect your network traffic from prying eyes or malicious modification, while the data is in transit.

## Solution

Use the Java Secure Socket Extension, JSSE, to encrypt your traffic.

## Discussion

Introduced in JDK 1.4, JSSE provides services at a number of levels, but the simplest way to use it is simply to get your ServerSocket from an SSLServerSocketFactory instead of using the ServerSocket constructor directly. SSL is the Secure Sockets Layer; a revised version is known as TLS. It is specific to use on the Web. To secure other protocols, you'd have to use a different form of the SocketFactory.

The SSLServerSocketFactory returns a ServerSocket that is set up to do SSL encryption. The code in Example 17-9 uses this technique to override the getServerSocket( ) method in Recipe 17.5. If you're thinking this is too easy, you're wrong!

*Example 17-9. JSSEWebServer0*

```
import java.net.ServerSocket;
import javax.net.ssl.SSLServerSocketFactory;
```

*Example 17-9. JSSEWebServer0 (continued)*

```java
/**
 * JSSEWebServer - subclass trivial WebServer0 to make it use SSL.
 * @version $Id: ch17,v 1.4 2004/05/04 18:04:54 ian Exp $
 */
public class JSSEWebServer0 extends WebServer0 {

    public static final int HTTPS = 8443;

    public static void main(String[] args) throws Exception {
        System.out.println("DarwinSys JSSE Server 0.0 starting...");
        JSSEWebServer0 w = new JSSEWebServer0();
        w.runServer(HTTPS);          // never returns!!
    }

    /** Get an HTTPS ServerSocket using JSSE.
     * @see WebServer0#getServerSocket(int)
     * @throws ClassNotFoundException if the SecurityProvider cannot be instantiated.
     */
    protected ServerSocket getServerSocket(int port) throws Exception {

        SSLServerSocketFactory ssf = (SSLServerSocketFactory)SSLServerSocketFactory.
getDefault();

        return ssf.createServerSocket(port);
    }

}
```

That is, indeed, all the Java code one needs to write. You do have to set up a Web Server Certificate. For demonstration purposes, this can be a self-signed certificate; the steps in Recipe 23.14 (Steps 1–4) will suffice. You have to tell the JSSE layer where to find your keystore:

```
java -Djavax.net.ssl.keyStore=/home/ian/.keystore -Djavax.net.ssl.
keyStorePassword=secrit JSSEWebServer0
```

The typical client browser raises its eyebrows at a self-signed certificate (see Figure 17-1), but, if the user OKs it, will accept the certificate. Figure 17-2 shows the output of the simple WebServer0 being displayed over the HTTPS protocol (notice the padlock in the lower right corner).

## See Also

JSSE can do much more than encrypt web server traffic; this is, however, sometimes seen as its most exciting application. For more information on JSSE, see the Sun web site *http://java.sun.com/products/jsse/* or *Java Security* by Scott Oaks (O'Reilly).

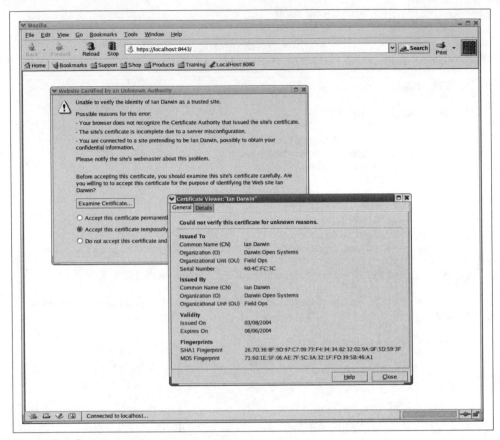

*Figure 17-1. Browser caution*

## 17.7 Network Logging

### Problem

Your class is running inside a server container, and its debugging output is hard to obtain.

### Solution

Use a network-based logger like the JDK 1.4 Logging API, Apache Logging Services Project's log4j, or the simple one shown here.

### Discussion

Getting the debug output from a desktop client is fairly easy on most operating systems. But if the program you want to debug is running in a "container" like a servlet engine or an EJB server, it can be difficult to obtain debugging output, particularly if

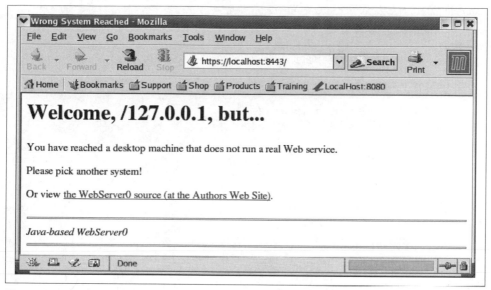

*Figure 17-2. With encryption*

the container is running on a remote computer. It would be convenient if you could have your program send messages back to a program on your desktop machine for immediate display. Needless to say, it's not that hard to do this with Java's socket mechanism.

Several logging APIs can handle this. As of JDK 1.4, Java has a standard logging API (discussed in Recipe 17.9) that talks to various logging mechanisms including Unix syslog. The Apache Logging Services Project produces log4j, which is used in most open source projects that require logging (see Recipe 17.8). And, before these became widely used, I wrote a small, simple API to handle this type of logging function. The JDK logging API and log4j are more fully fleshed out and can write to such destinations as a file, an OutputStream or Writer, or a remote log4j, Unix syslog, or Windows Event Log server.

The program being debugged is the "client" from the logging API's point of view—even though it may be running in a server-side container such as a web server or application server—since the "network client" is the program that initiates the connection. The program that runs on your desktop machine is the "server" program for sockets since it waits for a connection to come along.

Example 17-10 is a simple client program, NetLogSimple, using my simple Netlog API.

*Example 17-10. NetLogSimple.java*

```
/* A simple example of using the NetLog program.
 * Unrealistic in that it's standalone; this API is
 * intended for use inside another program, possibly
 * a servlet or EJB.
 */
```

*Example 17-10. NetLogSimple.java (continued)*

```java
public class NetLogSimple {

    public static void main(String[] args) throws java.io.IOException {

        System.out.println("NetLogSimple: Starting...");

        // Get the connection to the NetLog
        NetLog nl = new NetLog( );

        // Show sending a String
        nl.log("Hello Java");

        // Show sending Objects
        nl.log(new java.util.Date( ));
        nl.log(nl);

        // Show sending null and "" (normally an accident...)
        nl.log(null);
        nl.log("");

        // All done, close the log
        nl.close( );

        System.out.println("NetLogSimple: Done...");
    }
}
```

In Figure 17-3, I show both the server and client running side by side.

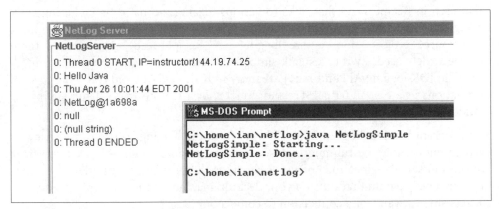

*Figure 17-3. NetLog server and client*

The client-side API and the server code are both online. Example 17-11 shows the code for the key parts of my NetLog server.

*Example 17-11. NetLogServer.java*

```java
public class NetLogServer {

    public static final int PORT = 65432;

    public static final int NUM_THREADS = 8;

    JFrame theFrame;
    JTextArea theTextArea;

    /** Main method, to start the servers. */
    public static void main(String[] av)
    {
        new NetLogServer(PORT, NUM_THREADS);
    }

    /** Constructor */
    public NetLogServer(int port, int numThreads)
    {
        ServerSocket servSock;
        Socket clientSocket;

        try {
            servSock = new ServerSocket(PORT);

        } catch(IOException e) {
            /* Crash the server if IO fails. Something bad has happened */
            System.err.println("Could not create ServerSocket " + e);
            System.exit(1);
            return;  /*NOTREACHED*/
        }

        // Build the GUI - must be before Handler constructors!
        theFrame   = new JFrame("NetLog Server");
        theTextArea = new JTextArea(24, 80);
        theTextArea.setEditable(false);
        theTextArea.setBorder(BorderFactory.createTitledBorder("NetLogServer"));
        theFrame.getContentPane().add(new JScrollPane(theTextArea));

        // Now start the Threads
        for (int i=0; i<numThreads; i++) {
            new Handler(servSock, i).start();
        }

        theFrame.pack();
        theFrame.setVisible(true);
        theFrame.setDefaultCloseOperation(JFrame.EXIT_ON_CLOSE);
    }

    public synchronized void log(int tid, String s) {
        StringBuffer sb = new StringBuffer();
        sb.append(tid);
        sb.append(": ");
```

*Example 17-11. NetLogServer.java (continued)*

```
        if (s == null) {
            sb.append("(null)");
        }
        else if (s.length( ) == 0) {
            sb.append("(null string)");
        }
        else
            sb.append(s);

        sb.append('\n');
        theTextArea.append(sb.toString( ));
        theTextArea.setCaretPosition(theTextArea.getText( ).length( ));
        theFrame.toFront( );
    }

    /** A Thread subclass to handle one client conversation. */
    class Handler extends Thread {
        ServerSocket servSock;
        int tid;

        /** Construct a Handler. */
        Handler(ServerSocket s, int i) {
            super( );
            servSock = s;
            tid = i;
            setName("Thread " + tid);
        }

        public void run( )
        {
            /* Wait for a connection */
            while (true){
                try {
                    // log(tid, getName( ) + " waiting");
                    Socket clientSocket = servSock.accept( );
                    log(tid,getName( ) + " START, IP=" +
                        clientSocket.getInetAddress( ));
                    BufferedReader is = new BufferedReader(
                        new InputStreamReader(clientSocket.getInputStream( )));
                    String line;
                    while ((line = is.readLine( )) != null) {
                        // System.out.println(">> " + line);
                        log(tid,line);
                    }
                    log(tid,getName( ) + " ENDED ");
                    clientSocket.close( );
                } catch (IOException ex) {
                    log(tid, getName( ) + ": IO Error on socket " + ex);
                    return;
                }
            }
        }
    }
}
```

## See Also

Better network loggers are available. The Apache Foundation Logging Services Project (*http://logging.apache.org*) offers log4j, which provides a similar service (see Recipe 17.8). JDK 1.4 includes an Event Logger mechanism, described in Recipe 17.9.

If you want to run any network-based logger, you need to be very aware of security issues. One common form of attack is a simple denial-of-service during which the attacker makes a lot of connections to your server in order to slow it down. If you had extended this program by writing the log to disk, the attacker could fill up your disk by sending lots of garbage. However, because this example displays the log on the screen, you would see this happening. Don't leave the server running while you're not around to watch it!

The simplest non-network logger around is probably my Debug class described in Recipe 1.11.

# 17.8   Network Logging with log4j

## Problem

You wish to write log file messages using log4j.

## Solution

Get a Logger and use its log( ) method or the convenience methods. Control logging by changing a properties file. Make it network-based by using the org.apache.log4j. net package.

## Discussion

Logging using log4j is simple, convenient, and flexible. You need to get a Logger object from the static method Logger.getLogger( ), pass in a configuration identifier that can either be a hierarchical name like com.darwinsys or a Class object (e.g., MyApp.class) that generates the full package and class name. This name can be used in the configuration file to specify the level of detail that you want to see from the logger. The Logger has public void methods—debug( ), info( ), warn( ), error( ) and fatal( )—each of which takes one Object to be logged. As with System.out.println( ), if you pass in anything that is not a String, its toString( ) method is called. A generic logging method is also included:

```
public void log(Level level, Object message);
```

The Level class is defined in the log4j package. The standard levels are in this order: DEBUG < INFO < WARN < ERROR < FATAL. So debug messages are least important, and fatal are most important. Each Logger has a level associated with it; messages whose level is less than the Logger's level are silently discarded.

A simple application can log messages using these few statements:

```
import org.apache.log4j.Logger;
import org.apache.log4j.PropertyConfigurator;

public class Log4JDemo {
    public static void main(String[] args) {

        Logger myLogger = Logger.getLogger("com.darwinsys");

        Object o = new Object();
        myLogger.info("I created an object: " + o);

    }
}
```

If you compile and run this program with no *log4j.properties* file, it complains and does not produce any logging output:

```
ant run.log4jdemo
Buildfile: build.xml
run.log4jdemo:
     [java] log4j:WARN No appenders could be found for logger (com.darwinsys).
     [java] log4j:WARN Please initialize the log4j system properly.
```

So we need to create a configuration file, whose default name is *log4j.properties*. You can also provide the log file name via System Properties: -Dlog4j.configuration=URL.

Every Logger has a Level to specify what level of messages to write, and an Appender, which is the code that writes the messages out. A ConsoleAppender writes to System. out, of course; other loggers write to files, operating system-level loggers, and so on. A simple configuration file looks something like this:

```
# Set root logger level to DEBUG and its only appender to APP1.
log4j.rootLogger=DEBUG, APP1

# APP1 is set to be a ConsoleAppender.
log4j.appender.APP1=org.apache.log4j.ConsoleAppender

# APP1 uses PatternLayout.
log4j.appender.APP1.layout=org.apache.log4j.PatternLayout
log4j.appender.APP1.layout.ConversionPattern=%-4r [%t] %-5p %c %x - %m%n
```

This file gives the root logger a level of DEBUG—write all messages—and an appender of APP1, which is configured on the next few lines. Note that I didn't have to refer to the com.darwinsys Logger; since every Logger inherits from the root logger, a simple application needs to configure only the root logger. The properties file can also be an XML document or you can write your own configuration parser (almost nobody does this). With the above file in place, the demonstration works better:

```
$ ant run.log4jdemo
Buildfile: build.xml

init:
```

```
build:

run.log4jdemo:
    [java] 1    [main] INFO  com.darwinsys  - I created an object: java.lang.
Object@bb6086

BUILD SUCCESSFUL
Total time: 1 second
```

A more typical use of logging might be to catch an Exception and log it, as shown in Example 17-12.

*Example 17-12. Log4j—catching and logging*

```
import org.apache.log4j.Logger;
import org.apache.log4j.PropertyConfigurator;

public class Log4JDemo2 {
    public static void main(String[] args) {

        Logger myLogger = Logger.getLogger("com.darwinsys");

        try {
            Object o = new Object();
            if (o != null) {    // bogus, just to show logging
                throw new IllegalArgumentException("Just testing");
            }
            myLogger.info("I created an object: " + o);
        } catch (Exception ex) {
            myLogger.error("Caught Exception: " + ex);
        }
    }
}
```

Much of the flexibility of the log4j package stems from its use of external configuration files; you can enable or disable logging without recompiling the application. A properties file that eliminates all logging might have this entry:

```
log4j.rootLogger=FATAL, APP1
```

Only fatal error messages print; all levels less than that are ignored.

To log from a client to a server on a remote machine, the org.apache.log4j.net package includes several Appenders and servers to connect them to.

For more information on log4j, visit *http://logging.apache.org/log4j/*. log4j is free software, distributed under the Apache Software Foundation license.

# 17.9   Network Logging with JDK 1.4

## Problem

You wish to write logging messages using the JDK 1.4 logging mechanism.

## Solution

Get a Logger, and use it to log your messages and/or exceptions.

## Discussion

The JDK 1.4 Logging API (package java.util.logging) is similar to, and obviously inspired by, the log4j package. You acquire a Logger object by calling the static Logger.getLogger( ) with a descriptive String. You then use instance methods to write to the log; these methods include:

```
public void log(java.util.logging.LogRecord);
public void log(java.util.logging.Level,String);
// and a variety of overloaded log() methods
public void logp(java.util.logging.Level,String,String,String);
public void logrb(java.util.logging.Level,String,String,String,String);

// Convenience routines for tracing program flow
public void entering(String,String);
public void entering(String,String,Object);
public void entering(String,String,Object[]);
public void exiting(String,String);
public void exiting(String,String,Object);
public void throwing(String,String,Throwable);

// Convenience routines for log() with a given level
public void severe(String);
public void warning(String);
public void info(String);
public void config(String);
public void fine(String);
public void finer(String);
public void finest(String);
```

As with log4j, every Logger object has a given logging level, and messages below that level are silently discarded:

```
public void setLevel(java.util.logging.Level);
public java.util.logging.Level getLevel();
public boolean isLoggable(java.util.logging.Level);
```

As with log4j, objects handle the writing of the log. Each logger has a Handler:

```
public synchronized void addHandler(java.util.logging.Handler);
public synchronized void removeHandler(java.util.logging.Handler);
public synchronized java.util.logging.Handler[] getHandlers();
```

and each Handler has a Formatter, which formats a LogRecord for display. By providing your own Formatter, you have more control over how the information being passed into the log gets formatted.

Unlike log4j, the 1.4 logging mechanism has a default configuration, so this is a minimal logging example program:

---

```
import java.util.logging.Logger;

public class Log14Demo {
    public static void main(String[] args) {

        Logger myLogger = Logger.getLogger("com.darwinsys");

        Object o = new Object();
        myLogger.info("I created an object: " + o);
    }
}
```

Running it prints the following:

```
C:> java Log14Demo
Mar 8, 2004 7:48:26 PM Log14Demo main
INFO: I created an object: java.lang.Object@57f0dc
C:>
```

As with log4j, the typical use is in logging caught exceptions; the code for this is in Example 17-13.

*Example 17-13. Log14Demo2—catching and logging*

```
import java.util.logging.Logger;
import java.util.logging.LogRecord;
import java.util.logging.Level;

public class Log14Demo2 {
    public static void main(String[] args) {

        Logger myLogger = Logger.getLogger("com.darwinsys");

        try {
            Object o = new Object();
            if (o != null) {     // bogus, just to show logging
                throw new IllegalArgumentException("Just testing");
            }
            myLogger.info("I created an object: " + o);
        } catch (Throwable t) {
            LogRecord msg = new LogRecord(Level.SEVERE,
                "Caught exception ");
            msg.setThrown(t);
            myLogger.log(msg);
        }
    }
}
```

# 17.10 Finding Network Interfaces

## Problem

You wish to find out about the computer's networking arrangements.

## Solution

Use the NetworkInterface class introduced in JDK 1.4.

## Discussion

Every computer on a network has one or more *network interfaces*. On typical desktop machines, a network interface represents a network card or network port and often some software network interfaces, such as the loopback interface. Each interface has an operating system-defined name. On most versions of Unix, these devices have a two- or three-character device driver name plus a digit (starting from 0); for example, de0 and de1 for the first and second Digital Equipment* DC21x4x-based Ethernet card, xl0 for a 3Com EtherLink XL, and so on. On Linux, these interfaces are typically named eth0, eth1, and so on, without regard for the manufacturer. The loopback interface is usually lo0, at least on Unix-like platforms.

So what? Most of the time this is of no consequence to you. If you have only one network connection, like a dialup or cable link to your ISP, you really don't care. Where this matters is on a server, where you might need to find the address for a given network, for example. The NetworkInterface class lets you find out. It has static methods for listing the interfaces and other methods for finding the addresses associated with a given interface. The program in Example 17-14 shows some examples of using this class. Running it prints the names of all the local interfaces. If you happen to be on a computer named *daroad*, it prints the machine's network address; if not, you probably want to change it to accept the local computer's name from the command line; this is left as an exercise for the reader.

*Example 17-14. NetworkInterfaceDemo.java*

```
/**
 * Show some uses of the new-in-1.4 NetworkInterface class.
 */
public class NetworkInterfaceDemo {
    public static void main(String[] a) throws IOException {
        Enumeration list = NetworkInterface.getNetworkInterfaces();
        while (list.hasMoreElements()) {
            // Get one NetworkInterface
            NetworkInterface iface = (NetworkInterface) list.nextElement();
            // Print its name
            System.out.println(iface.getDisplayName());
            Enumeration addrs = iface.getInetAddresses();
            // And its address(es)
            while (addrs.hasMoreElements()) {
                InetAddress addr = (InetAddress) addrs.nextElement();
                System.out.println(addr);
            }
```

---

\* Digital Equipment was absorbed by Compaq, which was then absorbed by HP, but the name remains de because the engineers who name such things don't care for corporate mergers anyway.

*Example 17-14. NetworkInterfaceDemo.java (continued)*

```
    }
    // Try to get the Interface for a given local (this machine's) address
    InetAddress destAddr = InetAddress.getByName("daroad");
    try {
        NetworkInterface dest = NetworkInterface.getByInetAddress(destAddr);
        System.out.println("Address for " + destAddr + "" is " + dest);
    } catch (SocketException ex) {
        System.err.println("Couldn't get address for " + destAddr);
    }
  }
}
```

# 17.11 Program: A Java Chat Server

This program implements a simple chat server (Example 17-15) that works with the chat applet from Recipe 16.10. It accepts connections from an arbitrary number of clients; any message sent from one client is broadcast to all clients. In addition to ServerSockets, it demonstrates the use of threads (see Chapter 24). Since there are interactions among clients, this server needs to keep track of all the clients it has at any one time. I use an ArrayList (see Recipe 7.3) to serve as an expandable list and am careful to use the synchronized keyword around all accesses to this list to prevent one thread from accessing it while another is modifying it (this is discussed in Chapter 24).

*Example 17-15. ChatServer.java*

```
/** Simple Chat Server to go with our Trivial Chat Client.
 */
public class ChatServer {
    /** What I call myself in system messages */
    protected final static String CHATMASTER_ID = "ChatMaster";
    /** What goes between any handle and the message */
    protected final static String SEP = ": ";
    /** The Server Socket */
    protected ServerSocket servSock;
    /** The list of my current clients */
    protected ArrayList clients;
    /** Debugging state */
    private boolean DEBUG = false;

    /** Main just constructs a ChatServer, which should never return */
    public static void main(String[] argv) {
        System.out.println("DarwinSys Chat Server 0.1 starting...");
        ChatServer w = new ChatServer();
        w.runServer();                 // should never return.
        System.out.println("**ERROR* Chat Server 0.1 quitting");
    }
```

*Example 17-15. ChatServer.java (continued)*

```java
/** Construct (and run!) a Chat Service */
ChatServer( ) {
    clients = new ArrayList();
    try {
        servSock = new ServerSocket(Chat.PORTNUM);
        System.out.println("DarwinSys Chat Server Listening on port " +
            Chat.PORTNUM);
    } catch(IOException e) {
        log("IO Exception in ChatServer.<init>" + e);
        System.exit(0);
    }
}

public void runServer( ) {
    try {
        while (true) {
            Socket us = servSock.accept( );
            String hostName = us.getInetAddress( ).getHostName( );
            System.out.println("Accepted from " + hostName);
            ChatHandler cl = new ChatHandler(us, hostName);
            synchronized (clients) {
                clients.add(cl);
                cl.start( );
                if (clients.size( ) == 1)
                    cl.send(CHATMASTER_ID,
                            "Welcome! you're the first one here");
                else {
                    cl.send(CHATMASTER_ID, "Welcome! you're the latest of " +
                        clients.size( ) + " users.");
                }
            }
        }
    } catch(IOException e) {
        log("IO Exception in runServer: " + e);
        System.exit(0);
    }
}

protected void log(String s) {
    System.out.println(s);
}

/** Inner class to handle one conversation */
protected class ChatHandler extends Thread {
    /** The client socket */
    protected Socket clientSock;
    /** BufferedReader for reading from socket */
    protected BufferedReader is;
    /** PrintWriter for sending lines on socket */
    protected PrintWriter pw;
    /** The client's host */
    protected String clientIP;
```

*Example 17-15. ChatServer.java (continued)*

```java
    /** String form of user's handle (name) */
    protected String login;

    /* Construct a Chat Handler */
    public ChatHandler(Socket sock, String clnt) throws IOException {
        clientSock = sock;
        clientIP = clnt;
        is = new BufferedReader(
            new InputStreamReader(sock.getInputStream( )));
        pw = new PrintWriter(sock.getOutputStream( ), true);
    }

    /** Each ChatHandler is a Thread, so here's the run( ) method,
     * which handles this conversation.
     */
    public void run( ) {
        String line;
        try {
            while ((line = is.readLine( )) != null) {
                char c = line.charAt(0);
                line = line.substring(1);
                switch (c) {
                case Chat.CMD_LOGIN:
                    if (!Chat.isValidLoginName(line)) {
                        send(CHATMASTER_ID, "LOGIN " + line + " invalid");
                        log("LOGIN INVALID from " + clientIP);
                        continue;
                    }
                    login = line;
                    broadcast(CHATMASTER_ID, login +
                        " joins us, for a total of " +
                        clients.size( ) + " users");
                    break;
                case Chat.CMD_MESG:          // Private message from one user to another.
                    if (login == null) {
                        send(CHATMASTER_ID, "please login first");
                        continue;
                    }
                    int where = line.indexOf(Chat.SEPARATOR);
                    String recip = line.substring(0, where);
                    String mesg = line.substring(where+1);
                    log("MESG: " + login + "-->" + recip + ": "+ mesg);
                    ChatHandler cl = lookup(recip);
                    if (cl == null)
                        psend(CHATMASTER_ID, recip + " not logged in.");
                    else
                        cl.psend(login, mesg);
                    break;
                case Chat.CMD_QUIT:
                    broadcast(CHATMASTER_ID,
                    "Goodbye to "  + login + "@" + clientIP);
                    close( );
```

*Example 17-15. ChatServer.java (continued)*

```
                        return;         // The end of this ChatHandler

                case Chat.CMD_BCAST:    // Message from one user to everybody.
                    if (login != null)
                        broadcast(login, line);
                    else
                        log("B<L FROM " + clientIP);
                    break;
                default:
                    log("Unknown cmd " + c + " from " + login + "@" + clientIP);
                }
            }
        } catch (IOException e) {
            log("IO Exception: " + e);
        } finally {
            // the sock ended, so we're done, bye now
            System.out.println(login + SEP + "All Done");
            synchronized(clients) {
                clients.remove(this);
                if (clients.size() == 0) {
                    System.out.println(CHATMASTER_ID + SEP +
                        "I'm so lonely I could cry...");
                } else if (clients.size() == 1) {
                    ChatHandler last = (ChatHandler)clients.get(0);
                    last.send(CHATMASTER_ID,
                        "Hey, you're talking to yourself again");
                } else {
                    broadcast(CHATMASTER_ID,
                        "There are now " + clients.size() + " users");
                }
            }
        }
    }

    protected void close() {
        if (clientSock == null) {
            log("close when not open");
            return;
        }
        try {
            clientSock.close();
            clientSock = null;
        } catch (IOException e) {
            log("Failure during close to " + clientIP);
        }
    }

    /** Send one message to this user */
    public void send(String sender, String mesg) {
        pw.println(sender + SEP + mesg);
    }
```

*Example 17-15. ChatServer.java (continued)*

```java
    /** Send a private message */
    protected void psend(String sender, String msg) {
        send("<*" + sender + "*>", msg);
    }

    /** Send one message to all users */
    public void broadcast(String sender, String mesg) {
        System.out.println("Broadcasting " + sender + SEP + mesg);
        for (int i=0; i<clients.size(); i++) {
            ChatHandler sib = (ChatHandler)clients.get(i);
            if (DEBUG)
                System.out.println("Sending to " + sib);
            sib.send(sender, mesg);
        }
        if (DEBUG) System.out.println("Done broadcast");
    }

    protected ChatHandler lookup(String nick) {
        synchronized(clients) {
            for (int i=0; i<clients.size(); i++) {
                ChatHandler cl = (ChatHandler)clients.get(i);
                if (cl.login.equals(nick))
                    return cl;
            }
        }
        return null;
    }

    /** Present this ChatHandler as a String */
    public String toString() {
        return "ChatHandler[" + login + "]";
    }
  }
}
```

I've used this code with a number of clients connected concurrently, and no difficulties were found.

## See Also

The server side of any network mechanism is extremely sensitive to security issues. It is easy for one misconfigured or poorly written server program to compromise the security of an entire network! Of the many books on network security, two stand out: *Firewalls and Internet Security* by William R. Cheswick, Steven M. Bellovin, and Aviel D. Rubin (Addison Wesley) and *Hacking Exposed* by Stuart McClure, Joel Scambray, and George Kurtz (McGraw-Hill).

This completes my discussion of server-side Java using sockets. Next, I'll return to the client side to discuss applets and some useful client-side recipes. Later, in Chapter 22, I show an alternate technology that can be used to implement both sides of the chat program in a more object-oriented manner. Finally, a chat server could also be implemented using JMS (Java Message Service), a newer API that handles store-and-forward message processing. This is beyond the scope of this book, but there's an example of such a chat server in O'Reilly's *Java Message Service* by Richard Monson-Haefel and David Chappell.

# CHAPTER 18

# Network Clients II: Applets and Web Clients

## 18.0 Introduction

In Chapter 16, I discussed straightforward client applications that communicate over a socket. Chapter 17 covered simple server topics. Now we turn our attention to a variety of other client topics. First let's look at Java-based web applet client programs. Applets are, as you probably know, small programs that run inside and under the control of a web browser. There's a discussion of `Applet` versus `JApplet` and the `Applet` methods. Deploying an applet is no different from deploying a web page—you simply copy it into the web server directory—but you need an HTML page to invoke it (discussed in Recipe 18.1). We then discuss some additional client-side topics, such as loading a URL, that apply both to applets and to applications. Other books talk about servlets, which are programs similar to applets but designed to run inside the process of a web server. Applet deployment requires some considerations; see Recipe 23.6 for a means of ensuring that a user's browser has a Java runtime compatible with your applet. Recipe 23.13 contains information on Java Web Start, which combines applet-like downloading with full application capabilities.

## 18.1 Embedding Java in a Web Page

### Problem

You need to deploy a Java applet.

### Solution

Use an `<applet>` tag in an HTML page.

### Discussion

While this is not the place for a dissertation on the details of HTML, you should at least know that HTML is a tag-based textual language for writing web pages. The tags (officially called *elements*) have short names, such as p for paragraph and a for anchor (hyperlink). Tag names can be written in uppercase or lowercase, with a preference for lowercase because the emerging standard XHTML[*] requires lowercase. Tags are surrounded by angle brackets, < and >. Modifiers, called *attributes*, go between the tag name and the close angle brackets. For example, the body of a web page might be introduced by `<body bgcolor="white">`, which gives that page the specified background color. Most tags, including body and p, have a corresponding end tag, consisting of a forward slash character (/) and the name of the tag. A paragraph, for example, should begin with `<p>` and end with `</p>`.

In days of yore, it was common to simply use `<P>` between paragraphs, but this mistake stems from not understanding the nature of HTML tags as containers. It was also common to omit the quotation marks around attribute values. You still see old pages done this way and old books or web pages recommending this. You may even see a few examples of that in old code of mine!

The most common way to embed a Java applet is using an `<applet>` tag. Other tags for applets include `<object>` and `<embed>`, which I discuss briefly in Recipe 23.6. The `<applet>` tag has three required parameters (`code`, `width`, and `height`) and several optional ones. Table 18-1 lists these parameters.

*Table 18-1. Applet parameters*

| Parameter | Description |
| --- | --- |
| code | Name of applet class to run |
| object | Name of serialized applet to run |
| width | Width in pixels for applet display |
| height | Height in pixels for applet display |
| codebase | Directory (URL) from which to load class file; needed only if different from place where the HTML page itself is loaded from |
| archive | List of JAR archives in which to look for applet and resources |
| alt | Alternate text to display if applet can't be loaded |
| name | Name of this applet instance |
| align | Horizontal alignment |
| vspace | Vertical space around applet, in pixels |
| hspace | Horizontal space around applet, in pixels |

You may also wish to pass some parameters in to the applet. Since an applet has no main method, there is no command-line communication with the applet. Hence, the applet parameters are included in the HTML page: the `<param>` tags go between the `<applet>` and `</applet>` tags. The following HTML file demonstrates many of these parameters:

---

[*] XHTML is HTML written as though it were XML; see Chapter 21 for XML information.

---

```
<applet
    code="DemoApplet.class" width="400 " height="75"
    codebase="http://www.darwinsys.com/applets/"
    >
    <param  name="text"  value="Java is fun!">
    <hr / >
    If you were using a Java-enabled browser,
    you would see the graphical results instead of this paragraph.
    <hr />
</applet>
```

# 18.2  Applet Techniques

## Problem

You need to write an applet.

## Solution

Write a class that extends java.applet.Applet or javax.swing.JApplet, and use some or all of the applet methods. Start with Applet if you want to use plain AWT and be portable to all browsers; use JApplet if you want Swing capabilities in your applet (see the See Also section at the end of this recipe).

## Discussion

The four Applet "lifecycle" methods that an applet writer can implement are init( ), start( ), stop( ), and destroy( ) (see Table 18-2). The applet's lifecycle is more complex than that of a regular application since the user can make the browser move to a new page, return to a previous page, reload the current page, etc. What's a poor applet to do?

*Table 18-2. Applet methods*

| Method name | Function |
| --- | --- |
| init( ) | Initialize the applet (takes the place of a constructor). |
| start( ) | The page is loaded, or reloaded, or revisited via the Back button... |
| stop( ) | The user is leaving this page, or the applet is scrolled off-screen... |
| destroy( ) | The applet is being unloaded. |

Applets normally use their init( ) method to initialize their state, the same functionality as a constructor in a nonapplet class. This may seem a bit odd for those used to constructors in an OO language. However, it is mandatory for any methods that call applet-specific methods, such as the all-important getParameter( ). Why? In brief, because the browser first constructs the applet—always with the no-argument constructor form, which is much easier for the browser (see Recipe 25.3 for the reasons)—

and then call its setStub( ) method.* The AppletStub is an object provided by the browser, which provides a getAppletContext( ) method, which of course returns an AppletContext object. These objects are both *delegates* (in the design patterns sense). The AppletStub object contains the actual implementation of important methods like getParameter( ), getCodeBase( ), and getDocumentBase( ). The AppletContext object contains the real implementations of most other applet-specific routines, including showStatus( ), getImage( ), and showDocument( ).

So, an applet's constructor can't call getParameter( ), getImage( ), or showStatus( ) because the AppletStub isn't set until the applet's constructor returns. About the most a constructor can do is add GUI elements. Therefore, it is generally preferable to do all the applet's initialization in one place, so it might as well be the init( ) method, which the browser calls only once for each applet instance. This is why, in practice, most applets don't have any constructors: the default (no-argument) constructor is the only one ever called.

The start( ) method is called when the browser has fully loaded the applet and it's ready to go. It may be called again when the user moves back onto the page, scrolls back so the applet is shown again, and so on. This is the normal time for your applet to start threads (Chapter 24), audio or video (see Chapter 13), or anything else that takes time. The stop( ) method is called when the user gets bored and leaves the page.

The least commonly used applet method is destroy( ); it is called when the browser removes your applet instance from memory and allows you to close files, network connections, etc. After that, it's all over.

All four methods are public, all return void, and all take no arguments. They are shown together in Example 18-1.

*Example 18-1. AppletMethods.java*

```
import java.applet.*;
import java.awt.*;
import java.net.*;

/** AppletMethods -- show stop/start and AudioClip methods */

public class AppletMethods extends Applet {
    /** AudioClip object, used to load and play a sound file. */
    AudioClip snd = null;

    /** Initialize the sound file object and the GUI. */
    public void init() {
        System.out.println("In AppletMethods.init()");
        try {
            snd = getAudioClip(new URL(getCodeBase(), "laugh.au"));
```

---

* It didn't have to be this way. At the beginning of Java browserdom, they could have said, "Let's just pass in the applet stub as an argument when constructing the applet." But they didn't "and now it's too late," as Dr. Seuss once said.

*Example 18-1. AppletMethods.java (continued)*

```
        } catch (MalformedURLException e) {
            showStatus(e.toString());
        }
        setSize(200,100);      // take the place of a GUI
    }

    /** Called from the Browser when the page is ready to go. */
    public void start() {
        System.out.println("In AppletMethods.start()");
        if (snd != null)
            snd.play();      // loop() to be obnoxious...
    }

    /** Called from the Browser when the page is being vacated. */
    public void stop() {
        System.out.println("In AppletMethods.stop()");
        if (snd != null)
            snd.stop();      // stop play() or loop()
    }

    /** Called from the Browser (when the applet is being un-cached?).
     * Not actually used here, but the println will show when it's called.
     */
    public void destroy() {
        System.out.println("In AppletMethods.destroy()");
    }

    public void paint(Graphics g) {
        g.drawString("Welcome to Java", 50, 50);
    }

    /** An alternate form of getParameter that lets
     * you provide a default value, since this is so common.
     */
    public String getParameter(String p, String def) {
        return getParameter(p)==null?def:getParameter(p);
    }
}
```

## See Also

Applets based on Applet and using AWT work on most browsers. Applets based on JApplet and/or using Swing components need the Java Plug-in (see Recipe 23.6) to ensure that a compatible runtime is available.

# 18.3   Contacting a Server on the Applet Host

## Problem

You want an applet to contact a socket-based server on the host from which it was loaded.

## Solution

Use the method getCodeBase( ) to retrieve a URL for the applet host, and call the URL's getHost( ). Use this to construct a client socket.

## Discussion

For very good security reasons, applets are not permitted network access to servers on hosts other than the one from which the applet was loaded.

To reach a server on the download host, call the applet method getCodeBase( ), which yields a URL for the applet host. Call this URL's getHost( ) method to get the hostname. Finally, use the hostname to open a client socket (see Recipe 16.1). For example:

```
URL u = getCodeBase( );
String host = u.getHost( );
Socket s = new Socket(host , MY_SERVER_PORT);
```

Of course, in real code you wouldn't create all those temporary variables:

```
Socket s = new Socket(getCodeBase( ).getHost( ), MY_SERVER_PORT);
```

And, of course, you need error handling. Example 18-2 shows an applet that constructs a sort of login dialog and passes the results to a socket-based server on the applet host using exactly this technique. Figure 18-1 shows the screen display.

*Example 18-2. SocketApplet.java*

```java
/** Initialize the GUI nicely. */
public void init( ) {
    Label aLabel;

    setLayout(new GridBagLayout( ));
    int LOGO_COL = 1;
    int LABEL_COL = 2;
    int TEXT_COL = 3;
    int BUTTON_COL = 1;
    GridBagConstraints gbc = new GridBagConstraints( );
    gbc.weightx = 100.0; gbc.weighty = 100.0;

    gbc.gridx = LABEL_COL; gbc.gridy = 0;
    gbc.anchor = GridBagConstraints.EAST;
    add(aLabel = new Label("Name:", Label.CENTER), gbc);
    gbc.anchor = GridBagConstraints.CENTER;
    gbc.gridx = TEXT_COL; gbc.gridy = 0;
    add(nameTF=new TextField(10), gbc);

    gbc.gridx = LABEL_COL; gbc.gridy = 1;
    gbc.anchor = GridBagConstraints.EAST;
    add(aLabel = new Label("Password:", Label.CENTER), gbc);
    gbc.anchor = GridBagConstraints.CENTER;
    gbc.gridx = TEXT_COL; gbc.gridy = 1;
```

*Example 18-2. SocketApplet.java (continued)*

```java
    add(passTF=new TextField(10), gbc);
    passTF.setEchoChar('*');

    gbc.gridx = LABEL_COL; gbc.gridy = 2;
    gbc.anchor = GridBagConstraints.EAST;
    add(aLabel = new Label("Domain:", Label.CENTER), gbc);
    gbc.anchor = GridBagConstraints.CENTER;
    gbc.gridx = TEXT_COL; gbc.gridy = 2;
    add(domainTF-new TextField(10), gbc);
    sendButton = new Button("Send data");
    gbc.gridx = BUTTON_COL; gbc.gridy = 3;
    gbc.gridwidth = 3;
    add(sendButton, gbc);

    whence = getCodeBase();

    // Now the action begins...
    sendButton.addActionListener(new ActionListener() {
        public void actionPerformed(ActionEvent evt) {
            String name = nameTF.getText();
            if (name.length() -- 0) {
                showStatus("Name required");
                return;
            }
            String domain = domainTF.getText();
            if (domain.length() == 0) {
                showStatus("Domain required");
                return;
            }
            showStatus("Connecting to host " + whence.getHost() +
                " as " + nameTF.getText());

            try {
                Socket s = new Socket(getCodeBase().getHost(),
                    SocketServer.PORT);
                PrintWriter pf = new PrintWriter(s.getOutputStream(), true);
                // send login name
                pf.println(nameTF.getText());
                // passwd
                pf.println(passTF.getText());
                // and domain
                pf.println(domainTF.getText());

                BufferedReader is = new BufferedReader(
                    new InputStreamReader(s.getInputStream()));
                String response = is.readLine();
                showStatus(response);
            } catch (IOException e) {
                showStatus("ERROR: " + e.getMessage());
            }
        }
    });
}
```

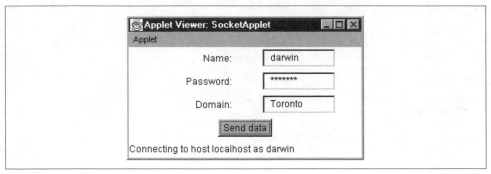

*Figure 18-1. SocketApplet in action*

# 18.4   Making an Applet Show a Document

## Problem

You want an applet to transfer control to another web page.

## Solution

Use the AppletContext method showDocument( ).

## Discussion

Any applet can request the browser that contains it to show a new web page by passing the new URL into the showDocument( ) method. Usually, the browser replaces the current page with the target page. This, of course, triggers a call to the applet's stop( ) method.

Note that the applet shown in Example 18-3 works correctly only in a full browser; the AppletViewer does not display HTML pages, so it ignores this method!

*Example 18-3. ShowDocApplet.java*

```
/** ShowDocApplet: Demonstrate showDocument( ).
 */
public class ShowDocApplet extends Applet {
    // String targetString = "http://www.darwinsys.com/javacook/secret.html";
    String targetString = "file:///c:/javasrc/network/ShowDocApplet.java";
    /** The URL to go to */
    URL targetURL;

    /** Initialize the Applet */
    public void init( ) {
        setBackground(Color.gray);
        try {
            targetURL = new URL(targetString);
        } catch (MalformedURLException mfu) {
```

*Example 18-3. ShowDocApplet.java (continued)*

```
            throw new IllegalArgumentException(
                "ShowDocApplet got bad URL " + targetString);
        }
        Button b = new Button("View Secret");
        add(b);
        b.addActionListener(new ActionListener( ) {
            public void actionPerformed(ActionEvent e) {
                getAppletContext( ).showDocument(targetURL);
            }
        });
    }

    public void stop( ) {
        System.out.println("Ack! Its been fun being an Applet. Goodbye!");
    }
}
```

Figure 18-2 shows the program in operation.

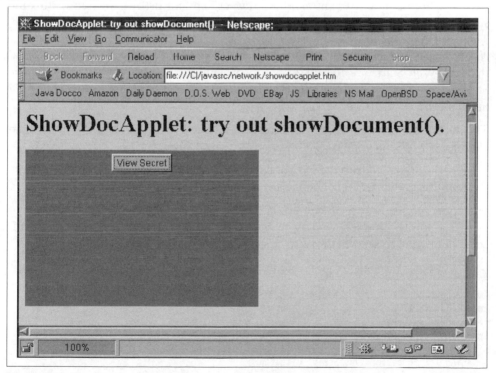

*Figure 18-2. ShowDocApplet program*

If the URL is unreachable, the browser notifies the user with a dialog, and the current page (including the applet) is left in view.

# 18.5 Making an Applet Run JavaScript

## Problem

You want to invoke JavaScript from within a browser applet.

## Solution

For browsers that support JavaScript, use the `netscape.javascript` package.

## Discussion

JavaScript is Netscape's browser client-side scripting language. It can be used on the client side by Java applets in some circumstances. The Netscape browser must include the optional support for Java. The package `netscape.javascript` includes a class called `JSObject`, a top-level class analogous to `java.lang.Object`.

To compile such an applet, you must include the appropriate JAR file in your class-path at compile time. At runtime, the browser supplies its own version of this file since it must be present in the browser-provided classpath to be run as trusted code. The exact name of this JAR file varies. For Netscape 4.x, it is *<netscapehome>/java/classes/java40.jar*. Netscape 7 does not include the file in its own path, deferring to the Java Web Start (see Recipe 23.13) to provide it. In this case, look for the file *netscape.jar* in your Java runtime; on Mac OS X, the file is */Library/Java/Home/lib/netscape.jar*.

This technique may not work with browsers such as KDE Konqueror, which use an external JVM to run applets.

Finally, the applet code in the HTML page must have the `mayscript="true"` attribute to grant this particular applet permission to use the JavaScript mechanism.

Still want to give it a try? Example 18-4 shows a code example using JavaScript to close the entire browser window in which the applet appears—drastic and anti-social, but you can see whether it works (I've tested it on Apple's Safari browser).

*Example 18-4. JScript.java*

```
import java.applet.*;
import java.awt.*;
import java.awt.event.*;
import netscape.javascript.*;

/* An Applet to perform JavaScript directly.
 * The import of netscape.javascript.* requires a JAR file.
 * EXPECT COMPILE ERROR unless you have the Netscape JAR file.
 * This may be e.g., $NETSCAPEHOME/java/classes/java40.jar.
 * The use of JavaScript requires <applet ... mayscript="true">
 */
```

*Example 18-4. JScript.java (continued)*

```java
public class JScript extends java.applet.Applet {
    JSObject jsObject;

    public void init() {
        jsObject = JSObject.getWindow(this);
        Button b = new Button("CLOSE BROWSER");
        b.addActionListener(new ActionListener() {
            public void actionPerformed(ActionEvent evt) {
                jsObject.eval("window.close()");
            }
        });
        add(b);
    }
}
```

## See Also

O'Reilly's *JavaScript & DHTML Cookbook* by Danny Goodman.

# 18.6   Making an Applet Run a CGI Script

## Problem

You want an applet to run a CGI script.

## Solution

Just use showDocument( ) with the correct URL.

## Discussion

It doesn't matter what type of target your URL refers to. It can be an HTML page, a plain text file, a compressed tar file to be downloaded, a CGI script, servlet, or a JavaServer Page. In all cases, you simply provide the URL. The Java applet for this appears in Example 18-5.

*Example 18-5. TryCGI.java*

```java
/**
 * Try running a CGI-BIN script from within Java.
 */
public class TryCGI extends Applet implements ActionListener {
    protected Button goButton;

    public void init() {
        add(goButton = new Button("Go for it!"));
        goButton.addActionListener(this);
    }
```

*Example 18-5. TryCGI.java (continued)*

```java
public void actionPerformed(ActionEvent evt) {
    try {
        URL myNewURL = new URL("http://server/cgi-bin/credit");

        // debug...
        System.out.println("URL = " + myNewURL);

        // "And then a miracle occurs..."
        getAppletContext().showDocument(myNewURL);

    } catch (Exception err) {
        System.err.println("Error! " + err);

        showStatus("Error, look in Java Console for details!");
    }
}
}
```

Since this is an applet, it requires an HTML page to invoke it. I used the HTML shown here:

```html
<html>
<head><title>Java Applets Can Run CGI's (on some browsers)</title></head>

<body bgcolor="white">
<h1>Java Applets Can Run CGI's (on some browsers)</h1>
<p>Click on the button on this little Applet for p(r)oof!</p>
<applet code="TryCGI" width="100" height="30">
<p>If you can see this, you need to get a Java-powered(tm) Web Browser
before you can watch for real.</p>
</applet>
<hr/>
<p>Use <a href="TryCGI.java">The Source</a>, Luke.</p>
</body>
</html>
```

# 18.7   Reading the Contents of a URL

## Problem

You want to read the contents of a URL (which can include a CGI script, servlet, etc.).

## Solution

Use the URL's openConnection( ) or getContent( ) method. This is not dependent upon being in an applet.

## Discussion

The URL class has several methods that allow you to read. The first and simplest, openStream( ), returns an InputStream that can read the contents directly. The simple

---

TextBrowser program shown here calls openStream( ) and uses this to construct a BufferedReader to read text lines from what is presumed to be a web server. I also demonstrate it reading a local file to show that almost any valid URL can be used:

```
$ java TextBrowser http://localhost/
*** Loading http://localhost/... ***
<html>
<head>
    <title>Ian Darwin's Webserver On The Road</title>
    <link rel="stylesheet" type="text/css" href="/stylesheet.css" title="Style"> </
head>
<body bgcolor="#c0d0e0">
<h1>Ian Darwin's Webserver On The Road</h1>
... (rest of body omitted) ...

$ java TextBrowser file:///etc/group
*** Loading file:///etc/group... ***
wheel:*:0:root
daemon:*:1:daemon
```

The next method, openConnection( ), returns a URLConnection object. This allows you more flexibility, providing methods such as getHeaderField( ), getLastModified( ), and other detailed methods. The third URL method, getContent( ), is more general. It returns an object that might be an InputStream, or an object containing the data. Use instanceof to determine which of several types was returned.

## See Also

O'Reilly's *Java Network Programming* by Elliotte Rusty Harold discusses this topic in considerable detail.

# 18.8 URI, URL, or URN?

## Problem

Having heard these terms, you want to know the difference between a URI, URL, and URN.

## Solution

Read on. Or see the Javadoc for java.net.uri.

## Discussion

A URL is the traditional name for a network address consisting of a scheme (like "http:") and an address (site name) and resource or pathname. But there are three distinct terms in all:

*URI*

Uniform Resource Identifier

*URL*

Uniform Resource Location

*URN*

Uniform Resource Name

Prior to 1.4, there was only a URL class; creating this class was primarily for purposes of reading from it. In 1.4, the URI class was introduced, primarily for manipulating resource identifiers, and a discussion near the end of the Java documentation for the new class explains the relationship among URI, URL, and URN. URIs form the set of all identifiers: URLs and URNs are subsets.

URIs are the most general; a URI is parsed for basic syntax without regard to the scheme, if any, that it specifies, and it need not refer to a particular server. A URL includes a hostname, scheme, and other components; the string is parsed according to rules for its scheme. When you construct a URL, an InputStream is created automatically. URNs name resources but do not explain how to locate them; typical examples of URNs that you will have seen include mailto: and news: references.

The main operations provided by the URI class are normalization (removing extraneous path segments including "..") and relativization (this should be called "making relative," but somebody wanted a single word to make a method name). A URI object does not have any methods for opening the URI; for that, you would normally use a string representation of the URI to construct a URL object, like so:

```
URL x = new URL(theURI.toString());
```

The program in Example 18-6 shows examples of normalization, making relative, and constructing a URL from a URI.

*Example 18-6. URIDemo.java*

```
public class URIDemo {
    public static void main(String[] args)
    throws URISyntaxException, MalformedURLException {

        URI u = new URI("http://www.darwinsys.com/java/../openbsd/../index.jsp");
        System.out.println("Raw: " + u);
        URI normalized = u.normalize();
        System.out.println("Normalized: " + normalized);
        final URI BASE = new URI("http://www.darwinsys.com");
        System.out.println("Relativized to " + BASE + ": " + BASE.relativize(u));

        // A URL is a type of URI
        URL url = new URL(normalized.toString());
        System.out.println("URL: " + url);
    }
}
```

# 18.9  Extracting HTML from a URL

## Problem

You need to extract all the HTML tags from a URL.

## Solution

Use this simple HTML tag extractor.

## Discussion

A simple HTML extractor can be made by reading a character at a time and looking for < and > tag delimiters. This is reasonably efficient if a BufferedReader is used.

The ReadTag program shown in Example 18-7 implements this; given a URL, it opens the file (similar to TextBrowser in Recipe 18.7) and extracts the HTML tags. Each tag is printed to the standard output.

*Example 18-7. ReadTag.java*

```
/** A simple but reusable HTML tag extractor.
 */
public class ReadTag {
    /** The URL that this ReadTag object is reading */
    protected URL myURL = null;
    /** The Reader for this object */
    protected BufferedReader inrdr = null;

    /* Simple main showing one way of using the ReadTag class. */
    public static void main(String[] args) throws MalformedURLException, IOException {
        if (args.length == 0) {
            System.err.println("Usage: ReadTag URL [...]");
            return;
        }

        for (int i=0; i<args.length; i++) {
            ReadTag rt = new ReadTag(args[0]);
            String tag;
            while ((tag = rt.nextTag()) != null) {
                System.out.println(tag);
            }
            rt.close();
        }
    }

    /** Construct a ReadTag given a URL String */
    public ReadTag(String theURLString) throws
            IOException, MalformedURLException {

        this(new URL(theURLString));
    }
```

*Example 18-7. ReadTag.java (continued)*

```java
/** Construct a ReadTag given a URL */
public ReadTag(URL theURL) throws IOException {
    myURL = theURL;
    // Open the URL for reading
    inrdr = new BufferedReader(new InputStreamReader(myURL.openStream( )));
}

/** Read the next tag.  */
public String nextTag( ) throws IOException {
    int i;
    while ((i = inrdr.read( )) != -1) {
        char thisChar = (char)i;
        if (thisChar == '<') {
            String tag = readTag( );
            return tag;
        }
    }
    return null;
}

public void close( ) throws IOException {
    inrdr.close( );
}

/** Read one tag. Adapted from code by Elliotte Rusty Harold */
protected String readTag( ) throws IOException {
    StringBuffer theTag = new StringBuffer("<");
    int i = '<';

    while (i != '>' && (i = inrdr.read( )) != -1) {
        theTag.append((char)i);
    }
    return theTag.toString( );
}

/* Return a String representation of this object */
public String toString( ) {
    return "ReadTag[" + myURL.toString( ) + "]";
}
}
```

When I ran it on one system (apparently part-way through converting to modern lowercase HTML tags), I got the following output:

```
darian$ java ReadTag http://localhost/
<html>
<head>
<title>
</title>
</head>
<FRAMESET BORDER="0" ROWS="110, *" FRAMESPACING="0">
<FRAME NAME="header" SRC="header.html" SCROLLING="NO" MARGINHEIGHT="0"
  FRAMEBORDER="0">
```

```
<FRAMESET COLS="130, *" FRAMESPACING="0">
<FRAME NAME="menu" SRC="menu.html" SCROLLING="NO" MARGINHEIGHT="0" FRAMEBORDER="0">
<FRAME NAME="main" SRC="main.html" MARGINHEIGHT="15" MARGINWIDTH="15"
FRAMEBORDER="0">
</FRAMESET>
</FRAMESET>
</html>
darian$
```

# 18.10  Extracting URLs from a File

## Problem

You need to extract just the URLs from a file.

## Solution

Use ReadTag from Recipe 18.9 and just look for tags that might contain URLs.

## Discussion

The program in Example 18-8 uses ReadTag from the previous recipe and checks each tag to see if it is a "wanted tag" defined in the array wantedTags. These include A (anchor), IMG (image), and APPLET tags. If it is determined to be a wanted tag, the URL is extracted from the tag and printed.

*Example 18-8. GetURLs.java*

```java
public class GetURLs {
    /** The tag reader */
    ReadTag reader;

    public GetURLs(URL theURL) throws IOException {
        reader = new ReadTag(theURL);
    }

    public GetURLs(String theURL) throws MalformedURLException, IOException {
        reader = new ReadTag(theURL);
    }

    /* The tags we want to look at */
    public final static String[] wantTags = {
        "<a ", "<A ",
        "<applet ", "<APPLET ",
        "<img ", "<IMG ",
        "<frame ", "<FRAME ",
    };

    public ArrayList getURLs() throws IOException {
        ArrayList al = new ArrayList();
        String tag;
```

*Example 18-8. GetURLs.java (continued)*

```
        while ((tag = reader.nextTag()) != null) {
            for (int i=0; i<wantTags.length; i++) {
                if (tag.startsWith(wantTags[i])) {
                    al.add(tag);
                    continue;          // optimization
                }
            }
        }
        return al;
    }

    public void close() throws IOException {
        if (reader != null)
            reader.close();
    }
    public static void main(String[] argv) throws
            MalformedURLException, IOException {
        String theURL = argv.length == 0 ?
            "http://localhost/" : argv[0];
        GetURLs gu = new GetURLs(theURL);
        ArrayList urls = gu.getURLs();
        Iterator urlIterator = urls.iterator();
        while (urlIterator.hasNext()) {
            System.out.println(urlIterator.next());
        }
    }
}
```

The `GetURLs` program prints the URLs contained in a given web page:

```
darian$ java GetURLs http://daroad
<IMG SRC="ian.gif">
<A ID="LinkLocal" HREF="webserver/index.html">
<A HREF="quizzes/">
<A HREF="servlets/IsItWorking">
<A HREF="demo.jsp">
<A ID=LinkRemote HREF="http://java.sun.com">
<A ID=LinkRemote HREF="http://www.openbsd.org">
<A ID=LinkRemote HREF="http://www.cpg.com">
<A ID=LinkRemote HREF="http://www.ssc.com">
<A ID=LinkRemote HREF="http://www.learningtree.com">
<A ID=LinkLocal HREF="javacook.html">
<A ID=LinkRemote HREF="http://java.oreilly.com">
<A ID=LinkLocal HREF="lookup/index.htm">
<A ID=LinkLocal HREF="readings/index.html">
<A ID=LinkLocal HREF="download.html">
<IMG SRC="miniduke.gif" BORDER=0>
darian$
```

The `LinkChecker` program in Recipe 18.13 extracts the HREF or SRC attributes and validates them.

# 18.11 Converting a Filename to a URL

## Problem

You require a URL, but you have a local file.

## Solution

Use getResource( ) or File.toURL( ).

## Discussion

Many operations require a URL, but it would be easier to refer to a file on the local filesystem or disk. For these, the convenience method getResource( ) in the class java.lang.Class can be used. This takes a filename and returns a URL:

```
public class GetResource {
    public static void main(String[] argv) {
        Class c = GetResource.class;
        java.net.URL u = c.getResource("GetResource.java");
        System.out.println(u);
    }
}
```

When I ran this code on my Windows system, it printed:

```
file:/C:/javasrc/netweb/GetResource.java
```

JDK 1.2 also introduced a toURL( ) method into the File class (Recipe 11.1). Unlike getResource( ), this method can throw a MalformedURLException. This makes sense, since a File object can be constructed with arbitrary nonsense in the filename. So the previous code can be rewritten as:

```
public class FileToURL
{
    public static void main(String[] argv) throws MalformedURLException {
        java.net.URL u = new File("GetResource.java").toURL( );
        System.out.println(u);
    }
}
```

Both programs print essentially the same result:

```
> java FileToURL
file:/usr/home/ian/javasrc/netweb/GetResource.java
> java GetResource
file:/usr/home/ian/javasrc/netweb/GetResource.java
```

# 18.12 Program: MkIndex

This little program has saved me a great deal of time over the years. It reads a directory containing a large number of files, harking back from a time when I kept all my demonstration Java programs in a fairly flat directory structure. MkIndex, shown in

Example 18-9, produces a better-formatted listing than the default directory that web servers generate. For one thing, it includes an alphabet navigator that lets you jump directly to the section of files whose names begin with a certain letter, saving a lot of scrolling time or iterations with the browser's find menu. This program uses a File object (see Recipe 11.1) to list the files and another to decide which are files and which are directories. It also uses Collections.sort (see Recipe 7.8) to sort the names alphabetically before generating the output. It writes its output to the file *index.html* in the current directory, even if an alternate directory argument is given. This is the default filename for most standard web servers; if your web server uses something different, of course, you can rename the file.

*Example 18-9. MkIndex.java*

```java
import java.io.*;
import java.util.*;
import com.darwinsys.io.FileIO;

/** MkIndex -- make a static index.html for a Java Source directory
 * <p>
 * Started life as an awk script that used "ls" to get
 * the list of files, grep out .class and javadoc output files, |sort.
 * Now it's all in Java (including the ls-ing and the sorting).
 *
 * @author    Ian F. Darwin, http://www.darwinsys.com/
 * @Version $Id: ch18,v 1.5 2004/05/04 20:13:14 ian Exp $
 */
public class MkIndex {

    class NameMap implements Comparable {
        String name, nameLC;
        String path;
        public NameMap(String nm, String p) {
            name = nm;
            nameLC = name.toLowerCase( );
            path = p;
        }
        public int compareTo(Object other) {
            return nameLC.compareTo(((NameMap)other).nameLC);
        }
    }

    /** The output file that we create */
    public static final String OUTPUTFILE = "index-byname.html";
    /** The string for TITLE and H1 */
    public static final String TITLE =
        "Ian Darwin's Java Cookbook: Source Code: By Name";
    /** The main output stream */
    PrintWriter out;
    /** The background color for the page */
    public static final String BGCOLOR="#33ee33";
    /** The File object, for directory listing. */
    File dirFile;
```

*Example 18-9. MkIndex.java (continued)*

```java
/** Make an index */
public static void main(String[] args) throws IOException {
    MkIndex mi = new MkIndex();
    String inDir = args.length > 0 ? args[0] : ".";
    mi.open(inDir, OUTPUTFILE);          // open files
    mi.begin();              // print HTML header
    System.out.println("** Start Pass One **");
    for (int i=0; i<args.length; i++)
        mi.process(new File(args[i]));    // "We do ALL the work..."
    mi.writeNav();       // Write navigator
    mi.writeList();      // Write huge list of files
    mi.end();            // print trailer.
    mi.close();          // close files
}

void open(String dir, String outFile) {
    dirFile - new File(dir);
    try {
        out = new PrintWriter(new FileWriter(outFile));
    } catch (IOException e) {
        System.err.println(e);
    }
}

/** Write the HTML headers */
void begin() throws IOException {
    println("<!DOCTYPE html PUBLIC '-//W3C//DTD XHTML 1.0 Transitional//EN'");
    println("    'http://www.w3.org/TR/xhtml1/DTD/xhtml1-transitional.dtd'");
    println(">");
    println();
    println("<html>");

    println("<head>");
    println("    <meta name='Generator' content-'Java MkIndex'/>");
    println("    <title>" + TITLE + "</title>");
    println("</head>");
    println();
    println("<body bgcolor=\"" + BGCOLOR + "\">");
    println("<h1>" + TITLE + "</h1>");
    if (new File("about.html").exists()) {
        FileIO.copyFile("about.html", out, false);
    } else {
        println("<p>The following files are online.");
        println("Some of these files are still experimental!</p>");
        println("<p>Most of these files are Java source code.");
        println("If you load an HTML file from here, the applets will not run!");
        println("The HTML files must be saved to disk and the applets compiled,");
        println("before you can run them!</p>");
    }
    println("<p>All files are Copyright (c): All rights reserved.");
    println("See the accompanying <a href=\"legal-notice.txt\">Legal Notice</a>.");
    println("May be used by readers of my Java Cookbook for educational purposes,");
    println("and for commercial use if certain conditions are met.");
```

*Example 18-9. MkIndex.java (continued)*

```java
        println("</p>");
        println("<hr />");
    }

    /** Array of letters that exist. Should
     * fold case here so don't get f and F as distinct entries!
     * This only works for ASCII characters (8-bit chars).
     */
    boolean[] exists = new boolean[255];

    /** List for temporary storage, and sorting */
    ArrayList list = new ArrayList();

    /** Do the bulk of the work */
    void process(File file) throws IOException {

        String name = file.getName();
        if (name.startsWith("index") ||
            name.endsWith(".class") ||
            name.endsWith(".bak")) {
            System.err.println("Ignoring " + file.getPath());
            return;
        } else if (name.equals("CVS")) {         // Ignore CVS subdirectories
            return;                              // don't mention it
        } else if (name.charAt(0) == '.') {      // UNIX dot-file
            return;
        }

        if (file.isDirectory()) {
            File[] files = file.listFiles();
            for (int i=0; i<files.length; i++) {
                String fn = files[i].getName();
                process(new File(file, fn));
            }
        } else {
            // file to be processed.
            list.add(new NameMap(name, file.getPath()));
            exists[name.charAt(0)] = true;
        }
    }

    void writeNav() throws IOException {

        System.out.println("Writing the Alphabet Navigator...");
        for (char c = 'A'; c<='Z'; c++)
            if (exists[c])
                print("<a href=\"#" + c + "\">" + c + "</a> ");
    }

    void writeList() throws IOException {
```

*Example 18-9. MkIndex.java (continued)*

```java
        // ... the beginning of the HTML Unordered List...
        println("<ul>");

        System.out.println("Sorting the list...");
        Collections.sort(list);

        System.out.println("Start PASS TWO -- from List to " +
            OUTPUTFILE + "...");
        Iterator it = list.iterator();
        while (it.hasNext()) {
            NameMap map = (NameMap)it.next();
            String fn = map.name;
            String path = map.path;
            // Need to make a link into this directory.
            // IF there is a descr.txt file, use it for the text
            // of the link, otherwise, use the directory name.
            // But, if there is an index.html or index.html file,
            // make the link to that file, else to the directory itself.
            if (fn.endsWith("/")) {       // directory
                String descr = null;
                if (new File(fn + "descr.txt").exists()) {
                    descr = FileIO.readLine(fn + "descr.txt");
                };
                if (new File(fn + "index.html").exists())
                    mkDirLink(fn+"index.html", descr!=null?descr:fn);
                else if (new File(fn + "index.htm").exists())
                    mkDirLink(fn+"index.htm", descr!=null?descr:fn);
                else
                    mkLink(fn, descr!=null?descr:fn + " -- Directory");
            } else // file
                mkLink(fn, path);
        }
        System.out.println("*** process - ALL DONE***");
    }

    /** Keep track of each letter for #links */
    boolean done[] = new boolean[255];

    void mkLink(String name, String path) {
        print("<li>");
        char c = name.charAt(0);
        if (!done[c]) {
            print("<a name=\"" + c + "\"/>");
            done[c] = true;
        }
        println("<a href=\"" + path + "\">" + name + "</a>");
    }

    void mkDirLink(String index, String dir) {
        // TODO  Open the index and look for TITLE lines!
        println("<a href='" + index + "'>" + dir + "</a>");
    }
```

*Example 18-9. MkIndex.java (continued)*

```
    /** Write the trailers and a signature */
    void end( ) {
        System.out.println("Finishing the HTML");
        println("</ul>");
        flush( );
        println("<p>This file generated by ");
        print("<a href=\"MkIndex.java\">MkIndex</a>, a Java program, at ");
        println(Calendar.getInstance().getTime().toString( ));
        println("</p>");
        println("</body>");
        println("</html>");
    }

    /** Close open files */
    void close( ) {
        System.out.println("Closing output files...");
        if (out != null)
            out.close( );
    }

    /** Convenience routine for out.print */
    void print(String s) {
        out.print(s);
    }

    /** Convenience routine for out.println */
    void println(String s) {
        out.println(s);
    }

    /** Convenience routine for out.println */
    void println( ) {
        out.println( );
    }

    /** Convenience for out.flush( ); */
    void flush( ) {
        out.flush( );
    }
}
```

# 18.13 Program: LinkChecker

One of the hard parts of maintaining a large web site is ensuring that all the hypertext links, images, applets, and so forth remain valid as the site grows and changes. It's easy to make a change somewhere that breaks a link somewhere else, exposing your users to those "Doh!"-producing 404 errors. What's needed is a program to automate checking the links. This turns out to be surprisingly complex due to the variety of link types. But we can certainly make a start.

---

Since we already created a program that reads a web page and extracts the URL-containing tags (Recipe 18.10), we can use that here. The basic approach of our new LinkChecker program is this: given a starting URL, create a GetURLs object for it. If that succeeds, read the list of URLs and go from there. This program has the additional functionality of displaying the structure of the site using simple indentation in a graphical window, as shown in Figure 18-3.

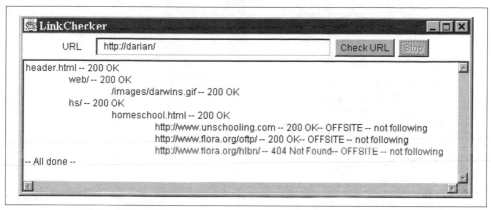

*Figure 18-3. LinkChecker in action*

So using the GetURLs class from Recipe 18.10, the rest is largely a matter of elaboration. A lot of this code has to do with the GUI (see Chapter 14). The code uses recursion: the routine checkOut( ) calls itself each time a new page or directory is started.

Example 18-10 shows the code for the LinkChecker program.

*Example 18-10. LinkChecker.java*

```java
/** A simple HTML Link Checker.
 * Need a Properties file to set depth, URLs to check. etc.
 * Responses not adequate; need to check at least for 404-type errors!
 * When all that is (said and) done, display in a Tree instead of a TextArea.
 * Then use Color coding to indicate errors.
 */
public class LinkChecker extends Frame implements Runnable {
    protected Thread t = null;
    /** The "global" activation flag: set true to halt. */
    boolean done = false;
    protected Panel p;
    /** The textfield for the starting URL.
     * Should have a Properties file and a JComboBox instead.
     */
    protected TextField textFldURL;
    protected Button checkButton;
    protected Button killButton;
    protected TextArea textWindow;
    protected int indent = 0;
        protected Map hash = new HashMap( );
```

*Example 18-10. LinkChecker.java (continued)*

```java
    public static void main(String[] args) {
        LinkChecker lc = new LinkChecker();
        lc.setSize(500, 400);
        lc.setLocation(150, 150);
        lc.setVisible(true);
        if (args.length == 0)
            return;
        lc.textFldURL.setText(args[0]);
    }

    public void startChecking() {
        done = false;
        checkButton.setEnabled(false);
        killButton.setEnabled(true);
        textWindow.setText("");
        doCheck();
    }

    public void stopChecking() {
        done = true;
        checkButton.setEnabled(true);
        killButton.setEnabled(false);
    }

    /** Construct a LinkChecker */
    public LinkChecker() {
        super("LinkChecker");
                        addWindowListener(new WindowAdapter() {
            public void windowClosing(WindowEvent e) {
            setVisible(false);
            dispose();
            System.exit(0);
            }
        });
        setLayout(new BorderLayout());
        p = new Panel();
        p.setLayout(new FlowLayout());
        p.add(new Label("URL"));
        p.add(textFldURL = new TextField(40));
        p.add(checkButton = new Button("Check URL"));
        // Make a single action listener for both the text field (when
        // you hit return) and the explicit "Check URL" button.
        ActionListener starter = new ActionListener() {
            public void actionPerformed(ActionEvent e) {
                startChecking();
            }
        };
        textFldURL.addActionListener(starter);
        checkButton.addActionListener(starter);
        p.add(killButton = new Button("Stop"));
        killButton.setEnabled(false);    // until startChecking is called.
        killButton.addActionListener(new ActionListener() {
```

*Example 18-10. LinkChecker.java (continued)*

```java
        public void actionPerformed(ActionEvent e) {
            if (t == null || !t.isAlive())
                return;
            stopChecking();
        }
    });
    // Now lay out the main GUI - URL & buttons on top, text larger
    add("North", p);
    textWindow = new TextArea(80, 40);
    add("Center", new JScrollPane(textWindow));
}

public void doCheck() {
    if (t!=null && t.isAlive())
        return;
    t = new Thread(this);
    t.start();
}

public synchronized void run() {
    textWindow.setText("");
    checkOut(textFldURL.getText());
    textWindow.append("-- All done --");
}

/** Start checking, given a URL by name.
 * Calls checkLink to check each link.
 */
public void checkOut(String rootURLString) {
    URL rootURL = null;
    GetURLs urlGetter = null;

    if (done)
        return;
    if (rootURLString == null) {
        textWindow.append("checkOut(null) isn't very useful");
        return;
    }
      if (hash.get(rootURLString) != null) {
        return; // already visited
      }
     hash.put(rootURLString, Boolean.TRUE);
    // Open the root URL for reading
    try {
        rootURL = new URL(rootURLString);
        urlGetter = new GetURLs(rootURL);
    } catch (MalformedURLException e) {
        textWindow.append("Can't parse " + rootURLString + "\n");
        return;
    } catch (FileNotFoundException e) {
        textWindow.append("Can't open file " + rootURLString + "\n");
        return;
```

*Example 18-10. LinkChecker.java (continued)*

```
        } catch (IOException e) {
            textWindow.append("openStream " + rootURLString + " " + e + "\n");
            return;
        }

        // If we're still here, the root URL given is OK.
        // Next we make up a "directory" URL from it.
        String rootURLdirString;
        if (rootURLString.endsWith("/") ||
            rootURLString.endsWith("\\"))
                rootURLdirString = rootURLString;
        else {
            rootURLdirString = rootURLString.substring(0,
                rootURLString.lastIndexOf('/'));     // TODO might be \
        }

        try {
            ArrayList urlTags = urlGetter.getURLs();
            Iterator urlIterator = urlTags.iterator();
            while (urlIterator.hasNext()) {
                if (done)
                    return;
                String tag = (String)urlIterator.next();
                System.out.println(tag);

                String href = extractHREF(tag);

                for (int j=0; j<indent; j++)
                    textWindow.append("\t");
                textWindow.append(href + " -- ");

                // Can't really validate these!
                if (href.startsWith("mailto:")) {
                    textWindow.append(href + " -- not checking\n");
                    continue;
                }

                if (href.startsWith("..") || href.startsWith("#")) {
                    textWindow.append(href + " -- not checking\n");
                    // nothing doing!
                    continue;
                }

                URL hrefURL = new URL(rootURL, href);

                // TRY THE URL.
                // (don't combine previous textWindow.append with this one,
                // since this one can throw an exception)
                textWindow.append(checkLink(hrefURL));

                // There should be an option to control whether to
                // "try the url" first and then see if off-site, or
                // vice versa, for the case when checking a site you're
```

*Example 18-10. LinkChecker.java (continued)*

```java
                    // working on on your notebook on a train in the Rockies
                    // with no web access available.

                    // Now see if the URL is off-site.
                    if (!hrefURL.getHost().equals(rootURL.getHost())) {
                        textWindow.append("-- OFFSITE -- not following");
                        textWindow.append("\n");
                        continue;
                    }
                    textWindow.append("\n");

                    // If HTML, check it recursively. No point checking
                    // PHP, CGI, JSP, etc., since these usually need forms input.
                    // If a directory, assume HTML or something under it will work.
                    if (href.endsWith(".htm") ||
                        href.endsWith(".html") ||
                        href.endsWith("/")) {
                            ++indent;
                            if (href.indexOf(':') != -1)
                                checkOut(href);             // RECURSE
                            else {
                                String newRef =
                                        rootURLdirString + '/' + href;
                                checkOut(newRef);           // RECURSE
                            }
                            --indent;
                    }
                }
            urlGetter.close();
        } catch (IOException e) {
            System.err.println("Error " + ":(" + e +")");
        }
    }

    /** Check one link, given its DocumentBase and the tag */
    public String checkLink(URL linkURL) {

        try {
            // Open it; if the open fails we'll likely throw an exception
            URLConnection luf = linkURL.openConnection();
            if (linkURL.getProtocol().equals("http")) {
                HttpURLConnection huf = (HttpURLConnection)luf;
                String s = huf.getResponseCode() + " " + huf.getResponseMessage();
                if (huf.getResponseCode() == -1)
                    return "Server error: bad HTTP response";
                return s;
            } else if (linkURL.getProtocol().equals("file")) {
                InputStream is = luf.getInputStream();
                is.close();
                // If that didn't throw an exception, the file is probably OK
                return "(File)";
            } else
                return "(non-HTTP)";
```

*Example 18-10. LinkChecker.java (continued)*

```
        }
        catch (SocketException e) {
            return "DEAD: " + e.toString( );
        }
        catch (IOException e) {
            return "DEAD";
        }
    }

    /** Extract the URL from <sometag attrs HREF="http://foo/bar" attrs ...>
     * We presume that the HREF is correctly quoted!!!!!
     * TODO: Handle Applets.
     */
    public String extractHREF(String tag) throws MalformedURLException {
        String caseTag = tag.toLowerCase( ), attrib;
        int p1, p2, p3, p4;

        if (caseTag.startsWith("<a "))
            attrib = "href";          // A
        else
            attrib = "src";           // image, frame
        p1 = caseTag.indexOf(attrib);
        if (p1 < 0) {
            throw new MalformedURLException("Can't find " + attrib + " in " + tag);
        }
        p2 = tag.indexOf ("=", p1);
        p3 = tag.indexOf("\"", p2);       // TODO should also handle single-quotes here!
        p4 = tag.indexOf("\"", p3+1);
        if (p3 < 0 || p4 < 0) {
            throw new MalformedURLException("Invalid " + attrib + " in " + tag);
        }
        String href = tag.substring(p3+1, p4);
        return href;
    }
}
```

## Downloading an Entire Web Site

It would also be useful to have a program that reads the entire contents of a web site and saves it on your local hard disk. Sounds wasteful, but disk space is quite inexpensive nowadays, and this would allow you to peruse a web site when not connected to the Internet. Of course much of the dynamic content (Servlets, CGI scripts) would no longer be dynamic in pages that you downloaded, but at least you could navigate around the text and view the images. The LinkChecker program contains all the seeds of such a program: you need only to download the contents of each non-dynamic URL (see the test for HTML and directories near the end of routine checkOut( ) and the code in Recipe 18.7), create the requisite directories (Recipe 11.9), and create and write to a file on disk (see Chapter 10). This final step is left as an exercise for the reader. Sites that use absolute references to their own pages would need to be normalized and relativized (see Recipe 18.8) during the download process.

# CHAPTER 19

# Java and Electronic Mail

## 19.0 Introduction

Sending and receiving email from a program is easy with Java. If you are writing an applet, you can simply trick the browser into composing and sending it for you. Otherwise, you can use the JavaMail Extension (package javax.mail) to both send and read mail. JavaMail provides three general categories of classes: Messages, Transports, and Stores. A Message, of course, represents one email message. A Transport is a way of sending a Message from your application into the network or Internet. A Store represents stored email messages and can be used to retrieve them as Message objects. That is, a Store is the inverse of a Transport, or, looked at another way, a Transport is for sending email and a Store is for reading it. One other class, Session, is used to obtain references to the appropriate Store and/or Transport objects that you need to use.

Being an extension, the JavaMail package must be downloaded separately from Sun's web site and is not part of the core API. It's worth it, though. For the cost of a few minutes' downloading time, you get the ability to send and receive electronic mail over a variety of network protocols. JavaMail is also included in the Java 2 Enterprise Edition (J2EE), so if you have J2EE you do not need to download JavaMail.

Finally, as you might have guessed from Chapter 16, it's not that big a stretch to write code that contacts an SMTP server yourself and pretends to be a mail program. Hey, why pretend? You really have a mail program at that point!

## 19.1 Sending Email: Browser Version

### Problem

You want an applet to permit the user to compose and send email.

## Solution

Use a mailto: URL, but hide it in some Java code.

## Discussion

Since most web browsers are now configured with either built-in or linked-in email clients, you can use the mailto: URL as a poor-person's email composer to have users contact you. Many people prefer this to a fill-in-the-blank "mail" form connected to a CGI script or servlet since they can use a specialized tool and save their own copy of the mail either in their log file or by CC'ing their own account. While you could use a mailto: URL directly in HTML, experience suggests that a species of parasite called a spam perpetrator will attach itself permanently to your mailbox if you do.

```
<H1>Test</H1> <P>Here is how to <A HREF="mailto:spam-magnet@darwinsys.
com?subject=Testing Mailto URL&cc=dilbert@office.comics">contact us</A>
```

My approach is to hide the mailto: URL inside a Java applet, where spam perps are less likely to notice it. The applet uses showDocument( ) to activate the mailto: URL:

```java
String theURL = "mailto:" + username;
URL targetURL = new URL(theURL);
getAppletContext.showDocument(targetURL);
```

Further, I break the email address into two parts and provide the @ directly, so it won't be seen even if the spam-spider is clever enough to look into the param parts of the applet tag. Since I know you won't actually deploy this code without changing Target1 and Target2—the param tags for the mail receiver's email name and host domain—you're fairly safe from spam with this. Example 19-1 is the Java applet class.

*Example 19-1. MailtoButton.java*

```java
import java.applet.*;
import java.awt.*;
import java.awt.event.*;
import java.net.*;
import java.util.*;

/**
 * MailtoButton -- look like a mailto, but not visible to spiders.
 */
public class MailtoButton extends Applet {
    /** The label that is to appear in the button */
    protected String label = null;
    /** The width and height */
    protected int width, height;
    /** The string form of the URL to jump to */
    protected String targetName, targetHost;
    /** The URL to jump to when the button is pushed. */
    protected URL targetURL;
```

*Example 19-1. MailtoButton.java (continued)*

```java
/** The name of the font */
protected String fontName;
protected String DEFAULTFONTNAME = "helvetica";
/** The font */
protected Font theFont;
/** The size of the font */
protected int fontSize = 18;
/** The HTML PARAM for the user account -- keep it short */
private String TARGET1 = "U";      // for User
/** The HTML PARAM for the hostname -- keep it short */
private String TARGET2 = "H";      // for Host
// Dummy
private String BOGON1 = "username";      // happy strings-ing, spam perps
private String BOGON2 = "hostname";      // ditto.
/** The string for the Subject line, if any */
private String subject;

/** Called from the browser to set up. We want to throw various
 * kinds of exceptions but the API predefines that we don't, so we
 * limit ourselves to the ubiquitous IllegalArgumentException.
 */
public void init( ) {
    // System.out.println("In LinkButton::init");
    try {
        if ((targetName = getParameter(TARGET1)) == null)
            throw new IllegalArgumentException(
                "TARGET parameter REQUIRED");
        if ((targetHost = getParameter(TARGET2)) == null)
            throw new IllegalArgumentException(
                "TARGET parameter REQUIRED");

        String theURL = "mailto:" + targetName + "@" + targetHost;

        subject = getParameter("subject");
        if (subject != null)
            theURL += "?subject=" + subject;

        targetURL = new URL(theURL);

    } catch (MalformedURLException rsi) {
        throw new IllegalArgumentException("MalformedURLException " +
            rsi.getMessage( ));
    }

    label = getParameter("label");      // i.e., "Send feedback"
    if (label == null)
            throw new IllegalArgumentException("LABEL is REQUIRED");

    // Now handle font stuff.
    fontName = getParameter("font");
    if (fontName == null)
        fontName = DEFAULTFONTNAME;
```

*Example 19-1. MailtoButton.java (continued)*

```
            String s;
            if ((s = getParameter("fontsize")) != null)
                fontSize = Integer.parseInt(s);
            if (fontName != null || fontSize != 0) {
                System.out.println("Name " + fontName + ", size " + fontSize);
                theFont = new Font(fontName, Font.BOLD, fontSize);
            }

            Button b = new Button(label);
            b.addActionListener(new ActionListener( ) {
                public void actionPerformed(ActionEvent e) {
                    if (targetURL != null) {
                        // showStatus("Going to " + target);
                        getAppletContext( ).showDocument(targetURL);
                    }
                }
            });
            if (theFont != null)
                b.setFont(theFont);
            add(b);
        }

        /** Give Parameter info to the AppletViewer, just for those
         * writing HTML without hardcopy documentation :-)
         */
        public String[][] getParameterInfo( ) {
            String info[][] = {
                { "label",      "string",      "Text to display" },
                { "fontname",   "name",         "Font to display it in" },
                { "fontsize",   "10-30?",      "Size to display it at" },

                // WARNING - these intentionally lie, to mislead spammers who
                // are incautious enough to download and run (or strings) the
                // .class file for this Applet.

                { "username",    "email-account",
                    "Where do you want your mail to go today? Part 1" },
                { "hostname",    "host.domain",
                    "Where do you want your mail to go today? Part 2" },
                { "subject",    "subject line",
                    "What your Subject: field will be." },
            };
            return info;
        }
    }
```

Example 19-2 shows the program in a simple HTML page to show you the syntax of using it.

*Example 19-2. MailtoButton.htm*

```
<HTML><HEAD>
<TITLE>Darwin Open Systems: Feedback Page</TITLE></HEAD>
<BODY BGCOLOR="White">
<H1>Darwin Open Systems: Feedback Page</H1>
<P>So, please, send us your feedback!</P>
<APPLET CODE=MailtoButton WIDTH=200 HEIGHT=40>
    <PARAM NAME="H" VALUE="www.darwinsys.com">
    <PARAM NAME="U" VALUE="wile_e_coyote">
    <PARAM NAME="subject" VALUE="Acme Widgets Feedback">
    <PARAM NAME="label" VALUE="Send Feedback by Mail">
    <PARAM NAME="font" VALUE="Helvetica">
    <PARAM NAME="fontsize" VALUE="16">
    <P>Your browser doesn't recognize Java Applets.
    Please use the non-Java CGI-based feedback form.</P>
</APPLET>
<P>You should get an acknowledgement by email shortly. Thank you
for your comments!</P>
<HR>
<P>Here is a traditional "CGI"-style form to let you to send feedback
if you aren't running Java or if your browser doesn't support
email composition.</P>
<FORM METHOD=POST ACTION="http://www.darwinsys.com/bin/feedback.cgi">
    <TEXTAREA NAME=message ROWS=5 COLS=60></TEXTAREA>
    <BR>
    <INPUT TYPE=SUBMIT VALUE="Send Feedback"></INPUT>
</FORM>
<P>Thank you for your comments.</P>
```

 Example 19-2 requires JavaMail API Version 1.2 or later due to a limitation in earlier versions.

Of course, not everybody uses a full-featured browser, and the light version doesn't include the email composer. Therefore, the page features a traditional CGI-based form for the benefit of those poor souls in need of a Java-based browser. Figure 19-1 is a screenshot in Netscape 4, showing the Compose window resulting from pressing the Feedback button.

The CGI form is a workaround, so it's better to provide a full-blown mail composer.

# 19.2   Sending Email: For Real

## Problem

You need to send email, and the browser trick in Recipe 19.1 won't cut it.

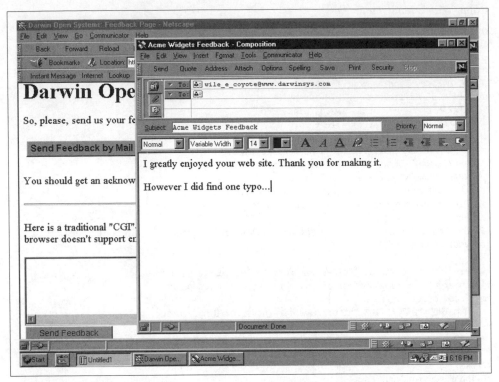

*Figure 19-1. MailtoButton*

## Solution

Provide a real email client.

## Discussion

A real email client allows the user considerably more control. Of course, it also requires more work. In this recipe, I'll build a simple version of a mail sender, relying upon the JavaMail standard extension in package `javax.mail` and `javax.mail.internet` (the latter contains classes that are specific to Internet email protocols). This first example shows the steps of sending mail over SMTP, the standard Internet mail protocol. The steps are listed in the sidebar.

As usual in Java, you must catch certain exceptions. This API requires that you catch the `MessagingException`, which indicates some failure of the transmission. Class Sender is shown in Example 19-3.

*Example 19-3. Sender.java*

```java
import java.io.*;
import java.util.*;
import javax.mail.*;
import javax.mail.internet.*;

/** sender -- send an email message.
 */
public class Sender {

    /** The message recipient. */
    protected String message_recip = "spam-magnet@darwinsys.com";
    /* What's it all about, Alfie? */
    protected String message_subject = "Re: your mail";
    /** The message CC recipient. */
    protected String message_cc = "nobody@erewhon.com";
    /** The message body */
    protected String message_body =
        "I am unable to attend to your message, as I am busy sunning " +
        "myself on the beach in Maui, where it is warm and peaceful. " +
        "Perhaps when I return I'll get around to reading your mail. " +
        "Or perhaps not.";

    /** The JavaMail session object */
    protected Session session;
    /** The JavaMail message object */
    protected Message mesg;

    /** Do the work: send the mail to the SMTP server.   */
    public void doSend( ) {

        // We need to pass info to the mail server as a Properties, since
        // JavaMail (wisely) allows room for LOTS of properties...
        Properties props = new Properties();
```

*Example 19-3. Sender.java (continued)*

```
        // Your LAN must define the local SMTP server as "mailhost"
        // for this simple-minded version to be able to send mail...
        props.put("mail.smtp.host", "mailhost");

        // Create the Session object
        session = Session.getDefaultInstance(props, null);
        session.setDebug(true);          // Verbose!

        try {
            // create a message
            mesg = new MimeMessage(session);

            // From Address - this should come from a Properties...
            mesg.setFrom(new InternetAddress("nobody@host.domain"));

            // TO Address
            InternetAddress toAddress = new InternetAddress(message_recip);
            mesg.addRecipient(Message.RecipientType.TO, toAddress);

            // CC Address
            InternetAddress ccAddress = new InternetAddress(message_cc);
            mesg.addRecipient(Message.RecipientType.CC, ccAddress);

            // The Subject
            mesg.setSubject(message_subject);

            // Now the message body.
            mesg.setText(message_body);
            // TODO I18N: use setText(msgText.getText( ), charset)

            // Finally, send the message!
            Transport.send(mesg);

        } catch (MessagingException ex) {
            while ((ex = (MessagingException)ex.getNextException( )) != null) {
                ex.printStackTrace( );
            }
        }
    }

    /** Simple test case driver */
    public static void main(String[] av) {
        Sender sm = new Sender( );
        sm.doSend( );
    }
}
```

Of course, a program that can only send one message to one address is not useful in the long run. The second version (not shown here, but in the source tree accompanying this book) allows the To, From, Mailhost, and Subject to come from the command line and reads the mail text either from a file or from the standard input.

---

# 19.3  Mail-Enabling a Server Program

## Problem

You want to send mail notification from within a program.

## Solution

Use the `javax.mail` API directly, or use this `Mailer` wrapper.

## Discussion

It is not uncommon to want to send email from deep within a non-GUI program such as a server. Here, I package all the standard code into a class called `Mailer`, which has a series of "set" methods to set the sender, recipient, mail server, etc. You simply call the `Mailer` method `doSend( )` after setting the recipient, sender, subject, and the message text, and `Mailer` does the rest. Very convenient! So convenient, in fact, that `Mailer` is part of the `com.darwinsys.util` package.

For extra generality, the lists of To, CC, and BCC recipients can be set in one of three ways:

- By passing a string containing one or more recipients, such as "ian, robin"
- By passing an `ArrayList` containing all the recipients as strings
- By adding each recipient as a string

A "full" version allows the user to type the recipients, the subject, the text, and so on into a GUI and have some control over the header fields. The `MailComposeBean` (in Recipe 19.9) does all of these, using a Swing-based GUI. `MailComposeBean` uses this `Mailer` class to interface with the JavaMail API. Example 19-4 contains the code for the `Mailer` class.

*Example 19-4. Mailer.java*

```
package com.darwinsys.mail;

import java.io.*;
import java.util.*;
import javax.mail.*;
import javax.mail.internet.*;

/** Mailer. No relation to Norman. Sends an email message.
 */
public class Mailer {
    /** The javamail session object. */
    protected Session session;
    /** The sender's email address */
    protected String from;
    /** The subject of the message. */
    protected String subject;
```

*Example 19-4. Mailer.java (continued)*

```java
/** The recipient ("To:"), as Strings. */
protected ArrayList toList = new ArrayList( );
/** The CC list, as Strings. */
protected ArrayList ccList = new ArrayList( );
/** The BCC list, as Strings. */
protected ArrayList bccList = new ArrayList( );
/** The text of the message. */
protected String body;
/** The SMTP relay host */
protected String mailHost;
/** The verbosity setting */
protected boolean verbose;

/** Get from */
public String getFrom( ) {
    return from;
}

/** Set from */
public void setFrom(String fm) {
    from = fm;
}

/** Get subject */
public String getSubject( ) {
    return subject;
}

/** Set subject */
public void setSubject(String subj) {
    subject = subj;
}

// LOTS OF OBVIOUS SETTERS/GETTERS NOT SHOWN HERE
// They are in the online source version.

/** Check if all required fields have been set before sending.
 * Normally called e.g., by a JSP before calling doSend.
 * Is also called by doSend for verification.
 */
public boolean isComplete( ) {
    if (from == null    || from.length( )==0) {
        System.err.println("doSend: no FROM");
        return false;
    }
    if (subject == null || subject.length( )==0) {
        System.err.println("doSend: no SUBJECT");
        return false;
    }
    if (toList.size( )==0) {
        System.err.println("doSend: no recipients");
        return false;
```

*Example 19-4. Mailer.java (continued)*

```
        }
        if (body == null || body.length( )==0) {
            System.err.println("doSend: no body");
            return false;
        }
        if (mailHost == null || mailHost.length( )==0) {
            System.err.println("doSend: no server host");
            return false;
        }
        return true;
    }

    public void setServer(String s) {
        mailHost = s;
    }

    /** Send the message.
     */
    public synchronized void doSend( ) throws MessagingException {

        if (!isComplete( ))
            throw new IllegalArgumentException(
                "doSend called before message was complete");

        /** Properties object used to pass props into the MAIL API */
        Properties props = new Properties( );
        props.put("mail.smtp.host", mailHost);

        // Create the Session object
        if (session == null) {
            session = Session.getDefaultInstance(props, null);
            if (verbose)
                session.setDebug(true);           // Verbose!
        }

        // create a message
        final Message mesg = new MimeMessage(session);

        InternetAddress[] addresses;

        // TO Address list
        addresses = new InternetAddress[toList.size( )];
        for (int i=0; i<addresses.length; i++)
            addresses[i] = new InternetAddress((String)toList.get(i));
        mesg.setRecipients(Message.RecipientType.TO, addresses);

        // From Address
        mesg.setFrom(new InternetAddress(from));

        // CC Address list
        addresses = new InternetAddress[ccList.size( )];
```

*Example 19-4. Mailer.java (continued)*

```
        for (int i=0; i<addresses.length; i++)
            addresses[i] = new InternetAddress((String)ccList.get(i));
        mesg.setRecipients(Message.RecipientType.CC, addresses);

        // BCC Address list
        addresses = new InternetAddress[bccList.size()];
        for (int i=0; i<addresses.length; i++)
            addresses[i] = new InternetAddress((String)bccList.get(i));
        mesg.setRecipients(Message.RecipientType.BCC, addresses);

        // The Subject
        mesg.setSubject(subject);

        // Now the message body.
        mesg.setText(body);

        // Finally, send the message! (use static Transport method)
        // Do this in a Thread as it sometimes is too slow for JServ
        new Thread() {
            public void run() {
                try {
                    Transport.send(mesg);
                } catch (MessagingException e) {
                    throw new IllegalArgumentException(
                    "Transport.send() threw: " + e.toString());
                }
            }
        }.start();
    }

    /** Convenience method that does it all with one call. */
    public static void send(String mailhost,
        String recipient, String sender, String subject, String message)
    throws MessagingException {
        Mailer m = new Mailer();
        m.setServer(mailhost);
        m.addTo(recipient);
        m.setFrom(sender);
        m.setSubject(subject);
        m.setBody(message);
        m.doSend();
    }

    /** Convert a list of addresses to an ArrayList. This will work
     * for simple names like "tom, mary@foo.com, 123.45@c$.com"
     * but will fail on certain complex (but RFC-valid) names like
     * "(Darwin, Ian) <ian@darwinsys.com>".
     * Or even "Ian Darwin <ian@darwinsys.com>".
     */
    protected ArrayList tokenize(String s) {
        ArrayList al = new ArrayList();
        StringTokenizer tf = new StringTokenizer(s, ",");
```

*Example 19-4. Mailer.java (continued)*

```
        // For each word found in the line
        while (tf.hasMoreTokens()) {
            // trim blanks, and add to list.
            al.add(tf.nextToken().trim());
        }
        return al;
    }
}
```

# 19.4   Sending MIME Mail

## Problem

You need to send a multipart, MIME-encoded message.

## Solution

Use the Part.

## Discussion

Way back in the old days when the Internet was being invented, most email was composed using the seven-bit ASCII character set. You couldn't send messages containing characters from international character sets. Then some enterprising soul got the idea to convert non-ASCII files into ASCII using a form of encoding known as UUENCODE (the UU is a reference to UUCP, one of the main transport protocols used for email and file transfer at a time when Internet access was prohibitively expensive for the masses). But this was pretty cumbersome, so eventually the Multi-media Internet Mail Extensions, or MIME, was born. MIME has grown over the years to support, as its name implies, a variety of multimedia types in addition to supporting odd characters. MIME typing has become very pervasive due to its use on the Web. As you probably know, every file that your web browser downloads—and a typical web page may contain from 1 to 20, 40, or more files depending on how hog-wild the graphics are—is classified by the web server; this "MIME type" tells the browser how to display the contents of the file. Normal HTML pages are given a type of text/html. Plain text is, as you might guess, text/plain. Images have types such as image/gif, image/jpeg, image/png, and so on. Other types include application/ms-word, application/pdf, audio/au, etc.

Mail *attachments* are files attached to a mail message. MIME is used to classify attachments so that they can be deciphered by a mail reader the same way that a browser decodes files it downloads. Plain text and HTML text are the two most popular, but something called Visual Basic Script, or VBS, was popularized (along with major weaknesses in the design of a certain desktop operating system) by several famous viruses including the so-called "love bug" virus.

The point of all this? The JavaMail extension is designed to make it easy for you to send and receive all normal types of mail, including mail containing MIME-typed data. For example, if you wish to encode a stream containing audio data, you can do so. And, as importantly for Java, if you wish to encode a Reader containing characters in an 8- or 16-bit character encoding, you can do that, too.

The API makes you specify each separate MIME-encoded portion of your message as a Part. A Part represents a chunk of data that may need special handling by MIME encoders when being sent, and MIME decoders (in your email client) when being read. Example 19-5 is an example of sending a text/html attachment along with plain text.

*Example 19-5. SendMime.java (partial listing)*

```
/** The text/plain message body */
protected String message_body =
    "I am unable to attend to your message, as I am busy sunning " +
    "myself on the beach in Maui, where it is warm and peaceful. " +
    "Perhaps when I return I'll get around to reading your mail. " +
    "Or perhaps not.";
/* The text/html data. */
protected String html_data =
    "<HTML><HEAD><TITLE>My Goodness</TITLE></HEAD>" +
    "<BODY><P>You <EM>do</EM> look a little " +
    "<font color=green>GREEN </FONT>" +
    "around the edges..." +
    "</BODY></HTML>";

/** Do the work: send the mail to the SMTP server.  */
public void doSend( ) throws IOException, MessagingException {

        // create a session and message as before

        // Addresses, Subject set as before

        // Now the message body.
        Multipart mp = new MimeMultipart( );

        BodyPart textPart = new MimeBodyPart( );
        textPart.setText(message_body);     // sets type to "text/plain"

        BodyPart pixPart = new MimeBodyPart( );
        pixPart.setContent(html_data, "text/html");

        // Collect the Parts into the MultiPart
        mp.addBodyPart(textPart);
        mp.addBodyPart(pixPart);

        // Put the MultiPart into the Message
        mesg.setContent(mp);

        // Finally, send the message as before
        Transport.send(mesg);
```

# 19.5  Providing Mail Settings

## Problem

You want a way to automatically provide server host, protocol, user, and password.

## Solution

Use a Properties object.

## Discussion

You may remember from Recipe 7.7 that java.util.Properties is a list of name/value pairs, and that my FileProperties extends Properties to provide loading and saving. In several places in this chapter, I use a FileProperties object to preload a large variety of settings, instead of hardcoding them or having to type them all on the command line. When dealing with JavaMail, you must specify the mail hostname, username and password, protocol to use (IMAP, POP, or mailbox for reading), and so on. I store this information in a properties file, and most of the programs in this chapter will use it. Here is my default file, *MailClient.properties*:

```
# This file contains my default Mail properties.
#
# Values for sending
Mail.address=ian@darwinsys.com
Mail.send.proto=smtp
Mail.send.host=localhost
Mail.send.debug=true
#
# Values for receiving
Mail.receive.host=localhost
Mail.receive.protocol=mbox
Mail.receive.user=*
Mail.receive.pass=*
Mail.receive.root=/var/mail/ian
```

The last two, pass and root, can have certain predefined values. Since nobody concerned with security would store unencrypted passwords in a file on disk, I allow you to set pass=ASK (in uppercase), which causes some of my programs to prompt for a password. The JavaMail API allows use of root=INBOX to mean the default storage location for your mail.

The keys in this list of properties intentionally begin with a capital letter since the property names used by the JavaMail API begin with a lowercase letter. The names are rather long, so they, too, are coded. But it would be circular to encode them in a Properties object; instead, they are embedded in a Java interface called MailConstants, shown in Example 19-6.

*Example 19-6. MailConstants.java*

```java
/** Simply a list of names for the Mail System to use.
 * If you "implement" this interface, you don't have to prefix
 * all the names with MailProps in your code.
 */
public interface MailConstants {
    public static final String PROPS_FILE_NAME = "MailClient.properties";

    public static final String SEND_PROTO = "Mail.send.protocol";
    public static final String SEND_USER  = "Mail.send.user";
    public static final String SEND_PASS  = "Mail.send.password";
    public static final String SEND_ROOT  = "Mail.send.root";
    public static final String SEND_HOST  = "Mail.send.host";
    public static final String SEND_DEBUG = "Mail.send.debug";

    public static final String RECV_PROTO = "Mail.receive.protocol";
    public static final String RECV_PORT  = "Mail.receive.port";
    public static final String RECV_USER  = "Mail.receive.user";
    public static final String RECV_PASS  = "Mail.receive.password";
    public static final String RECV_ROOT  = "Mail.receive.root";
    public static final String RECV_HOST  = "Mail.receive.host";
    public static final String RECV_DEBUG = "Mail.receive.debug";
}
```

The fields in this interface can be referred to by their full names; e.g., MailConstants. RECV_PROTO. However, that is almost as much typing as the original long string (Mail. receive.protocol).* As a shortcut, programs that use more than a few of the fields will claim to implement the interface, and then can refer to the fields as part of their class; e.g., RECV_PROTO. This is a bit of a trick on the compiler: the interface has no methods so anybody can implement it, but in so doing "inherit" all the fields (remember that fields in an interface can only be final, not nonfinal).

# 19.6  Sending Mail Without Using JavaMail

## Problem

You want to send mail, but don't want to require javax.mail.

## Solution

This is a Really Bad Idea. You *can* implement the SMTP protocol yourself, but you shouldn't.

---

* A bit like typing BorderLayout.NORTH instead of just North.

# Discussion

Implementing an Internet protocol from the ground up is not for the faint of heart. To get it right, you need to read and study the requisite Internet RFC* pseudo-standards. I make no pretense that this mail sender fully conforms to the relevant RFCs; in fact, it almost certainly does not. The toy implementation here uses a simpler send-expect sequencing to keep in sync with the SMTP server at the other end. Indeed, this program has little to recommend it for serious use; I can only say that I had it around, and it's a good illustration of how simple a mail sender can be. Reading it may help you to appreciate the JavaMail API, which handles not just SMTP but also POP, IMAP, and many other protocols. Do *not* use this code in production; use the JavaMail API instead!

The basic idea of SMTP is that you send requests like MAIL, FROM, RCPT, and DATA in ASCII over an Internet socket (see Recipe 16.1). Even if your mail contains 8- or 16-bit characters, the control information must contain only "pure ASCII" characters. This suggests either using the byte-based stream classes from java.io (see Recipe 10.1) or using Readers/Writers with ASCII encoding. Further, if the data contains 8- or 16-bit characters, it should be encoded using MIME (see Recipe 19.4) This trivial example uses only the ASCII character set to send a plain text message.

When I run this program, it traces the SMTP transaction in the same way sendmail does with the -v option under Unix (this resemblance is intentional). The <<< and >>> are not part of the protocol; they are printed by the program to show the direction of communication (>>> means outgoing, from client to server, and <<< means the opposite). Lines starting with these symbols are the actual lines that an SMTP client and server exchange. You may notice that the server sends lines with both a three-digit numeric code and a text message, while the client sends four-letter commands like HELO and MAIL to tell the server what do to. The data sent in response to the line beginning with code 354 (the actual mail message) is not shown.

```
daroad.darwinsys.com$ jr SmtpTalk localhost ian
+ jikes +E SmtpTalk.java
+ java SmtpTalk localhost ian
SMTP Talker ready
<<< 220 darwinsys.com ESMTP Sendmail 8.9.3/8.9.3; Thu, 23 Dec 1999 16:02:00
>>> HELO darwinsys.com
<<< 250 darwinsys.com Hello ian@localhost [127.0.0.1], pleased to meet you
>>> MAIL From:<MAILER-DAEMON@daroad.darwinsys.com>
<<< 250 <MAILER-DAEMON@daroad.darwinsys.com>... Sender ok
>>> RCPT To:<ian>
<<< 250 <ian>... Recipient ok
>>> DATA
<<< 354 Enter mail, end with "." on a line by itself
>>> .
```

---

* RFC stands for "Request For Comments," a reflection on the community-based standards process that was the norm when the Internet was young.

```
            <<< 250 QAA00250 Message accepted for delivery
            >>> QUIT
            <<< 221 darwinsys.com closing connection daroad.darwinsys.com$
```

The program, shown in Example 19-7, is straightforward, if not very elegant.

*Example 19-7. SmtpTalk.java*

```java
import java.io.*;
import java.net.*;
import java.util.*;

/**
 * SMTP talker class, usable standalone (as a SendMail(8) backend)
 * or inside applications such as JabaDex that need to send mail..
 *
 * OBSOLETE!! Use javax.mail instead, now that it's available!
 *
 */
public class SmtpTalk implements SysExits {
    // SysExits is a simple interface that just defines the
    // System.exit( ) codes to make this compatible with Sendmail.

    BufferedReader is;
    PrintStream os;
    private boolean debug = true;
    private String host;

    /** A simple main program showing the class in action.
     *
     * TODO generalize to accept From arg, read msg on stdin
     */
    public static void main(String[] argv) {
        if (argv.length != 2) {
            System.err.println("Usage: java SmtpTalk host user");
            System.exit(EX_USAGE);
        }

        try {
            SmtpTalk st = new SmtpTalk(argv[0]);

            System.out.println("SMTP Talker ready");

            st.converse("MAILER-DAEMON@daroad.darwinsys.com",
                argv[1], "Test message", "Hello there");
        } catch (SMTPException ig) {
            System.err.println(ig.getMessage( ));
            System.exit(ig.getCode( ));
        }
    }

    /** Constructor taking a server hostname as argument.
     */
```

*Example 19-7. SmtpTalk.java (continued)*

```java
SmtpTalk(String server) throws SMTPException {
    host = server;
    try {
        Socket s = new Socket(host, 25);
        is = new BufferedReader(
            new InputStreamReader(s.getInputStream( )));
        os = new PrintStream(s.getOutputStream( ));
    } catch (NoRouteToHostException e) {
        die(EX_TEMPFAIL, "No route to host " + host);
    } catch (ConnectException e) {
        die(EX_TEMPFAIL, "Connection Refused by " + host);
    } catch (UnknownHostException e) {
        die(EX_NOHOST, "Unknown host " + host);
    } catch (IOException e) {
        die(EX_IOERR, "I/O error setting up socket streams\n" + e);
    }
}

/** Send a command with an operand */
protected void send_cmd(String cmd, String oprnd) {
    send_cmd(cmd + " " + oprnd);
}

/* Send a command with no operand */
protected void send_cmd(String cmd) {
    if (debug)
        System.out.println(">>> " + cmd);
    os.print(cmd + "\r\n");
}

/** Send_text sends the body of the message. */
public void send_text(String text) {
    os.print(text + "\r\n");
}

/** Expect (read and check for) a given reply */
protected boolean expect_reply(String rspNum) throws SMTPException {
    String s = null;
    try {
        s = is.readLine( );
    } catch(IOException e) {
        die(EX_IOERR,"I/O error reading from host " + host + " " + e);
    }
    if (debug) System.out.println("<<< " + s);
    return s.startsWith(rspNum + " ");
}

/** Convenience routine to print message & exit, like
 * K&P error( ), perl die(1,), ...
 * @param ret Numeric value to pass back
 * @param msg Error message to be printed on stdout.
 */
```

*Example 19-7. SmtpTalk.java (continued)*

```java
    protected void die(int ret, String msg) throws SMTPException {
        throw new SMTPException(ret, msg);
    }

    /** send one Mail message to one or more recipients via smtp
     * to server "host".
     */
    public void converse(String sender, String recipients,
            String subject, String body) throws SMTPException {

        if (!expect_reply("220")) die(EX_PROTOCOL,
            "did not get SMTP greeting");

        send_cmd("HELO", "darwinsys.com");
        if (!expect_reply("250")) die(EX_PROTOCOL,
            "did not ack our HELO");

        send_cmd("MAIL", "From:<"+sender+">");    // no spaces!
        if (!expect_reply("250")) die(EX_PROTOCOL,
            "did not ack our MAIL command");

        StringTokenizer st = new StringTokenizer(recipients);
        while (st.hasMoreTokens()) {
            String r = st.nextToken();
            send_cmd("RCPT", "To:<" + r + ">");
            if (!expect_reply("250")) die(EX_PROTOCOL,
                "didn't ack RCPT " + r);
        }
        send_cmd("DATA");
        if (!expect_reply("354")) die(EX_PROTOCOL,"did not want our DATA!");

        send_text("From: " + sender);
        send_text("To: " + recipients);
        send_text("Subject: " + subject);
        send_text("");
        send_text(body + "\r");

        send_cmd(".");
        if (!expect_reply("250")) die(EX_PROTOCOL,"Mail not accepted");

        send_cmd("QUIT");
        if (!expect_reply("221")) die(EX_PROTOCOL,"Other end not closing down");
    }
}
```

# 19.7   Reading Email

## Problem

You need to read mail.

## Solution

Use a JavaMail Store.

## Discussion

The JavaMail API is designed to be easy to use. Store encapsulates the information and access methods for a particular type of mail storage; the steps for using it are listed in the sidebar.

---

### Ian's Basic Steps: Reading Email Using Store

Here is how you read email using Store:

1. Get a Session object using Session.getDefaultInstance( ). You can pass System.getProperties( ) as the Properties argument.
2. Get a Store from the Session object.
3. Get the root Folder.
4. If the root Folder can contain subfolders, list them.
5. For each Folder that can contain messages, call getMessages( ), which returns an array of Message objects.
6. Do what you will with the messages (usually, display the headers and let the user select which message to view).

---

Sun provides a Store class for the IMAP transport mechanism, and optionally for POP3.[*] In these examples I use the Unix mbox protocol[†] (when I started with Unix there was no POP3 protocol; it was traditional to access your mail spool file directly on a server). However, you could use all these programs with the POP or IMAP stores just by passing the appropriate protocol name where "mbox" appears in the following examples. I've tested several of the programs using Sun's POP store and several POP servers (CUCIpop and PMDF).

I delete most of the email I get on one of my systems, so there were only two messages to be read when I ran my first "mailbox lister" program:

```
daroad.darwinsys.com$ java MailLister mbox localhost - - /var/mail/ian
Getting folder /var/mail/ian.
Name: ian(/var/mail/ian)
No New Messages
irate_client@nosuchd  Contract in Hawaii
mailer-daemon@kingcr  Returned mail: Data format error
daroad.darwinsys.com$
```

---

[*] The POP3 Store classes must be downloaded and manually installed from *http://java.sun.com/products/javamail/*.

[†] This is free (GPL) software, which can be downloaded from the Giant Java Tree, *http://www.gjt.org*.

The main program shown in Example 19-8 takes all five arguments from its command line.

*Example 19-8. MailLister.java*

```java
import com.darwinsys.util.*;
import java.util.Properties;
import javax.mail.*;
import javax.mail.internet.*;

/**
 * List all available folders.
 */
public class MailLister {
    static StringAlign fromFmt =
        new StringAlign(20, StringAlign.JUST_LEFT);
    static StringAlign subjFmt =
        new StringAlign(40, StringAlign.JUST_LEFT);

    public static void main(String[] argv) throws Exception {
        String fileName = MailConstants.PROPS_FILE_NAME;
        String protocol = null;
        String host = null;
        String user = null;
        String password = null;
        String root = null;

        // If argc == 1, assume it's a Properties file.
        if (argv.length == 1) {
            fileName = argv[0];
            FileProperties fp = new FileProperties(fileName);
            fp.load();
            protocol = fp.getProperty(MailConstants.RECV_PROTO);
            host = fp.getProperty(MailConstants.RECV_HOST);
            user = fp.getProperty(MailConstants.RECV_USER);
            password = fp.getProperty(MailConstants.RECV_PASS);
            root = fp.getProperty(MailConstants.RECV_ROOT);
        }
        // If not, assume listing all args in long form.
        else if (argv.length == 5) {
            protocol = argv[0];
            host = argv[1];
            user = argv[2];
            password = argv[3];
            root = argv[4];
        }
        // Otherwise give up.
        else {
            System.err.println(
                "Usage: MailLister protocol host user pw root");
            System.exit(0);
        }

        boolean recursive = false;
```

*Example 19-8. MailLister.java (continued)*

```
        // Start with a Session object, as usual
        Session session = Session.getDefaultInstance(
            System.getProperties( ), null);
        session.setDebug(false);

        // Get a Store object for the given protocol
        Store store = session.getStore(protocol);
        store.connect(host, user, password);

        // Get Folder object for root, and list it
        // If root name = "", getDefaultFolder( ), else getFolder(root)
        Folder rf;
        if (root.length( ) != 0) {
            System.out.println("Getting folder " + root + ".");
            rf = store.getFolder(root);
        } else {
            System.out.println("Getting default folder.");
            rf = store.getDefaultFolder( );
        }
        rf.open(Folder.READ_WRITE);

        if (rf.getType( ) == Folder.HOLDS_FOLDERS) {
            Folder[] f = rf.list( );
            for (int i = 0; i < f.length; i++)
                listFolder(f[i], "", recursive);
        } else
                listFolder(rf, "", false);
    }

    static void listFolder(Folder folder, String tab, boolean recurse)
    throws Exception {
        folder.open(Folder.READ_WRITE);
        System.out.println(tab + "Name: " + folder.getName( ) + '(' +
            folder.getFullName( ) + ')');
        if (!folder.isSubscribed( ))
            System.out.println(tab + "Not Subscribed");
        if ((folder.getType( ) & Folder.HOLDS_MESSAGES) != 0) {
            if (folder.hasNewMessages( ))
                System.out.println(tab + "Has New Messages");
            else
                System.out.println(tab + "No New Messages");
            Message[] msgs = folder.getMessages( );
            for (int i=0; i<msgs.length; i++) {
                Message m = msgs[i];
                Address from = m.getFrom( )[0];
                String fromAddress;
                if (from instanceof InternetAddress)
                    fromAddress = ((InternetAddress)from).getAddress( );
                else
                    fromAddress = from.toString( );
                StringBuffer sb = new StringBuffer( );
                fromFmt.format(fromAddress, sb, null);
```

*Example 19-8. MailLister.java (continued)*

```
                sb.    append(" ");
                subjFmt.format(m.getSubject( ), sb, null);
                System.out.println(sb.toString( ));
            }
        }
        if ((folder.getType( ) & Folder.HOLDS_FOLDERS) != 0) {
            System.out.println(tab + "Is Directory");
        if (recurse) {
            Folder[] f = folder.list( );
            for (int i=0; i < f.length; i++)
                listFolder(f[i], tab + "", recurse);
            }
        }
    }
}
```

This program has the core of a full mail reader but doesn't actually fetch the articles. To display a message, you have to get it (by number) from the folder, then call methods like getSubject( ), getFrom( ), and others. The listFolder( ) method does this to obtain identifying information on each message, and formats them using the StringAlign class from Recipe 3.5.

If we add a GUI and a bit of code to get all the relevant header fields, we can have a working mail reader. We'll show the messages in a tree view, since some protocols let you have more than one folder containing messages. For this we'll use a JTree widget, the Swing GUI component for displaying text or icons in a tree-like view. The objects stored in a JTree must be Node objects, but we also want them to be Folders and Messages. I handled this by subclassing DefaultMutableNode and adding a field for the folder or message, although you could also subclass Folder and implement the Node interface. Arguably, the way I did it is less "pure OO," but also less work. Example 19-9 is my MessageNode; FolderNode is similar, but simpler in that its toString( ) method calls only the Folder's getName( ) method.

*Example 19-9. MessageNode.java*

```
import javax.mail.*;
import javax.mail.internet.*;
import javax.swing.tree.*;

/** A Mutable Tree Node that is also a Message. */
public class MessageNode extends DefaultMutableTreeNode {
    Message m;

    StringAlign fromFmt = new StringAlign(20, StringAlign.JUST_LEFT);
    StringAlign subjFmt = new StringAlign(30, StringAlign.JUST_LEFT);

    MessageNode(Message m) {
        this.m = m;
    }
```

*Example 19-9. MessageNode.java (continued)*

```java
    public String toString( ) {
        try {
            Address from = m.getFrom( )[0];

            String fromAddress;
            if (from instanceof InternetAddress)
                fromAddress = ((InternetAddress)from).getAddress( );
            else
                fromAddress = from.toString( );

            StringBuffer sb = new StringBuffer( );
            fromFmt.format(fromAddress, sb, null);
            sb.    append(" ");
            subjFmt.format(m.getSubject( ), sb, null);
            return sb.toString( );
        } catch (Exception e) {
            return e.toString( );
        }
    }
}
```

These are all put together into a mail reader in Recipe 19.8.

# 19.8   Program: MailReaderBean

Example 19-10 shows the complete MailReaderBean program. As the name implies, it can be used as a bean in larger programs but also has a main method for standalone use. Clicking on a message displays it in the message view part of the window; this is handled by the TreeSelectionListener called tsl.

*Example 19-10. MailReaderBean.java*

```java
import java.awt.*;
import java.awt.event.*;
import javax.swing.*;
import javax.swing.tree.*;
import javax.swing.event.*;
import javax.mail.*;
import javax.mail.internet.*;

/**
 * Display a mailbox or mailboxes.
 * This is the generic version in javasrc/email, split off from
 * JabaDex because of the latter's domain-specific "implements module" stuff.

 */
public class MailReaderBean extends JSplitPane {

    private JTextArea bodyText;
```

*Example 19-10. MailReaderBean.java (continued)*

```java
/* Construct a mail reader bean with all defaults.
 */
public MailReaderBean( ) throws Exception {
    this("smtp", "mailhost", "user", "nopasswd", "/");
}

/* Construct a mail reader bean with all values. */
public MailReaderBean(
    String protocol,
    String host,
    String user,
    String password,
    String rootName)
throws Exception {

    super(VERTICAL_SPLIT);

    boolean recursive = false;

    // Start with a Mail Session object
    Session session = Session.getDefaultInstance(
        System.getProperties( ), null);
    session.setDebug(false);

    // Get a Store object for the given protocol
    Store store = session.getStore(protocol);
    store.connect(host, user, password);

    // Get Folder object for root, and list it
    // If root name = "", getDefaultFolder( ), else getFolder(root)
    FolderNode top;
    if (rootName.length( ) != 0) {
        // System.out.println("Getting folder " + rootName + ".");
        top = new FolderNode(store.getFolder(rootName));
    } else {
        // System.out.println("Getting default folder.");
        top = new FolderNode(store.getDefaultFolder( ));
    }
    if (top == null || !top.f.exists( )) {
        System.out.println("Invalid folder " + rootName);
        return;
    }

    if (top.f.getType( ) == Folder.HOLDS_FOLDERS) {
        Folder[] f = top.f.list( );
        for (int i = 0; i < f.length; i++)
            listFolder(top, new FolderNode(f[i]), recursive);
    } else
            listFolder(top, top, false);

    // Now that (all) the foldernodes and treenodes are in,
    // construct a JTree object from the top of the list down,
```

*Example 19-10. MailReaderBean.java (continued)*

```
// make the JTree scrollable (put in JScrollPane),
// and add it as the MailComposeBean's Northern child.
JTree tree = new JTree(top);
JScrollPane treeScroller = new JScrollPane(tree);
treeScroller.setBackground(tree.getBackground( ));
this.setTopComponent(treeScroller);

// The Southern (Bottom) child is a textarea to display the msg.
bodyText = new JTextArea(15, 80);
this.setBottomComponent(new JScrollPane(bodyText));

// Add a notification listener for the tree; this will
// display the clicked-upon message
TreeSelectionListener tsl = new TreeSelectionListener( ) {
    public void valueChanged(TreeSelectionEvent evt) {
        Object[] po = evt.getPath( ).getPath( );    // yes, repeat it.
        Object o = po[po.length - 1];    // last node in path
        if (o instanceof FolderNode) {
            // System.out.println("Select folder " + o.toString( ));
            return;
        }
        if (o instanceof MessageNode) {
            bodyText.setText("");
            try {
                Message m = ((MessageNode)o).m;

                bodyText.append("To: ");
                Object[] tos = m.getAllRecipients( );
                for (int i=0; i<tos.length; i++) {
                    bodyText.append(tos[i].toString( ));
                    bodyText.append(" ");
                }
                bodyText.append("\n");

                bodyText.append("Subject: " + m.getSubject( ) + "\n");
                bodyText.append("From: ");
                Object[] froms = m.getFrom( );
                for (int i=0; i<froms.length; i++) {
                    bodyText.append(froms[i].toString( ));
                    bodyText.append(" ");
                }
                bodyText.append("\n");

                bodyText.append("Date: " + m.getSentDate( ) + "\n");
                bodyText.append("\n");

                bodyText.append(m.getContent( ).toString( ));

                // Start reading at top of message(!)
                bodyText.setCaretPosition(0);
            } catch (Exception e) {
                bodyText.append(e.toString( ));
```

*Example 19-10. MailReaderBean.java (continued)*

```
                }
            } else
                System.err.println("UNEXPECTED SELECTION: " + o.getClass());
        }
    };
    tree.addTreeSelectionListener(tsl);
}


static void listFolder(FolderNode top, FolderNode folder, boolean recurse)
throws Exception {
    // System.out.println(folder.f.getName() + folder.f.getFullName());
    if ((folder.f.getType() & Folder.HOLDS_MESSAGES) != 0) {
        Message[] msgs = folder.f.getMessages();
        for (int i=0; i<msgs.length; i++) {
            MessageNode m = new MessageNode(msgs[i]);
            Address from = m.m.getFrom()[0];
            String fromAddress;
            if (from instanceof InternetAddress)
                fromAddress = ((InternetAddress)from).getAddress();
            else
                fromAddress = from.toString();
            top.add(new MessageNode(msgs[i]));
        }
    }
    if ((folder.f.getType() & Folder.HOLDS_FOLDERS) != 0) {
        if (recurse) {
            Folder[] f = folder.f.list();
            for (int i=0; i < f.length; i++)
                listFolder(new FolderNode(f[i]), top, recurse);
        }
    }
}


/* Test unit - main program */
public static void main(String[] args) throws Exception {
    final JFrame jf = new JFrame("MailReaderBean");
    String mbox = "/var/mail/ian";
    if (args.length > 0)
        mbox = args[0];
    MailReaderBean mb = new MailReaderBean("mbox", "localhost",
        "", "", mbox);
    jf.getContentPane().add(mb);
    jf.setSize(640,480);
    jf.setVisible(true);
    jf.addWindowListener(new WindowAdapter() {
        public void windowClosing(WindowEvent e) {
        jf.setVisible(false);
        jf.dispose();
        System.exit(0);
        }
    });
}
}
```

It's a minimal, but working, mail reader. I'll merge it with a mail sender in Recipe 19.9 to make a complete mail client program.

## 19.9 Program: MailClient

This program is a simplistic GUI-based mail client. It uses the Swing GUI components (see Chapter 14) along with JavaMail. The program loads a `Properties` file (see Recipe 7.7) to decide which mail server to use for outgoing mail (see Recipe 19.2), as well as the name of a mail server for incoming mail and a `Store` class (see this chapter's Introduction and Recipe 19.7). The main class, `MailClient`, is simply a `JComponent` with a `JTabbedPane` to let you switch between reading mail and sending mail.

When first started, the program behaves as a mail reader, as shown in Figure 19-2.

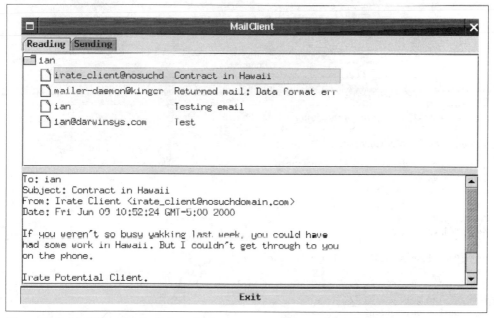

*Figure 19-2. MailClient in reading mode*

You can click on the Sending tab to make it show the Mail Compose window, shown in Figure 19-3. I am typing a message to an ISP about some spam I received.

The code reuses the `MailReaderBean` presented earlier and a similar `MailComposeBean` for sending mail. Example 19-11 is the main program.

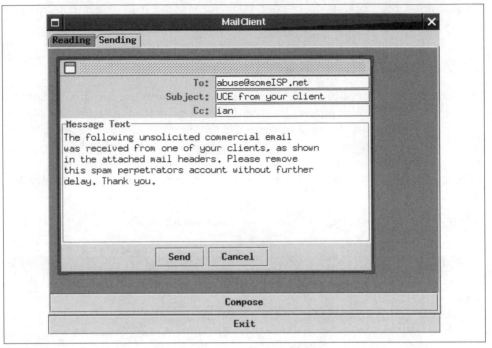

*Figure 19-3. MailClient in compose mode*

*Example 19-11. MailClient.java*

```java
import com.darwinsys.util.FileProperties;
import java.awt.*;
import java.awt.event.*;
import javax.swing.*;
import java.io.*;
import java.util.*;

/** Standalone MailClient GUI application.
 */
public class MailClient extends JComponent implements MailConstants {
    /** The quit button */
    JButton quitButton;
    /** The read mode */
    MailReaderBean mrb;
    /** The send mode */
    MailComposeFrame mcb;

    /** Construct the MailClient JComponent a default Properties filename */
    public MailClient() throws Exception {
        this(PROPS_FILE_NAME);
    }

    /** Construct the MailClient JComponent with no Properties filename */
    public MailClient(String propsFileName) throws Exception {
        super();
```

*Example 19-11. MailClient.java (continued)*

```
    // Construct and load the Properties for the mail reader and sender.
    Properties mailProps = new FileProperties(propsFileName);

    // Gather some key values
    String proto = mailProps.getProperty(RECV_PROTO);
    String user  = mailProps.getProperty(RECV_USER);
    String pass  = mailProps.getProperty(RECV_PASS);
    String host  = mailProps.getProperty(RECV_HOST);

    if (proto==null)
        throw new IllegalArgumentException(RECV_PROTO + "==null");

    // Protocols other than "mbox" need a password.
    if (!proto.equals("mbox") && (pass == null || pass.equals("ASK"))) {
        String np;
        do {
            // VERY INSECURE -- should use JDialog + JPasswordField!
            np = JOptionPane.showInputDialog(null,
            "Please enter password for " + proto + " user  " +
                user + " on " + host + "\n" +
                "(warning: password WILL echo)",
            "Password request", JOptionPane.QUESTION_MESSAGE);
        } while (np == null || (np != null && np.length() == 0));
        mailProps.setProperty(RECV_PASS, np);
    }

    // Dump them all into System.properties so other code can find.
    System.getProperties().putAll(mailProps);

    // Construct the GUI
    // System.out.println("Constructing GUI");
    setLayout(new BorderLayout());
    JTabbedPane tbp = new JTabbedPane();
    add(BorderLayout.CENTER, tbp);
    tbp.addTab("Reading", mrb = new MailReaderBean());
    tbp.addTab("Sending", mcb = new MailComposeFrame());
    add(BorderLayout.SOUTH, quitButton = new JButton("Exit"));
    // System.out.println("Leaving Constructor");
}

/** "main program" method - run the program */
public static void main(String[] av) throws Exception {

    final JFrame f = new JFrame("MailClient");

    // Start by checking that the javax.mail package is installed!
    try {
        Class.forName("javax.mail.Session");
    } catch (ClassNotFoundException cnfe) {
        JOptionPane.showMessageDialog(f,
            "Sorry, the javax.mail package was not found\n(" + cnfe + ")",
            "Error", JOptionPane.ERROR_MESSAGE);
```

*Example 19-11. MailClient.java (continued)*

```
        return;
    }

    // create a MailClient object
    MailClient comp;
    if (av.length == 0)
        comp = new MailClient();
    else
        comp = new MailClient(av[0]);
    f.getContentPane().add(comp);

    // Set up action handling for GUI
    comp.quitButton.addActionListener(new ActionListener() {
        public void actionPerformed(ActionEvent e) {
            f.setVisible(false);
            f.dispose();
            System.exit(0);
        }
    });
    f.addWindowListener(new WindowAdapter() {
        public void windowClosing(WindowEvent e) {
            f.setVisible(false);
            f.dispose();
            System.exit(0);
        }
    });

    // Set bounds. Best at 800,600, but works at 640x480
    // f.setLocation(140, 80);
    // f.setSize     (500,400);
    f.pack();

    f.setVisible(true);
    }
}
```

The MailReaderBean used in the Reading tab is exactly the same as the one shown in Recipe 19.8.

The MailComposeBean used for the Sending tab is a GUI component for composing a mail message. It uses the Mailer class from Recipe 19.3 to do the actual sending. Example 19-12 shows the MailComposeBean program.

*Example 19-12. MailComposeBean.java*

```
import com.darwinsys.util.*;
import java.awt.*;
import java.awt.event.*;
import javax.swing.*;
import java.util.*;
import java.io.*;
import javax.activation.*;
```

*Example 19-12. MailComposeBean.java (continued)*

```java
import javax.mail.*;
import javax.mail.internet.*;

/** MailComposeBean - Mail gather and send Component Bean.
 *
 * Can be used as a Visible bean or as a Non-Visible bean.
 * If setVisible(true), puts up a mail compose window with a Send button.
 * If user clicks on it, tries to send the mail to a Mail Server
 * for delivery on the Internet.
 *
 * If not visible, use add(), set( ), and doSend( ) methods.
 *
 */
public class MailComposeBean extends JPanel {

    /** The parent frame to be hidden/disposed; may be JFrame, JInternalFrame
     * or JPanel, as necessary */
    private Container parent;

    private JButton sendButton, cancelButton;
    private JTextArea msgText;          // The message!

    // The To, Subject, and CC lines are treated a bit specially,
    // any user-defined headers are just put in the tfs array.
    private JTextField tfs[], toTF, ccTF, subjectTF;
    // tfsMax MUST == how many are current, for focus handling to work
    private int tfsMax = 3;
    private final int TO = 0, SUBJ = 1, CC = 2, BCC = 3, MAXTF = 8;

    /** The JavaMail session object */
    private Session session = null;
    /** The JavaMail message object */
    private Message mesg = null;

    private int mywidth;
    private int myheight;

    /** Construct a MailComposeBean with no default recipient */
    MailComposeBean(Container parent, String title, int height, int width) {
        this(parent, title, null, height, width);
    }

    /** Construct a MailComposeBean with no arguments (needed for Beans) */
    MailComposeBean( ) {
        this(null, "Compose", null, 300, 200);
    }

    /** Constructor for MailComposeBean object.
     *
     * @param parent    Container parent. If JFrame or JInternalFrame,
     * will setvisible(false) and dispose( ) when
     * message has been sent. Not done if "null" or JPanel.
```

*Example 19-12. MailComposeBean.java (continued)*

```
 * @param title        Title to display in the titlebar
 * @param recipient    Email address of recipient
 * @param height     Height of mail compose window
 * @param width        Width of mail compose window
 */
MailComposeBean(Container parent, String title, String recipient,
        int width, int height) {
    super( );

    this.parent = parent;

    mywidth = width;
    myheight = height;

    // THE GUI
    Container cp = this;
    cp.setLayout(new BorderLayout( ));

    // Top is a JPanel for name, address, etc.
    // Centre is the TextArea.
    // Bottom is a panel with Send and Cancel buttons.
    JPanel tp = new JPanel( );
    tp.setLayout(new GridLayout(3,2));
    cp.add(BorderLayout.NORTH, tp);

    tfs = new JTextField[MAXTF];

    tp.add(new JLabel("To: ", JLabel.RIGHT));
    tp.add(tfs[TO] = toTF = new JTextField(35));
    if (recipient != null)
        toTF.setText(recipient);
    toTF.requestFocus( );

    tp.add(new JLabel("Subject: ", JLabel.RIGHT));
    tp.add(tfs[SUBJ] = subjectTF = new JTextField(35));
    subjectTF.requestFocus( );

    tp.add(new JLabel("Cc: ", JLabel.RIGHT));
    tp.add(tfs[CC] = ccTF = new JTextField(35));

    // Centre is the TextArea
    cp.add(BorderLayout.CENTER, msgText = new JTextArea(70, 10));
    msgText.setBorder(BorderFactory.createTitledBorder("Message Text"));

    // Bottom is the apply/cancel button
    JPanel bp = new JPanel( );
    bp.setLayout(new FlowLayout( ));
    bp.add(sendButton = new JButton("Send"));
    sendButton.addActionListener(new ActionListener( ) {
        public void actionPerformed(ActionEvent e) {
            try {
                doSend( );
```

*Example 19-12. MailComposeBean.java (continued)*

```
                } catch(Exception err) {
                    System.err.println("Error: " + err);
                    JOptionPane.showMessageDialog(null,
                        "Sending error:\n" + err.toString( ),
                        "Send failed", JOptionPane.ERROR_MESSAGE);
                }
            }
        });
        bp.add(cancelButton = new JButton("Cancel"));
        cancelButton.addActionListener(new ActionListener( ) {
            public void actionPerformed(ActionEvent e) {
                maybeKillParent( );
            }
        });
        cp.add(BorderLayout.SOUTH, bp);
    }

    public Dimension getPreferredSize( ) {
        return new Dimension(mywidth, myheight);
    }
    public Dimension getMinimumSize( ) {
        return getPreferredSize( );
    }

    /** Do the work: send the mail to the SMTP server.
     *
     * ASSERT: must have set at least one recipient.
     */
    public void doSend( ) {

        try {
            Mailer m = new Mailer( );

            FileProperties props =
                new FileProperties(MailConstants.PROPS_FILE_NAME);
            String serverHost = props.getProperty(MailConstants.SEND_HOST);
            if (serverHost == null) {
                JOptionPane.showMessageDialog(parent,
                    "\"" + MailConstants.SEND_HOST +
                        "\" must be set in properties"
                    "No server!",
                    JOptionPane.ERROR_MESSAGE);
                return;
            }
            m.setServer(serverHost);

            String tmp = props.getProperty(MailConstants.SEND_DEBUG);
            m.setVerbose(tmp != null && tmp.equals("true"));

            String myAddress = props.getProperty("Mail.address");
            if (myAddress == null) {
```

*Example 19-12. MailComposeBean.java (continued)*

```
                    JOptionPane.showMessageDialog(parent,
                        "\"Mail.address\" must be set in properties",
                        "No From: address!",
                        JOptionPane.ERROR_MESSAGE);
                    return;
                }
                m.setFrom(myAddress);

                m.setToList(toTF.getText());
                m.setCcList(ccTF.getText());
                // m.setBccList(bccTF.getText());

                if (subjectTF.getText().length() != 0) {
                    m.setSubject(subjectTF.getText());
                }

                // Now copy the text from the Compose TextArea.
                m.setBody(msgText.getText());
                // TODO  I18N: use setBody(msgText.getText(), charset)

                // Finally, send the sucker!
                m.doSend();

                // Now hide the main window
                maybeKillParent();

        } catch (MessagingException me) {
            me.printStackTrace();
            while ((me = (MessagingException)me.getNextException()) != null) {
                me.printStackTrace();
            }
            JOptionPane.showMessageDialog(null,
                "Mail Sending Error:\n" + me.toString(),
                "Error", JOptionPane.ERROR_MESSAGE);
        } catch (Exception e) {
            JOptionPane.showMessageDialog(null,
                "Mail Sending Error:\n" + e.toString(),
                "Error", JOptionPane.ERROR_MESSAGE);
        }
    }

    private void maybeKillParent() {
        if (parent == null)
            return;
        if (parent instanceof Frame) {
            ((Frame)parent).setVisible(true);
            ((Frame)parent).dispose();
        }
        if (parent instanceof JInternalFrame) {
            ((JInternalFrame)parent).setVisible(true);
            ((JInternalFrame)parent).dispose();
        }
    }
}
```

*Example 19-12. MailComposeBean.java (continued)*

```
    /** Simple test case driver */
    public static void main(String[] av) {
        final JFrame jf = new JFrame("DarwinSys Compose Mail Tester");
        System.getProperties().setProperty("Mail.server", "mailhost");
        System.getProperties().setProperty("Mail.address", "nobody@home");
        MailComposeBean sm =
            new MailComposeBean(jf,
            "Test Mailer", "spam-magnet@darwinsys.com", 500, 400);
        sm.setSize(500, 400);
        jf.getContentPane().add(sm);
        jf.setLocation(100, 100);
        jf.setVisible(true);
        jf.addWindowListener(new WindowAdapter() {
            public void windowClosing(WindowEvent e) {
            jf.setVisible(false);
            jf.dispose();
            System.exit(0);
            }
        });
        jf.pack();
    }
}
```

Further, the `MailComposeBean` program is a JavaBean, so it can be used in GUI builders and even have its fields set within a JSP. It has a `main` method, which allows it to be used standalone (primarily for testing).

To let you compose one or more email messages concurrently, messages being composed are placed in a JDesktopPane, Java's implementation of Multiple-Document Interface (MDI). Example 19-13 shows how to construct a multiwindow email implementation. Each `MailComposeBean` must be wrapped in a `JInternalFrame`, which is what you need to place components in the `JDesktopPane`. This wrapping is handled inside `MailReaderFrame`, one instance of which is created in the `MailClient` constructor. The `MailReaderFrame` method `newSend()` creates an instance of `MailComposeBean` and shows it in the `JDesktopFrame`, returning a reference to the `MailComposeBean` so that the caller can use methods such as `addRecipient()` and `send()`. It also creates a Compose button and places it below the desktop pane so that you can create a new composition window by clicking the button.

*Example 19-13. MailComposeFrame.java*

```
import java.awt.*;
import java.awt.event.*;
import javax.swing.*;

/** A frame for (possibly) multiple MailComposeBean windows.
 */
public class MailComposeFrame extends JPanel {
    JDesktopPane dtPane;
    JButton newButton;
    protected int nx, ny;
```

*Example 19-13. MailComposeFrame.java (continued)*

```
/** To be useful here, a MailComposeBean has to be inside
 * its own little JInternalFrame.
 */
public MailComposeBean newSend( ) {

    // Make the JInternalFrame wrapper
    JInternalFrame jf = new JInternalFrame( );

    // Bake the actual Bean
    MailComposeBean newBean =
        new MailComposeBean(this, "Compose", 400, 250);

    // Arrange them on the diagonal.
    jf.setLocation(nx+=10, ny+=10);

    // Make the new Bean be the contents of the JInternalFrame
    jf.setContentPane(newBean);
    jf.pack( );
    jf.toFront( );

    // Add the JInternalFrame to the JDesktopPane
    dtPane.add(jf);
    return newBean;
}

/* Construct a MailComposeFrame, with a Compose button. */
public MailComposeFrame( ) {

    setLayout(new BorderLayout( ));

    dtPane = new JDesktopPane( );
    add(dtPane, BorderLayout.CENTER);

    newButton = new JButton("Compose");
    newButton.addActionListener(new ActionListener( ) {
        public void actionPerformed(ActionEvent e) {
            newSend( );
        }
    });
    add(newButton, BorderLayout.SOUTH);
}
}
```

The file *TODO.txt* in the email source directory lists a number of improvements that would have to be added to the MailClient program to make it functional enough for daily use (delete and reply functionality, menus, templates, aliases, and much more). But it is a start and provides a structure to build on.

# See Also

Sun maintains a mailing list specifically for the JavaMail API. Read about the java-mail-interest list near the bottom of the main API page at *http://java.sun.com/products/javamail/*. This is also a good place to find other provider classes; Sun has a POP3 provider, and there is a list of third-party products. You can also download the complete source code for the JavaMail API from Sun's community source project through the link on the main API page.

There are now several books that discuss Internet mail. David Wood's *Programming Internet Email* (O'Reilly) discusses all aspects of Internet email, with an emphasis on Perl but with a chapter and examples on JavaMail. Similarly, Kevin Johnson's *Internet Email Protocols: A Developer's Guide* (Addison Wesley) covers the protocols and has appendixes on various programming languages, including Java. *The Programmer's Guide to Internet Mail: Smtp, Pop, Imap, and Ldap*, by John Rhoton (Digital Press) and *Essential E-Mail Standards: RFCs and Protocols Made Practical* by Pete Loshin (Wiley) cover the protocols without much detail on Java implementation. *Internet E-Mail: Protocols, Standards, and Implementation* by Lawrence E. Hughes (Artech House Telecommunications) covers a great deal of general material but emphasizes Microsoft technologies and doesn't say much about JavaMail. Finally, the books *Stopping Spam: Stamping Out Unwanted Email and News Postings* by Alan Schwartz and Simson Garfinkel (O'Reilly) and *Removing the Spam: Email Processing and Filtering* (Addison Wesley) by Geoff Mulligan aren't about JavaMail, but they discuss what is now perhaps the biggest problem facing Internet mail users.

# CHAPTER 20

# Database Access

## 20.0 Introduction

Java can be used to access many kinds of databases. A *database* can be something as simple as a text file or a fast key/value pairing on disk (DBM format), as sophisticated as a relational database management system (DBMS), or as exotic as an object database.

Regardless of how your data is actually stored, in many applications you'll want to write a class called an *accessor* to mediate between the database and the rest of the application. For example, if you are using JDBC, the answers to your query come back packaged in an object called a ResultSet, but it would not make sense to structure the rest of your application around the ResultSet because it's JDBC-specific. In a Personal Information Manager application, for example, the primary classes might be Person, Address, and Meeting. You would probably write a PersonAccessor class to request the names and addresses from the database (probably using JDBC) and generate Person and Address objects from them. The DataAccessor objects would also take updates from the main program and store them into the database.*

Java DataBase Connectivity (JDBC) consists of classes in package java.sql and some JDBC Level 2 extensions in package javax.sql. (SQL is the Structured Query Language, used by relational database software to provide a standard command language for creating, modifying, updating, and querying relational databases.)

Why was JDBC invented? Java is highly portable, but many databases previously lacked a portable interface and were tied to one particular language or platform. JDBC is designed to fill that gap.

---

* If this reminds you of Enterprise JavaBeans, you're right. If you're familiar with EJB, you can think of simple entity beans as a specialized kind of data accessor.

JDBC is patterned very loosely on Microsoft's Open DataBase Connectivity (ODBC). Sun's Java group borrowed several general ideas from Microsoft, who in turn borrowed some of it from prior art in relational databases. While ODBC is C- and pointer-based (void * at that), JDBC is based on Java and is therefore portable as well as being network-aware and having better type checking.

JDBC comes in two parts: the portable JDBC API provided with Java and the database-specific driver usually provided by the DBMS vendor or a third party. These drivers have to conform to a particular interface (called Driver, unsurprisingly) and map from the generic calls into something the existing database code can understand.

JDBC deals with *relational databases* only: no flat files (although several drivers have been written that map from flat files to the JDBC API) and no DBM files (though you could write a driver that used one DBM file for each table in a database). Through this clever division of labor, JDBC can provide access to any relational database, be it local or remote (remote databases are accessed using client sockets, as discussed in Chapter 17). In addition to the drivers from database vendors, there is also a JDBC-ODBC bridge in the standard JDK and JRE; this allows you to use JDBC with an existing Windows database. Its performance is weaker because it adds an extra layer, but it does work.

One fairly common form of database that I do not cover is the so-called Xbase format, which is implemented by several commercial databases (dBase, FoxBase, etc.) common in the MS-DOS and Windows world. If you wanted to decode such a database in Java, you'd probably start with the Xbase file format, documented at *http://www.e-bachmann.dk/docs/xbase.htm*. Alternately, you might find a useful driver in the Microsoft ODBC-32 software and use the JDBC-to-ODBC bridge to convert your data to a newer format such as a relational database.

Java Data Objects, or JDO, is an "accessor" layer that is much easier to use than invoking JDBC directly. One way to think of JDO is that it's a way of writing accessors automatically, leaving you more time to concentrate on your application logic.

This chapter overviews several database techniques, emphasizing JDBC, so that you know what this technology looks and feels like.

# 20.1   Easy Database Access with JDO

## Problem

You want an easy way to access your relational database.

## Solution

Use an implementation of the Java Data Objects specification.

## Discussion

As mentioned, JDO provides easy access to databases. JDO is a specification from Sun; there are many implementations of it. JDO works by inserting extra code into your data classes, a process it calls "enhancement." The extra code is what transparently interfaces with the database. The JDO spec is not tied to the relational model; JDO data can be stored in a local file, a relational database, an object database, or whatever else an implementation chooses to use.

The "Reference Implementation" from Sun uses a file store on local disks. Example 20-1 is the Serialization program from Chapter 10 (Recipe 10.18) implemented using JDO. Recall from that discussion that the save( ) method in the parent class calls the write( ) method implemented in this subclass to save a variety of objects.

*Example 20-1. SerialDemoJDO*

```
/**
 * A demonstration of serialization using JDO.
 */
public class SerialDemoJDO extends SerialDemoAbstractBase {

    public static void main(String[] args) throws IOException {
        SerialDemoJDO jd = new SerialDemoJDO( );
        jd.save( );
        jd.dump( );
    }

    public PersistenceManager getPM( ) {
        Properties p = new Properties( );
        try {
            p.load(new FileInputStream("jdo.properties"));
            PersistenceManagerFactory pmf =
                JDOHelper.getPersistenceManagerFactory(p);
```

*Example 20-1. SerialDemoJDO (continued)*

```
            return pmf.getPersistenceManager( );
    } catch (IOException ex) {
        throw new RuntimeException(ex.toString( ));
    }
}

public void write(Object o) {
    PersistenceManager pm = getPM( );
    pm.currentTransaction().begin( );
    if (o instanceof Collection) {
        pm.makePersistentAll((Collection)o);
    } else {
        pm.makePersistent(o);
    }
    pm.currentTransaction().commit( );
    pm.close( );
}

public void dump( ) {
    PersistenceManager pm = getPM( );
    Object[] data - new Object[3];
    pm.retrieveAll(data);
    for (int i = 0; i < data.length; i++) {
        System.out.println(data[i]);
    }
    pm.close( );
}
}
```

Two things are not shown here: how the `MyData` class used in the earlier recipe gets turned into a JDO class and how JDO knows how and where to store the data.

The Enhancement process requires an XML configuration file to tell it which classes are to be enhanced—that is, which are the data classes. This, and the actual class files, are read by the JDO enhancer, and new class files are generated. For example, a `setName( )` method that simply saves its argument in a field might be enhanced to also send it as an update to a database. The enhancement process consists of running an enhancer program provided with your implementation; for the Sun Reference Implementation, this can be as simple as:

```
java com.sun.jdori.enhancer.Main -s build/classdir build/com/darwinsys/Mydata.class
```

Naturally there is an Ant task for automating this step.

To tell JDO where to store its data, a properties file is loaded, which specifies a minimum of four parameters: the Service Provider to use, the database name, and a user name and password. The Reference Implementation provides an `FOStore` class that saves file objects on the local disk. A set of properties for this implementation could be the following:

```
javax.jdo.PersistenceManagerFactoryClass=com.sun.jdori.fostore.FOStorePMF
javax.jdo.option.ConnectionURL=fostore:database/javasrc.io
# For the JDO RI, it doesn't matter what name/passwd you use, but
# both MUST be specified as some value.
javax.jdo.option.ConnectionUserName=ian
javax.jdo.option.ConnectionPassword=anything
```

Once all these pieces are in place, the program in Example 20-1 can be run. The MyData objects are saved to disk and displayed by the program.

Where JDO really comes into its own is that it will just as easily access an SQL database, assuming that your JDO implementation supports this. All that is necessary is to extend the *jdo.properties* file to have a JDBC driver and a JDBC-style URL (details of these are discussed in Recipe 20.5). For example:

```
javax.jdo.option.ConnectionURL=jdbc:postgresql:ecom
javax.jdo.option.ConnectionDriverName=org.postgresql.Driver
```

## See Also

There is much more to JDO than I've covered here. The web site *http://www.jdocentral.com/* contains JDO information, articles, and links to many implementations. The O'Reilly book *Java Data Objects*, by David Jordan and Craig Russell (both of whom are on the JDO standards committee), covers JDO in detail.

# 20.2   Text-File Databases

## Problem

You wish to treat a text file as a database.

## Solution

Write an Accessor class that returns objects of the correct type.

## Discussion

The fictional JabaDot web site, like many web sites, has a list of registered users. Each user has a login name, full name, password, email address, privilege level, and so forth and is represented by a User object. These are stored in the User database.

This database has several versions, so I have an abstract class to represent all the user data accessors, called UserDB. UserDB and all its subclasses implement the Data Accessor Object (DAO) design pattern: use a class that encapsulates the complexity of dealing with a particular database. The DAO's main function is to read and write the database; in the text-based version, the reading can be done in the constructor or in the getUsers( ) method.

Of course, for efficiency, we want to do this reading only once, even though we may have many users visiting the site. As a result, the design pattern known as *singleton* (ensure one single instance exists; see Recipe 9.10) is used. Anybody wanting a UserDB object does not construct one (the constructor is private) but must call getInstance( ). Unsurprisingly, getInstance( ) returns the same value to anyone who calls it. The only implication of this is that some of the methods must be synchronized (see Chapter 24) to prevent complications when more than one user accesses the (single) UserDB object concurrently.

The code in Example 20-2 uses a class called JDConstants (JabaDot constants), which is a wrapper around a Properties object (see Recipe 7.7) to get values such as the location of the database.

*Example 20-2. UserDB.java*

```
package jabadot;

import java.io.*;
import java.util.*;
import java.sql.SQLException;      // Only used by JDBC version
import java.lang.reflect.*;        // For loading our subclass class.

/** A base for several DAOs for User objects.
 * We use a Singleton access method for efficiency and to enforce
 * single access on the database, which means we can keep an in-memory
 * copy (in an ArrayList) perfectly in synch with the database.
 *
 * We provide field numbers, which are 1-based (for SQL), not 0 as per Java.
 */
public abstract class UserDB {

    public static final int NAME      = 1;
    public static final int PASSWORD  = 2;
    public static final int FULLNAME  = 3;
    public static final int EMAIL     = 4;
    public static final int CITY      = 5;
    public static final int PROVINCE  = 6;
    public static final int COUNTRY    = 7;
    public static final int PRIVS     = 8;

    protected ArrayList users;

    protected static UserDB singleton;

    /** Static code block to intialize the Singleton. */
    static {
        String dbClass = null;
        try {
            dbClass = JDConstants.getProperty("jabadot.userdb.class");
            singleton = (UserDB)Class.forName(dbClass).newInstance();
```

*Example 20-2. UserDB.java (continued)*

```
        } catch (ClassNotFoundException ex) {
            System.err.println("Unable to instantiate UserDB singleton " +
                dbClass + " (" + ex.toString() + ")");
            throw new IllegalArgumentException(ex.toString());
        } catch (Exception ex) {
            System.err.println(
            "Unexpected exception: Unable to initialize UserDB singleton");
            ex.printStackTrace(System.err);
            throw new IllegalArgumentException(ex.toString());
        }
    }

    /** In some subclasses the constructor will probably load the database,
     *  while in others it may defer this until getUserList().
     */
    protected UserDB() throws IOException, SQLException {
        users = new ArrayList();
    }

    /** "factory" method to get an instance, which will always be
     * the Singleton.
     */
    public static UserDB getInstance() {
        if (singleton == null)
            throw new IllegalStateException("UserDB initialization failed");
        return singleton;
    }

    /** Get the list of users. */
    public ArrayList getUserList() {
        return users;
    }

    /** Get the User object for a given nickname */
    public User getUser(String nick) {
        Iterator it = users.iterator();
        while (it.hasNext()) {
            User u = (User)it.next();
            if (u.getName().equals(nick))
                return u;
        }
        return null;
    }

    public synchronized void addUser(User nu) throws IOException, SQLException {
        // Add it to the in-memory list
        users.add(nu);

        // Add it to the on-disk version
        // N.B. - must be done in subclass.
    }
```

*Example 20-2. UserDB.java (continued)*

```
    public abstract void setPassword(String nick, String newPass)
    throws SQLException;

    public abstract void deleteUser(String nick)
    throws SQLException;
}
```

In the initial design, this information was stored in a text file. The UserDB class reads this text file and returns a collection of User objects, one per user. It also has various "get" methods, such as the one that finds a user by login name. The basic approach is to open a BufferedReader (see Chapter 10), read each line, and (for nonblank, non-comment lines) construct a StringTokenizer (see Recipe 3.2) to retrieve all the fields. If the line is well-formed (has all its fields), construct a User object and add it to the collection.

The file format is simple, with one user per line:

```
#name:passwd:fullname:email:City:Prov:Country:privs
admin:secret1:JabaDot Administrator:ian@darwinsys.com:Toronto:ON:CA:A
ian:secret2:Ian Darwin:ian@darwinsys.com:Toronto:ON:Canada:E
```

So the UserDBText class is a UserDB implementation that reads this file and creates a User object for each noncomment line in the file. Example 20-3 shows how it works.

*Example 20-3. UserDBText.java*

```
package jabadot;

import java.io.*;
import java.util.*;
import java.sql.SQLException;

/** A trivial "database" for User objects, stored in a flat file.
 * <P>
 * Since this is expected to be used heavily, and to avoid the overhead
 * of re-reading the file, the "Singleton" Design Pattern is used
 * to ensure that there is only ever one instance of this class.
 */
public class UserDBText extends UserDB {
    protected final static String DEF_NAME =
        "/home/ian/src/jabadot/userdb.txt";

    protected String fileName;

    protected UserDBText() throws IOException,SQLException {
        this(DEF_NAME);
    }

    /** Constructor */
    protected UserDBText(String fn) throws IOException,SQLException {
        super();
        fileName = fn;
```

*Example 20-3. UserDBText.java (continued)*

```
            BufferedReader is = new BufferedReader(new FileReader(fn));
            String line;
            while ((line = is.readLine()) != null) {
                //name:password:fullname:City:Prov:Country:privs

                if (line.startsWith("#")) {            // comment
                    continue;
                }

                StringTokenizer st =
                    new StringTokenizer(line, ":");
                String nick = st.nextToken();
                String pass = st.nextToken();
                String full = st.nextToken();
                String email = st.nextToken();
                String city = st.nextToken();
                String prov = st.nextToken();
                String ctry = st.nextToken();
                User u = new User(nick, pass, full, email,
                    city, prov, ctry);
                String privs = st.nextToken();
                if (privs.indexOf("A") != -1) {
                    u.setAdminPrivileged(true);
                }
                users.add(u);
            }
        }

        protected PrintWriter pw;

        public synchronized void addUser(User nu) throws IOException,SQLException {
            // Add it to the in-memory list
            super.addUser(nu);

            // Add it to the on-disk version
            if (pw == null) {
                pw = new PrintWriter(new FileWriter(fileName, true));
            }
            pw.println(toDB(nu));
            // toDB returns: name:password:fullname:City:Prov:Country:privs
            pw.flush();
        }

        protected String toDB(User u) {
            // #name:password:fullName:email:City:Prov:Country:privs
            char privs = '-';
            if (adminPrivs)
                privs = 'A';
            else if (editPrivs)
                privs = 'E';
```

*Example 20-3. UserDBText.java (continued)*

```
        return new StringBuffer( )
            .append(u.name).append(':')
            .append(u.password).append(':')
            .append(u.fullName).append(':')
            .append(u.email).append(':')
            .append(u.city).append(':')
            .append(u.prov).append(':')
            .append(u.country).append(':')
            .append(u.privs)
            .toString( );
    }
}
```

This version does not have any "set" methods, which would be needed to allow a user to change his/her password, for example. Those will come later.

## See Also

If your text-format data file is in a format similar to the one used here, you may be able to massage it into a form where the SimpleText driver (see online source *contrib/ JDBCDriver-Moss*) can be used to access the data using JDBC (see Recipe 20.4).

# 20.3   DBM Databases

## Problem

You need to access a DBM file.

## Solution

Use my code, or SleepyCat's code, to interface DBM from Java.

## Discussion

Unix systems are commonly supplied with some form of DBM or DB[*] data file, often called a *database*. These are not relational databases but are key/value pairs, rather like a java.util.Hashtable that is automatically persisted to disk whenever you called its put( ) method. This format is also used on Windows by a few programs; for example, the Win32 version of Netscape keeps its history in a *history.db* or *netscape.hst* file, which is in this format. Not convinced?

```
daroad.darwinsys.com$ pwd
/c/program files/netscape/users/ian
daroad.darwinsys.com$ file *.hst
```

---

[*] DBM is the original format; DB is a newer, more general format. DBM is actually now a frontend to DB, but because it's a bit simpler, I've used it for this example. GDBM is the FSF's implementation.

```
netscape.hst: Berkeley DB Hash file (Version 2, Little Endian, Bucket Size 4096,
Bucket Shift 12, Directory Size 256, Segment Size 256, Segment Shift 8, Overflow
Point 8, Last Freed 36, Max Bucket 184, High Mask 0xff, Low Mask 0x7f, Fill Factor
54, Number of Keys 733)
daroad.darwinsys.com$
```

The Unix *file* command[*] decodes file types; it's what Unix people rely on instead of
(or in addition to) filename extensions.

So the DBM format is a nice, general mapping from keys to values. But how can we
use it in Java? There is no publicly defined mapping for Java, so I wrote my own. It
uses a fair bit of native code, that is, C code called from Java that in turn calls the
DBM library. I'll discuss native code in Recipe 26.5. For now it suffices to know that
we can initialize a DBM file by calling the relevant constructor, passing the name of
our DB file. We can iterate over all the key/value pairs by calling firstkey() once
and then nextkey() repeatedly until it returns null. Both byte arrays and objects can
be stored and retrieved; it is up to the programmer to know which is which (hint: use
one or the other within a given DBM file). Objects are serialized using normal Java
object serialization (see Recipe 10.18). Here is the API for the DBM class:

```
public DBM(String fileName) throws IOException;
public Object nextkey(Object) throws IOException;
public byte[] nextkey(byte[]) throws IOException;
public Object firstkeyObject() throws IOException;
public byte[] firstkey() throws IOException;
public void store(Object,Object) throws IOException;
public void store(byte[],byte[]) throws IOException;
public Object fetch(Object) throws IOException;
public byte[] fetch(byte[]) throws IOException;
public void close();
```

A simple program to print out the sites we have visited as listed in our Netscape history is shown in Example 20-4.

*Example 20-4. ReadHistNS.java*

```
import java.io.IOException;

/** Demonstration of reading the MS-Windows Netscape History
 * under UNIX using DBM.java.
 */
public class ReadHistNS {
    public static void main(String[] unused) throws IOException {
        DBM d = new DBM("netscape.hst");
        byte[] ba;
        for (ba = d.firstkey(); ba != null; ba = d.nextkey(ba)) {
            System.out.println("Key=\"" + new String(ba) + '"');
            byte[] val = d.fetch(ba);
            for (int i=0; i<16&&i<val.length; i++) {
```

---

[*] The version of file(1) in Linux and BSD systems was originally written by your humble scribe.

*Example 20-4. ReadHistNS.java (continued)*

```
            System.out.print((short)val[i]);
            System.out.print(' ');
        }
    }
  }
}
```

The DBM format is an emulation of an older format, built on top of the DB library. Because of this, the filename must end in *.pag*, so I copied the history file to the name shown in the DBM constructor call.

A longer program, which includes both storing and retrieving in a DBM file, is the DBM version of the UserDB class, UserDBDBM. This is shown in Example 20-5.

*Example 20-5. UserDBDBM.java*

```
package jabadot;

import java.io.*;
import java.util.*;
import java.sql.SQLException;

/** A trivial "database" for User objects, stored in a flat file.
 * <P>
 * Since this is expected to be used heavily, and to avoid the overhead
 * of re-reading the file, the "Singleton" Design Pattern is used
 * to ensure that there is only ever one instance of this class.
 */
public class UserDBDBM extends UserDB {
    protected final static String DEF_NAME =
        "/home/ian/src/jabadot/userdb";        // It appends .pag

    protected DBM db;

    /** Default Constructor */
    protected UserDBDBM() throws IOException,SQLException {
        this(DEF_NAME);
    }

    /** Constructor */
    protected UserDBDBM(String fn) throws IOException,SQLException {
        super();

        db = new DBM(fn);
        String k;
        Object o;

        // Iterate through contents of DBM, adding into list.
        for (o=db.firstkeyObject(); o!=null; o-db.nextkey(o)) {
            // firstkey/nextkey gives Key as Object; cast to String.
            k = (String)o;
            o = db.fetch(k);       // Get corresponding Value (a User)
            users.add((User)o);      // Add to list.
```

*Example 20-5. UserDBDBM.java (continued)*

```
        }
    }

    /** Add one user to the list, both in-memory and on disk. */
    public synchronized void addUser(User nu) throws IOException, SQLException {
        // Add it to the in-memory list
        super.addUser(nu);

        // Add it to the on-disk version: store in DB with
        // key = nickname, value = object.
        db.store(nu.getName(), nu);
    }
}
```

## See Also

SleepyCat software (*http://www.sleepycat.com*) provides an improved version of Berkeley DBM and includes a Java driver for it. The Free Software Foundation provides GDBM, another DBM-like mechanism.

# 20.4   JDBC Setup and Connection

## Problem

You want to access a database via JDBC.

## Solution

Use Class.forName( ) and DriverManager.getConnection( ).

## Discussion

While DB and friends have their place, most of the modern database action is in relational databases, and accordingly Java database action is in JDBC. So the bulk of this chapter is devoted to JDBC.

This is not the place for a tutorial on relational databases. I'll assume that you know a little bit about SQL, the universal language used to control relational databases. SQL has *queries* like "SELECT * from userdb", which means to select all columns (the *) from all rows (entries) in a database table named userdb (all rows are selected because the SELECT statement has no "where" clause). SQL also has *updates* like INSERT, DELETE, CREATE, and DROP. If you need more information on SQL or relational databases, many good books can introduce you to the topic in more detail.

JDBC has two Levels, JDBC 1 and JDBC 2. Level 1 is included in all JDBC implementation and drivers; Level 2 is optional and requires a Level 2 driver. This chapter concentrates on common features, primarily Level 1.

---

The first step in using JDBC 1 is to load your database's driver. This is performed using some Java JVM magic. The class java.lang.Class has a method called forName( ) that takes a string containing the full Java name for a class and loads the class, returning a Class object describing it. This is part of the introspection or reflection API (see Chapter 25) but can be used anytime to ensure that a class has been correctly configured into your CLASSPATH. This is the use that we'll see here. And, in fact, part of the challenge of installing JDBC drivers is ensuring that they are in your CLASSPATH at deployment time. The advantage of my slightly convoluted approach is that the drivers do not have to be on your CLASSPATH at compile time. In some cases, this can allow customers to use your software with database drivers that didn't even exist when your software was written; how's that for flexibility?

But wait, there's more! In addition to checking your CLASSPATH, this method also registers the driver with another class called the DriverManager. How does it work? Each valid JDBC driver has a bit of method-like code called a *static initializer*. This is used whenever the class is loaded—just what the doctor ordered! So the static block registers the class with the DriverManager when you call Class.forName( ) on the driver class.

For the curious, the static code block in a Driver called BarFileDriver looks something like this:

```
/** Static code block, to initialize with the DriverManager. */
static {
    try {
        DriverManager.registerDriver(new BarFileDriver());
```

```
        } catch (SQLException e) {
            DriverManager.println("Can't load driver" +
                                "darwinsys.sql.BarFileDriver");
        }
    }
}
```

Example 20-6 shows a bit of code that tries to load two drivers. The first is the JDBC-to-ODBC bridge described in the Introduction. The second is one of the commercial drivers from Oracle.

*Example 20-6. LoadDriver.java*

```
import java.awt.*;
import java.sql.*;

/** Load some drivers.  */
public class LoadDriver {

    public static void main(String[] av) {
        try {

            // Try to load the jdbc-odbc bridge driver
            // Should be present on Sun JDK implementations.
            Class c = Class.forName("sun.jdbc.odbc.JdbcOdbcDriver");
            System.out.println("Loaded " + c);

            // Try to load an Oracle driver.
            Class d = Class.forName("oracle.jdbc.driver.OracleDriver");
            System.out.println("Loaded " + d);
        } catch (ClassNotFoundException ex) {
            System.err.println(ex);
        }
    }
}
```

The first load succeeds; the second fails since I don't have the Oracle driver installed on my notebook:

```
daroad.darwinsys.com$ java LoadDriver
Loaded class sun.jdbc.odbc.JdbcOdbcDriver
java.lang.ClassNotFoundException: oracle/jdbc/driver/OracleDriver
daroad.darwinsys.com$
```

It is also possible to preregister a driver using the -D option to load it into the System Properties; in this case, you can skip the Class.forName( ) step:

```
java -Djdbc.drivers=com.acmewidgets.AcmeDriver:foo.bar.OhMyDriver MyClass
```

Once you have registered the driver, you are ready to connect to the database.

# 20.5  Connecting to a JDBC Database

## Problem

You need to connect to the database.

## Solution

Use `DriverManager.getConnection( )`.

## Discussion

The static method `DriverManager.getConnection( )` lets you connect to the database using a URL-like syntax for the database name (for example, *jdbc:dbmsnetproto:// server:4567/mydatabase*) and a login name and password. The "dbURL" that you give must begin with `jdbc:`. The rest of it can be in whatever form the driver vendor's documentation requires and is checked by the driver. The `DriverManager` asks each driver you have loaded (if you've loaded any) to see if it can handle a URL of the form you provided. The first one that responds in the affirmative gets to handle the connection, and its `connect( )` method is called for you (by `DriverManager. getConnection( )`).

Four types of drivers are defined by Sun (not in the JDBC specification but in their less formal documentation); these are shown in Table 20-1.

*Table 20-1. JDBC driver types*

| Type | Name | Notes |
| --- | --- | --- |
| 1 | JDBC-ODBC bridge | Provides JDBC API access. |
| 2 | Java and Native driver | Java code calls Native DB driver. |
| 3 | Java and Middleware | Java contacts Middleware server. |
| 4 | Pure Java | Java contacts (possibly remote) DB directly. |

Table 20-2 shows some interesting drivers. I'll use the ODBC bridge driver and InstantDB in examples for this chapter. Some drivers work only locally (like the JDBC-ODBC bridge), while others work across a network. For details on different types of drivers, please refer to the books listed at the end of this chapter. Most of these drivers are commercial products. InstantDB is a clever freeware[*] product; the driver and the entire database management system reside inside the same Java Virtual Machine as the client (the database is stored on disk like any other, of course). This eliminates the interprocess communication overhead of some databases. However, you can't have multiple JVM processes updating the same database at the same time.

---

[*] At this writing, it is also a freeware product in flux; use Google to see if you can find it.

*Table 20-2. Some JDBC drivers*

| Driver class | Start of dbURL | Database |
|---|---|---|
| `sun.jdbc.odbc.JdbcOdbcDriver` | `jdbc:odbc:` | Bridge to Microsoft ODBC (included with JDK) |
| `jdbc.idbDriver` | `jdbc:idb:` | Instant Database (IDB) |
| `oracle.jdbc.Driver.OracleDriver` | `jdbc:oracle:thin:`<br>`@server:port#:dbname` | Oracle |
| `postgresql.Driver` | `jdbc:postgres://`<br>`host/database` | PostGreSQL (freeware database; see *http://www.postgresql.org*) |
| `org.gjt.mm.mysql.Driver` | `jdbc:mysql://host/`<br>`database` | MySql (freeware database; see *http://www.mysql.com*) |

Example 20-7 is a sample application that connects to a database. Note that we now have to catch the checked exception SQLException since we're using the JDBC API. (The Class.forName( ) method is in java.lang, and so it is part of the standard Java API, not part of JDBC.)

*Example 20-7. Connect.java*

```
import java.awt.*;
import java.sql.*;

/** Load a driver and connect to a database.
 */
public class Connect {

    public static void main(String[] av) {
        String dbURL = "jdbc:odbc:Companies";
        try {
            // Load the jdbc-odbc bridge driver
            Class.forName("sun.jdbc.odbc.JdbcOdbcDriver");

            // Enable logging
            DriverManager.setLogWriter(new PrintWriter(System.err));

            System.out.println("Getting Connection");
            Connection conn =
                DriverManager.getConnection(dbURL, "ian", "");    // user, passwd

            // If a SQLWarning object is available, print its
            // warning(s).  There may be multiple warnings chained.

            SQLWarning warn = conn.getWarnings();
            while (warn != null) {
                System.out.println("SQLState: " + warn.getSQLState());
                System.out.println("Message:  " + warn.getMessage());
                System.out.println("Vendor:   " + warn.getErrorCode());
                System.out.println("");
                warn = warn.getNextWarning();
            }
```

*Example 20-7. Connect.java (continued)*

```
            // Process the connection here...

            conn.close();      // All done with that DB connection

        } catch (ClassNotFoundException e) {
            System.out.println("Can't load driver " + e);
        } catch (SQLException e) {
            System.out.println("Database access failed " + e);
        }
    }
}
```

I've enabled two verbosity options in this example. The use of DriverManager. setLogStream( ) causes any logging to be done to the standard error, and the Connection object's getWarnings( ) prints any additional warnings that come up.

When I run it on a system that doesn't have ODBC installed, I get the following outputs. They are all from the setLogStream( ) except for the last one, which is a fatal error:

```
Getting Connection
JDBC to ODBC Bridge: Checking security
*Driver.connect (jdbc:odbc:Companies)
JDBC to ODBC Bridge: Checking security
JDBC to ODBC Bridge 1.2001
Current Date/Time: Fri Jun 16 16:18:45 GMT-5:00 2000
Loading JdbcOdbc library
Unable to load JdbcOdbc library
Unable to load JdbcOdbc library
Unable to allocate environment
Database access failed java.sql.SQLException: driver not found: jdbc:odbc:Companies
```

On a system with JDBC installed, the connection goes further and verifies that the named database exists and can be opened.

## See Also

Performance will suffer if a program repeatedly opens and closes JDBC connections, because getting a Connection object involves "logging in" to the database. One solution is to use a *connection pool*: you preallocate a certain number of Connection objects, hand them out on demand, and the servlet returns its connection to the pool when done. Writing a simple connection pool is easy, but writing a connection pool reliable enough to be used in production is very hard. For this reason, JDBC 2 introduced the notion of having the driver provide connection pooling. However, this feature is optional—check your driver's documentation. Also, Enterprise JavaBeans (EJB) running in an application server usually provide connection pooling; for example, if a servlet is using EJBs and the servlet engine runs in the same "application server" process, this can be a very efficient solution. See the O'Reilly book *Enterprise JavaBeans* by Richard Monson-Haefel for information.

## 20.6  Sending a JDBC Query and Getting Results

### Problem

You're getting tired of all this setup and want to see results.

### Solution

Get a Statement and use it to execute a query. You'll get a set of results, a ResultSet object.

### Discussion

The Connection object can generate various kinds of statements. The simplest is a Statement created by createStatement( ), which is used to send your SQL query as an arbitrary string:

```
Statement stmt = conn.createStatement( );
stmt.executeQuery("select * from myTable");
```

The result of the query is returned as a ResultSet object. The ResultSet works like an iterator in that it lets you access all the rows of the result that match the query. This process is shown in Figure 20-1.

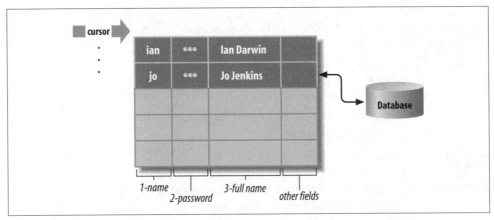

*Figure 20-1. ResultSet illustrated*

Typically, you use it like this:

```
while (rs.next( )) {
    int i = rs.getInt(1);        // or getInt("UserID");
```

As the comment suggests, you can retrieve elements from the ResultSet either by their column index (which starts at one, unlike most Java things, which typically start at zero) or column name. In JDBC 1, you must retrieve the values in increasing order by the order of the SELECT (or by their column order in the database if the query is SELECT *). In JDBC 2, you can retrieve them in any order (and, in fact, many JDBC 1 drivers don't enforce the retrieving of values in certain orders). If you want to learn the column names (a sort of introspection), you can use a ResultSet's getResultSetMetaData( ) method, described in Recipe 20.12. SQL handles many types of data, and JDBC offers corresponding methods to get them from a ResultSet. The common ones are shown in Table 20-3.

*Table 20-3. Data type mappings between SQL and JDBC*

| JDBC method | SQL type | Java type |
|---|---|---|
| getBit( ) | BIT | boolean |
| getByte( ) | TINYINT | byte |
| getShort( ) | SMALLINT | short |
| getInt( ) | INTEGER | int |
| getLong( ) | BIGINT | long |
| getFloat( ) | REAL | float |
| getDouble( ) | DOUBLE | double |
| getString( ) | CHAR | String |
| getString( ) | VARCHAR | String |
| getString( ) | LONGVARCHAR | String |
| getDate( ) | DATE | java.sql.Date |
| getTimeStamp( ) | TIME | java.sql.Date |
| getObject( ) | BLOB | Object |

Assuming that we have a relational database containing the User data, we can retrieve it as demonstrated in Example 20-8. This program retrieves any or all entries that have a username of ian and prints the ResultSets in a loop. It prints lines like:

```
User ian is named Ian Darwin
```

The source code is shown in Example 20-8.

*Example 20-8. UserQuery.java*

```
import jabadot.*;

import java.sql.*;
import java.io.*;
import java.util.*;

/** Look up one use from the relational database using JDBC.
 */
public class UserQuery {

    public static void main(String[] fn)
    throws ClassNotFoundException, SQLException, IOException {
```

*Example 20-8. UserQuery.java (continued)*

```
    // Load the database driver
    Class.forName(JDConstants.getProperty("jabadot.userdb.driver"));

    System.out.println("Getting Connection");
    Connection conn = DriverManager.getConnection(
        JDConstants.getProperty("jabadot.dburl"));

    Statement stmt = conn.createStatement();

    ResultSet rs = stmt.executeQuery(
        "SELECT * from userdb where name='ian'");

    // Now retrieve (all) the rows that matched the query
    while (rs.next()) {

        // Field 1 is login name
        String name = rs.getString(1);

        // Password is field 2 - do not display.

        // Column 3 is fullname
        String fullName = rs.getString(3);

        System.out.println("User " + name + " is named " + fullName);
    }

    rs.close();           // All done with that resultset
    stmt.close();         // All done with that statement
    conn.close();         // All done with that DB connection
    System.exit(0);        // All done with this program.
    }
}
```

Note that a ResultSet is tied to its Connection object; if the Connection is closed, the ResultSet becomes invalid. You should either extract the data from the ResultSet before closing it or cache it in a CachedRowSet (for more on RowSets, see Recipe 20.10).

# 20.7   Using JDBC Prepared Statements

## Problem

You want to save the overhead of parsing, compiling, and otherwise setting up a statement that will be called multiple times.

## Solution

Use a PreparedStatement.

# Discussion

An SQL query consists of textual characters. The database must first parse a query and then compile it into something that can be run in the database. This can add up to a lot of overhead if you are sending a lot of queries. In some types of applications, you'll use a number of queries that are the same syntactically but have different values:

```
select * from payroll where personnelNo = 12345;
select * from payroll where personnelNo = 23740;
select * from payroll where personnelNo = 97120;
```

In this case, the statement needs to be parsed and compiled only once. But if you keep making up select statements and sending them, the database mindlessly keeps parsing and compiling them. Better to use a *prepared statement,* in which the variable part is replaced by a parameter marker (a question mark). Then the statement need only be parsed (or organized, optimized, compiled, or whatever) once:

```
PreparedStatement ps = conn.prepareStatement(
    "select * from payroll where personnelNo = ?;")
```

Before you can use this prepared statement, you must fill in the blanks with the appropriate set methods. These take a parameter number (starting at one, not zero like most things in Java) and the value to be plugged in. Then use executeQuery( ) with no arguments since the query is already stored in the statement:

```
ps.setInt(1, 12345);
rs = ps.executeQuery( );
```

If there are multiple parameters, you address them by number; for example, if there were a second parameter of type double, its value would be set by:

```
ps.setDouble(2, 12345);
```

Example 20-9 is the JDBC version of the User accessor, UserDBJDBC. It uses prepared statements for inserting new users, changing passwords, and setting the last login date.

*Example 20-9. UserDBJDBC.java*

```
package jabadot;

import java.sql.*;
import java.io.*;
import java.util.*;

/** A UserDB using JDBC and a relational DBMS.
 * We use the inherited getUser ("Find the User object for a given nickname")
 * since we keep everything in memory in this version.
 */
public class UserDBJDBC extends UserDB {

    protected final static String DB_URL =
        JDConstants.getProperty("jabadot.userdb.url");
```

*Example 20-9. UserDBJDBC.java (continued)*

```java
    protected PreparedStatement setPasswordStatement;
    protected PreparedStatement addUserStmt;
    protected PreparedStatement setLastLoginStmt;
    protected PreparedStatement deleteUserStmt;

    /** Default constructor */
    protected UserDBJDBC( )
    throws ClassNotFoundException, SQLException, IOException {
        this(DB_URL);
    }

    /** Constructor */
    public UserDBJDBC(String fn)
    throws ClassNotFoundException, SQLException, IOException {
        super( );

        // Load the database driver
        Class.forName("jdbc.idbDriver");

        Connection conn = DriverManager.getConnection(fn,
            "www", "");    // user, password

        Statement stmt = conn.createStatement( );

        ResultSet rs = stmt.executeQuery("select * from userdb");

        while (rs.next( )) {
            //name:password:fullname:City:Prov:Country:privs

            // Get the fields from the query.
            String nick = rs.getString(1);
            String pass = rs.getString(2);
            String full = rs.getString(3);
            String email = rs.getString(4);
            String city = rs.getString(5);
            String prov = rs.getString(6);
            String ctry = rs.getString(7);
            int iprivs = rs.getInt(8);

            // Construct a user object from the fields
            User u = new User(nick, pass, full, email,
                city, prov, ctry, iprivs);

            // Add it to the in-memory copy.
            users.add(u);
        }
        stmt.close( );
        rs.close( );           // All done with that resultset

        // Set up the PreparedStatements now so we don't have to
        // re-create them each time needed.
        addUserStmt = conn.prepareStatement(
            "insert into userdb values (?,?,?,?,?,?,?,?)");
```

*Example 20-9. UserDBJDBC.java (continued)*

```
        setPasswordStatement = conn.prepareStatement(
            "update userdb SET password = ? where name = ?");
        setLastLoginStmt = conn.prepareStatement(
            "update userdb SET lastLogin = ? where name = ?");
        deleteUserStmt = conn.prepareStatement(
            "delete from userdb where name = ?");
    }

    /** Add one user to the list, both in-memory and on disk. */
    public synchronized void addUser(User nu)
    throws IOException, SQLException {
        // Add it to the in-memory list
        super.addUser(nu);

        // Copy fields from user to DB
        addUserStmt.setString(1, nu.name);
        addUserStmt.setString(2, nu.password);
        addUserStmt.setString(3, nu.fullName);
        addUserStmt.setString(4, nu.email);
        addUserStmt.setString(5, nu.city);
        addUserStmt.setString(6, nu.prov);
        addUserStmt.setString(7, nu.country);
        addUserStmt.setInt    (8, nu.getPrivs());

        // Store in persistent DB
        addUserStmt.executeUpdate();
    }

    public void deleteUser(String nick) throws SQLException {
        // Find the user object
        User u = getUser(nick);
        if (u -- null) {
            throw new SQLException("User " + nick + " not in in-memory DB");
        }
        deleteUserStmt.setString(1, nick);
        int n - deleteUserStmt.executeUpdate();
        if (n != 1) {     // not just one row??
            /*CANTHAPPEN */
            throw new SQLException("ERROR: deleted " + n + " rows!!");
        }

        // IFF we deleted it from the DB, also remove from the in-memory list
        users.remove(u);
    }

    public synchronized void setPassword(String nick, String newPass)
    throws SQLException {

        // Find the user object
        User u = getUser(nick);
```

*Example 20-9. UserDBJDBC.java (continued)*

```
        // Change it in DB first; if this fails, the info in
        // the in-memory copy won't be changed either.
        setPasswordStatement.setString(1, newPass);
        setPasswordStatement.setString(2, nick);
        setPasswordStatement.executeUpdate( );

        // Change it in-memory
        u.setPassword(newPass);
    }

    /** Update the Last Login Date field. */
    public synchronized void setLoginDate(String nick, java.util.Date date)
    throws SQLException {

        // Find the user object
        User u = getUser(nick);

        // Change it in DB first; if this fails, the date in
        // the in-memory copy won't be changed either.
        // Have to convert from java.util.Date to java.sql.Date here.
        // Would be more efficient to use java.sql.Date everywhere.
        setLastLoginStmt.setDate(1, new java.sql.Date(date.getTime( )));
        setLastLoginStmt.setString(2, nick);
        setLastLoginStmt.executeUpdate( );

        // Change it in-memory
        u.setLastLoginDate(date);
    }
}
```

Another example of prepared statements is given in Recipe 20.11.

# 20.8   Using Stored Procedures with JDBC

## Problem

You want to use a procedure stored in the database (a stored procedure).

## Solution

Use a CallableStatement.

## Discussion

A *stored procedure* is a series of SQL statements[*] stored as part of the database for use by any SQL user or programmer, including JDBC developers. Stored procedures are used for the same reasons as prepared statements: efficiency and convenience.

---

[*] And possibly some database-dependent utility statements.

Typically, the database administrator (DBA) at a large database shop sets up stored procedures and tells you what they are called, what parameters they require, and what they return. Putting the stored procedure itself into the database is totally database-dependent and not discussed here.

Suppose that I wish to see a list of user accounts that have not been used for a certain length of time. Instead of coding this logic into a JDBC program, I might define it using database-specific statements to write and store a procedure in the database and then use the following code. Centralizing this logic in the database has some advantages for maintenance and also, in most databases, for speed:

```
CallableStatment cs = conn.prepareCall("{ call ListDefunctUsers }");
ResultSet rs = cs.executeQuery();
```

I then process the `ResultSet` in the normal way.

## 20.9  Changing Data Using a ResultSet

### Problem

You want to change the data using a `ResultSet`.

### Solution

If you have JDBC 2 and a conforming driver, you can request an updatable `ResultSet` when you create the statement object. When you're on the row you want to change, use the update( ) methods and end with updateRow( ).

### Discussion

You need to create the statement with the attribute `ResultSet.CONCUR_UPDATABLE` as shown in Example 20-10. Do an SQL SELECT with this statement. When you are on the row (only one row matches this particular query because it is selecting on the primary key), use the appropriate update method for the type of data in the column you want to change, passing in the column name or number and the new value. You can change more than one column in the current row this way. When you're done, call updateRow( ) on the `ResultSet`. Assuming that you didn't change the autocommit state, the data is committed to the database.

*Example 20-10. ResultSetUpdate.java (partial listing)*

```
try {
    con = DriverManager.getConnection(url, user, pass);
    stmt = con.createStatement(
        ResultSet.TYPE_SCROLL_SENSITIVE, ResultSet.CONCUR_UPDATABLE);
    rs = stmt.executeQuery("SELECT * FROM Users where nick=\"ian\"");

    // Get the resultset ready, update the passwd field, commit
    rs.first();
```

*Example 20-10. ResultSetUpdate.java (partial listing) (continued)*

```
    rs.updateString("password", "unguessable");
    rs.updateRow( );

    rs.close( );
    stmt.close( );
    con.close( );
} catch(SQLException ex) {
    System.err.println("SQLException: " + ex.getMessage( ));
}
```

# 20.10 Storing Results in a RowSet

## Problem

You need to save some results in a JDBC form without maintaining a database connection. Or you want some JDBC results to have JavaBean semantics.

## Solution

Use a RowSet—in particular, a CachedRowSet.

## Discussion

The RowSet interface, a subinterface of ResultSet, was introduced with JDBC 2. Because a RowSet is a ResultSet, you can use any of the ResultSet processing methods previously discussed. But RowSets tend to be more self-contained; you typically do not need to specify a driver, and performing queries is done in a new way. You call setCommand( ) to specify the query and execute( ) to perform the query (this takes the place of creating a Statement and calling its executeQuery( ) method).

There five subinterfaces are listed in Table 20-4. For each of these, a reference implementation is provided in the com.sun.rowset package.

*Table 20-4. RowSet subinterfaces*

| Interface name | Implementation class | Purpose |
|---|---|---|
| CachedRowSet | CachedRowSetImpl | Caches results in memory; disconnected Rowset |
| FilteredRowSet | FilteredRowSetImpl | Implements lightweight querying, using javax.sql. rowset.Predicate |
| JdbcRowSet | JdbcRowSetImpl | Makes results available as a JavaBean component |
| JoinRowSet | JoinRowSetImpl | Combine multiple RowSets into one, like an SQL join |
| WebRowSet | WebRowSetImpl | Convert between XML data and RowSet |

But these, like the JDBC-ODBC bridge driver mentioned in Recipe 20.5, are in the com.sun package hierarchy, meaning that they are not fully supported. So although the Javadoc suggests using the new keyword to instantiate them, I prefer to use `Class.forName()` to avoid importing from "unsupported" packages, and so I can compile even if these classes are not available.[*]

The `CachedRowSet` looks the most interesting and useful. In Example 20-11, a `CachedRowSet` is created and populated with `setCommand()` and `execute()`. Then (hypothetically some time later) the user changes some data. After that is completed, we call `acceptChanges()`, which tells the `CachedRowSet` to put the changes back into the JDBC database.

*Example 20-11. CachedRowSetDemo*

```
import javax.sql.*;

/** Demonstrate simple use of the CachedRowSet.
 * The RowSet family of interfaces is in JDK1.5, but the Implementation
 * classes are (as of Beta 1) still in the unsupported "com.sun" package.
 */
public class CachedRowSetDemo {
    public static void main(String[] args) throws Exception {
        CachedRowSet rs;

        // Create the class with class.forName to avoid importing
        // from the unsupported com.sun packages.
        Class c = Class.forName("com.sun.rowset.CachedRowSetImpl");
        rs = (CachedRowSet)c.newInstance();

        rs.setUrl("jdbc:postgresql:tmclub");
        rs.setUsername("ian");
        rs.setPassword("secret");

        rs.setCommand("select * from members where name like ?");
        rs.setString(1, "I%");

        // This will cause the RowSet to connect, fetch its data, and
        // disconnect
        rs.execute();

        // Some time later, the client tries to do something.

        // Suppose we want to update data:
        while (rs.next()) {
            if (rs.getInt("id") == 42) {
                rs.setString("firstname", "Marvin");
                rs.updateRow();    // Normal JDBC

                // This additional call tells the CachedRowSet to connect
                // to its database and send the updated data back.
                rs.acceptChanges();
```

---

[*] Now that these classes have been added to JDK 1.5, this precaution is not as important.

*Example 20-11. CachedRowSetDemo (continued)*

```
            }
        }

        // If we're all done...
        rs.close();
    }
}
```

The `WebRowSet` has several uses that involve converting database results to or from XML. I have used a `WebRowSet` in conjunction with JUnit (see Recipe 1.14) to preload a `ResultSet` (since a `RowSet` is a `ResultSet`) to a known populated state before testing the SQL formatting code in Recipe 20.13. Because it writes data in a known format (public DTD), it could also be used with web services to exchange data across different vendors' systems.

## See Also

The documentation for JDBC that accompanies the JDK provides more details on the various `RowSet` implementations and their usages.

# 20.11 Changing Data Using SQL

## Problem

You wish to insert or update data, create a new table, delete a table, or otherwise change the database.

## Solution

Instead of using the `Statement` method `executeQuery( )`, use `executeUpdate( )` with SQL commands to make the change.

## Discussion

The `executeUpdate( )` method is used when you want to make a change to the database as opposed to getting a list of rows with a query. You can implement either data changes like `insert` or `update`, data structure changes like `create table`, or almost anything that you can do by sending SQL directly to the database through its own update command interface or GUI.

The program listed in Example 20-12 converts the `User` database from the text file format of Recipe 20.2 into a relational database. Note that I destroy the table before creating it, just in case an older version was in place. If there was not, `executeUpdate( )` simply indicates this line in its return code; it doesn't throw an exception. Then the program creates the table and its index. Finally, it goes into a loop reading the lines from the text file; for each, a prepared statement is used to insert the user's information into the database.

*Example 20-12. TextToJDBC.java*

```java
package jabadot;

import java.sql.*;
import java.io.*;
import java.util.*;

/** Convert the database from text form to JDBC form.
 */
public class TextToJDBC {

    protected final static String TEXT_NAME = "userdb.txt";
    protected final static String DB_URL = "jdbc:idb:userdb.prp";

    public static void main(String[] fn)
    throws ClassNotFoundException, SQLException, IOException {

        BufferedReader is = new BufferedReader(new FileReader(TEXT_NAME));

        // Load the database driver
        Class.forName("jdbc.idbDriver");

        System.out.println("Getting Connection");
        Connection conn = DriverManager.getConnection(
            DB_URL, "ian", "");      // user, password

        System.out.println("Creating Statement");
        Statement stmt = conn.createStatement();

        System.out.println("Creating table and index");
        stmt.executeUpdate("DROP TABLE userdb");
        stmt.executeUpdate("CREATE TABLE userdb (\n" +
            "name      char(12) PRIMARY KEY,\n" +
            "password char(20),\n" +
            "fullName char(30),\n" +
            "email    char(60),\n" +
            "city     char(20),\n" +
            "prov     char(20),\n" +
            "country  char(20),\n" +
            "privs    int\n" +
            ")");
        stmt.executeUpdate("CREATE INDEX nickIndex ON userdb (name)");
        stmt.close();

        // put the data in the table
        PreparedStatement ps = conn.prepareStatement(
            "INSERT INTO userdb VALUES (?,?,?,?,?,?,?,?)");

        String line;
        while ((line = is.readLine()) != null) {
            //name:password:fullname:city:prov:country:privs
```

*Example 20-12. TextToJDBC.java (continued)*

```
                if (line.startsWith("#")) {          // comment
                    continue;
                }

                StringTokenizer st =
                    new StringTokenizer(line, ":");
                String nick = st.nextToken( );
                String pass = st.nextToken( );
                String full = st.nextToken( );
                String email = st.nextToken( );
                String city = st.nextToken( );
                String prov = st.nextToken( );
                String ctry = st.nextToken( );
                // User u = new User(nick, pass, full, email,
                //    city, prov, ctry);
                String privs = st.nextToken( );
                int iprivs = 0;
                if (privs.indexOf("A") != -1) {
                    iprivs |= User.P_ADMIN;
                }
                if (privs.indexOf("E") != -1) {
                    iprivs |= User.P_EDIT;
                }
                ps.setString(1, nick);
                ps.setString(2, pass);
                ps.setString(3, full);
                ps.setString(4, email);
                ps.setString(5, city);
                ps.setString(6, prov);
                ps.setString(7, ctry);
                ps.setInt(8, iprivs);
                ps.executeUpdate( );
            }
        ps.close( );           // All done with that statement
        conn.close( );       // All done with that DB connection
        return;                // All done with this program.
    }
}
```

Once the program has run, the database is populated and ready for use by the UserDBJDBC data accessor shown in Recipe 20.7.

# 20.12 Finding JDBC Metadata

## Problem

You want to learn about a database or table.

## Solution

Read the documentation provided by your vendor or database administrator. Or ask the software for a MetaData object.

## Discussion

There are two classes relating to *metadata* (data about data) that you can ask for in the JDBC API: DatabaseMetaData and ResultSetMetaData. Each of these has methods that let you interrogate particular aspects. The former class is obtained from a get method in a Connection object; the latter from a get method in the given ResultSet.

### ResultSetMetaData

First, let's look at the class ResultsDecoratorHTML, a "generic query" formatter shown in Example 20-13. This is one of several "ResultSet Formatters" used in the SQLRunner program of Recipe 20.13 (the parent class ResultsDecorator, discussed with SQLRunner, simply defines a Constructor that saves the given PrintWriter as a field, as well as providing two abstract methods that ResultsDecoratorHTML implements). When a program using ResultsDecoratorHTML calls the write( ) method, the ResultSet is interrogated and formatted into a neat little HTML table, using the column names from the ResultSetMetaData as the headings for the HTML table. The nice part about this program is that it responds to whatever columns are in the ResultSet, which need not be in the same order as they are in the database. Consider the two queries:

```
select name, address from userdb
select address, name from userdb
```

Any code that depends upon knowing the order in the database would look very strange indeed if the user query requested fields in a different order than they were stored in the database.

*Example 20-13. ResultsDecoratorHTML..java*

```java
import java.io.PrintWriter;
import java.sql.ResultSet;
import java.sql.ResultSetMetaData;
import java.sql.SQLException;

/** Print ResultSet in HTML
 */
class ResultsDecoratorHTML extends ResultsDecorator {

    ResultsDecoratorHTML(PrintWriter out) {
        super(out);
    }

    public void write(ResultSet rs) throws SQLException {
        out.println("<br>Your response:");
```

*Example 20-13. ResultsDecoratorHTML.java (continued)*

```
        ResultSetMetaData md = rs.getMetaData( );
        int count = md.getColumnCount( );
        out.println("<table border=1>");
        out.print("<tr>");
        for (int i=1; i<=count; i++) {
            out.print("<th>");
            out.print(md.getColumnName(i));
        }
        out.println("</tr>");
        while (rs.next( )) {
            out.print("<tr>");
            for (int i=1; i<=count; i++) {
                out.print("<td>");
                out.print(rs.getString(i));
            }
            out.println("</tr>");
        }
        out.println("</table>");
        out.flush( );
    }

    /* (non-Javadoc)
     * @see ResultSetDecorator#write(int)
     */
    void write(int updateCount) throws SQLException {
        out.println("<br/>RowCount: updateCount = <b>" +
                    updateCount + "</p>");
    }
}
```

## DatabaseMetaData

Example 20-14 uses DatabaseMetaData to print out the name and version number of
the database product and its default *transaction isolation* (basically, the extent to
which users of a database can interfere with each other; see any good book on databases for information on transactions and why it's often really important to know
your database's default transaction isolation).

*Example 20-14. JDBCMeta.java*

```
import com.darwinsys.util.FileProperties;

import java.awt.*;
import java.sql.*;

/** A database MetaData query
 */
public class JDBCMeta {

    public static void main(String[] av) {
        int i;
```

*Example 20-14. JDBCMeta.java (continued)*

```java
    try {
        FileProperties fp = new FileProperties("JDBCMeta.properties");

        // Load the driver
        Class.forName(fp.getProperty("driver"));

        // Get the connection
        Connection conn = DriverManager.getConnection (
            fp.getProperty("dburl"),
            fp.getProperty("user"),
            fp.getProperty("password"));

        // Get a Database MetaData as a way of interrogating
        // the names of the tables in this database.
        DatabaseMetaData meta = conn.getMetaData( );

        System.out.println("We are using " + meta.getDatabaseProductName( ));
        System.out.println("Version is " + meta.getDatabaseProductVersion( ) );

        int txisolation = meta.getDefaultTransactionIsolation( );
        System.out.println("Database default transaction isolation is " +
            txisolation + " (" +
            transactionIsolationToString(txisolation) + ").");

        conn.close( );

        System.out.println("All done!");

    } catch (java.io.IOException e) {
        System.out.println("Can't load PROPERTIES " + e);
    } catch (ClassNotFoundException e) {
        System.out.println("Can't load driver " + e);
    } catch (SQLException ex) {
        System.out.println("Database access failed:");
        System.out.println(ex);
    }
}

/** Convert a TransactionIsolation int (defined in java.sql.Connection)
 * to the corresponding printable string.
 */
public static String transactionIsolationToString(int txisolation) {
    switch(txisolation) {
        case Connection.TRANSACTION_NONE:
            // transactions not supported.
            return "TRANSACTION_NONE";
        case Connection.TRANSACTION_READ_UNCOMMITTED:
            // All three phenomena can occur
            return "TRANSACTION_NONE";
        case Connection.TRANSACTION_READ_COMMITTED:
        // Dirty reads are prevented; non-repeatable reads and
        // phantom reads can occur.
```

*Example 20-14. JDBCMeta.java (continued)*

```
                return "TRANSACTION_READ_COMMITTED";
            case Connection.TRANSACTION_REPEATABLE_READ:
                // Dirty reads and non-repeatable reads are prevented;
                // phantom reads can occur.
                return "TRANSACTION_REPEATABLE_READ";
            case Connection.TRANSACTION_SERIALIZABLE:
                // All three phenomena prvented; slowest!
                return "TRANSACTION_SERIALIZABLE";
            default:
                throw new IllegalArgumentException(
                    txisolation + " not a valid TX_ISOLATION");
        }
    }
}
```

When you run it, in addition to some debugging information, you'll see something like this. The details, of course, depend on your database:

```
> java JDBCMeta
Enhydra InstantDB - Version 3.13
The Initial Developer of the Original Code is Lutris Technologies Inc.
Portions created by Lutris are Copyright (C) 1997-2000 Lutris Technologies, Inc.All
Rights Reserved.
We are using InstantDB
Version is Version 3.13
Database default transaction isolation is 0 (TRANSACTION_NONE).
All done!
>
```

# 20.13 Program: SQLRunner

The SQLRunner program is a simple interface to any SQL database for which you have a JDBC driver and a login name and password. Most databases provide such a program, and most of them are more powerful. However, this program has the advantage that it works with any database. The program reads SQL commands from a console window (up to a semicolon), passes them to the driver, and prints the results. If the result is a ResultSet, it is printed using a ResultsDecorator; otherwise, it is printed as a RowCount.

The abstract ResultsDecorator class (ResultsFormatter might have been a better name) is shown in Example 20-15. A text-mode decorator is used by default; an HTML decorator (discussed earlier in Example 20-13) and an SQL generator (potentially useful in dumping the data for insertion into another database) is also available. You can specify the decorator using command-line options or switch using the escape mechanism; for example, a line with \mh; sets the mode to HTML for the results of all following output.

To avoid hardcoding database parameters, they are fetched from a properties file, which defaults to *${user.home}/.db.properties*. For example, my *.db.properties* file contains entries like the following:

```
# Connection for the "lhbooks" database
lhbooks.DBDriver=org.postgresql.Driver
lhbooks.DBURL=jdbc:postgresql:ecom
lhbooks.DBUser=thisoneistopsecrettoo
lhbooks.DBPassword=fjkdjsj

# Connection for the "tmclub " database
tmclub.DBDriver=org.postgresql.Driver
tmclub.DBURL=jdbc:postgresql:tmclub_alliston
tmclub.DBUser=dontshowthereaderstherealpassword
tmclub.DBPassword=dlkjklzj
```

I wish I could connect to one of these databases just by saying:

```
java SQLRunner -c tmclub
```

But that won't work because I have to provide the driver jar files in the CLASS-PATH. So a Unix shell script *sqlrunner* runs this java command and sets the class-path to include my drivers. So I can say:

```
sqlrunner -c tmclub
```

This connects me to my Toastmasters* club database. In this example, I select all the meetings that are scheduled for the year 2004; just to show the use of different ResultsDecorators, I then switch to HTML and print the resultset as HTML, which I paste into an HTML page (in a web application, a servlet would get the results and call the ResultsDecorator directly):

```
SQLRunner: Loading driver org.postgresql.Driver
SQLRunner: Connecting to DB jdbc:postgresql:tmclub_alliston
SQLRunner: Connected to PostgreSQL
SQLRunner: ready.
select * from meetings where date > '2004-01-01';
Executing : <<select * from meetings where date > '2004-01-01'>>

id     date     theme    maxspeakers    roles_order
21    2004-01-07    Everything Old is New Again    7    null
22    2004-01-14    T.B.A.  7         null
23    2004-01-21    T.B.A.  7         null
24    2004-01-28    T.B.A.  7         null
25    2004-02-04    T.B.A.  7         null
26    2004-02-11    T.B.A.  7         null
27    2004-02-18    T.B.A.  7         null
28    2004-02-25    g Somehing New  7       null
29    2004-03-03    Spring is in the air?    null    null
2     2004-03-05    Peak Performance    null    null
```

---

* Toastmasters is an international nonprofit organization dedicated to public speaking and leadership; see *http://www.toastmasters.org/* for information on clubs and programs.

```
30      2004-03-10    Peak Performance      5        null
31      2004-03-17    Spring Break    null    null

\mh;
select * from meetings where date > '2004-01-01';
Executing : <<select * from meetings where date > '2004-01-01'>>
<table border=1>
<tr><th>id<th>date<th>theme<th>maxspeakers<th>roles_order</tr>
<tr><td>21<td>2004-01-07<td>Everything Old is New Again<td>7<td>null</tr>
<tr><td>22<td>2004-01-14<td>T.B.A.<td>7<td>null</tr>
<tr><td>23<td>2004-01-21<td>T.B.A.<td>7<td>null</tr>
<tr><td>24<td>2004-01-28<td>T.B.A.<td>7<td>null</tr>
<tr><td>25<td>2004-02-04<td>T.B.A.<td>7<td>null</tr>
<tr><td>26<td>2004-02-11<td>T.B.A.<td>7<td>null</tr>
<tr><td>27<td>2004-02-18<td>T.B.A.<td>7<td>null</tr>
<tr><td>28<td>2004-02-25<td>g Somehing New<td>7<td>null</tr>
<tr><td>29<td>2004-03-03<td>Spring is in the air?<td>null<td>null</tr>
<tr><td>2<td>2004-03-05<td>Peak Performance<td>null<td>null</tr>
<tr><td>30<td>2004-03-10<td>Peak Performance<td>5<td>null</tr>
<tr><td>31<td>2004-03-17<td>Spring Break<td>null<td>null</tr>
</table>
```

The code for ResultsDecorator and ResultsDecoratorText is shown in Example 20-15 and Example 20-16, respectively. These programs are quite general and have no dependency on SQLRunner.

*Example 20-15. ResultsDecorator.java*

```java
import java.io.PrintWriter;
import java.sql.ResultSet;
import java.sql.SQLException;

/** Base class for a series of ResultSet printers.
 * @version $Id: ch20,v 1.5 2004/05/04 20:13:30 ian Exp $
 */
public abstract class ResultsDecorator {
    ResultSet rs;
    PrintWriter out;
    ResultsDecorator(PrintWriter out){
        this.out = out;
    }
    abstract void write(ResultSet rs) throws SQLException;
    abstract void write(int rowCount) throws SQLException;
}
```

*Example 20-16. ResultsDecoratorText.java*

```java
import java.io.PrintWriter;
import java.sql.ResultSet;
import java.sql.ResultSetMetaData;
import java.sql.SQLException;

/**
 * Print a ResultSet in plain text.
 */
```

*Example 20-16. ResultsDecoratorText.java (continued)*

```java
class ResultsDecoratorText extends ResultsDecorator {

    ResultsDecoratorText(PrintWriter out) {
        super(out);
    }

    public void write(ResultSet rs) throws SQLException {
        ResultSetMetaData md = rs.getMetaData();
        int cols = md.getColumnCount();
        for (int i = 1; i <= cols; i++) {
            out.print(md.getColumnName(i) + "\t");
        }
        out.println();
        while (rs.next()) {
            for (int i = 1; i <= cols; i++) {
                out.print(rs.getString(i) + "\t");
            }
            out.println();
        }
        out.flush();
    }

    void write(int rowCount) throws SQLException {
        out.println("OK: " + rowCount);
        out.flush();
    }
}
```

Finally, the main program, SQLRunner, is shown in Example 20-17.

*Example 20-17. SQLRunner.java*

```java
import java.io.BufferedReader;
import java.io.File;
import java.io.FileReader;
import java.io.FileWriter;
import java.io.IOException;
import java.io.InputStreamReader;
import java.io.PrintWriter;
import java.sql.Connection;
import java.sql.DatabaseMetaData;
import java.sql.ResultSet;
import java.sql.SQLException;
import java.sql.Statement;

import com.darwinsys.database.DataBaseException;
import com.darwinsys.lang.GetOpt;
import com.darwinsys.sql.ConnectionUtil;

/** Class to run an SQL script, like psql(1), SQL*Plus, or similar programs.
 * Command line interface accepts options -c config [-f configFile] [scriptFile].
 * <p>Input language is: escape commands (begin with \ and MUST end with semi-colon), or
 * standard SQL statements which must also end with semi-colon);
```

*Example 20-17. SQLRunner.java (continued)*

```
 * <p>Escape sequences:
 * <ul>
 * <li> \m (output-mode), takes character t for text,
 * h for html, s for sql, x for xml (not in this version)
 * (the SQL output is intended to be usable to re-insert the data into an identical table,
 * but this has not been extensively tested!).
 * <li> \o output-file, redirects output.
 * <li> \q quit the program
 * </ul>
 * TODO: Fix parsing so escapes don't need to end with SQL semi-colon.
 * <p>This class can also be used from within programs such as servlets, etc.
 * <p>TODO: knobs to set debug mode (interactively & from getopt!)
 * <p>For example, this command and input:</pre>
 * SQLrunner -c testdb
 * \ms;
 * select *from person where person_key=4;
 * </pre>might produce this output:<pre>
 * Executing : <<select * from person where person_key=4>>
 *  insert into PERSON(PERSON_KEY, FIRST_NAME, INITIAL, LAST_NAME, ... )
 * values (4, 'Ian', 'F', 'Darwin', ...);
 * </pre>
 * @author     Ian Darwin, http://www.darwinsys.com/
 */
public class SQLRunner implements ResultsDecoratorPrinter {

    /** The set of all valid modes. Short, lowercase names were used
     * for simple use in \mX where X is one of the names.
     */
    enum mode {
        t, h, s, x;
    };
    mode outputMode = mode.t;

    /** Database connection */
    protected Connection conn;

    /** SQL Statement */
    protected Statement stmt;

    /** Where the output is going */
    protected PrintWriter out;

    private ResultsDecorator currentDecorator;

    private ResultsDecorator textDecorator;

    private ResultsDecorator sqlDecorator;

    private ResultsDecorator htmlDecorator;

    private ResultsDecorator xmlDecorator;

    boolean debug = false;
```

*Example 20-17. SQLRunner.java (continued)*

```
    private static void doHelp(int i) {
        System.out.println(
        "Usage: SQLRunner [-f configFile] [-c config] [SQLscript[ ...]]");
        System.exit(i);
    }

    /**
     * main - parse arguments, construct SQLRunner object, open file(s), run scripts.
     * @throws SQLException if anything goes wrong.
     * @throws DatabaseException if anything goes wrong.
     */
    public static void main(String[] args)  {
        String config = "default";
        String outputModeName = null;
        GetOpt go = new GetOpt("f:c:m:");
        char c;
        while ((c = go.getopt(args)) != GetOpt.DONE) {
            switch(c) {
            case 'h':
                doHelp(0);
                break;
            case 'f':
                ConnectionUtil.setConfigFileName(go.optarg());
                break;
            case 'c':
                config = go.optarg();
                break;
            case 'm':
                outputModeName = go.optarg();
                break;
            default:
                System.err.println("Unknown option character " + c);
                doHelp(1);
            }
        }

        try {

            Connection conn = ConnectionUtil.getConnection(config);

            SQLRunner prog = new SQLRunner(conn, outputModeName);

            if (go.getOptInd() == args.length) {
                prog.runScript(new BufferedReader(
                    new InputStreamReader(System.in)));
            } else for (int i = go.getOptInd(); i < args.length; i++) {
                prog.runScript(args[i]);
            }
            prog.close();
        } catch (SQLException ex) {
            throw new DataBaseException(ex.toString());
        } catch (IOException ex) {
            throw new DataBaseException(ex.toString());
```

*Example 20-17. SQLRunner.java (continued)*

```
        }
        System.exit(0);
    }


    /** Construct a SQLRunner object
     * @param driver String for the JDBC driver
     * @param dbUrl String for the JDBC URL
     * @param user String for the username
     * @param password String for the password, normally in cleartext
     * @param outputMode One of the MODE_XXX constants.
     * @throws ClassNotFoundException
     * @throws SQLException
     */
    public SQLRunner(String driver, String dbUrl, String user, String password,
            String outputMode)
            throws ClassNotFoundException, SQLException {
        conn = ConnectionUtil.createConnection(driver, dbUrl, user, password);
        finishSetup(outputMode);
    }

    public SQLRunner(Connection c, String outputMode) throws SQLException {
        // set up the SQL input
        conn = c;
        finishSetup(outputMode);
    }

    void finishSetup(String outputMode) throws SQLException {
        DatabaseMetaData dbm = conn.getMetaData();
        String dbName = dbm.getDatabaseProductName();
        System.out.println("SQLRunner: Connected to " + dbName);
        stmt = conn.createStatement();

        out = new PrintWriter(System.out);

        setOutputMode(outputMode);
    }

    /** Set the output mode.
     * @param outputMode Must be a value equal to one of the MODE_XXX values.
     * @throws IllegalArgumentException if the mode is not valid.
     */
    void setOutputMode(String outputModeName) {
        if (outputModeName == null ||
            outputModeName.length() == 0) { throw new IllegalArgumentException(
            "invalid mode: " + outputModeName + "; must be t, h, x or s"); }

        // Assign the correct ResultsDecorator, creating them on the fly
        // using the lazy evaluation pattern.
        ResultsDecorator newDecorator = null;
        outputMode = mode.valueOf(outputModeName);
        switch (outputMode) {
            case t:
```

*Example 20-17. SQLRunner.java (continued)*

```
                    if (textDecorator == null) {
                        textDecorator = new ResultsDecoratorText(this);
                    }
                    newDecorator = textDecorator;
                    break;
                case h:
                    if (htmlDecorator == null) {
                        htmlDecorator = new ResultsDecoratorHTML(this);
                    }
                    newDecorator = htmlDecorator;
                    break;
                case s:
                    if (sqlDecorator == null) {
                        sqlDecorator = new ResultsDecoratorSQL(this);
                    }
                    newDecorator = sqlDecorator;
                    break;
                case x:
                    if (xmlDecorator == null) {
                        xmlDecorator = new ResultsDecoratorXML(this);
                    }
                    newDecorator = sqlDecorator;
                    break;
                default:
                    String values = mode.values().toString();
                    throw new IllegalArgumentException("invalid mode: "
                                    + outputMode + "; must be " + values);
        }
        if (currentDecorator != newDecorator) {
            currentDecorator = newDecorator;
            System.out.println("Mode set to  " + outputMode);
        }

}

/** Run one script file, by name. Called from cmd line main
 * or from user code.
 */
public void runScript(String scriptFile)
throws IOException, SQLException {

    BufferedReader is;

    // Load the script file first, it's the most likely error
    is = new BufferedReader(new FileReader(scriptFile));

    runScript(is);
}

/** Run one script, by name, given a BufferedReader. */
public void runScript(BufferedReader is)
throws IOException, SQLException {
```

*Example 20-17. SQLRunner.java (continued)*

```java
        String stmt;
        int i = 0;
        System.out.println("SQLRunner: ready.");
        while ((stmt = getStatement(is)) != null) {
            stmt = stmt.trim();
            if (stmt.startsWith("\\")) {
                doEscape(stmt);
            } else {
                runStatement(stmt);
            }
        }
    }

    /**
     * Process an escape like \ms; for mode=sql.
     */
    private void doEscape(String str) throws IOException {
        String rest = null;
        if (str.length() > 2) {
            rest = str.substring(2);
        }
        if (str.startsWith("\\m")) {        // MODE
            if (rest == null){
                throw new IllegalArgumentException("\\m needs output mode arg");
            }
            setOutputMode(rest);
        } else if (str.startsWith("\\o")){
            if (rest == null){
                throw new IllegalArgumentException("\\o needs output file arg");
            }
            setOutputFile(rest);
        } else if (str.startsWith("\\q")){
            System.exit(0);
        } else {
            throw new IllegalArgumentException("Unknown escape: " + str);
        }

    }

    /** Set the output to the given filename.
     * @param fileName
     */
    private void setOutputFile(String fileName) throws IOException{
        File file = new File(fileName);
        out = new PrintWriter(new FileWriter(file), true);
        System.out.println("Output set to " + file.getCanonicalPath());
    }

    /** Set the output file back to System.out */
    private void setOutputFile() throws IOException{
        out = new PrintWriter(System.out, true);
    }
```

*Example 20-17. SQLRunner.java (continued)*

```java
    /** Run one Statement, and format results as per Update or Query.
     * Called from runScript or from user code.
     */
    public void runStatement(String str) throws IOException, SQLException {

        System.out.println("Executing : <<" + str.trim() + ">>");
        System.out.flush();
        try {
            boolean hasResultSet - stmt.execute(str);
            if (!hasResultSet)
                currentDecorator.write(stmt.getUpdateCount());
            else {
                ResultSet rs = stmt.getResultSet();
                currentDecorator.write(rs);
            }
        } catch (SQLException ex) {
            if (debug){
                throw ex;
            } else {
                System.out.println("ERROR: " + ex.toString());
            }
        }
        System.out.println();
    }


    /** Extract one statement from the given Reader.
     * Ignore comments and null lines.
     * @return The SQL statement, up to but not including the ';' character.
     * May be null if not statement found.
     */
    public static String getStatement(BufferedReader is)
    throws IOException {
        String ret="";
        String line;
        boolean found = false;
        while ((line = is.readLine()) != null) {
            if (line == null || line.length() == 0) {
                continue;
            }
            if (!(line.startsWith("#") || line.startsWith("--"))) {
                ret += ' ' + line;
                found = true;
            }
            if (line.endsWith(";")) {
                // Kludge, kill off empty statements (";") by itself, continue scanning.
                if (line.length() == 1)
                    line = "";
                ret = ret.substring(0, ret.length()-1);
                return ret;
            }
        }
        return null;
    }
```

*Example 20-17. SQLRunner.java (continued)*

```java
    public void close() throws SQLException {
        stmt.close();
        conn.close();
        out.flush();
        out.close();
    }

    /* (non-Javadoc)
     * @see DatabaseWriterImpl#println(java.lang.String)
     */
    public void print(String line) throws IOException {
        out.print(line);
    }

    public void println(String line) throws IOException {
        out.println(line);
        out.flush();
    }

    /* (non-Javadoc)
     * @see DatabaseWriterImpl#println()
     */
    public void println() throws IOException {
        out.println();
        out.flush();
    }

    /* (non-Javadoc)
     * @see ResultsDecoratorPrinter#getPrintWriter()
     */
    public PrintWriter getPrintWriter() {
        return out;
    }
}
```

I use this program fairly regularly, so it continues to evolve; the code in the online edition may differ from the version shown here.

## See Also

As an example of a more specific program, the online source code includes JDAdmin, an administrator's interface using Swing to display and modify the JabaDot user database used in some examples in this chapter.

The file *docs/guide/jdbc/getstart/introTOC.doc.html* is provided with the JDK and gives some guidance on JDBC. JDBC is given extensive coverage in O'Reilly's *Database Programming with JDBC and Java* by George Reese. Addison Wesley's *JDBC Database Access from Java: A Tutorial and Annotated Reference* by Graham Hamilton, Rick Cattell, and Maydene Fisher is also recommended. For general information on databases, you might want to consult *Joe Celko's Data and Databases* (Morgan Kaufman) or any of many other good general books.

---

# CHAPTER 21

# XML

## 21.0  Introduction

The Extensible Markup Language, or XML, is a portable, human-readable format for exchanging text or data between programs. XML is derived from the parent standard SGML, as is the HTML language used on web pages worldwide. XML, then, is HTML's younger but more capable sibling. And since most developers know at least a bit of HTML, parts of this discussion compare XML with HTML. XML's lesser known grandparent is IBM's GML (General Markup Language), and one of its cousins is Adobe FrameMaker's Maker Interchange Format (MIF). Figure 21-1 depicts the family tree.

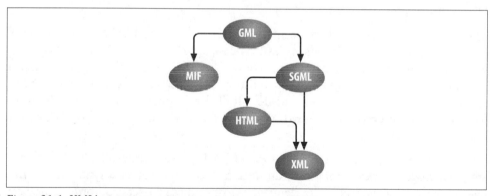

*Figure 21-1. XML's ancestry*

One way of thinking about XML is that it's HTML cleaned up, consolidated, and with the ability for you to define your own tags. It's HTML with tags that can and should identify the informational content as opposed to the formatting. Another way of perceiving XML is as a general interchange format for such things as business-to-business communications over the Internet or as a human-editable* description of things as diverse as word-processing files and Java documents. XML is all these things, depending on where you're coming from as a developer and where you want to go today—and tomorrow.

Because of the wide acceptance of XML, it is used as the basis for many other formats, including the Open Office (*http://www.openoffice.org*) save file format, the SVG graphics file format, and many more.

From SGML, both HTML and XML inherit the syntax of using angle brackets (< and >) around *tags*, each pair of which delimits one part of an XML document, called an *element*. An element may contain content (like a <P> tag in HTML) or may not (like an <hr> in HTML). While HTML documents can begin with either an <html> tag or a <DOCTYPE...> tag (or, informally, with neither), an XML file may begin with an XML declaration. Indeed, it must begin with an XML *processing instruction* (<? ... ?>) if the file's character encoding is other than UTF-8 or UTF-16:

```
<?xml version="1.0" encoding="iso-8859-1"?>
```

The question mark is a special character used to identify the XML declaration (it's syntactically similar to the % used in ASP and JSP).

HTML has a number of elements that accept attributes, such as:

```
<BODY BGCOLOR=white> ... </body>
```

In XML, attribute values (such as the 1.0 for the version in the processing instruction or the white of BGCOLOR) must be quoted. In other words, quoting is optional in HTML, but required in XML.

The BODY example shown here, while allowed in traditional HTML, would draw complaints from any XML parser. XML is case-sensitive; in XML, BODY, Body, and body represent three different element names. Yes, each XML start tag must have a matching end tag. This is one of a small list of basic constraints detailed in the XML specification. Any XML file that satisfies all of these constraints is said to be well-formed and is accepted by an XML parser. A document that is not well-formed is rejected by an XML parser.

Speaking of XML parsing, a great variety of XML parsers are available. A parser is simply a program or class that reads an XML file, looks at it at least syntactically, and lets you access some or all of the elements. Most of these parsers conform to the Java bindings for one of the two well-known XML APIs, SAX and DOM. SAX, the Simple API for XML, reads the file and calls your code when it encounters certain events,

---

* Although you can edit XML using *vi*, Emacs, notepad, or simpletext, it is considered preferable to use an XML-aware editor. XML's structure is more complex, and parsing programs are far less tolerant of picayune error, than was ever the case in the HTML world. XML files are kept as plain text for debugging purposes, for ease of transmission across wildly incompatible operating systems, and (as a last resort) for manual editing to repair software disasters.

such as start-of-element, end-of-element, start-of-document, and the like. DOM, the Document Object Model, reads the file and constructs an in-memory tree or graph corresponding to the elements and their attributes and contents in the file. This tree can be traversed, searched, modified (even constructed from scratch, using DOM), or written to a file.

An alternative API called JDOM has also been released into the open source field. JDOM, by Brett McLaughlin and Jason Hunter, has the advantage of being aimed primarily at Java (DOM itself is designed to work with many different programming languages). JDOM is available at *http://www.jdom.org* and has been accepted as a JSR (Java Standards Request) for the Sun Community Standards Process.

But how does the parser know if an XML file contains the correct elements? Well, the simpler, "nonvalidating" parsers don't—their only concern is the *well-formedness* of the document. *Validating parsers* check that the XML file conforms to a given Document Type Definition (DTD) or an *XML Schema*. DTDs are inherited from SGML; their syntax is discussed in Recipe 21.5. Schemas are newer than DTDs and, while more complex, provide such object-based features as inheritance. DTDs are written in a special syntax derived from SGML while XML Schemas are expressed using ordinary XML elements and attributes.

In addition to parsing XML, you can use an XML processor to transform XML into some other format, such as HTML. This is a natural for use in a web servlet: if a given web browser client can support XML, just write the data as-is, but if not, transform the data into HTML. We'll look at two approaches to XML transformation: transformation using a generic XSLT processor and then later some parsing APIs suitable for customized operations on XML.

If you need to control how an XML document is formatted, for screen or print, you can use XSL (Extensible Style Language). XSL is a more sophisticated variation on the HTML stylesheet concept that allows you to specify formatting for particular elements. XSL has two parts: tree transformation (for which XSLT was designed, though it can also be used independently, as we'll see) and formatting (the non-XSLT part is informally known as XSL-FO or XSL Formatting Objects).

XSL stylesheets can be complex; you are basically specifying a batch formatting language to describe how your textual data is formatted for the printed page. A comprehensive reference implementation is FOP (Formatting Objects Processor), which produces Acrobat PDF output and is available from *http://xml.apache.org*.

Prior to JDK 1.4, writing portable XML-based Java programs was difficult because there was no single standard API. JDK 1.4 introduced JAXP, the Java API for XML Processing, which provides standard means for accessing the various components discussed in this chapter. If you are still using JDK 1.3, you may need to acquire additional JAR files and/or change the examples somewhat.

# 21.1 Generating XML from Objects

## Problem

You want to generate XML directly from Java objects.

## Solution

Use the XML Object Serializers.

## Discussion

The Serialization demonstration in Recipe 10.18 showed an abstract base class that called upon abstract methods to write the file out in some format. Example 21-1 is the XML subclass for it.

*Example 21-1. SerialDemoXML.java*

```java
import java.beans.XMLDecoder;
import java.beans.XMLEncoder;
import java.io.*;

/** Show the XML serialization added to "java.beans.*" in JDK1.4.
 * Subclass "SerialDemoAbstractBase" to get most of the infrastructure
 */
public class SerialDemoXML extends SerialDemoAbstractBase {

    public static final String FILENAME = "serial.xml";

    public static void main(String[] args) throws IOException {
        new SerialDemoXML().save();
        new SerialDemoXML().dump();
    }

    /** Save the data to disk. */
    public void write(Object theGraph) throws IOException {
        XMLEncoder os = new XMLEncoder(          // NEEDS JDK 1.4
            new BufferedOutputStream(
                new FileOutputStream(FILENAME)));
        os.writeObject(theGraph);
        os.close();
    }

    /** Display the data */
    public void dump() throws IOException {
        XMLDecoder inp = new XMLDecoder(          // NEEDS JDK 1.4
            new BufferedInputStream(
                new FileInputStream(FILENAME)));
        System.out.println(inp.readObject());
        inp.close();
    }
}
```

# 21.2 Transforming XML with XSLT

## Problem

You need to make significant changes to the output format.

## Solution

Use XSLT; it is fairly easy to use and does not require writing much Java.

## Discussion

XSLT, the Extensible Stylesheet Language for Transformations, allows you a great deal of control over the output format. It can be used to change an XML file from one vocabulary into another, as might be needed in a business-to-business (B2B) application where information is passed from one industry-standard vocabulary to a site that uses another. It can also be used to render XML into another format such as HTML. Some open source projects even use XSLT as a tool to generate Java source files from an XML description of the required methods and fields. Think of XSLT as a scripting language for transforming XML.

This example uses XSLT to transform a document containing people's names, addresses, and so on—such as the file *people.xml*, shown in Example 21-2—into printable HTML.

*Example 21-2. people.xml*

```
<?xml version="1.0"?>
<people>
<person>
    <name>Ian Darwin</name>
    <email>http://www.darwinsys.com/contact.html</email>
    <country>Canada</country>
</person>
<person>
    <name>Another Darwin</name>
    <email type="intranet">afd@node1</email>
    <country>Canada</country>
</person>
</people>
```

You can transform the *people.xml* file into HTML by using the following command:

```
$ java JAXPTransform people.xml people.xsl people.html
```

The output is something like the following:

```
<html>
<head>
<META http-equiv="Content-Type" content="text/html; charset=UTF-8">
<title>Our People</title>
</head>
```

```
<body>
<table border="1">
<tr>
<th>Name</th><th>EMail</th>
</tr>
<tr>
<td>Ian Darwin</td><td>http://www.darwinsys.com/</td>
</tr>
<tr>
<td>Another Darwin</td><td>afd@node1</td>
</tr>
</table>
</body>
</html>
```

Figure 21-2 shows the resulting HTML file opened in a browser.

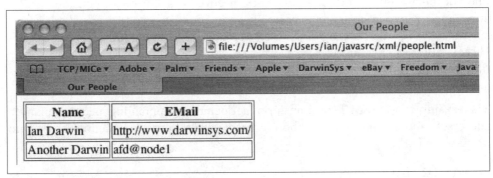

*Figure 21-2. XML to HTML final result*

Let's look at the file *people.xsl* (shown in Example 21-3). Since an XSL file is an XML file, it must be well-formed according to the syntax of XML. As you can see, it contains some XML elements but is mostly (well-formed) HTML.

*Example 21-3. people.xsl*

```
<?xml version="1.0"?>
<xsl:stylesheet xmlns:xsl="http://www.w3.org/1999/XSL/Transform" version="1.0">
<xsl:template match="/">

<html>
<head><title>Our People</title></head>
<body>

    <table border="1">
    <tr>
        <th>Name</th>
        <th>EMail</th>
    </tr>

    <xsl:for-each select="people/person">
        <tr>
```

*Example 21-3. people.xsl (continued)*

```
            <td><xsl:value-of select="name"/></td>
            <td><xsl:value-of select="email"/></td>
        </tr>
    </xsl:for-each>

    </table>

</body></html>
</xsl:template>
</xsl:stylesheet>
```

I haven't shown the JAXPTransform program yet. To transform XML using XSL, you use a set of classes called an *XSLT processor*. Java has included this since JDK 1.4, as part of JAXP. Another freely available XSLT processor is the Apache XML Project's Xalan (formerly available from Lotus/IBM as the Lotus XSL processor). To use JAXP's XSL transformation, you create an XSL processor by calling the factory method TransformerFactory.newInstance( ).newTransformer( ), passing in a StreamSource for the stylesheet. You then call its transform( ) method, passing in a StreamSource for the XML document and a StreamResult for the output file. The code for JAXPTransform appears in Example 21-4.

*Example 21-4. JAXPTransform.java*

```java
import java.io.File;

import javax.xml.transform.Transformer;
import javax.xml.transform.TransformerFactory;
import javax.xml.transform.stream.StreamResult;
import javax.xml.transform.stream.StreamSource;

/** Illustrate simple use of JAXP to transform using XSL */
public class JAXPTransform {
    public static void main(String[] args) throws Exception {
        if (args.length != 3) {
            System.out.println(
                "Usage: java JAXPTransform inputFile.xml inputFile.xsl outputFile");
            System.exit(1);
        }
        // Create a transformer object
        Transformer tx = TransformerFactory.newInstance( ).newTransformer(
            new StreamSource(new File(args[1]))); // not 0

        // Use its transform( ) method to perform the transformation
        tx.transform(
            new StreamSource(new File(args[0])),
            new StreamResult(new File(args[2])));
    }
}
```

If you prefer to use Xalan, see the version of this program called XSLTransform in the online source.

## See Also

A recent development is the use of *translets*. Sun has developed a program that reads a stylesheet and generates a `Translet` class, which is a compiled Java program that transforms XML according to the stylesheet. This eliminates the overhead of reading the stylesheet each time a document is translated. Translets have been incorporated under the name XSLTC into the Apache XML Xerces-Java project; see *http://xml. apache.org/xerces-j/*.

# 21.3   Parsing XML with SAX

## Problem

You want to make one quick pass over an XML file, extracting certain tags or other information as you go.

## Solution

Simply use SAX to create a document handler and pass it to the SAX parser.

## Discussion

The XML `DocumentHandler` interface specifies a number of "callbacks" that your code must provide. In one sense, this is similar to the `Listener` interfaces in AWT and Swing, as covered briefly in Recipe 14.4. The most commonly used methods are `startElement( )`, `endElement( )`, and `characters( )`. The first two, obviously, are called at the start and end of an element, and `characters( )` is called when there is character data. The characters are stored in a large array, and you are passed the base of the array and the offset and length of the characters that make up your text. Conveniently, there is a string constructor that takes exactly these arguments. Hmmm, I wonder if they thought of that....

To demonstrate this, I wrote a simple program using SAX to extract names and email addresses from an XML file. The program itself is reasonably simple and is shown in Example 21-5.

*Example 21-5. SAXLister.java*

```
import java.io.IOException;

import org.xml.sax.Attributes;
import org.xml.sax.SAXException;
import org.xml.sax.XMLReader;
import org.xml.sax.helpers.DefaultHandler;
import org.xml.sax.helpers.XMLReaderFactory;
import com.darwinsys.util.Debug;
```

*Example 21-5. SAXLister.java (continued)*

```java
/**
 * Simple lister - extract name and children tags from a user file. Version for SAX 2.0
 * @version $Id: ch21,v 1.5 2004/05/04 20:13:38 ian Exp $
 */
public class SAXLister {
    public static void main(String[] args) throws Exception {
        new SAXLister(args);
    }

    public SAXLister(String[] args) throws SAXException, IOException {
        XMLReader parser = XMLReaderFactory
                .createXMLReader("org.apache.xerces.parsers.SAXParser");
        // should load properties rather than hardcoding class name
        parser.setContentHandler(new PeopleHandler( ));
        parser.parse(args.length == 1 ? args[0] : "parents.xml");
    }

    /** Inner class provides DocumentHandler
     */
    class PeopleHandler extends DefaultHandler {
        boolean parent = false;
        boolean kids = false;
        public void startElement(String nsURI, String localName,
                String rawName, Attributes attributes) throws SAXException {
            Debug.println("docEvents", "startElement: " + localName + ","
                    + rawName);
            // Consult rawName since we aren't using xmlns prefixes here.
            if (rawName.equalsIgnoreCase("name"))
                parent = true;
            if (rawName.equalsIgnoreCase("children"))
                kids = true;
        }
        public void characters(char[] ch, int start, int length) {
            if (parent) {
                System.out.println("Parent:  " + new String(ch, start, length));
                parent = false;
            } else if (kids) {
                System.out.println("Children: " + new String(ch, start, length));
                kids = false;
            }
        }
        /** Needed for parent constructor */
        public PeopleHandler( ) throws org.xml.sax.SAXException {
            super( );
        }
    }
}
```

When run against the *people.xml* file shown in Example 21-2, it prints the listing:

```
$ java -classpath .:../jars/darwinsys.jar:../jars/xerces.jar SAXLister people.xml
Parent:  Ian Darwin
Parent:  Another Darwin
$
```

In Version 2 of the XML DOM API, you can use the new XMLReaderFactory. createXMLReader( ). One difficulty is that the SAX specification and code are maintained by the SAX Project (*http://www.saxproject.org*), not Sun. The no-argument form of createXMLReader( ) is expected first to try loading the class defined in the system property org.xml.sax.driver, and if that fails, to load an implementation-defined SAX parser. Unfortunately Sun's implementation (on 1.4 and on 1.5 Beta) does not do so; it simply throws an exception to the effect of System property org.xml.sax. driver not specified. An overloaded form of createXMLReader( ) takes the name of the parser as a string argument (e.g., "org.apache.xerces.parsers.SAXParser" or "org.apache.crimson.parser.XMLReaderImpl"). This class name would normally be loaded from a properties file (see Recipe 7.7) to avoid having the parser class name compiled into your application.

One problem with SAX is that it is, well, simple, and therefore doesn't scale well, as you can see by thinking about this program. Imagine trying to handle 12 different tags and doing something different with each one. For more involved analysis of an XML file, the Document Object Model (DOM) or the JDOM API may be better suited. (On the other hand, DOM requires keeping the entire tree in memory, so there are some scalability issues with extremely large XML documents.) And with SAX, you can't really "navigate" a document since you have only a stream of events, not a real structure. For that, you want DOM or JDOM.

# 21.4  Parsing XML with DOM

## Problem

You want to examine an XML file in detail.

## Solution

Use DOM to parse the document and process the resulting in-memory tree.

## Discussion

The Document Object Model (DOM) is a tree-structured representation of the information in an XML document. It consists of several interfaces, the most important of which is the *node*. All are in the package org.w3c.dom, reflecting the influence of the World Wide Web Consortium (*http://www.w3.org*) in creating and promulgating the DOM. The major DOM interfaces are shown in Table 21-1.

*Table 21-1. Major DOM interfaces*

| Interface | Function |
| --- | --- |
| Document | Top-level representation of an XML document |
| Node | Representation of any node in the XML tree |

*Table 21-1. Major DOM interfaces (continued)*

| Interface | Function |
|-----------|----------|
| Element | An XML element |
| Text | A textual string |

You don't have to implement these interfaces; the parser generates them. When you start creating or modifying XML documents in Recipe 21.6, you can create nodes. But even then there are implementing classes. Parsing an XML document with DOM is syntactically similar to processing a file with XSL, that is, you get a reference to a parser and call its methods with objects representing the input files. The difference is that the parser returns an XML DOM, a tree of objects in memory. XParse in Example 21-6 simply parses an XML document. Despite the simplicity, I use it a lot; whenever I have an XML file whose validity is in question, I just pass it to XParse.

*Example 21-6. XParse.java*

```
import java.io.File
import javax.xml.parsers.DocumentBuilder;
import javax.xml.parsers.DocumentBuilderFactory;

import org.w3c.dom.Document;
import org.xml.sax.SAXException;
import org.xml.sax.SAXParseException;

/** Parse an XML file using DOM, via JAXP.
 * @author Ian Darwin, http://www.darwinsys.com/
 * @version $Id: ch21,v 1.5 2004/05/04 20:13:38 ian Exp $
 */
public class XParse {

    /** Parse the file */
    public static void parse(String fileName, boolean validate) {
        try {
            System.err.println("Parsing " + fileName + "...");

            // Make the document a URL so relative DTD works.
            String uri = "file:" + new File(fileName).getAbsolutePath();

            DocumentBuilderFactory f = DocumentBuilderFactory.newInstance();
            if (validate)
                f.setValidating(true);
            DocumentBuilder p = f.newDocumentBuilder();
            // Get local copies of DTDs...
            p.setEntityResolver(new MyDTDResolver());
            Document doc = p.parse(uri);
            System.out.println("Parsed OK");

        } catch (SAXParseException ex) {
            System.err.println("+=================================+");
            System.err.println("|       *SAX Parse Error*        |");
```

*Example 21-6. XParse.java (continued)*

```
                System.err.println("+================================+");
                System.err.println(ex.toString());
                System.err.println("At line " + ex.getLineNumber());
                System.err.println("+================================+");
            } catch (SAXException ex) {
                System.err.println("+================================+");
                System.err.println("|            *SAX Error*         |");
                System.err.println("+================================+");
                System.err.println(ex.toString());
                System.err.println("+================================+");
            } catch (Exception ex) {
                System.err.println("+================================+");
                System.err.println("|            *XML Error*         |");
                System.err.println("+================================+");
                System.err.println(ex.toString());
            }
        }
    }

    public static void main(String[] av) {
        if (av.length == 0) {
            System.err.println("Usage: XParse file");
            return;
        }
        boolean validate = false;
        for (int i=0; i<av.length; i++) {
            if (av[i].equals("-v"))
                validate = true;
            else
                parse(av[i], validate);
        }
    }
}
```

DOM also provides tools to traverse the document. You can use the defined TreeWalker interface, or you can just use the algorithm shown in Example 21-7.

*Example 21-7. XTW.java*

```java
import java.io.File;
import java.io.Reader;

import javax.xml.parsers.DocumentBuilder;
import javax.xml.parsers.DocumentBuilderFactory;

import org.w3c.dom.Document;
import org.w3c.dom.Node;
import org.w3c.dom.NodeList;

import com.darwinsys.util.Debug;

/** XML Tree Walker
 * UPDATED FOR JAXP.
```

*Example 21-7. XTW.java (continued)*

```
 * @author Ian Darwin, http://www.darwinsys.com/
 * @version $Id: ch21,v 1.5 2004/05/04 20:13:38 ian Exp $
 */
public class XTW {

    public static void main(String[] av) {
        if (av.length == 0) {
            System.err.println("Usage: XTW file [...]");
            return;
        }
        for (int i=0; i<av.length; i++) {
            String name = av[i];
            new XTW().convert(name, true);
        }
    }

    /** Convert the file */
    protected void convert(String fileName, boolean verbose) {
        Reader is;
        try {
            if (verbose)
                System.err.println(">>>Parsing " + fileName + "...");
            // Make the document a URL so relative DID works.
            String uri = "file:" + new File(fileName).getAbsolutePath();

            DocumentBuilderFactory factory =
                DocumentBuilderFactory.newInstance();
            DocumentBuilder builder = factory.newDocumentBuilder();
            Document doc = builder.parse( uri );

            if (verbose)
                System.err.println(">>>Walking " + fileName + "...");
            doRecursive(doc);

        } catch (Exception ex) {
            System.err.println("+=============================+");
            System.err.println("|        XTW Error            |");
            System.err.println("+=============================+");
            System.err.println(ex.getClass());
            System.err.println(ex.getMessage());
            System.err.println("+=============================+");
        }
        if (verbose) {
            System.err.println(">>>Done " + fileName + "...");
        }
    }

    /* Process all the nodes, recursively. */
    protected void doRecursive(Node p) {
        if (p == null) {
            return;
        }
```

*Example 21-7. XTW.java (continued)*

```
        NodeList nodes = p.getChildNodes( );
        Debug.println("xml-tree", "Element has " +
            nodes.getLength( ) + " children");
        for (int i = 0; i < nodes.getLength( ); i++) {
            Node n = nodes.item(i);
            if (n == null) {
                continue;
            }

            doNode(n);

        }
    }

    protected void doNode(Node n) {

        switch(n.getNodeType( )) {
            case Node.ELEMENT_NODE:
                System.out.println("ELEMENT<" + n.getNodeName( ) + ">");
                doRecursive(n);
                break;
            case Node.TEXT_NODE:
                String text = n.getNodeValue( );
                if (text.length( ) == 0 ||
                    text.equals("\n") || text.equals("\\r")) {
                    break;
                }
                System.out.println("TEXT: " + text);
                break;
            default:
                System.err.println( "OTHER NODE " +
                    n.getNodeType() + ": " + n.getClass( ));
                break;
        }
    }
}.
```

# 21.5   Verifying Structure with a DTD

## Problem

Up to now, I have simply provided XML and asserted that it is valid. Now you want to verify the structure using a Document Type Definition (DTD).

## Solution

Write the DTD and refer to it in one or more XML documents.

## Discussion

This is not the place for a full dissertation on Document Type Definition syntax. Briefly, a DTD is a means of restricting the structure of an XML document by listing all the elements allowed, where they are permitted, and what attributes they have, if any. The DTD uses a special syntax inherited from SGML. Example 21-8 is *people.dtd*, a DTD for the *people.xml* file shown earlier in this chapter.

*Example 21-8. people.dtd*

```
<!ELEMENT people (person)*>
<!ELEMENT person (name, email, country)>

<!ELEMENT name (#PCDATA)>
<!ATTLIST email type CDATA #IMPLIED>
<!ELEMENT email (#PCDATA)>
<!ELEMENT country (#PCDATA)>
```

To verify that a file conforms to a DTD—that is, to validate the file—you do two things:

1.  Refer to the DTD from within the XML file, as is sometimes seen in HTML documents. The `<!DOCTYPE>` line should follow the `<?xml ...>` line but precede any actual data:

    ```
    <?xml version="1.0"?>
    <!DOCTYPE people SYSTEM "people.dtd">

    <people>
    <person>
            <name>Ian Darwin</name>
            <email>someone@someplace.dom</email>
            <country>Canada</country>
    </person>
    ```

2.  Pass `true` as a second argument to the `createXMLDocument( )` method; `true` means "enforce document validity":

    ```
    XmlDocument doc = XmlDocument.createXmlDocument(uri, true);
    ```

Now any elements found in the document that are not valid according to the DTD result in an exception being thrown.

## See Also

Document Type Definitions are simpler to write than XML Schemas. In some parts of the industry, people seem to be going on the assumption that XML Schemas will completely replace DTDs. But many other developers continue to use DTDs. There are other options for constraining structure and data types, including RelaxNG (an ISO standard).

# 21.6 Generating Your Own XML with DOM

## Problem

You want to generate your own XML files or modify existing documents.

## Solution

Use DOM or JDOM; parse or create the document and call its write method.

## Discussion

Sun's XmlDocument class has a write( ) method that can be called with either an OutputStream or a Writer. To use it, create an XML document object using the XmlDocument constructor. Create nodes, append them into the tree, and then call the document's write( ) method. For example, suppose you want to generate a poem in XML. Running the program and letting the XML appear on the standard output might look something like this:

```
$ java DocWrite
<?xml version="1.0" encoding="UTF-8"?>

<Poem>
  <Stanza>
    <Line>Once, upon a midnight dreary</Line>
    <Line>While I pondered, weak and weary</Line>
  </Stanza>
</Poem>
$
```

The code for this is fairly short; see Example 21-9 for the code using DOM. Code for using JDOM is similar; see *DocWriteJDOM.java* in the online source code.

*Example 21-9. DocWriteDOM.java*

```java
import java.io.IOException;

import javax.xml.parsers.DocumentBuilder;
import javax.xml.parsers.DocumentBuilderFactory;

import org.w3c.dom.Document;
import org.w3c.dom.Node;

/** Make up and write an XML document, using DOM
 * UPDATED FOR JAXP.
 * @author Ian Darwin, http://www.darwinsys.com/
 * @version $Id: ch21,v 1.5 2004/05/04 20:13:38 ian Exp $
 */
public class DocWriteDOM {

    public static void main(String[] av) throws IOException {
        DocWriteDOM dw = new DocWriteDOM( );
        Document doc = dw.makeDoc( );
```

*Example 21-9. DocWriteDOM.java (continued)*

```
        // Sadly, the write() method is not in the DOM spec, so we
        // have to cast the Document to its implementing class
        // in order to call the Write method.
        //
        // WARNING
        //
        // This code therefore depends upon the particular
        // parser implementation.
        //
        ((org.apache.crimson.tree.XmlDocument)doc).write(System.out);
    }

    /** Generate the XML document */
    protected Document makeDoc() {
        try {
            DocumentBuilderFactory fact = DocumentBuilderFactory.newInstance();
            DocumentBuilder parser = fact.newDocumentBuilder();
            Document doc = parser.newDocument();

            Node root = doc.createElement("Poem");
            doc.appendChild(root);

            Node stanza = doc.createElement("Stanza");
            root.appendChild(stanza);

            Node line = doc.createElement("Line");
            stanza.appendChild(line);
            line.appendChild(doc.createTextNode("Once, upon a midnight dreary"));
            line = doc.createElement("Line");
            stanza.appendChild(line);
            line.appendChild(doc.createTextNode("While I pondered, weak and weary"));

            return doc;

        } catch (Exception ex) {
            System.err.println("+=============================+");
            System.err.println("|         XML Error           |");
            System.err.println("+=============================+");
            System.err.println(ex.getClass());
            System.err.println(ex.getMessage());
            System.err.println("+=============================+");
            return null;
        }
    }
}
```

A more complete program would create an output file and have better error reporting. It would also have more lines of the poem than I can remember.

Sun's XmlDocument class is not a committed part of the standard, which is why the code casts the object to org.apache.crimson.tree.XmlDocument before calling its write method. However, other vendors' APIs have similar functionality.

# 21.7   Program: xml2mif

Adobe FrameMaker* uses an interchange language called MIF (Maker Interchange Format), which is vaguely related to XML but is not well-formed. Let's look at a program that uses DOM to read an entire document and generate code in MIF for each node. This program was used to create some earlier chapters of this book.

The main program, shown in Example 21-10, is called XmlForm; it parses the XML and calls one of several output generator classes. This could be used as a basis for generating other formats.

*Example 21-10. XmlForm.java*

```java
import java.io.*;
import org.w3c.dom.*;
import javax.xml.parsers.*;

/** Convert a simple XML file to text.
 * @version $Id: ch21,v 1.5 2004/05/04 20:13:38 ian Exp $
 */
public class XmlForm {
    protected Reader is;
    protected String fileName;

    protected static PrintStream msg = System.out;

    /** Construct a converter given an input filename */
    public XmlForm(String fn) {
        fileName = fn;
    }

    /** Convert the file */
    public void convert(boolean verbose) {
        try {
            if (verbose)
                System.err.println(">>>Parsing " + fileName + "...");
            // Make the document a URL so relative DTD works.
            //String uri = "file:" + new File(fileName).getAbsolutePath( );
            InputStream uri = getClass( ).getResourceAsStream(fileName);
            DocumentBuilderFactory factory =
                DocumentBuilderFactory.newInstance( );
            DocumentBuilder builder = factory.newDocumentBuilder( );
            Document doc = builder.parse( uri );
            if (verbose)
                System.err.println(">>>Walking " + fileName + "...");
            XmlFormWalker c = new GenMIF(doc, msg);
            c.convertAll( );

        } catch (Exception ex) {
            System.err.println("+================================+");
```

---

* Previously from Frame Technologies, a company that Adobe ingested.

*Example 21-10. XmlForm.java (continued)*

```
            System.err.println("|           *Parse Error*          |");
            System.err.println("+=================================+");
            System.err.println(ex.getClass());
            System.err.println(ex.getMessage());
            System.err.println("+=================================+");
        }
        if (verbose)
            System.err.println(">>>Done " + fileName + "...");
    }

    public static void main(String[] av) {
        if (av.length == 0) {
            System.err.println("Usage: XmlForm file");
            return;
        }
        for (int i=0; i<av.length; i++) {
            String name = av[i];
            new XmlForm(name).convert(true);
        }
        msg.close();
    }
}
```

The actual MIF generator is not shown here—it's not really XML-related—but is included in the online source code for the book.

## See Also

XML-related technology is an area of rapid change. New APIs (and acronyms!) continue to appear. XML-RPC and SOAP let you build distributed applications known as web services using XML and HTTP as the program interchange. The W3C has many new XML standards coming out. Several web sites track the changing XML landscape, including the official W3C site (*http://www.w3.org/xml/*) and O'Reilly's XML site (*http://www.xml.com*).

Sun's Java API for XML Parsing (JAXP), included with the JDK 1.4 and later, provides convenience routines for accessing a variety of different parsers. It also includes SAX, DOM, and XSLT in the standard set of Java APIs.

For an interesting historical perspective on HTML by the person who primarily invented the Web and HTML, see Tim Berners-Lee's book, *Weaving the Web* (Harper).

Many books compete to cover XML. These range from the simple *XML: A Primer* by Simon St.Laurent to the comprehensive *XML Bible* by the prolific Elliotte Rusty Harold. In between is *Learning XML* by Erik T. Ray (O'Reilly). O'Reilly's *Java and XML* by Brett McLaughlin covers these topics in more detail and also covers XML publishing frameworks such as Apache's *Cocoon* and developing XML information channels using RSS, often used for blogging.

# CHAPTER 22

# Distributed Java: RMI

## 22.0 Introduction

A *distributed system* is a program or set of programs that runs using more than one computing resource. Distributed computing covers a wide spectrum, from intra-process distributed applications (which Java calls threaded applications, discussed in Chapter 24), through intrasystem applications (such as a network client and server on the same machine), to applications where a client program and a server program run on machines far apart (such as a web application).

Distributed computing was around a long time before Java. Some traditional distributed mechanisms include RPC (remote procedure call) and CORBA. Java adds RMI (Remote Method Invocation), its own CORBA support, and EJB (Enterprise Java-Beans) to the mix. This chapter covers only RMI in detail, but these other technologies are discussed briefly.

At its simplest level, *remote procedure call* is the ability to run code on another machine and have it behave as much as possible like a local method call. Most versions of Unix use remote procedure calls extensively: Sun's NFS, YP/NIS, and NIS+ are all built on top of Sun's RPC. Windows implements large parts of the Unix DCE Remote Procedure Call specification and can interoperate with it. Each of these defines its own slightly ad hoc method of specifying the interface to the remote call. Sun's RPC uses a program called rpcgen, which reads a protocol specification and writes both the client and server network code. These are both Unix-specific; they have their place but aren't as portable as Java.

Java Remote Method Invocation (RMI) is a type of remote procedure call[*] that is network-independent, lightweight, and totally portable, as it's written in pure Java. I discuss RMI in this chapter in enough detail to get you started.

---

[*] Both RMI and CORBA should really be called "remote method calls," as they both emphasize remote *objects*.

CORBA is the Object Management Group's (OMG) Common Object Request Broker Architecture, a sort of remote procedure call for programs written in C, C++, Java, Ada, Smalltalk, and others to call methods in objects written in any of those languages. It provides a transport service called the Internet Inter-Orb Protocol (IIOP) that allows object implementations from different vendors to interoperate. One version of RMI runs over IIOP, making it possible to claim that RMI is CORBA-compliant.

Enterprise JavaBeans (EJB) is a distributed object mechanism used primarily for building reusable distributed objects that provide both business logic and database storage. Types of EJBs include *session beans*, which do something (a shopping cart bean is a good example), and *entity beans*, which represent something (usually the things stored in a database; in our shopping cart example, the entity beans would be the objects available for purchase).

CORBA and EJB are of interest primarily to enterprise developers; they are covered briefly in O'Reilly's *Java Enterprise in a Nutshell*. A more detailed presentation will have to wait until O'Reilly decides to develop an *Enterprise Java Cookbook*. You can read about EJB in *Enterprise JavaBeans* by Richard Monson-Haefel (O'Reilly).

---

### Ian's Basic Steps: RMI

To use RMI:

1. Define (or locate) the remote interface in agreement with the server.
2. Write your server.
3. Run *rmic* (Java RMI stub compiler) to generate the network glue.
4. Write the client.
5. Ensure that the RMI registry is running.
6. Start the server.
7. Run one or more clients.

---

# 22.1  Defining the RMI Contract

## Problem

You want to define the communications exchange between client and server.

## Solution

Define a Java interface.

# Discussion

RMI procedures are defined using an existing Java mechanism: interfaces. An interface is similar to an abstract class, but a class can implement more than one interface. RMI remote interfaces must be subinterfaces of java.rmi.Remote. All parameters and return values must be either primitives (int, double, etc.), or implement Serializable (as do most of the standard types like String). Or, as we'll see in Recipe 22.5, they can also be Remote.

Figure 22-1 shows the relationships between the important classes involved in an RMI implementation. The developer need only write the interface and two classes, the client application and the server object implementation. The RMI stub or proxy and the RMI skeleton or adapter are generated for you by the *rmic* program (see Recipe 22.3), while the RMI Registry and other RMI classes at the bottom of the figure are provided as part of RMI itself.

Example 22-1 is a simple RemoteDate getter interface, which lets us find out the date and time on a remote machine.

*Example 22-1. RemoteDate.java*

```
package darwinsys.distdate;

import java.rmi.*;
import java.util.Date;

/** A statement of what the client & server must agree upon. */
public interface RemoteDate extends java.rmi.Remote {

    /** The method used to get the current date on the remote */
    public Date getRemoteDate( ) throws java.rmi.RemoteException;

    /** The name used in the RMI registry service. */
    public final static String LOOKUPNAME = "RemoteDate";
}
```

This file must list all the methods that will be callable from the server by the client. The lookup name is an arbitrary name that is registered by the server and looked up by the client to establish communications between the two processes (when looked up by the client it will normally be part of an *rmi:* URL). While most authors just hardcode this string in both programs, I find this error-prone, so I usually include the lookup name in the interface.

"So interfaces can contain variables?" you ask. No variables indeed, but interfaces may contain nonvariable (final) fields such as the field LOOKUPNAME in Example 22-1. Putting the lookup name here ensures that both server and client really agree, and that is what this interface is all about, after all. I've seen other developers waste a considerable amount of time tracking down spelling mistakes in the lookup names of various remote services, so I prefer doing it this way.

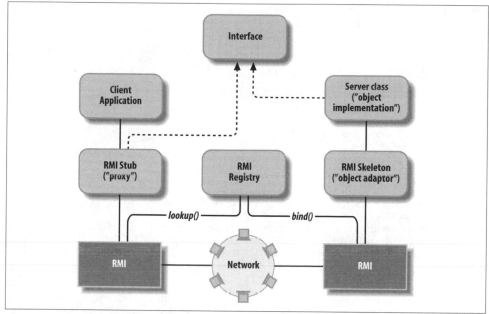

Figure 22 1. RMI overview

# 22.2 Creating an RMI Client

## Problem

You want to write a client to use an RMI service.

## Solution

Locate the object and call its methods.

## Discussion

Assume for now that the server object is running remotely. To locate it, you use `Naming.lookup()`, passing in the lookup name. This gives you a reference to a *proxy object*, an object that, like the real server object, implements the remote interface but runs in the same Java Virtual Machine as your client application. Here we see the beauty of interfaces: the proxy object implements the interface so that your code can use it just as it would use a local object providing the given service. And the remote object also implements the interface so that the proxy object's remote counterpart can use it exactly as the proxy is used. Example 22-2 shows the client for the `RemoteDate` service.

*Example 22-2. DateClient.java*

```
package darwinsys.distdate;

import java.rmi.*;
import java.util.*;

/* A very simple client for the RemoteDate service. */
public class DateClient {

    /** The local proxy for the service. */
    protected static RemoteDate netConn = null;

    public static void main(String[] args) {
        try {
            netConn = (RemoteDate)Naming.lookup(RemoteDate.LOOKUPNAME);
            Date today = netConn.getRemoteDate();
            System.out.println(today.toString()); // Could use a DateFormat...
        } catch (Exception e) {
            System.err.println("RemoteDate exception: " + e.getMessage());
            e.printStackTrace();
        }
    }
}
```

Also in the online source *rmi* directory are *DateApplet.htm* and *DateApplet.java*, which together provide an example of using the server. In DateApplet, the connection is set up in the applet's init() method. The actual RMI call to get the date is done in the action handler for the push button so that you can refresh it on demand.

# 22.3   Creating an RMI Server

## Problem

The client looks good on paper, but it will be lonely without a server to talk to.

## Solution

You need to write two parts for the server, an implementation class and a main method. These can be in the same class or separated for clarity.

## Discussion

The server-side code has to do a bit more work; see the sidebar.

This implementation divides the server into the traditional two parts—a main program and an implementation class. It is just as feasible to combine these in a single class. The main program shown in Example 22-3 simply constructs an instance of the implementation and registers it with the lookup service.

To implement an RMI server:

1. Define (or locate) the remote interface in agreement with the client.
2. Define the constructor for the remote object.
3. Provide implementations for the methods that can be invoked remotely.
4. Create and install a security manager.
5. Create one or more instances of a remote object.
6. Register at least one of the remote objects with the RMI remote object registry.

*Example 22-3. DateServer.java*

```
package darwinsys.distdate;

import java.rmi.*;

public class DateServer {
    public static void main(String[] args) {

        // You may want a SecurityManager for downloading of classes:
        // System.setSecurityManager(new RMISecurityManager());

        try {
            // Create an instance of the server object
            RemoteDateImpl im = new RemoteDateImpl();

            System.out.println("DateServer starting...");
            // Locate it in the RMI registry.
            Naming.rebind(RemoteDate.LOOKUPNAME, im);

            System.out.println("DateServer ready.");
        } catch (Exception e) {
            System.err.println(e);
            System.exit(1);
        }
    }
}
```

The `Naming.bind()` method creates an association between the lookup name and the instance of the server object. This method fails if the server already has an instance of the given name, requiring you to call `rebind()` to overwrite it. But since that's exactly where you'll find yourself if the server crashes (or you kill it while debugging) and you restart it, many people just use `rebind()` all the time.

The implementation class must implement the given remote interface. See Example 22-4.

*Example 22-4. RemoteDateImpl.java*

```java
package darwinsys.distdate;

import java.rmi.*;
import java.rmi.server.*;
import java.util.*;

public class RemoteDateImpl extends UnicastRemoteObject implements RemoteDate
{
    /** Construct the object that implements the remote server.
     * Called from main, after it has the SecurityManager in place.
     */
    public RemoteDateImpl() throws RemoteException {
        super();    // sets up networking
    }

    /** The remote method that "does all the work". This won't get
     * called until the client starts up.
     */
    public Date getRemoteDate() throws RemoteException {
        return new Date();
    }
}
```

### Using the server

Once you've compiled the implementation class, you can run *rmic* (the RMI compiler) to build some glue files and install the class files (for the interface, the stub, and any data classes) into the client's CLASSPATH:

```
$ jikes -d . RemoteDateImpl.java
$ ls darwinsys/distdate
DateApplet$1.class          DateClient.class          RemoteDate.class
DateApplet.class            DateServer.class          RemoteDateImpl.class
$ rmic -d . darwinsys.distdate.RemoteDateImpl
$ ls darwinsys/distdate
DateApplet$1.class          DateServer.class          RemoteDateImpl_Skel.class
DateApplet.class            RemoteDate.class          RemoteDateImpl_Stub.class
DateClient.class            RemoteDateImpl.class
$
```

You must also ensure that TCP/IP networking is running and then start the RMI registry program. If you're doing this by hand, just type the command **rmiregistry** in a separate window or start it in the background on systems that support this.

## See Also

See the JDK documentation in *docs/guide/rmi/getstart.doc.html*.

## 22.4  Deploying RMI Across a Network

### Problem

As shown so far, the server and the client must be on the same machine—some distributed system!

### Solution

Get the RMI registry to dish out the client stubs on demand.

### Discussion

RMI does not provide true *location transparency*, which means that you must at some point know the network name of the machine the server is running on. The server machine must be running the RMI registry program as well, though there's no need for the RMI registry to be running on the client side.

The RMI registry needs to send the client stubs to the client. The best way to do this is to provide an HTTP URL and ensure that the stub files can be loaded from your web server. This can be done by passing the HTTP URL into the RMI server's startup by defining it in the system properties:

```
java -Djava.rmi.server.codebase=http://serverhost/stubsdir/ ServerMain
```

In this example, serverhost is the TCP/IP network name of the host where the RMI server and registry are running, and stubsdir is some directory relative to the web server from which the stub files can be downloaded.

Be careful to start the RMI registry in its own directory, away from where you are storing (or building!) the RMI stubs. If RMI can find the stubs in its own CLASS-PATH, it assumes they are universally available and won't download them!

The only other thing to do is to change the client's view of the RMI lookup name to something like *rmi://serverhost/foo_bar_name*. And for security reasons, the installation of the RMI Security Manager, which was optional before, is now a requirement.

## 22.5  Program: RMI Callbacks

One major benefit of RMI is that almost any kind of object can be passed as a parameter or return value of a remote method. The recipient of the object will not know ahead of time the class of the actual object it will receive. If the object is of a class that implements Remote (java.rmi.Remote), the returned object will in fact be a proxy object that implements at least the declared interface. If the object is not remote, it must be serializable, and a copy of it is transmitted across the Net. The prime example of this is a String. It makes no sense to write an RMI proxy object for String.

Why? Remember from Chapter 3 that String objects are immutable! Once you have a String, you can copy it locally but never change it. So Strings, like most other core classes, can be copied across the RMI connection just as easily as they are copied locally. But Remote objects cause an RMI proxy to be delivered. So what stops the caller from passing an RMI object that is also itself a proxy? Nothing at all, and this is the basis of the powerful RMI callback mechanism.

An RMI callback occurs when the client of one service passes an object that is the proxy for another service. The recipient can then call methods in the object it received and be calling back (hence the name) to where it came from. Think about a stock ticker service. You write a server that runs on your desktop and notifies you when your stock moves up or down. This server is also a remote object. You then pass this server object to the stock ticker service, which remembers it and calls its methods when the stock price changes. See Figure 22-2 for the big picture.

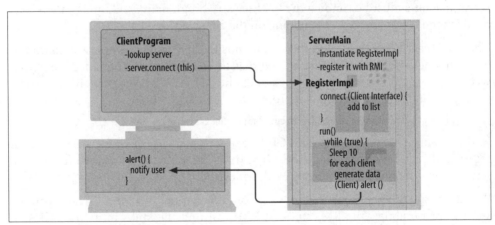

*Figure 22-2. RMI callback service*

The code for the callback service comes in several parts. Because there are two servers, there are also two interfaces. The first is the interface for the TickerServer service. There is only one method, connect( ), which takes one argument, a Client:

```
package com.darwinsys.callback;

import com.darwinsys.client.*;

import java.rmi.*;

public interface TickerServer extends Remote {
    public static final String LOOKUP_NAME = "TickerService";
    public void connect(Client d) throws RemoteException;
}
```

Client is the interface that displays a stock price change message on your desktop. It also has only one method, alert( ), which takes a String argument:

```
package com.darwinsys.client;

import java.rmi.*;

/** Client -- the interface for the client callback */
public interface Client extends Remote {
    public void alert(String mesg) throws RemoteException;
}
```

Now that you've seen both interfaces, let's look at the TickerServer implementation
(Example 22-5). Its constructor starts a background thread to "track" stock prices; in
fact, this implementation just calls a random number generator. A real implementation might use a third RMI service to track actual stock data. The connect( ) method
is trivial; it just adds the given client (which is really an RMI proxy for the client
server running on your desktop). The run method runs forever; on each iteration,
after sleeping for a while, it picks a random stock movement and reports it to any
and all registered clients. If there's an error on a given client, the client is removed
from the list.

*Example 22-5. TickerServerImpl.java*

```
package com.darwinsys.callback;

import com.darwinsys.client.*;

import java.rmi.*;
import java.rmi.server.*;
import java.util.*;

/** This is the main class of the server */
public class TickerServerImpl
    extends UnicastRemoteObject
    implements TickerServer, Runnable
{
    ArrayList list - new ArrayList( );

    /** Construct the object that implements the remote server.
     * Called from main, after it has the SecurityManager in place.
     */
    public TickerServerImpl( ) throws RemoteException {
        super( );    // sets up networking
    }

    /** Start background thread to track stocks :-) and alert users. */
    public void start( ) {
        new Thread(this).start( );
    }

    /** The remote method that "does all the work". This won't get
     * called until the client starts up.
     */
```

*Example 22-5. TickerServerImpl.java (continued)*

```java
    public void connect(Client da) throws RemoteException {
        System.out.println("Adding client " + da);
        list.add(da);
    }

    boolean done = false;
    Random rand = new Random( );

    public void run( ) {
        while (!done) {
            try {
                Thread.sleep(10 * 1000);
                System.out.println("Tick");
            } catch (InterruptedException unexpected) {
                System.out.println("WAHHH!");
                done = true;
            }
            Iterator it = list.iterator( );
            while (it.hasNext( )){
                String mesg = ("Your stock price went " +
                    (rand.nextFloat( ) > 0.5 ? "up" : "down") + "!");
                // Send the alert to the given user.
                // If this fails, remove them from the list
                try {
                    ((Client)it.next( )).alert(mesg);
                } catch (RemoteException re) {
                    System.out.println(
                        "Exception alerting client, removing it.");
                    System.out.println(re);
                    it.remove( );
                }
            }
        }
    }
}
```

As written, this code is not threadsafe; things might go bad if one client connects while we are running through the list of clients. I'll show how to fix this in Recipe 24.5.

This program's "server main" is trivial, so I don't include it here; it just creates an instance of the class we just saw and registers it. More interesting is the client application shown in Example 22-6, which is both the RMI client to the connect( ) method and the RMI server to the alert( ) method in the server in Example 22-5.

*Example 22-6. Callback ClientProgram.java*

```java
package com.darwinsys.client;

import com.darwinsys.callback.*;

import java.io.*;
import java.rmi.*;
import java.rmi.server.*;
```

*Example 22-6. Callback ClientProgram.java (continued)*

```
/** This class tries to be all things to all people:
 *     - main program for client to run.
 *     - "server" program for remote to use Client of
 */
public class ClientProgram extends UnicastRemoteObject implements Client
{
    protected final static String host = "localhost";

    /** No-argument constructor required as we are a Remote Object */
    public ClientProgram() throws RemoteException {
    }

    /** This is the main program, just to get things started. */
    public static void main(String[] argv) throws IOException, NotBoundException {
        new ClientProgram().do_the_work();
    }

    /** This is the server program part */
    private void do_the_work() throws IOException, NotBoundException {

        System.out.println("Client starting");

        // First, register us with the RMI registry
        // Naming.rebind("Client", this);

        // Now, find the server, and register with it
        System.out.println("Finding server");
        TickerServer server =
            (TickerServer)Naming.lookup("rmi://" + host + "/" +
            TickerServer.LOOKUP_NAME);

        // This should cause the server to call us back.
        System.out.println("Connecting to server");
        server.connect(this);

        System.out.println("Client program ready.");
    }

    /** This is the client callback */
    public void alert(String message) throws RemoteException {
        System.out.println(message);
    }
}
```

In this version, the client server alert() method simply prints the message in its console window. A more realistic version would receive an object containing the stock symbol, a timestamp, and the current price and relative price change; it could then consult a GUI control to decide whether the given price movement is considered noticeable and pop up a JOptionPane (see Recipe 14.7) if so.

## 22.6  Program: NetWatch

Here's a program I put together while teaching Java courses for Learning Tree (*http://www.learningtree.com*). In one exercise, each student starts the RMI registry on his or her machine and uses `Naming.rebind( )` (as in Recipe 22.3) to register with it. Some students come up with interesting variations on the theme of registering. This program contacts the RMI registry on each of a batch of machines and shows the instructor graphically which machines have RMI running and what is registered. A red flag shows machines that don't even have the registry program running; a black flag shows machines that are dead to the (networked) world.

This program also uses many ideas from elsewhere in the book. A Swing GUI (Chapter 14) is used. The layout is a `GridLayout` (discussed briefly in Recipe 14.2). A default list of machines to watch is loaded from a `Properties` object (Recipe 7.7). For each host, an `RMIPanel` is constructed. This class is both a `JComponent` (Recipe 14.13) and a thread (Chapter 24). As a `JComponent`, it can be run in a panel; as a thread, it can run independently and then sleep for 30 seconds (by default; settable in the properties file) so that it isn't continually hammering away at the RMI registry on all the machines (the network traffic could be awesome). This program combines all these elements and comes out looking like the display in Figure 22-3 (alas, we don't have color pages in this book).

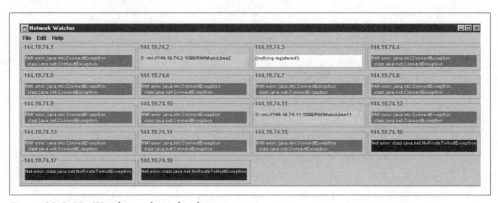

*Figure 22-3. NetWatch watching the class*

Example 22-7 is the main class, `NetWatch`, which creates the `JFrame` and all the `RMIPanels` and puts them together.

*Example 22-7. NetWatch.java*

```
public class NetWatch {
    public static void main(String[] argv) {

        Properties p = null;

        NetFrame f = new NetFrame("Network Watcher", p);
```

*Example 22-7. NetWatch.java (continued)*

```
    try {
        FileInputStream is = new FileInputStream("NetWatch.properties");
        p = new Properties();
        p.load(is);
        is.close();
    } catch (IOException e) {
        JOptionPane.showMessageDialog(f,
            e.toString(), "Properties error",
            JOptionPane.ERROR_MESSAGE);
    }

    // NOW CONSTRUCT PANELS, ONE FOR EACH HOST.

    // If arguments, use them as hostnames.
    if (argv.length!=0) {
        for (int i=0; i<argv.length; i++) {
            f.addHost(argv[i], p);
        }
    // No arguments. Can we use properties?
    } else if (p != null && p.size() > 0) {
        String net = p.getProperty("netwatch.net");
        int start = Integer.parseInt(p.getProperty("netwatch.start"));
        int end = Integer.parseInt(p.getProperty("netwatch.end"));
        for (int i=start; i<=end; i++) {
            f.addHost(net + "." + i, p);
        }
        for (int i=0; ; i++) {
            String nextHost = p.getProperty("nethost" + i);
            if (nextHost == null)
                break;
            f.addHost(nextHost, p);
        }
    }
    // None of the above. Fall back to localhost
    else {
        f.addHost("localhost", p);
    }

    // All done. Pack the Frame and show it.
    f.pack();
    // UtilGUI.centre(f);
    f.setVisible(true);
    f.addWindowListener(new WindowAdapter() {
        public void windowClosing(WindowEvent e) {
            System.exit(0);
        }
    });
    }
}
```

The per-machine class, RMIPanel, is shown in Example 22-8. This class is instantiated once for each machine being monitored. Its run method loops, getting the list of registered objects from the given machine's RMI registry, and checks the contents to see if the expected string is present, setting the state to one of several integer values defined in the parent class NetPanel (EMPTY, DUBIOUS, FINE, etc.) based on what it finds. This state value is used to decide what color to paint this particular RMIPanel in the setState() method of the parent class NetPanel, which we have no reason to override.

*Example 22-8. RMIPanel.java*

```java
/** Displays one machine's status, for RMI.
 */
public class RMIPanel extends NetPanel implements Runnable {

    public RMIPanel(String host, Properties p) {
        super(host, p);
    }

    /** Keep the screen updated forever, unless stop( )ped. */
    public void run( ) {
        String thePort = props.getProperty("rmiwatch.port", "");
        String theURL = "rmi://" + hostName + ":" + thePort;
        while (!done) {
            try {
                String[] names = Naming.list(theURL);
                ta.setText("");
                for (int i=0; i<names.length; i++) {
                    ta.append(i + ": " + names[i] + "\n");
                }
                // If we didn't get an exception, host is up.
                String expect = props.getProperty("rmiwatch.expect");
                String fullText = ta.getText( );
                if (fullText.length( ) == 0) {
                    ta.setText("(nothing registered!)");
                    setState(EMPTY);
                } else if (expect != null && fullText.indexOf(expect)==-1) {
                    setState(DUBIOUS);
                } else setState(FINE);
            } catch (java.rmi.ConnectIOException e) {
                setState(DOWN);
                ta.setText("Net error: " + e.detail.getClass( ));
            } catch (java.rmi.ConnectException e) {
                setState(NOREG);
                ta.setText("RMI error: " + e.getClass( ).getName( ) + "\n" +
                    "  " + e.detail.getClass( ));
                // System.err.println(hostName + ":" + e);
            } catch (RemoteException e) {
                setState(NOREG);
                ta.setText("RMI error: " + e.getClass( ).getName( ) + "\n" +
                    "  " + e.detail.getClass( ));
```

*Example 22-8. RMIPanel.java (continued)*

```
            } catch (MalformedURLException e) {
                setState(DOWN);
                ta.setText("Invalid host: " + e.toString( ));
            } finally {
                // sleep( ) in "finally" so common "down" states don't bypass.
                // Randomize time so we don't make net load bursty.
                try {
                    Thread.sleep((int)(sleepTime * MSEC * 2 * Math.random( )));
                } catch (InterruptedException e) {
                    /*CANTHAPPEN*/
                }
            }
        }
    }
}
```

The last part is NetPanel, shown in Example 22-9. Notice the state variable definitions, and the setState( ) method that calls setBackground( ) to set the correct color given the state.

*Example 22-9. NetPanel.java*

```
/** Displays one machine's status.
 * Part of the NetWatch program: watch the network
 * on a bunch of machines (i.e., in a classroom or lab).
 * <P>Each non-abstract subclass just needs to implement run( ),
 * which must, in a while (!done) loop:
 * <UL><LI>Try to contact the host
 * <LI>call setState( ); (argument below)
 * <LI>call ta.setText( );
 * <LI>Thread.sleep(sleepTime * MSEC);
 * </UL>
 */
public abstract class NetPanel extends JPanel implements Runnable {
    /** The name of this host */
    protected String hostName;
    /** The text area to display a list of stuff */
    protected JTextArea ta;
    /** Properties, passed in to constructor */
    protected Properties props;
    /** Default sleep time, in seconds. */
    protected static int DEFAULT_SLEEP = 30;
    /** Sleep time, in seconds. */
    protected int sleepTime = DEFAULT_SLEEP;
    /** Conversion */
    protected int MSEC = 1000;
    /** The constant-width font, shared by all instances. */
    protected static Font cwFont;
    /** The states */
    /** The state for: has "expect"ed name registered. */
    protected final static int FINE = 1;
```

*Example 22-9. NetPanel.java (continued)*

```
    /** The state for: does not have expected name registered. */
    protected final static int DUBIOUS = 2;
    /** The state for: Server has nothing registered. */
    protected final static int EMPTY = 3;
    /** The state for: host is up but not running RMI */
    protected final static int NOREG = 4;
    /** The state for: host unreachable, not responding, ECONN, etc. */
    protected final static int DOWN = 5;
    /** The color for when a machine is FINE */
    protected static final Color COLOR_FINE = Color.green;
    /** The color for when a machine is DUBIOUS */
    protected static final Color COLOR_DUBIOUS = Color.yellow;
    /** The color for when a machine is EMPTY */
    protected static final Color COLOR_EMPTY = Color.white;
    /** The color for when a machine has NOREG */
    protected static final Color COLOR_NOREG = Color.red;
    /** The color for when a machine is NOREG */
    protected static final Color COLOR_DOWN = Color.black;

    /** State of the monitored host's RMI registry, up or down.
     * Initially set 0, which isn't one of the named states, to
     * force the background color to be set on the first transition.
     */
    protected int state = 0;

    public NetPanel(String host, Properties p) {
        hostName = host;
        props = p;
        String s = props.getProperty("rmiwatch.sleep");
        if (s != null)
            sleepTime = Integer.parseInt(s);
        // System.out.println("Sleep time now " + sleepTime);

        // Maybe get font name and size from props?
        if (cwFont == null)
            cwFont = new Font("lucidasansTypewriter", Font.PLAIN, 10);

        // Gooey gooey stuff.
        ta = new JTextArea(2, 26);
        ta.setEditable(false);
        ta.setFont(cwFont);
        add(BorderLayout.CENTER, ta);
        setBorder(BorderFactory.createTitledBorder(hostName));

        // Sparks. Ignition!
        new Thread(this).start();
    }

    boolean done = false;
    /** Stop this Thread */
    public void stop( ) {
        done = true;
    }
```

*Example 22-9. NetPanel.java (continued)*

```java
/** Record the new state of the current machine.
 * If this machine has changed state, set its color
 * @param newState - one of the five valid states in the introduction.
 */
protected void setState(int newState) {
    if (state /*already*/ == newState)
        return;        // nothing to do.
    switch(newState) {
        case FINE:        // Server has "expect"ed name registered.
            ta.setBackground(COLOR_FINE);
            ta.setForeground(Color.black);
            break;
        case DUBIOUS:    // Server does not have expected name registered.
            ta.setBackground(COLOR_DUBIOUS);
            ta.setForeground(Color.black);
            break;
        case EMPTY:        // Server has nothing registered.
            ta.setBackground(COLOR_EMPTY);
            ta.setForeground(Color.black);
            break;
        case NOREG:        // host is up but not running RMI
            ta.setBackground(COLOR_NOREG);
            ta.setForeground(Color.white);
            break;
        case DOWN:        // host unreachable, not responding, ECONN, etc.
            ta.setBackground(COLOR_DOWN);
            ta.setForeground(Color.white);
            break;
        default:
            throw new IllegalStateException("setState("+state+") invalid");
    }
    state = newState;
    }
}
```

## See Also

The term *distributed computing* covers a lot of terrain. Here I've shown only the basics of RMI. For more on RMI, see *Java Distributed Computing* by Jim Farley (O'Reilly). Jim's book also offers some information on CORBA. It is possible to use RMI to access CORBA objects, or vice versa, using a mechanism called RMI-IIOP. See *http://java.sun.com/products/rmi-iiop/*.

The newest and potentially most important distributed mechanism for large-scale computing projects is Enterprise JavaBeans, part of the Java 2 Enterprise Edition (J2EE). See the O'Reilly book *Enterprise JavaBeans* by Richard Monson-Haefel.

You can also think of servlets and JSPs as a kind of distributed computing, used primarily as the gateway into these other distributed object mechanisms.

# CHAPTER 23
# Packages and Packaging

## 23.0  Introduction

One of the better aspects of the Java language is that it has defined a very clear packaging mechanism for categorizing and managing the external API. Contrast this with a language like C, where external symbols may be found in the C library itself or in any of dozens of other libraries, with no clearly defined naming conventions.* APIs consist of one or more packages; packages consist of classes; classes consist of methods and fields. Anybody can create a package, with one important restriction: you or I cannot create a package whose name begins with the four letters java. Packages named java. or javax. are reserved for use by Sun Microsystems' Java developers. When Java was new, there were about a dozen packages in a structure that is very much still with us; some of these are shown in Table 23-1.

*Table 23-1. Java packages basic structure*

| Name | Function |
| --- | --- |
| java.applet | Applets for browser use |
| java.awt | Graphical User Interface |
| java.lang | Intrinsic classes (strings, etc.) |
| java.net | Networking (sockets) |
| java.io | Reading and writing |
| java.util | Utilities (collections, date) |

Many packages have since been added, but the initial structure has stood the test of time fairly well. In this chapter, I show you how to create and document your own packages, and then discuss a number of issues related to deploying your package in various ways on various platforms.

---

* This is not strictly true. On Unix, at least, there is a distinction between normal include files and those in the *sys* subdirectory, and many structures have names beginning with one or two letters and an underscore, like pw_name, pw_passwd, pw_home, and so on in the password structure. But this is nowhere near as consistent as Java's java.* naming conventions.

# 23.1  Creating a Package

## Problem

You want to be able to import classes and/or organize your classes, so you want to create your own package.

## Solution

Put a package statement at the front of each file, and recompile with -d.

## Discussion

The package statement must be the very first noncomment statement in your Java source file—preceding even import statements—and it must give the full name of the package. Package names are expected to start with your domain name backward; for example, my Internet domain is *darwinsys.com*, so most of my packages begin with com.darwinsys and a project name. The utility classes used in this book are in one of the com.darwinsys packages listed in Recipe 1.5, and each source file begins with a statement, such as:

```
package com.darwinsys.util;
```

Once you have package statements in place, be aware that the Java runtime, and even the compiler, will expect the class files to be found in their rightful place, that is, in the subdirectory corresponding to the full name somewhere in your CLASS-PATH settings. For example, the class file for com.darwinsys.util.FileIO must *not* be in the file *FileIO.class* in my class path but must be in *com/darwinsys/util/FileIO.class* relative to one of the directories or archives in my CLASSPATH. Accordingly, it is customary to use the -d command-line argument when compiling. This argument must be followed by a directory name (often . is used to signify the current directory) to specify where to build the directory tree. For example, I often say:

```
javac -d . *.java
```

which creates the path (e.g., *com/darwinsys/util/*) relative to the current directory, and puts the class files into that subdirectory. This makes life easy for subsequent compilations, and also for creating archives, which I will do in Recipe 23.4.

Note that a change was made to the compiler in JDK 1.4 such that classes that do not belong to a package (the "anonymous package") cannot be listed in an import statement, although they can be referred to by other classes in that package.

# 23.2  Documenting Classes with Javadoc

## Problem

You have heard about this thing called "code reuse" and would like to promote it by allowing other developers to use your classes.

## Solution

Use Javadoc.

## Discussion

Javadoc is one of the great inventions of the early Java years. Like so many good things, it was not wholly invented by the Java folk; earlier projects such as Knuth's Literate Programming had combined source code and documentation in a single source file. But the Java folk did a good job on it and came along at the right time. Javadoc is to Java classes what "manpages" are to Unix or Windows Help is to Windows applications: it is a standard format that everybody expects to find and knows how to use. Learn it. Use it. Write it. Live long and prosper (well, perhaps not). But all that HTML documentation that you refer to when writing Java code, the complete reference for the JDK—did you think they hired dozens of tech writers to produce it? Nay, that's not the Java way. Java's developers wrote the documentation comments as they went along, and when the release was made, they ran Javadoc on all the zillions of public classes and generated the documentation bundle at the same time as the JDK. You can, should, and really must do the same when you are preparing classes for other developers to use.

All you have to do to use Javadoc is to put special "doc comments" into your Java source files. These begin with a slash and two stars (/**) and must appear immediately before the definition of the class, method, or field that they document. Doc comments placed elsewhere are ignored.

A series of keywords, prefixed by the at sign (@), can appear inside doc comments in certain contexts. These are listed in Table 23-2.

*Table 23-2. Javadoc keywords*

| Keyword | Use |
| --- | --- |
| @author | Author name(s) |
| @version | Version identifier |
| @param | Argument name and meaning (methods only) |
| @since | JDK version in which introduced (primarily for Sun use) |
| @return | Return value |
| @throws | Exception class and conditions under which thrown |
| @deprecated | Causes deprecation warning |
| @see | Cross-reference |

Example 23-1 is a somewhat contrived example that shows almost every usage of a javadoc keyword. The output of running this through Javadoc is shown in a browser in Figure 23-1.

*Example 23-1. JavadocDemo.java*

```java
import java.applet.*;
import java.awt.*;
import java.awt.event.*;

/**
 * JavadocDemo - a simple applet to show JavaDoc comments.
 * <P>Note: this is just a commented version of HelloApplet.
 * @author Ian F. Darwin, http://www.darwinsys.com/
 * @version $Id: ch23,v 1.5 2004/05/04 20:13:53 ian Exp $
 * @see java.applet.Applet
 * @see javax.swing.JApplet
 */
public class JavadocDemo extends Applet {

    /** init() is an Applet method called by the browser to initialize.
     * Init normally sets up the GUI, and this version is no exception.
     */
    public void init() {
        // We create and add a pushbutton here,
        // but it doesn't do anything yet.
        Button b;
        b = new Button("Hello");
        add(b);                         // connect Button into Applet
    }

    /** paint() is an AWT Component method, called when the
     * component needs to be painted. This one just draws colored
     * boxes in the Applet's window.
     *
     * @param g A java.awt.Graphics that we use for all our
     * drawing methods.
     */
    public void paint(Graphics g) {
        int w = getSize().width, h=getSize().height;
        g.setColor(Color.YELLOW);
        g.fillRect(0, 0, w/2, h);
        g.setColor(Color.GREEN);
        g.fillRect(w/2, 0, w, h);
        g.setColor(Color.BLACK);
        g.drawString("Welcome to Java", 50, 50);
    }

    /** Show makes a component visible; this method became deprecated
     * in the Great Renaming of JDK1.1.
     * @since 1.0
     * @deprecated Use setvisible(true) instead.
     */
    public void show() {
        setVisible(true);
    }
```

*Example 23-1. JavadocDemo.java (continued)*

```
    /** An Applet must have a public no-argument constructor.
     * @throws java.lang.IllegalArgumentException if the current day of the week is
Sunday.
     */
    public JavadocDemo( ) {
        if (new java.util.Date( ).getDay( ) == 0) {
            throw new IllegalArgumentException("Never On A Sunday");
        }
    }
}
```

The Javadoc tool works fine for one class but really comes into its own when dealing with a package or collection of packages. It generates thoroughly interlinked and crosslinked documentation, just like that which accompanies the standard JDK. There are several command-line options; I normally use -author and -version to get it to include these items, and often -link to tell it where to find the standard JDK to link to. Run **javadoc –help** for a complete list of options. Figure 23-1 shows one view of the documentation that the previous class generates when run as :

```
$ javadoc -author -version JavadocDemo.java
```

Be aware that one of the (many) generated files have the same name as the class, with the extension *.html*. If you write an applet and a sample HTML file to invoke it, the *.html* file is silently overwritten with the Javadoc output. For this reason, I recommend using a different filename or the filename extension *.htm* for the HTML page that invokes the applet. Alternately, use the –d directory option to tell Javadoc where to put the generated files if you don't want them in the same directory.

## See Also

Javadoc has numerous other command-line arguments. If documentation is for your own use only and will not be distributed, you can use the -link option to tell it where your standard JDK documentation is installed so that links can be generated to standard Java classes (like String, Object, and so on). If documentation is to be distributed, you can omit -link or use -link with a URL to the appropriate J2SE API page on Sun's web site. See the online tools documentation for all the command-line options.

The output that Javadoc generates is fine for most purposes. It is possible to write your own Doclet class to make the Javadoc program into a class documentation verifier, a Java-to-MIF or Java-to-RTF documentation generator, or whatever you like. Those are actual examples; see the Javadoc tools documentation that comes with the JDK for documents and examples, or go to *http://java.sun.com/j2se/javadoc/*.

Visit *http://www.doclet.com/* for a fabulous collection of other Javadoc-based tools.

Javadoc is for programmers using your classes; for a GUI application, end users will probably appreciate standard online help. This is the role of the Java Help API, which is not covered in this book but is fully explained in the O'Reilly book *Creating Effective JavaHelp*, which every GUI application developer should read.

---

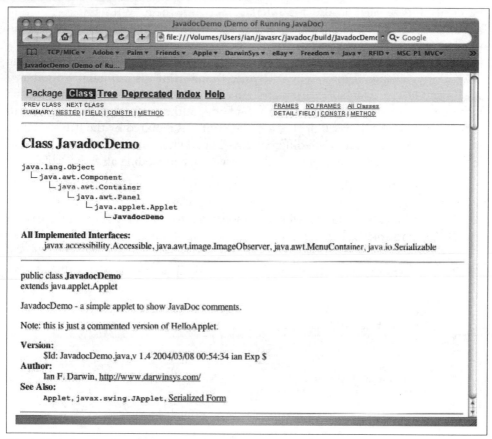

*Figure 23-1. Javadoc in action*

# 23.3   Beyond JavaDoc: Annotations/Metadata (JDK 1.5) and XDoclet

## Problem

You want to generate not just documentation, but also other code artifacts, from your source code. You want to mark code for additional compiler verification.

## Solution

Download and use XDoclet. Or, in 1.5, use the Annotations or Metadata facility.

## Discussion

XDoclet is a free tool that you can download from *http://xdoclet.sourceforge.net*. In addition to generating documentation, XDoclet can generate other "artifacts." For example, when writing an RMI program (see Chapter 22), you need to write not only the client and server but also the interface between them. With Enterprise Java-Beans, you need to write both a home and a remote interface. XDoclet reads additional @ tags in your source code and uses these to generate these little artifacts mechanically, the goal being to save you time and typing. For example, in generating Enterprise JavaBeans (EJBs), each Enterprise Bean—which is normally written as a single Bean class—may have a local and remote Home and Business interface. Each of these four artifacts is just an interface for some of the methods in the Bean itself. Also, at least one XML-based deployment descriptor is required by the EJB specification, in addition to one for each different brand of application server that you wish to deploy into. This makes for a great deal of busywork handcoding all these artifacts.

Enter XDoclet, the "attribute-oriented programming" tool.* XDoclet reads a variety of special @ tags in a "doc comment" before the class—and before methods and fields—describing, for example, which methods go into which interface in the case of an EJB. A slightly marked up EJB might begin like this (imports omitted):

```
/**
 * This  Shopping Cart Stateful Session bean is really an example of the XDoclet EJB
tags.
 * @see Product
 * @ejb.bean
 *      name="store/Cart"
 *      type="Stateful"
 *      jndi-name="store/Cart"
 * @ejb.interface
 *      remote-class="myejbs.Cart"
 * @version $Id: ch23,v 1.5 2004/05/04 20:13:53 ian Exp $
 */
public class XDocletDemo implements SessionBean {

        /** @ejb.interface-method
         */
        public void add(Product o) {
                cartItems.add(o);
        }

}
```

For both the class and the method, the @ejb... tags inform XDoclet how to fabricate the various EJB artifacts. This extra markup, and a series of Ant elements, are all that is needed to generate all the artifacts.

XDoclet has been successful and has grown immensely. Its EJB support now includes all major types, all major application servers, and even code for automatically implementing many EJB-related design patterns, such as Data Accessor Object (DAO). XDoclet also supports other types of classes such as JavaBeans, web applications, and others—in short, any time one class can be generated mechanically from another.

---

* Not to be confused with Aspect Oriented Programming (see *http://aopalliance.sourceforge.net/*). Aspect Oriented Programming aims to provide a simpler alternative to EJBs and other heavyweight frameworks. But I digress....

# The Annotations Mechanism (JDK 1.5)

The continuing success of XDoclet has led to a demand for a similar mechanism to be included as part of standard Java. The new 1.5 annotations are the result. The Annotations mechanism uses an interface-like syntax in which both declaration and use of Annotations see the name preceded by an at character (@). This was chosen, according to the designers, to be reminiscent of "Javadoc tags, a preexisting ad hoc annotation facility in the Java programming language." Javadoc is ad hoc only in the sense that its @ tags were never fully integrated into the language; most were ignored by the compiler, but @deprecated was always understood by the compiler (see Recipe 1.9).

Annotations can be read at runtime by use of the Reflection API; this is not discussed here (but see Chapter 25 for general information on the Reflection API). More commonly, annotations can be read before compile time by tools such as the RMI and EJB stub generators (and others to be invented, perhaps by you, gentle reader, in the post-1.5 release period!).

Annotations are also read by javac at compile time to provide extra information to the compiler. For example, a common coding error is overloading a method when you mean to override it, by mistakenly using the wrong argument type. Consider overriding the equals method in Object, if you mistakenly write:

```
public boolean equals(MyClass obj) {
}
```

then you have created a new overload, that will likely never be called, and the default version in object will be called. To prevent this, one of several new Annotations provided in java.lang is the Overrides annotation. This has no parameters but simply is placed before the method call. For example:

```
/** Simple demonstation of Metadata being used to verify
 * that a method does in fact override (not overload) a method
 * from the parent class. This class provides the method.
 */
abstract class Top {
    public abstract void myMethod(Object o);
}

/** Simple demonstation of Metadata being used to verify
 * that a method does in fact override (not overload) a method
 * from the parent class. This class is supposed to do the overriding,
 * but deliberately introduces an error to show how the 1.5 compiler
 * behaves (-source 1.5 required).
 */
class Bottom {
    @Overrides public void myMethod(String s) {     // EXPECT COMPILE ERROR
        // Do something here...
    }
}
```

Running this (with -source 1.5) results in a compiler error that the method in question does not override a method, even though the annotation says it does; this is a fatal compile-time error:

```
> javac OverridesDemo.java
OverridesDemo.java:16: method does not override a method from its superclass
        @Overrides public void myMethod(String s) {    // EXPECT COMPILE ERROR
        ^
1 error
>
```

A list of other annotations provided in 1.5 for use by Java developers is included in the online documentation that accompanies the release.

Finally, the Javadoc Doclet interface has been extended to allow reading of Annotations before compile time by programs that wish to generate other code artifacts. See the Doclet API documentation with JDK 1.5 for details on using this mechanism.

# 23.4   Archiving with jar

## Problem

You want to create a Java archive (JAR) file.

## Solution

Use *jar*.

## Discussion

The *jar* archiver is Java's standard tool for building archives. Archives serve the same purpose as the program libraries that some other programming languages use. Java normally loads its standard classes from archives, a fact you can verify by running a simple Hello World program with the -verbose option:

```
java -verbose HelloWorld
```

Creating an archive is a simple process. The *jar* tool takes several command-line arguments: the most common are c for create, t for table of contents, and x for extract. The archive name is specified with -f and a filename. The options are followed by the files and directories to be archived. For example:

```
jar cvf /tmp/MyClasses.jar .
```

The dot at the end is important; it means "the current directory." This command creates an archive of all files in the current directory and its subdirectories into the file */tmp/MyClasses.jar*.

Some applications of JAR files require an extra file in the JAR called a *manifest*. This file lists the contents of the JAR and their attributes. The attributes are in the form name: value, as used in email headers, properties files (see Recipe 7.7), and elsewhere.

Some attributes are required by the application, while others are optional. For example, Recipe 23.7 discusses running a main program directly from a JAR; this requires a `Main-Program` header. You can even invent your own attributes, such as:

```
MySillyAttribute: true
MySillynessLevel: high (5'11")
```

You store this in a file called, say, *manifest.stub,*\* and pass it to *jar* with the -m switch. *jar* includes your attributes in the manifest file it creates:

```
jar -cv -m manifest.stub -f /tmp/com.darwinsys.util.jar .
```

The *jar* program and related tools add additional information to the manifest, including a listing of all the other files included in the archive.

# 23.5 Running an Applet from a JAR

## Problem

You want to optimize downloading time for an applet by putting all the class files into one JAR file.

## Solution

*jar* the applet and supporting files. Deploy the JAR file in place of the class file on the web server. Use `<applet code="MyClass" archive="MyAppletJar.jar" ...>`.

## Discussion

Once you've deployed the JAR file on the web server in place of the class file, you need to refer to it in the applet tag in the HTML. The syntax for doing this is to use an `archive="`*name of jar file*`"` attribute on the applet tag.

## See Also

You can also store other resources such as GIF images for use by the applet. You then need to use `getResource( )` instead of trying to open the file directly; see Step 5 in the sidebar in Recipe 23.13.

# 23.6 Running an Applet with a Modern JDK

## Problem

You want to use an applet on an intranet or the Internet, but it needs a modern JDK to run.

---

\* Some people like to use names like *MyPackage.mf* so that it's clear which package it is for; the extension .mf is arbitrary, but it's a good convention for identifying manifest files.

## Solution

Use the Java Plug-in.

## Discussion

Sun's Java Plug-in allows your applet to run with a modern JDK even if the user has an ancient browser (Netscape 2, 3, or 4), or an anti-standard-Java browser (Internet Explorer might come to mind). For Netscape, the plug-in runs as a Netscape Plug-in. For Microsoft, the plug-in runs as an ActiveX control. The Java Plug-in was previously a separate download but is included in the Java Runtime Environment (JRE) in all modern JDK versions.

The HTML code needed to make a single applet runnable in either of those two modes rather boggles the mind. However, a convenient tool (which Sun provides for free) converts a plain applet tag into a hairy mess of HTML that is "bilingual": both of the major browsers interpret it correctly and do the right thing. Note that since browser plug-ins are platform-dependent, the Plug-in is platform-dependent. Sun provides versions for Solaris and Windows; other vendors provide it ported to various platforms. Learn more at Java's Plug-in page, *http://java.sun.com/products/plugin/*.

To try it out, I started with a simple JApplet subclass, the HelloApplet program from Recipe 25.8. Since this is a JApplet, it requires Swing support, which is not available in older Netscape versions or newer MSIE versions. Here are some screenshots, and the "before and after" versions of a simple HTML page with an applet tag run through the converter. Example 23-2 shows a simple applet HTML page.

*Example 23-2. HelloApplet.html*

```
<html>
<title>Hello Applet</title>
<body bgcolor="white">
<h1>Hello Applet</h1>
<hr>
<applet code=HelloApplet width=300 height=200>
        <param name="buttonlabel" value="Toggle Drawing">
</applet>
<hr>
</html>
```

When I run this under Netscape 4.x, it dies because Netscape 4 doesn't fully support Swing. So I need to convert it to use the Java Plug-in. Editing the HTML by hand is possible (there is a spec on the Java web site, *http://java.sun.com*), but messy. I decide to use the HTMLConverter instead. It pops up a simple dialog window (shown in Figure 23-2), in which I browse to the directory containing the HTML page. Note that the program will convert *all* the HTML files in a directory, so approach with caution if you have a lot of files. When I click on the Convert button, it chugs for a while and then pops up the window shown at the bottom of Figure 23-2 to show what it did.

---

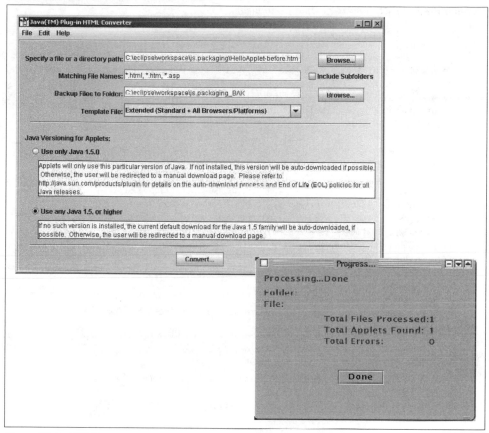

*Figure 23-2. HTML converter*

By the time the HTMLConverter is finished, the once-simple HTML file is simple no more (although the original is saved in _BAK). See Example 23-3 for the finished version of the HTML.

*Example 23-3. HTML converter output*

```
<html>
<head><title>Hello Applet</title></head>
<body bgcolor="white">
<h1>Hello Applet</h1>
<hr/>
<!--"CONVERTED_APPLET"-->
<!-- HTML CONVERTER -->
<script language="JavaScript" type="text/javascript"><!--
    var _info = navigator.userAgent;
    var _ns = false;
    var _ns6 = false;
    var _ie = (_info.indexOf("MSIE") > 0 && _info.indexOf("Win") > 0 && _info.
indexOf("Windows 3.1") < 0);
//--></script>
```

*Example 23-3. HTML converter output (continued)*

```
    <comment>
        <script language="JavaScript" type="text/javascript"><!--
        var _ns = (navigator.appName.indexOf("Netscape") >= 0 && ((_info.indexOf("Win") >
0 && _info.indexOf("Win16") < 0 && java.lang.System.getProperty("os.version").indexOf("3.
5") < 0) || (_info.indexOf("Sun") > 0) || (_info.indexOf("Linux") > 0) || (_info.
indexOf("AIX") > 0) || (_info.indexOf("OS/2") > 0) || (_info.indexOf("IRIX") > 0)));
        var _ns6 = ((_ns == true) && (_info.indexOf("Mozilla/5") >= 0));
//--></script>
    </comment>

<script language="JavaScript" type="text/javascript"><!--
    if (_ie == true) document.writeln('<object classid="clsid:8AD9C840-044E-11D1-B3E9-
00805F499D93" WIDTH = "300" HEIGHT = "200"  codebase="http://java.sun.com/update/1.5.0/
jinstall-1_5-windows-i586.cab#Version=1,5,0,0"><noembed><xmp>');
    else if (_ns == true && _ns6 == false) document.writeln('<embed ' +
        'type="application/x-java-applet;version=1.5" \
            CODE = "HelloApplet" \
            WIDTH = "300" \
            HEIGHT = "200" \
            buttonlabel ="Toggle Drawing" ' +
        'scriptable=false ' +
        'pluginspage="http://java.sun.com/products/plugin/index.html#download"><noembed>
<xmp>');
//--></script>
<applet  CODE = "HelloApplet" WIDTH = "300" HEIGHT = "200"></xmp>
    <PARAM NAME = CODE VALUE = "HelloApplet" >
    <param name="type" value="application/x-java-applet;version=1.5">
    <param name="scriptable" value="false">
    <PARAM NAME = "buttonlabel" VALUE="Toggle Drawing">

</applet>
</noembed>
</embed>
</object>

<!--
<APPLET CODE = "HelloApplet" WIDTH = "300" HEIGHT = "200">
<PARAM NAME = "buttonlabel" VALUE="Toggle Drawing">

</APPLET>
-->
<!--"END_CONVERTED_APPLET"-->

<hr/>
</body>
</html>
```

Sun's documentation makes the amusing claim that "this may look complicated, but it's not really." Your mileage may vary; mine did. In fairness to Sun, if you use the simpler templates you do get simpler converted output. But because I believe in choice, I used the "Extended" template to get a version of the file that can be used in almost any browser. The converter thus outputs the OBJECT version of the Applet for MSIE and the EMBED version for Navigator; other browsers can use one or the other. Both versions are cleverly interwoven to appear as ignorable comments to the other. Figure 23-3 shows this page running under Netscape, and Figure 23-4 shows it under MSIE.

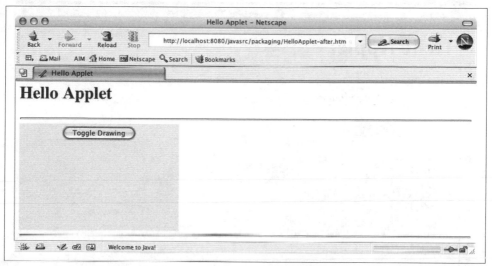

Figure 23-3. Applet working in Netscape using Java Plug-in

# 23.7   Running a Main Program from a JAR

## Problem

You want to distribute a single large file containing all the classes of your application and run the main program from within the JAR.

## Solution

Create a JAR file with a Main-Class: line in the manifest; run the program with the java –jar option.

## Discussion

The java command has a -jar option that tells it to run the main program found within a JAR file. In this case, it will also find classes it needs to load from within the same JAR file. How does it know which class to run? You must tell it. Create a one-line entry like this, noting that *the attribute fields are case-sensitive and that the colon must be followed by a space*:

```
Main-Class: HelloWorld
```

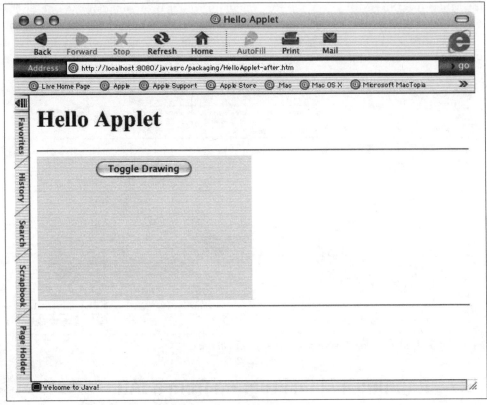

*Figure 23-4. Applet working in Microsoft Internet Explorer using Java Plug-in*

in a file called, say, *manifest.stub*, and assuming that you want to run the program HelloWorld. Then give the following commands:

```
C:> javac HelloWorld.java
C:> jar cvmf manifest.stub hello.jar HelloWorld.class
C:> java -jar hello.jar
Hello, World of Java
C:>
```

You can now copy the JAR file anywhere and run it the same way. You do not need to add it to your CLASSPATH or list the name of the main class.

On GUI platforms that support it, you can also launch this application by double-clicking on the JAR file. This works at least on Mac OS X and on Windows with the Sun Java runtime installed.

## Mac OS X Specifics

On Mac OS X, you can use the Jar Bundler (under */Developer/Applications/Java Tools/Jar Bundler.app*). This provides a windowed tool to specify the options set by my MacOSUI package (see Recipe 14.16) as well as CLASSPATH and other attributes. See Figure 23-5.

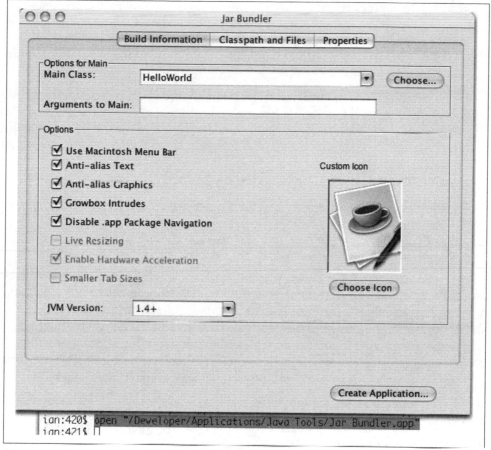

Figure 23-5. Mac OS Jar Bundler (OS X 10.3.2 version)

# 23.8 Preparing a Class as a JavaBean

## Problem

You have a class that you would like to install as a JavaBean.

## Solution

Make sure the class meets the JavaBeans requirements; create a JAR file containing the class, a manifest, and any ancillary entries.

## Discussion

Three kinds of Java components are called JavaBeans:

- Visual components for use in GUI builders, as discussed in this chapter.
- Components used in JavaServer Pages (JSPs).

- Enterprise JavaBeans (EJBs), containing features for building enterprise-scale applications. Creating and using EJBs is more involved than regular JavaBeans and would take us very far afield, so EJBs are not covered in this book. When you need to learn about EJB functionality, turn to the O'Reilly book *Enterprise JavaBeans*.

What all three kinds of beans have in common are certain naming paradigms. All public properties should be accessible by get/set accessory methods. For a given property Prop of type Type, the following two methods should exist (note the capitalization):

```
public Type getProp();
public void setProp(Type)
```

For example, the various AWT and Swing components that have textual labels all have the following pair of methods:

```
public String getText();
public void setText(String newText);
```

You should use this set/get design pattern (set/get methods) for methods that control a bean. Indeed, this technique is useful even in nonbean classes for regularity. The "bean containers"—the Bean Builders, the JSP mechanism, and the EJB mechanism—all use Java introspection (see Chapter 25) to find the set/get method pairs, and some use these to construct properties editors for your bean. Bean-aware IDEs, for example, provide editors for all standard types (colors, fonts, labels, etc.). You can supplement this with a BeanInfo class to provide or override information.

The bare minimum a class requires to be usable as a JavaBean in a GUI builder is the following:

- The class must implement java.io.Serializable.
- The class must have a no-argument constructor.
- The class should use the set/get paradigm.
- The class file should be packaged into a JAR file with the *jar* archiver program (see Recipe 23.9).

Here is a sample bean that may be a useful addition to your Java GUI toolbox, the LabelText widget. It combines a label and a one-line text field into a single unit, making it easier to compose GUI applications. A test program in the online source directory sets up three LabelText widgets, as shown in Figure 23-6.

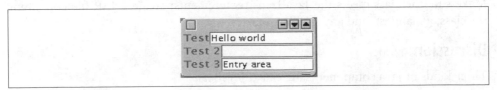

*Figure 23-6. LabelText bean*

The code for LabelText is shown in Example 23-4. Notice that it is serializable and uses the set/get paradigm for most of its public methods. Most of the public set/get methods simply delegate to the corresponding methods in the label or the text field. There isn't really a lot to this bean, but it's a good example of aggregation, in addition to being a good example of a bean.

*Example 23-4. LabelText.java*

```java
import java.awt.*;
import java.awt.event.*;
import javax.swing.*;

/** A label and text combination, inspired by
 * the LabelText control in Guy Eddon's ActiveX Components book
 * (2nd Edition, p. 203). But done more  simply.
 *
 */
public class LabelText extends JPanel implements java.io.Serializable {
    /** The label component */
    protected JLabel theLabel;
    /** The text field component */
    protected JTextField theTextField;

    /** Construct the object with no initial values.
     * To be usable as a JavaBean there MUST be a no-argument constructor.
     */
    public LabelText() {
        this("(LabelText)",  12);
    }

    /** Construct the object with the label and a default textfield size */
    public LabelText(String label) {
        this(label, 12);
    }

    /** Construct the object with given label and textfield size */
    public LabelText(String label, int numChars) {
        super();
        setLayout(new BoxLayout(this, BoxLayout.X_AXIS));
        theLabel = new JLabel(label);
        add(theLabel);
        theTextField = new JTextField(numChars);
        add(theTextField);
    }

    /** Get the label's horizontal alignment */
    public int getLabelAlignment() {
        return theLabel.getHorizontalAlignment();
    }

    /** Set the label's horizontal alignment */
    public void setLabelAlignment(int align) {
        switch (align) {
```

*Example 23-4. LabelText.java (continued)*

```
        case JLabel.LEFT:
        case JLabel.CENTER:
        case JLabel.RIGHT:
            theLabel.setHorizontalAlignment(align);
            break;
        default:
            throw new IllegalArgumentException(
                "setLabelAlignment argument must be one of JLabel aligners");
        }
    }

    /** Get the text displayed in the text field */
    public String getText( ) {
        return theTextField.getText( );
    }

    /** Set the text displayed in the text field */
    public void setText(String text) {
        theTextField.setText(text);
    }

    /** Get the text displayed in the label */
    public String getLabel( ) {
        return theLabel.getText( );
    }

    /** Set the text displayed in the label */
    public void setLabel(String text) {
        theLabel.setText(text);
    }

    /** Set the font used in both subcomponents. */
    public void setFont(Font f) {
        theLabel.setFont(f);
        theTextField.setFont(f);
    }

    /** Adds the ActionListener to receive action events from the textfield */
    public void addActionListener(ActionListener l) {
        theTextField.addActionListener(l);
    }

    /** Remove an ActionListener from the textfield. */
    public void removeActionListener(ActionListener l) {
        theTextField.removeActionListener(l);
    }
}
```

Once it's compiled, it's ready to be pickled into a JAR. JavaBeans people really talk like that!

# 23.9  Pickling Your Bean into a JAR

## Problem

You need to package your bean for deployment.

## Solution

"Pickle your bean into a JAR," that is, create a JAR archive containing it and a manifest file.

## Discussion

In addition to the compiled file, you need a manifest prototype, which needs only the following entries:

```
Name: LabelText.class
Java-Bean: true
```

If these lines are stored in a file called *LabelText.stub*, we can prepare the whole mess for use as a bean by running the *jar* command (see Recipe 23.4). Because the JAR file must contain the class files in their correct package location (see Recipe 23.1), and because LabelText is part of my com.darwinsys package (see Recipe 1.5), I start off in the source directory and refer to the class file by its full path (the Stub file can be anywhere, but I keep it with the source file so I can find it easily, thus I have to refer to it by its full path, too):

```
$ cd $js/darwinsys/src
$ jar cvfm labeltext.jar com/darwinsys/swingui/LabelText.stub \
        com/darwinsys/swingui/LabelText.class
added manifest
adding: com/darwinsys/swingui/LabelText.class(in =3D 1607) (out=3D
776)(deflated 51%)
$
```

Now we're ready to install *labeltext.jar* as a JavaBean. However, the curious may wish to examine the JAR file in detail. The x option to *jar* asks it to extract files:

```
$ jar xvf labeltext.jar
  created: META-INF/
extracted: META-INF/MANIFEST.MF
extracted: com/darwinsys/swingui/LabelText.class
$
```

The *MANIFEST.MF* file is based upon the manifest file (*LabelText.stub*); let's examine it:

```
$ more META-INF/MANIFEST.MF
Manifest-Version: 1.0
Created-By: 1.4.2_03 (Apple Computer, Inc.)
Java-Bean: true
Name: LabelText.class
```

Not much exciting has happened besides the addition of a few lines. But the class is now ready for use as a JavaBean. For a GUI builder, either copy it into the *beans* directory or use the bean installation wizard, as appropriate.

### See Also

Many good books on JavaBeans technology are available. O'Reilly's entry is *Developing JavaBeans* by Robert Englander. You can also find information on JavaBeans at Sun's web site, *http://java.sun.com/products/javabeans/*.

## 23.10 Packaging a Servlet into a WAR File

### Problem

You have a servlet and other web resources and want to package them into a single file for deploying to the server.

### Solution

Use *jar* to make a web archive (WAR) file.

### Discussion

Servlets are server-side components for use in web servers. They can be packaged for easy installation into a web server. A *web application* in the Servlet API specification is a collection of HTML and/or JSP pages, servlets, and other resources. A typical directory structure might include the following:

*index.html, foo.jsp*
> Web pages

*WEB-INF*
> Server directory

*WEB-INF/web.xml*
> Descriptor

*WEB-INF/classes*
> Directory for servlets and any classes used by them or by JSPs

*WEB-INF/lib*
> Directory for any JAR files of classes needed by classes in the *WEB-INF/classes* directory

Once you have prepared the files in this way, you just package them up with *jar*:

```
jar cvf MyWebApp.war .
```

You then deploy the resulting WAR file into your web server. For details on this, consult the web server documentation.

# 23.11 "Write Once, Install Anywhere"

## Problem

You want your application program to be installable on a variety of platforms by users who have not yet earned a Ph.D. in software installation.

## Solution

Use an installer.

## Discussion

The process of installing software is nontrivial. Unix command-line geeks are quite happy to extract a gzipped tar file and set their PATH manually, but if you want your software to be used by the larger masses, you need something simpler. As in, point and click. Several tools try to automate this process. The better ones will create startup icons on Mac OS, Windows, and even some of the Unix desktops (CDE, KDE, GNOME).

I've had good results with ZeroG Software's commercial InstallAnywhere. It ensures that a JVM is installed and has both web-based and application installation modes; that is, you can install the application from a web page or you can run the installer explicitly. See *http://www.zerog.com*.

Sitraka (formerly KL Group) DeployDirector is a newer entry that promises to automate deployment of client-side applications on hundreds or thousands of desktops. It works with Java Web Start (see Recipe 23.13). I haven't tried it. See *http://www. sitraka.com/deploy/*.

InstallShield has long been the leader in the Windows installation world, but they have had more competition in the Java world. They can be reached at *http://www. installshield.com*.

Recipe 23.13 discusses Java Web Start, Sun's new web-based application installer.

# 23.12 "Write Once, Install on Mac OS X"

## Problem

You want to install your Java program as a first-class application under Mac OS X.

## Solution

Structure your build directory as shown here. Or use a tool such as a commercial installer (Recipe 23.11) or the Eclipse IDE Export Mac OS Application wizard.

## Discussion

Mac OS X applications require a specific installation format, which is fairly easy to understand. Each Mac OS X Application, regardless of programming language, is installed in a separate directory called an "Application Bundle", whose name should end in ".*app*". This is the preferred way of installing applications under Mac OS X. Unlike simple JAR files, Application Bundles will be shown as icons in Finder ("explorer") windows and elsewhere, can be saved in the Dock for single-click startup, and can have file types associated with them (so that double-clicking or opening a file will launch your application and have it open the file).

Figure 23-7 shows a listing of the files in a simple Java application's directory.

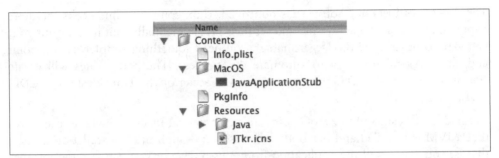

*Figure 23-7. Files in the Java application directory on Mac OS X*

As you can see, there is one directory *Contents* with two subdirectories: *MacOS* and *Resources*. *Contents/MacOS* contains the executable program, in the Java case *JavaApplicationStub*, a native-language Java launcher for Mac OS (provided with the Developer Tools package). *Contents/Resources/xxx.icns* contains icons in various resolutions for display by the Finder; this file can be created using the IconComposer program (found in */Developer/Applications/Utilities/Icon Composer.app*). The directory *Contents/Resources/Java* contains your Java classes and/or JAR files. *Contents/Info.plist* ties the whole thing together, specifying the names of the various files, the file types your application can open, and other information.

The better commercial installer tools (discussed in Recipe 23.11) generate this structure for you. You can create this structure using Ant. Eclipse 3.0 (since "Milestone 7") can generate a Mac OS X Application. Just select your Project in the Eclipse navigator, select Export Mac OS X application from the Export menu, and fill in two screens specifying the output destination and some other information, as shown in Figure 23-8. In the case of Ant or Eclipse, you probably want to use Disk Copy to build a *dmg* (disk image) file of your directory; *dmg* files can be downloaded by Mac OS X users and are normally expanded automatically upon download to recreate the Application Bundle.

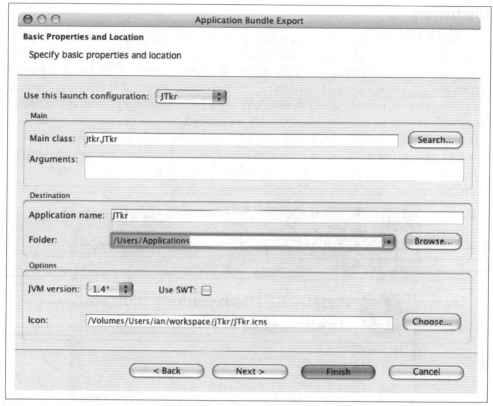

*Figure 23-8. Eclipse Application Bundle Export screen*

## See Also

Chapter 7 of the book *Mac OS X for Java Geeks*, by Will Iverson, covers Application Bundles. This book is recommended for any Java developer concerned with making good use of Java on OS X, and especially for anyone shipping applications who is concerned with making a good impression on OS X users.

# 23.13 Java Web Start

## Problem

You have an application (not an applet) and need to distribute it electronically.

## Solution

Sun's Java Web Start combines browser-based ease of use with applet-like "sandbox" security (which can be overridden on a per-application basis) and "instant update" downloading but also lets you run a full-blown application on the user's desktop.

## Discussion

Java Web Start (JWS[*]) provides application downloads over the Web. It is distinct from applets (see Chapter 18), which require special methods and run in a browser framework. JWS lets you run ordinary GUI-based applications. It is aimed at people who want the convenience of browser access combined with full application capabilities. The user experience is as follows. You see a link to an application you'd like to launch. If you've previously installed JWS (explained toward the end of this recipe), you can just click on its Launch link and be running the application in a few seconds to a few minutes, depending on your download speed. Figure 23-9 shows the startup screen that appears after clicking a Launch link for my JabaDex application.

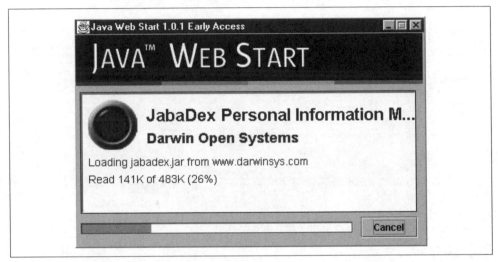

*Figure 23-9. Starting JabaDex as a JWS application*

After the application is downloaded successfully, it starts running. This is shown in slightly compressed form in Figure 23-10.

For your convenience, JWS caches the JAR files and other pieces needed to run the application. You can later restart the application (even when not connected to the Web) using the JWS application launcher. In Figure 23-11, I have JabaDex in my JWS launcher. JWS also allows you to create desktop shortcuts and start menu entries on systems that support these.

The basic steps in setting up your application for JWS are shown in the following sidebar.

---

[*] JWS used to stand for Java Web Server, which was discontinued, so the acronym has been recycled. Things recycle quickly on the Web.

---

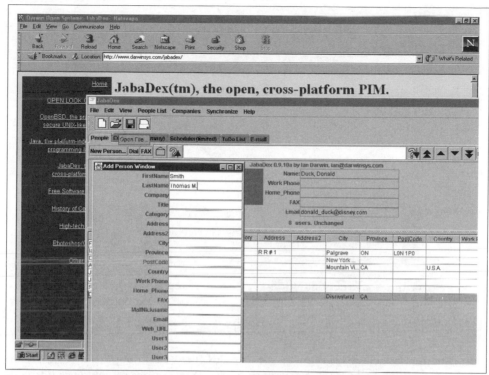

Figure 23-10. JabaDex up and running

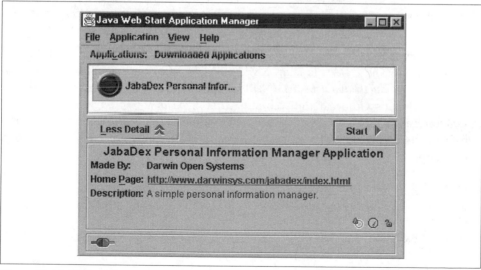

Figure 23-11. JWS application control screen

# Ian's Basic Steps: Java Web Start

To set up Java Web Start:

1. Package your application in one or more JAR files.
2. Optionally, provide icons to represent your application in JWS format.
3. Describe your application in a JNLP (Java Net Launch Protocol) description file.
4. If necessary, set your web server's MIME types list to return JNLP files as type `application/x-java-jnlp-file`.
5. If necessary, modify your application to use `ClassLoader`'s `getResource()` method instead of opening files.
6. If necessary, sign the application's JAR files.
7. Make links to your application's JNLP file and a download link for JWS itself.
8. Enjoy using your application locally with easy web downloading!

Let's go over these instructions in detail. The first step is to package your application in one or more JAR files. The *jar* program was described earlier in this chapter. The main JAR file should include the application classes and any resources such as properties files, images, and the like.

You should also include on the web site any JAR files containing extra APIs, such as JavaMail, `com.darwinsys.util`, or any other APIs. You can even include native code files, but they are platform-dependent.

Optionally, you can provide icons to represent your application in JWS format. The application icons should be in GIF or JPEG format and should be 64×64 bits.

The next step is to describe your application in a JNLP (Java Net Launch Protocol) description file. The JNLP file is an XML file. The official specification is at *http://java.sun.com/products/javawebstart/download-spec.html*; a less formal description is in the Developer's Guide at the web site *http://java.sun.com/products/javawebstart/docs/developersguide.html*. The file I used for enabling JabaDex to run with JWS is a subset of the allowable XML elements but should be moderately self-explanatory. See Example 23-5.

*Example 23-5. JabaDex.jnlp*

```
<?xml version="1.0" encoding="utf-8"?>
<!-- JNLP File for JabaDex Application -->
<jnlp spec="1.0+"
    codebase="http://www.darwinsys.com/"
    href="/jabadex/">
    <information>
      <title>JabaDex Personal Information Manager Application</title>
      <vendor>Darwin Open Systems</vendor>
      <homepage href="/"/>
```

*Example 23-5. JabaDex.jnlp (continued)*

```
        <description>JabaDex Personal Information Manager Application</description>
        <description kind="short">A simple personal information manager.</description>
        <icon href="images/jabadex.jpg"/>
        <offline-allowed/>
    </information>
    <security>
        <all-permissions/>
    </security>
    <resources>
        <j2se version="1.3"/>
        <j2se version="1.2"/>
        <jar href="jabadex.jar"/>
        <jar href="com-darwinsys-util.jar"/>
    </resources>
    <application-desc main-class="JDMain"/>
</jnlp>
```

If necessary, set your web server's MIME types list to return JNLP files as of type `application/x-java-jnlp-file`. How you do this depends entirely on what web server you are running; it should be just a matter of adding an entry for the filename extension *.jnlp* to map to this type.

Also if necessary, modify your application to get its ClassLoader and use one of its getResource( ) methods, instead of opening files. Any images or other resources that you need should be opened this way. For example, to explicitly load a properties file, you could use getClassLoader( ) and getResource( ), as shown in Example 23-6.

*Example 23-6. GetResourceDemo (partial listing)*

```java
// Find the ClassLoader that loaded us.
// Regard it as the One True ClassLoader for this app.
ClassLoader loader = this.getClass().getClassLoader();

// Use the loader's getResource() method to open the file.
InputStream is = loader.getResourceAsStream("widgets.properties");
if (is == null) {
    System.err.println("Can't load properties file");
    return;
}

// Create a Properties object
Properties p = new Properties();

// Load the properties file into the Properties object
try {
    p.load(is);
} catch (IOException ex) {
    System.err.println("Load failed: " + ex);
    return;
}
```

Notice that getResource() returns a java.net.URL object here while getResourceAsStream() returns an InputStream.

If you want the application to have "nonsandbox" (i.e., full application) permissions, you must sign the application's JAR files. The procedure to sign a JAR file digitally is described in Recipe 23.14. If you request full permissions and don't sign all your application JAR files, the sad note shown in Figure 23-12 displays.

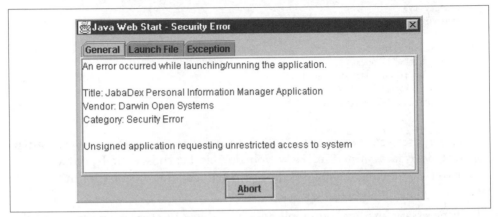

*Figure 23-12. Unsigned application failure*

If you self-sign (i.e., use a test certificate), the user sees a warning dialog like the one in Figure 23-13.

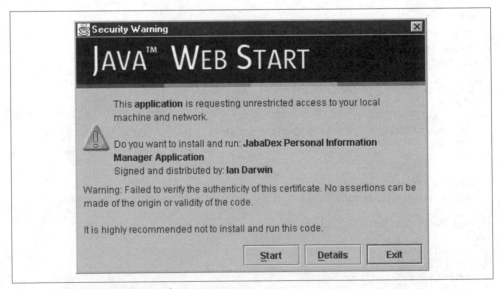

*Figure 23-13. Unverifiable certificate warning*

Finally, make links to your application's JNLP file in the web page and, optionally, a download link for JWS itself. JWS is a compiled program that must be loaded before the user can download any JWS-enabled applications; it runs as a "helper application" for the browsers. You can download it as a binary program from the JWS home page. In theory, you could write your own implementation of this helper from the *JNLP Specification*, if you needed to.

Actually, if the user has JWS installed, you don't need the download link; if they don't, the Launch link does not function correctly. The *Developer's Guide* shows how you can use client-side HTML scripting (JavaScript or VBScript) to make only one of these links appear. The Launch link must refer to the JNLP file:

```
If you have JWS installed, you can <a href="jabadex.jnlp">launch JabaDex<</a>
If not, you should <a href="http://java.sun.com/products/javawebstart/">
read about Java Web Start</a>.
```

You should now be ready to use your application in a downloadable fashion!

## See Also

See the JWS home page at *http://java.sun.com/products/javawebstart/*.

# 23.14 Signing Your JAR File

## Problem

You want to digitally sign your JAR file.

## Solution

Get or forge a digital certificate, and use the jarsigner program.

## Discussion

A JAR file can be digitally signed to verify the identity of its creator. This is very similar to digital signing of web sites: consumers are trained not to enter sensitive information such as credit card numbers into a web form unless the "padlock" icon shows that it is digitally signed. Signing JAR files uses the Security API in the core Java 2 platform. You can sign JAR files for use with Java applets (see Chapter 18) or JWS (Recipe 23.13). In either case, the jarsigner tool included in the JDK is used.

You can purchase a certificate from one of the commercial signing agencies when you are ready to go live. Meanwhile, for testing, you can "self-sign" a certificate. Here are the steps needed to sign a JAR file with a test certificate:

1. Create a new key in a new "keystore" as follows:

    ```
    keytool -genkey -keystore myKeystore -alias myself
    ```

    The alias myself is arbitrary; its intent is to remind you that it is a self-signed key so you don't put it into production by accident.

2. The program prompts you in the terminal window for information about the new key. It asks for a password for protecting the keystore. Then it asks for your name, department, organization, city, state, country, and so on. This information goes into the new keystore file on disk.

3. Create a self-signed test certificate:

   ```
   keytool -selfcert -alias myself -keystore myKeystore
   ```

   You enter the keystore password and keytool generates the certificate.

4. You may want to verify that the steps up to here worked correctly. You can list the contents of the keystore:

   ```
   keytool -list -keystore myKeystore
   ```

   The output should look something like the following:

   ```
   Keystore type: jks
   Keystore provider: SUN
   Your keystore contains 1 entry:

   myself, Mon Dec 18 11:05:27 EST 2000, keyEntry,
   Certificate fingerprint (MD5): 56:9E:31:81:42:07:BF:FF:42:01:CB:42:51:42:96:B6
   ```

5. You can now sign the JAR file with your test certificate:

   ```
   jarsigner -keystore myKeystore test.jar myself
   ```

The jarsigner tool updates the META-INF directory of your JAR file to contain certificate information and digital signatures for each entry in the archive. This can take a while, depending on the speed of your CPU, the number of entries in the archive, and so on. The end result is a signed JAR file that is acceptable to applet-enabled browsers, Java Web Start, and any other mechanisms that require a signed JAR file.

## See Also

For more information on signing and permissions, see *Java Security* by Scott Oaks (O'Reilly). For more information on the other JDK tools mentioned here, see the documentation that accompanies the JDK you are using.

# CHAPTER 24

# Threaded Java

## 24.0  Introduction

We live in a world of multiple activities. A person may be talking on the phone while doodling or reading a memo. A fax machine may scan one fax while receiving another and printing a third. We expect the GUI programs we use to be able to respond to a menu while updating the screen. But ordinary computer programs can do only one thing at a time. The conventional computer programming model—that of writing one statement after another, punctuated by repetitive loops and binary decision making—is sequential at heart.

Sequential processing is straightforward but not as efficient as it could be. To enhance performance, Java offers *threading*, the capability to handle multiple flows of control within a single application or process. Java provides thread support and, in fact, requires threads: the Java runtime itself is inherently multithreaded. For example, window system action handling and Java's garbage collection—that miracle that lets us avoid having to free everything we allocate, as we must do when working in languages at or below C level—run in separate threads.

Just as multitasking allows a single operating system to give the appearance of running more than one program at the same time on a single-processor computer, so multithreading can allow a single program or process to give the appearance of working on more than one thing at the same time. With multithreading, applications can handle more than one activity at the same time, leading to more interactive graphics and more responsive GUI applications (the program can draw in a window while responding to a menu, with both activities occurring more or less independently), more reliable network servers (if one client does something wrong, the server continues communicating with the others), and so on.

Note that I did not say "multiprocessing" in the previous paragraph. The term multitasking is sometimes erroneously called multiprocessing, but that term in fact refers to the less common case of two or more CPUs running under a single operating system. Actually, multiprocessing is nothing new: IBM mainframes did it in the 1970s,

Sun SPARCstations did it in the late 1980s, and Intel PCs did it in the 1990s. True multiprocessing* allows you to have more than one process running concurrently on more than one CPU. Java's support for threading includes multiprocessing under certain circumstances, if the operating system and the JVM support it as well. Consult your system documentation for details.

While most modern operating systems—POSIX P1003, Sun Solaris, the Distributed Computing Environment (OSF/DCE) for Unix, Windows, and Mac OS—provide threads, Java is the first mainstream programming language to have intrinsic support for threaded operations built right into the language. The semantics of java.lang. Object, of which all objects are instances, includes the notion of "monitor locking" of objects, and some methods (notify, notifyall, wait) that are meaningful only in the context of a multithreaded application. Java also has language keywords such as synchronized to control the behavior of threaded applications.

Now that the world has had a few years of experience with threaded Java, experts have started building better ways of writing threaded applications. The Concurrency Utilities, specified in JSR 166† and included in Java for the first time with JDK 1.5, are heavily based on the util.concurrent package by Professor Doug Lea of the Computer Science Department at the State University of New York at Oswego. This package aims to do for the difficulties of threading what the Collections classes (see Chapter 7) did for structuring data. This is no small undertaking, but they seem to have pulled it off. JSR 166 has been discussed as open source (since Professor Lea's package was open source), and a number of experts have worked over the code prior to its inclusion in the JDK.

The java.util.concurrent package includes several main sections:

- Executors, thread pools, and Futures
- Queues and BlockingQueues
- Locks and conditions, with JVM support for faster locking and unlocking
- Synchronizers, including Semaphores and Barriers
- Atomic variables

An implementation of the Executor interface is, of course, a class that can execute code for you. The code to be executed can be the familiar Runnable or a new interface Callable. One common kind of Executor is a "thread pool." A Future represents the future state of something that has been started; it has methods to wait until the result is ready.

---

* By which I mean SMP, *symmetric multiprocessing*, in which either the operating system or the application programs can be run on any of the available CPUs. At some point, the OS may be running on three of the four processors on a given system while at some later time all four processors may be running user processes. On systems such as Solaris, it is possible for one (threaded) process to be running on several CPUs concurrently.

† JSR stands for Java Specification Request. The Java Community Process calls standards, both proposed and adopted, JSRs. See *http://www.jcp.org* for details.

These brief definitions are certainly oversimplifications. Addressing all the issues is beyond the scope of this book, but I do provide several examples.

# 24.1  Running Code in a Different Thread

## Problem

You need to write a threaded application.

## Solution

Write code that implements Runnable; instantiate and start it.

## Discussion

There are several ways to implement threading, and they all require you to implement the Runnable interface. Runnable has only one method, whose signature is:

```
public void run( );
```

You must provide an implementation of the run( ) method. When this method returns, the thread is used up and can never be restarted or reused. Note that there is nothing special in the compiled class file about this method; it's an ordinary method and you could call it yourself. But then what? There wouldn't be the special magic that launches it as an independent flow of control, so it wouldn't run concurrently with your main program or flow of control. For this, you need to invoke the magic of thread creation.

One way to do this is simply to subclass from java.lang.Thread (which also implements this interface; you do not need to declare redundantly that you implement it). This approach is shown in Example 24-1. Class ThreadsDemo1 simply prints a series of "Hello from X" and "Hello from Y" messages; the order in which they appear is indeterminate since there is nothing in either Java or the program to determine the order of things.

*Example 24-1. ThreadsDemo1.java*

```
/**
 * Threaded demo application, as a Threads subclass.
 */
public class ThreadsDemo1 extends Thread {
    String mesg;
    int count;

    /** Run does the work: print a message, "count" number of times */
    public void run( ) {
        while (count-- > 0) {
            println(mesg);
            try {
                Thread.sleep(100);    // 100 msec
```

*Example 24-1. ThreadsDemo1.java (continued)*

```
            } catch (InterruptedException e) {
                return;
            }
        }
        println(mesg + " all done.");
    }

    void println(String s) {
        System.out.println(s);
    }

    /**
     * Construct a ThreadsDemo1 object.
     * @param m Message to display
     * @param n How many times to display it
     */
    public ThreadsDemo1(String m, int n) {
        count = n;
        mesg  = m;
        setName(m + " runner Thread");
    }

    /**
     * Main program, test driver for ThreadsDemo1 class.
     */
    public static void main(String[] argv) {
        // could say: new ThreadsDemo1("Hello from X", 10).run();
        // could say: new ThreadsDemo1("Hello from Y", 15).run();
        // But then it wouldn't be multi-threaded!
        new ThreadsDemo1("Hello from X", 10).start();
        new ThreadsDemo1("Hello from Y", 15).start();
    }
}
```

What if you can't subclass Thread because you're already subclassing another class, such as JApplet? There are two other ways to do it: have a class implement the Runnable interface, or use an inner class to provide the Runnable implementation. Example 24-2 is code that implements Runnable.

*Example 24-2. ThreadsDemo2.java*

```
public class ThreadsDemo2 implements Runnable {
    String mesg;
    Thread t;
    int count;

    /**
     * Construct a ThreadsDemo2 object
     *
     * @param    String m    Message to display
     * @param    int n       How many times to display it
     */
```

*Example 24-2. ThreadsDemo2.java (continued)*

```
    public ThreadsDemo2(String m, int n) {
        count = n;
        mesg  = m;
        t = new Thread(this);
        t.setName(m + " printer thread");
        t.start();
    }
```

The run method itself does not change, so I've omitted it from this listing. To complete the discussion, Example 24-3 is a version of this class that uses an inner class to provide the run method.

*Example 24-3. ThreadsDemo3.java*

```
public class ThreadsDemo3 {
    String mesg;
    Thread t;
    int count;

    /**
     * Main program, test driver for ThreadsDemo3 class.
     */
    public static void main(String argv[]) {
        new ThreadsDemo3("Hello from X", 10);
        new ThreadsDemo3("Hello from Y", 15);
    }

    /**
     * Construct a ThreadsDemo3 object
     * @param m message to display
     * @param n How many times to display it
     */
    public ThreadsDemo3(String m, int n) {
        count = n;
        mesg  = m;
        t = new Thread(new Runnable() {
            public void run() {
                while (count-- > 0) {
                    System.out.println(mesg);
                    try {
                        Thread.sleep(100);     // 100 msec
                    } catch (InterruptedException e) {
                        return;
                    }
                }
                System.out.println(mesg + " thread all done.");
            }
        });
        t.start();
    }
}
```

Here the run method is part of the anonymous inner class declared in the statement beginning t = new Thread(...). This runs with no interaction with other classes, so it's a good use of an inner class.

To summarize, you can create a Runnable in three ways:

- Extend Thread as ThreadsDemo1 did. This works best for standalone applications that don't need to extend another class.

- Implement the Runnable interface. This works for applets that extend JApplet and cannot extend Thread due to single inheritance.

- Construct a Thread passing an inner class that is a Runnable. This is best for tiny run methods with little outside interaction.

### Thread lifecycle methods

I should mention a few other methods briefly, starting with the Thread constructors: Thread(), Thread("Thread Name"), and Thread(Runnable). The no-argument and name-argument constructors are used only when subclassing. But what's in a name? Well, by default, a thread's name is composed of the class name and a number such as a sequence number or the object's hashcode; on Sun's JDK it uses sequence numbers, such as Thread-0, Thread-1, and so on. These names are not very descriptive when you need to look at them in a debugger, so assigning names like "Clock Ticker Thread" or "Background Save Thread" will make your life easier when (not if) you wind up having to debug your threaded application. Because of this, getName()/setName(String) methods return or change the thread's name, respectively.

We've seen already that the start() method begins the process of assigning CPU time to a thread, resulting in its run() method being called. The corresponding stop() method is deprecated; see Recipe 24.3, where I also discuss interrupt(), which interrupts whatever the thread is doing. The method boolean isAlive() returns true if the thread has neither finished nor been terminated by a call to its stop() method. Also deprecated are suspend()/resume(), which pause and continue a thread; they are prone to corruption and deadlocking, so they should not be used. If you've created multiple threads, you can join() a thread to wait for it to finish; see Recipe 24.4.

The methods int getPriority()/void setPriority(int) show and set the priority of a thread; higher priority threads get first chance at the CPU. Finally, wait()/notify()/notifyAll() allow you to implement classical semaphore handling for such paradigms as producer/consumer relationships. See the Javadoc page for the Thread class for information on a few other methods.

# 24.2  Displaying a Moving Image with Animation

## Problem

You need to update a graphical display while other parts of the program are running.

---

## Solution

Use a background thread to drive the animation.

## Discussion

One common use of threads is an *animator*, a class that displays a moving image. This "animator" program does just that. It draws a graphical image (see Recipe 13.8) at locations around the screen; the location is updated and redrawn from a Thread for each such image. This version is an applet, so we see it here in the AppletViewer (Figure 24-1).

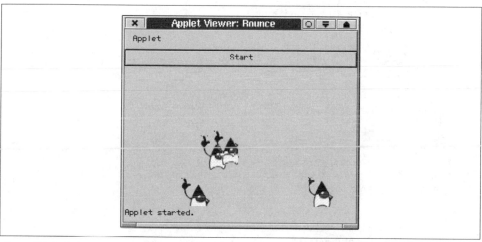

*Figure 24-1. Animator*

The code for the animator program consists of two classes, Sprite (Example 24-4) and Bounce* (Example 24-5). A Sprite is one image that moves around; Bounce is the main program.

*Example 24-4. Sprite.java (part of animator applet)*

```
import java.applet.*;
import java.awt.*;
import java.awt.event.*;
import java.util.*;

/** A Sprite is one Image that moves around the screen on its own */
class Sprite extends Component implements Runnable {
    protected static int spriteNumber = 0;
    protected Thread t;
    protected int x, y;
    protected Bounce parent;
```

---

* The title belies some unfulfilled ambitions to make the animations follow the bouncing curves seen in some flashier animation demonstrations.

*Example 24-4. Sprite.java (part of animator applet) (continued)*

```
    protected Image img;
    protected boolean done = false;

    /** Construct a Sprite with a Bounce parent: construct
     * and start a Thread to drive this Sprite.
     */
    Sprite(Bounce parent, Image img) {
        super();
        this.parent = parent;
        this.img = img;
        setSize(img.getWidth(this), img.getHeight(this));
        t = new Thread(this);
        t.setName("Sprite #" + ++spriteNumber);
        t.start();
    }

    /** Stop this Sprite's thread. */
    void stop() {
        System.out.println("Stopping " + t.getName());
        done = true;
    }

    /**
     * Run one Sprite around the screen.
     * This version is very stupid, and just moves them around
     * at some 45-degree angle.
     */
    public void run() {
        int width = parent.getSize().width;
        int height = parent.getSize().height;
        // Random location
        x = (int)(Math.random() * width);
        y = (int)(Math.random() * height);
        // Flip coin for x & y directions
        int xincr = Math.random()>0.5?1:-1;
        int yincr = Math.random()>0.5?1:-1;
        while (!done) {
            width = parent.getSize().width;
            height = parent.getSize().height;
            if ((x+=xincr) >= width)
                x=0;
            if ((y+=yincr) >= height)
                y=0;
            if (x<0)
                x = width;
            if (y<0)
                y = height;
            // System.out.println("Move " + t.getName() + " from " +
            //     getLocation() + " to " + x + "," + y);
            setLocation(x, y);
            repaint();
            try {
                Thread.sleep(250);
```

*Example 24-4. Sprite.java (part of animator applet) (continued)*

```
        } catch (InterruptedException e) {
            return;
        }
    }
}

/** paint -- just draw our image at its current location */
public void paint(Graphics g) {
    g.drawImage(img, 0, 0, this);
}
}

}
```

*Example 24-5. Bounce.java (part of animator applet)*

```
import java.applet.*;
import java.awt.*;
import java.awt.event.*;
import java.util.*;

/** This is the Bounce class; create and start Sprites, using Threads. */
public class Bounce extends Applet implements ActionListener {
    /** The main Panel */
    protected Panel p;
    /** The image, shared by all the Sprite objects */
    protected Image img;
    /** A Vector of Sprite objects. */
    protected Vector v;

    public void init( ) {
        Button b = new Button("Start");
        b.addActionListener(this);
        setLayout(new BorderLayout( ));
        add(b, BorderLayout.NORTH);
        add(p = new Panel( ), BorderLayout.CENTER);
        p.setLayout(null);
        String imgName = getParameter("imagefile");
        if (imgName == null) imgName = "duke.gif";
        img = getImage(getCodeBase( ), imgName);
        MediaTracker mt = new MediaTracker(this);
        mt.addImage(img, 0);
        try {
            mt.waitForID(0);
        } catch(InterruptedException e) {
            throw new IllegalArgumentException(
                "InterruptedException while loading image " + imgName);
        }
        if (mt.isErrorID(0)) {
            throw new IllegalArgumentException(
                "Couldn't load image " + imgName);
        }
        v = new Vector( );
    }
```

*Example 24-5. Bounce.java (part of animator applet) (continued)*

```java
    public void actionPerformed(ActionEvent e) {
        System.out.println("Creat-ing another one!");
        Sprite s = new Sprite(this, img);
        s.start();
        p.add(s);
        v.addElement(s);
    }

    public void stop() {
        for (int i=0; i<v.size(); i++) {
            ((Sprite)(v.get(i))).stop();
        }
        v.clear();
    }
}
```

# 24.3   Stopping a Thread

## Problem

You need to stop a thread.

## Solution

Don't use the `Thread.stop()` method; instead, use a `boolean` tested at the top of the main loop in the `run()` method.

## Discussion

While you can use the thread's `stop()` method, Sun recommends against it. That's because the method is so drastic that it can never be made to behave reliably in a program with multiple active threads. That is why, when you try to use it, the compiler will generate deprecation warnings. The recommended method is to use a `boolean` variable in the main loop of the `run()` method. The program in Example 24-6 prints a message endlessly until its `shutDown()` method is called; it then sets the controlling variable `done` to false, which terminates the loop. This causes the `run()` method to return, ending the thread. The `ThreadStoppers` program in the source directory for this chapter has a main program that instantiates and starts this class and then calls the `shutDown()` method.

*Example 24-6. StopBoolean.java*

```java
public class StopBoolean extends Thread {
    protected boolean done = false;
    public void run() {
        while (!done) {
            System.out.println("StopBoolean running");
            try {
                sleep(720);
```

*Example 24-6. StopBoolean.java (continued)*

```
            } catch (InterruptedException ex) {
                // nothing to do
            }
        }
        System.out.println("StopBoolean finished.");
    }
    public void shutDown() {
        done = true;
    }
}
```

Running it looks like this:

```
StopBoolean running
StopBoolean running
StopBoolean running
StopBoolean running
StopBoolean running
StopBoolean running
StopBoolean running
StopBoolean finished.
```

But what if your thread is blocked reading from a network connection? You then
cannot check a Boolean, as the thread that is reading is asleep. This is what the stop
method was designed for, but, as we've seen, it is now deprecated. Instead, you can
simply close the socket. The program shown in Example 24-7 intentionally dead-
locks itself by reading from a socket that you are supposed to write to, simply to
demonstrate that closing the socket does in fact terminate the loop.

*Example 24-7. StopClose.java*

```
import java.io.*;
import java.net.*;

public class StopClose extends Thread {
    protected Socket io;

    public void run() {
        try {
            io = new Socket("localhost", 80);     // HTTP
            BufferedReader is = new BufferedReader(
                new InputStreamReader(io.getInputStream()));
            System.out.println("StopClose reading");

            // The following line will deadlock (intentionally), since HTTP
            // enjoins the client to send a request (like "GET / HTTP/1.0")
            // and a null line, before reading the response.

            String line = is.readLine();     // DEADLOCK

            // Should only get out of the readLine if an interrupt
            // is thrown, as a result of closing the socket.
```

*Example 24-7. StopClose.java (continued)*

```
            // So we shouldn't get here, ever:
            System.out.println("StopClose FINISHED!?");
        } catch (IOException ex) {
            System.err.println("StopClose terminating: " + ex);
        }
    }

    public void shutDown() throws IOException {
        if (io != null) {
            // This is supposed to interrupt the waiting read.
            io.close();
        }
    }
}
```

When run, it prints a message that the close is happening:

```
StopClose reading
StopClose terminating: java.net.SocketException: Resource temporarily unavailable:
```

"But wait," you say. "What if I want to break the wait, but not really terminate the socket?" A good question, indeed, and there is no perfect answer. You can, however, *interrupt* the thread that is reading; the read is interrupted by a java.io. InterruptedIOException, and you can retry the read. The file *Intr.java* in this chapter's source code shows this.

# 24.4  Rendezvous and Timeouts

## Problem

You need to know whether something finished or whether it finished in a certain length of time.

## Solution

Start that "something" in its own thread and call its join() method with or without a timeout value.

## Discussion

The join() method of the target thread is used to suspend the current thread until the target thread is finished (returns from its run method). This method is overloaded; a version with no arguments waits forever for the thread to terminate, while a version with arguments waits up to the specified time. For a simple example, I create (and start!) a simple thread that just reads from the console terminal, and the main thread simply waits for it. When I run the program, it looks like this:

```
darwinsys.com$ java Join
Starting
Joining
```

```
Reading
hello from standard input # waits indefinitely for me to type this line
Thread Finished.
Main Finished.
darwinsys.com$
```

Example 24-8 lists the code for the join( ) demo.

*Example 24-8. Join.java*

```java
public class Join {
    public static void main(String[] args) {
        Thread t = new Thread( ) {
            public void run( ) {
                System.out.println("Reading");
                try {
                    System.in.read( );
                } catch (java.io.IOException ex) {
                    System.err.println(ex);
                }
                System.out.println("Thread Finished.");
            }
        };
        System.out.println("Starting");
        t.start( );
        System.out.println("Joining");
        try {
            t.join( );
        } catch (InterruptedException ex) {
            // should not happen:
            System.out.println("Who dares interrupt my sleep?");
        }
        System.out.println("Main Finished.");
    }
}
```

As you can see, it uses an inner class Runnable (see Recipe 24.1) in Thread t to be runnable.

# 24.5  Synchronizing Threads with the synchronized Keyword

## Problem

You need to protect certain data from access by multiple threads.

## Solution

Use the synchronized keyword on the method or code you wish to protect.

# Discussion

I discussed the synchronized keyword briefly in Recipe 17.4. This keyword specifies that only one thread at a time is allowed to run the given method in a given object (for static methods, only one thread is allowed to run the method at a time). You can synchronize methods or smaller blocks of code. It is easier and safer to synchronize entire methods, but this can be more costly in terms of blocking threads that could run. Simply add the synchronized keyword on the method. For example, many of the methods of Vector (see Recipe 7.3) are synchronized.* This ensures that the vector does not become corrupted or give incorrect results when two threads update or retrieve from it at the same time.

Bear in mind that threads can be interrupted at almost any time, in which case control is given to another thread. Consider the case of two threads appending to a data structure at the same time. Let's suppose we have the same methods as Vector, but we're operating on a simple array. The add( ) method simply uses the current number of objects as an array index, then increments it:

```
1 public void add(Object obj) {
2     data[max] = obj;
3     max = max + 1;
4 }
```

Threads A and B both wish to call this method. Now suppose that Thread A gets interrupted after line 2 but before line 3, and then Thread B gets to run. Thread B does line 2, overwriting the contents of data[max]; we've now lost all reference to the object that Thread A passed in! Thread B then increments max in line 3 and returns. Later, Thread A gets to run again; it resumes at line 3 and increments max past the last valid object. So not only have we lost an object, but we have an uninitialized reference in the array. This state of affairs is shown in Figure 24-2.

Now you might think, "No problem, I'll just combine lines 2 and 3":

```
data[max++] = obj;
```

As the game show host sometimes says, "Bzzzzt! Thanks for playing!" This change makes the code a bit shorter but has absolutely no effect on reliability. Interrupts don't happen conveniently on Java statement boundaries; they can happen between any of the many JVM machine instructions that correspond to your program. The code can still be interrupted after the store and before the increment. The only good solution is to use Java synchronization.

Making the method synchronized means that any invocations of it will wait if one thread has already started running the method:

```
public synchronized void add(Object obj) {
    ...
}
```

---

* The corresponding methods of ArrayList are not synchronized; this makes nonthreaded use of an ArrayList about 20 to 30 percent faster (see Recipe 7.17).

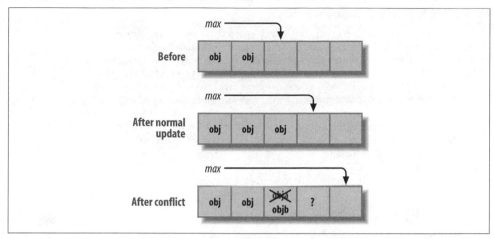

*Figure 24-2. Nonthreadsafe add method in operation: normal and failed updates*

Anytime you wish to synchronize some code, but not an entire method, use the `synchronized` keyword on an unnamed code block within a method, as in:

```
synchronized (someObject) {
    // this code will execute in one thread at a time
}
```

The choice of object is up to you. Sometimes it makes sense to synchronize on the object containing the code, as in Example 24-9. For synchronizing access to an `ArrayList`, it would make sense to use the `ArrayList` instance, as in:

```
synchronized(myArrayList) {
    if (myArrayList.indexof(someObject) != -1) {
        // do something with it.
    } else {
        create an object and add it...
    }
}
```

Example 24-9 is a web servlet that I wrote for use in the classroom, following a suggestion from Scott Weingust (*scottw@sysoft.ca*). It lets you play a quiz show game of the style where the host asks a question and the first person to press her buzzer (buzz in) gets to try to answer the question correctly. To ensure against having two people buzz in simultaneously, the code uses a synchronized block around the code that updates the Boolean buzzed variable. And for reliability, any code that accesses this Boolean is also synchronized.

*Example 24-9. BuzzInServlet.java*

```
import javax.servlet.*;
import javax.servlet.http.*;
import java.io.*;
```

*Example 24-9. BuzzInServlet.java (continued)*

```java
/** A quiz-show "buzzer" servlet: the first respondent wins the chance
 * to answer the skill-testing question. Correct operation depends on
 * running in a Servlet container that CORRECTLY implements the Servlet
 * spec, that is, a SINGLE INSTANCE of this servlet class exists, and it
 * is run in a thread pool. This class does not implement "SingleThreadModel"
 * so a correct Servlet implementation will use a single instance.
 * <p>
 * If you needed to work differently, you could synchronize on an object
 * stored in the Servlet Application Context, at a slight increased cost
 * in terms of system overhead.
 */
public class BuzzInServlet extends HttpServlet {

    /** This controls the access */
    protected static boolean buzzed = false;
    /** who got the buzz? */
    protected static String winner;

    /** doGet is called from the contestants web page.
     * Uses a synchronized code block to ensure that
     * only one contestant can change the state of "buzzed".
     */
    public void doGet(HttpServletRequest request, HttpServletResponse response)
    throws ServletException, IOException
    {
        boolean igotit = false;

        // Do the synchronized stuff first, and all in one place.
        synchronized(this) {
            if (!buzzed) {
                igotit = buzzed = true;
                winner = request.getRemoteHost() + '/' + request.getRemoteAddr();
            }
        }

        response.setContentType("text/html");
        PrintWriter out = response.getWriter();

        out.println("<html><head><title>Thanks for playing</title></head>");
        out.println("<body bgcolor=\"white\">");

        if (igotit) {
            out.println("<b>YOU GOT IT</b>");
            getServletContext().log("BuzzInServlet: WINNER " +
                request.getRemoteUser());
            // TODO - output HTML to play a sound file :-)
        } else {
                out.println("Thanks for playing, " + request.getRemoteAddr());
                out.println(", but " + winner + " buzzed in first");
        }
        out.println("</body></html>");
    }
```

*Example 24-9. BuzzInServlet.java (continued)*

```
/** The Post method is used from an Administrator page (which should
 * only be installed in the instructor/host's localweb directory).
 * Post is used for administrative functions:
 * 1) to display the winner;
 * 2) to reset the buzzer for the next question.
 * <p>
 * In real life the password would come from a Servlet Parameter
 * or a configuration file, instead of being hardcoded in an "if".
 */
public void doPost(HttpServletRequest request, HttpServletResponse response)
throws ServletException, IOException
{
    response.setContentType("text/html");
    PrintWriter out = response.getWriter();

    if (request.getParameter("password").equals("syzzy")) {
        out.println("<html><head><title>Welcome back, host</title><head>");
        out.println("<body bgcolor=\"white\">");
        String command = request.getParameter("command");
        if (command.equals("reset")) {
            // Synchronize what you need, no more, no less.
            synchronized(this) {
                buzzed = false;
                winner = null;
            }
            out.println("RESET");
        } else if (command.equals("show")) {
            synchronized(this) {
                out.println("<b>Winner is: </b>" + winner);
            }
        }
        else {
            out.println("<html><head><title>ERROR</title><head>");
            out.println("<body bgcolor=\"white\">");
            out.println("ERROR: Command " + command + " invalid.");
        }
    } else {
        out.println("<html><head><title>Nice try, but... </title><head>");
        out.println("<body bgcolor=\"white\">");
        out.println(
            "Your paltry attempts to breach security are rebuffed!");
    }
    out.println("</body></html>");
    }
}
```

Two HTML pages lead to the servlet. The contestant's page simply has a large link (<a href=/servlet/BuzzInServlet>). Anchor links generate an HTML GET, so the servlet engine calls doGet( ):

```
<html><head><title>Buzz In!</title></head>
<body>
<h1>Buzz In!</h1>
```

```
<p>
<font size=+6>
<a href="servlet/BuzzInServlet">
Press here to buzz in!
</a>
</font>
```

The HTML is pretty plain, but it does the job. Figure 24-3 shows the look and feel.

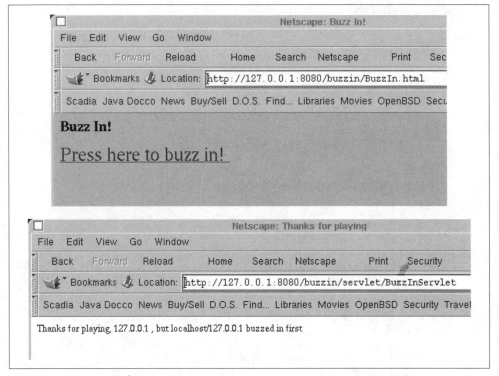

*Figure 24-3. BuzzInServlet in action*

The game show host has access to an HTML form with a POST method, which calls the doPost( ) method. This displays the winner to the game show host and resets the "buzzer" for the next question. A password is provided; it's hardcoded here, but in reality the password would come from a properties file (Recipe 7.7) or a servlet initialization parameter (as described in O'Reilly's *Java Servlet Programming*):

```
<html><head><title>Reset Buzzer</title></head>
<body>
<h1>Display Winner</h1>
<p>
<b>The winner is:</b>
<form method="post" action="servlet/BuzzInServlet">
    <input type="hidden" name="command" value="show">
    <input type="hidden" name="password" value="syzzy">
    <input type="submit" name="Show" value="Show">
</form>
```

```
<h1>Reset Buzzer</h1>
<p>
<b>Remember to RESET before you ask the contestants each question!</b>
<form method="post" action="servlet/BuzzInServlet">
    <input type="hidden" name="command" value="reset">
    <input type="hidden" name="password" value="syzzy">
    <input type="submit" name="Reset" value="RESET!">
</form>
```

The game show host functionality is shown in Figure 24-4.

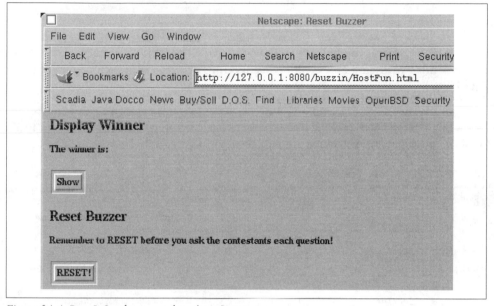

*Figure 24-4. BuzzInServlet game show host function*

For a more complete game, of course, the servlet would keep a Stack (Recipe 7.14) of people in the order they buzzed in, in case the first person doesn't answer the question correctly. Access to this would have to be synchronized, too.

# 24.6   Simplifying Synchronization with 1.5 Locks

## Problem

You want an easier means of synchronizing threads.

## Solution

Use the Lock mechanism, new in 1.5.

# Discussion

JDK 1.5 introduced the `java.util.concurrent.locks` package; its major interface is Lock. This interface has several methods for locking and one for unlocking. The general pattern for using it is:

```
Lock lock = ....
try {
    lock.lock();
    // do the work that is protected by the lock
} finally {
    lock.unlock();
}
```

The point of putting the `unlock()` call in the `finally` block is, of course, to ensure that it is not bypassed if an exception occurs (the code may also include one or more catch blocks, as required by the work being performed).

The improvement here, compared with the traditional synchronized methods and blocks, is that using a Lock actually looks like a locking operation! And, as I mentioned, several means of locking are available, shown in Table 24-1.

*Table 24-1. Locking methods of the Lock class*

| Return type | Method | Meaning |
| --- | --- | --- |
| void | `lock()` | Get the lock, even if you have to wait until another thread frees it first. |
| boolean | `tryLock()` | Get the lock only if it is free right now. |
| boolean | `tryLock(long time, TimeUnit units) throws InterruptedException` | Try to get the lock, but only wait for the length of time indicated. |
| void | `lockInterruptibly() throws InterruptedException` | Get the lock, waiting unless interrupted. |
| void | `unlock()` | Release the lock. |

The `TimeUnit` class lets you specify the units for the amount of time specified, including: `TimeUnit.SECONDS`, `TimeUnit.MILLISECONDS`, `TimeUnit.MICROSECONDS`, and `TimeUnit.NANOSECONDS`.

In all cases the lock must be released with `unlock()` before it can be locked again.

The standard Lock is useful in many applications, but depending on the application's requirements, other types of locks may be more appropriate. Applications with asymmetric load patterns may benefit from a common pattern called the "reader-writer lock"; I call this one a Readers-Writer lock to emphasize that there can be many readers but only one writer. It's actually a pair of interconnected locks; any number of readers can hold the read lock and read the data, as long as it's not being written (shared read access). A thread trying to lock the write lock, however, waits until all the readers are finished, then locks them out until the writer is finished (exclusive write access). To support this pattern, JDK 1.5 provides the ReadWriteLock interface and the implementing class ReentrantReadWriteLock. The interface has only two methods, readLock() and writeLock(), which provide a reference to the appropriate Lock implementation. *These methods do not, in themselves, lock or unlock the locks*; they only provide access to them, so it is common to see code like:

```
rwlock.readLock().lock();
...
rwlock.readLock().unlock();
```

To demonstrate ReadWriteLock in action, I wrote the business logic portion of a web-based voting application. It could be used in voting for candidates or for the more common web poll. Presuming that you display the results on the home page and change the data only when somebody takes the time to click on a response to vote, this application fits one of the intended criteria for ReadWriteLock—i.e., that you have more readers than writers. The main class, ReadersWritersDemo, is shown in Example 24-10. The helper class BallotBox is online; it simply keeps track of the votes and returns an invariant Iterator upon request. Note that in the run() method of the reading threads, I obtain the iterator while holding the lock but release the lock before printing it; this allows greater concurrency and better performance.

*Example 24-10. ReadersWriterDemo.java*

```java
import java.util.ArrayList;
import java.util.Iterator;
import java.util.List;
import java.util.concurrent.locks.ReentrantReadWriteLock;

/**
 * Simulate multiple readers
 */
public class ReadersWriterDemo {
    private static final int NUM_READER_THREADS = 3;
    public static void main(String[] args) {
        new ReadersWriterDemo().demo();
    }
    /** Set this to true to end the program */
    private boolean done = false;
    /** The data being protected. */
    private BallotBox theData;
    /** The read lock / write lock combination */
    private ReentrantReadWriteLock lock = new ReentrantReadWriteLock();

    /**
     * Constructor: set up some quasi-random initial data
     */
    public ReadersWriterDemo() {
        List questionsList = new ArrayList();
        questionsList.add("Agree");
        questionsList.add("Disagree");
        theData = new BallotBox(questionsList);
    }
```

*Example 24-10. ReadersWriterDemo.java (continued)*

```
/**
 * Run a demo with more readers than writers
 */
private void demo() {

    // Start two reader threads
    for (int i = 0; i < NUM_READER_THREADS; i++) {
        new Thread() {
            public void run() {
                while(!done) {
                    Iterator results = null;
                    try {
                        lock.readLock().lock();
                        results = theData.iterator();
                    } finally {
                        // Unlock in finally to be sure.
                        lock.readLock().unlock();
                    }
                    // Now lock has been freed, take time to print
                    print(results);
                    try {
                        Thread.sleep(((long)(Math.random()* 1000)));
                    } catch (InterruptedException ex) {
                        // nothing to do
                    }
                }
            }
        }.start();
    }
    // Start one writer thread to simulate occasional voting
    new Thread() {
        public void run() {
            while(!done) {
                try {
                    lock.writeLock().lock();
                    theData.voteFor(
                            (((int)(Math.random()*
                            theData.getCandidateCount())))));
                } finally {
                    lock.writeLock().unlock();
                }
                try {
                    Thread.sleep(((long)(Math.random()*1500)));
                } catch (InterruptedException ex) {
                    // nothing to do
                }
            }
        }
    }.start();

    // In the main thread, wait a while then terminate the run.
    try {
        Thread.sleep(10 *1000);
```

*Example 24-10. ReadersWriterDemo.java (continued)*

```
            } catch (InterruptedException ex) {
                // nothing to do
            } finally {
                done = true;
            }
        }

        /** print the current totals */
        private void print(Iterator iter) {
            boolean first = true;
            while (iter.hasNext()) {
                BallotPosition pair = (BallotPosition) iter.next();
                if (!first)
                    System.out.print(", ");
                System.out.print(pair.getName() + "(" + pair.getVotes() + ")");
                first = false;
            }
            System.out.println();
        }
    }
}
```

Since this is a simulation and the voting is random, it does not always come out 50-
50. In two consecutive runs, the following were the last line of each run:

```
Agree(6), Disagree(6)
Agree(9), Disagree(4)
```

## See Also

The `Lock` interface also makes available `Condition` objects, which provide even more
flexibility. Consult the documentation for the 1.5 release for more information.

# 24.7   Synchronizing Threads with wait( ) and notifyAll( )

## Problem

The synchronized keyword lets you lock out multiple threads but doesn't give you
much communication between them.

## Solution

Use `wait( )` and `notifyAll( )`. Very carefully.

## Discussion

Three methods appear in `java.lang.Object` that allow you to use any object as a synchronization target: `wait( )`, `notify()`, and `notifyAll( )`.

wait( )
> Causes the current thread to block in the given object until awakened by a notify( ) or notifyAll( ).

notify( )
> Causes a randomly selected thread waiting on this object to be awakened. It must then try to regain the monitor lock. If the "wrong" thread is awakened, your program can deadlock.

notifyAll( )
> Causes all threads waiting on the object to be awakened; each will then try to regain the monitor lock. Hopefully one will succeed.

The mechanism is a bit odd: there is no way to awaken only the thread that owns the lock. However, that's how it works, and it's the reason almost all programs use notifyAll( ) instead of notify( ). Also, note that both wait( ) and the notification methods can be used only if you are already synchronized on the object; that is, you must be in a synchronized method within—or a code block synchronized on—the object that you wish your current thread to wait( ) or notify( ) upon.

For a simple introduction to wait( ) and notify( ), I'll use a simple Producer-Consumer model. This pattern can be used to simulate a variety of real-world situations in which one object is creating or allocating objects (producing them), usually with a random delay, while another is grabbing the objects and doing something with them (consuming them). A single-threaded Producer-Consumer model is shown in Example 24-11. As you can see, no threads are created, so the entire program—the read( ) in main as well as produce( ) and consume( )—runs in the same thread. You control the production and consumption by entering a line consisting of letters. Each p causes one unit to be produced, while each c causes one unit to be consumed. So if I run it and type pcpcpcpc, the program alternates between producing and consuming. If I type pppccc, the program will produce three units and then consume them. See Example 24-11.

*Example 24-11. ProdCons1.java*

```java
public class ProdCons1 {

    /** Throughout the code, this is the object we synchronize on so this
     * is also the object we wait() and notifyAll() on.
     */
    protected LinkedList list = new LinkedList();

    protected void produce() {
        int len = 0;
        synchronized(list) {
            Object justProduced = new Object();
            list.addFirst(justProduced);
            len = list.size();
            list.notifyAll();
```

*Example 24-11. ProdCons1.java (continued)*

```
        }
        System.out.println("List size now " + len);
    }

    protected void consume() {
        Object obj = null;
        int len = 0;
        synchronized(list) {
            while (list.size() == 0) {
                try {
                    list.wait();
                } catch (InterruptedException ex) {
                    return;
                }
            }
            obj = list.removeLast();
            len - list.size();
        }
        System.out.println("Consuming object " + obj);
        System.out.println("List size now " + len);
    }

    public static void main(String[] args) throws IOException {
        ProdCons1 pc = new ProdCons1();
        int i;
        while ((i = System.in.read()) != -1) {
            char ch = (char)i;
            switch(ch) {
                case 'p':    pc.produce(); break;
                case 'c':    pc.consume(); break;
            }
        }
    }
}
```

The part that may seem strange is using `list` instead of the main class as the synchronization target. Each object has its own wait queue, so it does matter which object you use. In theory, any object can be used as long as your synchronized target and the object in which you run `wait()` and `notify()` are one and the same. Of course, it is good to refer to the object that you are protecting from concurrent updates, so I used `list` here.

Hopefully, you're now wondering what this has to do with thread synchronization. There is only one thread, but the program *seems* to work:

```
> javac +E -d . ProdCons1.java
> java ProdCons1
pppccc
List size now 1
List size now 2
List size now 3
```

```
Consuming object java.lang.Object@d9e6a356
List size now 2
Consuming object java.lang.Object@d9bea356
List size now 1
Consuming object java.lang.Object@d882a356
List size now 0
```

But this program is not quite right. If I enter even one more c than there are p's, think about what happens. The consume( ) method does a wait( ), but it is no longer possible for the read( ) to proceed. The program, we say, is *deadlocked*: it is waiting on something that can never happen. Fortunately, this simple case is detected by some versions of the Java runtime:

```
ppccc
List size now 1
List size now 2
Consuming object java.lang.Object@18faf0
List size now 1
Consuming object java.lang.Object@15bc20
List size now 0
Dumping live threads:
'gc' tid 0x1a0010, status SUSPENDED flags DONTSTOP
  blocked@0x19c510 (0x1a0010->|)
'finaliser' tid 0x1ab010, status SUSPENDED flags DONTSTOP
  blocked@0x10e480 (0x1ab010->|)
'main' tid 0xe4050, status SUSPENDED flags NOSTACKALLOC
  blocked@0x13ba20 (0xe4050->|)
Deadlock: all threads blocked on internal events
Abort (core dumped)
```

Indeed, the read( ) is never executed because there's no way for produce( ) to get called and so the notifyAll( ) can't happen. To fix this, I want to run the producer and the consumer in separate threads. There are several ways to accomplish this. I'll just make consume( ) and produce( ) into inner classes Consume and Produce that extend Thread, and their run( ) method will do the work of the previous methods. In the process, I'll replace the code that reads from the console with code that causes both threads to loop for a certain number of seconds, and change it to be a bit more of a simulation of a distributed Producer-Consumer mechanism. The result of all this is the second version, ProdCons2, shown in Example 24-12.

*Example 24-12. ProdCons2.java*

```java
import java.util.*;
import java.io.*;

public class ProdCons2 {

    /** Throughout the code, this is the object we synchronize on so this
     * is also the object we wait() and notifyAll() on.
     */
    protected LinkedList list = new LinkedList();
    protected int MAX = 10;
    protected boolean done = false; // Also protected by lock on list.
```

*Example 24-12. ProdCons2.java (continued)*

```
/** Inner class representing the Producer side */
class Producer extends Thread {

    public void run() {
        while (true) {
            Object justProduced = getRequestFromNetwork();
            // Get request from the network - outside the synch section.
            // We're simulating this actually reading from a client, and it
            // might have to wait for hours if the client is having coffee.
            synchronized(list) {
                while (list.size() == MAX) // queue "full"
                try {
                    System.out.println("Producer WAITING");
                    list.wait();      // Limit the size
                } catch (InterruptedException ex) {
                    System.out.println("Producer INTERRUPTED");
                }
                list.addFirst(justProduced);
                if (done)
                    break;
                list.notifyAll();      // must own the lock
                System.out.println("Produced 1; List size now " + list.size());
                // yield();     // Useful for green threads & demo programs.
            }
        }
    }

    Object getRequestFromNetwork() {     // Simulation of reading from client
        // try {
        //     Thread.sleep(10); // simulate time passing during read
        // } catch (InterruptedException ex) {
        //     System.out.println("Producer Read INTERRUPTED");
        // }
        return(new Object());
    }
}

/** Inner class representing the Consumer side */
class Consumer extends Thread {
    public void run() {
        while (true) {
            Object obj = null;
            int len = 0;
            synchronized(list) {
                while (list.size() == 0) {
                    try {
                        System.out.println("CONSUMER WAITING");
                        list.wait();     // must own the lock
                    } catch (InterruptedException ex) {
                        System.out.println("CONSUMER INTERRUPTED");
                    }
                }
```

*Example 24-12. ProdCons2.java (continued)*

```
                        if (done)
                            break;
                        obj = list.removeLast( );
                        list.notifyAll( );
                        len = list.size( );
                        System.out.println("List size now " + len);
                    }
                    process(obj);     // Outside synch section (could take time)
                    //yield( );
                }
        }

        void process(Object obj) {
            // Thread.sleep(nnn) // Simulate time passing
            System.out.println("Consuming object " + obj);
        }
    }

    ProdCons2(int nP, int nC) {
        for (int i=0; i<nP; i++)
            new Producer( ).start( );
        for (int i=0; i<nC; i++)
            new Consumer( ).start( );
    }

    public static void main(String[] args)
    throws IOException, InterruptedException {

        // Start producers and consumers
        int numProducers = 2;
        int numConsumers = 2;
        ProdCons2 pc = new ProdCons2(numProducers, numConsumers);

        // Let it run for, say, 30 seconds
        Thread.sleep(30*1000);

        // End of simulation - shut down gracefully
        synchronized(pc.list) {
            pc.done = true;
            pc.list.notifyAll( ); // Wake up any waiters!
        }
    }
}
```

I'm happy to report that all is well with this. It runs for long periods of time, neither crashing nor deadlocking. After running for some time, I captured this tiny bit of the log:

```
Produced 1; List size now 118
Consuming object java.lang.Object@2119d0
List size now 117
Consuming object java.lang.Object@2119e0
List size now 116
```

By varying the number of producers and consumers started in the constructor method, you can observe different queue sizes that all seem to work correctly.

# 24.8   Simplifying Producer-Consumer with the 1.5 Queue Interface

## Problem

You need to control producer-consumer implementations involving multiple threads.

## Solution

Use JDK 1.5's new Queue interface or the BlockingQueue subinterface.

## Discussion

As an example of the simplifications possible with 1.5's java.util.Concurrent package, consider the producer-consumer program in Recipe 24.7. Example 24-13, *ProdCons15.java,* uses the new java.util.BlockingQueue (itself a subinterface of the new-in-1.5 java.util.Queue interface) to reimplement the program ProdCons2 from Example 24-12 in about two-thirds of the number of lines of code. With these new features, the application need not be concerned with wait() or the vagaries of notify() and the use of notifyAll() in its place.

The application simply puts items into a queue and takes them from it. In the example, I have (as before) 4 producers and only 3 consumers, so the producers eventually wait. Running the application on one of my older notebooks, the producers' lead over the consumers increases to about 350 over the ten seconds or so of running it.

*Example 24-13. Prodcons15.java*

```
import java.util.*;
import java.io.*;
import java.util.concurrent.*;

/** Producer-Consumer in Java, for J2SE 1.5 using concurrent.
 */
public class ProdCons15 {

protected boolean done = false;

/** Inner class representing the Producer side */
class Producer implements Runnable {

    protected BlockingQueue queue;

    Producer(BlockingQueue theQueue) { this.queue = theQueue; }
```

*Example 24-13. Prodcons15.java (continued)*

```java
    public void run() {
        try {
            while (true) {
                Object justProduced = getRequestFromNetwork();
                queue.put(justProduced);
                System.out.println("Produced 1 object; List size now " + queue.size());
                if (done) {
                return;
                }
            }
        } catch (InterruptedException ex) {
            System.out.println("Producer INTERRUPTED");
        }
    }

    Object getRequestFromNetwork() {// Simulation of reading from client
        try {
                Thread.sleep(10); // simulate time passing during read
        } catch (InterruptedException ex) {
            System.out.println("Producer Read INTERRUPTED");
        }
        return(new Object());
    }
}

/** Inner class representing the Consumer side */
class Consumer implements Runnable {
    protected BlockingQueue queue;

    Consumer(BlockingQueue theQueue) { this.queue = theQueue; }

    public void run() {
        try {
            while (true) {
                Object obj = queue.take();
                int len = queue.size();
                System.out.println("List size now " + len);
                process(obj);
                if (done) {
                    return;
                }
            }
        } catch (InterruptedException ex) {
                System.out.println("CONSUMER INTERRUPTED");
        }
    }

    void process(Object obj) {
        // Thread.sleep(xxx) // Simulate time passing
        System.out.println("Consuming object " + obj);
    }
}
```

*Example 24-13. Prodcons15.java (continued)*

```
ProdCons15(int nP, int nC) {
    BlockingQueue myQueue = new LinkedBlockingQueue();
    for (int i=0; i<nP; i++)
        new Thread(new Producer(myQueue)).start();
    for (int i=0; i<nC; i++)
        new Thread(new Consumer(myQueue)).start();
}

public static void main(String[] args)
throws IOException, InterruptedException {

    // Start producers and consumers
    int numProducers = 4;
    int numConsumers = 3;
    ProdCons15 pc = new ProdCons15(numProducers, numConsumers);

    // Let the simulation run for, say, 10 seconds
    Thread.sleep(10*1000);

    // End of simulation - shut down gracefully
    pc.done = true;
}
```

# 24.9   Background Saving in an Editor

## Problem

You need to save the user's work periodically in an interactive program.

## Solution

Use a background thread.

## Discussion

This code fragment creates a new thread to handle background saves, as in most word processors:

```
public class AutoSave extends Thread {
    /** The FileSave interface is implemented by the main class. */
    protected FileSaver model;
     /** How long to sleep between tries */
    public static final int MINUTES = 5;
    private static final int SECONDS = MINUTES * 60;

    public AutoSave(FileSaver m) {
        super("AutoSave Thread");
        // setDaemon(true);          // so we don't keep the main app alive
        model = m;
    }
```

```
public void run() {
    while (true) {          // entire run method runs forever.
        try {
            sleep(SECONDS*1000);
        } catch (InterruptedException e) {
            // do nothing with it
        }
        if (model.wantAutoSave() && model.hasUnsavedChanges())
            model.saveFile(null);
    }
}
```

As you can see in the run( ) method, this code sleeps for five minutes (300 seconds), then checks whether it should do anything. If the user has turned autosave off, or hasn't made any changes since the last save, nothing needs to be done. Otherwise, we call the saveFile( ) method in the main program, which saves the data to the current file. It would be smarter to save it to a recovery file of some name, as the better word processors do.

What's not shown is that now the saveFile( ) method must be synchronized, and what's more, whatever method shuts down the main program must also be synchronized on the same object. It's easy to see why if you think about how the save method would work if the user clicked on the Save button at the same time that the autosave method called it, or if the user clicked on Exit while the file save method had just opened the file for writing. The "save to recovery file" strategy gets around some of this, but it still needs a great deal of care.

# 24.10 Program: Threaded Network Server

## Problem

You want a network server to be multithreaded.

## Solution

Either create a thread when you accept a connection or create a pool of threads in advance and have each wait on the accept( ) call.

## Discussion

Networking (see Chapter 16 and Chapter 18) and threads are two very powerful APIs that are a standard part of the Java platform. Used alone, each can increase the reach of your Java programming skills. A common paradigm is a threaded network server, which can either preallocate a certain number of threads or can start a new thread each time a client connects. The big advantage is that each thread can block on read without causing other client threads to delay.

One example of a threaded socket server was discussed in Recipe 17.4; another is shown here. It seems to be some kind of rite (or wrong) of passage for Java folk to write a web server entirely in Java. This one is fairly small and simple; if you want a full-bodied flavor, check out the Apache Foundation's Apache (written in C) and Tomcat (pure Java) servers (I may be biased because I coauthored O'Reilly's *Tomcat: The Definitive Guide*, recommended for administering Tomcat). The main program of mine constructs one instance of class Httpd. This creates a socket and waits for incoming clients in the accept( ) method. Each time there is a return from accept( ), we have another client, so we create a new thread to process that client. This happens in the main( ) and runserver( ) methods, which are near the beginning of Example 24-14.

*Example 24-14. Httpd.java*

```java
import java.net.ServerSocket;
import java.net.Socket;
import java.util.Properties;

import com.darwinsys.util.FileProperties;

/**
 * A very very simple Web server.
 * <p>
 * NO SECURITY. ALMOST NO CONFIGURATION. NO CGI. NO SERVLETS.
 *<p>
 * This version is threaded. I/O is done in Handler.
 */
public class Httpd {
    /** The default port number */
    public static final int HTTP = 80;
    /** The server socket used to connect from clients */
    protected ServerSocket sock;
    /** A Properties, for loading configuration info */
    private Properties wsp;
    /** A Properties, for loading mime types into */
    private Properties mimeTypes;
    /** The root directory */
    private String rootDir;

    public static void main(String argv[]) throws Exception {
        System.out.println("DarwinSys JavaWeb Server 0.1 starting...");
        Httpd w = new Httpd();
        if (argv.length == 2 && argv[0].equals("-p")) {
            w.startServer(Integer.parseInt(argv[1]));
        } else {
            w.startServer(HTTP);
        }
        w.runServer();
        // NOTREACHED
    }
```

*Example 24-14. Httpd.java (continued)*

```java
/** Run the main loop of the Server. Each time a client connects,
 * the ServerSocket accept() returns a new Socket for I/O, and
 * we pass that to the Handler constructor, which creates a Thread,
 * which we start.
 */
void runServer() throws Exception {
    while (true) {
        final Socket clntSock = sock.accept();
        Thread t = new Thread(){
            public void run() {
                new Handler(Httpd.this).process(clntSock);
            }
        };
        t.start();
    }
}

/** Construct a server object for a given port number */
Httpd() throws Exception {
    super();
    wsp=new FileProperties("httpd.properties");
    rootDir = wsp.getProperty("rootDir", ".");
    mimeTypes = new FileProperties(wsp.getProperty("mimeProperties",
                "mime.properties"));
}

public void startServer(int portNum) throws Exception {
    String portNumString = null;
    if (portNum == HTTP) {
        portNumString = wsp.getProperty("portNum");
        if (portNumString != null) {
            portNum = Integer.parseInt(portNumString);
        }
    }
    sock = new ServerSocket(portNum);
    System.out.println("Listening on port " + portNum);

}

public String getMimeType(String type) {
    return mimeTypes.getProperty(type);
}
public String getMimeType(String type, String dflt) {
    return mimeTypes.getProperty(type, dflt);
}
public String getServerProperty(String name) {
    return wsp.getProperty(name);
}

public String getRootDir() {
    return rootDir;
}
}
```

The Handler class—shown in Example 24-15—is the part that knows the HTTP protocol, or at least a small subset of it. You may notice near the middle that it parses the incoming HTTP headers into a Hashmap but does nothing with them. Here is a log of one connection with debugging enabled (see Recipe 1.11 for information on the Debug class):

```
Connection accepted from localhost/127.0.0.1
Request: Command GET, file /, version HTTP/1.0
hdr(Connection,Keep-Alive)
hdr(User-Agent,Mozilla/4.6 [en] (X11; U; OpenBSD 2.8 i386; Nav))
hdr(Pragma,no-cache)
hdr(Host,127.0.0.1)
hdr(Accept,image/gif, image/jpeg, image/pjpeg, image/png, */*)
hdr(Accept-Encoding,gzip)
hdr(Accept-Language,en)
hdr(Accept-Charset,iso-8859-1,*,utf-8)
Loading file //index.html
END OF REQUEST
```

At this stage of evolution, the server is getting ready to create an HttpServletRequest object, but it is not sufficiently evolved to do so. This file is a snapshot of work in progress. More interesting is the Hashtable used as a cache; to save disk I/O overhead, once a file has been read from disk, the program does not reread it. This means you have to restart the server if you change files; comparing the timestamps (see Recipe 11.1) and reloading files if they have changed is left as an exercise for the reader.

*Example 24-15. Handler.java*

```java
import java.io.*;
import java.net.*;
import java.util.*;

import com.darwinsys.util.Debug;

/** Called from Httpd in a Thread to handle one connection.
 * We are created with just a Socket, and read the
 * HTTP request, extract a name, read it (saving it
 * in Hashtable h for next time), and write it back.
 * <p>
 * TODO split into general handler stuff and "FileServlet",
 *    then handle w/ either user HttpServlet subclasses or FileServlet.
 * @version $Id: ch24,v 1.4 2004/05/04 20:14:01 ian Exp $
 */
public class Handler {

    /** inputStream, from Viewer */
    protected BufferedReader is;
    /** outputStream, to Viewer */
    protected PrintStream os;
    /** Main program */
    protected Httpd parent;
    /** The default filename in a directory. */
    protected final static String DEF_NAME = "/index.html";
```

*Example 24-15. Handler.java (continued)*

```java
/** The Hashtable used to cache all URLs we've read.
 * Static, shared by all instances of Handler (one Handler per request;
 * this is probably quite inefficient, but simple. Need ThreadPool).
 * Note that Hashtable methods *are* synchronized.
 */
private static Hashtable h = new Hashtable();
static {
    h.put("", "<html><body><b>Unknown server error</b>".getBytes());
}
/** Construct a Handler */
Handler(Httpd parent) {
    this.parent = parent;
}

protected static final int RQ_INVALID = 0, RQ_GET = 1, RQ_HEAD = 2,
    RQ_POST = 3;

public void process(Socket clntSock) {
    String request;        // what Viewer sends us.
    int methodType = RQ_INVALID;
    try {
        System.out.println("Connection accepted from " +
            clntSock.getInetAddress());
        is = new BufferedReader(new InputStreamReader(
            clntSock.getInputStream()));
        // Must do before any chance of errorResponse being called!
        os = new PrintStream(clntSock.getOutputStream());

        request = is.readLine();
        if (request == null || request.length() == 0) {
            // No point nattering: the sock died, nobody will hear
            // us if we scream into cyberspace... Could log it though.
            return;
        }

        // Use a StringTokenizer to break the request into its three parts:
        // HTTP method, resource name, and HTTP version
        StringTokenizer st = new StringTokenizer(request);
        if (st.countTokens() != 3) {
            errorResponse(444, "Unparseable input " + request);
            return;
        }
        String rqCode = st.nextToken();
        String rqName = st.nextToken();
        String rqHttpVer = st.nextToken();
        System.out.println("Request: Command " + rqCode +
                ", file " + rqName + ", version " + rqHttpVer);

        // Read headers, up to the null line before the body,
        // so the body can be read directly if it's a POST.
        HashMap map = new HashMap();
        String hdrLine;
```

*Example 24-15. Handler.java (continued)*

```
                while ((hdrLine = is.readLine()) != null &&
                        hdrLine.length() != 0) {
                    int ix;
                    if ((ix=hdrLine.indexOf(':')) != -1) {
                        String hdrName = hdrLine.substring(0, ix);
                        String hdrValue = hdrLine.substring(ix+1).trim();
                        Debug.println("hdr", hdrName+","+hdrValue);
                        map.put(hdrName, hdrValue);
                    } else {
                        System.err.println("INVALID HEADER: " + hdrLine);
                    }
                }

                // check that rqCode is either GET or HEAD or ...
                if ("get".equalsIgnoreCase(rqCode))
                    methodType = RQ_GET;
                else if ("head".equalsIgnoreCase(rqCode))
                    methodType = RQ_HEAD;
                else if ("post".equalsIgnoreCase(rqCode))
                    methodType = RQ_POST;
                else {
                    errorResponse(400, "invalid method: " + rqCode);
                    return;
                }

                // A bit of paranoia may be a good thing...
                if (rqName.indexOf("..") != -1) {
                    errorResponse(404, "can't seem to find: " + rqName);
                    return;
                }

                // XXX new MyRequest(clntSock, rqName, methodType);
                // XXX new MyResponse(clntSock, os);

                // XXX if (isServlet(rqName)) [
                //          doServlet(rqName, methodType, map);
                // else
                    doFile(rqName, methodType == RQ_HEAD, os /*, map */);
                os.flush();
                clntSock.close();
            } catch (IOException e) {
                System.out.println("IOException " + e);
            }
            System.out.println("END OF REQUEST");
        }

        /** Processes one file request */
        void doFile(String rqName, boolean headerOnly, PrintStream os) throws IOException {
            File f;
            byte[] content = null;
            Object o = h.get(rqName);
            if (o != null && o instanceof byte[]) {
```

*Example 24-15. Handler.java (continued)*

```
            content = (byte[])o;
            System.out.println("Using cached file " + rqName);
            sendFile(rqName, headerOnly, content, os);
        } else if ((f = new File(parent.getRootDir() + rqName)).isDirectory()) {
            // Directory with index.html? Process it.
            File index = new File(f, DEF_NAME);
            if (index.isFile()) {
                doFile(rqName + DEF_NAME, index, headerOnly, os);
                return;
            }
            else {
                // Directory? Do not cache; always make up dir list.
                System.out.println("DIRECTORY FOUND");
                doDirList(rqName, f, headerOnly, os);
                sendEnd();
            }
        } else if (f.canRead()) {
            // REGULAR FILE
            doFile(rqName, f, headerOnly, os);
        }
        else {
            errorResponse(404, "File not found");
        }
    }

    void doDirList(String rqName, File dir, boolean justAHead, PrintStream os) {
        os.println("HTTP/1.0 200 directory found");
        os.println("Content-type: text/html");
        os.println("Date: " + new Date().toString());
        os.println();
        if (justAHead)
            return;
        os.println("<html>");
        os.println("<title>Contents of directory " + rqName + "</title>");
        os.println("<h1>Contents of directory " + rqName + "</h1>");
        String fl[] = dir.list();
        Arrays.sort(fl);
        for (int i=0; i<fl.length; i++)
            os.println("<br/><a href=\"" + rqName + File.separator + fl[i] + "\">" +
                "<DEFANGED_IMG align='center' border='0' src='/images/file.jpg'>" +
                ' ' + fl[i] + "</a>");
    }

    /** Send one file, given a File object. */
    void doFile(String rqName, File f, boolean headerOnly, PrintStream os) throws
        IOException {
        System.out.println("Loading file " + rqName);
        InputStream in = new FileInputStream(f);
        byte c_content[] = new byte[(int)f.length()];
        // Single large read, should be fast.
        int n = in.read(c_content);
        h.put(rqName, c_content);
```

*Example 24-15. Handler.java (continued)*

```java
        sendFile(rqName, headerOnly, c_content, os);
        in.close();
    }

    /** Send one file, given the filename and contents.
     * @param justHead - if true, send heading and return.
     */
    void sendFile(String fname, boolean justHead,
            byte[] content, PrintStream os) throws IOException {
        os.println("HTTP/1.0 200 Here's your file");
        os.println("Content-type: " + guessMime(fname));
        os.println("Content-length: " + content.length);
        os.println();
        if (justHead)
            return;
        os.write(content);
    }

    /** The type for unguessable files */
    final static String UNKNOWN = "unknown/unknown";

    protected String guessMime(String fn) {
        String lcname = fn.toLowerCase();
        int extenStartsAt = lcname.lastIndexOf('.');
        if (extenStartsAt<0) {
            if (fn.equalsIgnoreCase("makefile"))
                return "text/plain";
            return UNKNOWN;
        }
        String exten = lcname.substring(extenStartsAt);
        String guess = parent.getMimeType(exten, UNKNOWN);

        return guess;
    }

    /** Sends an error response, by number, hopefully localized. */
    protected void errorResponse(int errNum, String errMsg) {

        // Check for localized messages
        ResourceBundle messages = ResourceBundle.getBundle("errors");

        String response;
        try { response = messages.getString(Integer.toString(errNum)); }
        catch (MissingResourceException e) { response=errMsg; }

        // Generate and send the response
        os.println("HTTP/1.0 " + errNum + " " + response);
        os.println("Content-type: text/html");
        os.println();
        os.println("<html>");
        os.println("<head><title>Error " + errNum + "--" + response +
            "</title></head>");
```

*Example 24-15. Handler.java (continued)*

```
        os.println("<h1>" + errNum + " " + response + "</h1>");
        sendEnd( );
    }

    /** Send the tail end of any page we make up. */
    protected void sendEnd( ) {
        os.println("<HR>");
        os.println("<address>Java Web Server,");
        String myAddr = "http://www.darwinsys.com/freeware/";
        os.println("<a href=\"" + myAddr + "\">" +
            myAddr + "</a>");
        os.println("</address>");
        os.println("</html>");
        os.println( );
    }
}
```

From a performance point of view, it may be better to precreate a pool of threads and cause each one to run the Handler when a connection comes along. This is how servlet engines drive ordinary servlets to high levels of performance; it avoids the overhead of creating a Thread object for each request. This can be done easily in JDK 1.5, using the Concurrency Utilities.

# 24.11 Simplifying Servers Using the Concurrency Utilities (JDK 1.5)

## Problem

You need to implement a multithreaded server.

## Solution

Use the JDK 1.5 Thread Pool implementation of the Executor interface.

## Discussion

The java.util.concurrent package includes Executors; an Executor is, of course, a class that can execute code for you. The code to be executed can be the familiar Runnable or a new interface Callable. One common kind of Executor is a "thread pool." The code in Example 24-16 subclasses the main class of the Threaded Web Server from Recipe 24.10 to use a pool of Threads to schedule multiple clients concurrently.

*Example 24-16. HttpdConcurrent.java*

```
import java.net.Socket;
import java.util.concurrent.*;
```

*Example 24-16. HttpdConcurrent.java (continued)*

```
/**
 * HttpConcurrent - Httpd Subclass using java.lang.concurrent
 */
public class HttpdConcurrent extends Httpd {
    Executor myThreadPool = Executors.newFixedThreadPool(5);

    public HttpdConcurrent() throws Exception {
        super();
    }

    public static void main(String[] argv) throws Exception {
        System.out.println("DarwinSys JavaWeb Server 0.1 starting...");
        HttpdConcurrent w = new HttpdConcurrent();
        if (argv.length == 2 && argv[0].equals("-p")) {
            w.startServer(Integer.parseInt(argv[1]));
        } else {
            w.startServer(HTTP);
        }
        w.runServer();
    }
    public void runServer() throws Exception {
        while (true) {
            final Socket clientSocket = sock.accept();
            myThreadPool.execute(new Runnable() {
                public void run() {
                    new Handler(HttpdConcurrent.this).process(clientSocket);
                }
            });
        }
    }
}
```

You can see this program in action in Figure 24-5.

## See Also

For details on java.util.concurrent, see the online documentation accompanying the JDK. For background on JSR 166, see Doug Lea's home page at *http://gee.cs.oswego.edu/* and his JSR 166 page at *http://gee.cs.oswego.edu/dl/concurrency-interest/index.html*.

I have not discussed several general Threads issues. Scheduling of threads is not necessarily preemptive; it may be cooperative. This means that, on some platforms, the threads mechanism does not interrupt the running thread periodically to give other threads a "fair" chance to get CPU time. Therefore, in order to be portable to all Java platforms, your code *must* use yield( ) or wait( ) periodically (or some other method that causes the thread to be suspended, such as reading or writing). I also didn't get into priorities. The priority model is more limited than that of some other thread models, such as POSIX threads.

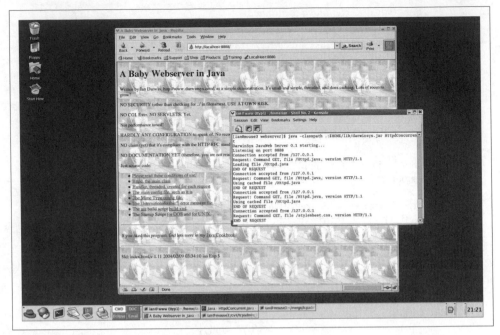

*Figure 24-5. HttpdConcurrent in action*

All in all, it's important to understand that *threaded classes require careful design*. For this reason, you should refer to a good book on threaded Java before unleashing anything threaded upon the world. Recommendations include *Concurrent Programming in Java* by Doug Lea (Addison Wesley), *Multithreaded Programming with Java Technology* by Lewis et al (Prentice Hall), and *Java Threads* by Scott Oaks and Henry Wong (O'Reilly).

# CHAPTER 25

# Introspection, or "A Class Named Class"

## 25.0  Introduction

The class java.lang.Class, and the reflection package java.lang.reflect, provide a number of mechanisms for gathering information from the Java Virtual Machine. Known collectively as *introspection* or *reflection*, these facilities allow you to load classes on the fly, to find methods and fields in classes, to generate listings of them, and to invoke methods on dynamically loaded classes. There is even a mechanism to let you construct a class from scratch (well, actually, from an array of bytes) while your program is running. This is about as close as Java lets you get to the magic, secret internals of the Java machine.

The JVM implementation is a large program, normally written in C and/or C++, that implements the Java Virtual Machine abstraction. You can get the source for Sun's and other JVMs via the Internet, which you could study for months. Here we concentrate on just a few aspects, and only from the point of view of a programmer using the JVM's facilities, not how it works internally; that is an implementation detail that varies from one vendor's JVM to another.

I'll start with loading an existing class dynamically, move on to listing the fields and methods of a class and invoking methods, and end by creating a class on the fly using a ClassLoader. One of the more interesting aspects of Java, and one that accounts for both its flexibility (applets, servlets) and part of its perceived speed problem, is the notion of *dynamic loading*. For example, even the simplest "Hello Java" program has to load the class file for your HelloJava class, the class file for its parent (usually java.lang.Object), the class for PrintStream (since you used System.out), the class for PrintStream's parent, and so on. To see this in action, try something like:

```
java -verbose HelloJava | more
```

To take another example, a browser can download an applet's bytecode file over the Internet and run it on your desktop. How does it load the class file into the running JVM? We discuss this little bit of Java magic in Recipe 25.3. The chapter ends with replacement versions of the JDK tools *javap* and AppletViewer—the latter doing what a browser does, loading applets at runtime—and a cross-reference tool that you can use to become a famous Java author by publishing your very own reference to the complete Java API.

# 25.1 Getting a Class Descriptor

## Problem

You want to get a Class object from a class name or instance.

## Solution

If the type name is known at compile time, you can get the class instance using the compiler keyword `.class`, which works on any type that is known at compile time, even the eight primitive types.

Otherwise, if you have an object (an instance of a class), you can call the java.lang. Object method getClass( ), which returns the Class object for the object's class (now that was a mouthful!):

```
import java.util.*;
/**
 * Show the Class keyword and getClass() method in action.
 */
public class ClassKeyword {
    public static void main(String[] argv) {
        System.out.println("Trying the ClassName.class keyword:");
        System.out.println("Object class: " + Object.class);
        System.out.println("String class: " + String.class);
        System.out.println("String[] class: " + String[].class);
        System.out.println("Calendar class: " + Calendar.class);
        System.out.println("Current class: " + ClassKeyword.class);
        System.out.println("Class for int: " + int.class);

        System.out.println( );

        System.out.println("Trying the instance.getClass() method:");
        System.out.println("Robin the Fearless".getClass());
        System.out.println(Calendar.getInstance( ).getClass( ));
    }
}
```

When we run it, we see:

```
C:\javasrc\reflect>java ClassKeyword
Trying the ClassName.class keyword:
Object class: class java.lang.Object
String class: class java.lang.String
String[] class: class [Ljava.lang.String;
Calendar class: class java.util.Calendar
Current class: class ClassKeyword
Class for int: int
```

```
Trying the instance.getClass( ) method:
class java.lang.String
class java.util.GregorianCalendar

C:\javasrc\reflect>
```

Nothing fancy, but as you can see, you can get the Class object for any class known at compile time, whether it's part of a package or not.

# 25.2   Finding and Using Methods and Fields

## Problem

You need more to find arbitrary method or field names in arbitrary classes.

## Solution

Use the reflection package java.lang.reflect.

## Discussion

If you just wanted to find fields and methods in one particular class, you wouldn't need this recipe; you could simply create an instance of the class using new and refer to its fields and methods directly. But this allows you to find methods and fields in any class, even classes that have not yet been written! Given a class object created as in Recipe 25.1, you can obtain a list of constructors, a list of methods, or a list of fields. The method getMethods( ) lists the methods available for a given class as an array of Method objects. Similarly, getFields( ) returns a list of Field objects. Since constructor methods are treated specially by Java, there is also a getConstructors( ) method, which returns an array of Constructor objects. Even though "class" is in the package java.lang, the Constructor, Method, and Field objects it returns are in java.lang.reflect, so you need an import of this package. The ListMethods class (Example 25-1) shows how get a list of methods in a class whose name is known at runtime.

*Example 25-1. ListMethods.java*

```java
import java.lang.reflect.*;

/**
 * List the Constructors and methods
 */
public class ListMethods {
    public static void main(String[] argv) throws ClassNotFoundException {
        if (argv.length == 0) {
            System.err.println("Usage: ListMethods className");
            return;
        }
    }
```

*Example 25-1. ListMethods.java (continued)*

```
        Class c = Class.forName(argv[0]);
        Constructor[] cons = c.getConstructors();
        printList("Constructors", cons);
        Method[] meths = c.getMethods();
        printList("Methods", meths);
    }
    static void printList(String s, Object[] o) {
        System.out.println("*** " + s + " ***");
        for (int i=0; i<o.length; i++)
            System.out.println(o[i].toString());
    }
}
```

For example, you could run Example 25-1 on a class like java.lang.String and get a fairly lengthy list of methods; I'll only show part of the output so you can see what it looks like:

```
> java ListMethods java.lang.String
*** Constructors ***
public java.lang.String()
public java.lang.String(java.lang.String)
public java.lang.String(java.lang.StringBuffer)
public java.lang.String(byte[])
// and many more...
*** Methods ***
public static java.lang.String java.lang.String.copyValueOf(char[])
public static java.lang.String java.lang.String.copyValueOf(char[],int,int)
public static java.lang.String java.lang.String.valueOf(char)
// and more valueOf() forms...
public boolean java.lang.String.equals(java.lang.Object)
public final native java.lang.Class java.lang.Object.getClass()
// and more java.lang.Object methods...
public char java.lang.String.charAt(int)
public int java.lang.String.compareTo(java.lang.Object)
public int java.lang.String.compareTo(java.lang.String)
```

You can see that this could be extended (almost literally) to write a BeanMethods class that would list only the set/get methods defined in a JavaBean (see Recipe 23.8).

Alternatively, you can find a particular method and invoke it, or find a particular field and refer to its value. Let's start by finding a given field, since that's the easiest. Example 25-2 is code that, given an Object and the name of a field, finds the field (gets a Field object) and then retrieves and prints the value of that Field as an int.

*Example 25-2. FindField.java*

```
import java.lang.reflect.*;
import java.util.*;

/** This class shows using Reflection to get a field from another class. */
public class FindField {
```

*Example 25-2. FindField.java (continued)*

```java
    public static void main(String[] unused)
    throws NoSuchFieldException, IllegalAccessException {

        // Create instance of FindField
        FindField gf = new FindField( );

        // Create instance of target class (YearHolder defined below).
        Object o = new YearHolder( );

        // Use gf to extract a field from o.
        System.out.println("The value of 'currentYear' is: " +
            gf.intFieldValue(o, "currentYear"));
    }

    int intFieldValue(Object o, String name)
    throws NoSuchFieldException, IllegalAccessException {
        Class c = o.getClass( );
        Field fld = c.getField(name);
        int value = fld.getInt(o);
        return value;
    }
}

/** This is just a class that we want to get a field from */
class YearHolder {
    /** Just a field that is used to show getting a field's value. */
    public int currentYear = Calendar.getInstance( ).get(Calendar.YEAR);
}
```

What if we need to find a method? The simplest way is to use the methods getMethod( ) and invoke( ). But this is not altogether trivial. Suppose that somebody gives us a reference to an object. We don't know its class but have been told that it should have this method:

```java
public void work(String s) { }
```

We wish to invoke work( ). To find the method, we must make an array of Class objects, one per item in the calling list. So, in this case, we make an array containing only a reference to the class object for String. Since we know the name of the class at compile time, we'll use the shorter invocation String.class instead of Class. forName( ). This, plus the name of the method as a string, gets us entry into the getMethod( ) method of the Class object. If this succeeds, we have a Method object. But guess what? In order to invoke the method, we have to construct yet another array, this time an array of Object references actually containing the data to be passed to the invocation. We also, of course, need an instance of the class in whose context the method is to be run. For this demonstration class, we need to pass only a single string, as our array consists only of the string. Example 25-3 is the code that finds the method and invokes it.

*Example 25-3. GetMethod.java*

```java
import java.lang.reflect.*;

/** This class is just here to give us something to work on,
 * with a println() call that will prove we got here. */
class X {
    public void work(String s) {
        System.out.println("Working on \"" + s + "\"");
    }
}

/**
 * Get a given method, and invoke it.
 */
public class GetMethod {

    public static void main(String[] argv) {
        try {
            Class clX = X.class; // or Class.forName("X");
            // To find a method we need the array of matching Class types.
            Class[] argTypes = {
                String.class
            };

            // Now find a Method object for the given method.
            Method worker = clX.getMethod("work", argTypes);

            // To INVOKE the method, we need its actual arguments, as an array.
            Object[] theData = {
                "Chocolate Chips"
            };

            // The obvious last step: invoke the method.
            worker.invoke(new X(), theData);
        } catch (Exception e) {
            System.err.println("Invoke() failed: " + e);
        }
    }
}
```

Not tiny, but it's still not bad. In most programming languages, you couldn't do that in the 40 lines it took us here.

A word of caution: when the arguments to a method are of a primitive type, such as int, you do not pass Integer.class into getMethod(). Instead, you must use the class object representing the primitive type int. The easiest way to find this class is in the Integer class, as a public constant named TYPE, so you'd pass Integer.TYPE. The same is true for all the primitive types; for each, the corresponding wrapper class has the primitive class referred to as TYPE.

# 25.3 Loading and Instantiating a Class Dynamically

## Problem

You want to load classes dynamically, just like browsers load your applets and web servers load your servlets.

## Solution

Use `class.forName("ClassName");` and the class's `newInstance( )` method.

## Discussion

Suppose you are writing a Java application and want other developers to be able to extend your application by writing Java classes that run in the context of your application. In other words, these developers are, in essence, using Java as an extension language, in the same way that Applets are an extension of a web browser. You would probably want to define a small set of methods that these extension programs would have and that you could call for such purposes as initialization, operation, and termination. The best way to do this is, of course, to publish a given, possibly abstract, class that provides those methods and get the developers to subclass from it. Sound familiar? It should. This is just how web browsers such as Netscape allow the deployment of applets.

We'll leave the thornier issues of security and of loading a class file over a network socket for now, and assume that the user can install the classes into the application directory or into a directory that appears in CLASSPATH at the time the program is run. First, let's define our class. We'll call it Cooklet (see Example 25-4) to avoid infringing on the overused word *applet*. And we'll initially take the easiest path from ingredients to cookies before we complicate it.

*Example 25-4. Cooklet.java*

```
/** A simple class, just to provide the list of methods that
 * users need to provide to be usable in our application.
 * Note that the class is abstract so you must subclass it,
 * but the methods are non-abstract so you don't have to provide
 * dummy versions if you don't need a particular functionality.
 */
public abstract class Cooklet {

    /** The initialization method. The Cookie application will
     * call you here (AFTER calling your no-argument constructor)
     * to allow you to initialize your code
     */
    public void initialize( ) {
    }
```

*Example 25-4. Cooklet.java (continued)*

```
    /** The work method. The cookie application will call you
     * here when it is time for you to start cooking.
     */
    public void work() {
    }

    /** The termination method. The cookie application will call you
     * here when it is time for you to stop cooking and shut down
     * in an orderly fashion.
     */
    public void terminate() {
    }
}
```

Now, since we'll be baking, err, making this available to other people, we'll probably want to cook up a demonstration version too; see Example 25-5.

*Example 25-5. DemoCooklet.java*

```
public class DemoCooklet extends Cooklet {
    public void work() {
        System.out.println("I am busy baking cookies.");
    }
    public void terminate() {
        System.out.println("I am shutting down my ovens now.");
    }
}
```

But how does our application use it? Once we have the name of the user's class, we need to create a Class object for that class. This can be done easily using the static method Class.forName(). Then we can create an instance of it using the Class object's newInstance() method; this calls the class's no-argument constructor. Then we simply cast the newly constructed object to our Cooklet class, and we can call its methods! It actually takes longer to describe this code than to look at the code, so let's do that now; see Example 25-6.

*Example 25-6. Cookies.java*

```
/**
 * This is the part of the Cookies application that loads
 * the user-defined subclass.
 */
public class Cookies {
    public static void main(String[] argv) {
        System.out.println("Cookies Application Version 0.0");
        Cooklet cooklet = null;
        String cookletClassName = argv[0];
        try {
            Class cookletClass = Class.forName(cookletClassName);
            Object cookletObject = cookletClass.newInstance();
            cooklet = (Cooklet)cookletObject;
```

*Example 25-6. Cookies.java (continued)*

```
        } catch (Exception e) {
            System.err.println("Error " + cookletClassName + e);
        }
        cooklet.initialize();
        cooklet.work();
        cooklet.terminate();
    }
}
```

And if we run it?

```
$ java  Cookies DemoCooklet
Cookies Application Version 0.0
I am busy baking cookies.
I am shutting down my ovens now.
$
```

Of course, this version has rather limited error handling. But you already know how to fix that. Your ClassLoader can also place classes into a package by constructing a Package object; you should do this if loading any medium-sized set of application classes.

# 25.4 Constructing a Class from Scratch

## Problem

You need to load a class and run its methods.

## Solution

Write and use your own ClassLoader.

## Discussion

A ClassLoader, of course, is a program that loads classes. One class loader is built into the Java Virtual Machine, but your application can create others as needed. Learning to write and run a working class loader and using it to load a class and run its methods is a nontrivial exercise. In fact, you rarely need to write a class loader, but knowing how is helpful in understanding how the JVM finds classes, creates objects, and calls methods.

ClassLoader itself is abstract; you must subclass it, presumably providing a loadClass() method that loads classes as you wish. It can load the bytes from a network connection, a local disk, RAM, a serial port, or anywhere else. Or you can construct the class file in memory yourself, if you have access to a compiler.

You must call this class loader's loadClass() method for any classes you wish to load from it. Note that it is called to load all classes required for classes you load (parent classes that aren't already loaded, for example). However, the JVM still loads classes that you instantiate with the new operator "normally" via CLASSPATH.

When writing a class loader, your loadClass( ) method needs to get the class file into a byte array (typically by reading it), convert the array into a Class object, and return the result.

What? That sounds a bit like "And Then a Miracle Occurs…" And it is. The miracle of class creation, however, happens down inside the JVM, where you don't have access to it. Instead, your ClassLoader has to call the protected defineClass( ) method in your superclass (which is java.lang.ClassLoader). This is illustrated in Figure 25-1, where a stream of bytes containing a hypothetical Chicken class is converted into a ready-to-run Chicken class in the JVM by calling the defineClass( ) method.

*Figure 25-1. ClassLoader in action*

**What next?**

To use your ClassLoader subclass, you need to instantiate it and call its loadClass( ) method with the name of the class you want to load. This gives you a Class object for the named class; the Class object in turn lets you construct instances, find and call methods, etc. Refer back to Recipe 25.2.

# 25.5  Performance Timing

## Problem

You need to know how long a Java program takes to run.

## Solution

Call System.currentTimeMillis( ) before and after invoking the target class dynamically.

# Discussion

The simplest technique is to save the JVM's accumulated time before and after dynamically loading a main program, and calculate the difference between those times. Code to do just this is presented in Example 25-7; for now, just remember that we have a way of timing a given Java class.

One way of measuring the efficiency of a particular operation is to run it many times in isolation. The overall time the program takes to run thus approximates the total time of many invocations of the same operation. Gross numbers like this can be compared if you want to know which of two ways of doing something is more efficient. Consider the case of string concatenation versus println( ). The code:

```
println("Time is " + n.toString( ) + " seconds");
```

creates a StringBuffer, appends the string "Time is ", the value of n as a string, and " seconds", and finally converts the finished StringBuffer to a String and passes that to println( ). Suppose you have a program that does a lot of this, such as a Java servlet that creates a lot of HTML this way, and you expect (or at least hope) your web site to be sufficiently busy so that doing this efficiently will make a difference. There are two ways of thinking about this:

- Theory A: This string concatenation is inefficient.
- Theory B: String concatenation doesn't matter; println( ) is inefficient, too.

A proponent of Theory A might say that since println( ) just puts stuff into a buffer, it is very fast and that string concatenation is the expensive part.

How to decide between Theory A and Theory B? Assume you are willing to write a simple test program that tests both theories. One way of proceeding might be to disassemble the resulting bytecodes and count the CPU cycles each uses. This is an interesting theoretical exercise, and a good subject for a computer science dissertation. But we need the results quickly, so we will just write a simple program both ways and time it. StringPrintA is the timing program for Theory A:

```
public class StringPrintA {
    public static void main(String[] argv) {
        Object o = "Hello World";
        for (int i=0; i<100000; i++) {
            System.out.println("<p><b>" + o.toString( ) + "</b></p>");
        }
    }
}
```

StringPrintAA is the same but explicitly uses a StringBuffer for the string concatenation. StringPrintB is the tester for Theory B:

```
public class StringPrintB {
    public static void main(String[] argv) {
        Object o = "Hello World";
        for (int i=0; i<100000; i++) {
```

```
            System.out.print("<p><b>");
            System.out.print(o.toString());
            System.out.print("</b></p>");
            System.out.println();
        }
    }
}
```

## Timing results

I ran `StringPrintA`, `StringPrintAA`, and `StringPrintB` twice, each on a single 400 MHz Intel Celeron. Here are the results:

| | |
|---|---|
| StringPrintA | 17.23, 17.20 seconds |
| StringPrintAA | 17.23, 17.23 seconds |
| StringPrintB | 27.59, 27.60 seconds |

Moral: Don't guess. If it matters, time it.

Another moral: Multiple calls to `System.out.print()` cost more than the same number of calls to a `StringBuffer`'s `append()` method, by a factor of roughly 1.5 (or 150%). Theory B wins; the extra `println` calls appear to save a string concatenation but make the program take substantially longer.

A shell script to run these timing tests appears in file *stringprinttimer.sh* in the online source.

## Timing program

It's pretty easy to build a simplified `time` command in Java, given that you have `System.currentTimeMillis()` to start with. Run my `Time` program, and, on the command line, specify the name of the class to be timed, followed by the arguments (if any) that class needs for running. The time that the class took is displayed. But remember that `System.currentTimeMillis()` returns clock time, not necessarily CPU time. So you must run it on a machine that isn't running a lot of background processes. And note also that I use dynamic loading (see Recipe 25.3) to let you put the Java class name on the command line.

*Example 25-7. Time.java*

```java
import com.darwinsys.util.QuickTimeFormat;
import java.lang.reflect.*;

/**
 * Time the main method of another class, for performance tuning.
 */
public class Time {
    public static void main(String[] argv) throws Exception {
        // Instantiate target class, from argv[0]
        Class c = Class.forName(argv[0]);
```

*Example 25-7. Time.java (continued)*

```
        // Find its static main method (use our own argv as the signature).
        Class[] classes = { argv.getClass() };
        Method main = c.getMethod("main", classes);

        // Make new argv array, dropping class name from front.
        String nargv[] = new String[argv.length - 1];
        System.arraycopy(argv, 1, nargv, 0, nargv.length);

        Object[] nargs = { nargv };

        System.err.println("Starting class " + c);

        // About to start timing run. Important to not do anything
        // (even a println) that would be attributed to the program
        // being timed, from here until we've gotten ending time.

        // Get current (i.e., starting) time
        long t0 = System.currentTimeMillis();

        // Run the main program
        main.invoke(null, nargs);

        // Get ending time, and compute usage
        long t1 = System.currentTimeMillis();

        long runTime = t1 - t0;

        System.err.println(
            "runTime-"  + QuickTimeFormat.msToSecs(runTime));
    }
}
```

Of course, you can't directly compare the results from the operating system `time` command with results from running this program. There is a rather large, but fairly constant, initialization overhead—the JVM startup and the initialization of `Object` and `System.out`, for example—that is included in the former and excluded from the latter. One could even argue that my `Time` program is more accurate since it excludes this constant overhead. But, as noted, it must be run on a single-user machine to yield repeatable results. And no fair running an editor in another window while waiting for your timed program to complete!

# 25.6  Printing Class Information

## Problem

You want to print all the information about a class, similar to the way *javap* does.

## Solution

Get a Class object, call its getFields( ) and getMethods( ), and print the results.

## Discussion

The JDK includes a program called *javap*, the Java Printer. Sun's JDK version normally prints the outline of a class file—a list of its methods and fields—but can also print out the Java bytecodes or machine instructions. The Kaffe package did not include a version of *javap*, so I wrote one and contributed it (see Example 25-8). The Kaffe folk have expanded it somewhat, but it still works basically the same. My version doesn't print the bytecodes; it behaves rather like Sun's behaves when you don't give theirs any command-line options.

The getFields( ) and getMethods( ) methods return arrays of Field and Method, respectively; these are both in package java.lang.reflect. I use a Modifiers object to get details on the permissions and storage attributes of the fields and methods. In many Java implementations, you can bypass this and simply call toString( ) in each Field and Method object (as I do here for Constructors). Doing it this way gives me a bit more control over the formatting.

*Example 25-8. MyJavaP.java*

```java
import java.lang.reflect.Constructor;
import java.lang.reflect.Field;
import java.lang.reflect.Method;
import java.lang.reflect.Modifier;

/**
 * JavaP prints structural information about classes.
 * For each class, all public fields and methods are listed.
 * "Reflectance" is used to look up the information.
 */
public class MyJavaP {

    /** Simple main program, construct self, process each class name
     * found in argv.
     */
    public static void main(String[] argv) {
        MyJavaP pp = new MyJavaP( );

        if (argv.length == 0) {
            System.err.println("Usage: MyJavaP className [...]");
            System.exit(1);
        } else for (int i=0; i<argv.length; i++)
            pp.doClass(argv[i]);
    }

    /** Format the fields and methods of one class, given its name.
     */
    protected void doClass(String className) {
```

*Example 25-8. MyJavaP.java (continued)*

```java
        try {
            Class c = Class.forName(className);
            System.out.println(Modifier.toString(c.getModifiers()) + ' ' + c + " {");

            int mods;
            Field fields[] = c.getDeclaredFields();
            for (int i = 0; i < fields.length; i++) {
                if (!Modifier.isPrivate(fields[i].getModifiers())
                  && !Modifier.isProtected(fields[i].getModifiers()))
                    System.out.println("\t" + fields[i]);
            }
            Constructor[] constructors = c.getConstructors();
            for (int j = 0; j < constructors.length; j++) {
                Constructor constructor = constructors[j];
                System.out.println("\t" + constructor);

            }
            Method methods[] = c.getDeclaredMethods();
            for (int i = 0; i < methods.length; i++) {
                if (!Modifier.isPrivate(methods[i].getModifiers())
                  && !Modifier.isProtected(methods[i].getModifiers()))
                    System.out.println("\t" + methods[i]);
            }
            System.out.println("}");
        } catch (ClassNotFoundException e) {
            System.err.println("Error: Class " +
                className + " not found!");
        } catch (Exception e) {
            System.err.println(e);
        }
    }
}
```

# 25.7  Program: CrossRef

You've probably seen those other Java books that consist entirely of listings of the Java API for version thus-and-such of the JDK. I don't suppose you thought the authors of these works sat down and typed the entire contents from scratch. As a programmer, you would have realized, I hope, that there must be a way to obtain that information from Java. But you might not have realized how easy it is! If you've read this chapter faithfully, you now know that there is one true way: make the computer do the walking. Example 25-9 is a program that puts most of the techniques together. This version generates a cross-reference listing, but by overriding the last few methods, you could easily convert it to print the information in any format you like, including an API Reference book. You'd need to deal with the details of this or that publishing software—FrameMaker, troff, TeX, or whatever—but that's the easy part.

This program makes fuller use of the Reflection API than did MyJavaP in Recipe 25.6. It also uses the java.util.zip classes (see Recipe 10.20) to crack the JAR archive containing the class files of the API. Each class file found in the archive is loaded and listed; the listing part is similar to MyJavaP.

*Example 25-9. CrossRef.java*

```java
import java.io.*;
import java.util.*;
import java.util.zip.*;
import java.lang.reflect.*;

/**
 * CrossRef prints a cross-reference about all classes named in argv.
 * For each class, all public fields and methods are listed.
 * "Reflectance" is used to look up the information.
 *
 * It is expected that the output will be post-processed e.g.,
 * with sort and awk/perl. Try:
 *   java CrossRef |
 *       uniq | # squeeze out polymorphic forms early
 *       sort | awk '$2=="method" { ... }' > crossref-methods.txt
 * The part in "{ ... }" is left as an exercise for the reader. :-(
 *
 */
public class CrossRef {
    /** Counter of fields/methods printed. */
    protected static int n = 0;

    /** A "Modifier" object, to decode modifiers of fields/methods */
    protected Modifier m = new Modifier();

    /** True if we are doing classpath, so only do java. and javax. */
    protected static boolean doingStandardClasses = true;

    /** Simple main program, construct self, process each .ZIP file
     * found in CLASSPATH or in argv.
     */
    public static void main(String[] argv) {
        CrossRef xref = new CrossRef();

        xref.doArgs(argv);
    }

    protected void doArgs(String[] argv) {

        if (argv.length == 0) {
            // No arguments, look in CLASSPATH
            String s = System.getProperties().getProperty("java.class.path");
            //  break apart with path sep.
            String pathSep = System.getProperties().
                getProperty("path.separator");
            StringTokenizer st = new StringTokenizer(s, pathSep);
```

*Example 25-9. CrossRef.java (continued)*

```
            // Process each classpath
        while (st.hasMoreTokens()) {
            String cand = st.nextToken();
            System.err.println("Trying path " + cand);
            if (cand.endsWith(".zip") || cand.endsWith(".jar"))
                processOneZip(cand);
        }
    } else {
        // We have arguments, process them as zip files
        doingStandardClasses = false;
        for (int i=0; i<argv.length; i++)
            processOneZip(argv[i]);
    }

    System.err.println("All done! Found " + n + " entries.");
    System.exit(0);
}

/** For each Zip file, for each entry, xref it */
public void processOneZip(String classes) {
        ArrayList entries = new ArrayList();

        try {
            ZipFile zippy =
                new ZipFile(new File(classes));
            Enumeration all = zippy.entries();
            // For each entry, get its name and put it into "entries"
            while (all.hasMoreElements()) {
                entries.add(((ZipEntry)(all.nextElement())).getName());
            }
        } catch (IOException err) {
            System.err.println("IO Error: " + err);
            return;
        }

        // Sort the entries (by class name)
        Collections.sort(entries);

        // Process the entries
        for (int i=0; i< entries.size(); i++) {
            doClass((String)entries.get(i));
        }
}

/** Format the fields and methods of one class, given its name.
 */
protected void doClass(String zipName) {
    if (System.getProperties().getProperty("debug.names") != null)
        System.out.println("doClass(" + zipName + ");");

    // Ignore package/directory, other odd-ball stuff.
    if (zipName.endsWith("/")) {
```

*Example 25-9. CrossRef.java (continued)*

```java
            System.err.println("Starting directory " + zipName);
            return;
        }
        // Ignore META-INF stuff
        if (zipName.startsWith("META-INF/")) {
            return;
        }
        // Ignore images, HTML, whatever else we find.
        if (!zipName.endsWith(".class")) {
            System.err.println("Ignoring " + zipName);
            return;
        }
        // If doing CLASSPATH, Ignore com.sun.* which are "internal API".
        if (doingStandardClasses && zipName.startsWith("com.sun")){
            return;
        }

        // Convert the zip file entry name, like
        //     java/lang/Math.class
        // to a class name like
        //     java.lang.Math
        String className = zipName.replace('/', '.').
            substring(0, zipName.length() - 6);    // 6 for ".class"
        if (System.getProperties().getProperty("debug.names") != null)
            System.err.println("ZipName " + zipName +
                "; className " + className);
        try {
            Class c = Class.forName(className);
            printClass(c);
        } catch (ClassNotFoundException e) {
            System.err.println("Error: Class " +
                className + " not found!");
        } catch (Exception e) {
            System.err.println(e);
        }
        // System.err.println("in gc...");
        System.gc();
        // System.err.println("done gc");
    }

    /**
     * Print the fields and methods of one class.
     */
    protected void printClass(Class c) {
        int i, mods;
        startClass(c);
        try {
            Object[] fields = c.getFields();
            Arrays.sort(fields);
            for (i = 0; i < fields.length; i++) {
                Field field = (Field)fields[i];
                if (!m.isPrivate(field.getModifiers())
```

*Example 25-9. CrossRef.java (continued)*

```
                && !m.isProtected(field.getModifiers()))
                    putField(field, c);
            else System.err.println("private field ignored: " + field);
        }

        Method methods[] = c.getDeclaredMethods();
        // Arrays.sort(methods);
        for (i = 0; i < methods.length; i++) {
            if (!m.isPrivate(methods[i].getModifiers())
             && !m.isProtected(methods[i].getModifiers()))
                putMethod(methods[i], c);
            else System.err.println("pvt: " + methods[i]);
        }
    } catch (Exception e) {
        System.err.println(e);
    }
    endClass();
}

/** put a Field's information to the standard output.
 * Marked protected so you can override it (hint, hint).
 */
protected void putField(Field fld, Class c) {
    println(fld.getName() + " field " + c.getName() + " ");
    ++n;
}
/** put a Method's information to the standard output.
 * Marked protected so you can override it (hint, hint).
 */
protected void putMethod(Method method, Class c) {
    String methName = method.getName();
    println(methName + " method " + c.getName() + " ");
    ++n;
}
/** Print the start of a class. Unused in this version,
 * designed to be overridden */
protected void startClass(Class c) {
}

/** Print the end of a class. Unused in this version,
 * designed to be overridden */
protected void endClass() {
}

/** Convenience routine, short for System.out.println */
protected final void println(String s) {
    System.out.println(s);
}
}
```

You probably noticed the methods startClass( ) and endClass( ), which are null. These methods are placeholders designed to make subclassing easy for when you need to write something at the start and end of each class. One example might be a fancy text formatting application in which you need to output a bold header at the beginning of each class. Another would be XML (see Chapter 21), where you'd want to write a tag like <class> at the front of each class, and </class> at the end. Example 25-10 is, in fact, a working XML-specific subclass that generates (limited) XML for each field and method.

*Example 25-10. CrossRefXML.java*

```java
import java.io.*;
import java.lang.reflect.*;

/** This class subclasses CrossRef to output the information in XML.
 */
public class CrossRefXML extends CrossRef {

    public static void main(String[] argv) {
        CrossRef xref = new CrossRefXML( );
        xref.doArgs(argv);
    }

    /** Print the start of a class.
     */
    protected void startClass(Class c) {
        println("<class><classname>" + c.getName( ) + "</classname>");
    }

    protected void putField(Field fld, Class c) {
        println("<field>" + fld + "</field>");
        ++n;
    }

    /** put a Method's information to the standard output.
     * Marked protected so you can override it (hint, hint).
     */
    protected void putMethod(Method method, Class c) {
        println("<method>" + method + "</method>");
        ++n;
    }

    /** Print the end of a class.
     */
    protected void endClass( ) {
        println("</class>");
    }
}
```

By the way, if you publish a book using either of these and get rich, "Remember, remember me!"

# 25.8 Program: AppletViewer

Another JDK tool that can be replicated is the AppletViewer. This uses the reflection package to load a class that is subclassed from Applet, instantiate an instance of it, and add() this to a frame at a given size. This is a good example of reflection in action: you can use these techniques to dynamically load any subclass of a given class. Suppose we have a simple applet like HelloApplet in Example 25-11.

*Example 25-11. HelloApplet.java*

```java
import java.applet.*;
import java.awt.*;
import javax.swing.*;
import java.awt.event.*;

/**
 * HelloApplet is a simple applet that toggles a message
 * when you click on a Draw button.
 */
public class HelloApplet extends JApplet {

    /** The flag which controls drawing the message. */
    protected boolean requested;

    /** init() is an Applet method called by the browser to initialize */
    public void init() {
        JButton b;
        requested = false;
        Container cp = (Container)getContentPane();
        cp.setLayout(new FlowLayout());
        cp.add(b = new JButton("Draw/Don't Draw"));
        b.addActionListener(new ActionListener() {
            /*  Button - toggle the state of the "requested" flag, to draw or
             *  not to draw.
             */
            public void actionPerformed(ActionEvent e) {
                String arg = e.getActionCommand();
                // Invert the state of the draw request.
                requested = !requested;
                do_the_work();
            }
        });
    }

    /** paint() is an AWT Component method, called when the
     * component needs to be painted.
     */
    public void do_the_work() {
        /* If the Draw button is selected, draw something */
        if (requested) {
            showStatus("Welcome to Java!");
        } else {
```

*Example 25-11. HelloApplet.java (continued)*

```
        showStatus("");    // retract welcome? :-)
    }
  }
}
```

If we run it in my `AppletViewer`,* it shows up as a window with just the Draw button showing; if you press the button an odd number of times, the screen shows the welcome label (Figure 25-2).

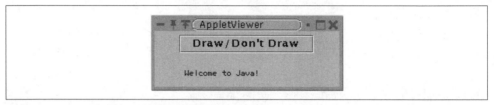

*Figure 25-2. My AppletViewer showing simple applet*

Example 25-12 is the code for the main part of the AppletViewer, which creates a `JFrame` and then loads the `Applet` class dynamically and adds it to the `JFrame`.

*Example 25-12. AppletViewer.java main program*

```java
import java.awt.*;
import java.awt.event.*;
import javax.swing.*;
import java.applet.*;
import java.lang.reflect.*;
import java.net.*;
import java.util.*;

/*
 * AppletViewer - a simple Applet Viewer program.
 */
public class AppletViewer {
    /** The main Frame of this program */
    JFrame f;
    /** The AppletAdapter (gives AppletStub, AppletContext, showStatus) */
    static AppletAdapter aa = null;
    /** The name of the Applet subclass */
    String appName = null;
    /** The Class for the actual applet type */
    Class ac = null;
    /** The Applet instance we are running, or null. Can not be a JApplet
     * until all the entire world is converted to JApplet. */
```

---

* My AppletViewer doesn't parse HTML like the real one does, so you invoke it with just the name of the Applet subclass on its command line. The size is therefore hardcoded, at least until somebody gets around to writing code to extract the class, width, and height attributes from the applet tag in the HTML page like the real McCoy does.

*Example 25-12. AppletViewer.java main program (continued)*

```java
Applet ai = null;
/** The width of the Applet */
final int WIDTH = 250;
/** The height of the Applet */
final int HEIGHT = 200;

/** Main is where it all starts.
 * Construct the GUI. Load the Applet. Start it running.
 */
public static void main(String[] av) {
    new AppletViewer(av.length==0?"HelloApplet":av[0]);
}

/** Construct the GUI for an Applet Viewer */
AppletViewer(String appName) {
    super();

    this.appName = appName;

    f = new JFrame("AppletViewer");
    f.addWindowListener(new WindowAdapter() {
        public void windowClosing(WindowEvent e) {
            f.setVisible(false);
            f.dispose();
            System.exit(0);
        }
    });
    Container cp = f.getContentPane();
    cp.setLayout(new BorderLayout());

    // Instantiate the AppletAdapter which gives us
    // AppletStub and AppletContext.
    if (aa == null)
        aa = new AppletAdapter();

    // The AppletAdapter also gives us showStatus.
    // Therefore, must add() it very early on, since the Applet's
    // Constructor or its init() may use showStatus()
    cp.add(BorderLayout.SOUTH, aa);

    showStatus("Loading Applet " + appName);

    loadApplet(appName , WIDTH, HEIGHT);    // sets ac and ai
    if (ai == null)
        return;

    // Now right away, tell the Applet how to find showStatus et al.
    ai.setStub(aa);

    // Connect the Applet to the Frame.
    cp.add(BorderLayout.CENTER, ai);
```

*Example 25-12. AppletViewer.java main program (continued)*

```
            Dimension d = ai.getSize( );
            d.height += aa.getSize( ).height;
            f.setSize(d);
            f.setVisible(true);        // make the Frame and all in it appear

            showStatus("Applet " + appName + " loaded");

            // Here we pretend to be a browser!
            ai.init( );
            ai.start( );
        }

    /*
     * Load the Applet into memory. Should do caching.
     */
    void loadApplet(String appletName, int w, int h) {
        // appletName = ... extract from the HTML CODE= somehow ...;
        // width =         ditto
        // height =        ditto
        try {
            // get a Class object for the Applet subclass
            ac = Class.forName(appletName);
            // Construct an instance (as if using no-argument constructor)
            ai = (Applet) ac.newInstance( );
        } catch(ClassNotFoundException e) {
            showStatus("Applet subclass " + appletName + " did not load");
            return;
        } catch (Exception e ){
            showStatus("Applet " + appletName + " did not instantiate");
            return;
        }
        ai.setSize(w, h);
    }

    public void showStatus(String s) {
        aa.getAppletContext( ).showStatus(s);
    }
}
```

For Applet methods to work, two additional classes must be defined: AppletStub and
AppletContext. The AppletStub is the tie-in between the applet and the browser, and
the AppletContext is a set of methods used by the applet. In a real browser, they are
probably implemented separately, but I have combined them into one class (see
Example 25-13). Note that the scope of applets that will work without throwing
exceptions is rather limited, since so many of the methods here are, at present, dum-
mied out. This AppletViewer is not a full replacement for Sun's AppletViewer; it has
been tested only with a basic Hello World applet, and it is simply provided as a starting point for those who want to fill in the gaps and make a full-blown applet viewer
program.

*Example 25-13. AppletAdapter.java, partial AppletStub, and AppletContext*

```java
import java.awt.*;
import java.awt.event.*;
import java.applet.*;
import java.net.*;
import java.util.*;

/*
 * AppletAdaptor: partial implementation of AppletStub and AppletContext.
 *
 * This code is far from finished, as you will see.
 *
 */
public class AppletAdapter extends Panel implements AppletStub, AppletContext {
    /** The status window at the bottom */
    Label status = null;

    /** Construct the GUI for an Applet Status window */
    AppletAdapter() {
        super();

        // Must do this very early on, since the Applet's
        // Constructor or its init() may use showStatus()
        add(status - new Label());

        // Give "status" the full width
        status.setSize(getSize().width, status.getSize().height);

        showStatus("AppletAdapter constructed");    // now it can be said
    }

    /****************** AppletStub *********************/
    /** Called when the applet wants to be resized.  */
    public void appletResize(int w, int h) {
        // applet.setSize(w, h);
    }

    /** Gets a reference to the applet's context.  */
    public AppletContext getAppletContext() {
        return this;
    }

    /** Gets the base URL.  */
    public URL getCodeBase() {
        return getClass().getResource(".");
    }

    /** Gets the document URL.  */
    public URL getDocumentBase() {
        return getClass().getResource(".");
    }

    /** Returns the value of the named parameter in the HTML tag.  */
    public String getParameter(String name) {
```

```
        String value = null;
        return value;
    }
    /** Determines if the applet is active.  */
    public boolean isActive() {
        return true;
    }


    /*********************** AppletContext ***********************/

    /** Finds and returns the applet with the given name. */
    public Applet getApplet(String an) {
        return null;
    }

    /** Finds all the applets in the document */
    public Enumeration getApplets()  {
        class AppletLister implements Enumeration {
            public boolean hasMoreElements() {
                return false;
            }
            public Object nextElement() {
                return null;
            }
        }
        return new AppletLister();
    }

    /** Create an audio clip for the given URL of a .au file */
    public AudioClip getAudioClip(URL u) {
        return null;
    }

    /** Look up and create an Image object that can be paint()ed */
    public Image getImage(URL u)  {
        return null;
    }

    /** Request to overlay the current page with a new one - ignored */
    public void showDocument(URL u) {
    }

    /** as above but with a Frame target */
    public void showDocument(URL u, String frame)  {
    }

    /** Called by the Applet to display a message in the bottom line */
    public void showStatus(String msg) {
        if (msg == null)
            msg = "";
        status.setText(msg);
    }
}
```

It is left as an exercise for the reader to implement getImage( ) and other methods in terms of other recipes used in this book.

## See Also

We have not investigated all the ins and outs of reflection or the ClassLoader mechanism, but I hope I've given you a basic idea of how it works.

Perhaps the most important omissions are SecurityManager and ProtectionDomain. Only one SecurityManager can be installed in a given instance of the JVM (e.g., to prevent a malicious applet from providing its own!). A browser, for example, provides a SecurityManager that is far more restrictive than the standard one. Writing such a SecurityManager is left as an exercise for the reader—an important exercise for anyone planning to load classes over the Internet! (For more information about security managers and the Java Security APIs, see *Java Security* by Scott Oaks.) A ProtectionDomain can be provided with a ClassLoader to specify all the permissions needed for the class to run.

I've also left unexplored some other topics in the JVM; see the O'Reilly books *The Java Virtual Machine* and *The Java Language,* or Sun's JVM Specification document (*http://java.sun.com/docs/books/vmspec/*) for a lifetime of reading enjoyment and edification!

The Apache Software Foundation maintains a variety of useful software packages that are free to get and use. Source code is always available without charge from its web site. Two packages you might want to investigate include the Commons BeanUtils and the Byte Code Engineering Library (BCEL). The Commons BeanUtils, available from *http://jakarta.apache.org/commons/beanutils/*, claims to provide easier-to-use wrappers around some of the Reflection API. BCEL is a third-party toolkit for building and manipulating "bytecode" class files. Written by Markus Dahm, BCEL has become part of the Jakarta Project and is available from *http://jakarta.apache.org/bcel/*.

# CHAPTER 26
# Using Java with Other Languages

## 26.0 Introduction

Java has several methods of running programs written in other languages. You can invoke a compiled program or executable script using Runtime.exec( ), as I'll describe in Recipe 26.1. Or you can drop down to C level with Java's "native code" mechanism and call compiled functions written in C/C++. From there, you can call to functions written in just about any language. Not to mention that you can contact programs written in any language over a socket (see Chapter 17), with HTTP services (see Chapter 18), or with Java clients in RMI or CORBA clients in a variety of languages (see Chapter 22).

There is an element of system dependency here, of course. You can only run Windows applications under Windows and Unix applications under Unix. So some of the recipes in this chapter aren't portable, although in a few cases I try to make them at least run on Windows *or* Unix.

## 26.1 Running a Program

### Problem

You want to run a program.

### Solution

Use one of the exec( ) methods in the java.lang.Runtime class. Or, on JDK 1.5, use the start( ) method of ProcessBuilder.

### Discussion

The exec( ) method in the Runtime class lets you run an external program. The command line you give is broken into strings by a simple StringTokenizer (Recipe 3.2) and passed on to the operating system's "execute a program" system call. As an example, here is a simple program that uses exec( ) to run kwrite, a windowed text editor program.* On Windows, you'd have to change the name to notepad or wordpad, possibly including the full pathname; e.g., *c:/windows/notepad.exe* (you can also use backslashes, but be careful to double them because the backslash is special in Java strings):

```
// file ExecDemoSimple.java
public class ExecDemoSimple {
    public static void main(String av[]) throws java.io.IOException {

        // Run an editor
        Process p = Runtime.getRuntime( ).exec("kwrite");

    }
}
```

When you compile and run it, the appropriate editor window appears:

```
$ jr ExecDemoSimple
+ jikes +E -d . ExecDemoSimple.java
+ java ExecDemoSimple # causes a KWrite window to appear.
$
```

This version of exec( ) assumes that the pathname contains no blanks because these break proper operation of the StringTokenizer. To overcome this potential problem, use an overloaded form of exec( ), taking an array of strings as arguments. Example 26-1 runs the Windows or Unix version of Netscape, assuming Netscape was installed in the default directory. It passes the name of a help file as an argument, offering a kind of primitive help mechanism, as displayed in Figure 26-1.

*Example 26-1. ExecDemoNS.java*

```
import java.awt.*;
import java.awt.event.*;
import javax.swing.*;
import java.io.*;
import java.net.*;
import java.util.*;

import com.darwinsys.util.Debug;

/**
 * ExecDemoNS shows how to execute a program from within Java.
 */
public class ExecDemoNS extends JFrame {
    /** The name of the help file. */
    protected final static String HELPFILE = "./help/index.html";

    /** A stack of process objects; each entry tracks one external running process */
    Stack<Process> pStack = new Stack<Process>( );
```

---

* kwrite is Unix-specific; it's a part of the K Desktop Environment (KDE). See *http://www.kde.org*.

*Example 26-1. ExecDemoNS.java (continued)*

```java
/** main - instantiate and run */
public static void main(String av[]) throws Exception {
    String program = av.length == 0 ? "netscape" : av[0];
    new ExecDemoNS(program).setVisible(true);
}

/** The path to the binary executable that we will run */
protected static String program;

/** Constructor - set up strings and things. */
public ExecDemoNS(String prog) {
    super("ExecDemo: " + prog);
    String osname = System.getProperty("os.name");
    if (osname == null)
        throw new IllegalArgumentException("no os.name");
    if (prog.equals("netscape"))
        program = // Windows or UNIX only for now, sorry Mac fans
            (osname.toLowerCase().indexOf("windows")!=-1) ?
            "c:/program files/netscape/communicator/program/netscape.exe" :
            "/usr/local/netscape/netscape";
    else
        program = prog;

    Container cp = getContentPane();
    cp.setLayout(new FlowLayout());
    JButton b;
    cp.add(b=new JButton("Exec"));
    b.addActionListener(new ActionListener() {
        public void actionPerformed(ActionEvent evt) {
            runProg();
        }
    });
    cp.add(b=new JButton("Wait"));
    b.addActionListener(new ActionListener() {
        public void actionPerformed(ActionEvent evt) {
            doWait();
        }
    });
    cp.add(b=new JButton("Exit"));
    b.addActionListener(new ActionListener() {
        public void actionPerformed(ActionEvent evt) {
            System.exit(0);
        }
    });
    pack();
}

/** Start the help, in its own Thread. */
public void runProg() {

    new Thread() {
        public void run() {
```

*Example 26-1. ExecDemoNS.java (continued)*

```
            try {
                // Get the URL for the Help File
                URL helpURL = this.getClass().getClassLoader().
                    getResource(HELPFILE);

                // Start Netscape from the Java Application.

                pStack.push(Runtime.getRuntime().exec(program + " " + helpURL));

                Debug.println("trace", "In main after exec " + pStack.size());

            } catch (Exception ex) {
                JOptionPane.showMessageDialog(ExecDemoNS.this,
                    "Error" + ex, "Error",
                    JOptionPane.ERROR_MESSAGE);
            }
        }
    }.start();

    }

    public void doWait() {
        if (pStack.size() == 0) return;
        Debug.println("trace", "Waiting for process " + pStack.size());
        try {
            pStack.peek().waitFor();
                // wait for process to complete
                // (does not work as expected for Windows programs)
            Debug.println("trace", "Process " + pStack.size() + " is done");
        } catch (Exception ex) {
            JOptionPane.showMessageDialog(this,
                "Error" + ex, "Error",
                JOptionPane.ERROR_MESSAGE);
        }
        pStack.pop();
    }

}
```

JDK 1.5 includes a new class, ProcesssBuilder, that is designed to replace most nontrivial uses of Runtime.exec(). ProcessBuilder uses the 1.5 Generic Collections discussed in Chapter 8 to let you modify or replace the environment. For details, see the Javadoc for java.lang.ProcessBuilder.

# 26.2  Running a Program and Capturing Its Output

## Problem

You want to run a program but also capture its output.

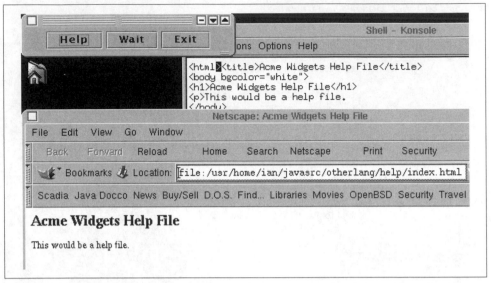

*Figure 26-1. ExecDemoNS in action*

## Solution

Use the `Process` object's `getInputStream( )`; read and copy the contents to `System.out` or wherever you want them.

## Discussion

A program's standard and error output does not automatically appear anywhere. Arguably, there should be an automatic way to make this happen. But for now, you need to add a few lines of code to grab the program's output and print it:

```
// part of ExecDemoLs.java
p = Runtime.getRuntime( ).exec(PROGRAM);

// getInputStream gives an Input stream connected to
// the process p's standard output (and vice versa). We use
// that to construct a BufferedReader so we can readLine( ) it.
BufferedReader is =
    new BufferedReader(new InputStreamReader(p.getInputStream( )));

while ((line = is.readLine( )) != null)
    System.out.println(line);
```

This is such a common occurrence that I've packaged it up into a class called `ExecAndPrint`, which is part of my package `com.darwinsys.lang`. `ExecAndPrint` has several overloaded forms of its `run( )` method (see the documentation for details), but they all take at least a command and optionally an output file to which the command's output is written. Example 26-2 shows the code for some of these methods.

*Example 26-2. ExecAndPrint.java (partial listing)*

```
/** Need a Runtime object for any of these methods */
protected static Runtime r = Runtime.getRuntime( );

/** Run the command given as a String, printing its output to System.out */
public static int run(String cmd) throws IOException {
    return run(cmd, new OutputStreamWriter(System.out));
}

/** Run the command given as a String, print its output to "out" */
public static int run(String cmd, Writer out) throws IOException {

    String line;

    Process p = r.exec(cmd);

    FileIO.copyFile(new InputStreamReader(p.getInputStream( )), out, true);
    try {
        p.waitFor( );      // wait for process to complete
    } catch (InterruptedException e) {
        return -1;
    }
    return p.exitValue( );
}
```

As a simple example of using exec( ) directly along with ExecAndPrint, I'll create three temporary files, list them (directory listing), and then delete them. When I run the ExecDemoFiles program, it lists the three files it has created:

```
-rw------- 1 ian  wheel  0 Jan 29 14:29 file1
-rw------- 1 ian  wheel  0 Jan 29 14:29 file2
-rw------- 1 ian  wheel  0 Jan 29 14:29 file3
```

Its source code is in Example 26-3.

*Example 26-3. ExecDemoFiles.java*

```
// Get and save the Runtime object.
Runtime rt = Runtime.getRuntime( );

// Create three temporary files
Process p = rt.exec("mktemp file1"); p.waitFor( );
p = rt.exec("mktemp file2"); p.waitFor( );
p = rt.exec("mktemp file3"); p.waitFor( );

// Run the "ls" (directory lister) program
// with its output printed back to us.
String[] args = { "ls", "-l", "file1", "file2", "file3" };
ExecAndPrint.run(args);

rt.exec("rm file1 file2 file3");
```

A process isn't necessarily destroyed when the Java program that created it exits or bombs out. Simple text-based programs will be, but window-based programs like kwrite, Netscape, or even a Java-based JFrame application will not. For example, our ExecDemoNS program started Netscape, and when ExecDemoNS' Exit button is pressed, ExecDemoNS exits but Netscape stays running. What if you want to be sure a process has completed? The Process object has a waitFor( ) method that lets you do so, and an exitValue( ) method that tells you the "return code" from the process. Finally, should you wish to forcibly terminate the other process, you can do so with the Process object's destroy( ) method, which takes no argument and returns no value. Example 26-4 is ExecDemoWait, a program that runs whatever program you name on the command line (along with arguments), captures the program's standard output, and waits for the program to terminate.

*Example 26-4. ExecDemoWait.java*

```
// A Runtime object has methods for dealing with the OS
Runtime r = Runtime.getRuntime( );
Process p;                    // Process tracks one external native process
BufferedReader is;     // reader for output of process
String line;

// Our argv[0] contains the program to run; remaining elements
// of argv contain args for the target program. This is just
// what is needed for the String[] form of exec.
p = r.exec(argv);

System.out.println("In Main after exec");

// getInputStream gives an Input stream connected to
// the process p's standard output. Just use it to make
// a BufferedReader to readLine( ) what the program writes out.
is = new BufferedReader(new InputStreamReader(p.getInputStream( )));

while ((line = is.readLine( )) != null)
    System.out.println(line);

System.out.println("In Main after EOF");
try {
    p.waitFor( );     // wait for process to complete
} catch (InterruptedException e) {
    return;
}
System.err.println("Process done, exit status was " + p.exitValue( ));
return;
```

## See Also

You wouldn't normally use any form of exec( ) to run one Java program from another in this way; instead, you'd probably create it as a thread within the same process, since this is generally quite a bit faster (the Java interpreter is already up and running, so why wait for another copy of it to start up?). See Chapter 24.

When building industrial-strength applications, note the cautionary remarks in the Java API docs for the Process class concerning the danger of losing some of the I/O due to insufficient buffering by the operating system.

# 26.3   Mixing Java and Scripts with BSF

## Problem

You want to interface Java components to an existing scripting language.

## Solution

Use the Bean Scripting Framework (BSF).

## Discussion

Many scripting languages are used in the computing field today: VB, Perl, Python, JavaScript, Tcl/TK, REXX, and others. A project that originated at IBM but has now been taken over by the Apache Foundation, the Bean Scripting Framework (BSF), aims to provide a way to allow a number of scripting languages to interoperate with Java.

The BSF consists of a management API, an engine API for driving different scripting languages, and a series of plug-ins for different scripting languages. The management API lets you either evaluate an expression in the given scripting language, such as "2+2" (which is so simple as to be valid in most supported languages), or run a script stored in a script file. In this example, I'll use Jython, a pure-Java (certified) implementation of the scripting language Python (see *http://www.python.org* and *http://www.jython.org* or the O'Reilly book *Learning Python*).

While it is convenient (and efficient) to run Jython in the same JVM as the calling program, this is not by any means a requirement; for example, it is possible to use BSF with scripting languages written in some native language. BSF and the scripting plug-in are responsible for dealing with whatever "plumbing"—external connections or processes—this requires. Among others, BSF currently supports the languages listed in Table 26-1.

*Table 26-1. Some languages supported by BSF*

| Language | Description |
| --- | --- |
| Jython | Java implementation of Python |
| Jacl | Java implementation/interface for Tcl |
| Xalan (LotusXSL) | XML stylesheets (see Recipe 21.2) |
| NetRexx | REXX variant |
| Mozilla | JavaScript implementation |
| Pnuts | Scripting language for accessing Java APIs |
| JScript, VBScript, PerlScript | Windows scripting languages |

BSF could also support Mac OS Apple Scripting or almost any other language, although I don't know of an implementation at present.

Example 26-5 uses Jython to evaluate and print the value of 22/7, a crude but time-honored approximation of Math.PI, using the management API's eval( ) function. The imports assume you are using BSF 2.3; prior to this, the namespace of com.ibm was used instead of org.apache.

*Example 26-5. BSFSample.java*

```
import org.apache.bsf.util.*;
import org.apache.bsf.*;
import java.io.*;

/** Sample of using Bean Scripting Framework with Jython */
public class BSFSample {
    public static void main(String[] args) {
        BSFManager manager = new BSFManager();

        // register scripting language
        String[] fntypes = { ".py" };
        manager.registerScriptingEngine("jython",
            "com.ibm.bsf.engines.jython.JythonEngine", fntypes);

        try {
            // try an expression
            Object r = manager.eval("jython", "testString", 0, 0, "22.0/7");
            System.out.println("Result type is " + r.getClass().getName());
            System.out.println("Result value is " + r);
        } catch (Exception ex) {
            System.err.println(ex.toString());
        }
        System.out.println("Scripting demo done.");
        return;
    }
}
```

This program prints the following output:

```
$ java BSFSample
'import exceptions' failed; using string-based exceptions
Result type is org.python.core.PyFloat
Result value is 3.142857142857143
Scripting demo done.
$
```

The exceptions failure is probably due to my having installed Jython in a nonstandard location and not setting the environment variable(s) needed to find it. Further, the first time you run it, Jython spits out a bunch of nattering about your CLASS-PATH, one line for each JAR file that it finds. These can be a bit surprising when they pop up from a script, but Jython doesn't seem to know or care whether it's being run interactively or dynamically:

```
packageManager: processing new jar, "/usr/local/java/swingall.jar"
```

The following longer example uses the LabelText bean from Recipe 23.8 and a push button to run a Python script that collects the text from the LabelText instance and displays it on the standard output. Here is the little script, *buttonhandler.py*:

```
print "Hello";
print bean.getText( );
```

When I ran this, I typed the famous words that Alexander Graham Bell apparently sent to his assistant Watson and had the Java program send them to the Python script.

Sure enough, when I clicked on the button, I got this on the standard output (as shown in Figure 26-2):

```
Script output: -->
Hello
Mr. Watson, come here
<-- End of Script output.
```

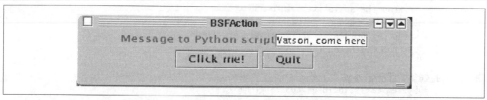

*Figure 26-2. BSFSample in action*

Nothing you couldn't do in Java, of course, but in this example, the LabelText bean is registered with the BSF as a bean, and the JButton's action handler runs a script that gets that text and displays it. Example 26-6 shows the source code for the script-using program.

*Example 26-6. BSFAction.java*

```
import org.apache.bsf.util.*;
import org.apache.bsf.*;
import javax.swing.*;
import java.awt.*;
import java.awt.event.*;
import java.io.*;

/** Longer sample of using Bean Scripting Framework with Jython */
public class BSFAction {
    protected String FILENAME = "buttonhandler.py";
    protected BSFManager manager;
    protected BSFEngine jythonengine;
    protected String language;
    protected String script;

    public static void main(String[] args) {
        new BSFAction( );
    }
```

*Example 26-6. BSFAction.java (continued)*

```
    BSFAction( ) {

        // Construct the Bean instance
        LabelText bean = new LabelText("Message to Python script");

        try {
            manager = new BSFManager( );

            // register scripting language
            String[] fntypes = { ".py" };
            manager.registerScriptingEngine("jython",
                "com.ibm.bsf.engines.jython.JythonEngine", fntypes);
            jythonengine = manager.loadScriptingEngine("jython");

            // Tell BSF about the bean.
            manager.declareBean("bean", bean, LabelText.class);

            // Read the script file into BSF
            language = manager.getLangFromFilename(FILENAME);
            script = IOUtils.getStringFromReader(
                new FileReader(FILENAME));

        } catch (Exception ex) {
            System.err.println(ex.toString( ));
            System.exit(0);
        }

        System.out.println("Scripting setup done, building GUI.");

        final JFrame jf = new JFrame(getClass( ).getName( ));

        Container cp = jf.getContentPane( );
        cp.setLayout(new FlowLayout( ));

        cp.add(bean);                   // add the LabelText

        JButton b = new JButton("Click me!");
        cp.add(b);                      // and the button under it.
        b.addActionListener(new ActionListener( ) {
            public void actionPerformed(ActionEvent evt) {
                try {

                    // When the button is pressed, run the script.
                    System.out.println("Script output: -->");
                    manager.exec(language, FILENAME, 0, 0, script);
                    System.out.println("<-- End of Script output.");
                } catch (BSFException bse) {
                    JOptionPane.showMessageDialog(jf,
                        "ERROR: " + bse, "Script Error",
                        JOptionPane.ERROR_MESSAGE);
                }
            }
        });
```

*Example 26-6. BSFAction.java (continued)*

```java
        // A Quit button at the bottom
        JButton qb = new JButton("Quit");
        cp.add(qb);
        qb.addActionListener(new ActionListener() {
            public void actionPerformed(ActionEvent evt) {
                System.exit(0);
            }
        });

        // Routine JFrame setup
        jf.pack( );
        jf.setVisible(true);
    }
}
```

## See Also

Information on the Bean Scripting Framework is located at the Jakarta Project's web site at *http://jakarta.apache.org/bsf/*.

Many other projects aim to blend Java with other languages. As a single example, check out the Omega Project's interface at *http://www.omegahat.org/RSJava/*. R, itself a clone of S, is the statistical package used to produce the charts back in Figure 5-1. This interface lets you use Java inside R or S and to call R or S from Java code.

# 26.4 Marrying Java and Perl

## Problem

You want to make use of your existing Perl code base from a Java application, or vice versa.

## Solution

Use the Perl `Inline::Java` module.

## Discussion

Perl is often called a "glue language" that can be used to bring together diverse parts of the software world. But, in addition, it is a full-blown language in its own right for creating software. A wealth of extension modules provide ready-to-run solutions for quite diverse problems, and most of these modules are available for free from CPAN, the Comprehensive Perl Archive Network (*http://www.cpan.org/*). Also, as a scripting language, it is ideally suited for rapid prototyping. On the other hand, while building graphical user interfaces is definitely possible in Perl, it is not exactly one of the language's strengths. So you might want to construct your GUI using Java Swing, and, at the same time, reuse business logic implemented in Perl.

Fortunately, among the many CPAN modules, Inline::Java makes the integration of Perl and Java a breeze. Let's assume first that you want to call into Java from Perl. For business logic, I have picked a CPAN module that measures the similarity of two strings (the so-called *Levenshtein edit distance*). Example 26-7 shows the complete source. You need at least Version 0.44 of the module Inline::Java; previous versions did not support threaded applications properly, so use of Swing wasn't possible.

*Example 26-7. Swinging.pl*

```perl
#! /usr/bin/perl
# Calling Java from Perl, and back again

use strict;
use warnings;

use Text::Levenshtein qw( );
  # Perl module from CPAN to measure string similarity

use Inline 0.44 "JAVA" => "DATA";  # pointer to the Inline java source
use Inline::Java qw(caught);  # helper function to determine exception type

my $show = new Showit;     # construct Java object using Perl syntax
$show->show("Just another Perl hacker");              # call method on that object

eval {
  # Call a method that will call back to Perl;
  # catch exceptions, if any.
  print "matcher: ", $show->match("Japh", shift||"Java"), " (displayed from Perl)\n";
};
if ($@) {
  print STDERR "Caught:", caught($@), "\n";
  die $@ unless caught("java.lang.Exception");
  print STDERR $@->getMessage( ), "\n";
}

__END__

__JAVA__
// Java starts here
import javax.swing.*;
import org.perl.inline.java.*;

class Showit extends InlineJavaPerlCaller {
  // extension only neeeded if calling back into Perl

  /** Simple Java class to be called from Perl, and to call back to Perl
   */
  public Showit() throws InlineJavaException { }

  /** Simple method */
  public void show(String str) {
    System.out.println(str + " inside Java");
  }
```

*Example 26-7. Swinging.pl (continued)*

```
/** Method calling back into Perl */
public int match(String target, String pattern)
    throws InlineJavaException, InlineJavaPerlException {

    // Calling a function residing in a Perl Module
    String str = (String)CallPerl("Text::Levenshtein", "distance",
        new Object [] {target, pattern});

    // Show result
    JOptionPane.showMessageDialog(null, "Edit distance between '" + target +
        "' and '" + pattern + "' is " + str,
        "Swinging Perl", JOptionPane.INFORMATION_MESSAGE);
    return Integer.parseInt(str);
}

}
```

In simple cases like this, you don't even need to write a separate Java source file: you combine all the code, Perl and Java alike, in one single file. You do not need to compile anything, either; just execute it by typing:

```
perl Swinging.pl
```

(You can also add a string argument.) After a little churning, a Java message box pops up, telling you that the distance between "Japh" and "Java" is 2. At the same time, your console shows the string "Just another Perl hacker inside Java." When you close the message box, you get the final result "matcher: 2 (displayed from Perl)."

In between, your Perl program has created an instance of the Java class Showit by calling its constructor. It then called that object's show( ) method to display a string from within Java. It then proceeded to call the match( ) method, but this time, something more complicated happens: the Java code calls back into Perl, accessing method distance of module Text::Levenshtein and passing it two strings as arguments. It receives the result, displays it in a message box, and finally, for good measure, returns it to the Perl main program that it had been called from.

Incidentally, the eval { } block around the method call is the Perlish way of catching exceptions. In this case, the exception is thrown from within Java.

If you restart the program, you will notice that startup time is much shorter, which is always good news. Why is that so? On the first call, Inline::Java took the input apart, precompiled the Java part, and saved it to disk (usually, in a subdirectory called *_Inline*). On subsequent calls, it just makes sure that the Java source has not changed and then calls the class file that is already on disk. (Of course, if you surreptitiously changed the Java code, it is recompiled just as automagically.) Behind the scenes, even stranger things are going on, however. When the Perl script is executed, a Java server is constructed and started unbeknownst to the user, and the Perl part and the Java bits communicate through a TCP socket (see Chapter 17).

Let's look at the other way around now: you conceive of your Java code as the "main program," and you want to call some Perl code. As the Perl folks have it, "TMTOWTDI" (for the uninitiated: "There's more than one way to do it"), but I think it is easiest to actually start from Perl, using a very simple stub that, besides supplying all the Perl business logic you need, basically just starts up your Java code and hands control over to Java.

*StringDistance.java* is a fairly short Swing application that displays the dialog shown in Figure 26-3.

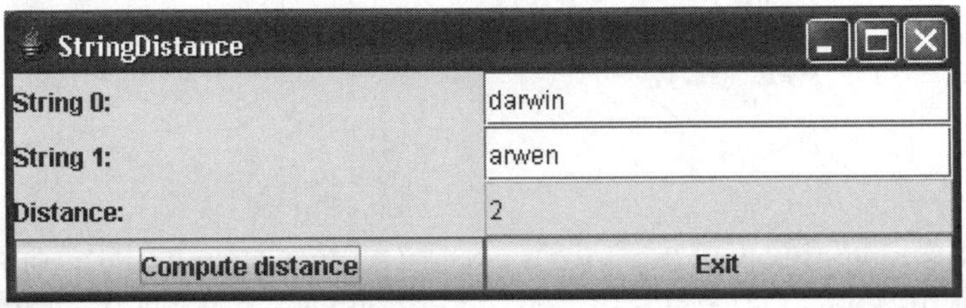

*Figure 26-3. StringDistance.java/.pl in action*

The full source is included online; Example 26-8 shows just the essential part that deals with Perl. This time, since it is a separate source file, you have to compile it yourself.

*Example 26-8. StringDistance.java (extract)*

```
// requires classpath to include InlineJavaServer.jar; usually something like
// .;<perldir>/site/lib/Inline/Java/InlineJavaServer.jar
public class StringDistance extends InlineJavaPerlCaller {
  JFrame frame;          // visual container
  JTextField tf[], dist;  // text input fields, result output field
  JButton go, exit;      // action buttons

  /* The constructor with possibly 2 initial strings */
  public StringDistance(String[] strs) throws InlineJavaException {
    // omitted from printed version
  }
  /** The central interface function to Perl. */
  public int match(String s0, String s1) {
    try {
      String str = (String)CallPerl("Text::Levenshtein", "distance",
                                     new Object [] {s0, s1});
      return Integer.parseInt(str);
    } catch (InlineJavaPerlException e) {
      System.err.println("Inline Java Perl Exception: " + e);
    } catch (InlineJavaException e) {
      System.err.println("Inline Java Exception: " + e);
    }
    return 0;
  }
}
```

Example 26-9 shows the full Perl code that is needed for getting things running—just 12 lines of code.

*Example 26-9. StringDistance.pl*

```perl
#! /usr/bin/perl
# Perl main program acting as a stub for callbacks from Java

use strict;
use warnings;

# all modules called from either Perl or from Java must go here:
use Text::Levenshtein qw();

use Inline "Java"  => "STUDY",          # glean interface from Java class file
           "AUTOSTUDY" => 1,            # glean more interfaces, too, just in case
           "STUDY" => ["StringDistance"], # name of our main Java class
           "CLASSPATH" => ".",          # needed in order to find main Java class
           ;

my $sd = StringDistance->new(\@ARGV);   # construct instance of main Java class
$sd->show();                            # call routine to show it
$sd->StartCallbackLoop();               # prepare to listen for threaded callbacks
```

Marrying two platform-independent languages, like Perl and Java, in a portable way skirts many portability problems. When distributing inlined applications, be sure to supply not just the source files but also the contents of the *_Inline* directory. (It is advisable to purge that directory and to rebuild everything just before distribution time; otherwise, old compiled versions left lying around might make it into the distribution.) Each target machine needs to repeat the magic steps of Inline::Java, which requires a Java compiler. In any case, the Inline::Java module must be installed.

Since Perl has Inline modules for a number of other languages (ordinary languages like C, but others as exotic as Befunge), one might even consider using Perl as glue for interoperation between those other languages, jointly or separately, and Java. I am sure many happy hours can be spent working out the intricacies of such interactions.

## See Also

Full information on Inline::Java can be found on CPAN (*http://search.cpan.org/*) or in the POD (plain old documentation) that is installed along with the module itself.

# 26.5  Blending in Native Code (C/C++)

## Problem

You wish to call native C/C++ functions from Java, either for efficiency or to access hardware- or system-specific features.

## Solution

Use JNI, the Java Native Interface.

## Discussion

Java lets you load *native* or compiled code into your Java program. Why would you want to do such a thing? One reason might be to access OS-dependent functionality. Another is speed: native code will likely run faster than Java, at least at present. Like everything else in Java, this mechanism is subject to security restrictions; for example, applets are not allowed to access native code.

The native code language bindings are defined for code that has been written in C or C++. If you need to access a language other than C/C++, write a bit of C/C++ and have it pass control to other functions or applications, using any mechanism defined by your operating system.

Due to such system-dependent features as the interpretation of header files and the allocation of the processor's general-purpose registers, your native code may need to be compiled by the same C compiler used to compile the Java runtime for your platform. For example, on Solaris you can use SunPro C or maybe gcc. On Win32 platforms, use Microsoft Visual C++ Version 4.x or higher (32 bit). For Linux and Mac OS X, you should be able to use the provided gcc-based compiler. For other platforms, see your Java vendor's documentation.

Also note that the details in this section are for the Java Native Interface (JNI) of Java 1.1 and later, which differs in some details from 1.0 and from Microsoft's native interface.

The steps to call native code are summarized in the following sidebar and detailed below.

---

### Ian's Basic Steps: Java Calling Native Code

To call native code from Java:

1. Write Java code that calls a native method.
2. Compile this Java code.
3. Create an .h file using *javah*.
4. Write a C function that does the work.
5. Compile the C code into a loadable object.
6. Try it!

---

The first step is to write Java code that calls a native method. To do this, use the keyword native to indicate that the method is native, and provide a static code block that loads your native method using System.loadLibrary( ). (The dynamically loadable module is created in Step 5.) Static blocks are executed when the class containing them is loaded; loading the native code here ensures it is in memory when needed!

Object variables that your native code may modify should carry the volatile modifier. The file *HelloWorld.java*, shown in Example 26-10, is a good starting point.

*Example 26-10. HelloWorld.java*

```
/**
 * A trivial class to show Java Native Interface 1.1 usage from Java.
 */
public class HelloWorld {
    int myNumber = 42;          // used to show argument passing

    // declare native class
    public native void displayHelloWorld( );

    // Application main, call its display method
    public static void main(String[] args) {
        HelloWorld hw = new HelloWorld( );
        hw.displayHelloWorld( );        // call the native function
        System.out.println("Back in Java, \"myNumber\" now " + hw.myNumber);
    }

    // Static code blocks are executed once, when class file is loaded
    static {
        System.loadLibrary("hello");
    }
}
```

The second step is simple; just use *javac HelloWorld.java* as you normally would. You probably won't get any compilation errors on a simple program like this; if you do, correct them and try the compilation again.

Next, you need to create an *.h* file. Use *javah* to produce this file:

**javah HelloWorld**          // produces HelloWorld.h

The *.h* file produced is a "glue" file, not really meant for human consumption and particularly not for editing. But by inspecting the resulting *.h* file, you'll see that the C method's name is composed of the name Java, the package name (if any), the class name, and the method name:

```
JNIEXPORT void JNICALL Java_HelloWorld_displayHelloWorld(JNIEnv *env,
    jobject this);
```

Then create a C function that does the work. You must use the same function signature as is used in the *.h* file.

This function can do whatever it wishes. Note that it is passed two arguments: a JVM environment variable and a handle for the this object. Table 26-2 shows the correspondence between Java types and the C types (JNI types) used in the C code.

*Table 26-2. Java and JNI types*

| Java type | JNI | Java array type | JNI |
|-----------|-----|-----------------|-----|
| byte | jbyte | byte[] | jbyteArray |
| short | jshort | short[] | jshortArray |
| int | jint | int[] | jintArray |
| long | jlong | long[] | jlongArray |
| float | jfloat | float[] | jfloatArray |
| double | jdouble | double[] | jdoubleArray |
| char | jchar | char[] | jcharArray |
| boolean | jboolean | boolean[] | jbooleanArray |
| void | jvoid | | |
| Object | jobject | Object[] | jobjectArray |
| Class | jclass | | |
| String | jstring | | |
| array | jarray | | |
| Throwable | jthrowable | | |

Example 26-11 is a complete C native implementation. Passed an object of type HelloWorld, it increments the integer myNumber contained in the object.

*Example 26-11. HelloWorld.c*

```c
#include <jni.h>
#include "HelloWorld.h"
#include <stdio.h>

/*
 * This is the 1.1 implementation of displayHelloWorld.
 */
JNIEXPORT void JNICALL Java_HelloWorld_displayHelloWorld(JNIEnv *env, jobject this)
{
    jfieldID fldid;
    jint n, nn;

    (void)printf("Hello from a Native Method\n");

    if (this == NULL) {
        fprintf(stderr, "Input pointer is null!\n");
        return;
    }
    if ((fldid = (*env)->GetFieldID(env,
        (*env)->GetObjectClass(env, this), "myNumber", "I")) == NULL) {
        fprintf(stderr, "GetFieldID failed");
```

*Example 26-11. HelloWorld.c (continued)*

```
        return;
    }

    n = (*env)->GetIntField(env, this, fldid);     /* retrieve myNumber */
    printf("\"myNumber\" value is %d\n", n);

    (*env)->SetIntField(env, this, fldid, ++n);     /* increment it! */
    nn = (*env)->GetIntField(env, this, fldid);

    printf("\"myNumber\" value now %d\n", nn);           /* make sure */
    return;
}
```

Finally, you compile the C code into a loadable object. Naturally, the details depend on platform, compiler, etc. For example, on Windows:

```
> set JAVA_HOME=C:\java                  # or wherever
> set INCLUDE=%JAVA_HOME%\include;%JAVA_HOME%\include\Win32;%INCLUDE%
> set LIB=%JAVA_HOME%\lib;%LIB%
> cl HelloWorld.c -Fehello.dll -MD -LD
```

And on Unix:

```
$ export JAVAHOME=/local/java    # or wherever
$ cc -I$JAVAHOME/include -I$JAVAHOME/include/solaris \
-G HelloWorld.c -o libhello.so
```

Example 26-12 is a makefile for Unix.

*Example 26-12. Unix makefile*

```
# Makefile for the Java Native Methods examples for
# Learning Tree International Course 471/478.
# Has been tested on Solaris both with "gcc" and with SunSoft "cc".
# On other platforms it will certainly need some tweaking; please
# let me know how much! :-)

# Configuration Section

CSRCS       = HelloWorld.c
JAVAHOME    = /local/jdk1.1.2
INCLUDES    = -I$(JAVAHOME)/include -I$(JAVAHOME)/include/solaris

all:        testhello testjavafromc

# This part of the Makefile is for C called from Java, in HelloWorld
testhello:       hello.all
        @echo
        @echo "Here we test the Java code \"HelloWorld\" that calls C code."
        @echo
        LD_LIBRARY_PATH='pwd':. java HelloWorld

hello.all:       HelloWorld.class libhello.so
```

*Example 26-12. Unix makefile (continued)*

```
HelloWorld.class: HelloWorld.java
        javac HelloWorld.java

HelloWorld.h:    HelloWorld.class
        javah -jni HelloWorld

HelloWorld.o::    HelloWorld.h

libhello.so:    $(CSRCS) HelloWorld.h
    $(CC) $(INCLUDES) -G $(CSRCS) -o libhello.so

# This part of the Makefile is for Java called from C, in javafromc
testjavafromc:    javafromc.all hello.all
    @echo
    @echo "Now we test HelloWorld using javafromc instead of java"
    @echo
    ./javafromc HelloWorld
    @echo
    @echo "That was, in case you didn't notice, C->Java->C. And,"
    @echo "incidentally, a replacement for JDK program \"java\" itself!"
    @echo

javafromc.all:    javafromc

javafromc:    javafromc.o
    $(CC) -L$(LIBDIR) javafromc.o -ljava -o $@

javafromc.o:    javafromc.c
    $(CC) -c $(INCLUDES) javafromc.c

clean:
    rm -f core *.class *.o *.so HelloWorld.h
clobber: clean
    rm -f javafromc
```

And you're done! Just run the Java interpreter on the class file containing the main program. Assuming that you've set whatever system-dependent settings are necessary (possibly including both CLASSPATH and LD_LIBRARY_PATH or its equivalent), the program should run as follows:

```
C> java HelloWorld
Hello from a Native Method        // from C
"myNumber" value is 42            // from C
"myNumber" value now 43          // from C
Value of myNumber now 43         // from Java
```

Congratulations! You've called a native method. However, you've given up portability; the Java class file now requires you to build a loadable object for each operating system and hardware platform. Multiply {Windows NT, 2000, XP, and 2003, Mac OS X, Sun Solaris, HP/UX, Linux, OpenBSD, NetBSD, FreeBSD} times {Intel, Intel-64, AMD64, SPARC, PowerPC, HP-PA} and you begin to see the portability issues.

Also note that native code can be used in server code and desktop applications but is normally not permitted in web browsers.

Beware that problems with your native code can and will crash the runtime process right out from underneath the Java Virtual Machine. The JVM can do nothing to protect itself from poorly written C/C++ code. Memory must be managed by the programmer; there is no automatic garbage collection of memory obtained by the system runtime allocator. You're dealing directly with the operating system and sometimes even the hardware, so, "Be careful. Be very careful."

## See Also

If you need more information on Java Native Methods, you might be interested in the comprehensive treatment found in *Essential JNI: Java Native Interface* by Rob Gordon (Prentice Hall).

# 26.6   Calling Java from Native Code

## Problem

You need to go the other way, calling Java from C/C++ code.

## Solution

Use JNI again.

## Discussion

Starting from 1.1, JNI provides an interface for calling Java from C, with calls to:

1.  Create a JVM
2.  Load a class
3.  Find and call a method from that class (e.g., main)

JNI lets you add Java to legacy code. That can be useful for a variety of purposes and lets you treat Java code as an extension language (just define or find an interface or class like Applet or Servlet, and let your customers implement it or subclass it).

# 26.7   Program: DBM

This program lets you use the original Unix DBM (database access method) routines from Java. DBM is actually emulated using the newer Berkeley Database (DB) routines, but the DBM interface is more traditional and simpler. DBM was used in Recipe 20.3 to provide a name-to-login database, which is similar to how many modern Unixes actually store name and password information. That recipe also showed how to use it to display your Netscape history, even under Windows.

I'll now show the Java version of the DBM library, *DBM.java*, in Example 26-13. To compile it, you need the DBM routines installed.

*Example 26-13. DBM.java*

```java
import java.io.*;

/** This class provides a dbm-compatible interface to the Unix-style
 * database access methods described in dbm(3) (which is on some Unixes
 * a front-end to db(3)).
 * <p>Each unique record in the database is a unique key/value pair,
 * similar to a java.util.Hashtable but stored on a persistent medium, not
 * kept in memory. Dbm was originally optimized for Unix for fast
 * access to individual key/value pairs.</p>
 */
public class DBM {
    /** Since you can only have one DBM database in use at a time due
     * to implementation restrictions, we enforce this rule with a
     * class-wide boolean.
     */
    protected static boolean inuse = false;

    /** Save the filename for messages, etc. */
    protected String fileName;

    /** Construct a DBM given its filename */
    public DBM(String file) {
        synchronized(this) {
            if (inuse)
                throw new IllegalArgumentException(
                    "Only one DBM object at a time per Java Machine");
            inuse = true;
        }
        fileName = file;
        int retCode = dbminit(fileName);
        if (retCode < 0)
            throw new IllegalArgumentException(
                "dbminit failed, code = " + retCode);
    }

    // Static code blocks are executed once, when class file is loaded.
    // This is here to ensure that the shared library gets loaded.
    static {
        System.loadLibrary("jdbm");
    }

    protected ByteArrayOutputStream bo;

    /** serialize an Object to byte array. */
    protected byte[] toByteArray(Object o) throws IOException {
        if (bo == null)
            bo = new ByteArrayOutputStream(1024);
        bo.reset();
```

*Example 26-13. DBM.java (continued)*

```java
        ObjectOutputStream os = new ObjectOutputStream(bo);
        os.writeObject(o);
        os.close();
        return bo.toByteArray();
    }

    /** un-serialize an Object from a byte array. */
    protected Object toObject(byte[] b) throws IOException {
        Object o;

        ByteArrayInputStream bi = new ByteArrayInputStream(b);
        ObjectInputStream os = new ObjectInputStream(bi);
        try {
            o = os.readObject();
        } catch (ClassNotFoundException ex) {
            // Convert ClassNotFoundException to I/O error
            throw new IOException(ex.getMessage());
        }
        os.close();
        return o;
    }

    protected native int dbminit(String file);

    protected native int dbmclose();

    /** Public wrapper for close method. */
    public void close() {
        this.dbmclose();
        inuse = false;
    }

    protected void checkInUse() {
        if (!inuse)
            throw new IllegalStateException("Method called when DBM not open");
    }

    protected native byte[] dbmfetch(byte[] key);

    /** Fetch using byte arrays */
    public byte[] fetch(byte[] key) throws IOException {
        checkInUse();
        return dbmfetch(key);
    }

    /** Fetch using Objects */
    public Object fetch(Object key) throws IOException {
        checkInUse();
        byte[] datum = dbmfetch(toByteArray(key));
        return toObject(datum);
    }
```

*Example 26-13. DBM.java (continued)*

```java
    protected native int dbmstore(byte[] key, byte[] content);

    /** Store using byte arrays */
    public void store(byte[] key, byte[] value) throws IOException {
        checkInUse();
        dbmstore(key, value);
    }

    /** Store using Objects */
    public void store(Object key, Object value) throws IOException {
        checkInUse();
        dbmstore(toByteArray(key), toByteArray(value));
    }

    protected native int delete(Object key);

    public native byte[] firstkey() throws IOException;

    public Object firstkeyObject() throws IOException {
        return toObject(firstkey());
    }

    public native byte[] nextkey(byte[] key) throws IOException;

    public Object nextkey(Object key) throws IOException {
        byte[] ba = nextkey(toByteArray(key));
        if (ba == null)
            return null;
        return toObject(ba);
    }

    public String toString() {
        return "DBM@" + hashCode() + "[" + fileName + "]";
    }
}
```

Notice how the methods toByteArray() and toObject(), the inverses of each other, convert between an object and an array of bytes using ByteArrayStreams. These provide the functionality of reading from or writing to a buffer that is in memory, instead of the usual buffer that has been read from or written to a disk file or socket.

## See Also

A more complete and widely used implementation of DBM for Java is available from SleepyCat Software, the heirs-apparent to the Berkeley DBM software. Their Sleepy-Cat DBM can be downloaded for free, in source form, under the Berkeley (University of California at Berkeley) software license. Check out *http://www.sleepycat.com*.

# Afterword

Writing this book has been a humbling experience. It has taken far longer than I had predicted, or than I would like to admit. And, of course, it's not finished yet. Despite my best efforts and those of the technical reviewers, editors, and many other talented folks, a book this size is bound to contain errors, omissions, and passages that are less clear than they might be. Please, let us know by email if you happen across any of these things. Subsequent editions will incorporate changes sent in by readers just like you!

It has been said that you don't really know something until you've taught it. I have found this true of lecturing, and find it equally true of writing.

I tell my students that when Java was very young, it was possible for one person to study hard and know almost everything about Java. When JDK 1.1 came out, this was no longer true. Today, anybody who tells you they "know all about Java" should cause your "bogosity" detector to go off at full volume. And the amount you need to know keeps growing. How can you keep up? Java books? Java magazines? Java courses? Conferences? There is no single answer; all of these are useful to some people. Sun's Java software division has several programs that you should be aware of:

- JavaOne, Sun's annual conference (*http://java.sun.com/javaone/*)
- The Java Developer Connection, a free web-based service for getting the latest APIs, news, and views (*http://developer.java.sun.com*)
- The Java Community Process (*http://jcp.org*), the home of open Java standardization and enhancement
- Java Developer Essentials, a fee-based CD-ROM subscription to all the Java APIS, tools, and other material (*http://www.sun.com/developers/tools/*)
- O'Reilly books (*http://java.oreilly.com*) and conferences (*http://conferences.oreilly.com*)—among the very best available!

As you know, the Java API is divided into packages. A package is normally considered "core" if its package name begins with java, and an optional extension if its package name begins with javax. But there are already exceptions to that rule, such as javax.swing.*, which is core.

As you can see, there is no end of Java APIs to learn about. And there are still more books to be written...and read.

# Index

## Symbols

( ) (parentheses), capture groups in regular
    expressions, 98
< and > (angle brackets)
    <? ... ?>, in XML processing
        instructions, 616
    > (greater than) operator, 166
    < (less than) operator, 166
    around HTML tags, 502
    around XML tags, 616
* (asterisk), use in regular expressions, 97
@ (at sign)
    annotations and, 659
    in doc comments, 654
    XDoclet reading of tags in source
        code, 658
\ (backslash)
    continuing lines with, 275
    escaping metacharacters in regular
        expressions, 92
    operating systems, differences in use, 40
    root directory, Microsoft platforms, 308
    string escapes, using in, 73
: (colon)
    after properties file key
        names/values, 188
    differences in use on operating
        systems, 40
- (dash)
    command arguments, use in, 43
    Unix option delimiter, 40
$ (dollar sign)
    end-of-line regex pattern matching, 107
    format codes, use in, 254

. (dot)
    .* in regular expression pattern
        matching, 97
    regular expressions, matching any regular
        character or the newline, 105
. (dot) commands, formatting control
    with, 82
– (equal sign)
    == (equals) operator, 166, 225
    after property file key names/values, 188
^ in beginning-of-line regex pattern
    matching, 91, 107
# or !, beginning comment lines in properties
    file, 188
% (percent sign), use in format codes, 254
+ (plus sign)
    +– (assignment) operator, 240
    ++ (increment) operator, 239
    +? non-greedy regex quantifier, 109
    +E option, Jikes compiler, 2
    multiplier or quantifier in regular
        expressions, 92
    string concatenation operator, 56
/ (slash)
    //+ and //- in special Java comments, 74
    /** (beginning doc comments), 654
    /**, in Javadoc comments, 223
    command arguments, use in, 43
    operating systems, differences in use, 40
    Unix root directory, 308
| (vertical bar), pipeline character, 271

We'd like to hear your suggestions for improving our indexes. Send email to *index@oreilly.com*.

## Numbers

## A

computeArea( ) (Shape), 238
concatenating strings, 56
    converting numbers to strings, 118
    example showing three methods of, 57
    println( ) method, 253
    timing, println( ) vs.), 735
concurrency, threads
    java.util.concurrent package, 684
    locks, 702–705
    Queue and BlockingQueue
        interfaces, 711–713
    simplifying servers with, 722–724
conditional compilation, 22
conditional statements, formatting plurals
        with, 136
connect( ), 443, 585
ConnectException, 446
ConnectFriendly class (example), 446
connecting to JDBC database, 585–587
    Connect class (example), 586
connection pools, 587
connections
    datagram (UDP), 453
    socket, encrypted (JSSE), 466
console, reading from, 248
ConsoleAppender class, 490
constants
    conditional debugging, use in, 22
    INFINITY, 123
constraints, layout manager, 415
constructors
    getting, 727
    no argument, calling for class, 732
    passing values, 239
container classes
    layout managers (see layout managers)
    nonparameterized, errors with, 213
containers
    adding components to, 374
    JFrame component, 373
    window layout, 375–377
        JTabbedPane, 378
contains( ), 196
containsKey( ), 196
containsValue( ), 196
ContentPane container, 373
continued lines, reading, 275–280
ContLineReader class, 277
control and message strings, getting localized
        versions, 422

controllers for movie players, 362
controls (user interface), configuring from
        resource bundle, 436–439
convenience routines, writing for
        internationalization, 425
converse( ) (example method), 335, 448
converting
    between primitives and object wrappers,
        using autoboxing, 214
    text to/from Unicode, 248, 273
    to/from Primitive to Object and vice
        versa, 208
Cookies class (example), 732
Cooklet class (example), 731
copying files, 266–269
    FileIO class (example), 266–269
CORBA (Common Object Request Broker
        Architecture), 635
core Java API, xxii
country codes, 430
CPAN (Comprehensive Perl Archive
        Network), 763
cpio utility, 292
CPUs
    running two or more with single operating
        system, 683
    time, assigning to threads, 688
    timing use of, clock time vs., 736
CREATE statement, SQL, 582
createFont( ) (Font), 352
createImage( ) (Graphics), 354
createNewFile( ) (File), 300
createStatement( ) (Connection), 588
createStatement( ) (Connection), 583
createTempFile( ) (File), 304
createXMLReader( ) (XMLReaderFactory
        class), 624
CrossRef class (example), printing Java API
        cross-reference, 739–744
CrossRefXML class (example), outputting
        class information in XML, 744
cryptography
    BigInteger class, creating prime pairs for
        public keys, 147
    SecureRandom class, using, 140
CSV (comma-separated values), 75–80
    CSV class (example), 75
        source code, 76
    parsing with regular expressions, 78–80
currencies, formatting, 128

jtest script, 30
JTree component, use in mail reader, 554
JUnit testing tool, 29–30
just-in-time (JIT) runtime system, 31
JVM (Java Virtual Machine) (see virtual
    machines)
JWindow component, default layout
    manager, 377
JWS (Java Web Start), 675–681
    download link for application,
        creating, 681
    home page (web site), 681
    JNLP (Java Net Launch Protocol)
        files, 678
    setting up application for, basic
        steps, 676
Jython, 759–763
    using with BSF, 760–763

**K**

Kaffe, Java implementation, 3
keySet( ) (Map), 210
key/value pairs
    DBM file format, 579
    mapping, TreeMap class, 194
    string, storing in Properties and
        Preferences, 186–190
keywords, javadoc, 654
Korn shell script, managing CLASSPATH
    with, 13
kwrite (windowed text editor program),
    running with Java, 753

**L**

L10N (see localization)
labels, GUI components, 346
LabelText bean, running with Python
    script, 761
LabelText class (example), 668–670
    packaging in JAR file, 671
language codes, 423, 430
languages
    creating properties files for, 428
    formatting messages in different, 432
    user.language system property, 431
large-scale number computing, Java web site
    for, 153
last modified dates, comparing for
    directories, 167

last( ), 194
last-in, first-out (LIFO) stack, 64, 201
lastIndexOf( ), 53
lastModified( ) (File), 167
Launch link, electronically distributed
    applications, 681
layout managers, 375–377
    BorderLayout, 7
    custom, creating, 414–420
        EntryLayout class (example), 417–420
    GridLayout, use in RMIWatch
        program, 646
    JTabbedPane class as, 378
layoutContainer( ) (LayoutManager), 415
LayoutManager interface, 376, 414
    methods, listed, 415
LayoutManager2 interface, 376
leading spaces
    continuing lines with, 275
    trimming from strings, 74
leading zeros, formatting numbers with, 128
Learning Tree, xxx
left-aligned strings, 60–62
length( ) (String), 59
length of text in pattern matches, 98
Level class (log4j), 489
levels of logging, 489
    fatal error messages, 491
lex (file scanning tool), 261
licensing
    Apache Software Foundation license, 491
    free software, understanding, 33
    GNU Public License, 3
    Sun Java Community Source License, 32
lifecycle methods
    Applet class, 503
    Thread, 688
LIFO (last-in, first-out) stack, 64, 201
line mode, reading/writing text in, 274
line numbers, preserving in stack
    tracebacks, 31
line termination characters, 274
    matching only \n in text strings, 107
LineNumberReader class, 277
line-oriented tools, Unix, 107
lines
    beginning with periods (dot
        commands), 82
    continued, reading, 275–280
    drawing, 343
LinkChecker class (example), 525–530

## About the Author

**Ian F. Darwin** divides his non-family time among writing (books, courses, and magazine articles), teaching Java and Unix courses, and consulting for Java and Unix projects. He is the original author of two four-day Java programming courses taught by Learning Tree International. He's also the author of *Checking C Programs with Lint*, published by O'Reilly in 1988. Of his second O'Reilly book, *X Window System User's Guide: Volume 3, OPEN LOOK*, little can be said except that he placed the final manuscript in Tim O'Reilly's hands the same week that Sun announced they were discontinuing OPEN LOOK in favor of the Common Desktop Environment; the ill-fated "Vol3OL" was published only in a CD-ROM compilation available from *http://www.darwinsys.com*. (Sun later announced its move from CDE to GNOME, which makes Ian glad he did not write a *Volume 3, CDE Edition*.) Ian's open source freeware contributions include the *file(1)* command used on Linux and BSD, a variety of Java programs, and contributions to various open source projects. He used to fly small airplanes and teach scuba diving, but he's been too busy lately as a computerist and family man to enjoy such ups and downs.

Ian's wife and three children raise Plymouth Barred Rock chickens. They believe that it complements Ian's book writing, since the Plymouth Barred Rock breed was "cooked up" by blending the Dominique and Black Java breeds.

## Colophon

Our look is the result of reader comments, our own experimentation, and feedback from distribution channels. Distinctive covers complement our distinctive approach to technical topics, breathing personality and life into potentially dry subjects.

The animal on the cover of *Java Cookbook*, Second Edition, is a domestic chicken (*Gallus domesticus*). Domestic chickens are descended from the wild red jungle fowl of India. Domesticated over 8,000 years ago in the area that is now Vietnam and Thailand, chickens are raised for meat and eggs, and the males for sport as well (although cockfighting is currently illegal in many places).

With their big, heavy bodies and small wings, these birds are well suited to living on the ground, and they can fly only short distances. Their four-toed feet are designed for scratching in the dirt, where they find the elements of their usual diet: worms, bugs, seeds, and various plant matter.

A male chicken is called a rooster or cock, and a female is known as a hen. The incubation period for a chicken egg is about three weeks; newly hatched chickens are precocial, meaning they have downy feathers and can walk around on their own right after emerging from the egg. They're also not dependent on their mothers for food; not only can they procure their own, but they also can live for up to a week after hatching on egg yolk that remains in their abdomen after birth.

The topic of chickens comes up frequently in ancient writings. Chinese documents date their introduction to China to 1400 B.C., Babylonian carvings mention them in 600 B.C., and Aristophanes wrote about them in 400 B.C. The rooster has long symbolized courage: the Romans thought chickens were sacred to Mars, god of war, and the first French Republic chose the rooster as its emblem.

Marlowe Shaeffer was the production editor and proofreader for *Java Cookbook*, Second Edition. Genevieve d'Entremont, Jamie Peppard, and Claire Cloutier provided quality control. Ellen Troutman Zaig wrote the index.

Hanna Dyer designed the cover of this book, based on a series design by Edie Freedman. The cover image is a 19th-century engraving from the Dover Pictorial Archive. Emma Colby produced the cover layout with QuarkXPress 4.1 using Adobe's ITC Garamond font.

David Futato designed the interior layout. This book was converted by Julie Hawks to FrameMaker 5.5.6 with a format conversion tool created by Erik Ray, Jason McIntosh, Neil Walls, and Mike Sierra that uses Perl and XML technologies. The text font is Linotype Birka; the heading font is Adobe Myriad Condensed; and the code font is LucasFont's TheSans Mono Condensed. The illustrations that appear in the book were produced by Robert Romano and Jessamyn Read using Macromedia FreeHand 9 and Adobe Photoshop 6. The tip and warning icons were drawn by Christopher Bing. This colophon was written by Leanne Soylemez.